George I
Elector and King

George I
Elector and King

RAGNHILD HATTON

Harvard University Press
Cambridge, Massachusetts
1978

© 1978 Thames and Hudson Ltd, London
Printed in Great Britain

For Harry, who had a Hanoverian great-grandmother

Library of Congress Cataloging in Publication Data
Hatton, Ragnhild Marie.
   George I, elector and king.

   Includes index.
   1. George I, King of Great Britain, 1660–1727.
2. Great Britain—Kings and rulers—Biography.
3. Great Britain—History—George I, 1714–1727.
DA501.A2H4   941.07′1′0924 [B]   77–15058
ISBN 0–674–34935–0

Contents

Contents

PREFACE

When in my *Europe in the Age of Louis XIV* I put George I on a list
of rulers from the early modern period in need of biographical
treatment based on recent scholarship, I had no intention of taking
on the task myself. Indeed, I hoped to tempt one of the young
historians who had done research on aspects of George's reign in
Britain, most of them pupils of Professor Plumb and all of them
indebted to his pioneering work, to embark on a full-scale study.
Alternatively, if none of these could be enticed to cope with the
Schrift of the German archives and with the masses of monographic
research published on Hanoverian history, might not one of the
pupils of Professor Schnath – himself the acknowledged expert on
the pre-1714 period – be willing to write of George as elector and
king? For one thing seemed essential: George would have to be
studied without the usual division between English and European
history. On the personal side it would be hard to understand him
without knowing his family background and the tasks he had faced
as elector; on the political side it would be impossible to evaluate him
as a European figure without considering him as king of Great
Britain as well as elector of Hanover. I found no takers. Instead it was
suggested that I, who had for a great many years concerned myself
with George I's foreign policy in Europe, might find it easier to fill
the gap.

Encouraged by Professors Schnath and Plumb, I decided to assess
George in his dual role within the framework of a biography. The
expansion of my research and reading which this necessitated has
brought me much pleasure in the last seven years. The rereading of
published documents, memoirs and letters with a new objective in
mind is always valuable and at times more rewarding than anticipated; and familiar British and continental official archives proved
happy hunting-grounds for information about a character which
had not before been at the centre of my interest. Moreover, I was

fortunate enough to be given access to the hitherto unused private collections of two of George I's most important Hanoverian advisers: Andreas Gottlieb von Bernstorff and Friedrich Wilhelm von Görtz. Both sets of papers yielded important and even exciting new material. I wish to express my gratitude to Graf Andreas von Bernstorff of Gartow for permission to use the Bernstorff archives and to the Görtz von Schlitz family for permission to consult the papers of their ancestor now deposited in the Darmstadt archives. In Great Britain the gracious permission of Her Majesty the Queen and of His Royal Highness the Prince of Wales enabled me to search, with some success, for new material in, respectively, the Royal Archives at Windsor and the Stanhope papers at Chevening. I am further indebted to Her Majesty the Queen for permission to reproduce paintings and engravings from the Royal Collection. For permission to reproduce paintings I wish also to thank Prince Philipp Ernst of Schaumburg-Lippe and Carl Graf von Kielmansegg. I gratefully acknowledge permission to use the Cowper (Panshanger) papers, now in the Hertford County Record Office, the Portland papers deposited at Nottingham University Library, and the Sir John Evelyn manuscript journal at Christ Church, Oxford. I owe a special debt to Their Royal Highnesses Prince and Princess Ernst August of Hanover. The Prince permitted me to use the family archives of the house of Hanover deposited in the Staatsarchiv; and the Prince and Princess gave generously of their time to guide me through their collections at Marienburg, Calenberg and the Fürstenhaus at Herrenhausen when I was choosing illustrations for this book. The courtesy and help of officials of museums, archives and libraries in Great Britain, France and Germany have been greatly appreciated. My debt to fellow-historians will be demonstrated in the notes to my text. I pay tribute to the historians of the past and thank those of the present: without their work mine could not have been undertaken.

SPELLING OF NAMES AND PLACES

A skilful critic justly blames
Hard, tough, crank, gutt'ral stiff names . . .
Hanover may do well enough,
but *Georg* and *Brunswic* are too rough,
Hesse-Darmstadt makes a rugged sound,
Guelph the strongest ear will wound

SWIFT

The spelling of names and places presented certain difficulties given the topic and period. It would be pedantic to attempt to distinguish systematically between George I, King of Great Britain after 1714, and Georg Ludwig who was Elector of Hanover from 1698 until his death in 1727. He signed himself, before 1714, as Georg Ludwig if he wrote in German, as George Louis if he wrote in French; after 1714 he always signed himself George R. and was styled *Königliche und Kurfürstliche Majestät* even when acting as elector. I have used the anglicized George throughout since this book is intended for the English reader, though I decided to call his son Georg August to avoid confusion except in the few instances when I speak of him as king George II; and for George's maternal grandfather and for his grandson I have – for obvious reasons – used Frederick. The name common to both George I's wife and daughter equally necessitated choice. The French form Sophie Dorothée is as usual among contemporaries as the German Sophie Dorothea, but I have chosen to use the anglicized Sophia Dorothea, Sophia – not Sophie – for George's mother, and Sophia Charlotte – not Sophie Charlotte – for George's sister and for his (illegitimate) half-sister. For other persons I have adopted German and English modern usage, with alternative contemporary forms given in brackets in the index. Where a person has two Christian names, but I have proof that the second of these was used exclusively in the intimate circle, as in the case of [Ehrengard] Melusine von der Schulenburg and her 'nieces' [Petronella]

Melusine von der Schulenburg and [Margarethe] Gertrud von Oeynhausen I have used in the text the second and preferred name, but in the index both baptismal names in their correct order.

For place-names I have followed the convention that if a non-English place has a well-established anglicized form it would needlessly complicate the text to use the foreign form, though I have given the national version in brackets in the index. The hybrid Brunswick-Lüneburg may offend the purist, but while Braunschweig is still too 'foreign', Lüneburg has been acceptable since the formal proclamation of George as king in 1714. The correct description of the electorate which was created in 1692 would be the Kurfürstentum zu Braunschweig und Lüneburg. But as even German contemporaries spoke and wrote of Kurhannover in daily parlance I have for simplicity's sake used the electorate of Hanover, though well aware that George I would have preferred the electorate of Brunswick and Lüneburg. It goes without saying that contemporaries would have been horrified at the use of the Christian names of royal and other main characters in the text and by the lack of proper noble titles and of titles of office where statesmen and courtiers are concerned (except at first mention and in the index), but present convention permits if indeed it does not demand this liberty. In titles of rank and office the lower case has been used in preference to capitals. Quotations in German have been avoided, though a few German titles have been used (with translations in the index). Some brief quotations in French have been included where it seemed important for the reader to have the exact words used; but the general sense of these quotations can be deduced from the context.

NOTE ON DATES

The reform of the calendar, issued by pope Gregory XIII in 1582, was adopted immediately in Catholic countries, but resisted for a considerable time by Protestant states. They stuck to Old Style (OS), which in the seventeenth was ten and in the eighteenth century eleven days behind the New Style (NS). As religious dividing lines became less important, Protestant states on the continent increasingly adopted the New Style. George, as elector of Hanover, decided to do so in 1700 when he decreed that eleven days be subtracted from the month of February: from 1 March 1700 Hanover therefore used NS. German historians of the nineteenth century caused much confusion by translating OS into NS for such dates as royal births and important political events without letting on what they were up to. I decided to keep OS for Hanoverian dates before 1700, not least because in England (where OS remained in force until the reform of 1752) such dates as the birthday of George as king and of Georg August as prince of Wales were celebrated according to the Old Style which both countries had used in the seventeenth century. After 1 March 1700 Hanoverian dates are given in NS, while dates for events in England are in OS. Both OS and NS are given for a few dates where confusion might arise and also in some notes when letters are cited as references. This is in accordance with contemporary usage since English correspondents with close professional or private ties to the continent preferred the double dating or indicated what style they were using. They increasingly tended to ignore the convention by which the English New Year began on 25 March OS, antedating it to 1 January OS, and I have therefore always given the New Year as starting on I January even where OS is used.

I

Parents and childhood

George's personality was undoubtedly influenced by his position as
a first-born son of fond but ambitious parents and by unfinished
business which he had been brought up to regard as his sacred duty
to complete when he succeeded his father Ernst August as elector of
Hanover in 1698. The dukes of Brunswick-Lüneburg had dreamt of
being raised to electoral rank ever since 1648, when the constitution
of the Holy Roman Empire of the German Nation had been changed
to accommodate eight electors, instead of the seven decreed in the
Golden Bull of 1356. The electoral dignity was the great dividing
line which separated the ordinary run of German ruling princes –
dukes, landgraves and margraves – from the chosen few who sat in
the Electoral College, shared between them the administrative
offices of the Empire, elected the emperor on the death of the incumbent of that highest ranking office in Europe and also the King
of the Romans if ever an emperor managed to persuade the electors
that it was in the best interests of the Empire that a successor (who
traditionally bore that title) should be designated in his own lifetime. In earlier times the electors had managed to obtain territorial
gains or large sums of money for their votes; and, conjunctures
permitting, they could still insist on a 'capitulation' which imposed
certain conditions or restraints on the new emperor, as had happened
in 1658 at the election of Leopold I. But the last election contested on
the grand scale had been in 1519,[1] and it was easier said than done to
keep an emperor to his *Wahlkapitulation* even if one had been
exacted.

Yet the electoral dignity, symbolized by the electoral cap or
bonnet, had many and real advantages. In matters of German
prestige and rank the electors came immediately below the emperor,
and their pre-eminence above other ruling German princes was
recognized in international diplomacy and fiercely upheld if contested.[2] The offices traditionally held by them were well-paid: when
George was made arch-treasurer of the Empire in 1710 he received
a salary of 48,000 Taler a year. If the Electoral College were agreed

in policy matters, it could exert pressure on the house of Habsburg which in its Austrian branch held the Imperial title between 1558 and 1740; and individual electors could and did receive concessions from the emperor for their cooperation on given issues. But the prestige of the Sacred Empire as such and the mystique surrounding the emperor's office counted for a good deal even with those electors who bargained for material advantages, while the ban of the Empire was feared. Loyalty to emperor and Empire was anyhow in the ascendant in the 1660s and 1680s when the Ottoman threat to Central Europe was at its fiercest, and waxed strong between 1689 and 1714 when France posed a serious problem on the western border of the Empire – a period therefore when the Habsburg 'Christian mission' in the east and its 'German mission' against France and Sweden, the victors of 1648, took on a new significance. This was part of a climate of opinion which had its effects on George as on other German princes, though his temperament was not a romantic or mystical one.

In the early days of her married life, Ernst August's wife Sophia, daughter of the Winter King and Queen, conscious of the fact that she was the granddaughter of James I of England as well as sister of Karl Ludwig, the elector palatine, of old the premier among the secular electors, proved sensitive to the scorn with which her relatives heard of the Brunswick-Lüneburg ambitions. How, Karl Ludwig asked, with a pointed reference to the family's emblem, the Saxon horse, could four dukes sit on one steed? Did the four brothers intend to wear the electoral cap in turn? Sophia, easily tempted into irony herself, took this in good part; but she became more concerned as soon as it seemed likely that her husband might emerge victorious in competition for the electoral dignity.[3] This had not seemed remotely possible when, in spite of his being inferior to her in rank, she had married him in 1658 out of a strong desire, as she frankly admitted in her memoirs, 'to get an establishment of my own'. She was then twenty-eight years old, relatively advanced at a time when princesses usually married young or not at all; and experiences in childhood had made her particularly inclined to value a settled state.

Sophia was born in exile, of deposed royal parents. Her father, the elector palatine, had lost after one year's war the Bohemian kingdom to which he had been called in 1619 by a country in rebellion against its Catholic Habsburg ruler: the epithet 'Winter King' has clung to Frederick V ever since the Protestants' defeat at the battle of the White Mountain justified the Habsburg prophecy that he would be but a winter king, gone with the melting snow. From the refuge offered him and his queen and children in the Dutch Republic he had to watch, helplessly at first, Spanish troops taking possession of his Rhine (or Lower) Palatinate and the emperor giving his Upper Palatinate (adjacent to Bohemia) and his electoral dignity to Maximilian of Bavaria as a reward for fighting on the Habsburg-Catholic side in the struggle known to us as the Thirty Years War. In November 1632, just as the tide seemed to have turned in his favour, with Gustavus Adolphus freeing the Rhineland and welcoming Frederick to his camp at Frankfurt, he died unexpectedly. He had been able to visit the Palatinate to confer with his brother (who was undertaking regency duties there) and was planning military action in cooperation with the Swedes when illness struck him. He lived long enough to hear of the great Protestant victory at Lützen, and his last wish was that his queen, Elizabeth, should devote herself to the re-establishment of their children – ten of whom survived him – in the Empire.

This proved no easy task. Gustavus Adolphus's death on the battlefield of Lützen brought temporary setbacks for the Protestants: the Palatinate was re-occupied by the enemy, and queen Elizabeth had to safeguard the interests of the Palatinate dynasty in difficult political and financial circumstances.

The Winter Queen's preoccupation with European diplomacy as well as her absorption in intellectual and artistic pursuits made Sophia, the twelfth and penultimate of the children, feel that she had been short of mother-love in her early years. Like all the children, she was brought up away from the parents, at a separate establishment in Leiden, till they reached years of discretion. They then (in the case of daughters) formed part of the parents' court or (in the case of sons) pursued their studies at universities or by travel or service in the armed forces of a foreign ruler. This was, however, part of a well-thought-out pattern. At Leiden a strict Palatinate etiquette was drilled into them so that they might be equipped to take their future rightful place in the world of princes and kings: that lesson could not be learnt in the capital of a republic. They benefited also from a programme of education carefully fashioned by their father in which the girls as well as the boys studied – apart from the living languages of French, German, English and Dutch – Latin and Greek, theology and history, mathematics and law. In retrospect Sophia looked upon her Leiden years as a horrible and unnatural banishment, and her resentful 'our mother cared more for her dogs and pet-monkeys than for her children' has been much quoted as evidence of Elizabeth's indifference to her role as a mother.[4] In reality Sophia was permitted to join her mother's

court in The Hague at an earlier age than her sisters, since on the
death in 1641 of the youngest brother, Gustavus, the Leiden nursery
was closed down. Those who read the full text of Sophia's memoirs –
written when she was fifty years old – will form a more charitable
judgment. With kindness, tact and understanding the queen is seen
to have eased the shy Sophia's entry into the circle of three self-
possessed and teasing older sisters. The young girl thought of herself
as thin and pale to the point of ugliness and possibly destined to die
young; had not a visitor, before he realized that she understood
English, commented on the good looks and health of Gustavus while
commiserating with her mother on Sophia's plainness and lack of
robustness? But in a court where intelligence was valued and learn-
ing encouraged, and where the shackles of excessive piety were
removed, her inquisitive mind expanded and her body thrived.
Soon she took what she deemed her rightful place in the competition with her sisters in looks and accomplishments: Elizabeth was
more learned and serious, Louise Hollandine more gifted as a
painter, Henrietta more beautiful; but Sophia was admired for her
wit and spirit, and her tendency to mock was usually forgiven
because people could not help liking her. Underneath lurked a
certain diffidence which made her treasure and remember praise,
especially of her attractiveness, repeated to her or overheard; a
diffidence which remained with her all her life but which she learnt
to hold in check by applications of robust common sense bidding her
accept 'things as they are'. That queen Elizabeth shared the general
high opinion of Sophia and the future she deserved is shown by her
sponsorship of this daughter as the prospective bride of Charles
Stuart,* proclaimed King of the Scots after his father's execution in
1649 and with prospects – so the royalists in exile maintained – of
making good his claim not only to Scotland but to England and
Ireland as well. Charles did appear to pay court to Sophia; her
pride, however, was deeply hurt when she discovered that his real
objective, without the strings of marriage, was financial help from
lord Craven whose fortune had long supported the Palatinate court
in exile and who was particularly attached to Sophia. She decided
to get away from The Hague as soon as possible and showed considerable shrewdness in engineering an invitation from her eldest
brother, Karl Ludwig, to make her home in Heidelberg, as well as
great determination in overcoming her mother's objections to her
plans.

The Palatinate princes had roamed Europe while their sisters had
stayed close to queen Elizabeth's apron-strings. At times it had
looked as if they would never be able to settle down. The two

* Sophia was the only one of her daughters younger than Charles, but Henrietta, four
years his senior, could have been the mother's choice. Elizabeth (b. 1618) and Louise
Hollandine (b. 1622) were probably too old to be seriously considered.

eldest, Karl Ludwig and Rupert, had terminated their studies at Leiden university upon their father's death and taken service with the army of Frederick Henry, prince of Orange. They paid an extended visit, from 1636 to 1638, to their uncle Charles I in England, gaining sufficient financial support to permit them to embark on military ventures in the Empire. Both proved unsuccessful and ended up as prisoners, though in 1640 they were released, respectively, from French and Imperial captivity. Moritz and Edward, the two middle brothers, who had visited France as part of their youthful education, returned with Karl Ludwig to The Hague. Rupert and Moritz served Charles I throughout the civil war on land and sea, but Karl Ludwig – after a brief stay with Charles in 1642 – remained on the continent to keep in touch with the Westphalia peace negotiations and further the restitution of at least part of the Palatinate inheritance. In 1645 Edward moved back to Paris and converted to Catholicism on his marriage to Anna Gonzaga, princess of Mantua-Nevers. Philip, the youngest surviving son, had accompanied Edward to benefit in his turn from a stay in France, and eventually entered the French army and died fighting the Spaniards.

The family was gradually being dispersed. Elizabeth and Louise Hollandine took refuge with Brandenburg relatives, having supported Philip in a quarrel with their mother;* and financial squabbles between queen Elizabeth and her eldest son, exacerbated rather than ameliorated by his restoration to the Rhine Palatinate at the general peace settlement of 1648, alienated them in reality if not in form. Negotiations which his two elder sisters promoted in Berlin for Henrietta's marriage to Sigismund Rákóczi, prince of Transylvania (Siebenbürgen), also met with Karl Ludwig's disapproval: he regarded the prince as unequal to his bride in rank.

In spite of her displeasure at Sophia's move to Heidelberg queen Elizabeth could find no valid reason to prevent it. Karl Ludwig had recently married and it was perfectly proper that Sophia should live with the head of the family whom she and Henrietta had long addressed as 'Papa'. Moreover, her main objection, that the chances of an English marriage for Sophia would be spoilt, was countered with the argument that negotiations for it – if they ever materialized – could be carried on as easily at Heidelberg as at The Hague. Sophia was even able to persuade others – though not her mother – that her chosen attendants (two English ladies, the Misses Carey) went with her at the express wish of the queen.

In theory Sophia should have been happy at Heidelberg. She was devoted to her brother, on good terms with his illegitimate son Louis

---

* Philip had been recalled to The Hague in 1646 to prevent his following Edward's example in turning Catholic, but he had to flee the Republic after stabbing to death the marquis d'Espinay.

von Rothenschild (created Freiherr von Selz as soon as Karl Ludwig
was restored to the Palatinate), delighted in his children by Charlotte
of Hesse-Cassel (Karl, born in 1651, and Elisabeth Charlotte, called
Liselotte for short, born in 1652), and tried her best to live peace-
fully with her sister-in-law whose capricious temper and suspicious
nature made this a difficult task. There was much to interest her:
the rebuilding and refurbishing of the electoral palaces and gardens;
the university with its learned men; the many visitors, including
Elizabeth and Rupert, who stayed for long periods entertained by
feasts, dances and plays; the opportunity to accompany Karl
Ludwig and Charlotte on their private and official journeys within
the Empire. She also had her own pastimes, her reading and needlework, her guitar-playing and singing lessons, the long walks which
she much preferred to riding and card-playing. But in practice
things did not work out as she had expected. The family visits gave
rise to family quarrels and though these were conducted with
Palatine decorum they were distasteful. Rupert departed with an
annuity to settle in England; Elizabeth began negotiations to enter
a German Protestant abbey; and Louise Hollandine – failing to
find a place in a Protestant establishment – converted to Catholicism
and entered the convent of Maubuisson near Paris. Two members of
the family had died since Sophia's coming to Heidelberg: Henrietta,
who married her prince without Karl Ludwig's blessing, already
in 1651, and Moritz in 1652. Worse, from Sophia's point of view, was
that Karl Ludwig's marriage came under intolerable strain. He had
fallen in love with Louise von Degenfeld, one of his wife's maids-of-
honour, and the attendant scenes and alarums when Charlotte
realized that he wanted a divorce in order to marry Louise morgan-
atically, were distressing if at times ludicrous. All this, on top of
Charlotte's insinuation that there was an incestuous relationship
between Karl Ludwig and Sophia, made her increasingly anxious
to get away by means of a marriage which would give her an
independent establishment. For a long time her pride prevented her
from considering a bridegroom who was not a ruling prince, but by
1656 she permitted negotiations to go ahead for her betrothal to
Adolf Johann of Zweibrücken – who was only regent of that duchy
on behalf of his brother king Charles X of Sweden – though she
found him singularly unattractive.[5]

She was saved by the necessary slowness of correspondence on
points of the marriage contract between Heidelberg and the battlefields of Poland where Charles X was on campaign. Adolf regarded
Sophia as his fiancée, but no contract had been signed when duke
Georg Wilhelm, of the house of Brunswick-Lüneburg, arrived at

Karl Ludwig's court late in 1656 and asked for Sophia's hand. He was accompanied by his youngest brother, Ernst August. Both had visited Heidelberg three years earlier. Sophia had then enjoyed playing duets with Ernst August, admiring also his skill at dancing and his good looks (he had beautifully shaped hands and fine blue eyes); but she never let herself think of him as a possible suitor. His only prospect was that, in time, he was sure to be the next prince-bishop of Osnabrück, a non-hereditary position;* and Sophia had therefore let the correspondence which Ernst August began after his departure lapse. As the cadet of cadets, the youngest of four sons of the junior branch of the Brunswick dukes (the line of Brunswick-Wolfenbüttel was senior to that of Brunswick-Lüneburg), he was not a good *parti*. His brother may have made her heart flutter on the earlier visit, for he was a man who found it easy to attract women; and his suit was, in any case, welcomed in 1656 because of his secure position. Since 1648 he had been ruling prince of the duchy of Calenberg-Göttingen, the second in importance of the two duchies into which the Brunswick-Lüneburg inheritance was divided by duke Georg's will; but he would be at liberty to choose to move to the duchy of Lüneburg-Grubenhagen if his elder brother, Christian Ludwig, died without a male heir of his own body. If this happened, the third son, Johann Friedrich, would inherit whatever duchy Georg Wilhelm wished to relinquish. Only in the unlikely event of two of his three brothers dying without sons would Ernst August – provided he survived them – become a ruling prince.

Sophia and her brother Karl Ludwig were both happy to accept Georg Wilhelm's offer and the marriage contract was signed before the two brothers continued their journey to Venice: the Brunswick-Lüneburgers, like the Brunswick-Wolfenbüttels, were frequent visitors to Italy (particularly in the carnival season) and drew most of their architects and musicians from the peninsula. The betrothal was kept secret for the time being since Georg Wilhelm hoped to be able to make a better financial arrangement with his Estates (they had pressed him to think of marriage and heirs) if the issue was still thought of as in the balance. Once in Italy, however, Georg Wilhelm had second thoughts. He enjoyed the freedom which his bachelor status gave him and found himself reluctant to give it up. To break his word would tarnish the honour of the house, but he thought he saw a way out. It was easy enough to persuade Ernst August to take his place as a prospective bridegroom. To make him acceptable to Karl Ludwig and Sophia, a convention was entered into (signed on 11/21 April 1658) between the two brothers, that Georg Wilhelm

---

* At the settlement of 1648 it had been agreed that the prince-bishopric should alternate between a Catholic and a Protestant ruler, and though Ernst August had been named coadjutor there was no knowing when he would succeed the present incumbent, nor was he, according to the settlement, at liberty to influence the choice of his successor.

would never marry, which meant that one or other of the two duchies might be more likely to devolve on Ernst August. Such an arrangement was nothing new in the family; their own father, duke Georg, had benefited from a drawing of lots among the six sons of duke Wilhelm (who reigned between 1559 and 1592) to decide who should be the one permitted legal marriage and inheritance of the undivided duchy of Calenberg-Göttingen.

The 1658 convention provided no guarantee that Ernst August would ever rule either the duchy of Hanover (as Calenberg-Göttingen was unofficially called after 1636 when duke Georg demolished the old Calenberg Schloss and moved his capital to Hanover) or that of Lüneburg-Grubenhagen (inherited by duke Georg from an uncle and referred to for brevity's sake as the duchy of Celle after its capital). But the convention was the best Georg Wilhelm could offer and would seem, by removing one brother from the race for inheritance, to give a measure of security to sons of Ernst August born in wedlock.

The Hanoverian envoy who pressed the substitution of bride-grooms at the Heidelberg court painted the future as brightly as he could. Christian Ludwig was married, but had no issue; Johann Friedrich, *der dicke Herzog*, was unmarried and thought incapable of producing children:* both the Brunswick-Lüneburg duchies would therefore come to Ernst August.[6] It is unlikely that Karl Ludwig and Sophia were convinced by his reasoning, but they were prepared to accept Georg Wilhelm's solution as the best that could be obtained for the jilted bride. Ernst August's family was old, descended from Heinrich *der Löwe*, the mightiest German prince of Friedrich Barbarossa's time until the emperor cut him down to size and confined his territories to the lands between the Weser and the Elbe. The fact that Heinrich had married the English princess Mathilde also appealed to them. But that the convention weighed most is indicated by Sophia's copying it into her memoirs (written in French) in its original German in full; it was the very foundation of the hoped-for 'establishment'. Sophia's *amour-propre* had been damaged by Georg Wilhelm's rejection but she was given to understand – or convinced herself – that he had contracted syphilis in Venice and was now 'unfit for marriage'.[7] Karl Ludwig comforted her by saying that he had all along liked Ernst August better than Georg Wilhelm, and the wedding ceremony was fixed for the end of September 1658. Her brother Edward came to Heidelberg to witness Karl Ludwig giving Sophia into marriage; and Sophia's minute description – some twenty years later – of all the arrangements, of what she wore and the entertainments provided, vividly

---

* In the event, his marriage (in 1668) produced four daughters of whom three survived infancy.

depicts the elegance and good taste of the Palatinate court and also her own intense pleasure at entering the married woman's estate. None of her husband's family was present. It would have been in bad taste for Georg Wilhelm to attend, and Johann Friedrich had much resented the April convention: why had he not been given the chance to substitute for Georg Wilhelm on such good terms?

Sophia felt no love for Ernst August before they became man and wife, though she found him 'amiable' and had resolved to make him a good wife. She assumed that he was indifferent, marrying her for the advantage that attended his bargain with Georg Wilhelm. She was therefore pleased when he proved a passionate lover and felt flattered rather than annoyed at his jealous guardianship of her once they had arrived in Hanover to make their home – until Osnabrück should materialize – with Georg Wilhelm. She got on well with the many new relatives by marriage assembled to welcome her to Hanover with grand processions and festivities, but her love and concern from her wedding night onwards were for Ernst August. In her eyes he could not do wrong. She, usually so sharp, exaggerated his virtues and ignored his weaknesses. To her he was the most industrious of men; if he left his duties to go on long and expensive vacations to Italy it was either for the sake of his health or to 'save money' by cutting down the court budget at home.

In middle age she marvelled that she could have been silly enough to imagine that her husband would remain physically attracted to her 'for the rest of his life'. Ernst August was a gallant, a great admirer of women, incapable of being faithful to his wife for more than the first few years of marriage. Once he had achieved an independent status as ruler of Osnabrück in 1661, minor adventures, more or less serious, became frequent; he found it hard to resist temptation that came his way either in the circle of his wife's ladies-in-waiting or on visits to Italy. At times Sophia suffered but saw to it that the marriage did not. Ernst August remained fond of her and was always ready to remind her what a delightful surprise she had been to him on their wedding night.[8] They had children and ambitions for their house in common. No affair of Ernst's was ever a serious threat to Sophia's position until the 1670s when Klara Elisabeth von Meysenbug, eighteen years younger than Sophia, monopolized Ernst August sufficiently to become known as his *maîtresse en titre*. Married in 1673 to Franz Ernst Baron von Platen, governor to Ernst's sons by Sophia,* Klara presented her husband with a son in 1674 but the daughter, Sophia Charlotte, born in 1675, was accepted in the family circle as Ernst August's child and treated as the half-sister of the legitimate children. When George I bestowed an English peerage

---

* His career as one of Ernst's talented advisers was advanced by his complaisance as a husband and in 1689 he was made a *Graf* of the Empire at Ernst's request.

on her in 1722 her coat of arms included that of the house of Brunswick with a bend sinister. Ernst's long and close relationship with
Klara caused Sophia much grief, particularly as the mistress knew
how to nettle the wife in such matters as copying her furs and
getting large sums of money out of Ernst which Sophia thought could
have been better spent 'on the family'. Sophia, however, learnt how
to control her tongue and was more than kind to Sophia Charlotte
whom she genuinely liked. She had her belated reward. After 1694,
when Ernst August's health deteriorated sharply, Sophia was the
only one he wished near him; Klara von Platen at best made up a
fourth at the game of cards which Sophia occasionally persuaded
him to play.*

*   *   *

There is no doubt that the early years of their married life were very
happy ones. They were well suited, in bed and out of bed. They
appreciated each other's intelligence as well as each other's taste.
Ernst was less curious intellectually than his wife and did not share
her interest in philosophy and theology; but he was the more
practical character who got things done. They met, however, in
joint absorption in music and opera, in building and decorating
their homes, in landscape-gardening and the pleasure of fountains.
If anything, Sophia was the more frivolous and less detached of the
two, though she has the reputation of a cool bluestocking, while Ernst
August is often considered as a self-indulgent lightweight given to
outbursts of temper. Such a view ignores Ernst August's political
acumen and his work to reform the administration in Osnabrück
and, after 1679, also in Hanover, and it fails to assess the evidence
of Sophia's published letters. Those to and from her brother Karl
Ludwig have survived from 1658 to his death in 1680, as have most
of those she exchanged with Leibniz from 1680 onwards. Those she
wrote to Karl Ludwig's daughters by Louise von Degenfeld after
1680 are also extant, as is the whole of her correspondence beginning
in 1684 with her relatives in Berlin, her daughter and granddaughter, who both married into the Hohenzollern family, and their
respective husbands. Her letters to Liselotte have been lost, but those
from Liselotte have been kept for the years 1672 to 1714 and, as the
niece invariably comments on Sophia's letters and even cites from
them, we get a fair idea of the missing side of the correspondence.
This uniquely rich series of letters is one of the historical and literary
treasures of the second half of the seventeenth century. They do not
tell us all we would like to know, as Sophia was both shrewd and
discreet when it suited her purposes. Yet they give sufficient indi-

---

* Sophia did not play; the other two were Mme Harling and *Kammerherr* Klencke
(Sophia, *Letters to the raugravines*: to Louise 4/14 Jan. 1677).

cations of her intensely personal attitude to people and events: she could hate with gusto and be patently unreasonable, but when times changed – and particularly as she reached the age when contemporaries began to die off – she tended to become reconciled and even quite attached to old enemies. Ernst August had a clearer and more impartial judgment, but he was more ruthlessly ambitious than his wife where the advancement of his house, and especially his own branch of it, was concerned.

They both wished for children as soon as possible to establish such a branch and their joy was great when the 'George Louys' of the memoirs was born on 28 May 1660. There had been hopes deferred and moments of despondence when Sophia thought she might prove barren for ever and that her 'only child' would be Liselotte, who had come with her governess, Katharine von Offeln, to stay with her aunt, away from the tense atmosphere of the Heidelberg court. Early in 1660, when Sophia knew for sure that she was pregnant but reckoned that a miscarriage was no longer likely, she and Liselotte paid a visit to queen Elizabeth at The Hague during the absence of Ernst August and Georg Wilhelm in Italy. The stay proved enjoyable, but Sophia took care to return to Hanover early enough not to risk a premature birth through the jolting of her carriage and to be there to welcome her husband back. She was always delighted to be reunited with Ernst August, even after short absences, and his presence and comfort helped her through a long and difficult birth: she could not have lived through the 'continuelles douleurs' of the three-day labour, she felt, without him.

The boy was big and healthy, and though some of his facial traits (especially as he got beyond middle age) were reminiscent of his mother, on the whole he took after his father in looks (though shorter in stature when grown). The clear blue Brunswick eyes were immediately noticed; later the finely modelled hands of Ernst August and his long and sharp nose were seen to be reproduced in the first-born. In Sophia's opinion George was 'beautiful as an angel', and she was glad to have him as an outlet for her *tendresse* during the next visit of Ernst August and Georg Wilhelm to Italy.[9] Soon after Christmas 1660 it was arranged that Sophia, pregnant once more, should visit her brother at Heidelberg, and Liselotte and George went with her. She had a pleasant enough stay, but was worried lest she make trouble for the Brunswick-Lüneburg dukes with their Hesse-Cassel neighbours by paying her respects to Louise von Degenfeld and her son and daughter while Charlotte was still living at court. She managed with her usual tact to please Karl Ludwig by doing this discreetly and found Louise's infants 'les plus jolies du monde'. Of the fourteen children born to Karl Ludwig and Louise, created a *Raugräfin* on her morganatic marriage to the elector, the eight who survived their parents – five sons and three daughters – eventually became Sophia's responsibility since they lost their mother in 1677 and their father in 1680. Though their status created precedence difficulties in Hanover,* the young raugraves and raugravines played an important role in the family's life, and one of them, raugrave Karl Moritz, became a particular friend of George's.

At Eastertime 1661 Ernst August and Georg Wilhelm arrived at Heidelberg to fetch Sophia, Liselotte and George. Karl Ludwig put two finely appointed ships at their disposal for their trip down the Rhine to the Netherlands where George was to be presented to his grandmother: this was done at Rotterdam where the Winter Queen was preparing her move to England. By the autumn of that year George was no longer an only child, his brother Friedrich August being born in early October. For nearly five years after his birth Sophia did not bear any live children; stillbirths and miscarriages were her lot. She fretted at this and blamed her misfortune on her having broken the customary six-week period in the lying-in chamber to move (at Ernst August's request) into her husband's bedroom after a mere fortnight. A severe chill which she then caught weakened her constitution, she argued; but she was careful to stress in her memoirs that she did not make the move reluctantly, but with 'la plus grande joie du monde'. Her ill-health, whatever caused it, was cured by her long visit to Italy in 1664–65 and after 1666 the children came in quick succession: Maximilian Wilhelm, the survivor of boy twins in 1666, Sophia Charlotte in 1668, Karl Philipp in 1669, Christian Heinrich in 1671, and, finally, Ernst August in 1674. By that time George, at fourteen, was reckoned old enough to stand godfather to his youngest brother. Sophia was wont to say in later years that fate had possibly given her too many children, but by that time she was thinking of how to provide suitably for them all.

Sophia was a good and devoted mother. Memories of her own joyless early childhood made her determined that her children should have a great deal of her time and personal care, and that the men and women who came into close contact with them, and especially those to whom she gave a measure of authority over them, should be of a loving and cheerful disposition. 'Excessively religious' people were anathema to her since she equated their devotion to their faith with too inflexible and strict an attitude towards small children. She was lucky to retain Katharine von Offeln as a member of her household even after Liselotte – to everyone's regret – had returned to the

* Some of the raugraves were touchy about the fact that in Hanover rank went by office and that privy councillors, even when they were not counts, took precedence over them; while in the case of the raugravines, Ernst August and George did not wish to offend Klara von Platen and Melusine von der Schulenburg respectively by treating them as inferior in rank to the Heidelberg relatives.

Palatinate in the summer of 1663 at her father's bidding. Liselotte had shared the excitement when Ernst August in December 1661 had succeeded to Osnabrück and the family had moved to the castle of Iburg. For Sophia, as well as for her husband, the new-found independence was delightful. There was a new palace to plan and build, and challenging activities for Ernst August in reforming the administration of the prince-bishopric. Sophia noted with pride that the revenues he drew, not more than 18–20,000 *écus* a year, were in stark contrast to the 40,000 which his predecessor 'had pressed out of his subjects'.[10] They could now enlarge their respective households and create the kind of court they wanted; and though Georg Wilhelm was a frequent guest who enjoyed playing with his nephews, the parents of Görgen and Gustchen – as the two boys were called in the family – were glad to be relieved of the strain of living *à trois*. But for the fact that Liselotte's governess married Ernst August's *Oberhofmeister* (chamberlain) Friedrich von Harling, Sophia might have lost a born educator for her children. Mme von Harling was energetic, optimistic, able to instil manners and the requisite measure of discipline while gaining the affection of her charges. In due course, as the boys of the family reached the ages between six and seven, they became the responsibility of governors and preceptors; but there was no lack of younger boys throughout the Osnabrück years and, apart from remaining in charge of the only girl of the family – nicknamed Figuelotte – until her marriage, Mme von Harling became Sophia's *Oberhofmeisterin*, and as head of her entire staff exercised a certain amount of general influence until her death in 1702.

It was her visit to Italy to join Ernst August and his brother Johann Friedrich which taught Sophia that her maternal instincts were strong enough to make her, in her own words, a 'nearly stupidly fond' mother.[11] She had been keen enough to set out in April 1664 to catch up with the advance party for the first long holiday Ernst August had arranged since becoming ruler of Osnabrück. She had settled the boys in Mme von Harling's care at Heidelberg where they would have plenty of young company with Liselotte and the Degenfeld children, and had arranged for good-looking ladies-in-waiting and fine dresses to please the husband whom she would 'gladly have followed to the antipodes'.[12] She found much to enjoy during the nearly year-long travels interspersed with longer stays in Venice and Rome. The sensuousness of the balmy southern evenings proved irresistible and she and her ladies danced in the streets with an abandonment which gave them the reputation of behaving 'é la moda franchese'.[13] Famous sights, art collections and interesting people attracted her. She was quick in making up her mind about everyone and everything and enjoyed indulging her prejudices: to find her Catholic brother-in-law in disagreement with the pope was one of the highlights of the journey. But she missed her children more than she had thought possible. She felt cheated when she realized that she had no share in significant stages of their natural growth and development. To think that George had come out of the skirts of infancy and into his first suit of breeches and had already learnt his first dance-steps! Was Katharine sure that Gustchen was made sufficient fuss of? The news that both had suffered an attack of smallpox alarmed her. Was the attack as slight as she had been told? Would the boys (like herself) become permanently scarred? Writing to Heidelberg she made no bones about wishing that her husband would soon take the road to Germany: she would rather gaze at the children's faces than at all the art-treasures of Italy; to watch them at play would please her more than the best theatre-performance abroad.

After her return in February 1665 Sophia never wished to be parted from her growing family for any length of time. Her husband complained in a moment of temper that she loved their children more than she loved him;[14] but conflict between them on the issue of foreign travel was minimized since Ernst August was tied to Osnabrück by his own duties and ambitions for roughly a decade* during which he found himself becoming preoccupied with his sons as soon as they could take an interest in things where he could be their guide. Görgen and Gustchen became his companions in riding and hunting, and his first-born began to share his own absorption with military matters. As the eldest son of an ambitious father, George had a vital role in Ernst August's plans for the future. Indeed, these plans shaped George's life from an early age and no other son was given as much of the father's time. That George held a special place in his mother's heart has often been denied. The fact that she once described Gustchen as a 'real Palatine' when compared to the 'Brunswick Görgen'[15] has been taken to imply that Sophia disliked George, presumably on the grounds that she, being of the Palatinate house, must have regarded those of her children who reminded her of the Palatinate family as preferable to those taking after her husband's side. Similarly, her confession to one of the raugravines after Karl Philipp had been killed in battle early in 1690 that this was the son she had secretly loved best has been interpreted as proof of a theory that George grew up cold and un-feeling because he was deprived of mother-love in his childhood. Neither hypothesis is borne out by the available evidence. In the

---

* In this period, Ernst August's only visit to Italy was in 1671–72. He and Sophia attended the wedding of Karl Ludwig's son and heir in Heidelberg in September 1671, and Sophia – who had given birth to Christian Ludwig on their arrival in the Palatinate – stayed at her brother's court until Ernst August returned to fetch her in the early spring of 1672.

very letter in which Sophia distinguished between the looks and characters of the two elder boys, she admits that George touches her heart more than Friedrich August. As a child he was so responsible, so conscientious in his lessons, and tried so hard to do her bidding and to please her that he set an example none of the others could emulate: Gustchen was naughty and moody, Maximilian had no *Geist* (lit. spirit), Karl Philipp was a reserved *Querkopf* (lit. oddhead), Figuelotte and Christian Heinrich were not keen to learn, and though Ernst August, the youngest, was 'the easiest of all my children' she did not think there was 'much to him'.[16]

These, and similar comments, were of course impressions of the moment passed on in letters to relatives. Certainly Sophia Charlotte developed into a young lady of powerful intellect, Karl Philipp became a charmer who wrote his mother well-turned and informative letters from the wars, Friedrich and Christian collected books more demanding than those bought by their elder brother, and George in adolescence went through a period of sullen reserve which drove his mother to distraction.[17] She never, however, changed her mind about George's temperament and character; and circumstances dictated that he was her main companion after her husband's death. Friedrich August had fallen in battle against the Turks at the end of the year (1690) which had already brought Karl Philipp's death at the hands of the infidel. Christian Heinrich was killed in 1703 when fighting the French and their Bavarian allies; Maximilian lived abroad and had become estranged from her even to the point of non-correspondence; Ernst August she had never really fathomed and could not get close to.[18] She and George, once he had succeeded as elector in 1698, had their occasional disagreements, over minor matters like invitations to the raugravines and major ones such as the best policy to be pursued in England, which annoyed Sophia and provoked caustic comments in her letters. But on the whole the two got on surprisingly well. He remained 'her Benjamin' – the phrase used by her husband in 1675 when the fifteen-year-old George first accompanied him into battle[19] – and she never tired of explaining to those who regarded him as cold and overserious that he could be *lustigh* (jolly), that he took things to heart, that he felt deeply and sincerely and was more sensitive than he cared to show. To her he combined the best of the Palatinate and the Brunswick strains; he worked hard, he had *mérite* and *savoir faire* and though not so easy in manner as her late brother Karl Ludwig he reminded her irresistibly of him by the neat and amusing way he told a story.[20]

Sophia often marvelled that children born of the same parents, 'from the same matrix so to speak', could differ so much. Under the blows of fortune Gustchen grew bitter and threw discretion to the winds; Karl Philipp got into debt; Maximilian vacillated, proved totally irresponsible in money matters and did not outgrow his laziness; Christian Heinrich showed himself overproud, yet would not exert himself and expected 'ready-roasted birds to fly into his mouth'.[21]

The happy days of the united family of the 1660s and 1670s seemed, in retrospect, to have passed so quickly: the joint family treats and outings, the fireworks on feast days . . . the five-year-old Gustchen and six-year-old Görgen coming as far as Celle with her and Ernst on their 1667 visit to Glückstadt to meet the Danish royal family . . . and, greeting them on their return, George drilling a company of sixty 'soldiers' formed from the young sons of Georg Wilhelm's ministers and officers – a splendid surprise prepared by a fond uncle . . . the two boys being regarded as old enough in 1671 to form part of her suite when she visited her sister Elizabeth at Herford and enjoyed getting the better in disputation with the fanatic Labadie with his gloomy pietist outlook on life.[22] Even when these and a host of other memories had been overlaid by current strife within the family, Sophia did not find if difficult to make allowances for those who were out of step. Every one of the children was as dear to her as the rest, she used to say, and her natural tendency to side with the underdog (or underdogs) of the moment disturbed her relationship in 1684–85 and, more seriously, in 1691–92 with her husband. That Ernst August should be involved in war to promote the interests and aggrandizement of his house Sophia, like her contemporaries, found natural. She realized with her mind that the constitutional reform, the introduction of primogeniture (worked out in 1682, approved by the emperor in 1683 and revealed to the family at large in 1684), formed part and parcel of these interests and ambitions; but the link between her own pride and her husband's ambitions, the drive which that pride imparted to him, she does not seem to have grasped. She, as well as Ernst August, helped to provoke those blows of fortune which hit the family once the primogeniture issue came into the open, setting sons against father and isolating George from all but one of his brothers. Even the death of three of Sophia's sons in battle can be said to have been rendered more likely by the family quarrel. The three who fell were those who had felt forced to take independent service with the Habsburg army; the three who survived were those who served with Hanoverian regiments. All were brave, but those who had to win promotion in foreign armies were more exposed to risks and lacked the support of officers and men devoted to the house.

II

The electoral cap

In 1665 Ernst August acquired the first piece of land, the *Grafschaft* of Diepholz, that could be passed on by inheritance. It came to him as a reward for two services he performed in that year for his brother Georg Wilhelm. Both had a connection with Georg Wilhelm's having fallen deeply in love with a beautiful and accomplished French lady of the Huguenot faith, Mlle Eléonore d'Olbreuse. He had first met her at Hesse-Cassel where she visited as maid-of-honour to a daughter of that house, Emilie princess of Tarente; and she as well as another maid-of-honour, Mlle de la Motte, were invited on his and Ernst August's recommendation to form part of Sophia's suite for her Italian journey of 1664–65. While Mlle de la Motte accepted, Mlle d'Olbreuse refused and went with the princess of Tarente to The Hague: a fact which explains Georg Wilhelm's decision not to go with his brothers to the south but to spend the winter of 1664–65 in the Netherlands. He ignored messages that his brother Christian Ludwig of Celle was seriously ill and wished to see him, and even after the duke's death was known to him he was reluctant to leave for Germany. By contrast, Johann Friedrich, who received the news of Christian Ludwig's death on his return journey from Italy, rode posthaste to Celle and prepared to proclaim that duchy his inheritance in spite of their father's will giving Georg Wilhelm, his senior, the choice between Celle and Hanover. In the quarrel that ensued Ernst August took Georg Wilhelm's side and put a regiment of Osnabrück troops at his disposal. Matters were eventually settled amicably, though – to make Johann Friedrich climb down and accept Hanover – Georg Wilhelm separated Grubenhagen from the duchy of Celle and let it be incorporated in Hanover.[1]

To Sophia, Diepholz seemed a magnificent reward for the loan of a regiment that had not even seen action; but she was less pleased with the second half of her husband's bargain with Georg Wilhelm. A legal marriage to Eléonore d'Olbreuse was denied him by the 1658 convention. She came of a decent family and Georg Wilhelm wished to make things as easy as possible for her, and to have her accepted by his own relatives. He persuaded Ernst August, who in his turn persuaded Sophia, to invite Eléonore to Osnabrück as a lady-in-waiting. In this capacity she accompanied the Osnabrück couple to Celle, where she entered into 'a marriage of conscience' with Georg Wilhelm, once the 1658 agreement had been suitably confirmed and expanded to make clear that no son of their union could ever inherit Celle. She was known as Mme de Harburg (or Harbourg) after one of the two estates which Georg Wilhelm settled on her; she was well provided for financially,* and the duke promised to be faithful to her for the rest of his life. The daughter born to them in September 1666 and christened Sophia Dorothea was much loved by both parents and her illegitimate status naturally grieved them. Being a girl, she posed no immediate threat to Ernst August and Sophia; and she seemed – providentially, from their point of view – destined to remain an only child, Eléonore's later pregnancies resulting in miscarriages or in the birth of daughters who were stillborn or did not survive infancy. But a nagging worry had come into the life of the Osnabrücks. Eléonore was known to hope for a legal marriage and was said to have told friends that the duke had promised to arrange one if she had a son. Questioned on this point by Sophia, Georg Wilhelm denied it in writing;[2] but she – even more than her husband – feared that the convention of 1658 might be overturned if not by Georg Wilhelm then on his death by his son-in-law, it being assumed that Sophia Dorothea would marry. Might not the armed forces of Celle and its riches be used to defeat the prospects of Sophia and Ernst August's children?

In spite of this family tension the two brothers kept a common front in politics, to some extent directed against Johann Friedrich. They resented his efforts, with French help, to achieve the electoral dignity for his branch of the house and did what they could to counteract them. Georg Wilhelm, a personal friend of William of Orange, speedily joined the anti-French coalition in the European war, known as the Dutch War, which escalated from Louis XIV's attack on the United Provinces in 1672. In the early years of this war Ernst August sat on the fence, having signed a treaty of neutrality with France for two years, the subsidies of which enabled him to build up the Osnabrück army. When Austria and Spain came into the war as allies of the Dutch, he joined Georg Wilhelm in a personal capacity for the campaign of 1674 and in December of that year entered into an alliance whereby, against Dutch subsidies, he would furnish 6,000 Osnabrück troops for the rest of the war. In 1675, therefore, Ernst August's troops joined those of Celle to fight, first

* She had an income of 2,000 Taler a year, to be increased to 6,000 if she survived him.

with the Rhine army of some 30,000 men under the command of
Georg Wilhelm, and next – by detachments of both Osnabrück and
Celle troops – in Bremen and Verden against Sweden which, as an
ally of France, had been manoeuvred into making a diversionary
move against Brandenburg in the Empire.[3]

THE FATHER'S PLANS FOR HIS SON

At this time George and his future prospects became the central
focus of Ernst August's calculations. Georg Wilhelm was utilizing
the goodwill which his anti-French stance earned him with emperor
Leopold. In 1671 he had prevailed upon Leopold to make Eléonore
a *Reichsgräfin* and to agree that Sophia Dorothea would be permitted
to display the arms of the house of Brunswick-Lüneburg without
the bend sinister if she married into the family of a ruling prince.
In April 1675 he went further and, with Imperial blessing, married
Eléonore in a church ceremony which retrospectively removed the
stigma of illegitimacy from Sophia Dorothea and, worse still from
the Osnabrück point of view, would unquestionably render any
future sons legitimate. The next month, to allay the fears of Ernst
August and Sophia, Georg Wilhelm once more confirmed and
strengthened the 1658 convention, but this seemed jeopardized by
the simultaneous announcement of the engagement of Sophia
Dorothea to the son and heir of duke Anton Ulrich of Brunswick-
Wolfenbüttel of the prestigious elder branch of the house. The
prospective match, in any case very much a future event in view of
the bride's age (she was nine at the time), was speedily nullified by
young Friedrich August's death in the siege of Philippsburg the next
year.

From this time onwards Ernst August made up his mind that
George would have to be married to Sophia Dorothea if suitable
terms could be arranged; any other bridegroom for the girl presented
too much of a risk for the prospects of his own family.[4] He had never
felt robust in middle age. He had put on weight and suffered from
catarrh and coughs; he feared he might not have long to live. There
was also the possibility of death in battle. It seemed desirable, apart
from giving George experience of active service, to introduce him to
the facts of the political power game which could lead to Ernst
August's goal: the electoral cap, the purple ermine-trimmed
bonnet surmounted by a golden arch, representing the highest
German dignity below the emperor – far more impressive, therefore,
than the crown of a reigning Brunswick–Lüneburg duke. Not that
such a crown was yet his, but either he or his boy would inherit one

of the Brunswick-Lüneburg duchies if the 1658 convention could be upheld; two if Johann Friedrich (married in 1668) continued to produce only daughters.

It was a blessing that George was so obedient. His mother was convinced that he would 'marry a cripple if he could serve the House'.[5] It was even more providential that he had a liking for the military life. Only by skilful deployment of his armed forces, and a constant increase of them by means of subsidy treaties, could the prince-bishop of Osnabrück advance the position of his branch of the house. And only if the troops were well trained and well led could profits, both in terms of hard cash to maintain and increase the army and in terms of prestige, be maximized. In a real sense the army was the capital with which a prince in his position had to gamble if he wished to further his ambitions. Thus it was with the deliberate purpose of testing and training the boy under battle conditions that Ernst August took George with him on the 1675 campaign.

George had been well drilled at home. He was a good horseman, had steady nerves and plenty of physical courage. His behaviour at the battle of Conzbrücke (at the junction of the Moselle and the Saar), and in the ensuing operations which forced the French to abandon the important base they had established at Trier, earned high praise from Ernst August. 'Your Benjamin was worthy of you,' he wrote to Sophia, 'he stuck to my side through thick and thin.' When Sophia visited Versailles in 1679 Louis XIV congratulated her on the victory of 1675 when two battalions of his *Maison du Roi* had been cut down by the Osnabrück guards regiment.[6] Much as Sophia feared war for the dangers it brought to husband and sons, she could not help glorying in them when they distinguished themselves in battle. In spite of her anguish she regarded this as their métier as members of royal and princely houses and was not above paying gazetteers to have their praises sung.[7]

*   *   *

During the four campaigns in which he took part in the Dutch War, George grew to maturity and became a capable officer. In 1675 his father had kept him close throughout, not only to test and train him but also to see, to the best of his ability, that he was protected from taking unnecessary risks. The fact that George served under Georg Wilhelm at the siege of Maestricht in 1676 indicates a measure of parental confidence; and by 1677 and 1678 George was reckoned experienced enough to be sent wherever he was needed and given increasingly more independent responsibilities. He got to know

the Rhine frontier and the Netherlands, made friends and acquaintances, met or heard tales of famous commanders on the allied side
and on that of the enemy. When at Osnabrück between campaigns
he was treated as a grown man. His formal education, with von
Platen as his governor and Johann von dem Bussche as his preceptor,
came to an end. He had good French, German and Latin, some
Dutch and Italian. His interests tended towards the practical, and
participation in campaigns at an early date channelled them into
maps, books on travel, geography and recent history and into a
study of the art of war. Throughout his life he remained eager to
read and hear of such matters. The books he bought as a young man
fall within these fields.[8] News fresh from the Turkish front in the
1716–18 war had to be reserved for his perusal before anyone else
had a chance to lay their hands on it.[9] He read with close attention
diplomats' accounts of their missions or of the countries they had
visited and negotiations in which they had participated.[10]

From 1679 onwards his education continued by precept and
practice. In that year Ernst August, on Johann Friedrich's death,
became duke of Hanover and began deliberately to prepare George
for his future as a ruling prince; first by visits abroad on his own,
then by fully independent command of Hanoverian troops in the
Turkish wars, and finally by discussion of aspects of the government and administration of Hanover as a prelude to his actual
participation during the years after 1694 when Ernst August became
an invalid.

With the departure of governors and preceptors after 1675 came
sexual freedom, but only after a serious quarrel in the autumn of
1676 when George was found to have put Figuelotte's under-
governess in the family way. Ernst August stormed at the embarrassment that might follow, since the lady concerned had come to them
from the Heidelberg court; Sophia took the matter more calmly.
Both parents expressed doubts whether the prospective mother was
as innocent as she claimed and hinted broadly that she had been
free with her favours; but the son she bore was the spit image of
George. Karl Ludwig's intervention on his nephew's behalf mollified
Ernst August, and George was now told that he could take to his
bed whom he wished as long as he remained circumspect enough not
to have his name bawled from the housetops as the progenitor of
bastards.[11] The child was not acknowledged and nothing is known of
its fate or that of its mother.

It would seem that George took the lesson to heart. In later years,
none of his illegitimate daughters by Melusine von der Schulenburg
was publicly admitted to be his. And if ladies, rumoured to have

been his mistresses in the late 1670s and early 1680s, brought children of his into the world, no one was any the wiser. Even the names of the mistresses have not come down to us with any certainty, though one, Maria Katharine von Meysenbug – Klara von Platen's younger sister – is so frequently mentioned in contemporary correspondence as George's companion that it has been assumed that she was, before her marriage, George's mistress. This may well have been so. It was customary for royal and princely parents to arrange (more or less discreetly) for their sons at the age of sixteen to find a trustworthy and healthy sexual partner. Louis XIV was even younger when his mother picked a lady of her choice for him,[12] and it would be in character for Ernst August to create a situation whereby the sister of his own mistress became the mistress of his son. Through Klara he could control Mlle von Meysenbug. She was good-looking and lively but of an age to be sensible (some five years older than George) and could be relied on not to create trouble when the time came for George's marriage.[13]

Ever since the death of young Friedrich August of Brunswick-Wolfenbüttel, Ernst August had put out feelers, or had entertained feelers put out by Georg Wilhelm, on terms for a dynastic union via George and Sophia Dorothea. The conditions he set were tough and stuck in his brother's throat, especially the demand for Osnabrück's occupation of at least two Celle fortresses as security for the future implementation of the 1658 convention.[14] Sophia was at this stage less keen than her husband. The thought of a *mésalliance* for her first-born grieved her. For one as conscious of *le bon sang* as she, it was frightful even to contemplate the quarterings of Sophia Dorothea's arms on her mother's side, though there was some comfort in recalling that William of Orange had done even worse by his marriage in 1677 to princess Mary of England: her mother had been a commoner, while Eléonore d'Olbreuse was of noble, if not exalted, rank. She was, however, anxious to attract other offers for George and reported him to her correspondents as 'not anxious' to marry Sophia Dorothea.[15]

Upon the return of European peace in 1678/9 there seemed less urgency and the negotiations lapsed for some considerable time. Ernst August's life was no longer in perpetual danger, and everyone's thoughts turned to foreign travel. Gustchen had taken part in the later stages of the Dutch War and the three middle boys had been to France with their tutors at varying times from 1676 to 1678. Now it was the parents' turn. Ernst August planned a visit with Johann Friedrich to Italy for the late autumn of 1679.

Relations between these two had improved ever since Johann

Friedrich's refusal to fight Osnabrück and Celle troops in the Empire as requested by Louis XIV during the Dutch War. Moreover, Ernst August wished to take the opportunity of their travelling together to discover what terms Johann Friedrich would offer to secure George as a bridegroom for one of his daughters. As they were mere children, these overtures were clearly intended to increase Georg Wilhelm's keenness. In any case, Johann returned a non-committal answer: he would think the matter over.

It had been agreed before the brothers' departure that Sophia should take Figuelotte to France to visit Louise Hollandine, now abbess at Maubuisson, and Liselotte, married to Louis XIV's brother (Philippe, duc d'Orléans) since 1671. She travelled incognito and took care to assure Georg Wilhelm that she did so in order not to bring shame on his house by submitting to rules of precedence which he might deem humiliating.[16] The duke of Celle was the laxest of rulers in respect of etiquette, Sophia was the one intent on avoiding hurt to her own pride. When queen Marie Thérèse handed her the hem of her royal skirt to be kissed, Sophia pretended not to notice and was much amused at the dodge whereby Liselotte's son (the post-1715 regent of France) avoided that particular ceremony: he bent over the hem but kissed only his own hand.[17] Sophia's hope that Figuelotte might be considered a suitable bride for the dauphin came to naught (the girl, at eleven, was far too young in view of Louis XIV's desire to secure the succession in the second generation as soon as possible); but she prepared the ground for a visit to Versailles by George and for the rest enjoyed herself greatly at the French court. Louis XIV and Philippe went out of their way to honour her and make her welcome at the ceremonies connected with the marriage by proxy of Monsieur's daughter by his first marriage to Carlos II of Spain.

THE FAMILY'S ADVANCEMENT AND GEORGE'S MARRIAGE

Sophia's own status, like that of the whole family, underwent a great change on 21 December 1679 when Johann Friedrich died unexpectedly, after two days' illness, in Ulm on his way to Italy. Since Johann Friedrich left no son, Ernst August – who had chosen another route to their Italian rendezvous and had already reached Swiss territory – now succeeded him as reigning duke of Hanover. In theory Georg Wilhelm, if he so wished, could have demanded to exchange Celle for Hanover, but there was no reason for him to do so. Celle had a rather better income; he had built himself a magnificent palace, and had perfected the hunting-grounds in the forests of Göhrde so that its *Parforcejagd* was the best in northern Europe.[18] He had also, as a reward for his participation in the Dutch War, obtained a strip of land in Bremen-Verden before these duchies were restored to Sweden – a small but significant expansion northwards which gave an impetus to further expansion at the cost of Sweden during George's reign as elector. Ernst August's words to Sophia on first meeting her after Johann's death – 'I am glad it is not I who died' – have been much quoted. It would, however, be a mistake to interpret them as proof only of callous greed. The rest of Sophia's entry shows how grieved and shaken they both were at this first death in the closer family circle, far removed from the complacent joy of those letters of 1661 in which she had given news of the long-desired death of the old prince-bishop of Osnabrück.[19]

Ernst August's succession brought the two duchies of Hanover and Celle closer together in ways which had not been possible during Johann's lifetime. Though Johann had not fought during the Dutch War,* the decidedly anti-French Georg Wilhelm had much resented the fact that Celle and Hanover were on opposite sides in European politics. Now the armies of both duchies, as well as the troops of Ernst August as prince-bishop of Osnabrück, worked together as one unit, and in the diplomatic field the two brothers were represented by the same diplomat. Regular house-conferences took place between their ministers at Engensen, halfway between their two capitals, to co-ordinate policies after due discussion. This was, in part, also intended to prepare for the future unification of the two duchies according to the 1658 convention and proved of the greatest value to George when he inherited Celle in 1705: the ministers, officers and diplomats were so well acquainted that the two administrations easily coalesced, though some struggles for the ear of the ruler could not be avoided.

In 1679 Ernst August retained in office the Hanoverian ministers and officials of his late brother, integrating his own Osnabrück courtiers and advisers into their ranks. He saw no need to make abrupt changes. Johann Friedrich's Catholicism had not influenced his overwhelmingly Protestant Hanoverians; and Ernst August was in any case used to rule over Catholic and Protestant subjects, free exercise of religion having been stipulated for Osnabrück at the end of the Thirty Years War as a necessary condition for the system of alternating rulers of the two faiths. He had tried, but in vain, to obtain the emperor's consent – on the grounds of his services to the anti-French coalition in the Dutch War – to two successive rulers in Osnabrück of his family against a provision that two Catholic bishops should next follow: an insurance policy which would have

---

* Louis XIV had appreciated his delicate position and had continued to pay him subsidies in return for his neutrality.

given George a power-base from which to safeguard his position should Ernst August die before Johann Friedrich and Georg Wilhelm. Upon Ernst August's accession to Hanover this failure became less important, though it would have been pleasant to be able to provide for one of the younger sons. His branch of the house was now firmly established and he could begin to utilize the skill and experience of the ministers he had inherited from Johann Friedrich, the most prominent of whom was the able diplomat Otto Grote, and to exploit to the full the reputation which his and Georg Wilhelm's troops had won in the Dutch War. Marlborough, who had fought under Turenne on the French side, was at that time sufficiently impressed with the Brunswick-Lüneburgers to ask for a particular regiment, known as the Parrots because of their green and red uniforms, to serve under him in the War of the Spanish Succession; and a Swedish commander, court-martialled for losses in Bremen-Verden, had argued in his defence that only the devil could withstand the Hanoverians.[20] From his position of strength Ernst August could afford to be less tough in his marriage negotiations on George's behalf. With a frontier contiguous with Celle, he could drop his demand for fortresses inside Georg Wilhelm's duchy, and with a much better income from Hanover (more than 100,000 Taler a year), he could ease his pressure in respect of money.

He was in no hurry, however, and had nothing against his wife's assessing alternative opportunities for George since this might stir Georg Wilhelm into action. While George paid his visit to France, Sophia took up a suggestion – originating with her brother Rupert – that the duke of York's younger daughter, princess Anne, might prove a suitable bride for the duke of Hanover's eldest son; and, after attending the solemn October ceremony whereby the Estates of the duchy swore loyalty to Ernst August, George went to England early in December 1680. William of Orange, whom George visited *en route*, was in favour of this match; as for the rich Celle girl, he suggested to his diplomats, she might make a suitable bride for Gustchen.[21] Even so, too much has certainly been made of George's suit and the consequences of its assumed failure. One version has it that George took a dislike to Anne and that her later enmity towards the house of Hanover can be attributed to her feelings of humiliation; another that George met with a rebuff and therefore bore a grudge towards England and the English for ever after.[22] There certainly were rumours in London and on the continent of an impending engagement. Prince Rupert may well have gossipped and to London polite society it seemed natural to assume that the young foreign prince, related to the house of Stuart on his mother's side, had come to woo an English bride, following the example of William of Orange in 1677. From speculation in contemporary journals and letters that George was bidding for Anne's hand, historians have concluded that the match was seriously pursued. This does not accord with evidence now at hand which shows that George, who was introduced to Charles II by prince Rupert, lodged at court and treated *en cousin,* was empowered to listen to proposals made to him but not to make any overtures himself or have them made on his behalf. He met princess Anne, but matrimonial prospects were not discussed. It is possible that George was not taken fully into his parents' confidence during his visit to London. Certainly, after his uncle Rupert's death, at the time of the announcement of his engagement to Sophia Dorothea, he gracefully parried the question of an earlier proposed marriage with princess Anne which Rupert's assumed wife put to him: nobody had told him of such plans at the time suggested; he had found Anne charming and would have been much honoured if a match had been proposed; now, he implied, he was happily contemplating matrimony with his Celle cousin and wished princess Anne the best of husbands whenever she decided to enter the matrimonial state.[23]

It is worth noting that one of the English observers who commented on the rumoured negotiations remarked that they were broken off when George was called home to enter into a German marriage contracted for him by his father.[24] In this the observer was premature, or possibly he conflated events in retrospect, for Ernst August was in Italy (on the vacation postponed because of Johann Friedrich's death) and nothing had been fixed with Celle when George came back to Hanover in March 1681. After Ernst August's return, a visit to Berlin in the spring of 1682, on which George and Figuelotte accompanied their parents, was more openly in search of partners. Figuelotte, it was hoped, would attract interest at the Hohenzollern court and catch one of its younger princes; and the opportunity could be taken to inspect princess Maria to see if she would serve for George. She was, however, deemed unhealthy, not at all suitable to perpetuate the line; and the duke and duchess of Hanover now began to negotiate in earnest for Sophia Dorothea.

By September 1682 everything was settled. Ernst August abandoned his claim to fortresses and declared himself satisfied with a once-only dowry of 100,000 Taler (over six years) and an annual income for the bride – to be at the husband's disposal – of 4,000. Moreover, George had stayed at Celle and found himself much pleased with Sophia Dorothea. Three letters (hitherto unknown) from Sophia to Georg Wilhelm, expressing her happiness at the union of the two families and reporting George's favourable reaction to his bride-to-be,[25] may come as a surprise in view of the general assumption that Sophia was at best resigned to the marriage and George indifferent. Sophia was not above dissimulation but parts at least of these letters carry conviction. She had reached the age when the prospect of grandchildren promises a new and rewarding experience; and her hope that she, as well as Georg Wilhelm, would have the joy 'de voir germer nos enfants ensemble comme les Sedres de Lebanon' rings true and renders it likely that her prayer to 'le grand Dieu de voloir benis son [*i.e.*, George's] mariage et nous en faire goûter toute la satisfaction que nous souhaitons d'un couple si bien assorti' was sincerely meant. Sophia might well be suspected of some exaggeration when she writes in the last letter of the three, the one of 13/23 September, of the passion which George has conceived for Sophia Dorothea: never had she believed him capable 'd'une si forte passion comme iay remarque en luy pour elle, ie crois qu'il seroit enrage s'il l'auroit venue entre les mains d'un autre'. But, taken in combination with the fact that an expression of Sophia's has been consistently misinterpreted, it must be said to prove that George could not actively have disliked Sophia Dorothea at this time. In a letter of September 10/20 (long since in print), giving news of the engagement, Sophia informs her correspondent that George is now 'avec sa maitresse'.[26] This has always been taken to mean 'mistress' in the usual sense of the word since no one has noted the fact that Sophia uses *maîtresse* in the sense of the betrothed, the affianced bride: she writes in 1671, for example, of the Danish princess Wilhelmine as the *maîtresse* of her nephew Karl of the Palatinate.[27] George, contrary to what has been accepted and hitherto taken as proof of his indifference and even contempt for the approaching marriage,[28] was not with his current 'mistress' on September 10/20 but in Celle with his bride-to-be.

The failure of the marriage of George and Sophia Dorothea was therefore not so much on the cards as has been argued with the benefit of hindsight; though those who gaze at the horoscope cast for George at his birth may be struck by the prediction that the months of June and July 1694 would be extremely adverse in his relations with the opposite sex.[29] George found Sophia Dorothea attractive and was not an unwilling bridegroom. Sophia Dorothea, sixteen when the marriage was celebrated on 22 November 1682, was thrilled at that rise in the world which her parents had so much wanted for her; but she was probably too immature, too spoilt and too undisciplined to realize what she was letting herself in for. The bridegroom's family was pleased. Sophia had decided that recognition of Mme de Harbourg as duchess of Celle was a small price to pay for the advantages gained both for the family and for *l'Etat*: for Georg Wilhelm now ceded to Hanover part of the *Grafschaft* of Hoya which made for better communications with Osnabrück.[30] She looked forward to a young companion for Figuelotte, and – as recent biographers of Sophia have realized – went out of her way to be kind and helpful to her daughter-in-law.[31] Ernst August was much taken with her, and those of George's brothers who were of an age to appreciate female beauty and high spirits thought him lucky: Sophia Dorothea was the *bellissime* of Friedrich August's letters; Maximilian was her devoted (at times she felt too devoted) escort whenever he had the chance; and Karl Philipp her adoring swain who, by chance, brought count Königsmarck to see her one morning in 1689.[32]

THE PRIMOGENITURE STRUGGLE

Long before that date the family had been torn apart by the primogeniture struggle. The new duke of Hanover, who thanks to the 1658 convention with Georg Wilhelm saw himself or his eldest son within sight of reuniting the Brunswick-Lüneburg duchies, was determined to introduce primogeniture by a will recognized by the emperor in his lifetime in order that constitutional change might stand a better chance to survive his own death. Legal preparations began as soon as Ernst August succeeded Johann Friedrich but secretly, since the ultimate goal – the achievement of electoral rank – must not be divulged too early. The opportunity to exploit circumstances in such a way that the emperor might be induced to elevate Hanover to an electorate must be awaited and the struggle to have this dignity recognized by the existing electors might prove long and hard; but until primogeniture had become the law of the land it would be far more difficult to make use of any chances that came his way. The marriage of George and Sophia Dorothea, though not constitutionally essential, formed an integral part of Ernst August's plan. It would, firstly, make it more certain that, on Georg Wilhelm's death, Celle would be joined to Hanover (there being no non-Hanover son-in-law to challenge the convention on behalf of Sophia Dorothea) and thus help convince the emperor that the new electorate would reach the necessary size and income to be able to serve the house of Habsburg usefully. Secondly, it would be easier to persuade Georg Wilhelm – if Ernst August's chance should come within the elder brother's lifetime – to stand aside and let the electoral title, to which he as the senior might lay claim, go to his cadet: after all, the dignity would mean additional honour and rank for his daughter and for his prospective grandchildren. Finally, the better the financial settlement connected with the marriage, the greater its contribution to the expensive years that lay ahead. Compensation would have to be paid to Ernst August's five younger sons for their loss of territorial expectations. Costly diplomatic missions, and valuable presents, would be needed to obtain Imperial recognition of the primogeniture and for the canvassing of the electoral cap. Treasure would have to be spent in rendering military service on a scale which, in the emperor and the Empire's opinion, would justify the innovation of a ninth electorate.

During 1682 the necessary legal drafting was completed. Primogeniture was to be decreed by Ernst August's will; and in July 1683 emperor Leopold, conscious of his need for military aid against the Turks, consented to this against a promise of Hanoverian contingents, at Ernst August's own cost, for the campaigns on the Habsburg eastern frontier. George and Gustchen were sent as volunteers to the siege of Vienna of 1683 as an earnest of the Hanoverian contingents to come.

Sophia Dorothea was pregnant when George left for the 1683 campaign and he was home, covered with glory, in time to be present at the birth of their first child in December, a boy, christened Georg August. The succession into the second generation was thus assured; and when Figuelotte's marriage to the recently widowed Friedrich, electoral prince of Brandenburg,* had been celebrated in October 1684 and Sophia and George had returned from escorting her to Berlin, Ernst August judged the time ripe to let his family know of the momentous change. He was planning a spring visit to Italy, partly as a vacation and partly to make arrangements for the Hanoverian regiments he was sending, against subsidies, to the Republic of Venice to fight the Turks. He wished to announce the primogeniture and have it accepted by his family before he left for the south. At Christmas 1684 Friedrich August and Maximilian Wilhelm were informed that every son, as he came of age, would be asked to sign an undertaking which gave him a yearly income commensurate with his position in return for acceptance of the constitutional innovation.

Friedrich August, who as the second son had to sacrifice greater prospects than the rest, would receive the largest compensation. The *Grafschaft* of Diepholz, Ernst August's personal possession, might be earmarked for him after his father's death. He would eventually have 60,000 Taler a year; in the meantime he would

---

* He was not the bridegroom angled for during the 1682 visit (who had in the meantime died), but better from the point of view of Ernst August and Sophia: as a future elector he would be in a position to help Hanover achieve recognition of the hoped-for electorate in the Empire.

receive a yearly allowance of 12,000.[33] Much to his father's annoyance, he refused this offer and would not listen to any terms. He had made something of a reputation in the later stages of the Dutch War and had, like George, distinguished himself against the Turks in the 1683 and 1684 campaigns. He felt dispossessed, his honour damaged: 'Je me vois perdus et mal heureux toute de ma vie.' Sophia's preaching and pleadings were pushed aside, as were her promises to work with Grote to have his eventual income nearly doubled. What he wanted was not assurance of his father's sympathy for him in his wild grief, but that Sophia should help him change Ernst August's mind. This she could not do, nor did she try. Her ultimate loyalty was to her husband and to his house; she could not press him to give up the chance to remedy the damage his own father had done by decreeing the splitting of the Brunswick-Lüneburg duchies contrary to the spirit of earlier attempts to work towards primogeniture. When he realized this, Gustchen took active steps at foreign courts to overturn Ernst August's plans. He found support with Anton Ulrich of Brunswick-Wolfenbüttel, anxious to stifle Hanoverian primogeniture lest it lead to a Hanoverian electorate; and with the help of the senior branch he agitated, if in vain, to have his father forced to confirm the will of duke Georg.

The break between father and son soon became complete. From Venice on 3/13 April 1685 Ernst August accused Friedrich August of attempting to govern him by disputing 'le pouvoir de père sur ses enfants' in matters which affected the conservation of the family and the state.[34] In the spring of that year Friedrich August chose to take service with an Imperial regiment, while Maximilian – his junior – was given command of the Hanoverian troops in Venetian pay. Gustchen continued to correspond with Sophia and she, anxious to minimize hostility between her first-born and her second son, urged him to see George during the 1685 campaign. He did so, but the bitterness with which he contrasted George's *bel equipage et cartiers* [*i.e.*, quarters] and his own *vie de hazarre*, dependent on gambling at cards in the hope of improving the miserable state of his finances, hurt Sophia to the quick. Karl Philipp – by insisting that his father buy an Imperial regiment for him – showed that he shared Gustchen's views, though he did not break openly with Ernst August.[35]

Maximilian signed the primogeniture clause in 1687, but after the death of Friedrich August in battle towards the end of 1690 he reneged. He was now the second surviving son and in his turn regarded the primogeniture as unjust. History repeated itself. Max got in touch with Anton Ulrich and tried to collect other allies.

He found more sympathizers inside Hanover than Friedrich August had done, and two members of the von Moltke family became heavily implicated in his machinations. It is a debatable point whether Sophia's activities on behalf of Maximilian amounted to treason.[36] Her preoccupation, intensified by her grief at losing both Karl Philipp and Friedrich August in battle in a single year (1690), was with pacifying those who felt themselves disinherited. She attempted this in two ways: by stressing the need for submission to the father's reform and advising settlement on the terms offered, and by attempting to help the rebels to positions and/or marriages which would enable them to enjoy honourable status in the world. In 1691/92 her situation was more delicate than in 1685; and though the present writer would not accept the treason charge, it has been proved that Sophia was not totally ignorant of Max's contacts with foreign courts. Certainly, when Max's collaborators were jailed, and he himself put under house-arrest in February 1692, suspicion touched her: had she condoned Max's treasonable activities?

In 1685 she had declined Ernst August's invitation to come with him to Italy, mainly because she wished to stay closer to home. Figuelotte was expecting a child. Sophia wanted to go to Berlin for the confinement,* and she also felt useful in keeping an eye on George and Sophia Dorothea's boy (in the care, as his father had been, of Mme von Harling) when her daughter-in-law travelled to Italy to see the sights and be reunited with her husband after the 1685 campaign. Ernst August had sympathized with his wife's reasoning; he did not take umbrage at her refusal and did not connect it with her support of Gustchen. But in 1692 Sophia had to defend herself against accusations of direct implication in Maximilian's plans. The fact that she addressed her defence to privy councillor Albrecht Philipp von dem Bussche shows that Ernst August's suspicions were strong enough to cause a temporary interruption of all communication between the spouses. The breach was not made public and was in any case brief. Maximilian saved himself – with the help of Georg Wilhelm – by a fresh signature of the primogeniture, and Ernst August accepted that Sophia had been ignorant of the extent of their son's treachery.[37]

The crowning of their joint hopes, the electoral cap, helped to restore their good relations. Ernst August and his ministers, and especially Otto Grote, had played their cards cleverly at the outbreak in 1688 of the so-called Palatinate War† of emperor and Empire against Louis XIV. French diplomacy had worked hard to keep Hanover neutral and the duke had been able to play off

---

* Sophia was present at the birth of Figuelotte's first son who died in infancy (as did her second son); the first to survive was Friedrich Wilhelm, born in 1688.
† In English present-day historiography usually labelled the Nine Years War, the older label of the War of the League of Augsburg having proved inaccurate (some of the members of that league remained neutral in the war). From the German point of view,

Versailles against Vienna.[38] George was sent as a volunteer to help
defend the gates of the Empire against France; Ernst August,
Maximilian and Christian Heinrich put in appearances on the
western front at various times and places; but full military commitment of the Hanoverian forces was to be had only at the price of the
electoral dignity signed and sealed.

Meanwhile, Ernst August made overtures to the Maritime Powers
and the German electors, sending auxiliary contingents (against
subsidies) for the 1690 and 1692 campaigns and promising Hanover's formal entry into the war if they would agree to the ninth
electorate and, preferably, agitate for it with Leopold. To the
Catholic electors he did not scruple to hint – unknown to the Protestant courts – that he was considering conversion to the Church of
Rome, hoping that this might make them willing to accept his
candidature. His troops were needed. Georg Wilhelm was brought
to agree that, if and when the electoral dignity should come to the
house of Brunswick-Lüneburg, Ernst August should achieve the
honour at first hand and not, as the duke of Celle would have preferred, succeed his elder brother in the rank. William III, as king of
England and stadholder of the Dutch Republic, arranged for subsidies and put his diplomatic weight behind the claim for the ninth
electorate. Spasmodic support came also from Ernst August's son-
in-law, since 1688 elector of Brandenburg and thus able to influence
other electors. The emperor, hard-pressed – though aware of and
not averse to the fact that Hanover's introduction into the Electoral
College would be a matter for further lengthy negotiations – gave in.
In December 1692 Grote, kneeling before Leopold, had the honour
of delivering on Ernst August's behalf the oath of allegiance as
elector, and preparations for Hanoverian participation in the next
campaign began in earnest. In March 1693 an Imperial envoy
arrived in Hanover with the electoral cap which the ninth elector
placed on his own head in a grandly staged ceremony.

This was a moment of triumph for Sophia and Ernst August. The
role which they had envisaged for their court and worked for after
1679 had not proved over-ambitious. The Leineschloss, forbidding
and dark after the new Osnabrück palace, had been greatly improved. Old buildings had been torn down to give Sophia an
uninterrupted view of the Leine river and private access to its islands.
The Rittersaal, the great presence chamber, had been embellished
with portraits and coats of arms of Guelph ancestors, and the present
family had been depicted for posterity between 1684 and 1690.[39]
The theatre built by Johann Friedrich had been transformed into the
grandest opera house in northern Europe, with a seating capacity of

the Palatinate War is the best choice, since Louis XIV resented Leopold's close ally,
Philipp Wilhelm of Pfalz–Neuburg, succeeding Sophia's childless nephew, Karl; Louis
started what he hoped would be a limited diversion in the Palatinate also because he
wished to encourage the Turks to continue their war against the Austrian Habsburgs.

2,000. At its inauguration in 1689 Steffani's *Enrico Leone* (with libretto by Mauro) had been performed to glorify the house by reminding Europe of its descent from Heinrich *der Löwe*. Leibniz, the librarian and intellectual factotum of Johann Friedrich, had been commissioned to write the *Historia Domus*.[40] Progress was to be slow, in spite of the farming-out of specific enquiries to minor diplomatic agents; Beyrie in London, for example, was sent to the Tower to go through the old records in the hope of finding material relating to the Mathilde marriage.[41] In the process, however, Sophia and Leibniz became well acquainted. Sophia always enjoyed the company of learned men. At Heidelberg Spanheim had been a particular friend and adviser;[42] and in Hanover – apart from Leibniz – she especially valued Georg Wolters Molanus, rector of the renowned secular abbey at Loccum. She liked exposing her children to religious and philosphical discussion in the hope that they might come to share their mother's latitudinarian and ecumenical views. She was happy to report to Leibniz that her eldest son had, to her mind, got the better of Molanus in argument: George, she stressed, was as much a materialist (*i.e.*, a rationalist) as she herself and her comment that Figuelotte was as yet 'of no religion' is well known.[43] Sophia's marriage contract had stipulated that she should have the right to exercise 'in private' the Calvinist religion in which she had been brought up, but in practice she did not think it mattered whether one worshipped according to the Lutheran, Calvinist or Catholic creed.

The religious tolerance of both parents gave a cosmopolitan character to their court. In their Osnabrück days they had employed Catholic Italians as architects and gardeners, composers and musicians, painters and poets; and others, often related to those who already served, were taken over from Johann Friedrich. Several bore church titles and office: Mauro was an abbé, Steffani became a bishop. As part of Ernst August's diplomatic preparations for the electorate he agreed that a Catholic church should be built in Hanover; and in George's reign as elector a Calvinist church was built for the French Huguenot community, which numbered about 1,000, most of whom had settled in Hanover after Johann Friedrich's death, and another for the German Calvinists.[44]

Quite a few Huguenots were in court service, the most famous of them in Ernst August's reign being the landscape gardener Martin Charbonnier who had worked for Sophia in Osnabrück and was called to Hanover in 1682; and in George's time the painter La Fontaine, the son of a Huguenot connected with the court theatre. Charbonnier, and his son after him, were much used at Herrenhausen, the summer court residence established by Johann Friedrich (on the site of a small hunting-lodge of duke Georg's), and enlarged and embellished by Ernst August's Italian architect from his Osnabrück days, Quirini. The Osnabrück stock of orange trees was transferred to Herrenhausen and rare plants and exotic shrubs were bought abroad; sculptures (of sandstone painted white, since marble would not stand the northern climate) by the Dutch artist Pieter van Empthusen were put in place; cascades, grottoes and fountains were fashioned or improved; green apartments enclosed by clipped hornbeam and linden 'walls', but open to the sky, took shape; and an open air theatre, the *Gartentheater* (still in use) was created between 1689 and 1692.[45]

At Herrenhausen the court spent each summer from May till October. It did not, however, totally remove itself from the capital even during these months. Sunday church service in Hanover was obligatory for members of the ducal family and those of the courtiers and ministers who had built summer residences near Herren-hausen, and frequently Saturday as well as Sunday found the court in Hanover. This enabled contact to be maintained with those officials and ministers who had stayed in the capital during the week or who had their country estates – where they hoped to spend at least part of the summer – at a greater distance. It also kept the ducal family popular with the townspeople.

So did the carnival which Ernst August had introduced on the Venetian pattern to enliven the season before the annual move to Herrenhausen. Relatives of Ernst August and Sophia, foreign diplomats and visitors, came from far and wide, and tradespeople found the carnival season profitable.[46] Some of the entertainments offered were open to burghers and non-noble visitors; and the masques, mythological plays and parades could be enjoyed at several levels. To see the ducal family and their relatives dressed up as gods and goddesses in intricate and lavish tableaux was sufficient amuse-ment for some; others sensed the message of glorification of the ruling house which the masques were meant to convey; and for the connoisseurs the professional singers, actors and musicians put on performances of a high standard.

GEORGE'S DIVORCE

The carnival of 1693 was particularly magnificent to celebrate worthily the Hanoverian electorate. It opened immediately after the Rittersaal ceremony, in which – as in all the public and private entertainments that followed – Ernst August and Sophia's surviving children and all members of their two families who approved of the ninth electorate were either present or had sent representatives. George, as the electoral prince, had a prominent place with his wife, now styled electoral princess, and their children: Georg August, nine years old, and Sophia Dorothea, named after her mother and the fruit of the Italian rendezvous, nearly six. Their marriage, however, was no longer a happy one. Sophia Dorothea, who in 1683 had accompanied her husband part of the way when he set out to help defend Vienna and who had – on the evidence of the first gentleman of her household, Hans Kaspar von Bothmer – been longing for his return,[47] had by 1686 become indifferent to him, according to her lady-in-waiting Eleonore von dem Knesebeck.[48] Whether this was George's fault or her own is difficult to decide. Her husband, conscious of his duties to the house and absorbed by the responsibilities which came his way as commander of the Hanoverian forces sent to fight the Turks in 1684 and 1685, was absent for the better part of the year; and Sophia Dorothea had insufficient resources in herself not to be bored. She was too different in outlook and interests to make friends, at any significant level, with either Figuelotte or Sophia. In middle age she took up Sophia's habit of stitching chair-seats and found it soothing to jangled nerves, but in her youth her mother-in-law seemed to her stuffy and dull and Figuelotte a bluestocking, not interested in 'externals'. To them she seemed undisciplined, forever impatient of etiquette and forms which they took for granted, and stupidly superficial in her constant preoccupation with dressing to kill, or at least to outshine, countess von Platen whose privileged position at court she resented. Sophia was disturbed enough by her daughter-in-law's behaviour to comfort herself when Figuelotte left home for Berlin at the age of fifteen that she would no longer risk being spoilt by Sophia Dorothea's example.[49] The difference which Aurora von Königsmarck noted in 1693 between the two sisters-in-law – whom she had ample chance to observe at the ceremonies and carnival entertainments of that year – is shrewdly described. Figuelotte is characterized as 'beauté charmante', Sophia Dorothea as 'beauté tyrannique'.[50]

While Sophia Dorothea's boredom with life in Hanover and with George soon spilt over into tantrums and scenes, it was George who first sought comfort outside marriage. Melusine von der Schulenburg (christened Ehrengard Melusine, but always known by her second name as her signature to letters and its use in her will shows) had become a *Hoffräulein* to George's mother in 1690; and she became George's mistress not later than 1691, since their first daughter was born January 1692. It was also in 1690 that Sophia Dorothea began her clandestine correspondence with the Swedish count Philipp Christoph von Königsmarck, a colonel in the Hanoverian army since 1689; but it was not until 1692 that they became lovers. Circumstances and family connections played their part in forging new emotional relationships for both George and his wife. Melusine came of an illustrious Altmark family who traced their ancestors back to the thirteenth century. Her own branch had long been settled in the Magdeburg region, after it had become part of the Hohenzollern state in 1648, and owned estates and held offices there.[51] Her eldest brother, Johann Matthias (the later field marshal), was in Brunswick-Wolfenbüttel service; this and the Brandenburg connection made Melusine appreciated at the Hanover court. For Sophia Dorothea, Königsmarck meant a link with Celle; one of his sisters was married to a Swedish count in her father's military service and was well known to her, and Königsmarck was able to remind her that he had visited the court of her parents before her move to Hanover. She was attracted by his high spirits and his good looks; above all, his attention flattered her at a time when she sensed that she was losing her hold over her husband. Even if her own indifference had helped to bring this about, it was galling for one of her temperament and beauty to hear that her husband was paying attention to a lady-in-waiting who, though slightly younger than herself, was her inferior in looks as in rank.

Melusine was tall and thin enough to be called a *malkin* (a hop-pole or scarecrow) by George's mother, annoyed at the complications which her son's love affair was bringing into her life, and the 'Maypole' in England after 1714* where she was contrasted to the 'Elephant', George's half-sister, Sophie Charlotte von Kielmansegg, who by then had become quite matronly in figure.[52] The one known portrait, head and shoulders only, from Melusine's youth shows a most attractive, if shy, face; but compared with the petite and charmingly plump Sophia Dorothea, there may well have been something awkward and gawkish in Melusine's carriage caused by her consciousness of being taller than most women and certainly taller than George. In temperament she differed strongly from Sophia Dorothea. She was pliant and patient, a welcome relief to George from his wife's petulant and stormy personality. She tried to please and to soothe, she shared his interest in music and the theatre, she studied him and his moods, and learnt to manage him. That she was useful to George after 1714 is clear from the way she took the initiative in making friends with English ladies known to have influence with their husbands in high positions, and in the manner in which he permitted her to become a kind of sounding-board for ministers in mat-

* Melusine was born in 1667 and was thus seven years younger than George, not – as English historiography has it – one year older. In her later years she did put on weight, as confirmed by a three-quarter length portrait recently become available.

ters where they were reluctant to approach him directly.[53] Her devotion to George was never doubted by his family, or by hers. It is implied in the letters of George's mother and youngest brother and in those of Melusine's eldest brother; it is made explicit in the section which George's Prussian granddaughter, Wilhelmine, devoted in her memoirs to the lady she was brought up to accept as her grandfather's morganatic wife.[54] Wilhelmine's characterization of Melusine as a person 'without either vices or virtues' must of necessity be second-hand, derived from her mother – George's daughter – who often visited Hanover and was friendly with Melusine (using her at times, like the British ministers, to figure out the best way to broach a subject with the king-elector), and from the many courtiers, men and women, who travelled between Hanover and Berlin on various missions. It is in any case curiously incomplete. Melusine's kind disposition is not in doubt. The *Gräfin* zu Schaumburg-Lippe, who knew her well both in Hanover and in England, praised her concern 'to do all the good she can',[55] but Melusine was not as meek and mild as both descriptions might seem to imply. She was intelligent and well-educated, though clearly not as clever as either George's mother or sister. Her French spelling was near perfect, far better than that of George's daughter-in-law, Caroline, and she wrote well also in English. She knew how to sum up people and amused George by cleverly cut paper figures of ministers and others at court which she sometimes exaggerated to the point of caricature.[56] She was, or became with experience, shrewd, and her letters are not without their pointed remarks when she deemed this necessary. In 1720 she let Aislabie know, if politely, that she felt he had mismanaged her South Sea Company stock; and in 1730 she asked Robert Walpole, somewhat tartly, to transfer to her, since she 'had need of it', the whole of the sum which had been left in trust with him on her behalf by the late king.[57]

But before 1714, and particularly before George's divorce in 1694, her position was less assured. Three daughters were born of their union, [Anna] Louise in 1692, [Petronella] Melusine, who like her mother always used her second baptismal name, in 1693, and [Margarethe] Gertrud, known in the family as Trudchen or Trutjen, in 1701 – beautiful enough to earn the soubriquet *die schöne Gertrud* among Hanoverian courtiers in England. The eldest daughter was also reckoned a great beauty; as for the middle girl, our sources tell us that she was good-looking and that she was spirited enough to speak her mind to George on issues, even political ones, where she disagreed with him. That they formed part of George's close family circle even before all three came to England with Melusine is clear

from the letters which George's youngest brother, Ernst August,
wrote to a friend between 1703 and 1726. From 1707 onwards he
makes a number of references to them: Louise goes to the opera with
Melusine; young Melusine becomes a *Hoffräulein* with the dowager
electress; Trutjen at the age of six reads the newspaper to George
at Pyrmont with the gravity of an adult, at twelve she – always
George's favourite – is permitted to join his hunting-party at Göhrde,
she is a real tomboy, hoping to be a soldier when she grows up.[58]

Yet none of the daughters was ever legitimized or even publicly
acknowledged. The first two were registered as the children of
Melusine's sister Margarethe Gertrud, married to a Schulenberg relative, Friedrich Achaz; and the youngest – since Margarethe Gertrud
was no longer alive in 1703 – as the child of another sister, Sophie
Juliane, and her husband, Rabe Christoph von Oeynhausen. They
were all three known as Melusine's nieces, though in the case of the
two younger there are contemporary direct references to rumours
that they were Melusine's children by George and, in the case of the
eldest, expressions in the Ernst August letters mentioned above which
show that he did not include Melusine among Louise's 'aunts'.[59] In
recent years German historians have concluded with 'near certainty'
from a variety of evidence – such as the financial support Melusine
gave the putative parents, the girls' move to England in 1714, and the
titles and/or marriages George arranged for them – that they were
George's daughters by Melusine.[60] This conclusion is strengthened
by an analysis of the Ernst August letters and rendered inescapable
by Melusine's will of 1743. By that time Trudchen had long been
dead; but Louise and young Melusine were both alive. In the will
the beneficiaries are strictly defined by relationship (her one surviving sister, her many nephews and nieces individually named),
while in the cases of Louise, countess of Delitz, and Melusine,
dowager countess of Chesterfield, only their formal titles preface
the financial arrangements made for them. We know that the
duchess of Kendal (the title by which Melusine was known in
England after 1719) was a regular churchgoer, at least in her later
years, and the phraseology of the religious preamble to the will is
less stereotyped than those usually encountered. It would seem,
therefore, that the solemnity of the occasion made it impossible for
her to perpetuate the lie which had been forced upon her by circumstances. Whether the daughters themselves were ever informed of
their true parentage is impossible to decide with certainty. The
requests in the wills of the countess of Delitz (1773) and the dowager
countess of Chesterfield (1778) that they be buried with the remains
of the duchess of Kendal in the family fault in the South Audley

Street chapel* sustain the assumption that they had been told; so
do the lightly veiled references to George being the father of Gertrud
in the letters of her mother-in-law, the *Gräfin* zu Schaumburg-
Lippe.[61] There is also, however, an adverse indication: Louise in
her own will disposes of a sum of money she has inherited from a
Schulenburg 'brother' (a 'cousin' if she had wanted to reveal her
true parentage); but this may be explained by her concern for the
proprieties.

That George refrained from legitimizing, or even acknowledging,
his daughters with Melusine is at first sight surprising. Acknowledged
illegitimate children were common in princely houses. They had the
right to the arms of their father – though pierced with the bar
sinister. Care and money were often lavished on them. Within the
Brunswick-Palatinate circle one can think of the much-loved son of
Karl Ludwig mentioned above, and of Buccolini (in Germany
known as Buccow), the son of duke Georg Wilhelm from his pre-
Eléonore days – the object, Sophia Dorothea recalled, of the worst
quarrel she had ever witnessed between her parents.[62] If an illegitimate child was legitimized, as Sophia Dorothea herself had been,
its position improved dramatically since legitimization brought full
acceptance in the princely or royal family. Contemporaries were
well aware of the influence wielded at Versailles by Louis XIV's
children by La Vallière and Mme de Montespan. Nearer home –
from the Hanoverian point of view – was the case of Maurice, the
son of Aurora von Königsmarck (one of Philipp Christoph's sisters) by Augustus of Saxony-Poland. Maurice had been well received
at George's court even before his legitimization since his military
education had been entrusted to Melusine's brother, Johann
Matthias; but when in his sixteenth year he was legitimized and
given the title comte de Saxe, his social position became secure all
over Europe.[63] The court of Hanover showed a lively interest in
relatives on the wrong side of the blanket, but legitimized, whom
George discovered when he was campaigning in the Netherlands
during the Nine Years War.[64] A morganatic marriage with the
mother of the illegitimate children, legitimized or soon to be legitimized, often brought great happiness, as did Karl Ludwig's marriage
to the left hand with Louise von Degenfeld and the consequent elevation of their sons and daughters to raugraves and raugravines; but
– from the children's point of view – their exclusion from the succession
at times caused jealousy of the legitimate heirs to titles and crowns.

In George's case there were, however, strong inhibitions against
the acknowledgement or legitimization of his daughters by Melusine.
The two elder ones were born before his divorce, and his father

---

* [Petronella] Melusine ordered in her will that the vault should be closed up after her
own funeral, conscious that she and her elder sister, both childless, were the last of the
line in England. The youngest girl, married in 1721 to *Graf* Albert Wolfgang zu Schaumburg-Lippe and dead – to George's and Melusine's great grief – in 1726, had two sons.
Of these the elder died, unmarried, before his father, and the younger who succeeded to
the government of the *Grafschaft* in 1748 died without male issue in 1777.

demanded discretion as long as he lived. The divorce itself became (as we shall see) inextricably intertwined with concern that scandal should not besmirch the newly-won – but not yet generally accepted – electoral title. Once the electoral status was safe (security having been gained in two stages, in 1708 and in 1713/14), great inconveniences and much embarrassment would have been caused by introducing the subject of George's paternity of girls who had long been known as Melusine's nieces. In England after 1714 public acknowledgment and/or legitimization would have served to rake up the old story of Königsmarck's disappearance and Sophia Dorothea's imprisonment. The very fact that all three were daughters also rendered the matter less of a problem. They had not – like sons – to make their own way in the world; they would marry or, if not, live protected within the family circle.

*   *   *

Whether Sophia Dorothea knew that [Anna] Louise and [Petronella] Melusine were Melusine's daughters is impossible to tell; but George's growing attachment to his mother's young lady-in-waiting, *La Schulenburg* or *die Schulenburgin*, was common knowledge in court circles: Königsmarck in his letters to Sophia Dorothea openly referred to Melusine as George's mistress, and Sophia Dorothea in conversation claimed that her husband cared as little for her as she did for him.[65] He cared, however, for the proprieties and for his reputation. It was a commonplace of the age that ruling princes demanded virtuous wives: how else could the succession be preserved without debasing the line and mixing bastards with those who possessed the true hereditary right of succession? This view ultimately derived from the concept of the ruler as chosen by God; but it was held even by those who did not consciously accept the religious reasoning: the whole system would be upset if a ruler could not be sure that his heir was the fruit of his own loins.

If Sophia Dorothea had been discreet, or if she had been content to have an admirer of the precious and mannered kind permitted to fashionable ladies, tragedy might not have overwhelmed her. But her feelings proved too strong for her. At first she lightheartedly thought that she could control her flirtation with Königsmarck, permitting him to write to her (his first letter is dated July 1690) without sending him letters in return. From there she passed to consenting to and even encouraging secret meetings when he came to Hanover at the end of that year's campaign. His temperament – ardent, poetic – contrasted with George's matter-of-fact attitudes. He was dashing and persuasive, adoring yet imperious, sensuous rather than sensible. His jealousy of George was intoxicating. She began to write to him when he was absent from Hanover.

About half of their correspondence has survived. They were in the habit of sending their letters for safe-keeping, every half-year or so, to Philipp's sister Aurora. On her death these passed to their elder sister, Amalia Wilhelmine, married to count Lewenhaupt (the one in Celle service), and remained in the possession of Lewenhaupt descendants until the nineteenth century when they were donated to Lund University library and made available to scholars. The letters missing from this set turned up in the Prussian royal archives, having been sent in 1754 by queen Lovisa Ulrika of Sweden to her brother Friedrich II, who marked the file in his own hand 'Lettres d'Amour de la Duchesse D'allen au Conte Königsmarc'. Other portions of the correspondence must be presumed lost. Those from the second half of 1693 and the first half of 1694 were sent to safety by Königsmarck's secretary after the count's disappearance; but we lack any information about their fate after the 1720s when they were offered, in vain, for sale successively to George and to Sophia Dorothea. Letters intercepted at Hanover, and those which were found in Sophia Dorothea's room in 1694 (sewn into curtain linings or hidden at the bottom of playing-card boxes), have now disappeared and may have been destroyed by George II.[66]

With the major part of the Sophia Dorothea-Königsmarck correspondence as evidence, we can watch how the tone between the two letter-writers changes as their relationship develops. Mutual attraction clearly swept them off their feet and from March 1692 the letters prove that they were lovers in the physical sense. They also convince us that they loved each other and had come to believe that they could not live without planning for a future when their devotion should be open and permanent. Since Sophia Dorothea insisted – as long as she lived – that she had not been unfaithful to her husband (the most she would admit, long after the divorce, was that she might have 'offended' him), and Eleonore von dem Knesebeck, her lady-in-waiting, would testify only to 'amitié et conversation familiale' between her mistress and Königsmarck, the letters, when published, created quite a stir.[67] Historically it is of no significance whether Sophia Dorothea committed adultery or not (though historians have not failed to take sides, sympathy usually being given to Sophia Dorothea),[68] for – as we shall see – her divorce from George was at her own wish, on the grounds that she refused cohabitation and the restitution of conjugal rights. But the letters also help to show how and why the love affair between George's wife and Königsmarck became a matter of state.

From the very first their affair was talked about. When they were in the same place, in Hanover or in Celle, they had to take too many people into their confidence – or half-confidence – to preserve total secrecy. Pre-arranged signals and even their glances betrayed them; notes left for Königsmarck by Eleonore von dem Knesebeck in his hat or gloves could be spotted; Königsmarck's servants were not always careful or silent. When they were apart, which was more often than not, in spite of Königsmarck's leaving the 1692 campaign without permission and contriving to remain in Hanover for most of the 1693 campaign, the volume of their correspondence made them vulnerable: quite apart from their own need to write to bridge the distance that separated them, the practical arrangements for secret meetings meant frequent letters and messages. Philipp's sisters and brother-in-law helped them a good deal, as did Eleonore von dem Knesebeck; but less careful go-betweens often had to be trusted. That they managed to meet was a measure of the risks they were willing to take; but they were also assisted by the preoccupations of Sophia Dorothea's Hanover and Celle relations with urgent political matters: the campaigns in the west, the Maximilian conspiracy, the electoral issue and, not least, the Danish attack on Ratzeburg in 1693 which kept Celle in fear of invasion.

Warnings were administered to both of them that the affair must come to an end: to Sophia Dorothea by her own mother, by Sophia, by Figuelotte on her visits to Hanover; to Philipp by George's brothers, by his fellow-officers and by the head of the Hanoverian army, field marshal von Podewils. The lovers tried to bluff. They lied. Philipp gave Podewils his word that there was 'nothing in it', and this gained them some time. Ernst August was sufficiently worried to bar Aurora von Königsmarck from visiting Hanover and broad hints were dropped to Philipp that he had better look for employment elsewhere. Attempts were made to keep Sophia Dorothea with her husband's family when he was on campaign, so that there should be fewer opportunities for her to meet Philipp; but she knew how to defeat them by all kinds of stratagems. A favourite one was to complain that her brother-in-law Maximilian was lodged too near her at Linsburg and Herrenhausen to be decent during her husband's absence, another was feigned illness. She also engineered appeals from her parents that she might stay with them at Celle where she felt freer. George had to consent to such visits, for the sake of Hanover's relations with the duke of Celle, though in his letters to his wife he suggested (with no effect) that her stay should be as short as possible. When absent on campaign, George wrote regularly to his wife. Indeed, once when Sophia

Dorothea wanted to rile Königsmarck, she stressed that her husband's letters were more frequent than his. The one fragment which has survived (because Sophia Dorothea quotes it to Philipp) is dry to the point of irony on the subject of her 'Maximilian excuse' for leaving his parents' roof: George congratulates her on being 'a veritable Lucretia' with whom his honour is 'very safe'. Taken in conjunction with other bits from George's letters which Sophia Dorothea passes on to Philipp, this may be interpreted as a warning to his wife; he takes care to inform her, for instance, of the gambling debts which Königsmarck has run up in Flanders during earlier campaigns and hints that this may be a reason for his not wishing to serve there in 1693.[69]

The warnings, though Sophia Dorothea made light of them to Eleonore von dem Knesebeck, did get through to the lovers. The theme of arrest and imprisonment for both of them, and death for Königsmarck, becomes one of the three recurring topics of the correspondence, the other two being intense jealousy that the beloved bestows affection elsewhere,* and the planning and plotting how to start a new life together. Here, money was the rub. Philipp had run through a sizable fortune by gambling and by his urge to cut a fine figure: a bachelor, he kept twenty-nine servants when the average, even for the households of great Hanoverian ministers, was twenty. And though he had expectations, his present financial affairs were in total disarray. Reading through her marriage contract, Sophia Dorothea was disagreeably surprised to find that she had nothing she could call her own; she began agitating to get an independent income from her parents, though without divulging her ultimate objective. She had no success. Celle's conflict with Denmark channelled her father's cash resources into the army. Her mother could only dispose of her jewellery and did not think it worth risking her husband's displeasure by selling it for no apparent immediate need. She knew that Sophia Dorothea hoped to end her marriage to George, but neither parent approved of this and they tried their best to dissuade her. In 1694, on the accession of Augustus of Saxony,† Königsmarck went to Dresden to claim a gambling debt of 30,000 Taler which the new elector owed him from the Netherlands campaign of 1691. Augustus, hard up for cash since the funeral of the late elector had to be paid for, offered his friend a Saxon regiment instead. This was accepted, and gave Königsmarck a measure of security.

An elopement was indeed much feared at the Hanoverian

---

* Though Philipp hated the thought of George's *monter à cheval* (a euphemism for sexual intercourse) with Sophia Dorothea, he urged submission to her husband's embraces lest they be discovered. His jealousy was more inflamed by rumours of her flirtations, and she – who flew into passionate anger when she heard he had been to or given parties where ladies were present – was not above taunting him by pretending to have become attracted to one of her other admirers.

† His electoral title was Friedrich August I, but he is so well known as Augustus II, king of Poland from 1697, that it would be pedantic to use any other name.

court. With the freedom which Königsmarck's Saxon appointment
implied, he might make arrangements to send Sophia Dorothea to
Saxony or even further afield; or – worse still – he might persuade
her to take refuge with Anton Ulrich of Brunswick-Wolfenbüttel.
Much would depend on his behaviour when he returned to resign
his commission and make up the accounts of his regiment; and also
on Sophia Dorothea's reactions to his presence. If the two had come
to their senses, well and good; if not, it was time for sterner measures.
Sophia Dorothea had stayed with her parents during part of the
summer of 1694, but she was back in Hanover before Königsmarck
returned there. George had gone to Berlin, to visit his sister and to
discuss the political situation with his brother-in-law. It is impossible
to say if George's journey was engineered by his parents to coincide
with the time when Königsmarck was expected back; whether
fortuitous or not, it served the purpose of keeping him abroad in a
period when delicate problems might arise. It is significant
that George was left uninformed of the events which followed
the night of 1/11 July 1694 for several weeks. Sophia's comment
to one of the raugravines, 'Meanwhile George is with his sister
in Berlin and knows nothing of what has passed here,' sounds too
pat.[70]

Accounts deriving in part from contemporary romances but also
from consciously misleading reports supplied by Hanover and Celle
authorities (though without, as will be seen below, any mention of
Königsmarck) assume a firm plan by the lovers to elope on Philipp's
return to Hanover. We now know that this was not so. Königsmarck
had to join his Saxon regiment on the Rhine and had given orders to
his household that all should be ready for his departure on 5/15
July. Quite apart from this, there was a total lack of money to set up
Sophia Dorothea in a style she would have been willing to accept.
What sealed the fate of both was their behaviour when Königsmarck
arrived in Hanover. He avoided all company, paid no calls, took no
steps to resign his commission or to put the affairs of his regiment in
order. Measured against Sophia Dorothea's attitude on her return
from Celle, this caused alarm: she had neglected to stop at Herrenhausen, where the electress expected her, and had driven straight
to Hanover where she shut herself up in her own apartments,
pleading illness. Both suspects were watched, and Ernst August –
contrary to custom – took up residence at the Leineschloss even
though it was full summer. During the night of July 1/11 Königsmarck was seen to enter the palace and make his way to Sophia
Dorothea's apartments. We have no certainty whether he ever
reached them; according to Eleonore von dem Knesebeck's testimony

(and she was threatened with torture by count Platen to make her tell the truth), he did not.[71]

That he was killed that night is beyond doubt, but whether the murder was accidental or planned we do not know. His arrest only might have been intended, but assassination seems more likely. Information received from Hanover by Anton Ulrich of Wolfenbüttel, and passed on by him to a Danish diplomat, Otto Mencken, named four courtiers as the perpetrators of the murder and gave the name of Montalban as the one who had given the killing thrust with his sword. Though the duke of Wolfenbüttel's sources of information were exceptionally good, historians would be wary of accepting his version as the likeliest explanation for Königsmarck's disappearance but for Professor Schnath's discovery that Don Nicolò Montalbano (usually called Montalban), the Italian who had endeared himself to the family during the work on the new Osnabrück palace, had settled on him shortly after 1/11 July the sum of 150,000 Taler from Ernst August's coffers. A princely reward, indeed, if it is taken into account that Montalban's salary was 200 Taler a year and that of the highest-paid electoral minister 1,500. Reward for what? It seems inescapable that this was payment for his services on 1/11 July and, at the same time, silence-money: the sum was to be paid by regular quarterly instalments. The other courtiers mentioned in Mencken's despatch were also devoted to the house: von Stubenvol was a Palatinate-born *Kammerjunker* who had married a natural daughter of Ernst August's; von Klencke was *Oberkammerjunker* to Ernst August; and Freiherr von Eltz was *Hofmeister* to young Georg August. All were men who could be expected to take firm action lest the newly-won dignity be besmirched by the scandal of an elopement.* The identification of Nicolò Montalban (for there were several of that family name at the Hanoverian court) made by Schnath lends strong credence to the correctness of the rest of Anton Ulrich's information: the names of the other courtiers involved and the method of disposing of Königsmarck's body, sunk in the Leine river in a sack weighted with stones.[72]

Once the deed was done, swift action followed. Sophia Dorothea was confined to her apartments and these were searched, revealing letters from Königsmarch, Eleonore von dem Knesebeck, anxious to get away and offered escape by a brother-in-law, was persuaded by her mistress to stay. 'If you flee,' Sophia Dorothea implored her, 'I'll be judged guilty; if you stay you can swear to my innocence and, when freed, make your way to Wolfenbüttel': advice which shows that Sophia Dorothea knew where she, and those who were

---

* Courtiers, as Schnath observes, would be more likely to be used in a murder plot than officers or soldiers, in view of Königsmarck's commission in the Hanoverian army. Montalban died in 1696, Stubenvol eventually left Hanover, but Eltz and Klencke remained in Hanoverian service, and we shall meet the former again entrusted with diplomatic missions and rising to ministerial rank.

on her side, could expect refuge.[73] In the event Eleonore was put under arrest and Ernst August and Georg Wilhelm (confronted with the evidence of the correspondence between Königsmarck and his daughter) agreed that a divorce must be arranged which suppressed Königsmarck's name altogether and concentrated on Sophia Dorothea's refusal to cohabit with George. She was removed to Ahlden, in Celle territory, and the few foreign diplomats who were told anything at all were led to believe that she had been caught in flight from Hanover to Bruchhausen to throw herself on her parents' mercy. Sophia Dorothea, initially in ignorance about Königsmarck's fate and believing that divorce would open the gates to freedom and to reunion with him, was only too keen to be divorced and firmly refused the genuine and prolonged attempts at conciliation which the court, composed of experienced Hanoverian and Celle jurists, tried to bring about. On 28 December 1694 (OS) the marriage was dissolved and Sophia Dorothea, as the guilty party, was denied re-marriage while it was specifically permitted for George. By a private arrangement between Ernst August and Georg Wilhelm, the so-called *Acte de disgrâce*, it was agreed that Sophia Dorothea should be relatively strictly confined by her father, who would give her an adequate income,* and that George should keep her dowry for the use of their children. It was not until she was a virtual prisoner, back in Ahlden after the divorce proceedings which took place in Hanover, that Sophia Dorothea realized she would not be allowed access to her children, her father did not wish to see her, and her contact with the outer world would be severely circumscribed.

Königsmarck's disappearance created a furore. Augustus of Saxony, his own family and especially the indefatigable Aurora von Königsmarck, pursued diligent inquiries to the intense embarrass-ment of the Hanoverian court. Eleonore von dem Knesebeck had been incarcerated in the fortress of Scharzfels for 'having helped to alienate her mistress's affection from George', in reality to prevent gossip. Sophia, usually so busy a correspondent, rested her quill for an unprecedented length of time. When she did take it up again, she assured her relatives that nothing was known in Hanover of Königsmarck's whereabouts. As for Sophia Dorothea, the electress was of the opinion that if a wife did not wish to live with her husband both were better apart. Brunswick-Lüneburg diplomats who tried to get information on Königsmarck's fate to satisfy the curiosity of the courts to which they were accredited drew blanks with Hano-verian and Celle superiors: there was nothing to tell.[74]

English anti-Hanoverian propaganda after 1714 blamed Sophia Dorothea's imprisonment (usually thought much harsher than it

---

* 8,000 Taler a year, to be increased on her father's death to 12,000, and to 18,000 on her entering her forty-first year.

was) on George I; it was assumed that the divorce had been at his insistence and that Königsmarck's disappearance must be laid at his door, whether the wife's lover had been murdered and laid under the floorboards at the Leineschloss or plastered into a niche or whether – as other stories had it – he had been allowed to flee the country.[75] Such various surmises are natural in view of the conspiracy of silence begun in 1694 and maintained till the mid-nineteenth century. Even the divorce suit papers were destroyed (it is thought by order of George II) and only reconstructed, at the request of the duke of Cambridge in 1826, from the detailed notes kept by one of the judges. The reasons for Sophia Dorothea's continued imprisonment are not difficult to find and amply documented in the diplomatic correspondence of the period. Between 1694 and 1708 the fate of the ninth electorate was in the balance, and Sophia became the centre round which a web of diplomatic intrigues were spun; Denmark and Wolfenbüttel were persistent enemies of Hanover, until 1700 and 1706 respectively; Saxony and Brandenburg participated in anti-ninth electorate propaganda whenever there was friction between Dresden and Hanover or Berlin and Hanover. France was mightily feared, but it is now known that Louis XIV – though he opposed the ninth electorate until 1714 – refused to stoop to intrigues: he would be willing to receive Sophia Dorothea in France if she converted to Catholicism, but he did not wish to take an active part in ensuring her escape. Nor did the duchess of Celle's efforts to alienate William III and queen Anne from Hanover by making them espouse Sophia Dorothea's cause have any effect.[76] By 1708, when Hanover was admitted to the Electoral College, the immediate danger may be said to have been over; but George's involvement after 1715 in the Great Northern War in his capacity as elector breathed new life into plans in which Sophia Dorothea could be used as a political counter in the Empire and in Britain. Jacobitism provided the connecting link. Jacobite agents tried to resuscitate the Königsmarck affair to embroil Charles XII of Sweden with Britain,[77] and three Scottish gentlemen tried as late as 1718 to gain access to Ahlden to greet Sophia Dorothea as 'Queen of Great Britain'.[78]

In the circumstances George proved firm but not vindictive. In 1698 he gave a written promise to Georg Wilhelm that the terms of Sophia Dorothea's confinement and her financial support should not be made stricter on her father's death. He sent her good financial advisers and permitted her to keep all surpluses derived from the domains she inherited from Georg Wilhelm in 1705: at the time of her death her fortune stood at 277,000 Taler, and her silver and jewellery were valued at 15,528 and 23,774 respectively. He relaxed the censoring of her correspondence and made it easier for her to receive visitors. He sanctioned visits (denied by the agreement of 1694) to Ahlden by Georg Wilhelm though none took place for reasons unconnected with George I, and permitted the widowed duchess of Celle to move from her dower-house in Lüneburg to the castle of Celle so that she might have a less strenuous journey for the many and long visits she paid to her daughter. He was seriously disturbed by the petition to be set free that she sent him on his becoming elector in 1698, but the political dangers attendant on release dictated his refusal.

Circumstances changed, however, after 1714 with the successive defeats of Jacobite invasions and plots. When in 1725, before her visit to Hanover, Sophia Dorothea, now queen of Prussia, was approached by her mother's representative, count Bar, to negotiate her liberty, the outlook seemed bright. But she found to her dismay that the plan for an amnesty which was in her mind and, she felt sure, also in that of her father was totally unacceptable at Ahlden: what George's divorced wife wanted was not forgiveness by grace, but a repudiation of the 1694 verdict to show that she had been unjustly treated. Compensation for wrongs suffered would, she wrote to her daughter, be essential for the sake of her *gloire*. If this was not freely offered, she would prefer to rely on 'the plans of her trusted friends' to gain her freedom. This was ominous news: who were these 'trusted friends' but Jacobites? The daughter told her mother that she dared not speak 'even about the amnesty' until the project she and her husband had at heart, the double marriage between two of their children with two of her brother's, was secured.[79]

After her dramatic escape from Scharzfels Eleonore von dem Knesebeck, bitterly disappointed at Sophia Dorothea's indifference, turned against her former mistress 'who wasted vast sums on clothes and luxuries while forgetting her promises to one who had risked all for her'. In 1710, casting about for taunts with which to prod Sophia Dorothea in her quest for financial support, she praised the generosity of George in refusing to listen to those who wished to betray her whereabouts as a prelude to her re-arrest, and threatened to go to Hanover to throw herself at the feet of the elector and Mlle von der Schulenburg, 'my good friend'. She received no reply. In effect, Knesebeck did not test her luck in the ninth electorate; and when she 'told all' in a letter to Sophia Dorothea's chaplain, her accusations were confined to those of ingratitude and broken promises. Sophia Dorothea may have been shrewd enough to gamble on the fact that Knesebeck would take care not to charge her with adultery and thus stand before the world as one who had committed perjury in 1694. It is equally possible, however, that, like George, she wanted to bury the past. Anything that brought 1694 to the forefront of consciousness was avoided. She refused, for instance, the offer from Königsmarck's Swedish relatives to buy those of her letters which had come into their possession.[80]

Between George I and his children the divorce was a forbidden subject: George 'froze' at any mention of Sophia Dorothea. Legend has it that Georg August as a young boy tried to get in touch with his mother and that he displayed her portrait in his house immediately upon his father's death. His presumed change of attitude to her memory in his own reign has been attributed to his reading of a document after 1727 in the Hanover archives which convinced him of her adultery.[81] Hervey, in his memoirs, has testified that George II, in a period of tension when he found relief in talk, was voluble on his own past and on his relationship with his father, but never once referred to his mother.[82]

According to continental law George I could have remarried legally if he had so wished; and, as we have seen, his granddaughter Wilhelmine firmly states in her memoirs that Melusine von der Schulenburg was George's morganatic wife, presumably in the same publicly unacknowledged way as Mme de Maintenon was married to Louis XIV. The friendly correspondence which empress Elisabeth-Christine – a Brunswick relative of George's – carried on with Melusine, and the fact that emperor Charles VI made her a *Reichsfürstin** (princess) in 1722, seem to point in the same direction.[83] The remark of Robert Walpole that the duchess of Kendal was as much 'Queen of England as anyone ever was'[84] might be taken to support the contention; but on balance the present writer concludes that the then English church law, which precluded marriage while the divorced spouse was alive, deterred George I, both before and after 1714, from making their union a formal one.

Whether legally married to Melusine or not, George formed a stable and lasting relationship with *la Schulenburg* which brought the joy of daughters close to him as well as, in time, of grandsons through Gertrud. This gave him, throughout his life after 1694, an emotional balance which increased the happiness he found in his grandchildren by his legitimate descendants, the children of Georg August and Caroline. Such comfort of the continuity of life on earth was largely denied to Sophia Dorothea, confined to the point of suffocation. She had a court of her own and lived in style with costly clothes in the latest fashion, a good table and a fine cellar. Eighty-one portraits of relatives – including George I – by blood and

---

* She was already, since October 1715, a *Reichsgräfin*, the emperor having included Johann Matthias von der Schulenburg's brothers and sisters in his elevation.

marriage hung on her walls. She could drive her carriage under observation a given distance, but she could not walk on foot outside the courtyard at Ahlden.[85] She was essentially lonely, George was not.

Yet the divorce had marked him too. We know, from a reference in a letter he wrote to Georg Wilhelm, that he was familiar with the contents of at least some of the letters from Sophia Dorothea to Königsmarck which had been intercepted or secured in July 1694.[86] It is likely therefore that he read sentences that would make the least sensitive person wince: his wife's intense desire for his death in battle, and her poor opinion of him as a lover when compared to Philipp Christoph.

Politically, though more passive than Friedrich August and Maximilian in intrigues against the ninth electorate, Sophia Dorothea had more potential power: the very size of her fortune rendered her a tempting object of foreign machinations, whether German or Jacobite. Through his relationship to Sophia Dorothea, George was taught a lesson in the danger of keeping incriminating letters; at a deeper level, after 1694, his fear of rebellion was reinforced by the intrigues in which she was involved, more or less willingly. He was made more conscious than before of his duty to the electorate as the first-born who had to secure gains already made and reach the goals set for him by his parents.

1   George I as a young man. Since the painting is attributed to Kneller, it probably dates from George's first visit to England (1680–81), when he was still
electoral prince and the possibility of his marrying Anne, later queen of England,
was a matter of speculation.

2, 3   The Palatinate grandparents, Frederick and his wife Elizabeth, through whom the British succession came to George.

4   George's father, Ernst August of Brunswick-Lüneburg.

5   George's mother, Sophia of the Palatinate. Note the pearls which were part of her inheritance from her mother. In 1714 George brought 'The Hanover Pearls' to England.

27 Kensington Palace, largely extended and re-decorated by George I, as indicated by the grey areas on the plan.

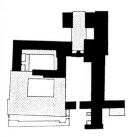

☐ NEW STATE APARTMENTS, 1718-21
COURTYARDS, 1717-26.

28 Kensington Palace: the south-west walls of the cupola room furnished and decorated by William Kent. Note the bas-relief by Rysbrack over the fireplace (*The Roman Marriage*).

29 Table in gesso at Hampton Court executed for George I. The royal cipher has unfortunately been damaged.

30, 31 A handwritten letter from George to the regent of France. Dated St James's, January 1718, it deals with important political matters.

32 'The beautiful Gertrud',
George's youngest daughter
by [Ehrengard] Melusine.
She was a constant com-
panion to her father from
her childhood onwards, and
her death in her early
twenties caused the king
great grief.

33, 34 Gertrud's children
by Albrecht Wolfgang zu
Schaumburg-Lippe. The
portraits were ordered by
George from Lafontaine,
who was in Britain to paint
the king's portrait (see
plate 40). Left, Georg
August, the elder of the
two, who died as a young
man. Right, [Friedrich
Ernst] Wilhelm, who suc-
ceeded his father as ruling
Graf of Schaumburg-Lippe.
He gained fame both for his
military talents and for his
patronage of music.

35 George's legitimate grand-children. The six younger children of the prince and princess of Wales: Anne, Amalie and Caroline, born in Hanover; William Augustus, Mary and Louisa, born in England.

36 The Prussian grand-children, Wilhelmine and Friedrich, a double portrait sent to George by his daughter, Sophia Dorothea, queen of Prussia.

37 George I shown in Roman dress: a statue, commissioned for the Rolls House, for which the king gave sittings. It now stands at the entrance to the Public Records Office Museum.

38, 39 Threat to the succession. A medal showing the Pretender, James Edward Stuart, after the birth of his son, Charles Edward Stuart (the Young Pretender). On the reverse, the symbolic Hanoverian horse is shown trampling on the lion and the unicorn. Note the effective and almost totally correct representation of London in 1721.

40 The last known portrait of George, painted by Lafontaine between 1725 and 1727, now in St James's Palace.

III

Experience gained

THE KÖNIGSMARCK MYTH

Though George did not lift a finger to save his wife from divorce and confinement, the murder of Königsmarck cannot be laid at his door: his absence in Berlin is incompatible with stories that he caught his wife and her lover *in flagranti* and killed the latter in the former's presence. Ernst August, however, must have been an accessory either before or immediately after the count's death. Tradition has ascribed a prominent share in a plot to murder Königsmarck to countess Platen and, as in all aspects of the whole affair, the few known facts have been embroidered with sensational details. We know that Eleonore von dem Knesebeck had worried lest the countess discover the lovers' secret correspondence and make trouble. We also know that Sophia Dorothea's thoughts, once she was told that Philipp was missing, flew to the countess as a possible jailer. 'Je tremble,' she wrote in an undated note to a Hanover minister whom she trusted, 'si C[omte] K[önigsmarck] est entre les mains de la dame que vous savez, que cela ne fasse tort a sa vie.'[1]

The fears of both ladies are reasonable and explicable in the circumstances. They had acted in ways which they knew would be resented by the elector; they had the memory of Maximilian's imprisonment and the execution of his chief accomplice fresh in mind;* they knew of Klara von Platen's influence over Ernst August. The general awareness of this influence, and rumours of great tension between Sophia Dorothea and her father-in-law's mistress who was assumed also to have seduced Philipp Christoph are at the base of stories which — though interesting as ingredients of popular mythology – would not be worth mentioning here but for the fact that one or more of them are still repeated in recent

---

* Otto Friedrich von Moltke, Ernst August's *Oberjägermeister* (master of the hunt) for Göttingen and Grubenhagen, had been executed in July 1692; his cousin, lieutenant-colonel Joachim von Moltke, Maximilian's adjutant, had his death sentence commuted to life-long exile as he had not taken an oath of fealty to Ernst August.

British books touching on George I: countess Platen, jealous because Königsmarck has deserted her bed for Sophia Dorothea's, determines to kill him, hires some officers to intercept him in the Leineschloss, grinds her heel in his face as he lies dying on the floor; Ernst August being informed only after the deed is done.[2]

These tales derive, with a host of others, from contemporary treatments of Königsmarck's life and death circulated in manuscript or print, with which the anonymous author of the *Histoire secrette de la duchesse d'Hanovre* (published in 1732 with many later editions and translations) spiced his concoction. His main source, volume seven of duke Anton Ulrich's *Römische Octavia*, was so discreet that it did not even hint at Königsmarck's murder. In the first version (1707), the book ends with *Aquilius* leaving court of his own will so as to save the reputation of his beloved; in the second version (1712), *Petilius Cerealis* (a clearer pseudonym for the Königsmarck figure) returns to free his beloved from unjust imprisonment and then nobly disappears from her life.[3] In both versions the lovers are innocent, the romance totally chivalric in tone.

The unlikelihood of the countess Platen figure of tradition does not need much labouring. For anyone moderately familiar with the historical background to the Königsmarck affair, the myth's lack of political content renders it suspect. On the personal level it would seem improbable that the countess would have risked her position with Ernst August by a love affair with Königsmarck; though she may, before the extent of the young man's financial inaptitude was known, have considered him a suitable bridegroom for her daughter by Ernst August. And it is incredible that she should have organized Königsmarck's murder without the elector's previous consent, given Ernst August's firm control of his entourage. It would be a reasonable assumption, however, that Ernst August discussed with her possible countermeasures, as an elopement scandal seemed imminent, and she may therefore have been an accessory to a murder plan. But the throwing of all blame on the countess, thus postulating Ernst August's innocence, may also point to an inspired story meant to divert attention from the person of the elector.[4]

What is worth stressing is that Anton Ulrich of Wolfenbüttel, when writing his romantic novel, knew more about the Königsmarck affair than anyone else outside the narrowest circle at Ernst August's court. He had excellent sources of information at Hanover: we have already seen that it was through him that the Danish diplomat Mencken learnt that Montalban was Königsmarck's assassin. He was on friendly terms and in correspondence with Sophia Dorothea's mother and thus in indirect contact with the 'Prinzessin von Ahlden'.

It was to his castle in Brunswick that Eleonore von dem Knesebeck fled on her escape from Scharzfels in November 1696, and it was to his duchy that she returned in January 1698 after she had obtained in Vienna (on his advice and with his help) a measure of Imperial protection. Bitter at an imprisonment which she considered unjust, and which certainly was irregular, she poured out stories to blacken the Hanover court, 'choses si extravagantes et exécrables' that Mencken was reluctant to put them on paper.[5] The duke may well have disbelieved some of them. But he made no use even of information which he considered reliable, though he was diplomatically most active in opposing the ninth electorate. His formal reconciliation with George in 1706 may be thought to furnish an explanation for this; but it seems more likely that he considered it incompatible with his *gloire* to pillory publicly – even in the guise of a novel – any branch of the house of Brunswick.

That Eleonore von dem Knesebeck contributed to the popular mythology of the Königsmarck affair in all its ramifications is certain. What she said in Wolfenbüttel, and probably also in Vienna, leaked out; what diplomats reported home also tended to become general knowledge. Her conviction that she had heard Königsmarck sing in a cell below hers in Scharzfels strengthened rumours that he might still be alive; and the dirt she flung at the Platens, especially at the countess, stuck. It is improbable, however, that it would have become part of 'tradition' unless it had satisfied something more than salacious curiosity. Popular mythology does pander to envy and voyeurism, but the rumours that fly about may also give expression to a sense of outrage that men and women who hold political and social power should put themselves above the moral laws by which they expect their inferiors to live. And where there is a suspicion that crimes or misdemeanours have gone unpunished, a tendency can be noted to read a fitting punishment into what happens later: the saga receives, so to speak, another instalment in which the person cast as the villain receives his or her just deserts.

Countess Platen and Ernst August are no exceptions. The elector's health began to fail in the spring of 1695, only a few months after Sophia Dorothea's divorce suit had been decided. Though various cures were attempted, he became an invalid and died in late January 1698. It has been suggested that he suffered from syphilis caught from countess Platen – the disease which was supposed to have caused her own death two years later. The only evidence for this 'fitting-punishment' theory would seem to be the stories, deriving mainly from Eleonore von dem Knesebeck, of the countess's love-affairs with younger men, including Königsmarck, and the sexual

orgies she was supposed to have organized at Linden, the Platen
country house halfway between Hanover and Herrenhausen.[6] A
recent writer, on the basis of medical advice, has diagnosed Ernst
August's illness as 'nervous debility', presumably from the symptoms
described by the electress in her letters: Sophia, while firm that
countess Platen suffered a stroke, at times ascribed her husband's
illness to 'his nerves'.[7] To a layman the symptoms (difficulty with
speech and movement) might – in view of Ernst August's corpulence
in late middle age – indicate a series of small strokes, ending in
partial paralysis. But it is not inconceivable that the strain of the
Königsmarck affair helped to bring about his illness, and that the
vexations which followed on Eleonore von dem Knesebeck's escape
from Scharzfels contributed to the worsening of his condition.[8]
Sophia's reference her husband's nerves, if set beside a cryptic comment of hers in 1694[9] just after Königsmarck's disappearance,* would
seem to bear this interpretation rather than the non-specific 'nervous
debility'. It must remain a matter of conjecture, however, whether
Ernst August's illness had a psychosomatic component. From what
we know of his temperament and general behaviour, he would, on
the level of rationalization, have found little difficulty in regarding
the Königsmarck murder as necessary for reasons of state or as a
somewhat irregular duel in which an officer who had as yet not
formally resigned his Hanoverian commission was challenged and
cut down.[10] That he considered himself justified in having Eleonore
von dem Knesebeck imprisoned is shown by the last order he signed,
on 16 November 1697, to the effect that she should be re-arrested if
caught on Hanoverian territory, and by the efforts made to have her
intercepted on her way to Vienna.[11]

By this time Ernst August had already handed over the day-to-day
government, including the signature of papers, to George. Expectations that visits to take the cure at Pyrmont and Wiesbaden would
restore the elector to health had been disappointed; and medical
advice from far and wide, eagerly followed in spite of Sophia's
disbelief in the wisdom of doctors, was no longer sought. His difficulty in articulating words embarrassed him, and in the last year of
his life he would tolerate no other company than Sophia's. She
read to him or sat by his side with her needlework day in and day
out, hardly able to escape for brief walks in the garden when he had
dozed off or for such occasions as the (informal) visit of tsar Peter of
Russia in 1697. In the autumn of 1697 the elector was so weak that
the court could not make its customary move from Herrenhausen
to Hanover, and it was at Herrenhausen that he died. Sophia,
weary, felt something akin to relief. It was not the invalid Ernst

* To the raugravine Louise to the effect that, although it was given out that Königsmarck has disappeared, 'we know what hour the clock has struck'.

August she wished to remember; disciplined as always, she directed her thoughts to when her husband 'had been himself.'[12]

GEORGE AT THE HELM

His father's illness had meant that George did not go to the front in 1695, nor in the remaining campaigns of the Nine Years War. His place was in Hanover and, increasingly, the whole direction of policy became his. Home affairs were, to a large extent, a matter of routine with experienced ministers and bureaucrats at his side.

In foreign affairs, however, the most important of Ernst August's advisers, Grote, had died already in 1693; and in this field un- expected events and the need for quick decisions were in the nature of things. In February 1696 danger seemed to threaten when inter- cepted correspondence revealed that William III's accredited representative to the ninth electorate, James Cresset, was intriguing with the duchess of Celle to embroil Ernst August and George with his master. The plan of the conspirators might seem innocent enough to us. The duke of Celle had arranged to visit William in the Netherlands in the summer of 1696. The duchess wished him to urge his old friend to intercede with Hanover on Sophia Dorothea's behalf: could she not be set free or at least be permitted to live at Celle with her parents? Cresset encouraged this, possibly persuaded by his wife who was related to the duchess. But from the Hanoverian point of view, to put Sophia Dorothea at liberty was tantamount to furthering the plans of Wolfenbüttel and Denmark and all other enemies of the ninth electorate. And any wedge driven between the stadholder-king and the elector could have fatal results, since diplo- matic good-will and financial support (in the form of subsidies for the Hanoverian army) were deemed essential for the very survival of the electorate in these critical years. That William looked upon Eléonore's efforts as mischievous is clear from his avowal in 1701 that she had so pestered him since 1694, by correspondence and in person, to put pressure on Hanover on Sophia Dorothea's behalf that he had been forced to forbid her to mention the subject again. William's reaction was not altruistic. He dared not run the risk of Hanover's taking umbrage and denying him its regiments in case of need. This was the main reason why the Hanoverian counter-measure of May 1696 – the mission of Friedrich Wilhelm, Freiherr von Görtz, to William III as soon as he had arrived on the continent from England – succeeded so easily. Görtz explained why Cresset had become *persona non grata* in Hanover; William assured him of his determination not to meddle in Ernst August's family affairs and, discreetly, found Cresset another posting.[13]

Bernstorff, Georg Wilhelm's first minister, had long supported Hanover in keeping the duke of Celle to the agreement entered into at the time of Sophia Dorothea's divorce, despite the duchess's efforts to the contrary. That he also had a word with William III on the subject seems likely since in August 1696 he preceded his master to the Netherlands and sought an interview with the stadholder-king. Bernstorff's career, like that of other Celle ministers, could be said to be tied to that of the ninth electorate: on the death of Georg Wilhelm, already in his seventies, Celle would join Hanover. But Bernstorff was also ambitious for the electorate and wished to see Hanover-Celle play an important role in north Germany. He was a skilled diplomat, intensely absorbed by foreign policy problems, who had a wide circle of correspondents (including the earl of Portland, greatly in William III's confidence) and was building up a network of news-writers and agents.[14]

That George took the danger to his house seriously and did not tamely follow the lead either of his father or of his father's and uncle's ministers is shown by the fact that in 1698, when he had become elector of Hanover, he employed Görtz on a similar mission. In the autumn of that year William III was visiting Celle for the hunting season and George, fearful of the duchess's persuasive powers, sent Görtz to intercept William at Bruchhausen – before he arrived in Celle – to stress that the stadholder-king would be doing his old friend Georg Wilhelm no service if he let that honourable prince break his word. And in 1701, when Georg Wilhelm again visited William in the Netherlands, this time accompanied by the electoral prince, Georg August, the task of fortifying William against the duchess's machinations fell to the young prince's governor, Philipp Adam, Freiherr von Eltz.[15]

THE PROSPECT OF ENGLAND

By the time of George's wholly personal initiatives in September 1698 and September 1701, more was at stake than the electorate: the prospect of the royal crown of England beckoned. It has long been customary to assert that George had no interest in the English succession, though a few specialists have realized that after the death of princess Anne's heir, the duke of Gloucester, in July 1700 the elector reckoned with and was keener on that succession than he wished the world to know.[16] There is also certain proof that as early as 1698 George, at the same time as he was warning William III against the duchess of Celle through one emissary, urged that duchess via other channels to remind William of the claims of his mother, himself and his son in the line of the Protestant succession and pressed to have them publicly named as being in the line of succession. The duchess, who probably knew nothing of Görtz's mission, did so with a will and would probably not have acted otherwise even if she had been aware of its purpose. She was ambitious for her grandson and clearly hoped that he would one day be able to intervene in favour of Sophia Dorothea.[17] The Hanover court complained that Eléonore, during her visits to Hanover and Georg August's visits to Celle, caused trouble by talking too freely to her grandson about his mother's plight. And certainly, when in September 1702 the duchess implored queen Anne's help to have Sophia Dorothea freed, she made use of the argument that her daughter's *condition présente* was not fitting for the mother of a future king of England.[18]

The ninth electorate and the English prospects were endangered also by members of George's own branch of the house of Brunswick. Immediately after Ernst August's death Maximilian reverted to his position of 1691 and '92, withdrawing his recognition of the constitutional change to primogeniture. Christian Heinrich adopted a similar position. Of the two defections George took Max's most to heart; he persisted in believing that it was Christian Heinrich who had misled the older brother rather than the other way round.[19] Christian never conspired with foreign courts against George, but Max – again with Wolfenbüttel's help – did so; and until George was able to bring Hanover into the Grand Alliance of 1701 and gain renewed guarantees of military help for the electoral dignity if needed, Max's negotiations were more than a nuisance.[20] Sophia tried her best to reconcile the brothers with George, using much the same arguments as during the earlier phases of the *Prinzenstreit*, by appeals to their sense of duty to the house and promises of financial support if they complied. In Christian's case she had no success, and in Maximilian's only a partial one: he refused to reside in, or even visit, Hanover but agreed to desist in his agitation against the primogeniture in return for payment of the allowance Ernst August had stipulated for him, 12,000 Taler a year. Characteristically, Sophia chided Max for not having settled with George at the time when his foreign contacts had alarmed Hanover and when he could have held out for an increased appanage.[21]

Max's conversion to Catholicism, which took place after this settlement, had repercussions on the succession prospects and became an issue in Anglo-Hanoverian negotiations. Sophia never fully grasped this, probably because her whole attitude to Maxi-

milian's change of faith became emotional enough to blind her even
to the fact that it was, in part, dictated by his hopes of promotion
in the Imperial army. She developed a hatred for the member of the
Order of Jesus on whom she put the blame not only for the conversion but for keeping Maximilian away from Hanover and for the
decline in, and eventually total stop of, his correspondence with her.
She became so vitriolic in her correspondence on the subject of this
Jesuit that Liselotte felt bound to remind her aunt of Sophia's
share in her own conversion to Catholicism: did Sophia not recall
having stressed the worldly advantages that would follow for
Liselotte?[22] Rumours of Max's change of faith, before it was publicly
acknowledged, were sufficient to cause despondency among those in
England and the Dutch Republic who favoured the Hanoverian
succession. And when Christian's conversion also became a matter of
public speculation the situation grew serious. In September 1701,
i.e., after the Act of Settlement of June of that year which had fixed
the succession on Sophia and the heirs of her body if Protestants,
William III pointedly asked Eltz whether the rumours concerning
the brothers had substance. Eltz had to admit that, though he was
sure Christian was not a Catholic, he could not be as positive about
Maximilian.[23] The assurance in Christian's case was some comfort.
The defection of two of George's brothers would have given a handle
to those who wished to undermine the credibility of the succession,
since George had only one son and the remaining brother, Ernst
August,[24] was reckoned unlikely to marry.* Hanoverian and Celle
diplomats at The Hague and in London wrote home on the damage
which gossip about Maximilian's coming adoption of the Catholic
faith had done to the *gloire* of the house: it was necessary not only
for the house to show itself Protestant, but to act as a champion of
Protestantism.[25]

Sophia herself was capable of creating problems for the ministers
and diplomats who had their eyes firmly fixed on the succession
prospects, and for George also. Mother and son were at one in not
wishing to appear over-eager; she from a sense of decorum, he
(while also concerned with the look of things) mainly from shrewd
calculation and a habitual need to keep his cards close to his chest
until he could judge the best time to play them.

In Ernst August's lifetime Sophia had, naturally enough, been permitted great freedom to handle English matters as she saw fit, and
George, out of filial respect, did not wish to upset her by too strict
a control once he became elector. His purposes could usually be
achieved via his mother's activities and correspondence; and it was
not till it became absolutely necessary, in June 1706, that he

---

* Liselotte held that he 'was attracted to neither sex', a rare occurrence in her
experience, but homosexuality has been inferred by historians from his letters to a brother-
officer.

challenged her and ordered her to desist in steps which he judged harmful to the house and to his own policies. But long before this, Sophia's way of handling matters, and her very personal and some-what thoughtless way of putting things, had caused trouble. The worst crisis had been in October 1700 when she visited William III's Het Loo palace with her daughter, the electress of Brandenburg. She was aware of the political significance of her conversations with the stadholder-king and with Dutch men of influence: the death of the duke of Gloucester the previous July had created a new situation in the succession-stakes. But what she said, and what she had written just prior to her arrival (in a letter to Stepney, the British representative at The Hague), alarmed Hanoverian diplo-mats and ministers. Why did she spread the story that George was indifferent to the crown of England? Even if it were true, it ought not to be divulged, since the very prospect of the elector being given a place in the English succession would improve the bargaining position of the electorate at a time of delicate and important negoti-ations. No wonder that William began to think of alternative candidates to George (had not Sophia herself invited it?), and that the son of the electress of Brandenburg was now reckoned to be ahead of his uncle. Sophia's letter to Stepney, which became widely known on both sides of the Channel, caused more permanent damage than her talk. It was neither correct nor politic to stress that George was 'absolute' in Hanover and that he would be too set in his ways when the time came for him to be king of England, in contrast to James II's son (whom she referred to as the prince of Wales) who was young enough and keen enough to be moulded into the kind of ruler most Englishmen wanted. Quite apart from the displeasing picture she painted of George, her virtual recommendation of James Edward Stuart was interpreted as insufficient abhorrence of the Catholicism in which this prince was brought up, while her use of the title 'Prince of Wales' was not to the liking of the Whigs.[26]

Sophia's attitude should not be looked upon as the outcome of ill will towards George nor of a desire to make mischief. She had under-taken the journey to The Hague for the very purpose of securing the succession, but she wished to do so without appearing greedy or unmindful of the claims of James II's son. She had been annoyed when the first diplomatic offensive in London* between the autumn of 1688 and February 1689 miscarried and she was not specifically named in the Bill of Rights and Succession as the nearest Protestant heir after Mary and Anne, and – failing heirs of their own bodies – children of a hypothetical second marriage by William III.[27] William's excuse, that it would needlessly offend princess Anne and

* By the Brunswick agent Guillaume Beyrïe and the Osnabrück councillor Johann von der Reck, sent specifically for the purpose; from April 1689 onwards the Celle diplomat Ludwig Justus Sinold genannt von Schütz took over.

her husband at a time when they were expecting a child, only partly mollified her; after all, the six children born to them earlier had all died, why should one expect the seventh to survive? But William, born in July 1689 and created duke of Gloucester, seemed destined to be luckier than the rest, and at an official level the succession issue was now regarded as less urgent. Sophia, though she bore no ill will towards the child duke and sincerely wished William III joy of the boy in his lonely years as a widower, had enough correspondents in England to be informed of Gloucester's lack of robust health: Margaret Hughes, the assumed widow of her brother Rupert, and the raugravine Caroline, married to one of William's trusted officers, Meinhard von Schomberg, duke of Leinster. These, and others, kept reminding her of her own prospects. So did visiting Englishmen and Englishwomen, either out of politeness or in the hope of present or future employment, and diplomats en route, or accredited to, the elector, both before and after 1698, who sought in her a channel of information about Hanoverian policies.

Even if Gloucester should not grow to maturity, there was always a chance that one of the fifty-four Catholics originally closer by hereditary claim than Sophia and her issue might turn Protestant for the sake of the British inheritance. There seemed little possibility of those of the Palatinate house doing so;* but what of the Savoy prince whose grandmother was Henrietta, daughter of Charles I? Sophia's sense of obligation to her relatives of the house of Stuart therefore helps to explain her suggestion – frequently made in correspondence with Liselotte and put before William III and a wider audience by her Stepney letter in the autumn of 1700 – that the 'Prince of Wales' might prove a more acceptable candidate to the English nation than herself and her children. She had never hidden from William and Mary her sympathy for her cousin James II in exile, nor her conviction that James Edward Stuart was not a suppositious child.[28] When older and freer of parental control, she argued, he might well turn Protestant in order to become king of England and Scotland. Others took up this idea and suggested to James II that William might make James Edward heir to the crown, after Anne, on the condition that the boy be sent to England and brought up in the Protestant faith.[29] James II refused to countenance efforts in this direction, and in June 1701 the Act of Settlement naming Sophia and the heirs of her body, 'being Protestants', as successors was passed in order to end English and European speculation about the succession. Sophia had tried to convince herself that if James Edward should be preferred she would feel neither

---

* Liselotte, the only remaining child of Karl Ludwig, elector palatine; Anne and Benedicte, daughters of Edward, prince palatine, from his marriage to Anna Gonzaga.

regret nor envy; but her indignation and agitation in September 1701 when Louis XIV, on James II's death, recognized James Edward as 'James III' indicates that in some measure she deceived herself.[30] So does the intense pleasure she experienced (though outward decorum was preserved) at being specifically named in the Act, and the splendid welcome she prepared for the English embassy which arrived in Hanover in August 1701 to present her with a copy of the Act and invest George with the Garter. Her thoughts are most clearly revealed in her correspondence with Leibniz at this time. She wanted to act royally and was spurred into uncharacteristic extravagance. The Mathilde medal she had struck for the occasion showed her profile on one side and that of Heinrich *der Löwe*'s English wife on the other; and, quite apart from the entertainments and presents given by George as elector, she herself was put to great expense in providing for the leaving-presents to lord Macclesfield and his suite.[31]

William III's death in March 1702 made Sophia queen Anne's immediate heir. From that time onwards she hoped for a regular allowance from parliament and was not above insinuating, even pressing, that this should be voted. The reason she gave, that such a grant would set the seal on her position as 'Princess of Wales', was genuine enough; but she had also a private reason divulged to none but the raugravines. She had not been left badly off at her husband's death, but her income never sufficed to satisfy Maximilian and Christian. Max, always careless in money matters, got into fresh debts however often she helped him out, and there was less to spare for Christian than she could wish: if only parliament would provide for her, she would use the money to buy him a large estate.[32] His being killed in action in 1703 put an end to this objective; but even if he had survived that campaign, Sophia would still have refused the private pension queen Anne offered her as late as May 1714: the recognition mattered as much as the money.

It is difficult to free oneself from an impression (though it can be no more than an impression) that losses in the family circle, and especially the death of Figuelotte in 1705 when on a visit to Hanover, intensified Sophia's absorption with the English succession. In theory she subscribed to a belief, spread by herself, that she was too old to expect ever to succeed to the crown in person or even to travel to England in the near future. Just after the passing of the Act of Settlement in 1701 she had, true to her ironic turn of phrase, stressed its comic aspects: fancy a procession in which she, in her seventy-first year, would walk behind those two 'children', William and Anne![33] Her oft-repeated 'I am of an age when I must prepare to

meet my maker rather than turn my thoughts to a worldly crown'
was sincerely meant, but her unconscious emphasis was on the *must*
(or on the *ought to* sometimes substituted).[34] She was in any case
so healthy and energetic that English visitors wanted to subtract
at least ten years from her age when describing the electoral court.[35]
She needed outlets for her energy. She needed to feel that she was
'useful' to George and his son. She craved some activity urgent
enough to drown her sorrows. She may have been goaded to some
extent by charges levied at the Hanoverian court of 'indifference to
the succession' by the new English resident Howe and his wife
Ruperta, the daughter of her late brother by Margaret Hughes.[36]
She was certainly nobly supported, and even pushed, by Leibniz who,
if anything, knew less of practical politics than Sophia did.

STRUGGLE OVER THE ENGLISH SUCCESSION BETWEEN GEORGE AND HIS MOTHER

From 1705, therefore, the dowager electress became involved in
succession politics in such a way that she (and Leibniz) moved on to
a collision course with George, the elector. Sophia had no desire to
be brought into English party struggles between Whig and Tory;
but this could not be avoided given her commitment to the succession
and her lack of a real grasp of the, at least superficially, confusing
politics of queen Anne's reign. To Sophia it was a matter of great
puzzlement that her response (suggesting that she was very willing,
in spite of her advanced age, to come to England 'if her friends so
wished') to a letter from the archbishop of Canterbury in November
1705 should bring a *Tory* motion before the House of Commons
that an invitation be issued for her to travel to London, only to
find this defeated by the *Whigs* when votes were counted. She did
not see the mischievousness of Tory attempts to forestall the Whigs,
nor realize the reasoning behind contemporaneous Whig measures,
such as the regency and naturalization bills, to secure the succession.
Indeed, she does not seem to have understood why queen Anne,
whose life was hectic enough in years of intense party strife and
stretched resources to meet the demands of the War of the Spanish
Succession, was determined to have no separate Hanoverian court
in England foisted upon her. Sophia assumed that the queen's
resistance was purely personal and took umbrage at the discreet
censure conveyed through Marlborough: how dared the younger
woman correct her?[37]

But Anne well remembered the time when she herself had been
the focus of an opposition court in William III's reign. The court of

Saint-Germain already provided one rallying point for the discontented, and to have another – in London itself – whether it was for the dowager electress Sophia or the electoral prince Georg August was more than she and her 'managers' could cope with. There was undoubtedly a personal element. Having any one of the Hanoverians at court, Anne was wont to say, would be tantamount to forcing her 'to look at her coffin every day that remained of her life'.[38] Quite apart from this emotional aspect of queen Anne's attitude, she may be said to have shown sound instinct based on the experience alluded to above. Certainly George I and George II found it difficult to cope with alternative courts when party struggles – more determinedly for power and office than in queen Anne's reign, though not exclusively so – could rally round, and use, a prince of Wales resident in England. Conversely, Sophia could not see the point of the regency bill which laid down interim measures for the period between the death of queen Anne and the arrival in England of her Hanoverian successor; nor of the bill which made her and those of her family in direct line of succession naturalized British subjects: was not the parchment of the Act of Settlement enough and should not the next step be to have a Hanoverian on the spot?

George, by contrast, had sufficient experience to grasp the issue at stake during the vital session of 1705–06. The Act of Settlement had forbidden the next heir after William from employing in any office of state or to give English rewards (land and titles implied) to men not English-born – a limitation dictated by the annoyance and envy at William's promotion of Dutch-born advisers; but the regency bill made amends by stipulating, first, that parliament (if not sitting) would automatically be recalled on queen Anne's death and, second, that a regency council – the majority of which was to be nominated from English-born subjects by the Hanoverian heir – should govern the country until the heir, whether Sophia or George, should arrive in person. This helped to solve a problem to which the most recent and authoritative study of British politics in the reign of queen Anne[39] has drawn attention: the Act of Settlement had fixed the succession, but how was the succession to be secured in practice? There was now a proper procedure laid down, and a later amendment (which increased the number to be nominated by the Hanoverian heir, the remaining members being – as before – the great officers of state at the time of the queen's death)* weighted the balance even more in favour of Hanover. At the same time, the naturalization bill for the Hanoverian family meant that no objection to them as 'foreigners' could be raised at a later date.

What has not been appreciated, however, is that the naturaliz-

---

* That is, the archbishop of Canterbury, the lord chancellor, the lord treasurer, the lord president, the lord privy seal, the first lord of the admiralty and the lord chief justice.

ation act immediately strengthened the hand of the next heir but one: George, now a naturalized Englishman, could feel on safer ground if moved to interfere with his mother's handling of the succession issue. The need for such interference came in 1706, and the crisis of the relationship between mother and son in June of that year. Sophia lent her tacit consent to a ploy by Leibniz, well-meant but misguided, in which a pamphlet criticizing the Whigs for their vetoing of the Tory invitation-motion was smuggled into London and widely distributed in the early months of 1706. Leibniz was the author, but the pamphlet (which had been printed in the Dutch Republic) was in the form of a letter signed by Sir Rowland Gwynne, an Englishman who was visiting Hanover at the time. Parliament censured the pamphlet as 'scandalous, libellous, false and malicious, tending to create a misunderstanding between Her Majesty and Princess Sophia'. Sophia may have been kept in ignorance of the actual details of composition and production, but only her general support could have emboldened Leibniz to take such a risk. In her private correspondence Sophia wrote that she could see 'nothing wrong' with the pamphlet, and her refusal to censure Sir Rowland shocked most observers in both England and Hanover.[40] George decided to put his foot down. He did not wish to mar the ceremonies attendant on lord Halifax's visit in March 1706 when, with a numerous embassy, he presented the regency and naturalization acts to Sophia and invested Georg August with the Garter, creating him on Anne's behalf baron Tewkesbury, viscount Tallerton, earl of Milford Haven, and duke of Cambridge. Soon afterwards, however, George made it clear to his mother and to Leibniz that they were not to act without his authority in the succession issue, ordered Schütz – the Hanoverian diplomat in London – to disassociate himself from the pamphlet, and forbade Sir Rowland to return to Hanover.[41] By June, the crisis was over; and from now on Sophia coordinated her policies in the succession issue with those of her son.

WIDER GERMAN HORIZONS

By this time a significant strengthening had taken place also in George's German position. His uncle Georg Wilhelm had died in 1705; Celle had been united with Hanover and George was now the ruler of a relatively important German state. Even in his father's reign Hanover had caught up with Celle in terms of income, and in the numbers of men under arms had surpassed it. Celle was, however, larger, more populous and compact than Hanover,* and Georg Wilhelm had made territorial gains during his reign which led

---

* See map 1 for Hanoverian and Celle territories: in 1705 the 12,500 sq. km. of Celle were added to Hanover's 7,000 sq. km. (in modern terms), and Hanover's population of some 200,000 was doubled.

contemporaries to predict that the Brunswick-Lüneburg dukes would eventually recapture all the possessions of their ancestor Heinrich *der Löwe* in north Germany.[42]

From his uncle, George also inherited a reputation for straight dealing with the Maritime Powers which stood him in good stead. His own father, though by far the more efficient ruler, had – deservedly – the name of a fairly tricky opportunist. He had never been fully trusted by William III, whereas Georg Wilhelm had been the stadholder-king's 'best and truest friend'.[43] On the European scene as a whole, however, George's father and uncle had complemented each other. Georg Wilhelm had been quick off the mark, keen to take risks, willing to commit his military resources without too much deliberation. Ernst August had taken his time, weighed advantages against disadvantages, but had in every case eventually come in on his elder brother's side, helping to turn his adventures into well-founded successes. Georg Wilhelm had shown the greater vision and optimism when he had backed William III's invasion of England in 1688 by sending Celle troops to the Republic to replace the regiments William had taken with him; the greater determination and forcefulness when he moved speedily to occupy Sachsen-Lauenburg in 1689 after the death of its ruler lest other German princes should steal a march on him; the greater insouciance and calm in the summer of 1693 when he accepted the challenge of Christian V of Denmark-Norway who laid siege to Ratzeburg, fortified by Celle, to sustain his own claim to at least part of Sachsen-Lauenburg. The Danish king had one of the largest armies in Europe, and if he wished he could have chased Georg Wilhelm's troops – even when strengthened by those of Ernst August – out of Sachsen-Lauenburg preparatory to an invasion of Celle itself. But Ernst August's military support and diplomatic pressure applied by William III won the day. Christian V acquiesced in the Brunswick occupation provided the town's fortifications (which he had already brought down by bombardment) were not restored; and, because of the war against Louis XIV, emperor and Empire accepted the sequestration by Brunswick troops of Sachsen-Lauenburg, with the exception of the county of Hadeln.*

Here was an important territorial gain, with an income of 46,000 Taler a year, 18,000 of which derived from tolls on the Elbe. After 1698 it became George's duty to convert the sequestration into a possession. He and Georg Wilhelm made great strides in that direction during their negotiations for entry into the Grand Alliance against France of 1701; and though George did not live to see the day when the emperor ceded the county of Hadeln to Hanover, the

* Hadeln was sequestered by the emperor, but was eventually ceded to Hanover in 1731.

incorporation of Sachsen-Lauenburg with Hanover was effected during his reign and did much to safeguard the position of Harburg, the Celle port, which was to play so significant a role in George I's commercial planning after 1714.

In north Germany, Georg Wilhelm and Ernst August were prominent among the princes who saw Denmark and Sweden as 'foreigners' in the Empire whose power ought to be circumscribed and, if possible, terminated. Ever since George had been in his father's and uncle's confidence the Brunswick position had been determined by hope of territorial gain at the expense of either of the Scandinavian powers, tempered by determination to erect a barrier against the more expansionist of the two at any given moment. During the Dutch War (1672–78) there had been hopes of conquering the greater part of the Swedish duchies of Bremen and Verden once Sweden had become a belligerent in 1675 in the war on the French side. The reward had, however, proved minimal (a small slip of land for Celle), thanks to Louis XIV's strong support of Charles XI during the peace negotiations. After the peace the king of Sweden was preoccupied with reforms at home, declaring his country a satiated power abroad; the king of Denmark now seemed to have a greater chance to make himself master of either Hamburg or Lübeck (or both) and to succeed in attempts to crush the dukes of Holstein-Gottorp whose alliance with Sweden had opened a back-door entry for possible enemies into Danish territory. For Sweden such access from its German dominions (Bremen and Verden in the west, Wismar and Swedish Pomerania in the east) was thought of as a precondition for retention of those Danish and Norwegian provinces on the Scandinavian peninsula which it had wrested from Denmark-Norway in the 1640s and '50s;* but for the Brunswick dukes the dominating motive in making common cause with Sweden in supporting Holstein-Gottorp lay in the need they felt to prevent the king of Denmark from becoming more powerful in the Empire, where he already possessed Oldenburg and Delmenhorst. Indeed, in the 1680s it was Ernst August, Georg Wilhelm, and the Brunswick-Wolfenbüttel dukes (Rudolf August, and his co-regent Anton Ulrich), who formed the main bulwark against expansionist Danish policies, since Charles XI of Sweden was concentrating at that time on domestic measures which would forge an army and a defensive system of fortresses strong enough to defend the country's great power position. It was the Brunswickers who foiled Christian V's designs on Hamburg in 1686; it was their argument that as 'watchdogs of the Empire' they must move into Sachsen-Lauenburg lest Denmark occupy it which won Leopold I's consent to the 1689

---

* Scania, Halland, Blekinge and Bohuslän on the Skagerak, the Sound and the Baltic; Jämtland and Härjedal commanding the non-coastal invasion routes between Norway and Sweden.

sequestration; and throughout the 1680s and '90s they declared themselves prepared to defend the *jus armorum* of the dukes of Holstein-Gottorp so that the land which those dukes held in their own right or in common with the kings of Denmark-Norway should not be lost to the 'barrier' round the neck of the Jutland peninsula.

It is interesting to note, and of significance when we consider George's heritage from his father and uncle, that Ernst August developed in the 1680s an alternative plan for a barrier against Denmark, a solution in tune with the ideas of the Early Enlightenment which pondered schemes whereby, via peaceful exchanges of territory, recourse to expensive wars could be avoided. This fully worked-out plan of exchanges on the 'equivalent' principle is the earliest (to my knowledge), though the barrier concept as such was much discussed in Europe in the 1670s and '80s. The ducal possessions, scattered throughout Holstein and Sleswig, and in particular the territories which were held in common between king and duke, were certain to create trouble in the future as in the past. The circumstance that Sleswig was outside the borders of the Empire while Holstein was inside added a further complication. The king of Denmark held his possessions in Holstein in his capacity as duke of Holstein and was – just as much as the duke of Holstein-Gottorp – subject to Imperial jurisdiction. Would it not be sensible to avoid conflict by a rational exchange of territories? What Ernst August envisaged was that duke Christian Albrecht should relinquish lands in Sleswig and Holstein (bar a small but strategically important corner of eastern Holstein) to king Christian V, receiving in return Oldenburg and Delmenhorst. This plan found no favour with Sweden (it would have rendered less feasible the kind of military operation which general Torstenson had undertaken in the 1640s and Charles X in the 1650s); and duke Christian Albrecht was unwilling to take the risk: might he not give up his undoubted rights and find himself less safe in the new state? Yet it should not be ignored by historians concerned with the reign of George I, for here we have the beginning of a tradition upon which he, Bernstorff, and Stanhope built on a European scale in their diplomacy after 1714.

It is equally typical of Ernst August – and of George after him – that once the 'exchange and equivalent' plan to solve the Holstein-Gottorp problem had misfired, Brunswick determination to uphold the barrier that did exist led to strong support for Christian Albrecht (and his son and successor duke Friedrich IV) until Hanover was drawn into the Great Northern War after 1709. Considerations of possible territorial gains as a reward for fighting Denmark in the good cause of 'the barrier' did play a part (Oldenburg, Delmenhorst, the fortress of Rendsburg and the town of Glückstadt which commanded strategic and commercially important waterways were discussed though not publicly admitted); but the maintenance of the barrier as such was the issue of greatest concern.[44] In the two crises of 1688–89 and 1699–1700 Brunswick showed military preparedness and willingness to fight Denmark to restore the duke (Christian Albrecht on the first occasion, Friedrich IV on the second) to ducal territories which the Danish king had occupied, and to such rights as the *jus armorum*, which had been confirmed to the duke by earlier treaties (and more particularly by that of 1675 which Denmark also had signed). In 1688–89 Hanover had 9,000 men, Celle 3,250 and Wolfenbüttel 1,000 on the borders of Holstein, ready to march with a Swedish army of 8,000; the pressure this exerted, helped on by the diplomacy of William III, effected the restitution of the duke to his lands and rights by the Altona recess of June 1689, guaranteed by the Maritime Powers as well as by the Brunswick dukes.[45] By the time the second crisis broke, Brunswick cooperation had been disturbed by the creation of the ninth electorate in 1692, and George had, in 1698, succeeded Ernst August as elector. It was he who took command of the army of the guarantors of Altona – Dutch, Swedish, Hanoverian and Celle contingents – which, by their march from the south into Holstein produced, in conjunction with the Swedish landing in Zealand (under the umbrella of, if not in cooperation with, a joint Anglo-Dutch fleet just outside the Sound), the peace of Travendal of August 1700: duke Friedrich, since 1698 an exile in Sweden, but now present with the army of the guarantors, was restored to his lands and rights.[46]

                              *   *   *

From June 1688 George had been admitted to the audiences which his father held each morning with his most important ministers,[47] those who formed the *Geheimrat* (the privy council), at this time Platen and Grote, coequal in influence since 1682 and concerned with both foreign and domestic policy; Ludolf Hugo, the legal expert who handled the technical work connected with the primogeniture and the electorate; Albrecht Philipp von dem Bussche, of an old Osnabrück family, the former governor of Ernst August's sons, especially trusted in the private affairs of the house; and the most recent recruit, from 1695, the Hesse-born Friedrich Wilhelm von Görtz, formerly in Holstein-Gottorp service, who was much used on diplomatic missions and increasingly given responsibility also for financial affairs. Ernst August never attended the meetings of the privy council as such. His ministers met on their own and reported to him in audiences (or in writing when he was absent) when they had discussed and clarified issues – a custom roughly similar to the distinction between the lords of the committee and the cabinet council in England. It is not known to what extent George had access to his father's *Kabinett*, to which only Ernst August had the key, a closet or study where he kept his private papers and where his secretaries worked; but it seems unlikely that he was given freedom of this sanctum until his father's illness. Individual ministers were invited into the *Kabinett* for private consultations with Ernst August; here despatches were drafted and signed; and the role, by 1688, of the chief private secretary, Johann Hattorf (assisted by two helpers, one for civil and one for military affairs), was important and well-rewarded.[48] It should be noted that the staff of the *Kabinett* had no formal relationship to the *Geheimrat*, a fact which made it easier for George to take with him to London in 1714 the *Deutsche Kanzlei* and to keep military matters in the *Kriegskanzlei* of Hanover in his own hands.

In the years when George learnt his métier the electoral audiences with the *Geheimrat* which he attended provided a good training. Here he met men on whose advice his father relied, and several of them, Platen and Grote (until his death in 1693, when he was succeeded by Görtz), formed a link between the *Geheimrat* and the so-called 'house conferences' between Hanover and Celle to which Georg Wilhelm without fail sent Bernstorff, and at times also other of his ministers. The dukes of Celle and Hanover met on frequent occasions and had many private talks, but their policies were worked out in detail during these ministerial conferences where the rulers were not present. Since the chief Hanoverian ministers, the members of the *Geheimrat*, were frequently entrusted with diplomatic missions during which they overrode ordinary accredited representatives, George also learnt a good deal about the European courts that mattered – Vienna, Paris, Berlin, Dresden, The Hague and London, Stockholm and Copenhagen – from his attendance at the audiences, especially after 1694 when his active war service in the Nine Years War came to an end. But even before that time, since negotiations tended to take place outside the campaigning season, he was well informed. Apart from sitting in on his father's council meetings, George accompanied him on several visits to Berlin, the purposes of which were diplomatic rather than social. He was also a regular member of the Brunswick-Lüneburg hunting parties, whether Ernst August was the host at Linsburg or – as was more usual – the Hanovers were the guests of Georg Wilhelm at Göhrde or at Ebstorf near Hamburg where they enjoyed the deerstalking.

George was thus largely in his father's confidence and experienced the tough problems of the 1688 to 1692 years, when Ernst August played Louis XIV and emperor Leopold off against one another, at second, if not first hand. He had the reputation of being less 'pro-French' than his father.[49] He may, therefore, have regretted that the need to keep the Hanoverian army in being at a time when assignations (money contributions levied by Imperial authority on those German states which kept no armed forces of their own) were drying up in north Germany drove Ernst August to sign the neutrality and subsidy treaty with France of November 1690.* Such treaties were normal in great-power diplomacy at the time, and especially in French diplomacy. It robbed France's enemies of Hanoverian troops for the coming campaigns of the Palatinate War (the treaty was meant to run for four years) and opened the road to the formation of a German 'third party', with Hanover as a nucleus which might help Louis XIV to achieve a compromise peace.[50] Once Ernst August, from the position of strength which an army in being gave him, had achieved his real objective (Leopold's binding promise of the electoral cap by the treaty of March 1692), he gave notice to Louis of his decision to break with France. In the summer of that year he re-entered the war on the allied side, having also committed himself to send some 6,000 men at his own cost to Hungary, to donate 500,000 gulden (equal to some 3,333 Taler) to the emperor's general war effort and to espouse Leopold's cause in the Spanish succession issue.[51]

From this time onwards the fate of the ninth electorate was inextricably interwoven with the fortunes of the first (1689) and second (1701) Grand Alliance against France, and the road which George had to follow between 1698 and 1714 – for the sake of the English succession no less than for the electorate – was clearly laid down. Because choice was removed, the terms which George and his uncle Georg Wilhelm could exact for their auxiliary troops in the War of the Spanish Succession during negotiations between 1701 and 1702 proved disappointing. That the lessons of 1688 to 1692 had not been wasted is, however, proved over and over again: by George's insistence that, though his entry into the second Grand Alliance was for the duration of the war, his commitment of troops was for each campaign only (so that he could exploit the opportunities which changing conjunctures might offer); by the way in which he proceeded cautiously, but with a ruthlessness which matched that of Ernst August, after 1715 when, as king of Great Britain, he had greater resources at his disposal; by the persistence with which he courted and secured eventual success.

* By it Louis XIV agreed to pay Ernst August subsidies of 400,000 Taler a month, with another 360,000 a month towards the paying off of arrears from Johann Friedrich's reign, against the duke's keeping 13,000 men in readiness while remaining neutral in the Palatinate War.

His close attention to Ernst August's example is less easily proved from direct documentation of the years of his pupillage (we have, for instance, no minutes of the Hanoverian *Geheimrat* meetings) than from his declarations and actions when he himself wielded power. Not that he slavishly followed his father's example. He pondered the lessons of Ernst August's reign and applied what he had learnt to the situations confronting himself. It is reasonable to deduce that his somewhat cynical appraisal of 'third parties' in wartime derived from his knowledge of how thoroughly Louis XIV had been deceived by his father; so did his disbelief in the efficacy of presents and pensions in foreign relations. The huge gratifications which France had paid to Hanoverian ministers seemed in retrospect to have had as little effect as those paid by Ernst August to Leopold's advisers:[52] in the end it was the willingness to use military force that counted. A similarity of temperament and circumstances, but also the example remembered, helps to explain the characteristic reluctance of Ernst August and George to commit themselves prematurely, and their equally characteristic aptitude to squeeze the last drop out of opportunities that came their way – though in George's case full freedom to exploit the conjunctures did not come until after his accession as king of Great Britain. Even here there is a striking parallel between father and son; just as the bishop of Osnabrück had been set free, by becoming duke of Hanover, to play a significant role in Germany, so George, on being transported across the Channel, was set free to make an impact on a European scale.

George benefited also from close cooperation with his uncle Georg Wilhelm after January 1698. This was, in some measure, a second tutelage; one that impressed upon him how much could be gained by cooperation with the Maritime Powers. William III's trust in Georg Wilhelm was such that he and his closest adviser, Bernstorff, were the first confidants (apart from Heinsius and the earl of Portland) who were fully informed of the partition treaty negotiations with Louis XIV. Robethon, one of the many French Huguenot refugees in Celle and a protégé of Bernstorff's, entered William's service as a confidential secretary to Portland on his 1698 mission to Versailles where Louis XIV's overtures to work out a compromise solution in the Spanish inheritance question were pursued in the hope of avoiding a new European war. Robethon sent newsletters to Bernstorff; but it was through Ludwig Sinold von Schütz, Bernstoff's brother-in-law, who represented both Celle and Hanover with William III and moved between London and The Hague in rhythm with the stadholder-king, that – as the Bernstorff archives prove – a channel of direct communication (first opened at the highest level during William's Celle visit in 1698) was maintained on this topic.[53]

The Brunswick-Lüneburg dukes were eager to throw their diplomatic and military weight on the side of the Spanish partition plan; and it was confidently expected that Louis XIV, as a reward for their accession to the second partition treaty (necessitated by the death of the electoral prince of Bavaria, the linch-pin of the first treaty of 1698), would recognize the ninth electorate.[54] Such hopes were, however, frustrated in November 1700 when Carlos II's will named Louis' grandson, the duc d'Anjou, heir to Spain's wide-flung possessions in Europe and the vast Spanish empire overseas, provided he agreed to prevent partition. Louis XIV, uncertain (and justifiably so) whether the Maritime Powers would be willing to impose the second partition treaty on emperor Leopold by force, accepted the will. In theory the door was kept open for the emperor to accede to the second partition treaty which would make his second son, archduke Charles, ruler of Spain, the Spanish Netherlands and New Spain. In reality the emperor was known to be totally opposed to any part of Spain's Italian territories (even if they were to be used by France for exchanges specified by treaties signed or in process of negotiation)* going outside the Austrian Habsburg family; and the Maritime Powers were equally adamant that unless Louis XIV, on his grandson's behalf, made sizable concessions concerning trade with the Spanish empire, and himself restored earlier French conquests in the Spanish Netherlands to serve as an enlarged buffer state or 'barrier' between the Republic and France, war would ensue.[55]

*   *   *

That war broke out in two stages: Leopold I, with the encouragement of William III, invaded Italy in 1701 but the Maritime Powers did not declare war on France till 1702, after William's death though the decision had been taken before that event. The delay was dictated by William's need to convince England that war was necessary (a task that became much easier once Louis had recognized James III in September 1701), and by the need to activate the German princes, many of whom would have preferred neutrality in what was thought of as a Habsburg dynastic issue.[56] In these circumstances the Brunswick-Lüneburg dukes should, on the pattern of the past, have been favourably placed to exact terms for joining the anti-French coalition, over and above the second Grand Alliance committing itself to enforce recognition of the ninth electorate on Louis XIV. In practice things worked out differently. The very fact that the Maritime Powers were sure of George and Georg Wilhelm worked

---

* Milan was to be exchanged for Lorraine; and negotiations were in progress to exchange Naples and Sicily for Victor Amadeus's north Italian state of Piedmont-Savoy.

against the Brunswick-Lüneburg dukes. So did Leopold's certainty of Anglo-Dutch support, since this would automatically entail that of the elector and his uncle.

Paradoxically, an important gain of the summer of 1702 for these dukes, obtained in cooperation with Sweden and the Maritime Powers, served to scale down the rate the latter were willing to pay for Brunswick-Lüneburg troops in the War of the Spanish Succession. The kings of Denmark had not been content to accept the Altona restitution of the duke of Holstein-Gottorp to his lands and rights any longer than they felt constrained to do so. Between 1698 and 1699 an anti-Swedish coalition had been formed (in which Christian V and, after his death, his son Frederik IV were the prime movers), and coordinated attacks on Sweden had been planned for the year 1700: Denmark would occupy ducal Holstein-Gottorp territory as a preliminary to an invasion of Scania; Augustus of Saxony-Poland would, in his capacity as elector (but with the connivance of some of his Polish advisers), invade Swedish Livonia; while tsar Peter had committed himself to march into Swedish Ingria as soon as he obtained a truce with the Turks.

William III and Heinsius, aware through their intelligence system in Denmark of what was coming, determined to keep the war out of the Empire lest trouble there should embolden Louis to become tougher in the negotiations over the Spanish partition. The conflict between Frederik IV and the duke of Holstein-Gottorp was public knowledge, even before the Danish march into Holstein, and Charles XII of Sweden and his ministers became willing to pay a high price in order to activate the guarantors of Altona: a Swedish guarantee of the treaty of Ryswick, in so far as that treaty dealt with the interests of the Maritime Powers, not only spelt the abandonment of the neutral balancing policy which Sweden had pursued during the Nine Years War, but also bound Charles XII to defend the Spanish Netherlands against French encroachment and to fight for the Protestant succession if Louis XIV were to support the Stuart cause. Since Sweden had already recognized the ninth electorate, there was nothing Charles XII could offer the Brunswick-Lüneburg dukes. George, however, was willing, and even keen, to fulfil his and Georg Wilhelm's obligations under the Altona recess in the hope that the ensuing settlement would force the king of Denmark to recognize the ninth electorate. This was duly done in the treaty of Travendal, a genuine gain for Hanover, since Denmark-Norway was, after France, the largest military power (and diplomatically more active than France) which had opposed Hanover's electoral title.

Yet the treaty of Travendal worked against Brunswick-Lüneburg interests in that the Maritime Powers, to make sure that Frederik IV did not break his word and rejoin Sweden's enemies, felt obliged to take as many Danish troops as possible into Anglo-Dutch service. This, as well as the fact that Augustus of Saxony-Poland (after his first defeat by Charles XII in the autumn of 1700) offered part of his army to the Maritime Powers, enabled these powers to obtain Brunswick-Lüneburg forces for the War of the Spanish Succession on the cheap. The subsidy terms were pressed down to a level which was insufficient to defray the total normal expense of the regiments in allied service, the military budgets of Hanover and Celle being balanced only by a reduction in the pay of officers and men when in winter-quarters.

Against this financial disappointment must be set a significant political gain. It had come to George's and Georg Wilhelm's notice that Anton Ulrich of Wolfenbüttel planned a conquest of the duchy of Celle as soon as the Brunswick-Lüneburg armies went to serve on the Rhine and in the Netherlands. Anton Ulrich had built up his army with the help of French subsidies and presented his Celle project as advantageous to Louis XIV: any move that increased the power of the anti-Hanoverian states in Germany would benefit France and harm the Grand Alliance. In reality Anton Ulrich, who had not taken his elder brother and co-regent, Rudolf August, fully into his confidence, was mainly concerned with depriving George of the Celle duchy; once he, Anton Ulrich, had conquered that duchy, the conventions which laid down George's succession on Georg Wilhelm's death could be regarded as null and void. As justification Anton Ulrich intended to use the argument that the senior branch of the house of Brunswick had a prior right to the duchy.

The danger to George was a real one. William III and Leopold realized this. Both agreed, once diplomatic pressure on Rudolf August had proved fruitless, to a pre-emptive strike by Hanover and Celle troops to force the abandonment of Anton Ulrich's pro-French stance. This operation was rightly seen as an essential precondition for the Allies' securing Brunswick-Lüneburg troops in the war against Louis XIV.

The diplomatic and military preparations for this venture, eventually fixed for the night of 19 and 20 March 1702, mark the decisive stage in George's training as an army commander and as a political leader. The coordination of the march into Wolfenbüttel (on a moonlit night to create the necessary element of surprise) with the timetable for the opening of the allied siege of Kaiserswerth was not easy, but the elector of Hanover showed maturity in his grasp of the Allies' difficulties and determination in fitting his and his uncle's plans into the all-over picture. The planning of the invasion routes, the working out of measures to avoid bloodshed and resistance by the population of Wolfenbüttel had to be thorough, and the most important orders for his troops were written by George himself: the invading forces were to make themselves masters of every church-tower as they progressed lest bells be rung in alarm; the soldiers should be warned that even the theft of a single chicken from Wolfen-büttel farms would be punished by death; it was strictly forbidden to damage any of Anton Ulrich's properties, and his beloved palace at Zahndam must be especially protected.

The operation was successful. Few lives were lost on either side. Anton Ulrich went into temporary exile, and Rudolf August abandoned Wolfenbüttel's French alliance. Wisely, George did not insist on Wolfenbüttel's recognition of the ninth electorate; he had no desire to let a 'selfish' Hanover aim detract from the official character of the Hanover-Celle action as one of obedience to Im-perial command to terminate the pro-French policy of Anton Ulrich.[57]

Relations between the two branches of the house of Brunswick did indeed improve rather than deteriorate after the 1702 operation. The invasion had shocked the Wolfenbüttel dukes into a realistic appraisal of their situation; and once their first anger had died down, they were impressed by the tact and moderation shown by George and Georg Wilhelm. Anton Ulrich returned, and when he became sole ruler (on Rudolf August's death in 1704) he accepted the Hanover-Celle merger of 1705; in 1706 he entered into a treaty of reconcili-ation with Hanover whereby he recognized the ninth electorate. Friendly visits between the two courts now resumed. That George harboured no ill-feelings towards the Wolfenbüttel branch of the *Gesamthaus* will become clear when his will of 1716 is discussed.

Meanwhile, quite apart from the main objective, the safeguarding of Celle, the Brunswick-Lüneburg dukes benefited in 1702 from Anglo-Dutch recognition of their possession of Sachsen-Lauenburg: a Wolfenbüttel share in the sequestration – which had been carried out in the name of the *Gesamthaus* – was deemed non-existent by the Maritime Powers while protection was promised for the Hanover-Celle claim, which (given Georg Wilhelm's advanced age) favoured George.

Brunswick-Lüneburg hopes, however, of improving on the terms of payment by the Allies for their troops once the War of the Spanish Succession had broken out, were doomed to disappointment. William

III's death – which had occurred during the Wolfenbüttel campaign – may have had some effect here. Queen Anne, while she had
immediately let George and Georg Wilhem know that she would
strictly keep all William's engagements, had a tough negotiator in
John Churchill, earl of Marlborough. He argued, and the Dutch
agreed with him, that George, who was now regarded as in charge of
his own and his uncle's foreign policy, must accept financial sacrifices
for the 'common cause' since he stood to benefit from Allied sponsorship of the Protestant succession in England, Scotland and Ireland.
Sophia of Hanover, queen Anne's heir, was old. It was more than
likely that George would succeed to the British crown, and the
Allies, it was argued, were fighting for George's future as well as
their own. Though mainly motivated at this stage by his concern for
the Empire's defence against France, George accepted their reasoning: he never pushed his yearly contract negotiations to the point of
disharmony within the Grand Alliance.[58]

LOSSES OF FRIENDS AND COMPANIONS

Georg Wilhelm had remained hale and hearty beyond what could
be expected for a man in his eighties. He still hunted vigorously, and
though he had of late become less active in politics, foreign and
domestic, he seemed so indestructible that his death in 1705 came
as a shock. According to Sophia's testimony, George took the loss of
his uncle greatly to heart.[59] He had seen much of him from his
earliest childhood and their joint interests, in politics as in hunting,
had formed a bond, especially after the death of George's father and
the death, or defection, of his elder brothers. Since then he had been
short of male company at home. Ernst August, the youngest of
Sophia's sons, followed the eldest 'like a dog', George having
carried responsibility for his military training from the campaign
of 1688 onwards. Ernst August's own letters between 1703 and 1714
show that, more often than not, he was wherever George was,
whether in Hanover, Herrenhausen, Pyrmont or Göhrde. But he
could not replace the male relative closest to George's heart, the
raugrave Karl Moritz, who died in 1702. In contrast to the elder
raugraves, Karl Moritz took no umbrage at the Hanoverian table
of ranks. While his brothers left Hanover to serve other princes, he
became a fixture at court, where his secret drinking was the despair
of Sophia, and his wit and conversation, based on wide reading, one
of the pleasures of George.*

* George, contrary to what is usually maintained, also enjoyed conversations with
Leibniz: see Sophia's letter of 17 March 1711 to George's daughter that her father is
not happy about Leibniz's many absences from Hanover, 'denn er liebt seine Unter-
haltung' (Sophia, *Correspondence with the Hohenzollerns*, p. 207).

The court of Hanover was abstemious; its moderation in the consumption of spirits, wines, and beer was commented on by all visitors, as were its polite manners.[60] Karl Moritz seldom, if ever, had the opportunity to get drunk at the electoral table, and great care was taken not to put temptation in his way. It proved impossible, however, to stop his solitary addiction to alcohol. Somehow or other, by cajoling or terrorizing servants, he had bottles smuggled into his quarters; and though he died from 'a sort of apoplexie' there was little doubt that it was drink that killed him. Sophia was absent from Herrenhausen at the time of Karl Moritz's illness, and George described his friend's death in letters to her. Until the very last day of his life the raugrave had been convinced that he would recover; then he was suddenly overcome by an *apprehension* of dying. To console him the elector had a clergyman brought to his bedside. This was not a success. Karl Moritz refused to conform. George's pride in his friend's stoicism is palpable in his report. Asked to repent his sins the raugrave 'kept silent'. Pressed to say whether he feared death, he returned a plain 'No'. When the clergyman insisted, ' "Mais Raugrave sy vous vennes deven [devant] la fasse du Seigneur que dirés vous", il repondit sechement, "je dirés rien".'

George missed Karl Moritz and mourned him: 'Comme j'ay eue d'amitié pour luy il m'est encore sy present.'[61] An even more deeply felt loss was that of George's sister, Sophia Charlotte, whose frequent visits to Hanover after her Hohenzollern marriage had sweetened life for her mother and eldest brother. She died after a brief illness at Herrenhausen in 1705 and, since Sophia herself was ill and confined to bed – too sick to be permitted by her doctors even to see her daughter to bid farewell – it was George who stayed with Figuelotte till the end. Again he admired his sister's stoic acceptance of death and the way in which she refused the proferred ministrations of clergy.[62] George, like many soldiers, held that fate decided the moment of entry and exit in the world and asserted, like them, that it was better to die suddenly than surrounded by wailing relatives and ineffectual medical men – an attitude, incidentally, which he shared with his mother.[63] Yet, the grief he experienced at the loss of Figuelotte nearly unnerved him. Years later his servant Mehemet recalled how his master, enraged at the seeming senselessness of his sister's death while still young and full of life, had paced his room for five days and nights, abstractedly kicking at the wainscoting ('as was his custom when upset'), trying to regain his composure, refusing food and company.[64] Georg Wilhelm's death, while sad, was easier to become reconciled to; reflection brought the realization that his uncle had been given much more than the biblical three score and ten. Compensation came also through the knowledge of the continuation of the house. In 1705 Georg August had married the intelligent and charming Caroline of Ansbach, and in 1707 the first grandson (christened Friedrich Ludwig, but in England always thought of as Frederick Louis) was born, a child to whom George felt particularly drawn.

IV

The royal crown

If George was now on his own and responsibility rested solely on his shoulders, there were challenges and opportunities ahead. The possibility of integrating Celle and Hanover more closely than the purely dynastic union demanded was within his grasp, and this was the first aim he set out to accomplish.

In the years of his electorship George had achieved greater insight into the administration and finances of Hanover than was possible when he had been the electoral prince. In the 1680s Ernst August and his advisers had reorganized the taxation system in collaboration with the Estates of Calenberg and Göttingen (those of Grubenhagen having to follow suit with less consultation). Taxation, which in Johann Friedrich's time had rested exclusively on land, was largely transferred to a number of important articles of consumption which enabled the duke to tax town and country alike. A salt tax had to be abandoned because it proved impossible to enforce, but the *Licent* was levied at a high rate on beer and malt, tobacco, grain, flour and bread, on cattle for slaughter and on meat in the butchers' shops, while clothes and luxuries were virtually exempt. The towns, which had earlier contributed only one-sixth of the income by taxation, now paid one-third. High nobility, *Ritterschaft* (the lesser nobility, of the *von* and *zu* variety), and clergy had, as elsewhere on the continent, managed to secure a measure of exemption, but were obliged by various means, such as the *don gratuit* and the near-forced loan, to contribute to the public exchequer.

The income of the duke of Hanover which came via the Estates in whatever form was allocated to the upkeep of the army, the need for which was keenly appreciated in a state where memories of invasion and occupations during the Thirty Years War were still alive. *Licent* money which exceeded expectations was paid into a special *Kasse* (literally, chest) for use in special contingencies. The

Estates' knowledge of and participation in the levying of this part of
the ducal revenue prepared George for the control which parliament
in Great Britain exercised over supply. But Ernst August and his son
were not as completely dependent as William III, queen Anne and
later George I himself on the money voted by parliament. Besides
the public exchequer Hanover had a *Kammer* (literally, chamber),
a treasury into which was paid the income from the ducal domains
and from the state's share in those Harz mines which belonged to
Hanover,* as well as foreign subsidies. This *Kammerkasse* was also
deployed for public expenditure, for the upkeep of the court, the
domestic administration, the diplomatic service and for defraying the
expenses levied on the duchy in its relationship to the Empire; but
the ruler felt fairly free to use it as he thought fit. The private ducal
income, derived from personal investment in mining and stocks, was
kept in yet another *Kasse*, the *Schatullkasse* (from *Schatulle*, literally
bureau-chest), and was spent for private purposes. The public
Kasse accounts (the *Kammerrechnungen*) were meticulously kept and
have survived; those for the *Kammerkasse* and the *Schatullkasse* have
not come down to us, though there are references to both in Ernst
August's will. It is clear that borrowing from one *Kasse* to another
was the rule of the day, at least in Ernst August's reign. From Professor Schnath's examinations of the budgets of the years after 1688
(when the new system was in full operation), it can be seen that
though the budgets balanced in theory, in practice the extent of
borrowing – to cover the extraordinary expenses connected with the
gaining of the electoral title, including the maintenance of un-
subsidized armies in Hungary during the 1692 and 1693 campaigns –
was significant.[1] In these transactions the Jewish court-financier
Elieser Lefmann Berens-Cohen, who had wide-ranging European
connections in Vienna, Prague, Amsterdam and Hamburg, was
especially important. That he grew rich is shown by his fine house in
the Neustadt and the synagogue which he built there.[2]

   After 1705 the Hanover taxation and financial system was extended to Celle. Integration of the administration also took place.
Bernstorff moved to Hanover, his ambition directed towards the
position of first minister whenever Platen, eighteen years his senior
and nowhere near as able as himself, should vacate it; but Weipart
Ludwig von Fabrice remained in Celle, where George established
the highest law-court† of the united duchies with this distinguished
legal expert as its chief administrator. The Celle Estates remained in
existence, on an equal footing with those of Calenberg-Göttingen;

---

* The mines of Lauterberg, Klausthal, Andreasberg, Altenau and Elbingerode belonged
to Hanover alone; those of Zellerfeld, Wildemann, Lautenthal, Grund and Gittelde were
owned jointly with the duke of Brunswick-Wolfenbüttel; the mines of Goslar (the most
important was that of Rammelsberg near Goslar) were also jointly owned. A French
diplomat (Rousseau de Chamoy) estimated in 1679 that Hanover owned four-sevenths
of all mining resources of the region, Wolfenbüttel three-sevenths. After 1679 Ernst
August also exploited the Upper Harz mines of Osterode and Herzberg.
† *Oberappellationsgericht.*

but the social unification of the duchies proceeded apace, and smoothly.

The amalgamation itself produced certain savings in the administration which benefited the population at large: the burdens on the common man in both duchies were lighter after 1705 than before. And for those in official positions, whether civil or military, the 1705 union brought better career prospects, especially since George, because of his place in the English succession, was destined to play a larger part on the European scene than Georg Wilhelm had in the last years of his reign. There was hardly any cause for friction. The newer administrative nobility in both duchies had, as elsewhere in Europe, begun to intermarry with the older feudal nobility possessed of large estates, while the younger members of the old noble families had increasingly sought court and administrative positions. Lampe's claim that the reigns of Ernst August and George were those in which the Hanoverian 'urban patriciate' was formed is largely justified;[3] though it should not be forgotten that the newer families, even before they were dignified with the Imperial titles of *Reichsfreiherr* or *Reichsgraf*, busily acquired land, and that the urbanized younger sons of the old feudal nobility took great pains to keep their links with the family estate, or estates, which through entails (*Fideikommis*) had gone to their elder brothers. They visited these estates when their duties permitted and rallied to the help of those members of the family who got into such serious money difficulties that the patrimony seemed threatened.

A good example of the first category, though more successful than most, is Andreas Gottlieb von Bernstorff. He came of a renowned family originating in Mecklenburg; but the early death of his father, an administrator in Ratzeburg, made him completely dependent on his official career. Immensely hard-working and ambitious, he invested in land all the money he could spare from his salary and the many perquisites that came his way as first minister of Celle. In 1694 he bought from Georg Wilhelm the district of Gartow, a purchase that was to involve him in later quarrels with the king of Prussia,* and he collected enough property in Mecklenburg to bring him, as a member of its *Ritterschaft*, into conflict with tsar Peter.[4] Both issues (as we shall see) were to have some influence on his later political stance.

From the second category, that of the court or urbanized sons of the landed nobility, the example of the von der Schulenburg family may be cited. The unmarried eldest son, Johann Matthias, and his sister Melusine spent more money than they could easily afford to pay the debts (occasioned by his obsession with expensive alchemy

---

* This long-standing conflict derived from the claim to superior rights over the Gartow district of the Hohenzollern dynasty as former grandmasters. In 1687 Georg Wilhelm dispossessed the then owners (of the von Bülow family) as they had been found guilty of felony by their support for the Hohenzollern claim.

experiments) of their brother, Daniel Bodo, the heir presumptive, lest he should endanger the family estates of his succession; and it was at Emden, at his mother's estate, that their half-brother in George's service, Friedrich Wilhelm, spent short leaves in 1718 and 1719 when the king-elector visited Hanover.[5]

The families already mentioned help to illustrate that George's ministers and courtiers were not drawn exclusively from Brunswick-Lüneburg: the von der Schulenburgs came – as we have seen – from Altmark and the Bernstorffs from Mecklenburg. Some families, such as the von Hattorfs and the von Bülows, were of Brunswick-Lüneburg nobility, while the von dem Bussches, of a distinguished old Osnabrück line, were reckoned equally close because of the Brunswick-Lüneburg connection with the bishopric of Osnabrück. But for the rest, George (like his father before him) put men into office and court posts from a variety of states. It should be noted, however, that in George's reign the majority of these were of north German or of Rhineland Protestant stock; and that he, in contrast to his father, employed very few non-Germans as diplomats. The bond of loyalty was service to the house, supported by a secondary loyalty to Empire and emperor with – at times – specific concern for the Protestant states within the north German circles.* An even more important criterion was previous experience; the Hesse-born Friedrich Wilhelm von Görtz, for instance, had held high office in Holstein before entering Hanoverian service in 1686.

There was naturally enough a measure of dynastic succession within the families who reached ministerial or *Kabinett* office. Bernstorff's career was eased – though his ability and capacity for hard work were recognized by all[6] – by his marriage to the daughter of the Celle chancellor Johann Helwig Sinold, Freiherr von Schütz. Two sons of von Schütz were employed on joint diplomatic missions by Celle and Hanover even before 1705; and when one of them (Ludwig Justus) died in 1710 while accredited to St James's he was replaced by his nephew (the son of Salentin Justus). Yet another of the younger members of the family was made *Kammerjunker* (later *Kammerherr*) to George in 1712 and went with him to England.[7] Otto Grote's son, Thomas, became a minister in 1712, but died in 1713. Johann von Hattorf, who had held important *Kabinett* positions (simultaneously *Geheimsekretär* and *Kriegssekretär*), decided in 1714 that he was too old to move to England; but his son, Johann Philipp, became George's *Kabinettsekretär* and remained in that position for the rest of George's life. Thomas Eberhard von Ilten, son of the Hanoverian minister Jobst Hermann, became a *Kriegsrat* and in 1715 joined George in England. Two of the von der Reiche family, Jobst

---

* Hanover was represented in two of these circles (see map 1), that of Westphalia and that of Lower Saxony, while the whole of Celle territory was within the Lower Saxon circle.

(who had already made his mark in Hanover) and his son Andreas, served in the *Deutsche Kanzlei* in London and were retained in their posts after George I's death. When younger men were appointed, like Friedrich Wilhelm von der Schulenburg and Friedrich Ernst von Fabrice, their family connections clearly helped, though their education and previous experience were equally important. Merit was, indeed, the deciding factor in administrative as well as military promotion and men could make their way without direct family influence. The career of Hans Kaspar von Bothmer is a convenient example of this. He started in diplomacy, became a courtier (a gentleman-in-waiting to Sophia Dorothea), was given increasingly important diplomatic missions and so ended up, after 1714, as one of George's most trusted Hanoverian ministers in London. He was less independent of mind than Bernstorff, but more ambitious socially. While Bernstorff refused to be created a *Reichsgraf* and contented himself in 1715 with accepting the title of *Reichsfreiherr*, Bothmer felt that his career was crowned by his patent as *Reichsgraf* and even stipulated in his will that his heir, a nephew, should institute the non-German custom of reserving the title of *Graf* for the head of the family, younger sons to be known by the title *Freiherr*.[8]

The concern that ministers and diplomats should be Protestants was linked to the prospect of the English succession, and even a courtier in high office who converted to Catholicism was expected to resign.[9] Exceptions were, however, made for artists of every kind, even if – like Quirini – they had court titles such as 'director of palaces and buildings'. Here the Italian-orientated tradition of the reigns of Johann Friedrich and Ernst August was largely maintained, though the growing influence of French Huguenot refugees in his father's reign was intensified in George's: the architect Rémy de la Fosse, employed from 1705 at Göhrde, is one instance. George used some Italian artists, most notable among them the painter Tommaso Giusti who decorated both Herrenhausen and Göhrde; and members of the Quirini family were made welcome even at George's English court.

One example of this is the private royal hospitality shown to a young diplomat of that name who represented the republic of Venice in London after 1714.[10] The appointment of Georg Friedrich Handel in 1710 as *Kapellmeister* in Hanover on Steffani's retirement marks, all the same, a shift towards a more northern Protestant orientation not unconnected with George's prospects in England. It is also worth stressing that, though the elector still sent his gardeners to France,[11] it was in the Dutch Republic that he ordered the tapestries and furniture and objets d'art in 1705 which he wanted for his refurbishing of Herrenhausen: thanks to the many Huguenot artists who had settled in the northern Netherlands French craftsmanship was available even to those who did not want to enrich Louis XIV's France by their purchases.[12]

George's patronage of Huguenot artists and craftsmen formed one bond with the duchy of Celle where the court, ever since Georg Wilhelm's marriage to Eléonore d'Olbreuse, had been a haven for French Protestants. More important for the Celle duchy as a whole was George's great interest in Göhrde. Here, on the site of Georg Wilhelm's hunting lodge, he built a minor palace after his own taste, with fine stables but also with a theatre where plays and ballets were performed.[13] The hunting was good, the comfort and entertainment of guests generous. British undersecretaries shook their heads at the extravagance of their ruler and expressed relief in 1723 that expenses for 60 guests and 300 horses were paid from George's Hanoverian pocket.[14] That year was, however, exceptional in that lavish Göhrde hospitality for large numbers was dictated by diplomatic considerations. The number of non-family visitors was usually more modest, though the standard of hospitality was equally high. George's predilection for the palace, quite apart from the fine hunting of the region, may have owed something to the fact that it was more 'his palace', and Melusine's, than Herrenhausen which Ernst August had left, with its surrounding villages, to Sophia during her widowhood.

GEORGE'S HOUSEHOLD AFTER 1698

George had, however, also begun to set his mark on Herrenhausen. Already in 1699 Sophia transferred the income willed to her for the upkeep of that palace to George on condition that he would take care of all expenses connected with it and its grounds. This was the start of a successful expansion programme of palace and gardens, in the main completed by 1708, but which did not end till George's death. The magnificent *Galerie*, with its huge ground-floor room for summer festivities, was now decorated and embellished with marble busts of Roman emperors. An outside orange garden was laid out and added to by transfer of trees from Celle in 1705 and later purchases: by 1720 the trees were so numerous that they could no longer be kept over the winter in the *Galerie*, and a new orangery was built. Fountains were improved, the 'Big Fountain' being completed by 1720; canals were dug and gondolas obtained; huge vases were ordered and skilfully placed; and the fine Herrenhausen allée, of more than 1300 linden trees, was planted.*

* It is clear that the *Galerie* and the *Orangerie* were intended as first stages towards a total rebuilding of Herrenhausen, a three-dimensional *Modell zum Herrenhausischen Bauwesen* having been made as early as 1689 by Johann Heinrich Wachter. The War of the Spanish Succession and George's move to England brought an end to major operations.

At Göhrde, and to some extent also at the Leineschloss and at Herrenhausen, Melusine was, after 1698, openly George's hostess. She was given precedence over all other ladies at court with the exception of the dowager electress and visiting royalty. Sophia did, in any case, usually keep to her own quarters, the magnificently decorated suite of rooms on the first floor of the *Galeriegebäude*, though she often took her meals with George. She was thrown more closely together with Melusine on visits to Göhrde, but all she would permit herself in her correspondence in the nature of complaint was that Mlle von der Schulenburg could 'hardly be reckoned to *her* court-ladies any more'.[15] She did resent, however, George's strict control – even when he was absent with the army during the War of the Spanish Succession – of the allocation of rooms at Herrenhausen lest the raugravines should steal a march on Melusine; Sophia's ruse, to permit visiting raugravines state rooms, was politely but firmly checkmated lest it prove a step up the ladder of precedence for them.[16]

The position at court of George's half-sister, Sophia Charlotte von Platen, married in 1701 to Johann Adolf von Kielmansegg, at times caused problems. We hear of some offence given by her to Georg August and of Ernst August smoothing over the difficulties that ensued. Here we may have the beginning of a certain tension between Sophia Charlotte and Caroline, which became noticeable in the post-1714 years to the extent that English ladies warned each other against praising one to the other and English statesmen tried to use either one or the other as a channel of communications, and it was hoped influence, with George I.[17] Johann Adolf shared an interest in opera and music with George, and in many ways typified the younger generation of servants that George brought into his household. He was given the post of *Oberstallmeister* in Hanover, moved with his family to England in 1714 and, though never formally English master of the horse, held most of the prerogatives – though not the salary – of that position from the autumn of 1714 till his death three years later.[18] Of an even younger generation we should note Melusine's half-brother, Friedrich Wilhelm, whose studies abroad George had sponsored and whom he used for a mission to 'Carlos III' during the War of the Spanish Succession, before bringing him formally into his household in England,[19] and Friedrich Ernst von Fabrice, the son of the jurist already mentioned, in whose services as a Holstein-Gottorp diplomat George took an interest before employing him as a semi-official diplomat and, eventually, finding him a Hanoverian court post in 1719.[20] As personal attendants on George two Turks, Mehemet and Mustafa, held long-established positions though they were, and remained, body-servants without political influence. Contrary to popular legend neither had been captured by George during his Hungarian campaigns: English historiography would seem to have confused them with a young Turkish boy whom George did capture and send home to his mother.[21] Mehemet was brought to Hanover by an officer under George's command, and Mustafa – after a period in the service of the Swedish officer who had captured him – was transferred to that of George. Of the two, both so much a fixture at George's court in England that they were depicted in the murals of Kensington Palace, Mehemet held the more responsible position and was in charge of George's private accounts, the *Schatullrechnungen* or *Quittungen* from 1699 until his death in 1726.[22] The surname he adopted on his ennoblement in 1716, von Königstreu (lit. true to the king), can be assumed to have been chosen by himself – since self-advertisement was against George's temperament – and tells us something of his attitude to his master.

THE WAR OF THE SPANISH SUCCESSION

Both before and after 1705, foreign affairs were of prime importance for George. He took an interest in the strategy and tactics of the War of the Spanish Succession, and kept a watchful eye on English affairs and on Hanover's relationship to the emperor and the Empire. His knowledge of the Rhine frontier as well as of the Netherlands battlefields explains a scheme which he pushed, with his uncle Georg Wilhelm, in the early stages of the war for massive deployment on the Middle and Upper Rhine of German troops independently maintained or in the pay of the Maritime Powers. Versions of this plan were never far from his thoughts. Once the danger to the Empire after the French victories of 1702 became apparent, he was one of those who urged a campaign in Bavaria by Marlborough and prince Eugène. There has been much discussion of the 'originator' of the 1704 Blenheim campaign. Recent English historians have been more inclined to give part at least of the glory, earlier reserved for Marlborough alone, to the Habsburg diplomat Wratislaw who persuaded Marlborough to go south.[23] But behind Wratislaw we can discern men of military experience on the Rhine, and George especially. Documents preserved in the Bernstorff archive show that he urged such a campaign as the only solution to the predicament of Leopold, ground between Hungarian revolt in the east and French advances in the west.[24]

Sophia, proud of her son's successful intervention in the Holstein-

Gottorp affair in 1700, hoped that the War of the Spanish Succession would give him an opportunity to add laurels to his fame. Might he not be made the leader of the coalition against Louis XIV, inheriting the mantle of William III? Individual Dutchmen suggested him as commander-in-chief for the army of the United Provinces: he had, in their opinion, all the qualities of a 'great general'.[25] Such dreams were, however, unrealistic. Hanover could not bear war costs in any way comparable to those undertaken by the Maritime Powers. Those who paid the piper felt entitled to call the tune and, by 1705, when George had inherited Celle and had more money at his disposal, the experience of Marlborough and Eugène in commanding large-scale forces far outweighed his. So did their ambitions. They had their way to make in the world and had no intention of letting the elector of Hanover take up any position which might detract from their search for glory and its rewards. This explains, in part, why George's hopes, limited to an independent command of part of the allied army, were frustrated. After 1705, he was willing to furnish sizable forces at his own cost to breach the French positions on the Middle and Upper Rhine. But he was not taken seriously; indeed, at times he was deceived by the chief allied commanders in the interests of the strategy on which they had privately agreed.

Quite apart from Marlborough's and Eugène's fears that George's rank would create problems (might he not try to impose his ideas on them?), the elector suffered from the lack of confidence of the Anglo-Dutch leadership in the emperor's willingness to put the Empire first. Leopold had his eyes firmly fixed on Italy; there, once troops could be spared from Hungary, he wanted to direct the main Habsburg war effort. Better things were expected from Joseph (who succeeded Leopold in 1705), but the *Reichsarmee* continued to be starved of troops. Its commander, margrave Ludwig of Baden, was known to be dissatisfied with the way the initiative was monopolized by Eugène, always concerned with the interests of the house of Habsburg. Marlborough for his part was content, after the successful campaign in Bavaria of 1704, to let the war in the Empire rest so that he might pursue vigorous campaigns in the Netherlands in the hope of a breakthrough into France.

The German princes, however, had war aims of their own. The allied occupation after 1704 of the territories of the two electors who had sided with Louis XIV, Bavaria and Cologne, excited the appetites of some of these princes; though it was realized that the emperor would demand the lion's share of Bavaria. All of them were vocal in demanding that Alsace and Strassburg and, if possible, also Franche-Comté (which, though a Spanish possession before 1678, had once formed part of the Imperial circles) should be regained for Germany as a barrier against France. The house of Habsburg was strongly in favour of such reconquests, which constituted its 'German mission'. But it held that they could be won at the negotiation table as long as the emperor made sure of conquering, with Anglo-Dutch naval help, all Spain's Italian possessions; much as Marlborough argued that Spain could be wrested from Philip V if France was beaten in the Netherlands. The Hofburg and Whitehall had nothing against diversionary military efforts on the Middle and Upper Rhine, and at times encouraged them. With financial resources stretched to the utmost on the other fronts, however, they regarded such efforts as bows at a venture: if they succeeded good and well, if they failed nothing much was lost.

This attitude was naturally galling to the Imperial field marshal, to his second-in-command Thüngen (to whom he increasingly left the thankless task of leading the *Reichsarmee*) and to all 'honnêtes gens' in the Empire.[26] When the margrave died in January 1707, it was not easy to find a successor. The Imperial diet unanimously chose prince Eugène so as to animate the Habsburg 'German mission'. But Joseph was not prepared to spare his best general: 1707 was the year of the allied Toulon attempt and the Austrian conquest of Naples.

In Germany that year's campaign gave cause for alarm. French invasions threatened all along a western frontier too thinly defended. The new *Reichsfeldmarschall*, the margrave of Brandenburg-Bayreuth, showed little or no initiative. The reputation of George, who with a Hanoverian contingent had command of one section of the western front, rocketed, however, during 1707 and he was generally lauded as 'the saviour of the fatherland'.[27]* It is now known that the French commander Villars' withdrawal to the left bank of the Rhine in July 1707 was the result less of George's military exploits than of the danger which threatened France from the Austro-Savoyard march towards Toulon; but the lustre which was added to the elector of Hanover's name explains why he was pressed to accept the Imperial field marshal's baton for the rest of the campaign and also why he acquiesced. He was fully aware of the difficulties under which his predecessors had laboured, but hoped that he could pin down Vienna and the Imperial diet firmly enough over money and men to make something of his command. He had little difficulty with the diet. Money and men were promised and George showed great energy and resourcefulness in making sure that these promises were kept.

Plans for the coming campaign were co-ordinated in April 1708 in Hanover with Marlborough and Eugène: the greatest strength

* *Retter des Reiches*

was to be concentrated on the Rhine-Moselle fronts, with George and Eugène in independent command of two separate armies, while Marlborough with Anglo-Dutch forces would act defensively to tie France down in the Netherlands. The prospect of offensive action was more important to George than the title of *Reichsfeldmarschall*; and the disillusionment he suffered later in the year, when it dawned upon him that Marlborough and Eugène had deliberately deceived him, was severe. They had privately agreed, long before April 1708, that the main allied effort was to be in the Netherlands and that by means of ostensibly confidential letters during the campaign, addressed to each other but meant to be passed on to George, they would pretend that a sudden emergency had occurred which made it necessary for Eugène's Moselle army to join Marlborough. The only other person who was privy to this secret, if in general terms, was the emperor Joseph; and he, like Marlborough and Eugène, judged the deceit of George essential so that the French might be lured to draw the major part of their forces to the Rhine and the Moselle. Only in this way could Marlborough and Eugène attempt to break Louis XIV's fortified lines to thrust at the heart of France. 'I do not like having to deceive the Elector', wrote Marlborough; but while the historian appreciates his and Eugène's motives, their natural desire to keep control in their own hands being strengthened by their disbelief in the efficacy of the *Reichsarmee*, he may conclude that the better course might have been to take the elector into their confidence. To judge from all evidence available, and especially from George's lack of rancour in his later cooperation with the two commanders, his consent would have been given. As it was, the resources of the Empire were needlessly wasted.[28]

The campaign of 1709, as far as the *Reichsarmee* was concerned, proved just as frustrating and more damaging to George's reputation. Again George did wonders in rallying the diet and obtained firm promises of money, especially from the Hanse towns. He worked out a plan which, though this time only diversionary, might make a real contribution to the allied war effort. Moreover, he made sure that the Maritime Powers, and prince Eugène personally, accepted the scheme as part of a strategy of encouragement for revolts inside France to facilitate allied invasions on several fronts. That the Allies hoped to use the revolt of the Camisards in the Cevennes to weaken Louis is well-known, 'the affair of Besançon' less so. Negotiations had long been afoot with discontented French subjects in Franche-Comté. It was assumed that if the *Reichsarmee* arrived there in strength in 1709, men of standing would make common cause with Louis' enemies or at least make occupation of the province easier and thus help build the western barrier against France. Swiss sympathizers with the Imperial cause had suggested a route for the *Reichsarmee* which, in part, traversed canton territory. Success was reckoned likely.

Habsburg measures, however, ruined George's prospects of carrying out his plan. Emperor Joseph appropriated the Hanse money for his own army to achieve his house's priority aims. This in its turn brought other defections in assignations, troops and quarters by German princes. The result was that the *Reichsfeld-marschall* had to open his campaign with too few troops to take the initiative. He could not even revenge the defeat at Rumersheim of general Mercy, one of his commanders who, during an exploratory manoeuvre, was surprised by the French. Whether George would have succeeded if he had been given a freer hand cannot be answered. It is, however, unlikely. French intelligence had got wind of the invasion scheme and had arrested some of its key men in Franche-Comté. George never blamed Mercy, a brave officer; though he let it be known among those who were closest to him that the general had acted without his knowledge. He himself was, however, held responsible for the defeat at Rumersheim; not by the German princes, who were well informed of the problems which any commander of the *Reichsarmee* faced, but by other allied commanders who sought a scape-goat. Later Jacobite propaganda even contrived to insinuate that it was George in person who had been defeated at Rumersheim.

For his part George felt he had had enough. In the given circum-stances it was impossible to deploy the *Reichsarmee* profitably and he laid down his field marshal's baton, never to go on active service again.[29] A significant gain had, however, come to Hanover in 1708; partly because of George's rise in reputation in the campaign of 1707 and partly because of his skilful use of the opportunity offered when all the chambers of the diet begged him to take on the com-mand of the Imperial army. As all electors, Catholic and Protestant, wished to secure his services, his suggestion that Hanover should, at last, be admitted to the Electoral College could not be refused. From 1708 onwards the ninth electorate took its seat in that college; and in 1710, when George was allotted one of the Imperial offices, the arch-treasureship, he could feel that he had completed the work of Ernst August.

DEATH OF QUEEN ANNE: THE 'ACT OF SETTLEMENT'
PUT INTO EFFECT

After the frustrations suffered in the 1708 and 1709 campaigns

George concentrated on the English succession. Since the crisis of 1705–06 he had kept control of Hanoverian policy in his own hands. He had taken a close interest in the negotiations for the Union between England and Scotland, well aware that only such a union could safeguard the Hanoverian succession in Scotland. The pro-Hanoverians were in a majority among the English members of the commission which negotiated the union; the secretary of the commission reported regularly to George and was later well rewarded.[30] The elector was greatly pleased with the Anglo-Dutch Treaty of Barrier and Succession of 1709 which promised Dutch military help if the Hanoverian cause seemed in danger; and Townshend, the Whig negotiator of that treaty, was marked for future promotion.

George was not merely a passive observer. He watched carefully that no interference which he thought prejudicial to the cause of his house should occur: James Scott – who had been in Sophia's service and who in 1707 paid a private visit to England – was told that he was no longer *persona grata* in Hanover as his private diplomacy to have Sophia invited to England counteracted that of the elector.[31]

George's decisive and open actions took place after queen Anne dropped Marlborough and Godolphin and made Harley her chief manager. The elector was initially motivated less by a belief that Anne and her ministers would bring in the Pretender (though this was widely rumoured in Europe, and Sophia was worried that this was the reason for the change of government in England)[32] than by his alarm at the English separate peace. George was convinced that the cause of Hanover and the Empire was best served by the Marlborough-Godolphin duumvirate and protested against the removal of the general who had become identified with the English war effort on the European continent.[33] The elector shared the general resentment of Britain's allies at being left in the lurch by Ormonde's 'restraining orders' of May 1712 (which forbade that commander to act against the French armies) and their indignation when it became clear that these orders had been secretly communicated to Louis XIV's general, Villars, permitting him to trap France's remaining enemies at Denain. George, like other German princes who had subsidy treaties with queen Anne, disassociated himself from her government and carried on the fight against Louis at his own expense, helped by the Dutch Republic. Their loyalty to emperor and Empire dictated their unanimous decision to stay put when Ormonde's British regiments left the field. So did their hope that such a demonstration might have some effect on Harley (now earl of Oxford)* and St John and halt them on their road to a separate peace. Their self-interest was naturally

---

* Harley had been created earl of Oxford in 1711; St John had to wait till July 1712 for his lesser title of viscount Bolingbroke.

involved: since the peace negotiations were conducted solely between Britain and France, specific Dutch, German and Habsburg objectives could only be achieved in so far as they suited queen Anne's government. It was the lack of consultation that rankled. The Dutch and the Germans, as war-weary as the British, found it galling to see the Grand Alliance break up after so many years of joint effort: they realized that without Britain it was unlikely that the other allies could for long avoid coming to terms with Louis, negotiating now from strength.

In the event George did not come out badly in the peace-makings of 1713–14. Queen Anne's new government repudiated the 1709 barrier treaty with the Dutch, but the treaty negotiated in 1713 still contained a Dutch guarantee of the Protestant succession; and in his treaty with the Empire of 1714 Louis XIV recognized the ninth electorate. The German barrier was not obtained, but this affected Hanover less than more west-lying states of Germany, and George was (as we shall see) at this time more concerned with developments in north Germany than with the west and south of the Empire.

Yet George protested at Britain's separate peace in firmer words than was relished by Anne and her ministry.[34] He did so from a variety of motives. Since he was in the line of succession he wished to take a clear stand. As a soldier he felt Britain's honour was besmirched by her defection and wanted no stain on his own reputation by seeming to condone it. He had little expectation that his action might restrain Anne's ministers, but it was worth giving notice of future displeasure lest worse should follow. We now know that queen Anne was no Jacobite, and that after March 1714 neither Oxford nor St John seriously expected that James Edward Stuart stood a chance of succeeding her. Up to then they had given guarded promises (always with the proviso that James would have to turn Anglican even if he remained a Catholic at heart) via the French foreign minister, Torcy, who skilfully hid from Saint-Germain the demand for a public change of religion until the Anglo-French peace was secure. The promises of the English ministers were no doubt greatly influenced by their desire for a peace with France: by holding out hopes that they would work for James they prevented Louis XIV from bringing the Dutch into the negotiations until they had tied France to a settlement which gave Britain the greater advantages. The need for reinsurance also operated with the two chief ministers. They were bound to offend George by their separation from the Grand Alliance, and who could tell what the future might bring? James, if he turned Anglican, would be far preferable to many Britons than the octogenarian Sophia and her German son.

The negotiations which touched upon James's succession, and in which Oxford played a greater role than St John (now Bolingbroke) did not remain a secret: at The Hague and in Hanover it was believed that the British ministry was plotting to subvert the Hanoverian succession even after James's declaration in March 1713 that he would never change his own religion, though he promised not to interfere with the Anglican beliefs of his subjects, had made Oxford and Bolingbroke good Hanoverians once more.[35]

The serious illness of queen Anne at the turn of the year 1713–14 caused general and growing speculation as to her successor, in Britain as in Europe. The fact that her speech from the throne on 2 March did not mention the Hanoverian succession was thought a bad omen by Bothmer, and George – whose hands were freer since the emperor (after a disappointing campaign) had made peace with Louis XIV – decided that the moment had come to act. Marlborough and his wife had left England in the hope of being able to delay the Habsburg-French peace which had implications for Marlborough in his capacity as prince of Mindelsheim.* George now arranged for Marlborough to have full powers from Hanover to defend the succession should James invade England on queen Anne's death. The British troops stationed in the Southern Netherlands as part of the Anglo-Dutch condominium forces could be used, and reinforced by Dutch and German regiments, if this became necessary. At the same time measures were concerted with the Whigs and the Hanoverian Tories in England. To give them a lever George sanctioned the question which young Schütz put on Sophia's behalf on 12/23 April 1714 'whether the electoral prince, as duke of Cambridge, should not have a writ enabling him to take his seat in the House of Lords'. In 1706 George had opposed his mother's desire to have Georg August go to England. Now necessity coincided with opportunity: an open move (cautiously phrased) would bring clarity in the succession issue or, at the very least, help the Whigs and the Hanoverian Tories to counteract measures which they feared were to be taken in favour of James. It certainly put Oxford on the spot. The privy council could find no legal grounds on which to refuse the writ. It was duly issued, but to mark the queen's displeasure Schütz was forbidden the court. Oxford's position was undermined: he had been seen to be powerless to save Anne from the prospect of having a Hanoverian coming to England. Bolingbroke – who was for refusing the writ – rose in favour.

George, however, was shrewd enough not to send his son over despite the pleas of Sophia, Caroline and Leibniz. He accepted the strictures implied in letters from the queen to his mother and his son

---

* The restoration of the electors of Cologne and Bavaria which Louis XIV obtained in the peace of Rastadt (March 1714) meant that Marlborough lost his principality (though not his title) of Mindelsheim in Bavaria.

and repudiated Schütz.* The actual move was no longer essential, he and his Dutch allies agreed, since he had succeeded in giving his supporters in England the lever they wanted: in June 1714 the Whigs, with Hanoverian Tory help, forced through parliament the promise of a reward for the capture of the 'pretended Prince of Wales'. [36]

The final touches to George's preparations were made after the death of Sophia on 8 June 1714 NS. The dowager electress's end was, as she had wished, mercifully quick. She felt faint during a walk in the Herrenhausen gardens, having hurried to shelter from sudden rain; she died in the arms of Gräfin Johanne Sophie zu Schaumburg-Lippe – one of her court ladies whom we shall meet again. Whether Sophia's death was hastened by the agitation she experienced on reading the censorious letters from queen Anne (as has often been claimed) is impossible to tell; what evidence we have is that she was only temporarily annoyed or agitated and that she soon mastered her irritation. Her last political act was to arrange for copies of the letters to herself and her grandson to be sent to Marlborough in the expectation that they should be published. It would have been out of character if, at this time, she had done so without consulting George; nor is it likely that Marlborough should have arranged for publication (as he did) if he had thought this would not be condoned by the elector. [37]

Upon his mother's death, George was the direct heir of queen Anne and as such he could and did revise the list of the Hanoverian chosen regents. The significance of the names on this list, as indications of George's thoughts on what kind of government he hoped to achieve in Britain, will be discussed in the next chapter. What needs stressing here is that during the final crisis at Anne's deathbed everything – in spite of George's careful preparations – depended on the way Anne's high officials used their power.

The dramatic sequence of events is well known. The queen dismissed Oxford as treasurer on 27 July/7 August. Like most of her remaining ministers, she was not keen to put Bolingbroke in supreme command and all agreed that the treasury should be put in commission. Discussions on the composition of the commission took time and Bolingbroke thought himself sure of being head of the government. His friends congratulated him and he began arrangements to send an emissary of his own to Hanover to assure George of his determination to promote the Hanoverian succession. Anne herself, weary unto death, expressed to her physician her desire to send to Hanover for George, so that he could take the responsibility off her shoulders. [38] The standard accounts have, however, assumed

---

* English historians have, therefore, assumed that Sophia was acting without her son's knowledge and have followed Trevelyan, *England under Queen Anne* III, pp. 278–79 in their accounts; a recent doctoral thesis based on new Hanover material by G. E. Gregg has demonstrated the elector's complicity.

that the decisive move, the securing of the treasurer's staff to the duke of Shrewsbury, was the work of Bothmer in cooperation with the dukes of Somerset and Argyll who, unbidden, went to Kensington Palace, burst into the privy council meeting and, with Shrewsbury, took control. A recent comparison by Professor Snyder of new material – the journal of the postmaster-general Sir John Evelyn who was related by marriage to the lord chancellor, Simon viscount Harcourt – with the *Diarium* of Bothmer for 30 July/10 August has shown that this was not so: the vital role was played by the lord chancellor. Once Harcourt had been told by the queen's doctors that she could not survive for more than a few hours, he called together those lords of the committee and members of the privy council who were already at Kensington and proposed to them that the council should advise the queen to make Shrewsbury lord treasurer. As soon as Anne 'came to her senses' after her stroke and could recognize people around her (though not articulate beyond Yes and No), a delegation consisting of Harcourt, Buckingham (lord president), Bolton (lord steward), Dartmouth, (lord privy seal) and Bolingbroke (secretary of state) went to give her their recommendation; on the queen's nodding her assent, Harcourt held her hand to direct the staff to the duke of Shrewsbury. Bothmer, fetched by the dukes of Somerset and Argyll at 12 noon, must have arrived at Kensington Palace too late to have influenced this event. Somerset had been alerted by a message, timed 11.30 a.m., sent from Kensington Palace by his wife, a lady of the bedchamber to the queen, conveying an invitation from Dartmouth and Bolton for him to come to Kensington. On his own authority he decided to bring Argyll and Bothmer along. Somerset and Argyll joined the council after Shrewsbury's appointment, and it was Harcourt who made preparations for the patent for Shrewsbury's appointment, brought it to Kensington for the queen's signature (or approval), and saw to it that it was enrolled. Only after that, in the evening, could Shrewsbury take his formal oath as lord treasurer.[39]

On the first day of August queen Anne died. The list of regents was opened. Those who were in London were sought out and sworn in, and just after one o'clock George I was proclaimed by the usual ceremony of heralds without any untoward incident. The proclamation, with one hundred and twenty-seven signatures, used the traditional forms (which included the British claim to France) and read

We therefore, the Lords Spiritual and Temporal of the Realm, being here assisted with those of her late Majesty's Privy Council, with numbers of other principal gentlemen of quality, with the Lord Mayor, Aldermen and Citizens of London, do now hereby with one full voice and consent of tongue and heart, publish and proclaim that the High and Mighty Prince George Elector of Brunswick Lüneburg is now by the death of our late sovereign of Happy Memory, become our lawful and rightful liege Lord, George by the Grace of God King of Great Britain, France and Ireland.[40]

V

Settling down

The Great Britain of which George became ruler on 1/12 August 1714 had, since 1688, been one of the great powers of Europe, intimately involved with the continent and yet – as several attempts at Jacobite invasions by those who favoured the restoration of James II and (after 1701) 'James III' had shown – sufficiently protected by its island position to render it invulnerable as long as the Protestant revolution had the support of the majority of the inhabitants. William III's determination to make England the arbiter of Europe had not been generally popular, but during the wars against Louis XIV between 1689 and 1713 this role had become accepted and even appreciated, sweetened by Marlborough's military victories between 1704 and 1708, and hardened by the singleminded ruthlessness of Oxford and Bolingbroke in settling Europe's affairs between 1710 and 1713 without consulting Britain's allies. The growth in national self-assertiveness was striking. The leading men of queen Anne's last ministry let Europe know that England felt free to make peace with France whenever it wanted and was in 'no need of a mediator'.[1]

Such behaviour reflected pride not only in the actual war-effort of Great Britain but in the skilful use of resources to finance the two long wars. William III had been a hard taskmaster at the treasury; he and his pupils, as well as French Protestant refugees and Dutch-trained bankers, had brought about the 'financial revolution' which enabled Britain to fit out large navies and pay considerable armies (the greater part of which consisted of foreign auxiliary troops) with less stress than was imposed on Louis XIV's France.[2] So complete was the success of this financial revolution that, though William himself had at times been forced to threaten abdication and announce his determination to 'retire to the Indies' unless money was forthcoming,[3] Oxford found it relatively easy to raise money even when the Bank of England opposed his policies: thanks to the support of Tory-minded financial men at home and abroad (John Drummond, the merchant and banker settled in the Dutch Republic, is a good example of the latter), and the foundation of the South Sea Company in 1711, he was able to weather the crisis of 1710 to 1712.[4]

Tories of the blue-water school who advocated concentration on seaward expansion and conquests in the West Indies and on the American continent (north and south), with consequent disengagement from European land warfare, and Whigs who argued that overseas gains could most easily be won if the European campaigns were pushed to the very gates of Paris and Madrid, were at one in stressing the primary importance of providing money, the sinews of war. The national debt rose between 1688 and 1714 from five to fifteen million pounds, but there was no doubt that the nation could carry it, though Tories – especially the landed gentry of that persuasion – grumbled that the land tax sucked them dry while the financiers of the capital grew bloated. Some of the gentry and many yeomen farmers were indeed ruined by the burdens they were asked to carry, but generally speaking the wars had tended to enrich the ruling sections of society. Foreigners who visited England never ceased to marvel at the number of palaces, in magnificently laid-out parks, which were built or remodelled in the immediate post-war years by moneyed men of town and country.

The resources of Britain – though poor in population, even after the union with Scotland (or North Britain as it was often called after 1707), when compared with France and the Austrian Habsburg dominions – were considerable. Its eight and a half million inhabitants were not impressive;* but its trade was highly profitable thanks to its favourable geographical position, its colonial possessions and overseas trading posts and, even more, to its skilful manipulation of navigation laws which gave preference, and monopoly when and where it was judged necessary, to British ships and British citizens.[5] The wars against France had given impetus to manufactures of all kinds, and towns like Manchester and Birmingham were thriving. Though the domestic market was the more important, exports continued to rise for a greater variety of goods than the pre-war dominant woollen cloth. The slave-contract obtained from Spain in 1713 led to rapid development for western ports, especially Bristol; these ports as well as the capital itself benefited from the increasing importance of Britain's role as an entrepot for extra-European produce – tobacco, coffee, sugar, and tea in particular. Dublin was booming, the second largest city after London in the realm, and Ireland (as a consequence of English restrictive laws

---

* Six million in England and Wales, one and a half in Ireland, one in Scotland.

which forbade the fattening of Irish cattle in England) had become an exporter of meat-products. Norwich was still the second largest city in England; but the east coast was, on the whole, declining in comparison with the centre and the west. Newcastle was important because of the domestic coal trade, carried by sea to London; and the ports in which naval dockyards were situated on the east and south coasts retained their significance because of the nation's strong naval commitment.

In the two houses of parliament – and especially in the House of Commons – Britain possessed a sensitive barometer for economic pressure. Vested interests were strong. The sensible Anglo-French commercial treaty signed by Bolingbroke in 1713 was denied ratification, partly because of remnants of political enmity towards France, but mainly because of the opposition of those who had profited from the monopoly position of Portuguese wines during the long years when the importation of French wines had been prohibited.[6] Great hopes were built on the restoration of trade with Old Spain and on the clause in the *asiento* which permitted limited trade in British manufactures with New Spain: that such trade was in theory restricted to one ship's load a year was not taken too seriously by optimistic merchants and speculators who reckoned with an expanding exchange of goods with Philip V's American subjects in return for Spanish gold and silver.[7] During the War of the Spanish Succession the gold discovered by the Portuguese in Brazil had largely found its way to Britain;[8] but the appetite of the western European powers for precious metal was insatiable. They needed currency to pay for the naval stores from the Baltic which were essential for the fitting-out of their fleets and to buy those silks and cottons and china goods from the Far East which were so fashionable in Europe that they amounted to near necessities.[9] The influence of those who traded with Spain and the Spanish empire (either through Spanish merchants in Castile or via the semi-legal smuggling trade which developed from the annual-ship clause of the *asiento*) was therefore considerable in parliament. Here again an element of competition with France is noticeable: Louis XIV had bought the *asiento* from a Portuguese company in 1701 and had aspired to a French domination of trade with Spain overseas; now it was Britain's turn.

This commercial confidence rested, in the last instance, on a conviction of financial and thus military, and especially naval, superiority. The French privateering warfare had hit hard at British shipping between 1704 and 1709, but the ability of Britain to continue her building programme of naval ships so that adequate convoys could be fitted out for both the Baltic and the Atlantic trade had left the country, when peace came, with a larger navy than France, which had been forced to concentrate on the expansion of its armies. It was realized that Spain, under the Bourbons, wanted to rebuild its navy so that the Castile monopoly of trade with New Spain should be maintained; but this would take time. The Dutch Republic – once so serious a rival in Baltic and Far East trade – was sufficiently exhausted from the late war not to be able to compete with Britain's naval programme; and though the Republic's economic prosperity continued far into the eighteenth century, its will for the pursuit of an aggressive economic policy had weakened.[10] As for the Austrian Habsburg dominions, whose ruler since 1711 was the emperor Charles VI,* the British were conscious of the fact that he needed Britain more than they needed him. He was reluctant to give up his claim to the whole of the Spanish Habsburg dominions; but sooner or later, the British felt sure, he would see reason since for the security of the share of those dominions which the peace-makings of 1713–14 had guaranteed to the house of Austria – the Southern Netherlands, the duchy of Milan, the kingdom of Naples with the Tuscan ports, the so-called *presidii*, and the island of Sardinia – he was dependent on their naval power: it was only too likely that Bourbon Spain should harbour plans for the reconquest of some, or all, of its former Italian possessions as no peace had been signed between Philip V and Charles VI.

Britain had already shown how easily it could transport troops to the Southern Netherlands; and the British gains, at Spain's expense, from the war – the island of Minorca and the fortress of Gibraltar – gave effective control of the western Mediterranean to the British navy. Austria's navy was virtually non-existent, though Charles VI and his Spanish-Italian advisers hoped to build a sizable fleet as soon as their financial situation would permit. Charles VI was also in need of British loans, or at least of payment of arrears of subsidies from the last war. The Austrian Habsburg state, in spite of the extent of its dominions and its large population, had not yet caught up with the administrative and financial organization of Britain.[11]

Britain's smaller size made it easier to govern than either France with its twenty million inhabitants or Habsburg Austria with its ten million: speedier action could be taken throughout the realm and control was surer than in the more centrally governed (in theory) state of Louis XIV and the geographically somewhat scattered dominions of Charles VI. Its taxation system was socially fairer and therefore less resented. The land tax was levied on all landowners, noble and commoner alike. Its method of raising income from

---

* The election of the emperor of the Holy Roman Empire had, by custom, become so firmly associated with the Austrian house of Habsburg that Louis XIV regarded its right as 'hereditary'.

indirect taxation was unusually flexible, capable of being changed in accordance with shifting economic and political needs. Its social cohesion was stronger, in spite of the gulf between rich and poor, since the sons of noblemen were legally commoners even though the eldest sons of high nobles held courtesy titles. Indeed, the nobility's only remaining privilege in law was its right to be tried by its peers in the House of Lords. The eldest son (who, in spite of his courtesy title, could be elected to the House of Commons in his father's lifetime) inherited his father's title, but the rest of the children did not – as on the continent – have noble status by hereditary right and had to find their place in society according to talents and luck. The move from commoner to nobleman was at least as difficult (or easy) as on the continent and took place for similar reasons: great services to the ruler or sufficient money – whether earned, inherited or achieved through marriage with an heiress – to live in the style and with the responsibilities of a landed nobleman. The pride of the English nobility was not usually behind that of its continental counterparts. Its members generally exceeded those of the continent in riches and political influence, for even if the individual nobleman held no ministerial or high court office he could bring pressure to bear through shire elections to the House of Commons.

There was in England also an intermediate class of social significance, consisting of those who obtained a knighthood. A knight was not a member of the peerage and therefore could not sit in the House of Lords (indeed he retained his right to stand for elections to the House of Commons), but he held the coveted title of Sir and his wife was styled Lady. From the government's point of view a distinction for merit or services could thus be bestowed without enlarging the peerage; from the point of view of the commoner, social mobility was made easier. Every educated and ambitious person considered it perfectly possible that he himself might be knighted and that his son (if not he himself) could aspire to even greater honours. It was realized that election to the House of Commons would facilitate the process for father as for son; it was so sure a route to influence that it was rated above that of service, whether at court, in the administration or in the army or navy. Courtiers and officials who wanted to get ahead, officers on the ladder of promotion, all coveted seats in the lower house. The very existence of the House of Commons, and the triennial parliaments established in 1694, was a cause of national pride among British commoners. The balance which it imparted to the constitution – holding in check not only the ruler but also the powerful House of Lords – was much admired by intellectuals abroad. 'How we praise your House of Commons', wrote Leibniz enthusiastically to a correspondent in England, 'how perfect is your constitution and how in accordance with the dictates of reason'.[12]

Leibniz's enthusiasm must not (in combination with the ever-present temptation to read history backwards) blind us to the fact that at the time of George I's accession, the House of Lords was very powerful indeed. Here sat, with rare exceptions, the important ministers of the crown, either because they were already peers when called to their posts or because of rapid promotion thereafter. The archbishops and bishops of the Anglican church took part by virtue of their office. The upper house was much smaller than the House of Commons, with some 200 to 250 members in the period with which we are concerned (compared with the 480-odd which composed the lower house); but it was in the House of Lords that the great issues of the reigns of William III and queen Anne had been decided. The standard of debate was high. So was the percentage of active members, explicable by the large proportion of peers who held office or court position and by the number of ambitious opponents who wished to challenge, and hoped to supplant, those in places of power and profit. Between 1702 and 1714 ministries had frequently been saved by the Lords from bills, passed by the Commons, deemed inimical to good government; and the need to control the Lords had on two occasions been acute enough for Anne's ministers to force the queen into mass-creation of peers.* In George's reign, as we shall see, the relationship between the two chambers changed a good deal, but management of the lords temporal and spiritual remained of crucial significance.

Wherever Britain looked, at home or abroad, the present looked acceptable and the future promising. The union with Scotland, though undertaken for political purposes, had eliminated a prospective economic rival as well as filling a gap in national security: the not inconsiderable Scottish mercantile and expansionist drives were henceforth channelled into the British community. Integration was implicit in the arrangement that sixteen Scottish peers – elected by the whole Scottish peerage – should sit in the House of Lords; forty-five seats were allocated for Scottish constituencies in the House of Commons. Scottish noblemen and commoners alike were eligible for any office and any title to be bestowed by the ruler of Great Britain. A secretary of state for Scotland was nominated to take charge of specifically Scottish affairs, but this proved to be an interim measure and George I – as we shall see – decided to abolish the post in the interest of integration. The integration of Ireland – of much older date – had become fixed within a dynastic union pattern,

---

* Four Tory peers were created in 1703 to redress the Whig balance, and in three days (29–31 Dec. 1711) a dozen peers were created to defeat Whig opposition to the government's peace moves.

and the union of Scotland and England in 1707 provoked no discussion as to whether change in Ireland was desirable or not. The Irish parliament continued to exist and had considerable autonomy; there was an Irish church establishment, a separate Irish peerage, and an Irish civil list to defray the king's expenses in ruling the country. But the presence of an English-nominated lord lieutenant, the claim of the central government to scrutinize acts passed by the Irish parliament, and the non-scrupling of the English House of Commons to enact laws which hit at Irish commercial interests if these came into conflict with those of England left no doubt which country was in control. In theory it might seem fair enough that Irish Catholics were unrepresented in the Irish parliament, that the Irish church was a purely Protestant (Anglican) one, and that no Irish Catholic could hold office under the crown. After all, English and Scottish Catholics suffered the same disabilities. But the far greater incidence of Catholicism in Ireland made this more of an injustice than in the rest of the kingdom, explicable only by the risk which haunted successive British governments, ever since Elizabeth I's time, of Irish Catholics cooperating with England's Catholic enemies abroad, first Spain and then France.

For political reasons William III, who was no bigot, had tried to minimize the harsher aspects of successive English conquests of Ireland. As the ally of Catholic powers, principally the house of Habsburg, the Spanish branch as well as the Austrian, he had promised 'no persecution' once James II's army (supported by Louis XIV with ships, men and money) had been defeated in 1692.[13] Instead of the blood-baths of previous reigns, the remnants of James's army were in that year given the choice of submitting to William III or going into exile in France. Nearly all (some 12,000) chose to leave Ireland. For several years these Irish regiments served as distinct units with the French army, owing allegiance to James II; but in time they were merged with Louis' forces, though they still retained a national character and received recruits from Scottish Jacobites seeking refuge on the continent because of their objection to the union of 1707. A considerable number of Irishmen and Scots settled in the western ports of France where the departure of the Huguenots in the 1670s and '80s had left gaps to be filled in the commercial and shipping life of that part of the country; after 1713 military men of both nations (and at times whole companies) took service with other Catholic monarchs, especially Philip V of Spain. The exiled court of James II and – after 1701 – of 'James III' could absorb only a portion of Scottish, Irish and English Catholics who offered their services; but a good many were employed as spies and agitators, working clandestinely in Britain and, more openly, at foreign courts opposed, for however short a period, to the policies of those whom the Jacobites considered after 1688 as usurpers. Here they often found support from non-military men who had, because of their sympathy with the Stuart cause, emigrated and made careers for themselves which brought them into contact with influential court circles, medical men, naval officers and financiers being prominent among them.[14]

From the point of view of the central government in London, the exodus of Irish, Scottish and even English Jacobites was beneficial, though successive governments remained acutely aware of Jacobite machinations abroad. This exodus removed the unruly elements and cemented the cohesion of those who remained, helped by the high reputation of the Irish and Scottish regiments which had fought for Britain during the wars against Louis XIV. There was also a sense in which all three kingdoms felt proud of the powerful state which emerged from the peace of Utrecht. The trading posts in India had not been enlarged; but in the West Indies the French island of St Christopher – renamed St Kitts – had become British, and on the North American continent Louis XIV had ceded Nova Scotia and Newfoundland, as well as French settlements in the Hudson Bay area, to queen Anne. But France had retained its right to participate in the cod-fisheries off the Newfoundland coasts with the privilege of drying and curing catches before transporting them to Europe; and there was considerable alarm lest French exploration from the St Lawrence river towards the Gulf of Mexico – the legendary exit for the North American river network – prevent expansion of Britain's colonies beyond the Alleghenies.[15]

France was indeed the joker in the pack. There was a healthy respect for Louis XIV's kingdom quite apart from its vigour overseas. Its great resilience in Europe had confounded wartime prophecies of the 'utter ruin' which Britain was to impose on the 'Christian Turk'.[16] Englishmen, travelling on the continent in the immediate post-Utrecht years, marvelled at France's prosperity[17] and in retrospect realized the fragility of English wartime propaganda. Statesmen in London, Tory and Whig, became aware that England's relationship to France was in need of redefinition. Would cooperation be more sensible than enmity? Bolingbroke had already made steps towards such cooperation by the time of queen Anne's death;[18] and the issue was one which was to confront the Whigs – and George I – not long after his accession. Such cooperation was strongly tied to plans to conjure away the black cloud on the European horizon which persisted after the peacemakings of Utrecht, Rastadt and

Baden, the Great Northern War which had raged ever since 1700. Commitment to resist Louis XIV had indeed denied Britain real influence in the Baltic since 1702. The Tories wished – if within the framework of their view that Charles XII was a hero whom fortune had deserted after 1709 and who must therefore accept sacrifices – to intervene on Sweden's side lest tsar Peter of Russia grow to exorbitant power in the north. For this purpose they aimed to recruit both French and Dutch support in the summer of 1714,[19] confident that wherever Britain inclined to preserve the balance of Europe after 1713, there it would prevail. A squadron was already fitted out, ostensibly for the sole purpose of safeguarding British trade, when queen Anne fell mortally ill. On her death it was diverted to escort George I to his kingdom. It would not do to dispose of the fleet without consultation with the new sovereign.

GEORGE AND THE PARTY SYSTEM

In 1714 George I became the ruler of a go-ahead, confident people, ambitious in domestic and foreign affairs, but he also inherited problems in governing it. The nation had a reputation for being changeable, dating from the civil wars of the 1640s, the submission to Cromwell's protectorate in the 1650s, the restoration of the Stuarts in 1660, and the revolt against James II in 1688. The radical element in Whig ideology had been much publicized on the continent; 1688 was widely thought to have made the monarchy, if not elective, wholly dependent on parliament. Republican principles took both aristocratic and democratic form. Some held that even if the nation would not yet stomach a republican constitution it could by degrees be brought to adopt the principle that the king could be 'sacked' – deemed to have abdicated, as had happened to James II – if he did not obey the dictates of the House of Lords. Others expressed agreement, though with the one important reservation that the preponderance of power should lie with the House of Commons. Neither Whig view was acceptable to George I who took care to let it be known that he came to Britain as a ruler by 'hereditary right', that right having been made extinct 'only for Catholic members of the House of Stuart'.[20] This declaration was meant to scotch any Whig interpretation that parliament had given him the kingdom. At the same time it was also intended to convince the Tories that he was no usurper. The Tory party, while firm on the traditional value of the royal prerogative, also held disadvantages for George. Quite apart from its desertion of the Grand Alliance, still in vivid memory, it was too closely identified with the Anglican church and its

intolerance towards Protestant dissenters to make a continental
ruler of the Early Enlightenment feel comfortable.

It is clear therefore that George agreed with those who urged that
the party-system should be kept in check whether the dividing line
went, as in periods of crisis when issues of principle were at stake,
between Whigs and Tories; or, in calmer periods, between 'court'
and 'country'; or, as continentals were wont to put it, between
strong and weak government. That George preferred strong government is shown by his suggestion in 1717 that the British succession
should be so modified that male heirs should take preference over
female heirs:[21] it would seem that he accepted Louis XIV's argument that England in queen Anne's reign had been a virtual republic.[22] In 1714 he hoped and expected to steer a moderate course,
independent of extremists of Whig and Tory persuasion, in short to
govern with a 'king's party' in the sense in which Schulenburg used
that term between 1717 and 1720.

George's list of regents,* to form the interim government until his
arrival, has hitherto been analyzed in terms of party affiliations only:
thirteen Whigs, four Hanover Tories and one 'unattached'. Such a
division is valid enough, but not sufficient for our purposes. Over
five names George had no control, since they were there by virtue
of offices held in queen Anne's last ministry; for the rest, the regents
are found to have been chosen for their opposition to the Oxford-
Bolingbroke betrayal of Britain's allies, for their ability to maintain
the union of Scotland with England, for their expertise in a special
field of administration or their strong influence in one or both
houses of parliament, and for their record of being 'court men' who
regarded it as their duty to work in the national interest as seen by
the crown. No one of extremist views was included, nor anyone
deemed too ambitious of power, though the element of reward for
services rendered was naturally present. In alphabetical order, and
apart from Charles Talbot, duke of Shrewsbury who, because of his
elevation to lord treasurer in the last hours of queen Anne's life,
also became *ex-officio* regent, they were: Montague Bertie, earl of
Abingdon, who controlled a Tory group in the House of Commons
and had strongly opposed the commercial treaty with France;
Arthur Annesley, earl of Anglesey, a sound High Church Tory who
had yet taken the Whig line in debates on peace negotiations in
1711–13; John Campbell, duke of Argyll, an army officer, influential in Scotland and known to George as committed to armed
opposition to a Stuart succession; Charles Powlet, duke of Bolton,
and Charles Howard, earl of Carlisle, both considerable borough
patrons, who might be classified as court Whigs, having been allies

* There were three copies of the list, one deposited with the archbishop of Canterbury,
one with the lord chancellor, and one with Bothmer, George's Hanoverian representative
in Britain; at a privy council meeting in the forenoon of Sunday August 1/12 the seals
were broken and the names made known.

or junior associates of the Whig junto during the War of the Spanish Succession rather than members of it; William Cowper, an experienced legal administrator (lord keeper 1705–07, lord chancellor 1707–10), one of the best speakers in the House of Lords and essentially fair-minded and moderate though – as will be seen – his religious toleration did not extend as far as George's; William Cavendish, duke of Devonshire, who, with Cowper, had been largely responsible for the adroit manoeuvring of the Whigs during the Oxford-Bolingbroke ministry; Charles Montagu, lord Halifax, who had long-established ties with Hanover and was – if vain and pompous – a skilled House of Lords debater with useful City connections; Henry Grey, duke of Kent, who had opposed Britain's separate peace with France, though he was by temperament a staunch court man holding that 'a quiet mind is better than to embroil myself amongst the knaves and fools about either Church or State';[23] James Graham, duke of Montrose, keeper of the privy seal in Scotland between 1703 and 1713, who had furthered the cooperation between the Whigs and the Scottish unionists; Daniel Finch, earl of Nottingham, a pro-Hanoverian Tory throughout a long ministerial career who had left queen Anne's ministry in 1711; Edward Russell, earl of Orford who, having been first lord of the admiralty between 1709 and 1711, had influence with admiralty officials and naval men, as well as with his Russell relatives in the House of Commons; Thomas Herbert, earl of Pembroke, also noted for admiralty experience; John Ker, duke of Roxburghe, strongly committed to the Hanoverian succession and to Scotland's remaining within the union; Richard Lumley, earl of Scarborough, classified as an 'independent Whig';[24] Charles Seymour, duke of Somerset, a household officer and great magnate controlling numerous seats in the House of Commons, who had prevented Scotland breaking out of the union during the so-called malt tax-riots;* Charles, viscount Townshend, who as negotiator of the Anglo-Dutch treaty of Barrier and Succession of 1709 had rendered services which George held to be of the greatest importance for the cause of Hanover.

Shrewsbury had earned his nomination on George's list by his consistent support for moderate measures as well as for his loyalty to the house of Hanover in parliamentary debates. A 'manager' of queen Anne's reign, he had a sense of his own importance, and he must have enjoyed the distinction of being both a nominated and an *ex-officio* regent. His membership of the Oxford-Bolingbroke ministry (as lord chamberlain since 1710 and lord lieutenant of Ireland after 1713) made him particularly useful to George as a link between the *ex-officio* and the nominated regents.

* The extension to Scotland of the English malt-tax had caused riots and loud demands for the repeal of the union in 1713.

It created some surprise that Marlborough was not among the
regents, nor his son-in-law Sunderland. It might be suspected that
George harboured ill-will towards Marlborough because of his
deceit in 1708, or – as is often said – that the duke was distrusted
because of his correspondence with the court of Saint-Germain.
George's first action as king (on 6/17 August, as soon as notification
of queen Anne's death reached him) disproves this, since he then
dismissed Ormonde and restored Marlborough to command of the
British army.[25] He had complete confidence in the duke's willingness
to defend the Hanoverian succession if James Edward should
challenge the proclamation of 1/12 August; but he may have had
some qualms about giving Marlborough – and his wife – political
power. Sunderland's exclusion was certainly deliberate; he had the
reputation of being an extreme and ambitious party man, a republican at heart. He was found a minor post in George's first
ministry, but the king continued wary of him; when it became
necessary to employ him in high political office after the crisis of
1716–17, he was, for a further two years, kept out of the court post
he most coveted, that of groom of the stole, which brought easy
access to the ruler. It is interesting to note that on his achieving a
place in the inner cabinet, one of his protégés found him inclined to
more moderate measures, 'being of late much come off from the
violence he shew'd in the last reign'.[26]

Of the *ex-officio* regents only two, apart from Shrewsbury, were
continued in office. Tenison, archbishop of Canterbury, a long-
standing correspondent of the house of Hanover, had disassociated
himself from the Oxford-Bolingbroke ministry, virtually immuring
himself in Lambeth Palace after 1711. His renewed activity after
1/12 August 1714 seemed to augur well for a tolerant and moderate
Anglican church; but he died in 1715 and his successor, William
Wake, though ecumenically minded in Europe, treasured the dominant position of the Anglican church at home. Thomas Parker, lord
chief justice since 1710, was confirmed by George even though
it was held that rulers on their accession were at liberty to dispense
with the 'tenure during good behaviour' act of William III's reign.
He was an able man (as well as one willing to support the king), who
was made chancellor in 1718 and created earl of Macclesfield in 1721.

The other *ex-officio* regents were not found places in George's first
government: Harcourt had to give room to Cowper as lord chancellor; Buckingham, lord president, to Nottingham; Dartmouth, lord
privy seal, to Wharton; Strafford, first lord of the admiralty, to
Orford. Four of the new men had been on George's list as regents;
the fifth, Wharton, had spoken vigorously against the separate peace.

George was not short of advice on the kind of men he should employ upon his arrival in England, nor on what policies were expected of him. He received solicited and unsolicited memoranda on the state of the parties, on the issues of the day, on which men to reward and which to punish. Traditionally Bothmer and Robethon are supposed to have decided 'everything' as the king has been held to be without either knowledge of or interest in English affairs.[27] In reality George had long weighed the problems and studied the men from whom he would draw his ministers. Englishmen were more important than Hanoverians in giving information. There are letters from Cowper and Nottingham in the Hanover state archives, and Bernstorff carefully preserved an undated and unsigned paper on 'La méthode dont s'est servir le dernier ministère pour faire casher le premier et se mettre eux mesmes dans la favour de la Reine'.[28] Via Bernstorff, Cowper did indeed become one of George's most prominent advisers. Building on the friendly relations that had existed between his brother-in-law Ludwig Justus von Schütz (the late Hanoverian envoy to St James's) and the Cowpers, Bernstorff entered into correspondence with lady Cowper as soon as news of queen Anne's death reached Hanover. Through Bernstorff, therefore, recommendations from the Cowpers reached the king, both before and after the move to England.[29] But George also listened to Friedrich Wilhelm von Görtz and Weipart Ludwig von Fabrice, who had friends and contacts in non-Jacobite Tory circles; and, since both ministers accompanied the king to England and continued there for several months, Cowper's 'Impartial History of Parties', in his wife's French translation, was not the only case of special pleading studied by George: the Tories also had their spokesmen and propagandists.[30]

The Whigs, however, found foreign advocates denied to the Tories. They knew that George would travel to England via The Hague and urged Dutch ministers to press the case for 'trusted Whigs only' in all offices. George had intended to spend only three days in the Republic, but contrary winds kept him there from 16 to 27 September. During this time he met Dutch statesmen and discussed with Bernstorff and Görtz (who had arrived already on 11 September) their conversations with Heinsius, the *raadpensionaris*, Slingelandt, the secretary of the council of state, and Duyvenvoorde, the son-in-law of Portland, well-versed in English affairs and with a good knowledge of the English nobility.[31]

George's declaration that during his reign he would not think of the names Whig and Tory but of merit only when choosing his advisers, made Heinsius cautious enough to recommend only those

Whigs he considered 'friends of the Dutch',[32] and to concentrate on the offices which bore most strongly on Britain's foreign relations. The ministers who dealt with domestic affairs – the lord chancellor, the lord chief justice, the lord treasurer and the lord privy seal – all belonged to the important small group of royal advisers known as the cabinet council. This met, on a specific day of the week, with the sovereign (and, at his bidding, at other times if required), and prepared matters by discussion in sittings of their own which were called 'meetings of the lords of the committee'. To this group, often labelled 'the inner cabinet' by historians,[33] the two specialists on foreign affairs, the secretaries of state, also belonged. It was these two posts which principally interested Heinsius and other Dutchmen who wished to restore the good relations with Britain largely lost during queen Anne's last ministry. Until the reform of 1782 which produced the Foreign Office and the Home Office, the two secretaries of state* were responsible for some domestic matters (shared between them partly by regions and partly by the nature of the business); but most of their time was spent on foreign affairs which were divided between them on a geographical basis. The 'Secretary for the South' covered relations with France, Spain and Portugal, the Italian states (with the exception of the Papal dominions), and the Ottoman empire; the 'Secretary for the North' dealt with Denmark-Norway, Sweden, Poland, Russia, the German states, and the Dutch Republic.[34] The senior secretary of the two, i.e., the one first appointed, tended to choose (or even change) office according to the relative urgency at any one time of problems in northern or southern Europe; he usually had some influence on the choice of his colleague since – though the ruler had the decisive say in matters of foreign policy – it was important that the two secretaries should pull together.

There was great joy therefore in the Republic when George announced from The Hague that Townshend would be his first secretary. Townshend was the architect of the treaty of 1709 whereby the Dutch had guaranteed the Protestant succession according to the Act of Settlement of 1701, receiving in return a guarantee for a given number of 'barrier' fortresses in the Southern Netherlands to be garrisoned by Dutch troops as a first defence against France. These garrisons were to be paid for by the future sovereign of this part of the Low Countries, governed – after the victory of Ramillies of 1706 – by an Anglo-Dutch condominium until that sovereign would be nternationally recognized and able to make his terms with the Maritime Powers.[35] Queen Anne's last ministry, fearing Dutch commercial exploitation of the Barrier, had in 1713 forced a renegotiation of the 1709 treaty which drastically cut the number of fortresses.

---

* Since the union with Scotland there was also a secretary for Scotland, but his office (which was abolished in 1724) had no share in foreign affairs.

Townshend's nomination made the Dutch confident, first, that he would choose the northern office, given the continuing unrest in the north and George's interest in the Northern War; and, second, that he would agree to restore at least some of the 'lost' fortresses when the Barrier was settled with the designated sovereign of the Southern Netherlands, the emperor Charles VI in his capacity as Austrian Habsburg ruler. He had only just (in March 1714) made his peace with Louis XIV and could not be expected to enter into negotiations for the Barrier until the peace between France and the Empire, on the point of conclusion at the congress of Baden in the Swiss Argau, had been signed.

The secretaryship of the south, in which Townshend could be assumed to have some say, also interested Dutch statesmen.[36] Bolingbroke had been dismissed and his papers sealed on George I's orders from Hanover, but whoever succeeded him would have to cope with a problem which had agitated him and the French foreign minister, Torcy: the non-existence of a formal peace between Charles VI as Habsburg ruler and Philip V of Spain. Technically these monarchs were still at war even if the treaty of neutrality for Italy (1713) had, temporarily at least, stopped hostilities between Spain and Austria in that contested area. The solution Bolingbroke had envisaged with Torcy and Victor Amadeus of Savoy-Sicily was that Charles VI should be made 'reasonable' towards Spain, at least to the extent of recognizing Philip V, and encouraged to keep the peace in the whole of Italy by strong Anglo-French support for Victor Amadeus: his royal title was to be confirmed, as were the terms of his 1703 treaty with the Grand Alliance in respect of Savoy's gains in the Milanese.[37] No conclusion had been reached at the time of queen Anne's death; but there is little doubt that Bolingbroke's project for 'the perfecting the Utrecht system' turned the thought of his successor Stanhope, and of George I, in a similar direction though the 'peace plan for the south' which was initiated in the autumn of 1716 was modified by Stanhope's personal knowledge of Spain and by George I's relationship to the regent of France.

Traditionally, Stanhope's appointment as second secretary has been attributed to Townshend's recommendation of him, which is supposed to have derived from Horatio Walpole, Robert's younger brother, who had served as secretary, in turn, to Stanhope in Spain and to Townshend at The Hague. This is not unlikely; but we know, from written contemporary evidence, that Stanhope was already known to George by reputation and had secretly been named as one of the triumvirate (with Cadogan and Argyll) charged with contingency planning for the armed defence of the Hanoverian succession while Marlborough was still on the continent.[38] Moreover, Stanhope was one of the few Englishmen who knew Europe well. He had spent a good deal of his youth there with his diplomat father and had on his own, when a military commander in Spain, handled negotiations with the Dutch, the Portuguese and, above all, with 'Carlos III' and his advisers when Charles VI had been the allied candidate for the Spanish crown.[39] Since young Schulenburg had also been accredited to 'Carlos III', George may have had an independent assessment of Stanhope.

George had his own line to Charles VI's Hofburg since he and some of his Hanoverian advisers corresponded with the widowed empress Wilhelmine (daughter of his late uncle Johann Friedrich) and with the empress Elisabeth, a younger Brunswick relative; but after 1714 he was keen to have Englishmen with a feel for European problems and situations at his side.

While successful in nominating two secretaries of state versed in continental affairs, George fared less well in his plans to form a mixed ministry, containing Whigs and Tories who would 'balance' each other. The king had no use for Bolingbroke or Oxford. Both were held guilty of pro-Pretender plans and their separate overtures to Hanover had been judged feints, though we now know that they were sincerely intended once both had become convinced that James Edward Stuart could not be brought to change his religion even as a mere outward gesture. Of the two, Oxford was most disliked by the allies who had felt betrayed by the separate Anglo-French negotiations after 1710. Bolingbroke was frank, and allied diplomats knew where they stood with him; his intelligence and concern for logic also earned their respect. Oxford was, however, hated once they found out that his bland, reassuring phrases to their faces concealed, or were meant to conceal, deceit as soon as his back was turned: if cornered, he cravenly denied responsibility. Dutch, Hanoverian and Austrian diplomats had suffered this humiliating experience; so had Heinsius who, by correspondence and by special emissaries, had tried to reach a compromise peace by cooperation with Oxford; so had prince Eugène during his visit to London in 1712.[40] The difference in attitude of George and his advisers towards the two ex-ministers is instructive. Bolingbroke retained a measure of respect and was permitted to return to England even after he had served the Pretender between 1715 and 1716. Oxford was impeached and though the suit against him was eventually dropped, because of a quarrel between the House of Lords and the House of Commons at a time when Robert Walpole was in opposition, he was not forgiven. The king certainly gave the Commons a chance to proceed with the impeachment process in 1717 and was greatly relieved when Oxford decided in 1718 to retire to the country and take no further part in political life.[41]

But George did hope to tempt moderate Tories into his first ministry. He offered posts to William Bromley, a one-time speaker of the House of Commons, who had been Bolingbroke's fellow-secretary, and to Sir Thomas Hanmer, the speaker of the outgoing house. Both refused, excusing themselves on grounds of party loyalty: nothing but half of all places for the Tories would satisfy them.[42] For their part many Whigs, and especially the younger Whigs called to office, thirsted for revenge against the Tories and were out of sympathy with the king's hopes.

They and the king were of one mind when it came to putting Whigs into particularly sensitive posts. Simon Harcourt, the lord chancellor, had to go since the chancellorship was so vital and a new incumbent was at hand in William Cowper; and Harcourt's relation by marriage, the postmaster-general, Sir John Evelyn, had to follow him into at least temporary wilderness since his office was crucial for the intelligence service – domestic and foreign – of the secretaries of state.[43] The intransigence of Bromley and Hanmer, however, even after they had been told that more posts would be found, if minor ones to start with, for the Hanover-Tories, saved the Whigs from a balanced ministry. They even resented that one important office, that of lord president, went to Nottingham whom they refused to regard as a 'loyal party man', and were not happy till they had hounded him out of office.

The death of the less revengeful Whigs, Halifax and Wharton, within the first year of George's reign brought able but even more forceful, less accommodating, younger men to the fore: in August 1715 Sunderland was promoted from the lord lieutenancy of Ireland to lord privy seal, and in October of the same year the paymaster-general, Robert Walpole, was transferred to the treasury. By this time party struggle had already been joined. Elections for the new parliament which met in March 1715 had produced a Whig majority estimated at 150 and emboldened the revenge-bent ministers to lay articles of impeachment for high treason against Oxford, Bolingbroke and Ormonde and for high crimes and mis-demeanours against Strafford – moves which contributed to James Edward Stuart's decision in September 1715 to challenge the Hanoverian succession.

It is useless to speculate whether the various crises that beset George on the home front between 1715 and 1718 could have been avoided if he had achieved a better balanced first ministry. In

theory the acceptance of Bromley and Hanmer might have helped
to offset the development of Whig predominance; in practice party
divisions and party loyalty proved stronger than George had expected, and cooperation of Hanover-Tories with Whigs had wilted
even before he arrived in his new kingdom. George was realistic
enough to accept this; but within the limits which circumstances
permitted he continued throughout his reign to work for ministries
that approached the one he had ideally aimed at. When the first
crisis of the reign, the Jacobite rebellion of 1715–16, effectively
destroyed the Tory party as a provider of viable alternative ministers, George pursued the idea of a balanced or mixed government by
having different groups from those broadly labelled Whigs cooperate
under his leadership in spite of personal rivalries or differing views
on the best means to achieve desired ends. Unfortunately George's
determination to shape royal foreign policy to suit Hanoverian ends
largely provoked the second crisis – that of 1716–17 – in which
ministerial tempers ran so high that the issues at stake were speedily
forgotten and the king was forced to reap what he had not wished to
sow: the resignations of Townshend and Robert Walpole. The third
crisis, not unconnected with the second, involved George's heir. It
broke early in 1718 and lasted for two years, years in which the
Whigs in opposition joined the prince of Wales in making frequent,
and effective, sorties against 'the King's party'. George learnt his
lessons, and after 1720 he managed his son and his ministers quite
skilfully and, on the whole, with success.

THE KING'S ENGLISH

Life in Britain was not all crises even in the early and more turbulent
years of the reign. George had brought Melusine and their three
daughters with him and installed them in St James's Palace. They
explored its park, made early visits to Kensington and its gardens,
and planned – as early as October 1715 – improvements to Hampton
Court.[44] Georg August, now prince of Wales, was also installed at
St James's with Caroline and their daughters – Anne born in 1709,
Amalie (Emily) in 1711, and Caroline in 1713. Their son Frederick,
seven years old in 1714, was left behind in Hanover with his tutors,
under the supervision of his great-uncle Ernst August, to follow
an educational programme laid down by George. It would not do to
deprive Frederick of knowledge of the electorate, and the Hanoverians might well feel deprived if the whole family departed for
London. Indeed, court life at Hanover, with the seasonal changes
from the capital to Herrenhausen, continued as before, with con-

certs, plays and entertainments.[45] George himself hoped to visit his
electorate as opportunity afforded, much as William III had managed
to visit the Netherlands and Celle. It could not have escaped him,
however, that William had had the valid excuse of the campaigns
of the Nine Years War for his presence on the continent; nor was he
unaware of the fact that according to a clause added to the Act of
Settlement Anne's successor had to ask permission from parliament
to go abroad. He realized that England would be his home from now
on, and planned accordingly. Given his enjoyment of the chase and
of driving, it is not surprising that among his permanent entourage
was Kielmansegg, his Hanoverian master of horse, nor that Kielmansegg's wife, George's half-sister Sophia Charlotte, and their
children, should soon follow.*

The prince and princess of Wales took part in the coronation
ceremony on October 20/31. George wore the crown made for
queen Anne, the old Stuart crown having been taken away by James
II and, so it was generally believed, lost in the Channel crossing.
The crown of William's reigning consort, Mary, was adapted for
Georg August: many generations had passed since a prince of
Wales had been present at a coronation ceremony, and there was no
time to have a special crown made. Immediately after the coronation
George ordered work to begin on a new royal crown. Jewels from
Anne's crown were transferred to the lighter crown (27 oz 16 dwt
6 g), and the frame of the discarded crown (weighing more than
40 oz) sold for the value of its gilt metal.[46]

The prince of Wales was brought into affairs of state, much as
George himself had been by his father, and took his seat in the cabinet
and the privy council. He did not share the secrets of the closet where
the king gave audiences to individual ministers, courtiers, private
petitioners and foreign diplomats, again on the pattern of George's
own Hanoverian upbringing. Queen Anne had also used the closet-
interview, but George seems to have relied on it more than she did,
particularly after 1717. The slight but perceptive distinction made
between king and heir can be seen in the last surviving fragments of
Cowper's diary. The chancellor records his audience at St James's
on his nomination as lord chancellor: the prince of Wales received
him in an anteroom, he then went on to meet the king, alone, in his
closet.[47]

It used to be held that George never attended cabinet meetings
because of his difficulty in communicating with his ministers.
Professor Plumb has, however, shown that the king continued to hold
cabinet meetings at least until April 1717 (his rudimentary knowledge of spoken English creating no serious problem, apart from the

* Rumours, still repeated in books on the period as facts, that Sophia Charlotte was
forced to remain on the continent because of her debts, have been refuted; she could not
leave as early as her husband as she had to organize the move. She did, indeed, take up a
loan (repaid within five years) to cover the expenses of the move: Kielmansegg, *Familien-
Chronik*, p. 453, n.1.

extra work of having papers submitted to him translated into French), and has surmised that the change towards a system whereby the king did not meet with his inner cabinet, but only with his prime minister, was effected over a longish period.[48] Later writers have, erroneously, interpreted the date-line 'April 1717' as the final date at which George presided over his cabinet and have explained this by the tension which developed between the king and his heir: without the prince of Wales as 'interpreter' at the meetings, it is argued, George floundered and took the easy way out.[49]

My own researches have established that George continued to hold cabinet councils throughout his reign, and that it was the prince of Wales who – in a bid for independent power – absented himself from them, and from the privy council, in the autumn of 1717. Schulenburg notes Thursday as being the fixed day for cabinet-councils at Hampton Court in 1718 and 1719;[50] Carteret in 1723 refers to a cabinet-council where a certain matter had been laid before the king and decided by him.[51]

George's knowledge of English was not extensive, but it was not as limited (or non-existent) as once believed. There may have been a measure of flattery when a subject of queen Anne's, 'who knew Hanover well', wrote in 1707 to George in English, stressing that he took this liberty because he knew the elector to be 'a master of the language'.[52] Certainly Oxford was more guarded when in 1710 he excused the use of his native tongue by the flattering conviction that he knew the elector had 'an English heart'.[53] But there are several incontrovertible pointers to George's grasp of English and occasional use of it, spoken and written. Cowper, à propos the October 1714 audience referred to above, notes that the prince of Wales spoke to him in French and English, and that the king – though Cowper himself used English – spoke to and answered him in French.[54] It is on record that George I opened his first parliament by a brief sentence in English: 'My Lords and Gentlemen, I have ordered my Lord Chancellor to declare to you, in my name, the causes of calling this Parliament.'[55] This sentence might, of course, have been learnt by heart parrot-fashion; but to it can be added evidence of George employing English phrases when talking French, of his speaking whole sentences in English in conversations after 1720, and even of his annotating, in English, a memorandum written in English.

Lady Cowper, in the early portions of her diary from George's reign, invariably quotes the king's remarks in French;[56] but in 1720 she records an English sentence which – it seems to me – must be a straight quote since it has a wrong plural of the kind often employed by Germans then and since. The topic of her conversation with

George was the Townshend-Walpole return to the king's ministry and the sentence, a somewhat grumpy one, runs as follows: 'What did they go away for? it was their own *faults*'.[57] That faulty plurals of this kind were a common error among contemporary Germans in England is shown by the following, probably apocryphal, story. Melusine and Sophia Charlotte shared a carriage which was stopped by an unfriendly mob. The following exchange then took place. *La Schulenburg*, 'Good people, why do you plague us so? We have come for your own goods.' Mob: 'Yes, and for our *chattels* too.'*

George's grasp of written English is implied in the circumstance that after 1714 Mehemet increasingly used English expressions and terms, and included English material – written and printed – without translations, in the king's private accounts which he knew would be carefully perused;[58] and of spoken English in his regular attendance at English plays. The Shakespeare performances he arranged at Hampton Court may not provide conclusive evidence;[59] but Schulenburg's report, at the height of the crisis of April 1718, that the king has a special 'envie' to hear in a given play a specific actor, now old, but 'fort renomé quie ne jouait pour faire Sa cour au Roy, etant Whig outré', is decisive.[60]

It also seems proved that George, at least after Stanhope's death, did not demand that memoranda from his British ministers should be written in French. In the Public Record Office there is a memorandum of 1723 in English by Townshend on which George has written in his own hand: 'I agree with you in everything contain'd in this letter, and desire you to communicate your opinion either to the Duke of Newcastle or H. Walpole, that the instructions to the Ambassadors may be sent according to your opinion.' GR.[61]

It is not strange, however, that George should have preferred to use French. French was the polite language of society in Europe and the one he had grown up with, using it, with German, in his correspondence with his mother, who herself wrote her memoirs in French. Germans, courtiers and diplomats, frequently used French. The Schulenburg correspondence with Görtz, for instance, is in French with the occasional Latin tag and German proverb. The Fabrice memoirs were written in French.[62]

Personal diffidence may be one explanation for George's sparing use of English; but concern for royal dignity, and for the dignity of the language of his kingdom, may have played its part. The dowager electress of Hanover had seen to it that the younger members of the family took English lessons after 1701 (though she discreetly refrains from mentioning her own sons in this context). Georg August's English was fairly fluent, but he had a strong Germanic accent which

---

* My italics for 'faults' and 'chattels'. My curiosity about the implication of *faults* was stimulated by an elderly German friend (the late learned Gertrud Koebner) who, in spite of many years' residence in England, persisted in saying *monthses* for *months* – a different type of mistake, yet providing grist to the historian's mill on so vexed a question as George's lack of English. Since then I have become aware of the linguistic idiosyncrasy of the faulty *s* even in persons more or less bilingual in English and German.

was much ridiculed just because he was so proud of his command of
the language.[63] The princess of Wales, who was fluent in speech,
avoided written use of English and increasingly employed her
daughters as secretaries when needing English.[64] On the whole it
was the women of the court who did best (though Bothmer was
praised for speaking English well). Melusine and Sophia Charlotte
received letters in English and wrote at times in English;[65] their
daughters – like those of the prince and princess of Wales – grew
up trilingual in French, German and English. The Gräfin zu
Schaumburg-Lippe's command of English was so perfect that her
correspondence with queen Caroline's ladies-in-waiting after her
retirement to Germany aroused astonishment and admiration in
nineteenth-century editors.[66] She herself noted from Twickenham
in 1727, with pride, that her grandsons (and George's), at the age of
five and three respectively could now read and understand all three
languages.[67]

THE ROYAL HOUSEHOLD

George's court, after the first year or two, had few Germans; but the
very fact that there were any at all offended English susceptibilities
and created mutual distrust in moments of crisis. So eminently
sensible and well-balanced a person as the Gräfin zu Schaumburg-
Lippe grew bitter and frantic when describing the scenes at the
several childbirths of the princess of Wales: why must the English
doctors use instruments before labour-pains had started, against the
more sensible German usage? No wonder the result of their interference was a still-born son or one that did not live long.[68]

The main English complaint against the king was that he kept to
himself too much and was never as intimate with his English
gentlemen-in-waiting as with his few German attendants. The layout
of English palaces had already been so fashioned as to impose a
spatial distance between ruler and subject, the privilege of access
being graded from the relatively public to the increasingly more
private rooms; but George removed the innermost sanctum, his
bedroom, even from those who claimed a traditional right to wait
on the king wherever he might be in his palace. In the presence
chamber he saw courtiers and members of the public; in his closet
he saw ministers, officials and foreign diplomats if he so wished; but
Mehemet and Mustafa guarded the privacy of his bedroom in a way
that was unexpected and disturbing. George had tried to avoid
unnecessary fuss and ostentation even as elector; he had, for instance,
forbidden the use of trumpets and drums to greet him on his return

from the campaigns of the War of the Spanish Succession, while
not begrudging the expense and traditional ceremonial at his
electoral coronation.[69] He had worked hard but he had also managed
to keep his private life his own, and he had no intention of abandon-
ing either habit. He was available for the necessary ceremonies,
but he wanted to read despatches and other documents in peace and
therefore usually did not leave his private apartments till nearly noon.
He preferred to see his ministers, English and German, at stated and
prearranged times except in emergencies. He liked exercise and when
there was no hunting, walked long distances either in the late
afternoon or, during the summer months, in the evenings. The
planning of improvements to the royal palaces and gardens – though
money was scarce until after 1720 – was one of his greatest relax-
ations. Though he frequently dined with his 'gentlemen' and with
visitors, his late suppers were taken with members of the closer
circle, with Melusine and their daughters, with his German *Kammerjunker* and other intimate friends. These suppers were informal and
Fabrice has left us a good description of how they were arranged.
Several small tables were laid, the servants withdrew after having
placed the food on buffets, everyone helped himself, and the conversation ranged widely.[70] Fabrice and Schulenburg have given us
samples of the topics which cropped up in the supper conversations:
the business at any given time in parliament, the military and diplomatic happenings in Europe, news of family and acquaintances,
mildly salacious gossip related from courts abroad.* Schulenburg
made a point of noting down the stories George himself contributed. Typical of these is one about a soldier and a *freeholder* (the
English phrase was kept though the story itself is given in French)
which had reached the court and aroused George's curiosity. A
soldier met a freeholder in an inn and invited him to drink the
health of the king. The freeholder refused and revealed his pro-
Stuart sympathies. He offered, however, to throw dice to decide the
issue: if the soldier won, the freeholder would drink to king George; if
the freeholder won, his prize would be the soldier's life. Luck was on
the side of the freeholder. The two men went outside in the dark
night where the soldier, intent on keeping his word, made no protest
when the freeholder grabbed an axe and set to his work as an
executioner till the unexpected arrival of other travellers saved the
soldier's life. The king was torn between his respect for the obstinacy
of both men and his amazement that they should take their respective
allegiances so seriously.[71]

Plans for outings and entertainments were also mooted at the
supper table. George liked to visit the houses of his ministers and

---

* Often from the French court, e.g., the story that tsar Peter, during his visit to Versailles,
demanded the bed of the late Louis XIV and Mme de Maintenon for himself and his
mistress.

courtiers if they were within reasonable distance; he enjoyed the layout of the gardens, the architecture of the buildings and the collections, especially those of paintings. He went regularly to the theatre, to operas and concerts, usually with Melusine and one or more of her 'nieces'. The masquerades arranged by the Swiss-born impresario, Heidegger, also appealed to him, reminiscent as they were of the Hanover carnival. He preferred, however, to leave the more lively entertainments to his son and daughter-in-law, though during his estrangement from them between 1718 and 1720 he carried the burden of being the sole host at Hampton Court, St James's and Kensington. The receptions for his birthday were always splendid and he took great pride in his granddaughters' growing skill in music and dancing, displayed on these as on more intimate family occasions. For the former Handel was responsible; in the latter, the princesses' governess after 1718, the countess of Portland, and the Gräfin zu Schaumburg-Lippe took a particular interest.[72] The seasonal moves from St James's to Kensington Palace, where the spring months were usually spent, and to Hampton Court, the summer residence, were accompanied with a certain amount of ceremonial, in particular that to Hampton Court when bells were rung in churches all along the route and surprisingly large presents of money – it would seem on a fixed scale – given in return. This was customary also when George made longer progresses to visit the country seats of noblemen, or to attend the races at Newmarket (a rare occurrence), or when he journeyed to and from the coast on his way between England and Hanover.[73] In all such moves his extended family accompanied him.

Inevitably the foreign aspect of their new king and his retinue, coupled with George's reserve in respect of his private life, gave rise to speculation and rumours. The fact that *La Schulenburg* and Sophia Charlotte von Kielmansegg often travelled in the same carriage probably started the story that they were both George's mistresses. The blood-relationship between George and Sophia Charlotte was not unknown in England. Lady Cowper notes in her diary that she had been told of it,[74] and in 1718 when Sophia Charlotte, after her husband's death, was naturalized and created countess of Darlington in the English peerage, a good many officials must have noticed that the king described her as of the *consanguineam nostram* (*i.e.*, of our common blood) on the parchment which announced the honour, and that the broken baton of illegitimacy appeared in her Brunswick coat of arms. There is of course no reason why a half-sister should not be a mistress. The publicity given to early nineteenth-century scandals of incest may help to account for the persistent characterization of Sophia Charlotte as George's mistress down to our own day, though some historians have assumed that incest had by then become fashionable because of the royal example set in the eighteenth century. Sophia Charlotte was, however, exceptionally devoted to her own husband, and incest was never imputed to George by anyone close to the royal circle. It should be noted that George's mother went out of her way in 1701 to deny to a correspondent the truth of rumours that the as yet un-married Sophia Charlotte von Platen was George's mistress: she stressed that, *to her certain knowledge, it was not so*, the nearest Sophia would go on paper with regard to the blood relationship between her son and his half-sister.[75] Others were less squeamish, Liselotte and Wilhelmine were both quite open about it in their letters and memoirs. In England the veiled hint of a physical relationship between them voiced by a confectioner of the royal household was regarded as scandalous by officials who found nothing shocking in the common talk of Melusine being the king's mistress. They urged that the man should be punished, but George, who thought him a good pastrycook, decided that dismissal sufficed.[76]

Gossip, deriving in part from ignorance of family relationships, ascribed several other mistresses to the king. In his lifetime the young countess Platen, Sophia Charlotte's sister-in-law, was often listed (and has continued to be so by historians) among George's mistresses; it was believed that only her Catholicism prevented him from bring-ing her to London. She certainly wielded some influence at the court of Hanover and – as she showed some enmity towards *La Schulenburg* – English ministers who espoused the cause of one or the other nourished these rumours or, possibly, believed in them. The fact that George was willing to pay for the dowry of her daughter was interpreted as proof that this daughter was his. Her husband's standing in Hanover offers, however, a sufficient explanation; and if guesses are hazarded (given the overall situation) it would be more sensible to assume that George believed Sophia Charlotte's brother to be his father's child.[77] Towards the very end of George's life a Miss Brett was said to have gained the king's favour and it was assumed that, but for George's death, she would have displaced Melusine; but the only foundation for this is a dispute between the young lady and the daughters of the princess of Wales about quarters at St James's which goes back to Horace Walpole's reminiscences and hardly bears the interpretation put on it.[78] Odder still* is the con-tention by Hervey, after George's death, that the Gräfin von Delitz had been the mistress of three members of the royal family: George

---

* Odd, since Hervey realized that Louise was the sister of young Melusine, but seems totally unaware of the real relationship of the two to *La Schulenburg*.

I, George II, and Frederick prince of Wales while he was resident in Hanover, seemingly on no other basis than that she had been lodged in Herrenhausen during George II's visit to Hanover in 1735 and lost her apartments because of a quarrel in 1736.[79] The pedestrian unravelling of kinship and connections, while less titillating, produces results which fit better George's sober, conscientious and controlled way of life after his early youth. He was, it would seem, faithful to Melusine and happy in his family life with her and their daughters and with his granddaughters by the prince and princess of Wales. The latter were 'the apples of his eye'; the former his and Melusine's constant companions, at concerts, operas and at masquerades and balls as well as at the supper table and on drives. English commentators usually mention only two nieces of *La Schulenburg*. The explanation for this is probably that Gertrud, the youngest, was only thirteen in 1714, and was not at first permitted to go to operas and concerts, and that when she became old enough to join the party, Louise had developed a more independent life-style. Trudchen, *die schöne Gertrud*, was especially dear to George; she was gay as well as beautiful and when the elder Melusine began to suffer from ill health it was the youngest daughter who went on drives with the king. At the age of twenty he married her to Graf Albrecht Wolfgang zu Schaumburg-Lippe and delighted in her happiness and in the two sons she bore. Her husband and his brother had been brought up in England (with studies abroad) because of the estrangement of their parents, and in 1720 Albrecht had entered into George's service, accompanying the elector-king on his visit to Hanover in that year. The letters of his mother, the Gräfin zu Schaumburg-Lippe, barely concealed her knowledge that Gertrud was George's child: she would not have permitted her elder son (due to inherit, as he did in 1728, the *Grafschaft* of Schaumburg-Lippe) to marry a mere *Hofdame*, even if the daughter of the duchess of Kendal's sister, except for the 'special circumstances'; the king is acting the father's part regarding the girl's dowry and trousseau; the king is so overjoyed and so concerned for the boy born in 1722 and christened Georg August Wilhelm 'as if the child was of the royal family'; the king insists that this boy and his younger brother born in 1724* shall be painted by La Fontaine.[80] Even more significant (though not revealed in the Gräfin's letters) is the fact that George promised in the marriage contract that he would support Albrecht Wolfgang's succession to Schaumburg-Lippe and that he and his Hanoverian successors would undertake to defend Schaumburg-Lippe against any attacker.[81] It was a terrible grief for the young husband, and for George, when Trudchen died of tuberculosis

---

* The elder boy died young (it was rumoured, in a duel) while studying at Leiden; the younger distinguished himself as an ally of Britain in the Seven Years War. His interest in military matters (he had been entrusted with the reorganization of the Portuguese army by Pombal; he wrote treatises on the art of war; and the fort he built as reigning Graf of Schaumburg-Lippe still stands) and his patronage of music remind us of George I, as do the 'Hanover' hands noticeable even in his portrait as a child.

in 1726, in spite of efforts for about two years to save her and visits to spas and specialists on the continent.[82]

Melusine was particularly attached to the second daughter, usually called young Melusine, who remained unmarried until 1733 and from whom she was hardly ever parted.[83] It is possible that she got on less well with the eldest, Louise; certainly in 1723, when George drew a money-order on the treasury from Hanover for the 'sister of Lady Walsingham', he asked that this should 'be done without the knowledge of the Duchess of Kendal'.[84] In 1726 he presented Louise with a beautiful little palace at Herrenhausen, known after her as the *Delitzsche Palais*,* presumably so that she should have a refuge if need be.[85] Possibly Melusine was less tolerant than George of Louise's way of life. She was witty and beautiful. An unnamed reader of a document, now in the Public Record Office, which mentions her by name has added a tribute to her pleasant personality in the margin.[86] But it is clear from Ernst August's letters that she was strong-willed,[87] and, according to Hervey, she not only had 'a thousand lovers' but her divorce was the result of being caught *in flagranti* by her husband.[88] She had been married young, into the Bussche-Ippenburg family; but all that is known for certain is that George arranged for her divorce before 1714,[89] and that he obtained for her – at the time when young Melusine was given an English title – an Imperial title as Gräfin von Delitz.[90] *La Schulenburg* clearly had strict standards. She disapproved so strongly of the gambling habits of Philip Dormer Stanhope 4th earl of Chesterfield, who married young Melusine, that he was too scared to confess his losses at cards during a visit to Bath: he pretended he had not played at all.[91]

Some tensions in family relationships are unavoidable; but the only one in George's nearest entourage of which we have specific knowledge is the envy which Sophia Charlotte is said to have felt at Melusine having the title of duchess while she had to be content with that of countess. When in Hanover she formed an anti-Schulenburg clique with her sister-in-law, the countess Platen; and there was sufficient vexation for Melusine in 1723 to confess to Townshend that she would not mind if, next summer, the parliamentary session went on long enough to save her from another visit to the electorate. George's Hohenzollern granddaughter Wilhelmine has a good deal to say of this rivalry in her memoirs – she, like her mother, taking the Schulenburg side.[92] The pressure exerted by Sophia Charlotte and countess Platen – on behalf of the latter's daughter – to have the father of her French husband-to-be raised to the rank of *duc et pair* caused George great embarrassment in 1723–24. His diplomats

* Now used as the Herrenhausen museum and known as the Fürstenhaus.

became involved and he himself lost some face in extricating himself from an awkward situation in which he was made to feel that he had interfered in French domestic affairs.[93]

But, except during visits to Hanover after 1719, harmony was the rule rather than the exception. The princess of Wales and Melusine got on well together and this kept Sophia Charlotte (who was disliked by the princess) in check. George always remained on good terms with his half-sister. His private accounts show that, as long as she lived, she was entrusted with the task of choosing presents for George's daughter, the queen of Prussia.[94] George's 'special concern' for her sons is noted in the instrument for the Imperial *Graf* titles which Charles VI bestowed on them in 1723.[95] Sophia Charlotte was more popular than Melusine among English women who moved in the royal circle. She was gregarious, well-read, a good conversationalist and had excellent taste:[96] Melusine, more retiring in society, was politically influential since she proved a useful 'breaker of ice' for topics which ministers wanted to put before George, particularly where personalities and promotions were concerned. She dined both English politicians and foreign diplomats of note,[97] and became involved – as discreetly as she could – in the struggles between George's British ministers after 1723.[98]

It is a measure of their adaptation to English life that Melusine and the daughters who survived George chose to live in England after 1727. The duchess of Kendal sold the Holstein estate which she had bought in the 1720s and settled at Twickenham; the Gräfin von Delitz disposed of the *Delitzsche Palais* (though her name clung for a generation or two to the Herrenhausen property) and bought a house in Paddington.[99] Sophia Charlotte remained in England after her husband's death in 1717, and though her sons made their careers in Germany, one daughter married in England.[100]

*   *   *

It is interesting to speculate on why this adaptation took place, but investigation suggests that it was just because these ladies were of the extended royal family that they did settle down in England. They had all, the countess zu Schaumburg-Lippe noted, cried 'bitter tears' when they left Hanover; but their fate was, like George's, tied to England from 1/12 August 1714 onwards. The very fact that they obtained Irish and English titles after naturalization created a particular bond with George's kingdom.

For the majority of Hanoverians who came over with George their years in England were limited. Those who stayed the shortest time were the courtiers and servants intended to cover the interim period until George's English court and household should be settled. Concern that the king-elector should arrive in state, dignifying Hanover's image, had influenced the composition of the suite and staff which arrived with, or shortly after, George in 1714. They numbered some seventy in all, ranging from ministers, officials and courtiers of high rank, physicians, apothecaries, tailors and trumpeters, to a complete kitchen staff. But most of them returned home in 1715 and 1716. After 1716 George's Hanoverian servants in England never exceeded twenty-five.[101]

Those who had business to conduct remained: all the important officials of the *Kanzlei*; a few courtiers in key positions, like Hardenberg and Kielmansegg and (for sentimental reasons) the general-adjutant Hammerstein who had saved George's life at Neerwinden in 1693; the body servants Mehemet and Mustafa; two pages and a few gentlemen of the bedchamber (Melusine's half-brother Friedrich Wilhelm having a privileged position among them between 1717 and 1720 and Fabrice from 1719 onwards); one or two medical men and, at times, a Hanoverian court-painter. There was also a court dwarf, Christian Ulrich Jorry (who entertained at George's supper-parties and is depicted in the Kensington Palace murals). He had been presented to the king by a German nobleman; but he does not seem to have received a Hanoverian salary, though his clothes were paid for by George.[102]

It should be noted that some staff, responsible for George's meals, remained: six cooks and three bakers and confectioners. George took a lively interest in his food though, contrary to what is generally believed, he did not put on much weight as he got older.[103] Like most German exiles among his contemporaries – Liselotte von der Pfalz must be especially mentioned – he enjoyed the typical dishes of his homeland; but whereas she had to rely on presents for sausages and hams prepared in the German manner,[104] George was in a position to command what he wanted. Fruit, of which he was a discriminating judge, presented no problem in England, though we do not find him praising the grapes of Hampton Court as highly as those grown at Herrenhausen.[105] There was game in plenty; we hear of George and his son shooting hare, pheasant, partridge, woodcock, and occasionally deer. Deer, especially stags and bucks, were, however, much rarer than in Hanover until George's improvements at Windsor and Walpole's at Richmond had taken effect in the 1720s. On visits to Germany, therefore, the king particularly enjoyed the hunting of large game, though the boar hunts of his youth and early manhood were not often his to enjoy: the parliamentary session in England opened before the best time for this sport. George grew to like English beer* and developed distinct preferences for individual brews

* So did Germans who had stayed in England for a while after 1714: presents of beer and cider were sent to Görtz and Oberg in Hanover by the duke of Kent and Hugh Boscawen: see Görtz Archive 121/6, letters for 11 and 20 July 1717.

served him in noble households. In 1717 Schulenburg reported him full of praise for lord Onslow's 'freeholder' or 'election' beer ('better even than the Cholmondeley brew'), but intimated to his correspondent that the royal palate was fickle: 'Je crois que cette préférence ne durera guerres et changera à la première que d'autres Luy offriroit.'[106] Of rare delicacies which were sent George as presents he particularly appreciated the truffles with which the French statesman Dubois regaled the royal table when in London for the Quadruple Alliance negotiations in 1718. Delicious truffles, Schulenburg tells us, then became 'more or less ordinary fare' at supper.[107]

In filling the posts for his English household, some 950 in all, George exhibited two peculiarities and one firm line of policy. His refusal to nominate a groom of the stole until 1719 (when his growing dependence on Sunderland left him no choice) was motivated by his desire to avoid an English courtier with unlimited access to himself; and his putting the mastership of the horse in commission after December 1715 was dictated by deference to his half-sister so that no one Englishman in charge of the royal stables should seem superior to her husband, the Hanoverian *Oberstallmeister*. It should be noted, however, that Kielmansegg was not paid from English funds and that the saving effected in the English household accounts was a real one, the money not being passed (as contemporaries believed) to one or other of the king's Hanoverian favourites. The distinct policy followed can be seen when George made new or confirmed old appointments as soon as the customary period of security of tenure after a royal demise was over. Changes were made mainly in the higher ranks, George putting in men of families who had strongly supported the war in Europe: Marlborough's sons-in-law, Godolphin's relatives, Cadogan and his protégés. Reward for past service can be seen also in appointments to the household of the prince of Wales (e.g., Argyll in return for his pre-1714 commitment to the house of Hanover). Most courtiers had some political influence, either via a government post or by membership of the House of Lords or the House of Commons. It is worth noting, however, that those who were promoted to the highest of the household offices (if the king was not under particular pressure from his ministers) were those who had proved themselves least ambitious politically. After Sunderland's death in April 1722, for instance, George waited a full year before filling his post as groom of the stole and then appointed Francis, earl Godolphin and Marlborough's son-in-law, who enjoyed the honour and profit of the place but was content not to exert political pressure on the king.

The most prestigious appointment within the household was that of the lord chamberlain, and all four holders of the office during George's reign were dukes. Shrewsbury was succeeded in 1715 by Bolton; Newcastle took over in 1717 and was followed by Grafton in 1724. This courtier was in charge of the whole household above stairs (some six hundred individuals) and of court ceremonial in its widest sense, arranging court entertainments and receptions for foreign diplomats, allocating lodgings in royal palaces and taking responsibility for the upkeep and improvement of buildings. He and his staff issued orders and arbitrated disputes, but powers were naturally delegated to various semi-autonomous departments: the wardrobe, the jewel office, the king's messengers and so on.

Closest to the king were in theory his English gentlemen of the bedchamber. Traditionally they were eleven in number, though George increased this between 1719 and 1720 to seventeen.* If George's private apartments remained closed to them (contrary to former practice and contrary to the custom followed by the prince of Wales), they were still his companions of the nobility on public occasions, his *seigneurs* in the French phraseology of the court, who on a rota basis attended him once he emerged from his private apartments, who introduced petitioners and other visitors at the closet door, who dined with him when he dined 'in public' and who at times walked with him, especially when he was at Hampton Court.[108] The fact that some of them combined their duties with administrative office and that others – like Charles Hamilton Douglas, earl of Selkirk[109] – were courtiers of long experience made them in their various ways useful to George, who liked conversation to focus on specific issues. The groom of the stole was, technically, the first gentleman of the bedchamber but his independence of the lord chamberlain (established in William III's reign) made him the second most important court official.

Most decorative at the court were the gentlemen-pensioners (all members of the nobility), the several sergeants-at-arms, the yeomen of the guard, the musicians and the watermen. The band of gentlemen-pensioners or gentlemen-at-arms had been formed in the sixteenth century as the personal bodyguard of the king and in their crimson uniforms with gold braid and lace, carrying axes, they added splendour and colour. On Sundays one officer and twenty gentlemen formed a guard in the presence chamber and marched in the chapel procession immediately after the king. On the king's birthday (and on certain festival days such as Easter and Christmas) the whole band of three officers and fifty gentlemen attended. Two sergeants-at-arms (there were four pairs in all who served one quarter

---

* In 1714 the dukes of Grafton, Kent and Richmond, the earls of Lincoln, Manchester, Orrery, Selkirk and Stair, and lord Carteret had been appointed; in 1719 the marquess of Lindsay and the earls of Bridgewater, Holderness and Warwick were added; and in 1720 the duke of Queensberry and lord Hardy.

of the year in turn) acted as mace-bearers in these Sunday and festival processions. The yeomen of the guard, less socially distinguished, were on guard rather than ceremonial duties in the first of the public rooms and at the head of the stairs of any palace in which the king stayed, to the number of forty under a non-commissioned officer. Two yeomen slept in the guardroom at night, and from their whole number – one hundred, commanded by a captain, a lieutenant and four corporals – an escort was provided whenever the king went out of the palace precincts. Twenty-four musicians and a 'Master of Musick' formed part of ceremonial court life, as did the sergeant-trumpeter with his twelve trumpeters, the kettle-drummer, the four drum-majors and the six hautboy players. To our mind the musicians of George's court are forever associated with Handel's 'Water Music.' The story that the king only became reconciled to Handel (who had 'deserted' Hanover for England before 1/12 August 1714 while still in the pay of the elector) because of the excellence of this composition and the way in which the King's Musick played it as George's barge, with attendant boats, was rowed over the waters of the Thames is not strictly correct: Handel had been 'forgiven' long before the water-music was composed.[110]

Also connected with the ceremonial side of court life was the staff of the chapel royal with its dean, its forty-eight chaplains and choir of gentlemen and boys; the principal painter and the painter in enamel; the keepers of the pictures and the armoury; the court poet, who composed odes to the king's birthday, the New Year and to other festive occasions; the writer and embellisher; the engraver of the seals and quite a few others with evocative titles.[111] These, like the physicians, surgeons and apothecaries to the person (with others for the household), the strewer of herbs, the mathematical instrument maker, the decipherer, the cardmaker, the printer, the ratkiller, the mole-taker, the keeper of the lions in the Tower, the tuner of organs, the master of the tennis court, the harpsichord maker, the furrier and the chocolate-maker, the gunsmith and the glover, and a host more, were all under the authority of the lord chamberlain.

The head of one offshoot of the chamber, the master of the robes, had become recognized as rather a privileged person, especially as the duchess of Marlborough had wielded such influence when she was queen Anne's mistress of the robes. During George's reign the master's post was a near sinecure, partly because William, earl Cadogan, who held the office till 1721, was busy, first in Scotland during the rebellion of 1715–16 and then on diplomatic missions in Europe; partly also because George let Mehemet arrange and pay for his hats, wigs and suits as can be seen from the *Schatull-*

Quittungen for the items supplied by tailors, hatmakers, embroiderers, lace- and shirt-makers.[112]

The lord steward was in charge of the household below stairs with its staff of nearly three hundred. Like the lord chamberlain he was of high rank,* and with his assistants (the treasurer, the comptroller, the master of the household, the cofferer) formed the 'board of the green cloth'. This board made contracts with victuallers for food, drink, fuel, candles; and the nomenclature below stairs indicates the many functions under the board's control: the spicery, the acatery, the confectionery, the scalding house, the poultry office, the ewry, the larder, the kitchen, the cellar, the woodyard, the bakehouse, the pantry, the buttery and so on. When 'public tables' were provided at court – that is, when the king did not dine or sup in private but entertained members of his household, his ministry and other guests – these were known as 'tables of the green cloth'. If the king gave orders that no such table was to be kept, as for instance during his stay in Hanover in 1716, extra expense fell on his chief ministers who felt obliged to provide tables of their own during the two public days a week when visitors, diplomats, and men and women on court business came to Hampton Court where the prince of Wales represented his father.[113]

The stables, as at every court in Europe, formed an important part of the household even if, as in George's reign, the mastership of the horse was in commission. Though George did not need as many horses, coaches, waggons, grooms and drivers in England as when he set out as elector on campaigns,[114] the list of surveyors of stables and highways, coachmen, postilions, grooms and helpers, saddlers and farriers was not negligible; and the equerries and pages of honour who (in turn) had the privilege of accompanying the king when he went riding or hunting valued the prestige of their office though they were paid much less than the gentlemen of the bedchamber.

The expense of the household was vast and consumed one-third of George I's civil list of £700,000 a year, some 15 per cent of the total budget of Great Britain.[115] Only one category of courtiers served without pay for the honour only, the gentlemen of the privy chamber.† Their duties were minimal, being restricted to attendance at great ceremonial occasions, but the posts were eagerly sought since, like all others at court, they carried exemption from various duties such as militia and jury service. From the king's point of view they enabled recognition to be given at no cost, and George permitted their numbers to increase from the forty-eight of queen Anne's reign to sixty-five in 1723. A similar purpose, that of re-

---

* Successively, in George's reign, the dukes of Devonshire, Kent, Argyll and Dorset.
† The paid ushers and grooms of the privy chamber, as of the guard chamber and the presence chamber – also referred to as the drawing room – had of course specific duties: opening of doors, seeing that fires were lit and candles replenished, and so on.

cognition of service, was effected by the revival of the Order of the Bath in 1725.[116]

It proved extremely difficult to cut down on household expenses, particularly on those below stairs. George, accustomed at Hanover to regular payments and sensible household management, did what he could. He achieved a measure of rationalization, but no savings to speak of. It is symptomatic of his interest in the contracts and accounts side of management that he tried to appoint comptrollers known for their experience of business, yet loyal to himself. He first asked James Brydges, paymaster-general of queen Anne's reign, to fill the post. Brydges was now rich enough to have no need to make money out of any office, though he had previously benefited greatly from the way in which the English system of late and infrequent audits permitted officeholders to enrich themselves by using government money for speculation. He had spent some years in his youth in Wolfenbüttel and Hanover, spoke German fluently and was on friendly terms with all the Hanoverians at court and in the *Deutsche Kanzlei*. But he refused, not wishing to tie himself to regular duties at a time when he wanted to enjoy the fruits of his fortune, the building and embellishing of Canons and the planning of concert performances by his own musicians. George therefore appointed Hugh Boscawen, Godolphin's nephew, a man of the same moral rectitude as the late treasurer and one who – as the Schulenburg correspondence shows – had George's confidence and could have occupied, if he so wished, high political office in 1717.[117]

Yet the system of perquisites, and even deliberate fraud, had grown and become so enmeshed over the centuries that it could neither be unravelled nor brought within reasonable bounds. It is possible that George, if he had not been faced with one crisis after another between 1715 and 1718, might have attempted a clean sweep. That he was irked and irritated even on a personal level is indicated by his ironic surprise that he could not take a carp from the lake in the park of St James's without the permission of one of his own officials and that – even when such permission had been obtained – he had to pay handsomely for 'taking his own carp from his own lake in his own park'.[118]

*   *   *

George had an income, the so-called civil list, made up from the 'hereditary revenues of the crown' (the customs, excise and the postal dues) granted by parliament. From this sum he had to defray all civil expenses of the administration and the royal household, with the exception of those incurred for the army and the navy, voted annually by parliament to provide a restraint on the sovereign's foreign policy: control of the ruler's ability to wage war was thus largely in the hands of the House of Lords and the House of Commons. From the civil list, therefore, the monarch had to pay the salaries of judges, ministers and officials, the outgoings for the diplomatic and the secret service, for the royal household and for the upkeep of all palaces – including the Palace of Westminster in which both houses of parliament sat. All pensions, whether agreed before 1714 or after that date, also fell on the civil list.

Until George's reign the income from the enumerated sources had fallen far short of the estimates, especially as during the Nine Years War and the War of the Spanish Succession appropriations for the war effort had been the rule rather than the exception. By 1713 the civil list debt stood at nearly one million pounds sterling. Parliament, in the euphoria engendered by the peaceful Hanoverian succession, paid off this debt in May 1715 and guaranteed George I the annual sum of £700,000 with the proviso that £100,000 of it should be earmarked for the prince of Wales. This arrangement disproves, incidentally, the contention that George 'hated' his son even before 1714: at this time he could easily have tied Georg August to his own purse-strings. Indeed, when conflict broke out between them in 1717, he wished he had been wise enough to have taken such a precaution. In 1715 parliament also decided that any surplus from the enumerated revenues should be paid into an aggregate fund. In the peaceful years after 1714 this fund grew fairly rapidly. In theory there was therefore a reserve from which new civil list debts could be met. In practice not only did George's total expenses outstrip the £700,000, but the aggregate fund was, first, earmarked for paying off the national debt and, later, raided by English ministers reluctant to increase the land tax.

In George's accounts a distinction was clearly made between the administrative expenses, pensions, and the royal household outgoings. At Windsor elaborate comparisons have survived between pension expenditure in the late queen's reign and in George's reign,[119] and in the British Museum I have found full details of all privy purse and secret service expenditure for the years 1721–25, marked 'to be laid before Parliament'.[120]

It is possible that this distinction derives from 1718 when the new civil list debts were examined by a parliamentary committee, and the expenses of the royal household came under particular scrutiny. It was noted that Melusine and Sophia Charlotte had drawn food, wine and beer, fuel and candles and furniture for their own apartments, from the royal kitchens and the Wardrobe, as had the prince and princess of Wales until their departure from George's court early in 1718. Some Hanoverian courtiers had also benefited in various ways at the expense of the royal household. In the case of the latter the privileges were withdrawn or severely curtailed, and George agreed that fixed sums of money should be given *La Schulenburg* and *La Kielmansegg* in lieu of kind (£3,000 for below stairs and £1,000 for the Wardrobe) so that the outgoings in respect of these two ladies could be properly budgeted for. Melusine, since George habitually took his supper in her apartment, was, however, still permitted to draw fuel and candles.[121]

The committee failed to tackle the far more numerous and much greater perks and frauds (which were not rooted out till the radical reforms of the 1780s) of the English members of the household; but the information which had come to light helped to fix the image of covetous Hanoverians 'who sucked the English dry' – George's ladies, as well as his electoral courtiers and ministers residing in England. This complaint, voiced from the early days of George's accession, raised an issue of principle in British politics and, in its turn, had some influence in directing George's thoughts towards the problem of how best to dissolve the dynastic union between Hanover and Britain.

VI

Two issues of principle

THE STRUGGLE FOR PLACE AND PROFIT

The accusation of Hanoverian greed for British money is one which
has reverberated from George I's own reign to the present day.[1]
Several facts need to be taken into account.

The position of George's electoral courtiers and ministers, and
even of Melusine and Sophia Charlotte, was not easy after 1714.
They all had commitments at home, estates or houses to keep up and
relatives to support, and this they had to do without the fees which
– within limits – had been available to the majority of them in the
electorate. Transfer to London meant a drop in earnings, and everything was found to be four times dearer than at home.[2] The chief
ministers had, in any case, been able to earn little above their salaries
and fees after 1698, in contrast to the reign of Ernst August when –
because of the international situation – von Platen and Otto Grote
increased their official salaries tenfold when gratifications from
Louis XIV and domestic presents flowed freely.[3] Bernstorff had
accumulated money before the union of Celle and Hanover in 1705,
but in his case riches had derived mainly from duke Georg Wilhelm's
generous rewards for his services and not from foreign gratifications.[4]

Leaner times had come with George's reign as elector; and, after
1714, the Hanoverians in England, even the most upright of them,
like Görtz and Bernstorff, looked about for ways either of economiz-
ing on expenditure or of maximizing their income. Görtz hoped for a
house paid for by the British crown during his stay and was surprised
when Sir John Vanbrugh, of the Office of Works, informed him that
there were none in the king's gift: English ministers paid for their
own homes.[5] On a more significant level, Brydges, who sought an
earldom for his father,* found that Melusine, Sophia Charlotte,
Bernstorff, Bothmer and Kreienberg (who had assisted Bothmer in
the London embassy before 1714) were willing to accept money-
presents in return for ensuring the success of his quest. His accounts,

---

* The father died before he was dubbed earl of Carnarvon, but the title – since it had been
bestowed – was deemed to have been inherited by Brydges, who was later created duke of
Chandos.

now in the Huntington library, show that between August 1715 and February 1720 he gave £9,545 to *La Kielmansegg*, £9,500 to *La Schulenburg*, £2,909 to Bernstorff, £1,350 to Bothmer and £750 to Kreienberg.

Whether these sums should be regarded as 'bribes' in the modern sense is open to question. The sale of offices or of the reversion of offices was part of the social system of Europe in an age when pensions or other provisions for one's old age were rare. In England places at court changed hands for money, as did army commissions, and the sale of votes was quite common. Numerous minor posts were sold by the chief clerk of the House of Commons and by officials of many kinds at the local as well as at the central level.[6] In France, Louis XIV's courtiers, male and female, were 'commission agents' selling services: effecting introductions, soliciting petitions, helping to procure places, titles, charters and grants.[7] Brydges certainly had some success in obtaining minor office for relatives: the deanship of Carlisle for his brother and the reversion to the office of clerk of the Hanaper for his son. His money-presents to Bernstorff and Bothmer may have eased these transactions. We know that he offered Robethon 400 guineas, in cash or lottery-tickets, for the reversion of a post in the salt office for a friend. We do not know if Robethon accepted; in any case this was a small sum when compared both with Brydges' fortune and with the going price for offices and positions: on her own admission, Sarah, duchess of Marlborough, sold the place of a page of the backstairs at the court of queen Anne for £400.[8]

In George I's reign no important place at court was for sale, and the evidence we possess tends to show a decline also in the sale of offices in general.[9] George's personal examination of all applications that touched the army is well known; but even where court or administrative office was concerned, his Hanoverian, like his British, advisers would have to take the king's prejudices into account – not only the person's fitness for the post and the influence of his patrons, but also his own past political behaviour and that of his family. Peter Wentworth, brother of the earl of Strafford, was told that he must 'be content yet awhile' when, supported by the duke of Shrewsbury and Friedrich Wilhelm von Görtz, he sought promotion; he did not rise beyond the rank of equerry until the reign of George II.[10] The earl of Strafford was never reinstated in any post. He was keen to be employed and humbled himself (for he was a proud man) to the extent of begging Görtz to assure George I, if current rumours should reach the king's ear, that he had not drunk the health of Ormonde on the latter's birthday.[11] Friedrich

Wilhelm von der Schulenburg's hints that it would be sensible to give Strafford a minor post to content him, or at least to tie him closer to the Hanoverian dynasty, also went unheeded.[12] Even men of impeccable antecedents had to wait their turn. Thomas Burnet, son of bishop Burnet and the author of pro-Hanoverian pamphlets both before and after George I's accession, assiduously solicited a post from September 1714. Not till May 1719 was he rewarded with a consulship in Lisbon, though it is fair to add that this exceeded his expectations.[13] Conversely others, sacked in 1714, who had become more or less reconciled to being out of office, were agreeably surprised to be brought back after the death of Stanhope in 1721 when Sunderland for a while had great influence on appointments – among them Sir John Evelyn, who became a commissioner of the customs.[14] It should be noted, however, that he was not restored to the sensitive post of postmaster-general; George's concern for the vital services of the state took precedence over ministerial recommendations.

While no firm evidence has been found beyond the sums actually spent by Brydges, it must be stressed that, quite apart from general gossip of the efficacy of bribes spent on the old Baron (as Bernstorff was often called), Bothmer and Robethon, or on 'the Germans' in general, important and responsible British ministers – Townshend, Robert Walpole and Craggs in particular – assumed and even claimed that George I's Hanoverian ministers lined their pockets with money-presents accepted in return for their recommending to the king candidates for British posts. Their accusations cannot be taken lightly.

In 1716, when George was in Hanover, Townshend complained to Stanhope that Bothmer and Robethon interfered in Scottish patronage and that Bothmer had 'every day some infamous project or other on foot to get money, having nothing in his view but raising a vast estate to himself'; and in 1717 he spread a story in London that Robethon, shortly after George's accession, had asked ministers for £40,000 to be shared among Bernstorff (£20,000), Bothmer (£10,000), Schütz and himself (£5,000 each).[15] In 1719, on hearing a rumour that Görtz might return to London, Craggs worried that this would mean 'filling a new purse' and charged the whole of George's Hanoverian entourage with excessive greed: 'I have remarked that there is no distinction of person or circumstances. Jacobites, Tories, Papists, at the Exchange or in Church, by Land or Sea, during the Session or in the Recess, nothing is objected to provided there is money.'[16]

It is of course true that both secretaries wrote at times when they feared that their political enemies would gain the upper hand through Hanoverian money-trafficking and that, from their point of view, the king's 'credit, interest and service' would then suffer. There is certainly an element of exaggeration in Craggs's letter and a shade of venom in Townshend's contention that Bothmer would not 'be satisfied till he has got the Ministry and Treasury into such hands that will satisfy his avarice'.[17]

Yet their concern to keep British patronage in British hands was natural since such patronage was part of political power, and George's rejoinder to Robert Walpole that he was sure the British ministers received *douceurs* for their recommendations fell on deaf ears.[18] Even if there was more smoke than fire in their accusations, a question of principle was raised, since any encroachment by Hanoverian ministers and courtiers in British affairs was deemed contrary to the spirit of the Act of Settlement. For this act, its authors bearing in mind the rewards of land, titles and political influence to William III's Dutch favourites (particularly Portland and Albemarle, but also prominent army officers), laid down that a future monarch should not be able to give land or office of any kind to those not British-born: even naturalized subjects could not qualify as recipients of royal bounty from any source but the ruler's private purse. That a minister or courtier of George I in his capacity as elector of Hanover should circumvent the act by using his proximity to and familiarity with the king to recommend even a single person for a British place was held to infringe the rights reserved for British-born subjects: an effrontery, a cheating of British subjects out of profits reserved solely for them, as well as a political danger. This explains the note of near-hysteria in the letters quoted above. The indignation was not directed at payment for recommendations to office as such. Walpole, Townshend and Craggs, and every other British statesman of the period, regarded this practice as normal to gain adherents and supporters, and used it without qualms; but they wanted the power associated with the practice to remain in British ministerial hands. The lesser officials shared the attitude of their superiors. News in 1723 of Bothmer's purchase of an estate in Mecklenburg set the secretarial staff of Townshend and Carteret speculating on the sum he paid for it. This was variously estimated, with £20,000 at its lowest and £36,000 at its highest; but all assumed that the purchase price had been amassed at the expense of the British and hotly resented this.[19] There is also some evidence from the German side (though admittedly from Fabrice, who was not well disposed towards Bernstorff and Bothmer) that he, Fabrice, did not intend to follow the example of those of George's

Hanoverian ministers who had harmed their reputation in England by cashing in on royal appointments: he did not wish to incur hatred as they had done; he hoped, eventually, to become a naturalized British subject and realized that he would need the support of George's British ministers and advisers.[20]

That the 'German ministers' had not profited to the extent their British colleagues assumed can be deduced from various circumstances: Bernstorff and Görtz had made their fortunes before 1714, and Bothmer and Robethon lived in relatively modest circumstances in London. Their wills do not indicate great wealth. Indeed, Robethon stresses that he had lost a good deal of money in the South Sea bubble and deplores the fact that all he can leave his wife is an annuity of £66 and the interest on the equivalent of £1,200 left him by an uncle in France.[21] His other bequests, to his son-in-law and to the son of a cousin, his 'universal heir' after his wife's death, amounted to £1,500. Bothmer's Mecklenburg estate, at Elmenhorst, was in the joint possession of himself and a nephew, though – since the whole revenue from the estate had accrued to Bothmer during his lifetime – it seems probable that Bothmer had provided the whole purchase-price. He assessed his own share at 100,000 Taler* and made arrangements for his wife and daughter to share a regular income of 4 per cent on that sum to be paid at stipulated times of the year, the daughter to have the whole interest on her mother's death. If the revenues of Elmenhorst could not bear that sum at any one time, the estate was to be mortgaged. Stipulation was also made that his daughter, a widow, should benefit from the repayment of 6,000 Taler which he had lent to one of his brothers. He wished her to buy a 'noble estate' in a Lutheran or Calvinist part of Germany and turn that into a *fideikommis* for her male descendants. As the nephew was the one who would carry on the Bothmer name and title of *Freiherr*, all movables at Elmenhorst were left to him, with arrangements for primogeniture in succession to the land.[22] While there was thus a considerable difference between Bothmer and Robethon in the way they were able to provide for those members of the family that survived them, there is a close similarity about the other clauses of their wills.

Both demanded simple funerals (though Bothmer asked to have his body sent to Germany); both made bequests to the poor or to hospitals of their choice; both had minor collections of plate, medals, linen, books and manuscripts to dispose of – but the only value revealed is that Bothmer's plate was worth 300 Taler.

Concern for those who survived is also shown in her will by Sophia Charlotte, countess of Darlington. A widow since 1717, she

* A Taler at this time was worth about one-third of a pound sterling.

had long been responsible for the four sons (the eldest of whom died before his mother) and two daughters of her marriage to Kielmansegg. The future in terms of rank for the boys had been arranged by George I's obtaining promotion from the *Freiherr* standing of their late father to that of *Graf*; when she herself became ill, she sold her Hanover estate (for 8,000 Taler) and put the exquisite contents of 'Fantaisie' into store, stipulating in her will[23] that all her furniture, paintings, books, objets d'art and jewellery should be sold for the pecuniary benefit of her descendants.* In London Sophia Charlotte had a reputation of being a spendthrift: it was said that she had soon squandered the £40,000 left her by her mother.[24] It seems likely, however, that Sophia Charlotte's main inheritance from Klara von Platen was in the form of jewellery. This was certainly valuable (even if it did not reach the figure recorded by Lady Mary Wortley Montagu); but it was not 'squandered' since it formed part of her effects sold after her death. The inheritance from her father was governed by entail regulations: she had no free access to the capital which was administered on her behalf. Though generous and impulsive, Sophia Charlotte kept regular accounts. We have already seen that she had to take up a loan on the von Platen *fideikommis* to move her family to England in 1714 and also that she repaid it by instalments. While her husband was alive and in receipt of his salary as Hanoverian master of the horse, the couple lived in some state in lodgings provided by George I with much of the furniture and hangings provided by the Wardrobe. As a widow, Sophia Charlotte received a pension of £2,000 from the king. She moved to a house in Great George Street, near Hanover Square. This was run with the help of a butler, a cook, a porter, two carriers for sedan chairs, four footmen and eight female servants – not an excessive staff, judged by the standards of the time, when one remembers the number of children and her family relationship to George. From her accounts it has been noted that she bought several tickets in the state lottery and that she recorded a win of £10,000. It has been assumed that from this prize she bought her South Sea stock.[25] That this is erroneous is clear from testimony given at the South Sea bubble inquiry to the effect that Sophia Charlotte had received, as a secret gift, stock to the value of £15,000: a *douceur* equal to that given to the duchess of Kendal – in the expectation that 'George I's ladies' would speak in the company's favour with the king and demonstrate their confidence in its future to the public, thus encouraging other investors.

This knowledge renders Sophia Charlotte's entry of £10,000 as a lottery prize somewhat suspect. The sum seems to tally with the

---

* The sale brought 51,100 Taler, to which her jewellery, valued at 22,000, contributed most. Her eldest surviving son, Georg Ludwig, bought back several items at the sale price, and these have remained in the Kielmansegg possession to the present day.

£9,545 which the duke of Chandos enters, in his accounts of 1720, as paid to the countess of Darlington as a reward for her support with king George for the title of duke of Chandos bestowed in 1719. But even if Sophia Charlotte's ticket brought a prize of £10,000 (while she did not enter the money-present from Chandos), the fact that her South Sea Company holding is noted at £15,000 in the list of her effects gives independent confirmation of the evidence given at the inquiry as to the sum she received. The chronicler of the Kielmansegg family history is mistaken in thinking that Sophia Charlotte was rewarded for keeping her head when the bubble burst. He argues that her refusal to sell increased her stock in the reconstituted company from £10,000 to £15,000 by the time of her death (May 1725).[26] On the contrary, the *douceur* she had received had much declined in value, though eventually the *fideikommis* benefited just because the stock had been a gift.

The duchess of Kendal and her two younger daughters were similarly unable to make the expected profit during the bubble, but for them also the slow rise of the stock, once the crisis of the company had been overcome, represented clear gain from the *douceur*. The only money apart from this South Sea Company stock which has been proved in the case of the elder Melusine is the gift of £9,500 from the duke of Chandos in 1720. This was for the same service in respect of his title as that performed by Sophia Charlotte; it rated fractionally higher as if Chandos was aware of their different relationships to the king. There were rumours of other presents to Melusine. She and young Melusine were supposed to have received 'something' in 1717 for helping the duke of Newcastle to the Garter and to have divided £12,000 between them when the duke of Kent obtained the same honour a little later. Melusine is also said to have pocketed £11,000 in 1725 for having persuaded George I to let Bolingbroke return to England.[27] This may well be so, even if in every case there were political reasons sufficient to explain George's actions; but direct proof is hard to come by where money presents are concerned.[28]

Melusine certainly needed money after 1714. She gave financial support to her brother of the alchemy experiments, as well as to the two brothers-in-law who were the putative fathers of her daughters by George. She seems to have been somewhat worried about her financial prospects if George I should die before her. An enigmatic letter from her brother, the field marshal, after George I's death makes the point that Melusine has only herself to blame if she is not now 'easy': she would never listen to her family's advice but kept her own counsel. If this means anything except a general grumble (and Johann Matthias was not given to them), it implies that

Melusine did not use her position at George's court to amass a fortune.[29] This estimate seems to fit the picture we have of Melusine from the side of George's family better than the money-grabbing harpy of English memoir literature.

In any case George was Melusine's financial mainstay. The pension he paid her was put at £7,500 a year by an Imperial diplomat, who had good contacts with the king's Hanoverian ministers.[30] George assuaged her vague worries over the future by granting her, in 1722, the patent for the Irish coinage which she was able to dispose of, at a profit of £10,000, to the contractor William Wood.[31] By this time she already held £10,000 in Bank of England stock,[32] and in 1720 she bought an estate in Holstein which she sold at a profit after the king's death.[33] George was clearly uneasy about her financial position; with her capital tied up in the estate she might be in need of ready money if she survived him. In 1723 he therefore made a last will and testament, witnessed by Robert Walpole, in which he left her £22,986. 2s. 2d.;* he let her know, as we can deduce from other evidence, the details of his bequest. As this will – only recently discovered in the British Museum[34] – makes no mention of anyone but Melusine, Hervey's story that George II suppressed a will of his father's in which the middle daughter, young Melusine, was left £20,000 and that the man she married in 1733, the earl of Chesterfield, was able to press this sum out of George II as the price for his keeping quiet about other aspects of the will, must be regarded with scepticism.[35] It is possible, however, that when the duchess of Kendal in 1730 demanded and received payment from Robert Walpole of the money he held in trust for her from the late king – in theory £12,986. 2s. 2d., but realizing, with dividends, only £6,993. 1s. 1d. – she did so in connection with marriage negotiations for young Melusine: discreet as ever, she just told Walpole that she had need of the money, all in one go, 'for a specific purpose'.[36] But it is more likely that she needed the cash to buy or build Kendal House at Twickenham where she lived for the rest of her life.[37] On her death in 1743 she made young Melusine, countess of Chesterfield since 1733, her main heir, with bequests both to Melusine's elder sister, the Gräfin Delitz, and to her nephews and nieces on the Schulenburg side. Her main charitable bequest, of £1,000, was to a missionary society in Africa.[38] The sums donated to nephews and nieces were quite modest (£300 to each); and the somewhat straitlaced attitude of Melusine as she got older (which we have already noticed in her dislike of gambling for high stakes) is evident in her leaving out one nephew from the list of bequests with the explanation that she did so because he had married against his parents' wishes. When the

* Made up of £10,000 worth of South Sea stock held in George I's own name and £12,986. 2s. 2d. worth of the same stock which had been transferred, the day before the will was signed, to Robert Walpole as a trustee for the duchess of Kendal.

dowager countess of Chesterfield had her own will drawn up in 1778, she noted that the residue of the duchess of Kendal's estate then stood at £17,164.[39] On the whole one is entitled to conclude that *La Schulenburg* did not amass a fortune commensurate with the rumours of her own lifetime. The pattern of the wills that I have been able to examine tends to be consistent: concern for relatives and especially for those expected to carry on the family rank and shoulder responsibility for its landed property; concern for servants in present or past employment; and small bequests to charitable institutions. That the family dynasty was more dominant than any other consideration is supported by arrangements made by those Hanoverians who had the misfortune to survive all their own sons and grandsons in the male line: in Bernstorff's case, this meant that his estates and fortune had to be entailed on the male descendants of a daughter who had, providentially, married a distant relative who also carried the Bernstorff name.[40]

That the 'Hanoverians sucked England dry' would therefore seem to be a gross exaggeration. George I clearly had some sympathy with those of his Hanoverian entourage who were willing to accept not only the usual presents of politeness (these the Hanoverians also bestowed on their English friends and connections),[41] but money-presents intended to influence him through them. The intention of bribing was thus present, and the secrecy connected with gratifications that could be deemed to be bribes was probably also present (*vide* the possible false entry in Sophia Charlotte's accounts). It would seem, however, from George's already quoted remark to Robert Walpole, that the king was *au courant* and this, according to the contemporary way of thinking, robbed the money-presents of the tinge of treason.[42]

In the cases of promotions to titles or minor office, where we have evidence of money-presents actually paid, we find them politically innocent, seen from George's point of view, since they were in tune with his policy of rewards for past services: Brydges had been pay-master-general during the War of the Spanish Succession and had punctually paid the Hanoverian auxiliary troops, in sharp contrast to the Tories who took over after him.[43] George therefore thought that Brydges and his family deserved rewards and did not mind his Hanoverian ministers benefiting from the largesse of so rich a British subject. And if, as rumoured, Melusine accepted money-presents for easing the path of the dukes of Newcastle and Kent to the Garter she was still working within George's concept of rewards: Kent, though a nobleman of 'indifferent parts',[44] was a staunch Whig who had rendered good service in queen Anne's reign,* while New-

---

* It is interesting to note that Kent's rise to the office of lord chamberlain in 1704 was rumoured to have been obtained by a bribe to the duchess of Marlborough of £10,000.

castle was a useful Whig of the younger generation – both were courtiers who would be given greater lustre by the blue ribbon. Again, if she helped Bolingbroke, for a fee, to return from exile, there may well have been an element of collusion between herself and the king who – as we have seen – wanted Bolingbroke in his 'party' at that particular moment.

That George himself felt, if not the need, then the desire to increase his private income from British sources in the early years of his reign can be traced in some detail from correspondence in the Bernstorff archives. At the peace of Utrecht Louis XIV had ceded the Caribbean island of St Christopher (the possession of which had been in dispute between France and England), and it was then renamed St Kitts. Via Bernstorff, George made inquiries whether he would be entitled to profit from certain land-sales there. This seems to have shocked Robert Walpole: only if the king publicly announced that he would use such money for a project that would please the nation, such as the rebuilding of Whitehall Palace, did he think there was any hope of success.[45] Busy as he was with Great Northern War issues, George let the matter drop; the time for London palace building had not yet come and he clearly had other ways of spending the St Kitts money (if it had materialized) in mind. Possibly the rebuttal taught him a lesson. It is worth noting that, though his ladies received stock in the South Sea Company as *douceurs*, he paid hard cash, and in full, for his own stock.

PROMOTION BY TITLE

While George, in the opinion of his British ministers, was not strict enough with Hanoverians who sought British money for recommendations to British posts and titles, he won their praise for meticulously keeping to the rules that forbade his giving British titles and posts to Hanoverians. Hereditary peerages were given only to legitimate male members of the house of Hanover: George's youngest brother, Ernst August, was made duke of York in 1716; and his grandson Frederick, at the age of eleven, was given the title duke of Gloucester.

For the royal ladies a halfway house was found – peerages for life after naturalization. Melusine, already naturalized in 1716, was in the same year created countess of Munster in the Irish peerage, progressing in 1719 to duchess of Kendal (a ducal title dormant since the death of the son of James II who bore it) in the English peerage. In 1722 young Melusine was given the title of countess of Walsingham.[46] Her elder sister Louise was not given an English title, but was in the same year made an Imperial countess in her own right, the Gräfin von Delitz (the name being taken from a property in the Schulenburg family). Trudchen was still too young to be honoured; and in the event she received high rank through marriage in 1721 to the heir of the ruling Graf zu Schaumburg-Lippe. George's half-sister, Sophia Charlotte, had, after her husband's death, to rely on George to complete arrangements for her sons to receive Imperial *Graf* rank, herself becoming a naturalized British subject preliminary to being granted the titles of countess of Leinster in 1719 and of Darlington in July 1722. Her younger daughter, Caroline, received naturalization at the same time; her elder daughter, named after herself, had become British by her marriage in 1719 to Emanuel Scrope, viscount Howe.[47]

This was the sum total of those whom George honoured by British titles, all members of his family or regarded as such. It is interesting to find, however, that discussions took place between Townshend and Robert Walpole in 1723 as to whether Sophia Charlotte's sister-in-law, wife of Ernst August, count von Platen, could be made a life-member of the English peerage. Townshend makes it clear that George had never hinted that he contemplated such a step (indeed, the secretary of state confessed that he was not certain whether the king would favour it or not): the query arose from his idea that he and Robert Walpole might, if it were legally possible, use the bait of the title to wean Sophia Charlotte from her friendship with Carteret, their feared rival for George's favour. The realization that the countess in question was of the Catholic religion (a fact which Townshend in his eagerness had overlooked) put an end to this particular pursuit, though not to their rivalry with Carteret.[48]

THE HANOVERIAN SUCCESSION

Surprisingly early in his reign as king, George I began to contemplate what we may call the Hanoverian succession, that is, the putting an end to the dynastic union between Britain and Hanover: already in February of 1716 he had a will drawn up which stipulated its future dissolution. That this was not a passing fancy is shown by his discussion of the problem with Hanoverian and British advisers, including legal experts, and also by a codicil to the will in 1720. Furthermore, he broached the subject with the person most concerned, his grandson Frederick; he also made strenuous efforts in Vienna to obtain Imperial cooperation; finally, he deposited three copies of the will, signed and witnessed: one in Britain, one in Vienna, and one in Wolfenbüttel.[49]

The reasons why he took these steps were various. The most immediate was the impact of the Jacobite menace as shown in the Fifteen. As an experienced soldier, George had no doubt that James Edward's invasion, and others that might follow, would be unsuccessful; but he argued that as long as the dynastic union between Britain and Hanover lasted there would be an element of division between 'Stuart' and 'Hanoverian', while Britain's enemies at any given time might be tempted to render assistance in money, arms, soldiers, or ships to the Stuart pretender to the British throne. Conversely, if the dynastic union between the electorate and the kingdom could be dissolved, then the accusations that the 'Hanoverian' line was 'foreign' would become muted, support for the Pretender and his descendants would die away and the country would have civil peace.

Secondly, he was concerned for Hanover and the Hanoverians. The separation of families brought problems and at times sorrows which he saw at close quarters. He himself had felt the pangs of parting and saw to it that the clause in the Act of Settlement of 1701 which forbade the monarch to leave the confines of the kingdom without express permission from parliament was repealed as early as 1715. He planned to visit Hanover 'frequently', to breathe familiar air and see familiar faces and places, to take the waters at Pyrmont for his health's sake, to hunt for pleasure, to watch the growth and development of his grandson Frederick, and – as he wrote to his daughter, the queen consort of Prussia – to give him the opportunity to meet her.[50]

In the event George was able to pay only five visits to Germany (in 1716, 1719, 1720, 1723 and 1725), but during four of these he met Sophia Dorothea and also, on one occasion in Berlin, his Prussian grandchildren, including Wilhelmine and the future Frederick the Great. The prince and princess of Wales and their younger children never went with George on his continental visits since their absence from London would have created serious constitutional problems: it was enough of a nightmare for the British ministers that the king went abroad at all and more often than not returned so late that parliament had to be prorogued again and again if politics, pleasure, or merely adverse winds on the Dutch side of the water delayed his return to London. Melusine was always of the royal party, as were her daughters and also Sophia Charlotte in her widowhood. Some of the London-based Hanoverian ministers and courtiers accompanied the king, though at

least one – usually Bothmer – was left behind to take care of Hanoverian interests. George's physician and a royal chaplain of the
Church of England formed part of his suite on every visit, and
individual British courtiers attended as and when it suited them and
George. The presence of at least one British secretary of state with
his staff was essential since much diplomatic business was transacted
during George I's stays on the continent; and, at times of tension
between his British ministers, two members of the inner cabinet made
the journey to Hanover with the king.

George was naturally disappointed, as was his Hanoverian entourage, in those years when circumstances did not permit a continental
visit. In 1715 news of the Pretender's approaching invasion made it
unthinkable that the king should leave Britain for however short a
time; and even in the summer of 1716, when George decided to
travel to Hanover, he did so in spite of the grave doubts expressed
by his British ministers as to the wisdom of the journey so soon
after the defeat of the Jacobite rebellion. In 1717 and 1718 the
unsettled domestic situation was sufficiently serious for George to
accept that he could not go abroad, even if important diplomatic
negotiations in progress during those years would have benefited
from his presence on the continent.* Hanoverians close to George
felt convinced that the king stayed in England at a significant risk
to his health during these two years; by the spring of 1719 it was
judged medically imperative that the king go to Germany to take
the Pyrmont waters as soon as possible and he left England already
at the end of May. Again there had been strong opposition from
most of his British ministers, though Stanhope realized the advantage
of George's being able to confer in person with his volatile son-in-law,
Friedrich Wilhelm I of Prussia, and win his cooperation for a
'peace plan for the north' now Charles XII of Sweden had been
removed from the European scene.

Once George's cure had been completed, attention was concentrated on the role of Prussia within the northern peace plan. Success
was hard to come by. Not only did Bernstorff remain suspicious of
Prussia's ultimate objectives, but Friedrich Wilhelm was in a difficult
position – wooed by George as elector of Hanover and by Britain,
but fearful of tsar Peter's reaction to any cooperation between
Prussia and George I. The Prussian king's vacillations kept the
British party longer on the continent than contemplated: it was
already mid-November when Friedrich Wilhelm and Sophia
Dorothea arrived at Herrenhausen, thus intimating that the Prusso-
Hanoverian and the Anglo-Prussian treaties already signed would
be implemented.

* The disadvantages of George's remaining in England were, in great part, compensated
for by the willingness of the French statesman Dubois to make an extended stay in England
– about half a year with one interruption – and by briefer visits by high-ranking diplomats
from other states concerned with the peace plan for the south.

For political and sentimental reasons, George was reluctant to cut his Hanover stays short and when he at last embarked on his Channel crossing, suitably escorted by British naval vessels, he often encountered terrible storms on the voyages back to his kingdom. In 1726 the ships were scattered and rumours spread all over Britain that the king had perished at sea. There was general relief when it became known that his yacht had got safely into Rye harbour, but the need to have carriages sent to his unexpected landing-place along snow-bound January roads made for further delay. The modest house in which the king stayed while in Rye can still be seen. Contemporary gazettes made much of the fact that the owners gave up their own bedroom to George, and that George – in return – stood godfather to the child born to the wife of his host during his stay: the boy was named after him and given 100 guineas as a christening gift.[51]

In 1720 George had the smoothest passage ever in arranging his visit to Hanover with his ministers. Stanhope was firmly in the saddle and as anxious as the king to exert influence on negotiations still in progress to end the Great Northern War in ways which suited Hanover and Britain. Moreover, the reconciliation, in February 1720, of the prince of Wales with his father gave assurance of domestic tranquillity, as did the re-entry of Townshend and Robert Walpole into George's government: Sunderland therefore felt free to go with the king and Stanhope.

That summer's visit to Germany was especially festive and George was so *lustig*, by all the reports Liselotte received from Hanover, that she could hardly believe this was the same person whom she remembered as *froid* and *sérieux* from his stay in France as a young man.[52] Ernst August, prince-bishop of Osnabrück since 1716, joined George's party at Göhrde, as did young Frederick of Hanover and prince Wilhelm of Hesse, the brother of king Fredrik I of Sweden.* When Friedrich Wilhelm of Prussia arrived with ministers and courtiers, it was estimated that George was at the expense of feeding seven hundred people (guests, their suites and servants, as well as his own staff) and of keeping over 1,000 horses for transport, riding and the hunt. The weather was fine. The days settled into a routine. At 8 o'clock in the morning the royal and princely guests and the more important ministers, courtiers, and officers met in the king's anteroom to take hot chocolate before hunting deer, foxes and hares. Dinner was served in the big hall at three large tables for those of high rank and office, and at six smaller tables in adjoining rooms for those who, in Fabrice's words, 'did not trust themselves to eat with royalty'.[53] Some of the twenty ladies (the number of George's

---

* His wife, Ulrika Eleonore, had succeeded her brother Charles XII in 1718, but in 1720 had abdicated in favour of her husband, Friedrich of Hesse, who adopted the Swedish form of his name on becoming king.

usual female entourage having been swelled by ladies of the electoral court, including one of Melusine's sisters) followed the hunt, Trudchen the keenest among them. In the afternoon all the ladies came into their own when courtiers and officers repaired to Melusine's apartments to drink coffee, gossip and flirt; and concerts, plays and dances were arranged in the evenings. At least one romance blossomed. The elder Schaumburg-Lippe son was of the party and must have found favour with both *die schöne Gertrud* and George: her marriage to Albrecht Wolfgang was celebrated in October 1721.

The afternoons, and often the evenings as well, were filled with work for the rulers and their ministers. Their secretaries and other trusted staff had been busy since early morning, deciphering sections of incoming despatches and enciphering parts of outgoing instructions, drafting treaty clauses and copying documents.

A similar routine, if with fewer guests in residence, was followed when George returned to Herrenhausen. There were balls and other entertainments. Increasingly, however, unease about the affairs of the South Sea Company transmitted itself to Hanover, affecting British and Hanoverian ministers and George and Melusine as well, necessitating a speedy return on both private grounds and reasons of state. It was therefore particularly galling for the king and the ministers to be held up in the Dutch port of Helvoetsluys for eleven days by contrary winds; but Fabrice (though worried about his own losses) depicts the king's dinner and supper tables during the waiting period, with Stanhope, Sunderland and the earl of Stair, from the British side, Hardenberg, Ilten and himself from the Hanoverian, as well as Sophia Charlotte and Melusine with the two younger daughters, as at least superficially jolly.[54]

The next two years George could not possibly get away from Britain: in 1721 the Bubble crisis had not yet been overcome, nor had George's ministry been re-established on a stable enough basis after Stanhope's death. And in 1722 the Jacobite invasion project, the so-called Atterbury plot, planned to take advantage of the general outcry against the South Sea Company directors and George I's government, was taken seriously enough by the British ministers to make them more or less veto the king's going abroad: news of a Stuart plot to assassinate George during his journey to Hanover was also given some credence.[55]

But in 1723 came another protracted visit to Germany, this time taking in Prussia as well as Hanover. Both British secretaries of state, Townshend and Carteret, accompanied the king with their respective under-secretaries and staff. This was in part a result of tension between the Townshend-Walpole group in the cabinet and Carteret who – on the death of Sunderland in 1722 – had gathered round him the remnants of the Stanhope-Sunderland group. More importantly, the presence of both secretaries demonstrated the predominance of British issues in George I's foreign policy negotiations: a significant shift (which will be discussed in due course) had taken place after 1719 in the relative priority for George of his electorate and his kingdom.

The 1723 visit followed the usual pattern of Pyrmont, Herrenhausen and Göhrde, and finally Hanover. At Göhrde there were a great many visitors who were lavishly entertained. Again the king, like his ministers, worked hard and hunted vigorously. For his visit to the court of Sophia Dorothea and Friedrich Wilhelm he drove, as he liked to do, his own light chaise with strong horses changed at every relay.[56] It was on 9 October NS, the first day of his stay at Charlottenburg, that he suffered a fainting-fit at the festive feast of welcome. This has been regarded as a slight stroke, though probably because the king died of a stroke in 1727.[57] In any case, George's indisposition was brief. He enjoyed meeting the Prussian grandchildren and discussing their future. In principle he accepted the double-marriage project which Sophia Dorothea had long desired, to marry her daughter Wilhelmine to Frederick of Hanover and her son Friedrich to a daughter, preferably the eldest, of the prince of Wales, though the king thought the cousins too young for any public announcement.[58]

The fainting-fit may have given Melusine a fright. Her plotting with Townshend to avoid a visit to Hanover in 1724 possibly had other reasons than unpleasantness with Sophia Charlotte and the von Platen clan: she may have started to worry about George's health and to think the journey and its festivities too tiring for him two years running. In the event she was the one who was seriously ill in 1724,[59] whereas George, during his 1725 visit to Hanover, was well and active enough – three to four hours in the saddle at hunts – to impress the British officials who reported to Whitehall.[60]

Biennial visits to Hanover became the pattern for the rest of the reign. No pressure can be traced from George or his electoral entourage in Britain for journeys to Germany in either 1724 or 1726. Conversely, there were urgent political reasons in 1725, as in 1727, why British ministers concerned with foreign policy should encourage the king to travel to the continent. In 1725 the build-up of two opposed political systems of alliances in which vital British interests were at stake necessitated a move, so to speak, of Whitehall to Hanover. In 1726 the diplomatic scene remained unstable enough for the ministry to prefer the king to stay at home, since the Spanish blockade and projected siege of Gibraltar, and the fear of large-scale war, turned their thoughts to defensive and contingency offensive military and naval preparations. By the summer of 1727 the threat of war had vanished – due more to George and his cooperation with Robert Walpole and French statesmen than to a bellicose Townshend; and there was general agreement that George's desire to finalize the double-marriage project with Prussia would serve British political ends. On 15 June (NS) the usual large party, spread over several yachts and other ships, left the British coast. Townshend and his officials stayed on for a short while at The Hague to concert measures with the Dutch, while George hurried ahead towards Hanover. On the way he suffered a stroke, and, hardly conscious, was taken to the palace of Osnabrück where he died during the night of 21-22 June.

*   *   *

During his five visits to Hanover George found time to look into electoral affairs. Indeed, he worked those Hanoverian ministers and officials whom he met only at rare intervals so hard that they were apt to feel they 'had no time to breathe' during the king-elector's stays.[61] Not that control was lax when George resided in his kingdom. All threads of foreign policy remained in his hands, and no army promotion could take place without reference to him. Extra-ordinary expenditure above a given sum – set as low as 50 Taler – had to be submitted to him for authorization. So did all petitions for pensions and other financial help, such as a dowry to permit the daughter of a former official to enter a Protestant convent.[62] In routine matters George relied on Görtz, the president of the *Kammer*, who had great expertise in financial matters. His incorruptibility was a byword; yet he remained uneasy lest his distance from the king-elector should work in his disfavour. His correspondence with young Schulenburg abounds with requests that he, or Melusine, should intercede for him with George when he suspected that his enemies in Hanover, or Bernstorff in London, were trying to make mischief in law-suits in which he was involved, or weaken his authority by arranging appointments in the *Kammer* directly with the king-elector.[63] Görtz was pro-Swedish in his views on foreign policy and had therefore an additional cause for worry: could Bernstorff use this to bring him into disfavour? Again and again Schulenburg had to stress that Görtz was the minister who had His Majesty's greatest trust in the realm of domestic Hanoverian affairs and to assure him that George would respect his views on foreign affairs as long as he did not take measures to undermine the king-elector's foreign policy.[64]

The greater opportunity which the separation of his Hanoverian ministers gave for misunderstandings and jealousies affected George's thinking on the Hanoverian succession. So did the suspicions and resentment (more or less strong) that his British ministers harboured of Bernstorff, Bothmer and Robethon. Of these, Robethon was the least important or influential. To call him George's 'private secretary' is somewhat misleading.[65] His official title was secretary of embassies and as such he was entrusted with much of the drafting of foreign despatches for Hanoverian diplomats. Research has established that instructions issued by him at critical moments of the Great Northern War touched upon British affairs. Yet he played no independent role; what he wrote was at Bernstorff's dictation and derived ultimately from George, who was not above exploiting his position as king for electoral purposes in the early years of his reign.[66] George increasingly distrusted Robethon. He had the reputation of a gossip, of not being *sage*, and in 1718 had to be taken to task (receiving *une bonne Mercuriale* in Schulenburg's phraseology) for having spread a rumour that the king planned to bring his grandson Frederick to England.[67] This hit George on a sensitive spot. British advisers, especially bishops, were apt to recommend that Frederick should come to Oxford or Cambridge to be trained for his future role as king;[68] while for the sake of Hanover it was essential for George to keep Frederick in the electorate to maintain loyalty and to serve as the rallying point for resistance if Hanover should suffer enemy invasion: a not unlikely prospect as long as the Great Northern War lasted.

If British contemporaries were deceived in overestimating Robethon's importance, they were right in ascribing to Bernstorff a greater influence with George than his fellow *Geh. Rat* in London, Bothmer. Bothmer, valued for his diplomatic experience, remained an adviser rather than a forceful minister willing to argue with his master when he disagreed with him.[69] Bernstorff, by contrast, held strong views and was not afraid to press them strongly on the king. It would be a mistake, however, to assume that he decided George's foreign policies whether as elector or king: there is much evidence to show that George sought a variety of opinions from British and Hanoverian subjects and took ultimate decisions himself. Nor is it correct to speak of Bernstorff's 'fall from grace' in the summer of 1719 (as a result of Stanhope's victory over him) and to assume that he never set foot in England again after that date; he was in England during 1720 and his influence with George was then thought 'as great as ever'.[70] He was, however, conscious of his advancing age, and wished to spend his remaining years at Gartow; he did not go back to London after the king's Hanover visit of 1720. From then on he kept in touch with London *Kanzlei* business through correspondence with Bothmer and with foreign affairs in general by letters from and meetings with Hanoverian and British diplomats.[71] He remained prominent enough in George's councils to make Townshend embark in 1723 on a campaign to have him excluded from any participation in the politics of George as king of Great Britain; and Townsend, Robert Walpole and Newcastle reckoned it a great victory when George in that year named Christian Ulrich von Hardenberg, his *Hofmarschall*, as *Geh. Rat* in Bernstorff's place.[72]

The resentment and fear of successive British ministers felt by his Hanoverian advisers could not but reinforce George's desire to dissolve the dynastic union between the electorate and the kingdom. It is noteworthy that the king's codicil of 1720, which reinforced the will of 1716, was signed after the Stanhope-Bernstorff tussle of 1719. George himself had increasingly become more British in outlook, but it was as if his British ministers would not believe this and distrusted him: Stanhope's toughness with Bernstorff in 1719 was mirrored (and even enlarged) when Townshend crowed in 1723 that he had forced the king to promise that he would not sign any document touching on British foreign policy issues except in his, Townshend's, presence.[73]

*   *   *

But how to effect a dissolution? George was not afraid of drastic changes. In 1700 he had accomplished the reform of the Hanoverian calendar in one fell swoop; in that year he discarded the Julian calendar and adopted the Gregorian by lopping off eleven days after 28 February.[74] On his accession in Britain he dropped the practice (as William III had done, though it had been revived by queen Anne) of touching for scrofula – the king's evil – not (as has been suggested) because he felt himself a usurper who had no right to lay on hands for healing but because he was in tune with the ideas of the early enlightenment and regarded the custom as mere superstition.[75] In political thinking he was a follower of Pufendorf and admired the latter's concept that the general good was the highest law. The fact that Pufendorf's translator dedicated the German version of *Of the duty of Man and Citizen* to George is no proof of this; but the range of the conversation George encouraged at his table and his support for a variety of scholars attuned to Pufendorf's ideas justify this conclusion.[76]

It should therefore cause no surprise that George adopted a

rationalist attitude to the problem that faced him. He realized that the obstacles would be formidable and that his solution could not be applied in the near future. He had only one son and, so far, only one grandson, Frederick, by that son.* Recalling the wounds which the quarrel over primogeniture had inflicted on his parents, his brothers and himself, George had no wish to rob anybody of his legal expectations. He insisted that Georg August and Frederick, having been brought up in the expectation that they would become kings of Great Britain as well as rulers of the electorate of Hanover, must not be deprived of either succession. What he stipulated was that, if Frederick should have more than one son, the first-born should inherit the royal crown and the second the electoral cap. If Frederick had only one son, that son should become king of Great Britain, while the electorate would pass into the Brunswick-Wolfenbüttel branch of the house of Brunswick.

The wisdom and maturity of this solution is striking: his own Brunswick-Lüneburg branch was to continue in Hanover if fate so decreed; if not, he had no thoughts of revenge on the enemy of 1692–1706, but harked back to the far older unity of the *Gesamthaus*. The priority given to Great Britain is even more significant. By accepting the Act of Settlement, the house of Hanover had taken on a responsibility for the Protestant succession which George did not think it right to abandon. Though not of a religious temperament, he held it 'a point of honour' to maintain this succession for himself and for his descendants.[77] George was also sure that his will would help Hanover. The electorate had greatly benefited from his accession to the crown and power of Great Britain: the terms he had secured from Sweden's enemies in 1715 can only be explained by the royal resources he now had and used with skill and ruthlessness to obtain Bremen and Verden for Hanover. Whichever branch of the *Gesamthaus* stood to inherit Hanover when the time came for the will to take effect, his personal *gloire* was assured as the elector who had fulfilled the Brunswick ambitions of expansion in north Germany.

He did not expect difficulties from the Hanoverian advisers whom he took into his confidence – Bernstorff, for one, agreed with him – nor with Frederick when the boy was old enough to discuss the issue. That George did so, and that he won his grandson's support for the will is shown by Frederick, on his deathbed in 1751, revealing his grandfather's wishes to his own eldest son† and imploring him to act in accordance with George I's will.[78] George also sent a copy of his will to the Wolfenbüttels in case Frederick should have only one son, so that they might make their claim heard. It was essential, if he should not fail in his duty to Hanover, for George to gain Im-

---

* The second son of the prince and princess of Wales to survive, William Augustus, was born in 1721.
† George, born in 1738; Frederick had four younger sons, three of whom reached adulthood.

perial consent to break the primogeniture rule for the electorate without having to sacrifice the electoral dignity. Efforts to achieve this were made after 1719; and though there was much discussion in Vienna as to the legality of what George wanted the emperor to do, the pressure which the king of Great Britain could put on Charles VI in the political negotiations of the 1720s gave hope of eventual success. The emperor and his closest advisers promised their consent (if in somewhat guarded terms), and a copy of George I's will was lodged at the Hofburg. A third copy was deposited with the archbishop of Canterbury.

George I put his plan before his British ministers and legal advisers, but these proved less pleased than he had anticipated. The ministers had quickly got used to the connection with Hanover which had some advantages, and promised more, in matters of British trade with the continent. More immediately, they feared that the will, if news of it should leak out, might have an unsettling effect on parliament and the country: could it not be used either by the Jacobites or by their own non-Jacobite political opponents to make mischief? Not wishing to offend the king, they remained non-committal and referred him to the jurists. In 1719 George submitted two propositions to a committee of legal experts under the chairmanship of Macclesfield, the lord chief justice. The first expressed his desire to give males preference over females in the British succession. Here the committee was not discouraging. The king had not asked to have females excluded from the succession, but was willing to contemplate a queen regnant if the male line failed. They gave as their opinion that this 'could be arranged if the king so willed'.[79] But when it came to the second submission, an examination of the will George had framed in 1716, they were deeply disturbed. They found that the prospect of an 'interregnum' was inseparable from George's plan for the dissolution of the dynastic union. Immediate succession was the English principle, expressed in the formula, 'The King is dead, long live the King!' There would be no time in law, they argued, for an heir to divest himself of his electoral title without prejudicing his royal title, since the formalities connected with that renunciation would create an interregnum, however short, and the nation 'abhorred an interregnum'. And even if some way could be found round this problem, what guarantee was there that the ruler would not go back on any promise, however solemn, he had made in order to become king according to George I's will, and at a later date claim the electorate, even going to war to displace his younger brother? And how could a second son who had inherited Hanover with the consent of the elder brother be prevented, on the death of that brother, from reopening his claim to the British succession? In either case there would be uncertainty. The jurists' conclusion was that any dissolution of the dynastic union would bring such dangers to Great Britain that the Protestant succession itself would be at risk.[80]

That this pessimistic report did not make George drop his plan is evidence of his attachment to the principle of dissolution of the union for the benefit of both kingdom and electorate. European developments between 1716 and 1720 (when he signed the codicil confirming the will) had indeed reinforced his determination to do all he could to bring about the intended separation: Hanover was now secure in possession of Bremen and Verden and specifically British and European interests dictated his and his ministers' policies to the near exclusion of electoral concerns. After 1720 this process gathered ever greater momentum, to the point where one Hanoverian minister could write – if in confidence – to another, 'Hanover will soon be a province of Great Britain, much as Ireland is now.'[81] George was well aware of this. His main attempt to find a solution to the problems raised by the Macclesfield committee were directed towards Vienna. If the emperor and the relevant Imperial authorities agreed to confer the electorate on the *second* great-grandson of his dynastic line, then the dissolution could safely take place. The prestige and power of the Empire would guarantee the safety of the new elector, while the knowledge that such an agreement had been won ought to make it possible for the *first* great-grandson to succeed in Great Britain without the interregnum envisaged by English legal experts.

Another solution, a more practical one in English terms, also presented itself and won George's conditional approval. The king must have discussed his will with his son and heir, for we find the prince and princess of Wales suggesting a revision of the will once the son born to them in 1721, William Augustus, seemed likely – to the delight of his parents and his grandfather – to survive infancy.* Their proposal was that this boy, born and brought up in England, should succeed his father in the kingdom, while his elder brother, Frederick, should rest content with the electorate of Hanover. George could see the advantages of this scheme. First, it would bring a quicker end of the Jacobite threat than his own will envisaged; secondly, it would revitalize a fully independent electorate more speedily; thirdly, it would create no complications in the Empire since primogeniture would persist in Hanover. George made his consent, however, conditional on Frederick accepting this solution of his own free will: he would not, in his will, rob Frederick of his birthright.[82] It is significant that there is no further codicil to

---

* It will be recalled that princess Caroline had a stillborn son in November 1716, and that George William, born in October 1717, had died in February 1718.

George's will after William Augustus's birth. We have no evidence that the king broached the subject of the revised plan with Frederick: it would seem that he waited for Georg August and Caroline to speak to the elder son about their intention in respect of the succession as he drew closer to manhood.

It is against this background, and possibly also the unexpectedness of George I's death, that we must see George II's suppression of his father's will in 1727. His pocketing of that document when the archbishop of Canterbury handed it to him in his first privy council, without communicating it according to custom to the members of that council, is well-documented.[83] Less well-known are George II's successful efforts to retrieve the copies of George I's will from Vienna and Brunswick. George II's having two sons strengthened his hand in negotiations with both Charles VI and the young duke of Brunswick-Wolfenbüttel:* against concessions on European issues, he persuaded the emperor to disgorge the Hofburg copy of the will; against financial compensation he brought the young duke of Brunswick-Wolfenbüttel – oppressed by debts left by his father – to surrender the Wolfenbüttel copy. Both copies were deposited in the Hanover archives, and it is indeed from these that historians in the twentieth century have been able to reconstruct the fate of George I's will of 1716 and its codicil of 1720.[84]

George I's plan for a dissolution of the dynastic union thus came up against not only British fears of an interregnum, but also his own son's dislike of the will as framed. If Frederick had lived longer than George II, or at least long enough to be able to discuss the proposed change at a more adult level than was possible with his own heir, a boy of twelve, George I's will might have come to fruition at the time he had envisaged.

What concerns us here is not so much the vicissitudes of George's will as the light it throws on his personality and on the way in which he attempted to solve problems along rational lines. News about his will which leaked out during his own lifetime and after his death was garbled and therefore misinterpreted or misunderstood. This explains the comments in English history books down to our own day that George I, out of hatred for his son, wished to rob Georg August of the royal throne.[85] Nothing could be farther from the truth. George I had settled in Britain and accepted that Britain had the first claim on the Hanoverian family. The greater power and glory of the kingdom, as against the electorate, no doubt played some part in his calculations; but his concern for justice, equity and rational solutions of political problems can be read in every line of the will. There is rancour against none.

---

* Anton Ulrich had died in March 1714 and been succeeded by his eldest surviving son, August Wilhelm (1662–1731).

VII

Three crises

GEORGE I'S IMAGE

George did not impress his new subjects by looks or majestic behaviour. He was on the short side (*de taille mediocre*) but had largely kept the figure of his youth, described in 1684 by a French diplomat as *fine et aisée*,[1] by vigorous exercise on horseback and by daily walks long enough to tire his entourage. His hands were strikingly fine, the fingers exceptionally long. His blue eyes, the rather hard Hanoverian 'china-blue', were arresting, though by his fifties pouches had developed beneath them. His mouth was well shaped and his chin was dimpled. The dominating feature was the long and pointed Ernst-August nose (not thick or heavy, as is often assumed)[2] which showed up well in profile, as can be seen in medals and in the interesting portrait in profile by Kneller in the possession of the Kielmansegg family. (A copy of this, 'from the studio of Kneller', is in the National Portrait Gallery.) The truest impression of George's looks during the early years of his reign as king is derived from this portrait in combination with a statue in Roman dress by the Flemish sculptor, Delvaux, from 1717. This statue is huge, made for the Rolls House. It was rediscovered as recently as 1954 and is now placed in the corridor leading to the Public Record Office Museum. The figure and face are slightly idealized as befits a heroic statue; but the features known from literary descriptions are clearly recognizable, and the fact that George does not wear a wig here establishes an immediate rapport with the modern viewer who can see the shape of his head.* The Kneller portrait, which one might be tempted to label a sketch or a study but for the fact that Sophia Charlotte had it put in the magnificently carved frame in which it is still found, tells us a good deal more of the person. It is livelier than the official portraits of the king, and catches the somewhat ironic smile that fits his personality in middle age. It conveys determination and ambition, but also maturity and tolerance.

Some of the official portraits, and even copies of them, are well

---

* It is possible that this work became the model for the face and figure of the several equestrian statues of George. Of these, at least two are extant: one in the grounds of Stowe School; the other (originally set up in Dublin and now rescued from a junk-yard) put in position in front of the Barber Institute of Fine Arts in Birmingham.

painted and give a sympathetic likeness. In Britain the Cholmondeley Kneller conveys George's watchful, shrewd intelligence as well as displaying his nicely turned ankles and the beautiful hands. More intimate, in spite of its royal appurtenances, is a huge portrait of George now in the Osnabrück Rathaus, the countenance open and trusting. Since this painting is on loan from the Bar family, two members of which served the Prinzessin von Ahlden in the highest posts at her private court after 1694, it is possible that it derives from the collection of Sophia Dorothea: we have literary evidence that this contained portraits of George as king of Great Britain. But usually, when pictured in his state or coronation robes, George seems disinclined to reveal anything of his persona; a memory of woodenness remains on the retina even if one realizes that this is produced by the sitter's unwillingness or inability to lower his guard. In the many equestrian portraits, as can be seen in the fine example in the Gorhambury collection, the very pose suits George better; and the riding-habit, simple in cut however grand in material, looks as if it has a body beneath it and not a dummy. None of the later portraits hides that slackening of the cheeks and jaw in his fifties in which George took after his mother. In Sophia's case this did not (however much she deplored the ravages of time when she looked into her mirror) mar the liveliness of paintings done of her from late middle-age onwards; in George's it contributes to a certain dullness of expression.

Relatively few portraits of George before 1714 have come down to us; but there is a striking continuity between the portrait of the young George, now in the Herrenhausen museum, and the last portrait, now in the Queen's collection, painted between 1725 and 1727 by La Fontaine, the son of a Huguenot refugee settled in Hanover, who came to London at George's request to paint him and other members of his family (including the two sons of *die schöne Gertrud*). The basic shyness is there, also the kindness: the child is clearly father to the man even if the man has aged. Incidentally, this portrait makes identification of an anonymous painting in the Royal collection of an elderly, very plump, gentleman as 'George I' very doubtful indeed.[3]

The many engravings, both before and after 1714, are less illuminating for the personality, though they are interesting for their contemporary propaganda value and richly illustrate the symbolism of the age. We find the handsome George, as hero from his early wars; we find the *Retter des Reiches* of the War of the Spanish Succession; we find him in his office as arch-treasurer of the Empire; we find him in Garter robes, and with all the attributes of power, the electoral cap, the baton of the commander, the crown, orb and sceptre of the monarch. Some are very fine indeed; others almost primitive. The falsification attendant on the engraver's using part of an older frame or even part of other figures is in evidence: I have seen engravings where the coat of arms is not George's, where his head has been put on to a body that ill fits it, and even one where he wears incongruous beribboned boots of extreme elegance only to find the self-same boots on the slim legs of an early Stuart monarch. Few of the engravings tell us much about George as a person; but at times we see, presumably for propaganda purposes, the firmness and determination in political affairs which we know from other evidence that he possessed.

Since he wears a wig (usually dark brown) in all the portraits which have survived, we are indebted to Sophia's information about the colour of his hair. It was fair in infancy and early childhood but turned Palatinate dark before 1676. The illegitimate son he then fathered was thought to be so like him, including 'black hair', that there could be no doubt of paternity. George's skin, sunburnt and windswept from campaigns, had by then become so dark that, in his mother's words, he 'could have passed for a Spaniard',[4] and this weatherbeaten skin colour remained – if somewhat toned down – because of his liking for fresh air and exercise.

The literary descriptions of people who observed him, but did not know him well, in 1714 and the years immediately after that date reinforced the impression of woodenness in public, a mask which betrayed lady Mary Wortley Montagu into thinking him a blockhead also in intelligence. Her assessment has largely been accepted by British historians without independent evidence; the easily accessible printed memoirs and letters of this period, while invaluable for giving us the feel of the past, are full of traps for the unwary and more important for the development of myths where third persons are concerned than for historical insight.[5] But even lady Mary, who did not know George well, gives instances of his ready wit; and lady Cowper – with more opportunities for close observation – conveys the flavour of his verbal pleasantries at court, tinged, if they were not mere compliments, by the ironic turn of phrase so reminiscent of his mother. George, like most men and many women of the age, appreciated a bawdy joke and the *double entendre*. There are examples of the first in his correspondence with the Hanoverian statesman von Ilten as early as the 1680s. His light touch in the latter category is epitomized in his remark (repeated by Schulenburg) to a certain courtier who in 1717 presented his wife to the king while his conversation ran exclusively on the praise of Irish horses.

It was to the effect that if the courtier 'connoissoit aussi bien en cheveaux qu'en femmes il ne pourroit manquer d'etre bien monté.'[6]

What those outside the inner circle at court saw, however, was the dutiful mask without much animation. George was not a glamorous figure. His accession had been received with jubilation in some quarters, especially by the dissenters who were hopeful that he would end the persecution they had suffered under the last ministry of queen Anne. It is said that when dissenting ministers presented themselves in their sober black to George on his arrival he – or one of his Hanoverian entourage – asked why they were in mourning. They answered that the object of burial was the Schism Act which would not now be enforced and that they rejoiced that it was George who came to bury it.[7] The very impact of majesty, the awe which the mythology surrounding the sovereign imposed even in the age of the Early Enlightenment,[8] explains the cheers which greeted George on his arrival in London in 1714. In reality the people at large reserved their judgment. Times had changed since the Restoration period when Charles II entertained on a scale large enough to embrace all the educated and socially privileged orders of society, while the mob was enthralled by ceremonial and by court scandal. George visited British magnates more or less as a private individual, and he attended public performances of theatres, operas and concerts rather than making the court a focus of such entertainments. His greatest claim to European fame, his military career, was not one that appealed to a war-weary country; and George – intent on accepting the peacemakings of 1713–14, if only to give him a free hand in the Great Northern War – was not the man to reminisce. Some of the pamphlets written to glorify the Hanoverian succession did refer to George's services in the wars against the Turks and Louis XIV,[9] but Jacobite pamphlets easily managed to take the shine off his achievements by denigrating them and fathering Mercy's defeat at Rumersheim on him: the 'Sultan' (a transparent synonym for George) had met with a reverse which impaired his *gloire* forever.[10] While it remained true that George had contributed to the planning of the 1704 campaign and that the behaviour of his Hanoverian contingent at Blenheim had evoked Marlborough's praise, the British were in general too insular to wish to assess the share of foreign troops – Dutch, German, Danes – in glories they reckoned specifically their own even though their British national regiments had formed but a minor part of the whole. George's share, and that of the Hanoverians, thus made no proper impact, especially as the elector's services had never been on the spectacular scale of Marlborough's and Eugène's.

THE JACOBITE 'FIFTEEN'

Conversely, as soon as George's first ministry began to use the over-whelming victory it had won in the elections of March 1715 to punish Tories at the national and local level, the image of young James Edward Stuart was shown to possess magnetic qualities. He was untried and therefore unspotted. He was good-looking and reputedly brave (he had fought with the French after the failure of the invasion attempt of 1708). The glamour of tradition was his, from the convivial toast 'To the [English-born] King across the waters' to the strong allegiance which many Scots felt for him as the lawful king of Scotland. With the Whigs weeding out Tory justices of the peace, mayors and members of corporations, putting their own men into even minor posts, and advertising their intention to be revenged by the impeachment processes which they began against Oxford, Bolingbroke, Ormonde and Strafford, the image of an alternative king began to take substance. Contacts were made with Saint-Germain, where James's mother still resided, and with Lorraine where James himself lived, and raised hopes of success for invasion plans which had been formulated but which had not till then seemed feasible. James's reliance on open support from Louis XIV had collapsed during 1714 and early 1715. That monarch, anxious to be seen to keep the treaty of Utrecht, had yet expressed his willingness to give underhand help if James could obtain an important ally. Charles XII of Sweden, besieged in Stralsund after his dramatic return from Turkey in October 1714, was approached by both Louis and the Jacobites: if James could gain the Protestant sister of Charles XII as a bride – so reckoned the Jacobites – his chances of general acceptance in Britain would be increased; if Charles XII would use his Swedish army (not negligible even if luck seemed to have deserted him since 1709) to take revenge on George I at war with Sweden in his capacity as elector of Hanover – so calculated Louis – then James would get the military support by trained troops which he needed to wrest George's kingdom from him.[11]

Both hypotheses proved unfounded. Charles had no intention of making George I, in his capacity as king of Great Britain, a bel-ligerent in the Great Northern War and buttressed his refusal to help 'James III' by the promise he had given the late queen Anne in 1712 never to give sustenance to the Jacobites; as for the marriage, it was out of the question that a Lutheran Swedish princess, the heir to the Swedish crown as long as Charles had no heirs of his own body, should marry a Catholic. Louis XIV drew the right conclusions from these various interchanges and in his turn forbade James Fitzjames, duke of Berwick (James III's half-brother on the wrong side of the blanket and a marshal of France), to put his military skill at the disposal of the Jacobites. The most Louis would do was to recommend his grandson, Philip V of Spain, to give or lend James money from the treasure expected from Spanish America, and to connive himself at James's collecting some hired ships and arms which his followers had been able to buy in French ports.[12] Such limited activity suited French policy. There was as yet no certainty whether George I and the Whigs wished to overturn the Utrecht settlement; at a time of a rumoured *grande liaison* between the British, the Dutch and the Emperor, it would be in Louis' interest to foment unrest in Britain.

George's British ministers had not been aware of inviting a Jacobite invasion. Their concern had been with muzzling their important opponents in parliament and with keeping promises made to local supporters during the elections. They were pleased rather than otherwise at Bolingbroke's flight in April 1715: it could be interpreted as proof of his guilt and would smear others by implication. Yet it was their impeachment proceedings which fanned the flames of unrest and brought many who would not have contemplated open rebellion to adopt that very course: the Whigs showed that they meant to carry into action their threat to punish men who had by their 'secret practices' encouraged the Pretender in the late queen's reign. Others, while not sympathizing with the rebels, resented Whig implacability and doubted whether treason or even high crimes and misdemeanours could be proved.[13] The weapons of revenge, forged mainly by Robert Walpole smarting under the memory of his own imprisonment in the Tower,[14] seemed to be turning against George I's ministry.

Bolingbroke's acceptance of the post as James III's secretary of state rebounded on the Whigs in the sense that it brought James the services of a highly intelligent and gifted man, far better informed on the English situation than the Jacobite exiles of longer standing, and one, moreover, with a high reputation in England. From mid-July, when certain news of the Pretender's invasion plans was received from lord Stair (the British ambassador in Paris who had a good intelligence network), Bolingbroke appeared to be more of a liability abroad than at home, and preparations to repel the coming attack were begun in earnest.[15]

Ormonde's flight in August 1715 was due to a loss of nerve and proved an unmixed blessing for the Whigs. Since March he had committed himself to support the Pretender's cause and had planned risings in the south and west of England and in Wales, all areas where he had great influence. His precipitate departure (under fear of arrest) robbed the English Jacobites of a leader and made James III too dependent on a Scottish rising. The slowness of communications with Scotland added to the difficulties of the conspirators. John, earl of Mar, the leader of the Scottish Jacobites, found himself unable to comply with orders from Ormonde in France to postpone his revolt so that it could be synchronized with an October attempt of Ormonde's to bring Devon into rebellion while James landed elsewhere on the southern shores of England: on 6/17 September Mar raised the Jacobite standard in Scotland. Nor was Ormonde successful in persuading James to issue the kind of popular appeal which Ormonde – fresh from Britain – was sure would bring the masses out and rouse them from their 'desponding submission to Hanover'; his, like Bolingbroke's, advice was either ignored or accepted too late. Ormonde's own efforts to rouse Devon (the first in October, the second in December) brought no response. When James, having given up the idea of invading England, joined Mar in Scotland in December the chances of success were so minimal that he set sail for France again in February 1716 to save his supporters from annihilation.

The danger of the Jacobite rebellion was, however, greater than this brief summary may indicate.[16] That Ormonde remained loyal to James for the rest of his life and that Oxford, from the Tower and when freed, favoured the Jacobites and worked for them is not surprising; but that Marlborough and Shrewsbury in the crisis of 1715–16 reinsured by helping the Pretender with money is an indication of the severity of the crisis.[17]

So is George I's decision to apply, after Ormonde's flight, to the States General for the 6,000 troops available under the treaty of Barrier and Succession. He did so reluctantly since, quite apart from the expense involved, it permitted Dutch statesmen to exert unwelcome pressure on negotiations in progress. Ever since George's accession a 'barrier treaty'* between the Maritime Powers and Charles VI had been sought so that the Anglo-Dutch condominium of the Southern Netherlands could be terminated and the emperor permitted to take possession of the now Austrian Netherlands on conditions which satisfied all parties. George, mindful of his need for Imperial support for his northern policy, had hitherto put a brake on Dutch demands. Now he was forced to put more of his weight on the Republic's side than intended, first, to obtain Dutch consent to bring the British regiments occupying Ostend and Nieuwport in

* That is, a treaty which allowed the Southern Netherlands to be used as a barrier against France by Dutch garrisons, at Austrian expense, in strategic fortresses.

the condominium area back to England and, then, to hurry the despatch of the 6,000 Dutch troops. He offered payment for these troops (though it could be argued that the Republic ought to bear the cost of them) from their day of embarkation till the day they set foot once more on Dutch soil, a generous offer beyond the terms of the 1713 treaty – in sharp contrast to the haggling which he him-self had suffered from the Maritime Powers in 1701–02 over pay for his electoral troops. Further expenditure was incurred by the purchase of 10,000 muskets and bayonets from the arsenal of the province of Holland. The Dutch were willing enough to supply the 6,000 troops; the epithet of 'Saviour' of Britain was balm after the London vilification of the Republic during queen Anne's last ministry.[18] But they took care not to let the troops sail till 16 Novem-ber, the day after the barrier treaty had been signed; and though this treaty fell far short of their hopes, its terms were much better than those they would have had to accept but for George's need of their regiments to suppress the Jacobite rebellion.[19] Before the end of the month the Dutch soldiers were on the march north. The very presence of so large a body of well-trained troops helped to quell the risings, though the Dutch were not involved in any major battle.

George and his ministers had in the meantime been active at home. A suspension of the *Habeas Corpus* act was decreed for a period of six months; known Jacobites were arrested and Roman Catholics suspected of disloyalty had their arms and horses impounded; the standing army was doubled and garrisons put into towns judged to be Jacobite in sympathy (Oxford and Bath were two of these); a strong squadron under admiral Byng was sent to control the Channel and intercept the Pretender; and Argyll – a member of the prince of Wales' household as a reward for his pro-Hanoverian stance before 1714 – was sent to Scotland with a small force to cope with Mar until the arrival of the Dutch. The Jacobite thrust expected in the south was inhibited by the government's measures (as shown by Ormonde's disappointments in October and December); but in the north-east of England a sizable number rallied round Thomas Forster, a county member of the House of Commons, and the Jacobite lords Derwentwater and Widdrington. Though they failed to take Newcastle by surprise, they were joined by lowlanders under the Scottish lords Kenmuir, Nithsdale, Carnwath and Wintoun and a detachment of highlanders sent by Mar. Failing to make any impact in the lowlands, this force – counting nearly 5,000 – marched to the north-west in the hope of capturing Cumberland, Westmor-land and Lancashire for James III and, if possible, to secure the port of Liverpool and link up with the Welsh Jacobites. On 13

November it was attacked at Preston in Lancashire and defeated by a much smaller but more disciplined army under two experienced generals (Wills and Carpenter) sent north by Stanhope: 1,600 rebel privates were taken prisoner as were seven English and Scottish lords; the rest dispersed.

On that very day Mar, whose plans to take Edinburgh had miscarried, fought the battle of Sheriffmuir with some 10,000 men against Argyll and his 3,300 regular troops. The outcome was indecisive, but could be reckoned a government victory since Mar withdrew to Perth and there, inactive, awaited the arrival of James III. His original force had grown from 1,300 to 10,000 and he had hopes – if James III arrived with arms and money – of eventual success. But James came too late and with too little cash and too few weapons, since by that time (22 December) Argyll had been reinforced by the 6,000 Dutch troops. Argyll, influenced by sympathy for his countrymen and by his conviction that if left alone they would 'melt away', did not take the offensive. This created some suspicion of him in the British ministry and Cadogan, who had returned to England from the continent after signing the barrier treaty of 15 November 1715, was only too eager to show his paces. In February Stanhope sent him north to replace Argyll as commander-in-chief. On his arrival Cadogan found that the Pretender, Mar, and his brother James Keith, had left Scotland for France. All that was left was for him to hunt down remnants of Mar's forces, who (as Argyll had prophesied) were rapidly making their way home, either to live and fight another day or to forget all about the Fifteen. Relieved, George cancelled his secret request to the Dutch pensionary to keep another 3,000 troops in readiness if reinforcements were needed.[20]

James III had not made a favourable impression on the Scots. His advertised coronation – set for 23 January in the palace of Scone – had not taken place. He had failed to animate his followers: 'if he was disappointed in us, we were tenfold more so in him'. George and his ministry proved magnanimous in victory. For this George must take most of the credit. He proved a moderating influence on those, notably Robert Walpole, who wished to take revenge. Cadogan, for his part, permitted many Scottish prisoners to escape from jail; and some who had been taken at Preston, including Forster, managed to flee from English imprisonment. Eventually, of the rank and file from Preston and the Scottish skirmishes, 700 were brought to trial and sentenced to be indentured as servants on West Indian plantations. The seven lords captured at Preston were sentenced to death, but only two, Kenmuir and Derwentwater (the only English noblemen of their number), were executed, two – Nithsdale and Wintoun – escaped and Carnwath, Nairne and Widdrington were released under the Act of Grace passed in 1717. Given the standards of the time, such clemency* has been pronounced 'unprecedented and certainly wise and politic'.[21] Walpole had worked hard to ensure that all seven should go to the block and carried the House of Commons, though with a small majority (seven only); the House of Lords, from class solidarity and unease that seven should suffer the death sentence when so many had been guilty of rebellion, urged leniency and petitioned the king 'to show mercy [to] such as he judged might deserve it'. This enabled George to defy the Whig interpretation of that clause of the Act of Settlement which laid down 'That no pardon under the Great Seal of England be pleadable to an impeachment by the Commons of England': he upheld the death sentence for three (one of whom was Nithsdale) and respited the rest.

The price he had to pay to the Whigs was the dismissal of Nottingham as lord privy seal and loss of places for his relatives. Shrewsbury had already resigned.[22] The sacrifice of those who, like Nottingham and Shrewsbury, had been a thorn in the flesh of the Whigs ever since the new king's accession limited George's freedom of action; but it was a necessary concession if he wished to keep the confidence of those of his ministers who had been most active in defeating the rebellion.

In London, where Jacobite agitation had started as soon as Oxford had been committed to the Tower, George also urged leniency. On 23 April 1715, the anniversary of queen Anne's coronation – which was also St George's day – crowds marched the streets shouting 'God bless the queen' and 'High Church'. By 28 May, George's birthday, the cry of 'High Church and Ormonde' had become the slogan of the Jacobites who cut the bellropes of at least one church to prevent the customary tribute of ringing, and spent the evening breaking windows illuminated in the king's honour. These and similar incidents George wished to ignore, explaining to his somewhat agitated Hanoverian entourage that punishment would only serve to aggravate popular unrest.[23] Mar's raising of the standard for James III had, however, repercussions in London, where – from November 1715 onwards – sporadic gang-fights between 'Jacks' and 'loyalists' took place, particularly on anniversaries into which a political connotation could be read: the birthday of George, prince of Wales, for 'Jack' attacks; the accession anniversaries of Charles II, James II and queen Anne for 'Jack' celebrations which developed into raids on inns and ale-houses regarded as loyalist strongholds.

* Note also George's decision that income from the forfeited Jacobite estates, up to a sum of £20,000, be allocated to provide schools in the Highlands; the rest to be used to reduce the public debt of Britain (*Treasury Books*, vol. XXX, I).

These were allowed to run their course for a time, even where 500 'Jacks' were involved; but eventually law-abiding citizens tired of the looting and burning and general terrorizing which became a feature of these occasions and demanded action by the authorities. After an attack on Read's Mug-house off Fleet Street in July 1716, five 'Jacks' were arrested, sentenced to death and hanged. The Jacobite agitation in London then came to an abrupt stop, but it should be noted that this was long after the rebellion in the north had been defeated.[24] The consequences of the Fifteen were many and important. It strengthened, as we have seen, the hold of the Whigs in the ministry. It also turned George I's thoughts towards the will he composed in February 1716, which had as one of its purposes to rob the Jacobite Stuarts of the claim that the Hanoverian succession would remain forever 'foreign' and unacceptable because of the dynastic union with the electorate. If this dynastic union would be known to have a terminus as soon as George died and his will was published (and even earlier if he obtained the consent of the emperor and of the British parliament), James Edward Stuart and his descendants* would be less likely to foment civil wars which George judged 'ruinous' for the country.[25] More immediately, the restraint shown first by Louis XIV and then by the regent of France (for the child-king Louis XV), Philippe d'Orléans, son of George's cousin Liselotte von der Pfalz, impressed George and influenced his foreign policy. Like his British ministers, George resented the way in which the French were trying to circumvent the Utrecht clause which bade them destroy the harbour of Dunkirk by building canals and fortifying Mardyk close by. Whatever their sophisticated arguments to explain away what they were doing, he insisted, they were in reality replacing a round port with an oblong one.[26] But he was impressed by the fact that the regent, who had promised before Louis XIV's death that he would not give succour to the Pretender, had kept his word when in a position of power. If George now spurned his proferred hand, might not the regent be tempted to embrace James III's cause in the future? The French denial of support for the Pretender in 1715–16 thus made it possible, and even imperative, for George to show willingness to negotiate on the Mardyk issue and others – such as the removal of James Edward Stuart from France.†

EUROPEAN ISSUES 1716–17

Confidence in French good will, and the need for negotiations with France, had been urged on George by his Dutch allies ever since the death of Louis XIV. The Republic had indeed been courted by

---

* James married in 1719 and his son Charles (the young Pretender) was born in 1720.
† The duke of Lorraine having refused him refuge on his return from Scotland, James stayed at various places in France while negotiating for asylum elsewhere.

Louis XIV from the moment the States General had signed their peace with France in 1713, but Dutch statesmen and especially the *raadpensionaris* Heinsius had thought it best to take no decisive step until George I's accession and politic to avoid putting pressure on him until the barrier treaty between the Maritime Powers and the emperor had been signed. Ideally the Dutch would have liked to follow up a French suggestion for a guarantee of the neutrality of the Southern Netherlands to be signed by France, the Maritime Powers and the emperor; but finding that Charles VI would never agree to this they concentrated on what came to be known as the *simul-et-semel* policy, which implied that the Maritime Powers and France should sign a treaty of mutual guarantee of rights and possessions at the same time that the Maritime Powers signed a similar treaty with the emperor. Dutch efforts, motivated by the need of the Republic to avoid involvement in European warfare, thus concentrated on having the treaties of Utrecht and Rastadt confirmed within the context of a post-Anne and post-Louis XIV world. The death of a sovereign traditionally demanded a renewal of treaties for guarantees to remain valid. If the *simul-et-semel* policy succeeded, the French regent would be made to guarantee the Protestant Succession and Charles VI would be forced to repeat his promise not to disturb the *status quo* in Italy.

Dutch labours bore some fruit in bringing George and the regent closer together between the end of March and the beginning of May 1716 when a Dutch ambassador on a special mission, Arent baron van Wassenaer, sieur de Duyvenvoorde, mediated in London – by carrying messages from one side to the other – between the French envoy Iberville and the British ministers, principally Townshend. By pressing Townshend to discuss the issue with George I, Duyvenvoorde elicited British terms for an alliance between the Maritime Powers and France: the alliance must be defensive, guaranteeing the French and the Protestant successions alike and the possessions of all three contracting parties according to the treaties of Utrecht; the Pretender must move 'beyond the Alps'; French and British commissioners must be appointed to supervise the destruction of the Mardyk canals and fortifications lest the new port should replace the now unfortified Dunkirk as a possible haven for naval and privateering action against Britain. That the Dutch eagerly continued their negotiations with the regent on the basis of these demands, while paying too little attention to the British ministers' warning that George I wanted the alliance with the emperor signed before that with France, concerns us less here than an argument against the French alliance which Townshend put to Duyvenvoorde at an early stage of their conversations. A large standing army, the secretary postulated, would be necessary for years to checkmate the Pretender and his followers. If George concluded with France, the opposition in parliament could successfully argue that this army was no longer necessary: thus the alliance with the regent would turn out to be disadvantageous for the British government.[27]

Here we have a clue to one of the several misunderstandings which accumulated between Townshend and Walpole on the one hand and George, supported by Stanhope and Sunderland, on the other, during the king's absence from Britain from late July 1716 to mid-January 1717. The two ministers who stayed at home were suspected of dragging their feet in the matter of the French alliance which – once the treaty with the emperor had been signed on 5 June – became, for a variety of reasons, urgent for George as king and elector. Stanhope, travelling with the king and handling the details of the negotiations with the regent's representative, the abbé Dubois, both at The Hague and in Hanover, moved at the same pace as George. Townshend and Walpole lagged behind and every delay, accidental or not, in procuring the necessary full powers in correct form for the Anglo-French treaty (signed by Stanhope and Dubois on 9 October in Hanover, but not formally at The Hague by Dubois and Cadogan till 28 November), was interpreted by George as wilful opposition to himself and excessive deference either to the Townshend-Walpole concept of parliamentary management or to the Dutch Republic, or both. George, impatient to complete his alliance system, was determined to deny the Dutch any real influence on his negotiations. It was not the time-consuming task of getting resolutions passed by the various provinces of the Republic which worried him. Experience had taught that when Dutch statesmen wished to act speedily (as in the case of the troops provided for Britain to fight the 'Fifteen') they found ways and means to do so. But they had clearly shown that their objective – the maintenance of the *status quo* of the peace settlements of 1713–14 – was one which would hamper George's freedom of action in achieving formulations desirable for his policies as elector. Townshend, Robert Walpole and his brother Horatio (Townshend's under-secretary) were anxious to keep as much in step with the Dutch Republic as possible. Their overriding motive was to ensure that the Republic shared Britain's treaty commitments lest the Dutch should benefit from trading as a neutral in any war in which Britain became involved. But they also valued Anglo-Dutch friendship as part of the 'Old System', that of the Grand Alliances of the wars against Louis XIV after 1688 when the Maritime Powers and the emperor had worked in close cooperation.

The restoration of the Old System, and especially the healing of that breach with the emperor which had occurred in 1712 when Leibniz in Vienna had turned out propaganda pamphlets against the Tory ministry on Charles VI's behalf (as virulent as Swift's on the conduct of the Dutch and Britain's other allies),[28] had been a joint objective of George, his British and his Hanoverian ministers throughout the first half of 1716. The first step was easy. An Anglo-Dutch treaty was signed in London on 6/17 February 1716. In form it was a simple renewal of alliances, which re-guaranteed the Protestant Succession and the territorial terms of the Utrecht settlement. The second step planned by the British ministers, that of inducing the emperor to accede to this alliance, proved impossible. It suited neither Charles VI's pride nor his ambitions in Italy where he resented having been robbed, as he put it, of Sicily and made to accept Sardinia in its place. More importantly, it did not suit George and his Hanoverian ministers, who were keen to leave the emperor some loophole for achieving his Italian objectives provided he looked kindly on Hanoverian goals of expansion in the Empire. A formal Imperial investiture for Hanover of the newly occupied Swedish provinces of Bremen and Verden was the ultimate aim, but even approval of the elector's participation in the Great Northern War would be welcome as a first earnest of the investiture to come.

Here we can discern another knot in the tangle which led to the crisis of 1716–17 between the king and the Townshend-Walpole group. Townshend was as anxious as the Dutch to avoid entanglements in Italy and the draft project which he and the other British ministers in January 1716 presented to count Otto Christoph von Volkra, Charles VI's special ambassador to London, left out the ominous *Prétensions et Titres* for which the emperor had desired a guarantee. The Republic's persistence in its *simul-et-semel* policy, however, gave the king and the Hanoverians a chance to take control. Both sets of ministers agreed that they could not wait for the Dutch and that a separate Anglo-Imperial alliance must be concluded before George left on his proposed summer visit to Hanover. The king pushed matters himself. On 30 May he ordered Townshend to approach Volkra; by 2 June agreement had been reached and on 5 June the treaty was signed on terms which were more favourable to Charles VI than to George I. It is significant that, though the treaty was one entered into by George solely in his capacity as king of Great Britain, Bernstorff and Bothmer, as well as Townshend, Stanhope and Marlborough had formed the team which negotiated with Volkra and Hoffmann; and also that the British ministers had reluctantly included in clause 2 a guarantee of

the emperor's *Honor, Dignitas et Jura* as well as of his actual possessions. From the Hanoverian point of view this left scope for future
support of Charles VI's Italian ambitions if he in return would
further George's Hanoverian objectives. Townshend chose to look
upon the treaty as foolproof against entanglements in Italy since the
guarantee of the emperor's 'honour, dignities and rights' had been
embedded in the very clause which emphasized the defensive
character of the agreement. His interpretation, freely voiced, could
be seen to work against George's intentions as elector.[29] He thus
became a less valuable secretary than Stanhope, who proved more
dynamic, not hidebound, in his attitude to his master's foreign
policy problems. As early as September 1716 Stanhope discussed
with George and his Hanoverian ministers ways and means whereby
a settlement of the Italian problems pleasing to the emperor could
be achieved without provoking a European war: the main lines of
what became known as the peace plan for the south were now
sketched in. But the chief reason for the undermining of Townshend
and Walpole's position was the rapid, and unexpected, developments in Baltic affairs during the summer and autumn of 1716. The
speed of changing events was such that they caught the British
ministers at home, beset with their own problems, unawares and
increasingly incapable of following the king's reaction to these
events. And George, whose Hanoverian policies had prospered
greatly in the 1715 campaign, thanks to the 'British navy' trump
card he held, was unprepared for the dilemmas of the 1716 campaign
and became – like his German ministers – distinctly rattled.

Before his accession to the English throne, George had taken secret
but decisive steps which sooner or later would bring him into
conflict with Sweden. Charles XII's defeat at Poltava in the summer
of 1709 and his subsequent, initially unintentional, stay in Turkey
until the autumn of 1714, meant that Sweden's German provinces
would be parcelled out. Though Hanover had been a firm ally of
Sweden since the 1680s, there was – as we have seen – an older
tradition of expansion at the expense of Sweden. It would have been
against the most fundamental principle of Brunswick policy to let
Denmark collect the duchies of Bremen and Verden as its share of
the Swedish spoils: Danish control of the Elbe duchies would put a
stranglehold on the electorate. For as long as possible George played
a waiting game, balancing between the pro-Swedish party led by
Görtz and the expansionist party, led by Bernstorff. He offered the
Swedish council, in need of money to fit out the ships and equip the
troops which Charles XII demanded, a sizable loan if he were
permitted to occupy Bremen and Verden for a period of twenty-five

years. The council was tempted but from Turkey Charles XII vetoed the plan: twenty-five years carried a danger of permanent cession. From this time onwards the anti-Swedish party in Hanover gained the upper hand and George might well have taken earlier positive action if the major part of his forces had not been committed to the War of the Spanish Succession. All he could do in 1712 when Frederik IV of Denmark occupied the duchy of Bremen was to move Hanoverian troops into the smaller duchy of Verden under an amicable agreement with the Swedish commander on the spot by which the elector signed a written promise to withdraw his forces as soon as the Danes evacuated Bremen. In 1713, during the congress of Brunswick called by the emperor in an attempt to mediate between Charles XII and his enemies, George (without the knowledge of the pro-Swedish party in Hanover) formulated his terms for entry into the anti-Swedish coalition: the occupation of Bremen and Verden by his troops, and guarantees that both duchies should become Hanoverian possessions at the peacemakings, before his own declaration of war against Sweden. George could hardly have expected compliance with his high demands; at this stage it was sufficient to state his price.[30]

The elector's promotion to king of Great Britain – celebrated with a fine medal showing the feet of the Saxon horse firmly planted in Hanover and its forelegs reaching to southern England – shifted the balance in George's favour. The Northern allies* badly wanted British naval help, directly or indirectly. George's son-in-law, Friedrich Wilhelm I of Prussia, who had committed himself in June 1714 to Sweden's enemies by a treaty with tsar Peter, acted as a willing go-between. Already in November 1714 he and George agreed to collaborate in a share-out of Sweden's provinces in the Empire which would suit them and serve the Imperial 'German mission' which urged the expulsion from Germany of the victors of 1648: France in the south-west and Sweden in the north. Between April and October 1715 a series of separate treaties, Prusso-Hanoverian, Dano-Hanoverian, Prusso-Danish and Russo-Hanoverian, was made. The vital one for George was that of 2 May between himself as elector and Frederik IV whereby he agreed that Denmark should be permitted to absorb the duke of Holstein-Gottorp's lands in Sleswig in return for (a) Bremen being handed over to Hanover on payment of 300,000 Taler and (b) a guarantee for Hanover's possession of Bremen and Verden *in perpetuum*. His own declaration of war against Sweden was to follow within a fortnight of his troops being permitted into Bremen. George further bound himself to contribute Hanoverian troops to the siege of Wismar, and

---

* Frederik IV of Denmark–Norway, Augustus of Saxony–Poland and tsar Peter of Russia.

to pay Denmark stipulated subsidies (fixed at 50,000 Taler a quarter) for one year from May 1716 if the war against Sweden had not then come to an end. The other treaties ensured that Denmark's share of Sweden's German possessions was shifted east to Pomerania, with Stralsund and Rügen, up to the river Peene; that Prussia's part would be Pomerania beyond the Peene river; that tsar Peter would be permitted to keep his conquests of the Swedish East Baltic provinces (though some allies made specific guarantees of Karelia, Ingria, Estonia and Livonia while others, among them George, omitted a guarantee for Livonia). All the contracting parties guaranteed Bremen and Verden to Hanover.[31]

The very foundation of the arrangements made with George as elector was not formally embodied in any of the above treaties, but there is ample proof in the diplomatic documents of the period that George pledged his 'royal word' that the British navy should assist the conquest of Pomerania during the 1715 season. It was also understood that George would continue to contrive British naval help every year until Sweden was forced to comply with the terms of the treaties he had signed as elector. There has been much discussion about whether George kept his pledge. Some historians have claimed that he trampled roughshod over the British constitution to gain objectives that were solely Hanoverian; others that the British navy undertook its Baltic cruises to serve only British aims and was never used for electoral purposes, George being content to trick his allies with glib promises.[32] In recent years all the relevant archives have been studied by Scandinavian, German, Russian, American and British scholars and the sum of their researches shows that George's behaviour was neither as black nor as white as in the respective simplistic views.[33] There was a large area of overlapping British-Hanoverian interests. The use of convoys to escort British merchantmen to the Russian-held ports of the East Baltic was essential in view of Britain's need for naval stores and after Charles XII's privateering ordinance of February 1715. Nor were the squadrons larger – as has sometimes been suggested – than were needed for convoying purposes.[34] Furthermore, most of George's British ministers held that British men-of-war in the Baltic would deter Sweden from making common cause with the Pretender. We now know that Charles XII never committed himself to give James Edward Stuart either military or naval support, but he was not above letting George believe that he might do so: a secondary objective of his invasions of Norway (in 1716 and 1718), though directed against Frederik IV of Denmark-Norway, was to tie down British warships to the defence of Scotland so that fewer might be sent to the Baltic.[35] It should also

be taken into account that George, when he came to make his peace
with Sweden as elector, took care to obtain commercial advantages
for his British subjects.

On the other hand, it is clear that George used the British navy to
further specific Hanoverian purposes and that his British ministers
connived at his cooperation with his electoral allies. One of their
main concerns was that the Dutch – who also sent men-of-war to
protect their Baltic convoys – should do so in concert with the British
or at least be thought to do so, both as a screen against criticism by
parliament and to ensure that the Dutch did not steal a commercial
march on the British. To achieve this goal (never perfectly accomplished between 1715 and 1719) British ministers, not excluding
Townshend in 1715 and 1716, prevaricated, indulged in double talk
and, on occasions, lied. They also gave promises which they and
George later broke. In 1718, for instance, Stanhope promised in
return for the Dutch commander's convoying the merchant ships of
both nations to the East Baltic – thus leaving admiral Norris free to
support the Danes with all his men-of-war – that the Republic
would share all trade advantages which George might procure for
Britain at the final peacemakings with Sweden. When the time came
the Dutch were left out in the cold, king and minister justifying
themselves by Dutch 'selfishness' and 'unreasonableness' in past and
present affairs in the Baltic as elsewhere in Europe.[36]

If the British ministers of George I experienced most difficulties
in bringing the Dutch into line, George himself had great trouble in
making his electoral allies grasp his delicate position. The most
critical year for George was 1715, when Charles XII was besieged
in Stralsund by Danes, Prussians and Saxons and when the services
of the British fleet were vital to prevent, in cooperation with the
Danish fleet, Pomerania being reinforced and supplied from Sweden.

We promise the King of Prussia, [George wrote in that year] that the
said squadron [*i.e.*, the British ships sent to the Baltic] shall in every way
second operations in Pomerania against Sweden, and hope his Prussian
Majesty will believe Our word, that there will be no want in the fulfilling
of this promise. But we could not give a written engagement, since the
providing of the squadron pertains to us as King, and if We gave a
written engagement we could not use our German Ministers, but We
should have to give it by the hands of Our English ministers. [37]

This quotation, though well known, gives a clue to the solution
adopted and also explains why historians who consult only British
sources tend to assume that exclusively British interests were served.
British commanders were given two sets of orders: one written which
could bear scrutiny, one verbal which either amplified the sense in

which such seemingly innocuous words and phrases as 'reprisals'
and 'chase the Swedes back to their ports that the British merchantmen may not be attacked' could be interpreted to fulfil the king's
'other purposes'; or they were referred to further instructions which
would follow from the king. These were usually given by George's
Hanoverian diplomats in Copenhagen by word of mouth, or transmitted in writing by one of George's Hanoverian ministers or via a
British minister or diplomat prepared to work fully with George as
elector.

Space does not permit (and I have in any case dealt with this
elsewhere)* a detailed reconstruction of the ways in which in 1715
first the whole squadron under admiral Norris – without neglecting
the interests of the merchantmen he convoyed – and then the eight
men-of-war which he was ordered to detach on his own departure
to join the Danish fleet under a 'discreet officer, not of flag-rank',
contributed to the success of the anti-Swedish coalition. The role of
the eight ships under captain Hopson during late September and
October was crucial for the conquest of Rügen. Suffice it to say that
Frederik IV, who was in no mood to relinquish his hold on Bremen
unless the British naval help had been substantial, handed over that
duchy to Hanover on 4/15 October. George, as elector, declared
war on Sweden on that very day, and on 2 November the first
Hanoverian contingent joined the Danes and the Prussians in their
siege of Wismar.

The war, however, would have to be continued. George and his
Hanoverian ministers had hoped that impetuous action by Charles
XII would have led to a naval battle in which the British could
participate as defenders of their convoy; but the Swedish king,
having no wish to add to his enemies, had given orders that this was
to be avoided. Moreover, the Swedish fleet which came too late to
relieve Stralsund continued to Wismar where it landed men, food
and ammunition, and Charles XII himself escaped from Stralsund
in December to take command of the peninsular Swedish war effort
in person. For the 1716 campaign the northern allies therefore
planned an invasion of Scania, meant to force Charles XII to sue
for peace on their terms. Frederik IV and tsar Peter were willing to
provide the necessary cavalry and infantry, some transports were
hired from Prussia, and George promised to let the British navy act
in such a way that the naval superiority necessary for success should
be achieved.[38]

Townshend, who had given George no reason for complaint by
his conduct during the 1715 campaign, did not obstruct the early
stages of that of 1716. The fact that Charles XII had invaded

* See my *Charles XII of Sweden* (1968), pp. 403–06.

Norway in February 1716 and maintained himself there till late summer caused speculation whether he might send help to James Edward Stuart in Scotland, either from Gothenburg or from west Norway if he penetrated that far. Townshend, embarrassed by his contretemps with the Dutch in 1715, left the negotiations with Danish and Russian missions sent to London in the spring of 1716 to George's Hanoverian ministers; but he connived at Norris's leaving before the end of May, more than a month before the Dutch squadron, and supported the invasion of Scania once it became clear Charles XII would not capitulate. His real concern was, however, with the re-establishment of peace and with the balance of power; he wished that the Anglo-Dutch squadrons could be used to enforce a settlement that did not leave Russia too powerful.[39] The tsar held all Sweden's east Baltic provinces with Narva, Reval and Riga – ports important to British trade. He had acted highhandedly towards Danzig, a free city whose independence ranked high among British priorities. He controlled Courland more or less directly* and the Polish-Lithuanian Commonwealth to the extent that Augustus of Saxony-Poland had been reduced to a powerless puppet. In April 1716 he had married his niece, Katarine Ivanovna, to duke Karl Leopold of Mecklenburg-Schwerin and put Russian troops at the duke's disposal in his long-standing struggle with the Mecklenburg nobility.[40]

It was therefore somewhat ironic that George's distrust of Townshend was caused by the secretary's refusal to share the violent anti-Russian feeling aroused in the king and his Hanoverian ministers at the tsar's abandonment on 19 September of the Scania plan and his proposal (in official expectation that the project might be revived for the 1717 season) that his army should winter in the duchy of Mecklenburg. This was too close to Hanover for comfort. Much has been made of the fact that Bernstorff, and other noblemen in electoral service, possessed estates in Mecklenburg which had suffered from the billeting of Russian soldiers while the Scania invasion forces gathered. Yet tsar Peter had specifically promised to exempt these estates from the 1716–17 winter quartering. Undoubtedly the military support which Russia was giving duke Karl Leopold of Mecklenburg created conflict, but greater issues were at stake. The tsar wished to make Mecklenburg a client state and planned to by-pass the Sound by cutting a canal from the Baltic to the North Sea which would permit direct Russian trade with the west of Europe. Such plans cut across Hanoverian hopes of developing Bremen and Verden for the electorate's benefit. There was also a more general concern lest the tsar should use his great military

---

* In 1710 his niece Anna Ivanovna had married the duke of Courland; she became a widow early in 1711 and from then onwards Peter governed through her.

power to gain a permanent footing in the Empire. The very fact that he had refused to carry out the Scania descent bred suspicion. From the tsar's point of view the postponement made some sense. Charles XII's maintaining himself so long in Norway had tied down a good part of the Danish navy which did not join the allied fleet (including Norris's squadron) till 8 August.* The season was far advanced and tsar Peter's reconnaisance of the well-fortified Swedish coast convinced him that the odds were in Charles XII's favour. Norris, directed from Hanover, tried hard to get the invasion moving. When this proved impossible, George and his Hanoverian ministers toyed with the idea of keeping Norris in the Baltic for the winter and more or less forcing the tsar (with Danish help) to quarter his troops 'beyond the Vistula'.[41] Stanhope and Sunderland do not seem to have dissuaded George from this risky venture, which collapsed, however, when the Danes decided not to break with the tsar in the hope of cooperation in 1717. Stanhope contented himself with reporting to Townshend that the central motive of George's foreign policy was his desire to 'divert the Tsar from attempts which would immediately throw all Germany into a flame'.[42] It was left to Townshend, and Robert Walpole, to protest. On 4 October (NS) the former wrote to Stanhope

My chief design is to beg you not to consent to Sir John Norris staying any longer than the first of November in the Baltic, nor to the king's engaging openly in the affair about the Tsar. This Northern war has been managed so stupidly, that it will be our ruin—would it not therefore be right for the king to think immediately how to make peace with Sweden even tho' he shou'd be obliged to make some sacrifice in obtaining it.

Here was the rub. Whether Stanhope showed the letter to the king or whether he, or Sunderland, only passed on Townshend's sentiments in general, George took umbrage that his British secretary should advise him to sacrifice the Hanoverian gains achieved in 1715.[43]

Hanover's falling out with tsar Peter made the conclusion of the French alliance a more urgent matter for George: he needed France's guarantees for Bremen and Verden now that the Russian underwriting had become doubtful. Again circumstances – or rather the combination of circumstances – worked in Townshend's disfavour. He had gone along with the decision that the Dutch should be denied a share in setting the terms for the French alliance and had even sent Horatio Walpole ostensible instructions (at variance with the real ones) to show 'in confidence' to Dutch statesmen in order to hide that very decision.[44] He had been kept informed of the Stanhope-Dubois negotiations at The Hague at the end of July and had

---

* Norris remained with the coalition fleet throughout the season, though detaching some British men-of-war to help the Dutch commander convoy the combined Anglo-Dutch merchant fleets to and from the East Baltic ports.

approved them. He was also correct in his argument that the pro-
cedural difficulties which Dubois made in October-November
emanated more from the French statesman than from Whitehall.
With Stanhope's signature of 6 October on the document safe in his
pocket, it was in Dubois' interest to wait for the Republic to sign*
and thus spare France the charge of having betrayed the Dutch.[45] In
the meantime, however, Stanhope acquired a hold on the Anglo-
French negotiations and on George's gratitude. The secretary for
the south, not as irascible as Townshend, was more interested in
politics on a Europe-wide scale, had great skill in negotiations and
was fertile in expedients leading to worthwhile compromises. He
enjoyed his sparring with the subtle Dubois. The Frenchman, knowing that Stanhope (with whom he was acquainted) would accompany
George to Hanover, spun a story to explain his own presence at
The Hague just as Stanhope and Bernstorff passed through the
town: he had been ordered by his doctor to take the waters at
Valenciennes and had been tempted to Leiden by an important
book sale. He would like the pleasure of calling on Stanhope.
Having fixed their interview for 8 o'clock in the morning of 29 July,
Stanhope took pleasure in being blunt and came straight to the
point: 'Vous et mois ferions plus en une heur qu'il ne s'en ferait en
six mois dans des conferences'. Advantages must accrue to both
Great Britain and Hanover. Dubois expressed his conviction that the
problems of the Pretender and Mardyk were easy of solution and
hinted broadly that expedients could be found whereby France
would guarantee Bremen and Verden to George. It was agreed that
Dubois should, after consultation with the regent in Paris, travel
secretly to Hanover so as not to cause George embarrassment with
the emperor. By 19 August Dubois was lodged in Stanhope's own
apartments.

Both men have left reports (fuller in Dubois' case) of their negotiations. Each prides himself on clever ploys; Stanhope on having made
Dubois drunk and loquacious, Dubois on his pretence of being taken
suddenly ill so that he might listen from a bed in an adjoining room,
through a door left slightly ajar, to Stanhope's conversation with
George's Hanoverian ministers. Comparison between the two accounts shows that neither took in the other and that both had their
wits about them at all times. On the whole, Stanhope got the better
bargain. The Pretender was to go 'beyond the Alps';† the Mardyk
details would be settled in London (on Dubois' assurance that all
would be made easy); Louis XIV's alliance with Sweden (of April
1715) would be sacrificed; and the French guarantee of the Protestant succession would be so worded that George's possessions as elec-

---

* By some minor concessions to the Republic, Dubois was able to obtain Dutch accession
to a Triple Alliance on 4 January 1717; once this had been signed Dubois, Châteauneuf
and Cadogan burnt the Anglo-French treaty of 28 November which they had succeeded
in keeping secret: see my *Diplomatic Relations*, pp. 132–43.
† In 1717 he left Avignon, the papal enclave in France, for Rome.

tor, including Bremen and Verden, would be comprised within it.
The French counterdemand, that all the peace treaties signed at
Utrecht should be guaranteed in full, could not be conceded since
these had included Victor Amadeus's possession of Sicily. George and
the Hanoverians did not want to be robbed of the loophole for a re-
settlement of Italian issues which they had created by the phrase
Honor, Dignitas et Jura in the Anglo-Imperial treaty of 1716. An
expedient, suggested by Stanhope, solved the problem. Not the full
treaties, but only those clauses which dealt with the possessions of
the Maritime Powers and France and with the French and British
successions, would be guaranteed. The loophole which permitted
changes in Italy was not closed, while the regent achieved his main
personal objective, the promise of military support if Philip V of
Spain should go back on his renunciation of his rights to inherit the
French crown. Philippe d'Orléans was a conscientious, loyal regent
and a fond uncle to Louis XV; but he was ambitious enough for his
own branch of the royal family to wish to make sure – if Louis XV
did not leave heirs of his own body – of the place in the French
succession which the peace of Utrecht had settled on him and his
descendants.

At midnight on 24 August Dubois and Stanhope signed the
alliance preliminaries. They were immediately sent to Whitehall by
express messenger with certain queries designed to test the opinion
of the lords of the council, and especially Townshend, as to whether
a formal signature without the Dutch would not be preferable to
risking discussion of sensitive issues which might cause delays and,
possibly, undo the Anglo-French agreement. Townshend's response
was negative, partly because he did not see the need for any great
hurry, partly because he had a policy of his own for the north that
he wished to further. He authorized Horatio Walpole to make the
terms of the preliminaries known in general to the Dutch; but
Horatio Walpole, on his own responsibility and without instructions,
went further and presented the terms as 'conditional upon Dutch
consent'. The ensuing misunderstandings and the prospect of further
delays caused intense irritation in Hanover. Townshend was clearly
out of touch with the situation as George saw it, and the moment
reports were received that the French diplomat in London, Iberville,
had consented (with amazing rapidity, it was thought) to measures
which in the opinion of British naval experts would effectively
prevent Mardyk from serving as a port for men-of-war and privateers,
George acted. On 9 October he ordered Stanhope to sign with
Dubois, and Townshend's dismissal as secretary of state for the north
was a foregone conclusion.[46]

THE MINISTERIAL CRISIS

It was not the 'Dutch business', nor the French alliance (which Townshend wanted), which brought George to this decision and to the ministerial crisis which followed, but a divergence of views on the balance of power in the north which came into the full light of day only in the crucial months of August and September 1716. In the spring and early summer Townshend had voiced his concern lest a successful invasion of Scania should upset the balance of power. He had found little comfort in the Hanoverian argument that Russian preponderance would prove transient: the tsarevich, he was reminded, was 'a Muscovite' and in the next reign Russia would turn its back on Europe. What the secretary for the north wanted, and what seemed feasible once the tsar had backed out of the 1716 invasion of Sweden, was for the Maritime Powers and the emperor to agree on peace terms which would re-establish a balance between Sweden and Russia and then force all belligerents in the Great Northern War to accept them: parliament, he argued as late at 16 October (OS) 1716, would be willing to bear Britain's share of the costs involved in this.[47] To George such advice, and Townshend's harping on the glory which would come to him as king of Great Britain if he mediated peace in the north, was at this time irrelevant and unrealistic. The emperor was at war with the Turks; the Dutch Republic was unwilling to take risks; while for the electorate of Hanover, Bremen and Verden were at stake and a Russian invasion from Mecklenburg was a distinct possibility unless George could obtain a binding agreement with France. The differing attitudes of the king and Townshend, which led to George's decision to remove him from his secretaryship,* where he could not but be concerned with foreign policy problems, led to a conflict which became political and even constitutional: a struggle by the king for his right to fill the ministerial posts as he thought best.

The struggle was not trivial and not – as is so often assumed – based merely on personal rivalries. It was natural for Townshend and Robert Walpole to feel that they had been betrayed by Hanoverian enemies, by Stanhope and Sunderland cooperating with these enemies, and by ill-wishers in England who pictured them as subservient to the prince of Wales and thus 'unfaithful' to the absent king. It is easy to see why historians have stressed the personal aspect since Townshend's and Walpole's printed letters[48] – casting about to find where they had offended – are full of such conjectures and of explanations for minor things that had gone wrong between

* This was done on 12 December (OS) 1716; Stanhope replaced him in the northern department.

them and the king, e.g., the delay in payment for German troops (those of Saxe-Gotha and of Münster) bespoke before the Fifteen rebellion had been defeated, their advice that George should not seek to draw private benefit from the sale of land in St Christopher, and their reputed wooing of the prince of Wales during his father's absence. But for those conversant with the unprinted documents of the period, there are significant clues even in these letters to the real issues. Furthermore the Schulenburg correspondence with Görtz from 12 February (NS) 1717 onwards enables us to follow and throws new light on the way the conflict developed and spread from day to day once George had returned to London.

George liked and respected Townshend and he was aware, like many of his Hanoverian ministers and courtiers, of the sterling worth of Robert Walpole. Walpole's reputation as a manager of the House of Commons was already well known, while Stanhope – 'on his own admission', Schulenburg assures us – knew that this was not his own *forte*.[49] Moreover, Walpole had also been a good administrator as chancellor of the exchequer and first commissioner of the treasury since October 1715. It was in the king's interest to keep all three men in his ministry. Stanhope had shown himself a secretary of state after George's own heart: frank and independent in speech, but understanding of George's dual responsibilities as elector and king. He was already at work, stimulated by his talks with Dubois, on a peace plan for the south to reconcile the emperor and Spain, and his general conversations with George's Hanoverian ministers, including Görtz, looked forward to a time when a peace plan for the north could be constructed.[50]

Once the Anglo-French agreement had resolved the immediate problem, everybody's efforts – bar, possibly, Sunderland's – were directed towards the preservation of the ministry. George, essentially fair-minded and just, accepted Horatio Walpole's explanations during his visit to Hanover in late October of the several misunderstandings connected with the French alliance and the various domestic issues, and apologized for any unjust suspicions he may have held of Townshend's behaviour.[51] Yet there was clearly an element of rivalry between Stanhope and Sunderland on the one hand and Townshend and Robert Walpole on the other. Sunderland had not forgiven the brothers-in-law* for his own relegation to the lord lieutenancy of Ireland, and the suggestion that this would be a fitting post for Townshend, leaving him in the cabinet but without a right to interfere in foreign policy, may well have derived from him. But Stanhope, though naturally pleased at his growing independence from Townshend, differed from him also in his concept

---

* Townshend had married Dorothy Walpole in 1713.

of a minister's duty to the king. There is no specific proof that his military past determined or even influenced this, but I consider this likely: it certainly made it easier for him to grasp George's problems in the Great Northern War. Conversely, the British ministers' feeling of betrayal at Stanhope's lack of total support is explicable. The dignified and moving letter which Robert Walpole wrote to Stanhope when the Irish post was suggested for Townshend, his pleading with his old friend to put things right and play fair with his colleagues at home, makes an immediate impact even today and channels the reader's sympathy to the home team. Stanhope's defence is lame in comparison, but he makes his point – valid at the time – that ministers, having given their advice, should not put themselves above the king. If Townshend should refuse Ireland, he argued, this would be tantamount to a demand that he be 'viceroy over father, son and their three kingdoms'. As for the dues of friendship, Stanhope wrote, 'I think more is not required from a man in behalf of his friend than in behalf of himself: I can't tell the king I won't serve him unless . . .'[52]

George journeyed back to England eager and determined to work for reconciliation and harmony within the council and the cabinet. He had sent messages to that effect via Horatio Walpole when he permitted him to leave the Republic and return to London so that he would not have to break his word by signing the French alliance without the States General. Dutch statesmen, informed by Townshend of the crisis, took the opportunity during the king's brief stay in the Republic to stress the European importance of British tempers being calmed; and from The Hague on 16 January (NS) George let Robert Walpole know – via Stanhope – that if Townshend would pay him the 'mark of duty and obedience' of accepting the lord lieutenancy for half a year or more, the king would at the end of that period give him a post more commensurate with his own wishes.[53] On his arrival at St James's, George called Townshend and Stanhope together in the closet and spoke to them *fortement* for an hour and a half; and Townshend, on being explicitly assured that he need not go to Ireland while lord lieutenant, kissed hands on the appointment. It says something of the strength of the ties of friendship which still bound the two secretaries, and also of George's powers of persuasion, that Townshend forced himself to swallow his pride and accept Stanhope in his own place as premier secretary. To make Townshend and Walpole forgive Sunderland proved harder, and George's success, won by threats as well as appeals to the urgency of the king's business, proved more apparent than real. He let Stanhope administer the threat in its crudest form, with Cadogan present as a witness: Townshend and Walpole were told that unless they reached an accommodation with the lord privy seal within three days, Sunderland would be given the secretaryship for the north while Stanhope would be put at the head of the treasury. George, though he hid the iron fist in a velvet glove, spoke to Townshend along similar lines and gave all his ministers his 'ordre du Roy' to work together without animosity and cabals.[54] Bernstorff and Bothmer did their best to promote reconciliation. The former spoke in favour of Townshend, the latter gave a dinner to celebrate the promise of Townshend and Walpole to cooperate with Sunderland. But court gossip had it that there were dangers ahead. Schulenburg told Görtz that Sunderland was 'hated' by the two brothers-in-law and that, though they had agreed to work with him, they were determined to show their distrust of him by neither visiting him nor receiving his visits. That Sunderland found an excuse to absent himself from the dinner which Stanhope in his turn gave on 23 February to celebrate the re-established harmony was also taken as a bad omen. By 2/13 March the council divided into two 'partis assez echauffés' against one another, unable to agree on the drafting of the king's speech for the opening of parliament, bickering at this and every following council meeting.[55] 'What one lot of ministers proposes the other opposes,' became an established pattern; but it is significant that Sunderland, not Stanhope, was reckoned head of the group opposed to Townshend and Walpole.[56] At court, men speculated on what *parti* would win the tussle for the king's confidence, while George – still hoping to keep both united in a king's party – tried throughout March and early April to ride the storm by consultations in the closet with individual ministers and by avoiding any comment outside the closet that might seem to favour either group.[57] At the supper table his talk was of indifferent matters, of stories from the French court culled from Liselotte's letters to the princess of Wales, and he continued to show himself to be in the 'meilleure humeur du monde'. Schulenburg was reduced to reporting the small change of court scandal: we learn of the plight of the poor lady-in-waiting in the circle round the princess of Wales during a drawing room reception, glued to her place by etiquette, who had to urinate where she stood – a puddle 'the size of a table to seat ten' threatened to lap the shoes of the princess and transfixed the eyes of the courtiers present.[58]

Judging by straws in the wind, such as the amount of time ministers spent with George in the closet, Schulenburg expected that Townshend and Walpole would win. He knew for a fact that Townshend was fully re-established in the king's confidence and prophesied that if only he would show 'un peu de menagement' for Sunderland's party, he would restore his position as George's most influential British minister. But if Townshend was too demanding, if – as rumoured – he wanted to force Sunderland to quit the ministry, then Schulenburg was convinced he would lose: the king would not be dictated to. Schulenburg does not seem to have known Townshend well, but he met Walpole during this period (at a dinner given by general Hammerstein) and followed proceedings in parliament closely. He had a great admiration for Robert Walpole's handling of the House of Commons and was well aware of the fact that the name of the firm was Townshend and Walpole: if Townshend decided to go, or was dismissed, Walpole would resign.[59]

It was at this delicate stage, the last week in March and the first week of April according to the New Style, that the interference of the prince of Wales in politics, independent of his father and in part in open opposition to him, aggravated the situation. The prince had been somewhat restive before his father's departure from Hanover. He knew of the talks that had taken place between George I and his British ministers on how the government was to be carried out during the king's absence and felt humiliated that his father did not trust him with full powers. It would indeed have been strange if George had done so. What the king visualized was the kind of arrangement which operated for Hanover when he himself was in England: minor matters to be settled in London, everything else to be referred to himself. The prince was to preside over cabinet meetings, but he had no control over important appointments, and could not create peers. The dislike of his son which is usually read into this arrangement does not stand up to examination: George's letter of instructions for the prince is affectionate in tone and sensible in approach. The word *regent* is used (the prince's official title being the age-old 'guardian and lieutenant of the realm'); *all imaginable regard* is promised for his recommendations to posts and places and for his advice in general; assurances are given that the king is *perfectly persuaded* that he might *without the least risk* confide to his son *the full and entire exercise* of the powers he has reserved for himself, but for the sake of precedence it has been necessary to set an example lest in the future *great inconveniences to our posterity* should follow.* The king was well aware of the need to train Georg August for his future role; he could not but benefit from discussions with Townshend and Walpole and from presiding at cabinet meetings. The prince was specifically given the right of appointment of officers in the army up to a certain rank. He had powers of suspension for all officers and governors of towns, places and fortresses in Great Britain, Ireland

---

* The italicized portions of this paragraph are direct quotes from the king's letter to his 'Dearest Son' dated 5 July (OS) 1716 from St James's; translated from the French and printed by William Coxe, *Memoirs of the Life and Administration of Sir Robert Walpole*, vol. I (1816 ed.) 282–84.

and the plantations on complaints of misconduct. He could issue pardons in all cases but those of high treason, and even here he was empowered to grant respites. He was also permitted to authorize payments for secret service and bounty money and to open a parliamentary session if this should be judged necessary, though not to sign any public act without the king's approbation and express consent. All in all, a sensible arrangement, reminiscent of George's introduction to business at a similar age.

On one point, however, the prince of Wales had cause for resentment: just before his departure for Hanover, the king forced the dismissal of Argyll as the prince's groom of the stole. Argyll had lost favour with the ministry after his dilatory campaign in Scotland and it was natural that Cadogan, and not Argyll, should be made (in all but name) commander-in-chief when Marlborough's first stroke (November 1716) proved serious enough to make him incapable of exercising his duties. Argyll's annoyance at being passed over was such that George I's ministers took alarm. They would in any case have preferred to keep the king in England for the summer and autumn of 1716 and had pleaded long and insistently that he forego his visit to Hanover, 'for the time being'. They had, however, robbed themselves of compulsive powers since that clause in the Act of Settlement which laid down that the ruler needed parliament's permission to leave his royal dominions had – in the emotional atmosphere of the Fifteen – been repealed to please George and show the nation's gratitude for his share in the speedy victory over the Jacobites. Unless Argyll was dismissed, Townshend and Walpole argued, he might intrigue against them, backed by the prince, once the king was in his electorate. George therefore had to take responsibility for Argyll's dismissal and, via Bernstorff, he resorted to threats to quieten the prince's protests at losing a servant to whom he was devoted. The thing could not be undone, the prince was told: unless he acquiesced, the king would call Ernst August to England to act as guardian of the realm. This threat brought Georg August to heel; he pronounced himself 'resolved to sacrifice everything to please and live well with the king'.[60]

Superficially things went better during George's absence than Townshend and Walpole had expected. They met with 'civil reception' from the prince of Wales who showed himself keen to discuss business with them. For their part, they went out of their way to be polite to Argyll (who remained at Hampton Court throughout the summer in spite of his dismissal) and his brother Islay. The suspicions of a compact among the four which this caused in Sunderland's mind were unjustified.* On the contrary,

* Sunderland is said to have made much of this supposed compact when he arrived in Hanover in September 1716, but even if this were so, I am not convinced that it had any great effect on George. It is certain, however, that Sunderland's suspicions – which he hinted at in a letter to Townshend of 11 November 1716 – caused bad blood between himself and the secretary.

Townshend and Walpole remained alert and reported to Hanover signs which pointed to a plan (behind which they saw Argyll) for the prince 'to keep up an interest of his own in Parliament independent of the King's'. They continued to hope, however, that it would prove possible 'to bring the Prince into other and better measures'.[61]

Unfortunately, by the time George returned it was too late. The prince and his wife had set their course and nothing would make them alter it by a single degree. The break in the royal family was postponed until December 1717 because George I strained every nerve to bring home to the young couple the serious effects that disunity would have on public business. He tried appeals and appeasement, was concerned to gain time and avoided threats. Policy issues of importance to George were at stake. He had promised his first privy council and a large deputation of non-conformist ministers in the autumn of 1714 that he would repeal two statutes of the reign of queen Anne: (i) the Tory amendment of 1711 to the Occasional Conformity Act, which forced dissenters to take the sacrament more than once a year, according to the rites of the Church of England, if they wished to hold office or a commission in the army or navy, and (ii) the Schism Act passed in 1714 which in theory if not in practice impaired their freedom to teach in schools and dissenting academies. Since the Fifteen had absorbed the government's energies, action on these two matters had been postponed until the king's return from Hanover. It soon became known, however, that the prince of Wales would side with those bishops who opposed freeing the dissenters from their disabilities in the hope of ingratiating himself – it was assumed – with the Anglicans.[62] The prince again tried to show that he was more British in sentiment than his father when, in January 1717, the Swedish envoy Gyllenborg was arrested, his papers seized, and extracts of his correspondence published to demonstrate the Jacobite contacts of himself and Charles XII's financial and diplomatic adviser, Georg Heinrich *Freiherr* von Görtz (a kinsman of George's Hanoverian minister Friedrich Wilhelm). George certainly hoped to make capital out of the 'Gyllenborg plot': parliament was to be asked for a large money supply as well as for a total prohibition of British trade with Sweden. By contrast, Georg August, wishing 'to make himself agreeable to the Nation', let it be known that he 'thought little of Bremen and Verden'.[63]

The prince's opposition to his father was at first clandestine. He absented himself from parliament while encouraging his supporters in both Houses to vote against the ministry. His absence, however, was generally interpreted as a sign of a rift between father and son. Most damaging was his staying away from cabinet meetings, since this brought dissension into the very heart of the government.[64] The princess of Wales was known to dislike Townshend, and this probably explains George I's choice of Stanhope for his emissary to the princess late in February 1717. The secretary appealed to her on the king's behalf to use her influence with her husband to make him return to cabinet and parliament. Stanhope lost his temper as the interview proceeded. He reminded the princess that her husband was a subject of George I, 'just as much as I myself', and that for his part – though he had been one of those who helped to settle £100,000 a year directly on the prince – he would not scruple to bring about a change by act of parliament to make this income dependent on the king's grace. The princess remained cool and teased him mercilessly: would he perhaps add his father-in-law's great diamond* to the new act to tempt the prince?[65]

Stanhope's hot temper was also in evidence in the critical debates in parliament on 8 and 9 April 1717 when supply was asked so that George I could concert measures with foreign princes and states to prevent future Swedish designs on Britain. Townshend now clearly worked against the king in the Lords, and Walpole – though he personally voted with the court – chose not to exercise his full influence over the Commons. Whether the brothers-in-law did so because Townshend had decided to show George I the amount of power they could wield is uncertain, but it seems likely. Their behaviour caused the king nerve-racking days, especially as the prince's men in Lords and Commons failed to support the *maison*. On the first day of the debate Stanhope, in the heat of the moment, used expressions that the Commons deemed menacing. He apologized, but was plainly told by the country members (the *Gentil-hommes Campagnards* of Schulenburg's letters) that it was no good his trying to force them to pay up: if he used such methods, he showed that he did not need a parliament and they might as well stay at home. During the debate George's Hanoverian ministers were accused of using subterfuges to push their German war against Sweden with British money to conserve Bremen and Verden, which were of no importance to Britain. The court was grateful that Stanhope on 8 April scraped home with fifteen votes – including that of Robert Walpole himself – but it was realized that Walpole had secretly encouraged his followers to defy the crown and that the prince of Wales had done likewise. The Tories, Schulenburg reported, gloated as if over a military victory since fifty-three Whigs had voted with them against the court. George immediately sent Bernstorff to his son to express his surprise at the behaviour of his *Gens*. Georg August was evasive. He informed Bernstorff that he had given orders that

---

* Thomas Pitt, known as 'Diamond Pitt', had returned from the East Indies with a fabulous diamond which eventually found its way into the collection of the regent of France.

his household and clients should either vote with the court or leave the respective chambers, and he therefore denied that he had 'acted against the king'.[66]

QUARREL IN THE ROYAL FAMILY

The next day, 9 April, the position worsened. The prince of Wales's men abstained as a body. Townshend and Walpole were clearly not bothering to pull their weight, for in spite of Walpole's vote for George I's government, *le party du Roy* in a single day saw its majority diminished by eleven, plummeting from fifteen to a mere four. Stanhope has often been blamed for this, but an indiscretion of his, though much publicized, had repercussions abroad rather than at home. In an attempt to show that George's friendship was valued in Europe, he stressed in his speech that the regent of France had defied 'his own Council and the [French] Nation' to enter into an alliance with Great Britain – a remark not likely to be relished by Philippe d'Orléans since it gave his opponents a chance to criticize him and his adviser Dubois. The domestic situation, however, was worrying since Bernstorff's visit to the prince of Wales could be seen not to have achieved its objective. 'Voilà une rupture ouverte entre Père et le Fils, et une grande division parmy les Whigs du Parlement', Schulenburg commented. Townshend would clearly have to go. His defiance in having voted against the passing of the Mutiny bill – the very foundation of the king's annual permission to keep a standing army – could not be condoned; but Schulenburg still hoped that Walpole might remain and that George, anxious to introduce a general amnesty for Jacobites involved in the rebellion, might get this measure through, weather the session and then 'lie low till next winter'. While still in the process of writing his long report to Görtz of the happenings of the past two days, Schulenburg heard that Townshend would be dismissed from the lord lieutenancy that very evening and before he finished his letter he had been informed that Walpole's resignation would come on the morrow: 'Voila ce Parlement perdu pour le Roy'.

If this summing-up was unduly pessimistic, the months until parliament rose on 15 July proved difficult and unpleasant. The king did his best not to antagonize Townshend and Walpole needlessly. He thanked the former, in writing and by word of mouth, for his past services and told the latter in a separate interview in the closet that he would like to keep him in office as long as he would *bien servir*. Walpole, as expected, returned the answer that he could not work with *ceux qui etoient en place* and resigned.[67] So did Orford of the admiralty; Methuen, Stanhope's successor as secretary for the south; Pulteney, the secretary-at-war since the accession; and – as soon as he returned to town – the lord steward, the duke of Devonshire, who now became the nominal leader of a group variously referred to by later historians as the dissident Whigs or the Walpolian Whigs. The members of this group often acted with the Tories against the government, but the most dangerous support for the rebels, from the point of view of the court, derived from the group's collaboration with the prince of Wales. The names of the above-named members of the group (bar that of Pulteney) figure in the right-hand column of a list drawn up by Schulenburg for Görtz's guidance, headed *Le Prince*. The left-hand column, that of *Le Roi*, names the dukes of Kingston (made lord privy seal in 1718), Kent (lord steward 1716–19), Roxburghe (secretary of state for Scotland since December 1716), Sunderland, nominated as secretary of state for the north while remaining lord president of the council, Marlborough, and Stanhope, now first commissioner of the treasury and chancellor of the exchequer.[68] Every one of the group, apart from Stanhope, had some influence over votes in the Commons, and it is significant that Bolton's successor as lord chamberlain, the duke of Newcastle, had great powers of patronage and knew how to use them skilfully. All the same the king's party was weak in the Commons and the ministry was short of able men. The important post of secretary of state for the south was filled by Joseph Addison, a fine writer but a man without administrative experience in high office.

In the hope of avoiding conflict, king and ministry accepted a cut in the army, and agreed that the bills to grant social justice to the dissenters, a measure of toleration for Roman Catholics and Jews, and reform of the universities would have to be postponed till easier times. Even so, George had to hear harsh words reported from the Commons. Heneage Finch, a member for Surrey, had shouted that it was a shame that Britain should be governed by 'a Mecklenburg squire'; Pulteney – though he later apologized to George for having been carried away in the heat of the debate – cried out that the present king would never love Britain.[69] Walpole, anxious to demonstrate – as his biographer has shown – both his worth and his nuisance value, would let through only those bills which he considered essential. The general amnesty bill was passed; the consolidation of the national debt and the establishment of the sinking fund, which Walpole himself had planned in the summer of 1717, got through when Stanhope introduced this measure; supply was voted, much to the court's relief, there having been concern lest Walpole would make it impossible for George to carry out his foreign policy objectives.[70] But for the rest Walpole opposed for the sake of opposition even measures of which he had whole-heartedly approved when in office; the Septennial bill was criticized and the impeachment process against Oxford – on which Walpole had been keener than anyone else – halted.[71] Accusations of malver-sation of funds, of corruption, and every other charge that could be thought of, came hot and fast against those in office, skilfully presented by men who had inside knowledge. The king was not spared, Pulteney hinting broadly that he could tell many a tale of German objectives being put first and German ministers listened to where British should have had the first say. Stanhope bore the brunt of the session and found it intolerable. He was well aware of his lack of skill in managing the Commons and told the king (as we now know, thanks to the Schulenburg letters) before parliament was prorogued that he must either be permitted to go to the House of Lords or resign. George and Sunderland did their best to persuade him to soldier on for just one more session; but when he pleaded on health grounds for *cette Grace*, the king gave in and created him viscount Mahon and later earl Stanhope.

Stanhope's elevation raised the problem of the management of the Commons for the next session. Hugh Boscawen, comptroller of the household, with whom George got on well – he had been a member of the king's entourage for Hanover in 1716 – had long experience as an M.P. and was now approached. He was offered an annual pension of £4,000 if he would lead the government in the Commons but declined on the grounds that no ministerial post which would give him weight and credit to grapple with Walpole went with the offer. In private he told Schulenburg that the situation in the Commons was worse than the ministers had let the king know: he clearly had no stomach for the task George wished him to take on.[72]

In the circumstances king and ministry felt bound to reach an understanding with at least some of their opponents and, when this failed, decided to undermine them as best they could. Contact was made with Bolingbroke in France to forestall any attempt by Walpole to recruit this brilliant Tory for his own group. Politicians and courtiers as yet uncommitted were assiduously cultivated. The greatest coup would be to win back the prince of Wales. In late March Stanhope had taken tea with princess Caroline in the hope of using her as a go-between, and from April onwards regular negotiations were carried on via Bernstorff and Bothmer who were at times called in by the prince and princess and at other times sent to the young couple by the king. The problem was that George had very little to offer. When the prince complained of the 'shocking things' Sunderland had said about him, the secretary offered to write a submissive letter apologizing if he had in any way offended the prince, but he could not, as *un honnête homme*, confess himself a liar when he knew himself innocent. In this George supported him. Conversely, any suggestion that the prince should sacrifice 'some of his friends' was regarded by Georg August as a capitulation to the king which he refused out of hand. Melusine found herself unable to help. The princess was, as always, gracious and pleasant to her but proved unwilling to influence her husband in the direction George wanted. The prince, though he seems to have been on quite good terms with *La Schulenburg* and showed her 'every respect' even after his father's death, chose at this time to keep his distance.[73]

Unable to achieve a speedy *accommodement* with the prince, George had to sacrifice his plan to go to Hanover for the summer and autumn. This, quite apart from the king's personal disappointment, meant that European negotiations, and especially those concerning the Northern War, which could more easily have been pursued on the continent, would have to be carried out by emissaries, public and clandestine, coming to Britain. The decision was now taken to make the king's summer stay at Hampton Court splendid beyond anything that had so far been his custom. This would enable him to advertise his support for his ministry and show his determination to govern. He also hoped to turn waverers into supporters of 'the king's party'. Throughout the more than three months at Hampton Court there was a regular weekly 'cabinet-day', Thursday, and this day as well as Sunday was a public day when the king kept open table for guests he wished to flatter and influence, usually for some dozen to twenty, but at times for thirty, forty and even fifty.[74] The king was generous with his time as well as his money. Though busy with negotiations which he in part handled alone – even without the help of Bernstorff – he dined with his British gentlemen-in-waiting every day, walked in the gardens with them and with visitors, arranged for morning levées and special 'ladies' days', and attended evening receptions at which he mingled and talked freely to his guests. In short, he behaved royally to the delight of his subjects. There was music, plays, billiards and card games. The celebrations on 2 August, for the anniversary of his accession, formed the climax of the entertainments. After chapel there was a reception in the Raphael cartoon gallery, which was packed, and in the evening the king led the princess of Wales to the pavilion at the end of the terrace for dancing and to the card tables. On non-public days George was freer to follow his ordinary routine of work and to take his suppers with Melusine and Hanoverian courtiers. Alexander Pope once espied the king in Hampton Court gardens with no other company than his vice-chamberlain and with the evening birdsong the only music.[75]

The Devonshire Whig group stayed away. There had been great fear at court that the prince and princess of Wales would do the same, and there was corresponding relief when they arrived at Hampton Court.

The princess was in the king's company more than the prince; she walked in the gardens with George while the prince tended to avoid his father. Georg August did not take part in the one shoot that George organized at the end of August but went out with his own people. It was realized that he no longer contemplated reconciliation, his friends having flattered him that his party could topple George's ministry when parliament reconvened in November. This, at least, was what court and ministry believed; and George's British advisers now counselled sterner measures since 'la voye de douceur', which the king had hitherto pursued, had not had the desired effect. Sunderland in particular was for seeing what threats might do, and the idea of turning the prince out of the royal palaces was mooted.[76] The king, however, wished to postpone a confrontation for as long as possible. The princess of Wales was expecting a child in the late autumn and the whole royal family hoped for a boy, to make up for the disappointment of the stillborn son in November 1716. It was noticed, however, that the king behaved to Georg August in a way which denoted displeasure – the kind of half-measure which may explain why, when king, George II remembered his father as a weak character.[77]

Early in September, though it was kept secret even from the British ministers, George's Hanoverian courtiers had a sharp fright. The king had been active, busy and cheerful throughout the summer. He had taken the cure with bottled Eger water (from Richmond) to make up for missing the opportunity of German spa treatment and joked that if only his British ministers would follow his example they would feel more optimistic about the outcome of the present crisis. But, without confiding in others, he suffered from time to time from haemorrhoids (as did George II when older); and late in August symptoms developed which seemed to indicate an anal fistula. Louis XIV's operation for this complaint in 1686 was still remembered and its dangers appreciated. George was wary of doctors both for himself and for his family. Though Schulenburg wrote to Görtz of the *grand peur* of the few in the know, and of their prayers that God would preserve the king, a good deal of planning and subterfuge was needed before the Hanoverian courtiers nerved themselves to authorize Mehemet to recommend a medical examination. Fortunately examination and tests established that there was no fistula* and George resumed his activities though he refrained from hunting for a while.[78] In his enforced tranquillity he took the opportunity to visit country estates not too far from Hampton Court; he admired, for instance, the magnificent furniture at lord Orkney's house near Windsor and dined with Newcastle at Claremont. In October, after the princess of Wales had returned to town, he visited Newmarket for the racing season where he also displayed lavish hospitality. He went out of his way to be affable to the many politicians and courtiers who congregated there, though he turned his back on Townshend and Robert Walpole.[79] This was part of a deliberate policy of letting them know that he disapproved of their politics and to give warning that the only way they could hope to get back – during his lifetime – was for them to 'come into his measures'.[80]

* * *

The conflict which broke out in the royal family after the birth to the prince and princess of Wales of a son, *bien fait* and apparently healthy† on 20 October, was therefore to some extent in the air and even engineered by king and ministry, determined to break the link between the prince of Wales and the real leaders of the opposition in parliament, Townshend and Walpole, who – it was rumoured at court – had boasted that they would be able to prevent the king sending a fleet to the Baltic for the 1718 season.[81] It was natural that the opposition should rally round the heir to the throne; but if this heir would no longer be permitted to concert policies directed against George I's interests – if he were, for instance, exiled from the royal palaces and thus shown to be in disgrace – might not Walpole, and possibly Townshend too, be forced to reconsider their attitudes? The ministry was keener than the king to find an excuse for the quarrel to come into the open. When the name of the new grandchild was being discussed George, without consulting his British ministers, deferred to his daughter-in-law's wish that 'William' should be chosen rather than 'George'; while the ministers insisted that since the king was one of the godfathers the name must be George. As a compromise the king decided on George William and sent the duke of Newcastle, the lord chamberlain, with a message to this effect. The duke was also involved in the next stage of the quarrel which arose over whether the duke should be one of the child's godfathers. The prince and princess wanted the child's

---

* The examination revealed '*un morceau de chair en emponge qui s'etoit formé en dehors autour des hemeroides et faisoit couler tant de matière*; it was opened (by purging) and it was then ascertained that there was no fistula.

† The autopsy in February 1718 showed that he had been born with the growth (a polyp) in the heart which caused his death.

grand-uncle, Ernst August, created duke of York in 1716, as godfather – a bachelor who might take an interest in the boy and possibly make him his heir. The British ministers stressed that it was customary in England for the lord chamberlain to be one of the godfathers; and the princess's compromise suggestion, that Newcastle should act at the ceremony as proxy for Ernst August, found no favour. Caroline next requested a postponement of the baptism, presumably in the hope of finding a way out; but there was now no one close to George willing to work for peace. The Hanoverian ministers agreed that it was necessary to go to extremes with a prince of Wales *qui ne garde plus aucune mesure de respect pour le Roy*; and the Hanoverian courtiers, never easy about George's health after the fistula scare, urged a quick decision and a short parliamentary session so that the king could depart for Hanover in the spring of 1718 to take the cure.[82]

It seems clear, therefore, that policy considerations brought about the third and final stage of events, and that deliberate use was made of the Newcastle incident at the christening ceremony.* The Schulenburg letters amplify our knowledge of this third stage. After the christening, which took place in the evening of 28 November, the prince of Wales, in accordance with etiquette, escorted his father some steps outside the room. When he returned, the prince took the lord chamberlain aside and accused him of having acted 'en cette affaire en malhonnête homme'. He used other 'strong, injurious expressions', among which may well have been the legendary 'I'll find you', interpreted as 'I'll fight you'. The next morning George I sent a deputation to his son to ascertain, first, whether he had made an offensive slur on Newcastle's honour and, second, whether he wanted to fight a duel with the lord chamberlain. The deputation consisted of the dukes of Roxburghe, Kent and Kingston. The prince agreed that he had spoken the words complained of, but denied that he wished to challenge Newcastle to a duel, the distance in rank between himself and the duke making this unthinkable. From the report of this deputation in the Chevening Papers, and from a further meeting with the prince of Cowper, Kingston and Kent acting on George's behalf (reported by Schulenburg), it is clear that the prince was enraged that the king had not given him the liberty of choosing the godparents for his own son. He felt it necessary to remind the duke of Newcastle, a mere subject, that he had shown a lack of respect to himself in agreeing to stand godfather against his, the prince's, will; he could very well have made some excuse to avoid doing so. The prince expressed his respect for his father and was clearly surprised at the

---

* In the standard accounts the issue is depicted as a crisis originating in Newcastle's nervous reaction when verbally attacked by the prince.

way in which the quarrel had escalated. When the king told him on 2 December to leave St James's, he refused to obey until George had given him the command in his own writing. The king for his part had expected the princess to stay, at least for the time being, since he had commanded the prince to leave his children in the royal care, and was disagreeably surprised on being told that Caroline had left with her husband.[83] She was given access to the three princesses and the baby prince, all of whom were left in the care of the countess zu Schaumburg-Lippe. But the king took umbrage when the prince, without asking permission and without calling on himself, visited the children. He forbade him to do so in future without giving due notice.[84] Georg August appealed to the law to have his children returned to his care, but the decision went against him: the royal grandchildren, according to English law, belonged to the crown and the prince would therefore have to leave their education in George I's hands.[85]

The prince and princess of Wales found temporary refuge in a rented house in Leicester Square where they later bought Leicester House, which became their permanent home until George I's death.[86] The expulsion caused heartbreak for Caroline and created problems for families, Hanoverian and British, who wished to be loyal to both the king and the young couple once George let it be known that he did not wish to receive those who frequented the prince's court. Particularly hard hit were Caroline's ladies-in-waiting, lady Cowper and Mrs Clayton, who for the sake of their husbands' careers had, officially, to follow the king's ruling. Subterfuges were, however, employed to keep in contact, including letters by safe hands and meetings at masked balls.[87] Sympathy for the prince and princess, especially because they had been forced to leave their children at St James's, was general in London since nearly everyone was unaware of the steps the king had taken to permit Caroline clandestine access. William Cowper resigned his post as lord chancellor in 1718, supposedly over the issue of the royal grand-children being left in the king's care; but from Cowper's own papers (and those of his wife) it would seem that private affairs, added to a dislike of the king's and Stanhope's religious tolerance policy, caused his resignation. George, who valued Cowper highly, attempted during a long talk in the closet to make him change his mind. When he refused, the king rewarded his past services with an earldom, while Bernstorff, Bothmer, Stanhope, Sunderland and Cadogan gave a dinner in his honour to show that they bore him no ill will.[88]

The strain of the family quarrel told on George I. His health began to give serious cause for concern. He felt the shame and sorrow of the public quarrel with his son and daughter-in-law, and was at this time also saddened by the grief of his half-sister for her husband who had died in November 1717. The ordinary business, the important foreign policy negotiations in which he was involved, interested and absorbed him and was therefore not burdensome; but the 'solicitations' – the clamouring for office – of his ministers for themselves and their relatives and clients bothered him at this time. He did not feel physically ill, or at least he never mentioned any one symptom which would give the courtiers a clue to what was wrong, but they argued that 'l'abondance des affaires fâcheuses' had undermined his health to the extent that they regarded a visit to Hanover essential for 1718, the earlier in the spring the better. To Schulenburg the king seemed 'quite altered', and there is some pictorial evidence of a suffering face, arresting in its unhappiness, from Kneller's hand, from this period.[89]

* * *

Politically the catharsis of November-December 1717 strengthened the king's party and the king's hand in dealing with his ministry. The prince did not, as generally expected, speak against the Mutiny bill but walked out of the chamber of the House of Lords before the vote was taken. This lost him sympathy with those Tories who had contemplated making him their leader now that George I's amnesty had reconciled them to the Hanoverian succession. When Townshend and Walpole left the government, the Tories had hoped that George I would turn to them but, as his ministry remained exclusively Whig under Stanhope and Sunderland, they had next pinned their hopes on the prince of Wales.[90] To the court, however, the prince's restraint seemed a good omen, and it was also assumed that Townshend and Walpole had been rendered *plus sage* by the showdown between father and son.[91] Plans were therefore laid to bring at least some of the dissident Whigs and/or the prince's men back into the king's party. Secret soundings were taken with Walpole, Argyll, Devonshire and others. Results were not achieved until 1719 and 1720; yet already in the early spring of 1718 there was a general feeling within the ministry that the expulsion of the prince of Wales from St James's had, by forcing him into the open, weakened his position.[92] In this they were justified. Georg August's court made a sorry and dull impression and could in no way compete with that which George I kept up whether at St James's, Kensington or Hampton Court until the reconciliation of the royal family in 1720. Only after that date did Leicester House begin to shine, the king being happy to escape expense and the fatigue of being contantly on show.

By March-April 1718 George I felt strong enough to get his own way in reshaping the ministry. He wanted Stanhope back in the secretaryship for the north and a more experienced administrator than Addison in that of the south. James Craggs, secretary-at-war since April 1717, was easily slotted into Addison's post. Though Stanhope was only too glad to leave the treasury and return officially to where he belonged, at the heart of foreign affairs, Sunderland put a price on his move. He wished to obtain a post he much coveted, that of the king's groom of the stole, in return for giving up the secretaryship. George would not hear of it, and in the end, though 'avec bien de la peine', Sunderland was persuaded to take one of the places* Stanhope vacated, that of first commissioner of the treasury. His rumoured expectation, about this time, of marrying a niece of *la Schulenburg* also came to naught.[93]

While Sunderland, a man of higher rank than Stanhope, was the undoubted leader of the group opposing Townshend and Walpole in the cabinet in 1717, it would be misleading to think of him (as is usually done) as the one and only head of the new ministry. Intelligent and witty though he was, he was not in personal favour with George; nor did he stand sufficiently high in the king's respect since – as Bothmer put it – he did 'not excel in foreign affairs'.[94] From the purely domestic British point of view Sunderland was clearly of greater importance than Stanhope. He carried more weight in parliament, controlled the greater share of patronage (subject to George's approval), and had stronger political ambitions: the peerage bill, for instance, is unthinkable without Sunderland's intense concern to secure himself against future revenge by the prince of Wales. But as far as the king was concerned, Stanhope was undoubtedly his most important and influential minister from April 1717 (and arguably from October 1716) till his death in February 1721. And during the years the 'Stanhope ministry' lasted, co-operation between king and minister influenced the political scene of Europe so significantly that they form a watershed in British as in European history.

---

* The other, that of chancellor of the exchequer, was given to Aislabie.

VIII

The watershed 1718–21

The three crises of 1715–18 had beneficial, if at times unexpected, repercussions in Britain and resulted in that measure of stability which enabled George I and Stanhope to play so significant a role in European affairs after 1718. The Fifteen rebellion showed that the Hanoverian dynasty, even if it was not generally popular, was there to stay, since it was much preferred to the unrest and anarchy implicit in James Edward Stuart's claim to the crown. George I's amnesty,* which went back to the date of his accession, helped reconcile the English Tories to the house of Hanover and made possible a distinction between the still numerous Tories and the relatively few firm Jacobites. All along George and his successive ministries had cause to be grateful to the sixteen Scottish representative lords sitting in Britain's upper chamber and the forty-five Scottish members of the lower house; and the king's leniency towards the Scottish Jacobites who had taken up arms, coupled with their disillusionment at the resources of James III, pacified the Scots in general for three decades. For Scotland the Hanoverian dynasty was in one sense peculiarly fitted to make the union work: a dynasty alien to both countries, if disliked by both, was yet looked upon as more likely to be fair to both.[1]

The aftermath of the Fifteen produced an important constitutional change, the Septennial Act. It was passed for the convenience of a ministry which did not want to risk the election due in 1718: the country was considered too excitable to produce a Whig majority. But there was much truth in the ministry's argument that the triennial parliaments of the post-1689 years had proved disruptive and expensive. The benefit of holding elections, with their time-consuming if essential settling of contested results, at longer intervals was immediately appreciated; and constitutional historians are now agreed that the Septennial Act contributed to greater political stability[2] and to the growth of the influence of the House of Commons:

* The few exceptions to the amnesty included Strafford and Harcourt.

since its members, far outnumbering those of the upper house, gained greatly in experience and self-assurance with the longer time-span of each parliament.[3] In retrospect the decision of Townshend and Walpole to go into opposition has also been reckoned a blessing. Between 1717 and 1720 the dissident Whigs, so it is now argued, helped to establish the modern concept of His Majesty's loyal opposition. The Tories could not do this since they – in spite of the amnesty – were tainted with potential Jacobitism, while the Walpolian Whigs could not be suspected of fundamental disloyalty to the Hanoverian dynasty.[4] George I, naturally enough, did not regard the dissident Whigs in this light, although he was well aware of their commitment to the house of Hanover. Since his son's opposition became politically significant only after the Walpolian Whigs had begun collaborating with the prince, George looked on them as disloyal to himself and his ministry. The prince of Wales had too few followers in the Lords and Commons to wreak havoc with government policies. But with skilled politicians of the Townshend-Walpole stamp in the prince's party, the heir to the throne provided a focus which the opposition to George I's ministry needed and used as long as it proved convenient for their purposes.

This was nothing new. It followed, rather than established, a tradition which had operated in parliament whenever there was an adult heir residing in the country. Those who had opposed William III and his policies had rallied round princess Anne. Nor did the process stop when George II succeeded his father: in his turn he was faced with the intractable problem of the opposition to his ministries using and being made use of by Frederick, prince of Wales.[5] The alternative government implied in the modern concept of His Majesty's loyal opposition was, however, largely missing during George I's reign. Robert Walpole opposed the king and his ministry in order to demonstrate his political power in the House of Commons and force George to restore him to office and the inner cabinet. If this could be achieved, he was quite willing to force the prince of Wales to become reconciled, at least superficially, to his father. He did so by April 1720, but he did not come back with an alternative government, that of 'the opposition', being content for himself and a few others to share power with George's ministry-in-being. But while Walpole always knew where he was going, Townshend and George I learnt valuable lessons between 1717 and 1720. Townshend was basically more indifferent to office than Walpole and far prouder.* We have seen that he was the real wrecker of the ministry in 1717 when he proved determined not to work with Sunderland, whom he no longer trusted. His bluff defence of the British point of

---

* He resigned a second time and for good in 1730 when he came into conflict with Robert Walpole.

view in Baltic issues is very attractive. It should be remembered, however, that it was not on a foreign policy issue that he resigned, but on a trial of strength concerning the composition of George's ministry. Opposition taught him, first, that he liked office better than he had assumed and, second, that he must take George's prejudices and principles into account. When he came back, first as lord president of the council and then (after Stanhope's death) as secretary of state for the north, he was a wilier creature than before though still less flexible and Europe-minded than Stanhope.

George I learnt from both Townshend and Walpole, and modified his attitude accordingly. Townshend's delineation of a specifically British point of view helped the king to a greater understanding of and respect for British susceptibilities; and Walpole, by the demonstration of his power in the House of Commons, taught George that what he needed was not so much 'managers' in parliament (as in William III's and Anne's reigns) as a 'mediator' between himself and the Commons in the shape of a minister who had the confidence both of the lower house and of the king.

George's behaviour during the crises of 1715–18 deserves a more balanced judgment than it is usually given. He steered a wise, moderate course in 1715–16 and gained a more stable position not only at home but abroad: as he had weathered the rebellion he was clearly a European ally to be valued. After his momentary panic in Hanover in the early autumn of 1716 he tried hard, in cooperation with Stanhope and his Hanoverian advisers, to show men he liked and respected that they ought not to resign for reasons of pride and personal pique. He did not mind admitting his own mistakes and showed maturity and sense in being willing to apologize to Townshend for suspicions wrongly entertained. When he failed, he had recourse to tougher tactics which – once they paid off – were replaced by genuine cooperation which lasted for the rest of his life. In 1720 Townshend and Walpole had to come back on the king's terms, but when the reconciliation (which George – contrary to standard accounts – used both his British and Hanoverian advisers to bring about)[6] had taken place, the king put past differences behind him and his working relationship with both was exceptionally harmonious. When the quarrel with his son had to come into the open – mainly because ministerial and family problems fused – the king behaved with as much moderation and kindness as the situation permitted. Faced with the fact that the princess of Wales immediately and unexpectedly left her children to go with her husband, he agreed that the countess of Schaumburg-Lippe (who wished to end the *Verwirrung* – the confusion – in the royal family) should visit

Caroline in her new home every evening to give her news of the
three daughters and the baby boy. When the infant was taken ill,
he was sent in the countess's care to Kensington Palace, which
provided neutral ground where both parents could see him. The
countess, who looked after the child for four weeks, day and night,
notes that the prince and princess suffered much during his illness
and at his death and that the king was *herzlich betrübt*. Long before
the official reconciliation the princess was allowed to come to St
James's 'every night' to see her daughters while George, whose
interest and pleasure in the granddaughters was strong, kept
discreetly out of sight.[7]

The king turned down the wild and vindictive schemes of men like
Sunderland who suggested that the prince should be transported on
a British man-of-war to the plantations overseas as punishment for
his revolt. Letters embodying such advice were found by George II
and queen Caroline in 1727, when they went through the late king's
papers. In 1735 Caroline showed two of the letters, or read extracts
from them,* to lord Hervey, and our knowledge of them derives
from his memoirs.[8] Why George I preserved these letters is a matter
for conjecture. It is possible that he wished to justify himself
posthumously to his son, the only person who had the right to
examine the papers in the closet upon the king's death. I would
suggest that this is likely because of the difficulty George experienced
in achieving a genuine reconciliation with his son in 1720. Matters
gradually improved after that date. The pleasure of the young
couple's court at the restoration of 'unison' had its effect on the
prince and princess. The king shared their joy at the birth of another
son in 1721, christened William – in itself a sign of reconciliation if
we recall the trouble over naming George William. Though the
three elder daughters remained in the king's care at St James's,
George took the sting out of this by permitting his son and daughter-
in-law to bring up William and Mary and Louisa (born in 1723 and
1724) at Leicester House and Richmond Lodge. For their part, the
prince and princess honoured the baptism of Trudchen's first son
and consented to the inclusion of August among his names. The
severe illnesses of the duchess of Kendal in 1724 and of the princess
Amalie in 1726, as well as the loss of Trudchen† in the same year,
also contributed to the retying of family bonds. There is evidence,
both in 1725 and in 1727, that George was much moved at parting
from the prince and princess and their children before leaving for
Hanover.[9]

* The extracts copied by him run as follows: (i) 'It is true that he [the prince of Wales]
is your son, but the Son of God himself was sacrificed for the good of mankind.'; (ii) 'He
[the prince of Wales] must be carried off and my Lord Berkeley will take him on board and
carry him to any part of the world Your Majesty will order him, whence he would never
be heard of more.' Hervey is often an unreliable witness, but in this case there is corroborative evidence from Schulenburg that Sunderland advocated stern measures.
† She had suffered from tuberculosis since 1723, and had in vain been treated by the
famous Dr Brunner.

But in 1720 it had not been easy. His son's rebellion had awakened bitter memories in George of the Hanoverian *Prinzenstreit* when he had been a powerless spectator. It is curious that the words he directed to Georg August – 'c'est le Monde renversé quand le Fils veut prescrire au Père quel Pouvoir il doit luy donner' – should be so reminiscent of those which his father had written to Friedrich August in 1685. The similarity of outlook, fashioned by the prevailing idea of the responsibility of rulers to the dynasty, may be a sufficient explanation for this; but it is possible that George had read Ernst August's letter either in draft or in copy, or had seen the original when Gustchen's belongings were sent back to Hanover. In any case George added a sentence specifically slanted to the English experience: 'Je voudrais savoir quel Droit vous avez de faire des Messages à la Chambre contre mon Intention'.[10]* What George seems to have longed for at the time of their reconciliation was a word of affection, a blotting out of the past troubles which – as we have seen – he had tried to minimize for as long as possible. But Georg August – though secretly pleased to have his disgrace ended – was determined to be correct but distant when he came to the closet on 23 April to make his submission to his father. Our only account of this private interview derives from what the prince of Wales told his wife. It is clear that the king was moved and could speak only in broken sentences, and the only phrase Georg August caught (or wanted to catch) was the accusatory *Votre conduite, votre conduite*, repeated several times. They made no real contact and the next day – the day of the formal reconciliation between the king and the dissident Whigs – it was noticed that George and his son avoided speaking to each other when they met in public.[11] George became convinced that his son had been dragged unwillingly to St James's by Townshend and Walpole, and this rankled. To his daughter, the queen of Prussia, he could not forbear pointing out how much more honourable it would have been if Georg August had sought a reconciliation of his own free will.[12]

The element of self-righteousness in this letter – the only one of his letters to Sophia Dorothea to show this trait – is not uncharacteristic of George when he had been given years to ponder over what seemed to him an unnecessary wrong done him, one which had wasted energies needed elsewhere. We meet it also in his gruff private comment on Townshend and Walpole in 1720. When the two, with the other dissident Whigs of former cabinet rank, waited on the king on 24 April, they received a brief but pleasant speech of welcome in answer to the address of their nominal leader, Devonshire – George expressing his genuine pleasure at the restored harmony. But to

* Equally significant is Georg August's remark to his father's emissaries that it was the right of 'every subject in England to chuse who should be Godfathers to their Children' (Chevening MSS 84/10).

Mary, countess Cowper, who paid him a compliment on the improved state of affairs, he (as we have noted in another context) grumbled, 'What did they go away for? It was their own Faults'.

EUROPEAN PEACE PLANS

Between 1717 and 1720 lay years of great endeavour and great success for George in the field of European politics, the main concern of rulers and ministers in the early modern period. What is so striking about the achievements is the range of vision involved in the peace plan for the south and the peace plan for the north. Only the first was brought to full fruition along lines laid down by George I and his advisers in cooperation with Philippe d'Orléans and his chief minister, Dubois. Though the northern settlement was only partially realized (mainly because of the temporary incapacity of British and French governments during the South Sea bubble and the Mississippi crash), it demonstrates a breadth of European concern which successfully counteracted exclusively German aspirations. On the evidence hitherto available it has been difficult, not to say impossible, to estimate George I's share in these achievements. It has therefore been assumed, even by scholars of the period, that England's contributions to the important experiments in solving European problems, by a system of interlocking guarantees embodying mutual gains and mutual concessions, owe everything to Stanhope and nothing to George; while for Hanoverian policies Bernstorff has been reckoned to 'rule' George rather than the other way round.

Luckily, access to the Görtz and Bernstorff archives has produced new material which permits an evaluation of George I's participation in the formulation of British and Hanoverian foreign policies for the crucial years 1717 to 1720. The king can now be seen to have been at the very centre of decision-making in foreign policy during these years, at times carrying on important negotiations virtually single-handed. The documentation for these years is so detailed as to render it unlikely that his role in the foreign policy field was a lesser one at any other time in his reign. Paradoxically, we owe most of this documentation to the fact that George was not able to leave England during the summer and autumn either in 1717 or in 1718. If he had been on the continent in either year, his foreign policy would have been conducted through conferences, thus leaving little, if any, proof of his personal intervention and control. The geographical position of Hanover in Europe made for ease of communication and speedy posts. Emissaries could come and go more secretly than in England, and the men – whether Hanoverian or British –

with whom the king wished to discuss issues were on the spot.

Like all historical material which has survived, there is an element of chance involved. If Bernstorff's correspondence with the Saxon field marshal and minister Jakob Heinrich Graf von Flemming had not been preserved more fully than any other in the Bernstorff archives after 1705, we should know much less of George's methods in foreign policy negotiations than will be shown below; but it was the very fact that George and Bernstorff were in England in 1717 which made it necessary for Flemming, acting on behalf of his master Augustus of Saxony-Poland, to put in writing his request of 27 September (NS) that a Hanoverian emissary be sent to Dresden for confidential talks, since it was impossible to reveal his master's thoughts to the English resident in Saxony who was 'purement anglois'.[13] If George and Bernstorff had been in Hanover in 1717 it would have been easy enough for Flemming to send a discreet person there; nor would it have been necessary to continue the correspondence into 1718 if the king had been able to stay in his electorate for part of that year. As far as the Schulenburg correspondence with Friedrich Wilhelm von Görtz is concerned, we also owe something to the accident of history in that Görtz proved so avid a treasurer of his papers and that the papers themselves escaped destruction and are now deposited in the Darmstadt archives; but, again, if George had not stayed in England through all of 1717 and 1718 there would have been no need for Schulenburg to report the comings of emissaries like Fabrice and Dubois and the discussions which took place during their visits: Görtz himself would have been at the centre of affairs in Hanover where, if the royal visits had materialized as planned, the negotiations would have been conducted. As things turned out, the Schulenburg correspondence now confirms and amplifies the Fabrice memoirs[14] on the subject of George's northern policies in 1717 and 1718. Fabrice wrote later and often without giving specific dates (though he based his narrative on journals, letters and notes); Schulenburg wrote contemporaneously with Fabrice's two visits (between August 1717 and February 1718) to George I. Furthermore, he reported royal reactions and intentions which were not fully communicated to Fabrice; and he kept Görtz up to date with the king's thinking on Great Northern War issues also during February–June 1718 when Fabrice was absent on a mission to Sweden.* Similarly Schulenburg enriches and expands, as far as George I's attitudes and decisions are concerned, what we know of Dubois' two stays in England, one in 1717, and the other in 1717–18, from the French statesman's reports to the regent and from other sources.[15]

---

* After his return he remained in England and before the end of the year he entered George I's service as his Hanoverian *Kammerherr*. From then on, he never left the king's side.

George I's negotiations on northern and southern problems intertwined once he had concluded the British alliance with France in
October 1716. At times one area provided a crisis which drove the
other temporarily into the background; but throughout the rest of
the regent's lifetime (he died in 1723) collaboration with France
remained a linch-pin of George's policy and the alliance remained
important even after that date. Naturally the cooperation presented
some difficulties, particularly in its early stages. The regent found
several of his advisers opposed to the alliance with Britain, and
Stanhope's *faux pas* in the House of Commons on 9 April 1717
hampered the progress of the peace plan for the south for months.[16]
For his part, George was suspicious of French efforts to include
Prussia in the Triple Alliance between the Maritime Powers and
France: Friedrich Wilhelm had taken Russia's part rather than
Hanover's in the tense situation created by the abandonment of the
1716 invasion plan.[17] But during the first half of 1717 George I
received several proofs of the regent's willingness to help him in
northern affairs, while unforeseen events in the second half of the
year (in particular Philip V's invasion of Sardinia) eased the problems
which both he and the regent faced in promoting the peace plan for
the south.

It is not strange that the affairs of the north should have been
uppermost in the minds of George I and his ministers in the first half
of 1717. Most of the Russian troops were still in Mecklenburg, and
the tsar's prolonged sojourn in the west, first in Amsterdam from
December 1716 till March 1717, then in France from May till July
1717, then once more back in the Dutch Republic, created un-
easiness: what was he up to? The exploitation by George and his
ministry of the Gyllenborg plot had to some extent misfired. The
Dutch proved unwilling to impose a prohibition of trade with
Sweden to match that agreed to by the British parliament, and
frustrated all British attempts to get access to the papers of Charles
XII's adviser Georg Heinrich von Görtz which – it was hoped in
Whitehall – would provide clearer proof than the Gyllenborg papers
of Swedish support for the Jacobites. Görtz and his secretary were
put in provisional Dutch custody, 'on account of the friendship and
treaties of the Republic with George I', but their papers were left
undisturbed. Moreover, the supervision of Görtz was lax enough to
permit him to carry on negotiations with Russian, Saxon and
Prussian statesmen and diplomats even before his release (without
previous consultation with Britain) on 2 August 1717.[18] And though
the Republic – fearing an Anglo-Swedish war – decided not to send
a convoy to the Baltic during the 1717 season, Swedish iron shipped

by Dutch merchantmen or bought by Dutch middlemen in Königsberg was resold, at a profit, to British manufacturers who could not do without this raw material.[19]

Clearly Sweden would not be brought to its knees by the combined Anglo-Dutch economic pressure which George had hoped for in 1717. Nor did Charles XII take the expected aggressive anti-British stance, and parliamentary criticism of the Baltic policy of George and his ministry grew rather than diminished. The Swedish king behaved sensibly, having no desire to find himself at war with Britain. He did not publicly protest, as the London diplomatic corps had predicted,[20] that the arrest of Gyllenborg was a breach of international law, but disavowed – through the good offices of the regent of France – both Gyllenborg and Görtz. At the same time he threw his diplomatic net widely to initiate peace negotiations with as many members of the anti-Swedish coalition as possible.[21] Already in his Turkey years Charles XII had laid down the main lines of a policy of simultaneous negotiations with his enemies to see which could be bought off against temporary sacrifice of territory; he would even accept total sacrifice of land in return for watertight arrangements whereby Sweden obtained military, naval and financial help to fight the rest of the coalition.[22] Not only Georg Heinrich von Görtz, but a fair number of Swedish, Polish and German officials and officers had been engaged in promoting this policy since Charles's return to his own dominions. The tension and discord among his enemies after the abandonment of the Scania project in 1716 naturally eased the task of Swedish diplomacy.[23]

The peace feelers did not exclude George I in his electoral capacity. Indeed, for Charles XII George I – because of his British naval and financial resources – became as vital a target in the peace offensive as tsar Peter of Russia: Denmark-Norway, Prussia, and Saxony-Poland were now far less powerful than the two giants of the coalition. For contact with George, Charles used two routes of approach. The first was via Georg Heinrich's kinsman, Friedrich Wilhelm von Görtz, who was friendly with the former Swedish governor of Bremen and Verden, count Mauritz Vellingk,[24] and in touch with Conrad Ranck, a Swedish officer in Hessian service who had become influential as the go-between in Friedrich of Hesse's successful negotiations for the hand of Charles XII's sister, Ulrika Eleonora.[25] The second route, which became the more important one because of George's fear that Ranck might pass information to the tsar, was built round the contacts of the elder Fabrice with Mauritz Vellingk. Here the young Friedrich Ernst von Fabrice became the principal messenger and, at a later date, chief negotiator. He was

persona grata with Charles XII, having been part of the royal entourage in Turkey from June 1710 onwards in his capacity as a
Holstein-Gottorp diplomat. In that capacity he also had an entrée to
Georg Heinrich von Görtz and was thus doubly useful to George I
in the race for a northern peace.[26]

Fabrice's first visit to George I took place in late August (the 23rd
or the 24th August seems the most likely date of his arrival, to judge
from the Schulenburg correspondence) at Hampton Court. After a
brief meeting with Bernstorff and Bothmer in the late afternoon, his
audience with the king was fixed for 11 o'clock at night – 'in the
little gallery' so that they might be alone and undisturbed. There
the two walked up and down for two hours, Fabrice informing
George of the Swedish offers of peace and George giving him
instructions how to test these offers more closely. Fabrice managed
to stall the curiosity of *La Kielmansegg*, whom he met accidentally
while waiting to see George I; but to the embarrassment of Bernstorff
– who hoped to hide the tension within the royal family – he insisted
on seeing the prince of Wales the next morning to tell him the
purpose of his visit. He allowed himself a day or two in London,
disguised in a black wig, to see the sights (including St James's) and
to pursue an amorous adventure or two, before hurrying back to
Hanover.[27] Some six weeks elapsed while couriers passed between
Germany, Sweden and England to press Charles XII beyond his
offer of alienation of Bremen and Verden for a limited period only
(twenty to twenty-five years at the most) in return for a military –
preferably naval – and financial commitment to work against
Sweden's enemies.

These terms (transmitted by Fabrice during his August visit) were
unacceptable to George for a variety of reasons. His own position
to some extent eased once tsar Peter had begun in July the evacuation
of his troops from Mecklenburg, thanks mainly to French diplomatic
pressure.[28] This was the second service* which Philippe d'Orléans
rendered George, achieved by his promising the tsar not to renew
France's subsidy treaty of 1715 with Sweden when it expired in
April 1718. Its termination was already implied in the Stanhope-
Dubois agreement of 1716, but the regent skilfully used it during
the tsar's visit to Paris and also gained Russian acceptance of
French mediation in the Great Northern War.[29] At the same time,
unbeknown to either George or Peter, the regent softened the blow
to Charles XII by paying outstanding arrears of subsidies and
promising Sweden support in keeping a foothold in the Empire.[30]

With less fear of a Russian invasion of Hanover from Mecklenburg,
George did not worry excessively at his own failure to achieve a

---

* The first was the regent's successful mediation in the Gyllenborg–Görtz affair which
saved face for George at a difficult moment.

reconciliation with the tsar. He had sent admiral Norris, well liked by Peter, to negotiate with the tsar on his return to the Republic from France. It was soon made clear that the cost of regaining Russian friendship was prohibitive: the British fleet could not possibly be put at the tsar's disposal for an invasion of Sweden from Finland.[31] Yet the Jacobite influence in Peter's entourage was making itself felt, and – until the death of Charles XII in late 1718 – there was always a danger that the separate Russo-Swedish peace for which the Jacobites worked might bring with it joint action against George as elector and as king.[32] George had to calculate carefully. Dare he run the risk of letting the tsar win the race for peace with Sweden? Fabrice, on his return to England in October 1717, gave hopes of the outright cession of part of Bremen and Verden; and correspondence carried on between Fabrice and Georg Heinrich von Görtz during Fabrice's second, and longer, stay in England brought further encouragement. Bernstorff was never as eager for peace with Sweden, which he regarded as precipitate, as were Friedrich Wilhelm von Görtz and the two Fabrices. George's decision, after long discussions alone with Fabrice, was to steer a middle course.[33] This was based on his own long experience of diplomatic negotiations and of his close study of the present situation. He did not believe, given Charles XII's Protestant stance and his disavowal of the Gyllenborg-Görtz deal with the Jacobites in 1716,* that the Swedish king would openly support the Pretender. Nor, in view of the tough terms which Charles asked of Hanover, did he reckon it likely that Sweden would make sacrifices in the East Baltic sufficient to satisfy the tsar. He tended therefore to discount rumours of an imminent Russo-Swedish peace with its dangers of a James Edward Stuart invasion better sustained than that of 1715–16. He agreed, however, to send Friedrich Ernst von Fabrice to Sweden early in 1718 to pursue the Hanoverian peace negotiations. This mission was un-official: if the young man succeeded he could be properly accredited; if the Swedes continued their dilatory game his visit could be pre-sented as a private one.[34]

Nor did George neglect any other opening that might help him to counteract Russian initiatives. He eagerly responded to an over-ture by Augustus II's Saxon minister Flemming who, in a letter to Bernstorff of 27 September (NS) 1717, suggested that his master was anxious to concert measures with George I for a northern peace and would like to have a Hanoverian diplomat sent to Dresden for confidential talks. The negotiations which ensued, though unpro-ductive until after George I had achieved his own treaty with Sweden as elector and king, form an episode well worth studying. First, they

---

* Charles XII, apart from the disavowal, had returned the money which Görtz obtained from the Jacobites, choosing to regard it as a short-term loan: see my *Charles XII*, pp.416–17, 438.

demonstrate the tight control which George exercised over foreign policy decisions. Bernstorff did not act on Flemming's proposal that he (Bernstorff) should send an emissary of his own choice, but handed Flemming's letter to the king, who decided to send one of his 'Brunswick secretaries' secretly to Dresden with assurances that Flemming could confide by word of mouth or by dictation whatever he wanted to convey in the sure knowledge that whatever he said or wrote would become known to George I only.[35] Secondly, they display Bernstorff's great diplomatic gifts in keeping the negotiations going after the Saxon minister had learnt (through his own intelligence network) of George's direct and undivulged negotiations with Sweden. His letters are masterpieces of tact and subtle mollification.[36] Finally, they give proof of the devious skill with which king and minister made use of British 'excuses' to further George's Hanoverian policies: a Saxon request that the directorship of the Lower Saxon circle of the Empire should be open to Catholic as well as to Protestant rulers was refused on the grounds that a *directoire interevangelicos* would make George suspect and *odieux* with all Protestants, 'pour ne point parler des interpretations sinistres qu'on donneroit en Angleterre à une pareille conduite'.[37] The lesson of 1701, when the house of Hanover had been accused of insufficient regard for the Protestant cause, had been taken, but it now served to exclude the electoral prince of Saxony – who had embraced Catholicism in the hope of succeeding his father in Poland – from influence in north German affairs.

The element of risk in George's northern policy was fully realized. If the king were wrong in his calculations and the tsar did make peace with Sweden, Schulenburg mused, the court would be 'bien embarrasés'.[38] But, as events showed, George's instinct had been right in predicting time-consuming difficulties in the Russo-Swedish negotiations, while his military experience had made him deduce (correctly) that Charles XII was using his diplomatic negotiations – which were seriously intended – to give Sweden time to recover sufficient military power to negotiate from strength. Northern negotiations therefore languished and were for a considerable time overshadowed by those of the south.

*   *   *

George I, Stanhope and the Hanoverian ministers had been extremely quick in communicating to all interested parties the main outlines of the southern peace plan conceived in Hanover during the late summer and early autumn of 1716. It had, as we have seen, been mooted during Dubois' visit and was built round an intimation from Victor Amadeus of Savoy to Stanhope in February 1716 that he might, in the interests of peace and to gain the friendship of Charles VI, be willing to exchange Sicily for Sardinia. The king of Sicily (Victor Amadeus's title after the peace of Utrecht) was not safe in his possession of that island or in his royal title until the emperor – so powerful in Italy after the settlements of 1713–14 – had guaranteed both: given Charles VI's attachment to the Spanish concept of the Two Sicilies (Naples and Sicily), he was not likely to do so. Without a navy, Charles VI could not attack Victor Amadeus in Sicily, but with his army he could invade the king of Sicily's main territories, built round Savoy-Piedmont in the north of Italy, and thus force him to sacrifice the island. It would therefore be in Victor Amadeus's interests to exchange Sicily for the less prosperous Sardinia, provided he kept the prestigious royal title, against an Austrian guarantee for all his territories, and if possible some expansion into the duchy of Milan.[39]

Stanhope's genius in expanding a settlement of this limited issue into a plan for completing the unfinished business of the 1713–14 settlements – a peace between Charles VI and Philip V of Spain who were still technically at war – is undoubted. His own experience in the Iberian peninsula and his acquaintance with Charles VI (when he had been Carlos III of Spain) was invaluable. The Hanoverian tradition of pacification by exchanges and equivalents, and George's desire to cooperate with the emperor for the sake of both the Imperial ideal and Hanoverian objectives, provided the second half of the equation. It is significant that, though Dubois' visit to Hanover in 1716 had been kept as secret as possible, the emperor had been informed by George I's German advisers and had been invited to send a diplomat in Charles VI's confidence to Hanover to coincide with the Frenchman's stay. It is typical of the slowness with which Hofburg diplomacy operated that only in late November, after news of the Anglo-French agreement of 6 October had leaked out and Dubois had long since left for France, did the emperor send Christoph Freiherr von Pentenrriedter to Hanover on a secret mission. Charles VI's advisers attacked the Anglo-French treaty, which they claimed prejudiced Charles VI's rights to the Spanish crown, 'whatever George I might say'; and Bernstorff and Bothmer were blamed for not having prevented it. Yet Pentenrriedter's visit enabled Stanhope to sound him on a large-scale southern peace plan based on mutual advantages and mutual concessions.[40] Charles VI would gain by obtaining Spanish renunciation of the Italian territory which Philip V had lost *de facto* by 1713; Philip, it was argued, would feel safer once Charles VI had given up his claim to the Spanish crown, though it was realized that something more positive would have to be added as an incentive, namely Anglo-French support for the claims which don Carlos, Philip's son by his second wife, Elisabeth Farnese, had from his mother's side to the successions of Parma, Piacenza and Tuscany; the regent would benefit from a renewed renunciation by Philip V of the French crown; George I in his electoral capacity would, it was expected, gain Imperial goodwill and thus facilitate the investitures of Bremen and Verden (and even Hadeln); while Britain would obtain a European-wide guarantee for its Mediterranean gains of the War of the Spanish Succession.[41]

The plan was influenced by Pufendorf's ideas of international relations: that peace, not war, was the natural state of man and that the use of reason could devise schemes to ensure settlements of problems without recourse to war. The concept, conveyed not only in Pufendorf's philosophical works but also in his widely read *Introduction to the History of the Principal Kingdoms and States of Europe* (written in 1682, published in German in 1693, with an English translation in 1699 and a French one in 1703), that statecraft consisted in analyzing, recognizing and reconciling the various interests of the European states, had made a great impression on a generation weary of the many and long conflicts of Louis XIV's reign. We have already noted the Palatinate interest in Pufendorf's work (in 1661 he had been called to fill the first European chair of international law established at Heidelberg) and the dedication to George of one of his works in its German translation.[42] It is significant that Stanhope had a copy of the *History* at Chevening though we cannot pinpoint the date when he acquired the volume (as we can from a surviving library acquisition list for *An Account of Sweden* and *An Account of Denmark*, both of which he bought in 1718).[43]

It is even more interesting to note that both George and Stanhope envisaged, as discussion of the peace plan for the south progressed, the sacrifice of Gibraltar to salve Spanish pride. In their opinion Minorca, with its excellent harbour Port Mahon, would be sufficient safeguard for British Mediterranean interests. Stanhope's local knowledge – he had conquered Port Mahon and was the architect of the treaty with 'Carlos III' which had first secured Minorca – lent weight to this decision and suggests that the restitution of Gibraltar was acceptable, taking an impartial view of the European situation at that time. In the event, British parliamentary opposition made it impossible to implement promises made by Stanhope and the regent on George I's behalf in 1718 and 1719. The bulldog tenacity with which parliament stuck to what had been gained came as a surprise to Stanhope and to George, since the interpretation of the Gibraltar clause in the Anglo-Spanish treaty of 1713 had led to tiresome difficulties, and the cost of the garrison was deemed excessive if the usefulness of the Rock (when compared to Minorca) was taken into account. The king and his chief British minister were only relieved from the obligation to carry out what amounted to firm verbal promises by the fact that a brief war broke out between Spain and Britain during the negotiations, nullifying all peace-time commitments and enabling suitable hedging (on the lines 'provided parliament agrees') when talks reverted to the topic after this war in 1720. Even so, it would seem that George and Stanhope did not give up hopes of persuading parliament to hand over Gibraltar to Spain. The draft treaty which Stanhope sent in July 1720 to White-hall from Hanover, and which was endorsed by George and Sunderland, suggested that the city and fortress of Gibraltar should be restored without a specific equivalent as soon as all former treaties between Spain and Britain had been renewed; and the written promise by George I to Philip V of 12 June 1721 – the one Philip kept in his bed in a locked box to which he had the only key – was couched positively although it did contain the safeguards on which the rest of the inner cabinet had insisted:

I do no longer balance to assure Your Majesty of my Readiness to satisfy you with regard to your Demand touching the Restitution of Gibraltar, promising you to make use of the first favourable Opportunity to regulate this article with the Consent of my Parliament.[44]

Townshend was thus being disingenuous (to say the least) when he suggested in 1725 to William Stanhope, George's ambassador in Madrid, that the offers the late earl Stanhope had made in relation to Gibraltar 'were done absolutely without the King's orders'; his correspondence with Newcastle shows that he was well aware of the written promise quoted above and ordered a search for it so that it might be copied to refresh the king's memory. To Newcastle, his fellow secretary, he was in any case more open as to his own views. Since Philip V, at the instigation of his queen, had signed an alliance (1725) with the emperor without informing Britain of his intentions,

We must take this opportunity (which their own Madness and Indiscretion has put into our hands) of getting rid of this Affair [the Gibraltar issue], and of silencing them [Philip and his queen], their Heirs and Successors for ever upon this head.[45]

Had a solution along the Stanhope-George line been possible, Anglo-Spanish relations might not have deteriorated to the extent they did during the eighteenth century. This hypothesis is incapable

of proof, but it is undeniable that Britain had obtained good commercial treaties with Spain in 1715 and 1716, rectifying omissions
and clarifying points in the 1713 treaty, and that further concessions
to Britain had been given during the early stages of the negotiations
for the Quadruple Alliance as the peace plan for the south was often*
called in contemporary diplomatic parlance.[46]

During Stanhope and Sunderland's stay at The Hague in December 1716, Dubois had been further consulted on the actual details of
the peace plan, while *raadpensionaris* Heinsius and the Spanish
ambassador, Beretti Landi, were informed in general terms that
George was eager to effect a reconciliation of Spain and Austria by
obtaining mutual concessions from Philip V and Charles VI. The
Dutch leaders were delighted – nothing could more decisively remove
the spectre of war in Europe. The reaction from Spain was in principle
favourable. Philip V, while professing himself 'wholly indifferent as
to the accommodation with the Emperor who can not attack him
in Spain and is much inferior in his Sea forces', expressed willingness
to refer his differences with Charles VI to the arbitration of George I
and the Republic, 'provided a just balance be thereby settled'.[47]

Here we meet another phrase, much used by the statesmen of the
period, including George, Stanhope, and Bernstorff, based on a
concept they all shared and which they all tried to achieve whether
they called it the just balance or the equilibrium of Europe. But the
look of the balance varied according to the point of view of the
observer. From Madrid the emperor seemed too powerful in Italy,
a view which was shared by many princes and statesmen on the
peninsula, including Giulio Alberoni, the Parma-born adviser of
Philip V who had become influential in Spain after Philip's marriage
to Elisabeth Farnese.[48] It was, however, late May 1717 before
Spain's answer quoted above reached George I; and the five-months
gap between invitation and response owed a good deal to Philip's
desire to put himself in a position to negotiate from strength. He
regarded the loss of Spain's Italian possessions as a blot on his *gloire*
and was determined, once the emperor had become involved in war
with Turkey,† to redress the Mediterranean balance with the help
of the naval forces he had so speedily built up after 1713.[49] Alberoni,
though he restrained his master to some extent, hoped for British
connivance at an attack on Sardinia (to be used as a bargaining
counter in future negotiations) and had for that reason obtained
trade concessions for Britain, on the principle that one good service
deserves another. Since a state of war still existed between Philip V
and Charles VI it could technically be argued that Spain was not
the aggressor if the Spanish fleet attacked one or other of the

* But not exclusively, it was also labelled the peace plan, the *accommodement*, or simply
'the plan'.
† In 1716 Charles VI intervened in the war which had broken out in 1714 between
Turkey and the republic of Venice.

territories held by the Austrians in Italy and the Mediterranean. If Philip acted without provocation, however, Spain could be held responsible for disturbing the neutrality of Italy which several powers, including Britain, had guaranteed. The Spanish king had therefore to await a favourable moment. When the Austrians obliged by their unwarranted arrest in Milan of the new Spanish grand inquisitor, Molinez, on his way from Rome to Spain, Alberoni gave Philip the go-ahead. Charles VI could now be accused of having broken the neutrality of Italy while Spanish action could be represented as a just reprisal.[50] A strong Spanish fleet collected at Barcelona and, as soon as Alberoni had obtained the cardinal's hat he had long coveted, proceeded to the conquest of Sardinia.

The flare-up between Spain and Austria caught Europe, and George, by surprise. British diplomacy had been taken in by Alberoni's friendly and apparently pacific intentions and when George, secretly, so as not to offend the emperor by making too much out of the incident, offered Philip V his mediation in the matter of Molinez' arrest,[51] he did not expect any warlike action. There was slight unease at Spanish fleet concentration in Barcelona harbour; but inquiries only elicited the answer that it was intended against the infidel, a reasonable explanation in view of the Austro-Venetian struggle with the Ottomans.[52] This war had engaged George I's interest ever since Charles VI had entered the field on the side of the republic of Venice. News 'from Hungary' was eagerly discussed at the king's supper table with Hanoverian officers and courtiers; a plan of Belgrade and the siege journal of one of Friedrich Wilhelm von Görtz's sons were closely studied.[53] The successful Spanish landing on Sardinia in the late summer of 1717 (22 August NS) came as a bolt from the blue: how would the emperor fare, preoccupied as he was on his eastern frontier?

Schulenburg once spoke of George I's 'lucky star' and expressed his strong belief in it.[54] This time it was certainly in evidence, for hot on the heels of Spanish aggression came the news of the fall of Belgrade (known at Hampton Court on 3 Sept. NS). This glorious success, Schulenburg reported to Görtz, will help our master 'on all sides'.[55] It was supposed to render Philip V more sensible of the need for negotiations, while the Spanish attack would impress on the emperor his need for British naval support in the Mediterranean and thus make him more amenable to a mixture of pressure and promises. Invitations were immediately sent to France, Austria and Spain for consultations in England on the details of the peace plan for the south. Philip refused to send a representative, but this proved a blessing in disguise as, on the one hand, it avoided an Austro-

Spanish confrontation under George I's auspices and, on the other, it left George and Stanhope much freer in working out compromises between Dubois, representing the regent, and Pentenrriedter who negotiated on behalf of Charles VI. There was no desire to keep Spain outside the negotiations, however, and Stanhope's cousin, William Stanhope, was sent to Madrid to keep in close touch with Alberoni. Dubois arrived promptly, before the end of September (NS), but it was more than a month before Pentenrriedter joined them. Even to achieve this much, George had to 'bribe' Charles VI by settling the Austrian claim to arrears of British subsidies from the War of the Spanish Succession.[56]

The interim period gave Dubois an opportunity to make closer contact with George I, since he was given rooms first at Hampton Court and then in a house next to the one the king occupied at Newmarket when he attended the races in the early autumn. The fact that, for a good part of the time, Stanhope was ill 'of a fever' (that vague seventeenth- and eighteenth-century term which might indicate anything from a virus infection to nervous exhaustion, and which we now know to have been caused by the strain of the House of Commons session) also helped to widen the circle in which Dubois moved. He knew how to entertain with culinary delicacies and amused George with anecdotes of the tsar's stay in France. But he also took the opportunity of impressing on the king, on Melusine and on Schulenburg, the need not to weight the peace plan too heavily in the emperor's favour as this would make the regent's position at home untenable: whatever strain there might be between Philip V and Philippe d'Orléans, French opinion would always favour Bourbon Spain against the Austrian Habsburgs.[57] It may be that the idea of Britain's sacrificing Gibraltar – as compensation for Philip V's having to renounce all the former Spanish territories in Italy – was first mooted at this time, though rumours of such a cession did not become current until January 1718 and the offer was not made till Stanhope's mission to Madrid between 12 and 26 August 1718. That it derived from the French side is highly probable since the regent kept coming back to it again and again, long after George had been forced to hedge the offer with demands for an equivalent, Spanish Florida being mentioned as 'particularly suitable'.[58]

With Pentenrriedter's arrival and Stanhope's recovery, negotiations for 'the plan' began in earnest. The objective, 'to find an equitable basis for perpetual peace between his Imperial Majesty and his Catholic Majesty and between his Imperial Majesty and the King of Sicily', was clear enough; but the road to success was not easy.[59]

The gap between Imperial and French demands was great and the British ministers had to act as mediators, dealing with the two emissaries separately until a reasonable amount of common ground had been established. The more extravagant claims on behalf of Charles VI – that the British fleet should conquer Majorca for Austria, or that Mexico and other Spanish territories overseas should be given him in return for his renunciation of the Spanish crown – were easily brushed aside. Yet his consent to make a 'perpetual renunciation' of the Spanish crown could only be bought at a high price: the duchies of Parma, Piacenza and Tuscany specified for don Carlos to inherit would be made Imperial fiefs; and Philip V's demand (put by Dubois) that Spanish garrisons should be admitted into the duchies on the signature of the peace plan was scaled down to neutral garrisons without a specific time set for their entry. That these concessions cut close to the Spanish bone was fully realized. Stanhope confessed to Stair (who represented George I in Paris) on 17 February (OS) 1718 that Charles VI was gaining, 'without striking a stroke', three fiefs, 'one of which is unquestionably a fief of the Crown of Spain and as such guaranteed to that Crown by us in a secret article of the Treaty of Utrecht; and the other is as undoubtedly a fee of the see of Rome'.[60] Spain naturally took great offence at the prospect of don Carlos taking an oath of fealty to the emperor and this, as well as the loose wording of the garrison clause, created problems which outlived the signature of the peace plan by all parties. The concessions were not, however, proof of excessive British or Hanoverian subservience to the emperor, as Dubois at times suspected,[61] but of British pragmatism. Stanhope argued that as long as the vital principles of the plan were accepted, minor adjustments could be left to the passing of time and the cooling of tempers;[62] and the regent was assured that if 'the emperor should endeavour to exceed his bounds, he would find Britain and the princes of the North of Germany ready to oppose him in conjunction with France'.[63]

The navy was the trump card of George and Stanhope in their efforts to gain Charles VI's consent to the peace plan. Both realized that the emperor could not be brought to sign without a firm assurance of a British naval presence in the Mediterranean for the 1718 season to protect him against further Spanish attacks; after all, Philip V's troops were in full control of Sardinia. But both were determined that such help would not be given until Charles VI had signed the detailed plan now worked out Its main points were as follows:

(*i*)   Sardinia to be exchanged for the far more desirable Sicily.

(*ii*)   Charles to renounce, unequivocally, the Spanish crown.

(*iii*)   Philip to renounce reconquest of Spain's former possessions in Italy.

(*iv*)   Don Carlos's rights to the Farnese succession (Parma and Piacenza) and the Medici succession (Tuscany) to be recognized and secured by neutral garrisons (Swiss or British were contemplated) on condition that the duchies be treated as Imperial fiefs.

(*v*)   The guarantees implicit in the peace plan to be worded in such a way that Philip's renunciation of the French crown would be upheld and George's electoral possessions of Bremen and Verden safeguarded.

(*vi*)   Problems arising from the settlement to be dealt with at congresses called for the specific purpose of solving them.

In form the peace plan, in its first stage, was envisaged as a Quadruple Alliance by the admission of the Dutch Republic once the emperor had accepted the plan; while secret articles, committing the signatories to use force, if necessary, to bring Philip to accept, formed an integral part of it. In the event the Dutch never signed, or more correctly, when they were ready to sign George and Stanhope were no longer willing to pay the price of Dutch accession.[64] The name was, however, justified when in November 1718 – after the emperor's formal signature of August – Victor Amadeus joined. A brief limited war with Spain fought by the British navy and the French army could not be avoided, but in February 1720 Philip V acceded to the Quadruple Alliance and the peace plan of the south was realized.

SUCCESS IN THE SOUTH

The amount of work involved had been formidable, for the ministers and diplomats of George I as well as for those of the regent of France. The main burden of drafting had fallen to Stanhope, helped by younger men, Craggs and Carteret, who benefited greatly from being exposed to problems that were both complex and important. Sunderland, though technically in charge of one of the foreign policy departments, left matters largely to Stanhope.[65] The German ministers, Bernstorff and Bothmer (and, at times at least, Robethon), took part in all crucial meetings. Luke Schaub, the Swiss-born diplomat in British service, sat in on all meetings, according to Stanhope's own evidence, so that he might familiarize himself with every detail and be able to handle the Hofburg's questions when he arrived in Vienna with the draft of the peace plan.[66]

That George kept control, discussed all aspects of the plan, and followed day-to-day developments is clear from a variety of surviving documentation: from his correspondence with his *Frère et Cousin* Philippe d'Orléans now in the Chevening papers,[67] from the memoirs of Bothmer for 1718,[68] and – most consistently – from the long run of Schulenburg letters. He waited eagerly for the return of Dubois from his November-December 1717 visit to France to persuade the regent to accept the 'Imperial fief and neutral garrison' compromise; he worried about the outcome of the parliamentary debates on supply for the vital Mediterranean squadron for 1718. Furthermore, he refrained from fixing a date for a visit to Hanover: unless Stanhope returned with satisfactory answers from his missions to France and Spain (late June–late September), George would have to stay at his post in London.[69]

All had gone well so far. The House of Commons voted the necessary supply, much to the court's relief, in spite of Walpole's warnings that the despatch of a fleet to the Mediterranean might bring war with Spain.[70] The element of Spanish aggression in Europe in 1717 was exploited by the government, as well as indignation at Philip V's attempts to limit British encroachments on Spain's monopoly of trade with its colonial empire in America.[71] There was, however, no desire on George and Stanhope's parts to use the squadron offensively unless absolutely necessary. The secretary of state counted Britain's favourable commercial treaties with Spain of 1715 and 1716 among his proudest achievements;[72] and the king was by temperament and experience inclined to achieve his objectives with the least possible expenditure of armed force. Prince Eugène's taunt that George I was trying to obtain Bremen and Verden 'on the cheap' was not undeserved. The diplomatic and naval measures planned by king and minister bear the stamp of George's Baltic tactics of 1715 and 1716. Byng, who sailed in June with a fleet of fine ships, had firm orders to protect Naples and the emperor's other territories in Italy, and also Victor Amadeus's Sicily – the secret linch-pin of the peace plan – with the official excuse that if the Spaniards should 'endeavour to make themselves masters of the kingdom of Sicily [it] must be with a design to invade the kingdom of Naples'. These orders (of 26 May OS 1718) were not communicated to Charles VI. Indeed, in order to make him convert his April acceptance in principle of the peace plan into a binding signature, George led the emperor and his diplomats to believe that orders for active protection of his Italian territories would be authorized only after the Hofburg's formal accession to the Quadruple Alliance. Once Charles VI had complied, Pentenrriedter signing for him in London on 7 August, Byng received fresh orders (communicated to Vienna) to defend Austrian Italy against Spain: a successful diplomatic gambit in a good cause.[73]

A mixture of promises and threats, in the form of hints that George's Mediterranean squadron might side with Spain if Charles VI did not speed up his decision, was effective with the Imperial court, but proved unsuccessful in Spain. Byng had been told to send, as soon as he touched a Spanish port, a copy of his May instructions to William Stanhope for transmission to Philip V in the hope that their perusal would put a stop to new aggressive Spanish measures. By the time they reached the Spanish court, however, the die had been cast; and it does not seem likely that they would have been effective, however early Philip had known of George's intentions. News of the fitting out of the British squadron had caused the Spaniards to speed up their own naval preparations and on 18 June a sizable fleet sailed from Barcelona for a 1718 campaign which Philip hoped would be as successful as that of 1717. The Spanish king would have preferred to attack Naples, but was persuaded by Alberoni that it would be more sensible to invade Sicily: there was a chance that Britain might look upon this as less objectionable than an assault on Naples. Alberoni further argued that possession of Sicily could be used – with Sardinia – to achieve a modification of the peace plan in Spain's favour. What was stipulated for don Carlos would benefit the royal family in its private capacity but not Philip V as ruler of Spain, and it was Philip's Spanish prestige that mattered most. The answer returned to William Stanhope was therefore brief and uncompromising: *le Chevalier Byng peut executer les ordres qu'il a du Roy son Maitre*.[74] The visit of Stanhope to Madrid in August made little or no impression. His argument that Spain ought to be grateful that don Carlos's duchies had been made Imperial (rather than Austrian Habsburg) fiefs fell on deaf ears: the legal protection implied against Austrian interference in the duchies seemed minute against the humiliation of a son of Spain's swearing fealty to the emperor. The offer of the restitution of Gibraltar, which he was authorized to make on George's behalf, was reckoned insufficient by a court jubilant at the news of the successful invasion of Sicily. Gibraltar would be welcome, but there must be something for Spain in Italy as well: what about Sicily?

Unknown to Stanhope and Alberoni, that issue had already been decided before the British secretary of state – still optimistic that Alberoni had the power and the willingness to knock some sense into Philip V and get him to sign the peace plan – left Madrid.[75] On

11 August (NS) Byng's squadron had fought a battle with the Spanish fleet off Cape Passaro which ended with the near-destruction of the symbol of Spain's regeneration after its late seventeenth-century military and naval weakness. The new fleet had splendid well-built ships, but its officers were less experienced than the British, and the element of surprise, with advantage of wind and station, had favoured the attacker. The news, when it reached Stanhope on his way to Paris once more, cannot have caused surprise; after all, he had himself helped to frame Byng's original orders. His next task was to help Dubois calm the regent and concert Anglo-French measures if Philip should declare war on George I, or if further action would be necessary before Philip V could be brought to accept the peace plan.

The debate which ensued over the justification or otherwise of the battle of Cape Passaro* does not concern us here, nor does the detailed – and oft told – story of the stages whereby Philip was brought to dismiss Alberoni in December 1719 and sign the Quadruple Alliance in January 1720. The war which Britain and France had declared on Spain on 28 December 1718 played its part since the British occupied Vigo, and blockaded Spanish-held Sardinia and Sicily; while the French armies which marched into north-western Spain in April 1719 and Catalonia in October 1719 made easy progress in areas unprepared for invasion. But the war was not pushed with great vigour as this would have been against the basic ideas of the peace plan. The most effective weapon was a diplomatic threat: a binding Anglo-French agreement entered into with Charles VI in October 1719 that unless Philip V joined the Quadruple Alliance within three months don Carlos would forfeit his expectations in Italy and the signatories proceed to nominate alternative princes for the Parma, Piacenza and Tuscany successions.[76]

Some general points can, however, usefully be made. First, the element of ruthlessness which can be seen in the treatment of Spain can also be noted – though without resource to force – in the treatment of Victor Amadeus of Savoy and of the Dutch Republic. The king of Sicily had blotted his copybook as far as George and Stanhope were concerned by withdrawing his offer of Sicily for Charles VI and playing off one side against the other in the hope of making further gains. He made enough of a nuisance of himself to earn the epithet at George's court of *Arche-Machiavall de la Siècle*;[77] and when he joined the Quadruple Alliance in November 1718 he received no advantage, beyond the guarantee of his territories, from the exchange of his title to the kingdom of Sicily for that of Sardinia.[78] The Dutch

---

*Byng maintained, for form's sake, that the Spaniards had started the action; the Spaniards complained bitterly of the 'barbaric behaviour of Britain' in attacking their fleet when the two countries were at peace.

also felt hard done by. George I and Stanhope wanted to bring them into the peace plan partly because of their desire to put European-wide moral pressure on Philip V, but also because of an axiom of British foreign policy which forbade the risk of involvement in war unless the Dutch Republic, the main trade rival, should be similarly committed. But as secrecy was difficult to maintain in the United Provinces it was thought best to postpone negotiations with Dutch statesmen on the details of the Quadruple Alliance till agreement had been reached between the three main signatories; and the secret articles of the Quadruple Alliance became known to the Dutch only through a leak. The result was Anglo-Dutch distrust. Various concessions and promises were made to gain Dutch accession, but the Republic – bent on avoiding involvement in war – proceeded deviously enough to be accused of trickery.[79] Robethon's exasperated 'The behaviour of the Dutch towards his Majesty is perfidious and detestable' was not wholly unmerited; and for their part Dutch statesmen thought it grossly unfair and even treacherous that George I, when they (in December 1719) agreed to sign the alliance with its secret articles, refused to accept their signature to avoid complying with promises made at an earlier date.[80]

Secondly, it should be noted that George's willingness to be ruth-less was part of the reason for the successful conclusion of the peace plan for the south, as was the trust he had established between the British and French governments. A previous experiment in solving a European problem (that of the Spanish succession) without recourse to large-scale war, the so-called partition treaties entered into by Louis XIV and the Maritime Powers in 1698 and 1700, had failed because of a lack of trust and because of William III's un-willingness to be ruthless with the emperor.[81] The ruthlessness towards Spain was in any case more apparent than real, given the need to procure a peace between Charles VI and Philip V without upsetting the balance of power established by the 1713–14 settle-ments. From Philip's point of view the emperor had the best of the bargain, and the setback to the Spanish navy by the British attack was galling in the extreme. Yet it must be admitted that to let Philip reconquer Spain's former Italian territories would have rendered the pacification of the Mediterranean scene more difficult, if not impossible.

Finally, there was another sense in which the statesmen and rulers of the day had learnt from the mistakes of the past and from the lively discussion about war and peace since the closing years of the War of the Spanish Succession.[82] The greatest care was taken to make the peace plan foolproof, though with the possibility of future modifications as long as the main principles were not infringed. That is why it endured. Whatever adjustments had to be made after 1720 were effected within the framework that Italian territories ruled by sons of Philip V's second marriage should never be united to Spain: the duchies would remain secundogenitures even if fate decreed (as it did in 1762) that one of Philip's descendants by Elisabeth Farnese should succeed to the crown of Spain. The laying-down in the treaty of the Quadruple Alliance that problems arising out of the peace plan should be settled at congresses of the contracting parties also represented an advance on earlier projects: what had been no more than pious phraseology was now turned into a binding commitment on present and future signatories. It had, as we shall see, beneficial effects on European diplomacy for the rest of George I's reign and was not without influence on the theory of international relations. George's share in this decisive and successful innovation is shown not only by the documentary evidence already mentioned, but by the very fact that while Stanhope was abroad for three months on peace plan business in 1718 the king remained at home, at the centre of control, working with Craggs at Hampton Court to send out orders, including those to Stanhope. During Stanhope's absence important letters to Craggs, those marked secret, were written in French, showing that they were intended for George's perusal. More than conventional flattery is therefore implied in Schulenburg's comment that the establishment of the *Tranquilité du cote de Midy*, which had been nearly despaired of before Stanhope and George got to work, added *un grand Lustre à la Gloire du Roy notre Maitre*.[83]

PARTIAL SUCCESS IN THE NORTH

The years 1718 and 1719 were also crucial in northern affairs.* Naval expenditure in the south in 1718 automatically entailed a diminution in ships available for the Baltic; as early as April of that year it was realized that at most ten ships would be available for the north. To leave Norris free to cooperate with the Danes, a bargain was struck with the Dutch whereby they agreed to convoy British merchantmen as well as their own to the East Baltic ports against a promise to partake in the advantages George expected to gain at the peace-making for British trade in Sweden.[84] This promise was, naturally enough in view of the trade rivalry between the two Maritime Powers, reluctantly given and, as naturally, greatly treasured. The Dutch took care to include it among their conditions for accession to the Quadruple Alliance, and though it passed muster at a time

---

* George had less freedom of action here than in the South since tsar Peter in a personal letter of 5 January 1718 categorically refused the king's appeals for a congress to settle northern problems: the tsar would not enter into any negotiation 'dans un Congrès Publique' (copy in Bernstorff Archive: AG 62).

when Dutch accession seemed highly desirable, George and Stanhope – since the Republic's binding consent came so late in the day – preferred, as we have seen, to drop the question of Dutch participation rather than remain bound to fulfil this promise. Dutch statesmen and the merchant oligarchy of the Republic were incensed: after all, they had kept the bargain made for the Baltic in 1718. But the English counter-argument, that George had in the meantime been at the expense not only of a war with Spain but also of equipping a fleet for the north in 1719 – a year when the Dutch sent not a single warship to the Baltic – had considerable force. It was also a fact that George, as elector, had made his peace with Sweden (a treaty which comprised commercial advantages for his British subjects) before the Republic pronounced itself ready to sign the Quadruple Alliance.[85]

Before this peace of Stockholm of 1719 had been achieved, as the first step in the peace plan for the north, much had happened. As early as February 1718 Fabrice had been sent to Sweden, as suggested by Georg Heinrich von Görtz, so that conferences at Lund (then Charles XII's headquarters) should counterbalance those agreed with the Russians at Lövö in the Åland islands. He was well received and took part in the family reunion of the Swedish king and his close relatives at Kristinehamn between 21 March and 3 April. A Hanoverian accredited diplomat, Schrader, joined him on Charles XII's return to Lund in case agreement should be reached. But it soon became clear that Charles XII was not willing to commit himself either to George or to tsar Peter until he had seen the outcome of the campaign which he planned for the late summer of 1718. That military offensive envisaged an initial attack on Norway, with a later invasion of Denmark and a move thence into Germany, aiming at Hanover in the first place. If it was even partially successful the Swedish king had hopes that Russia would content itself with Ingria, and Hanover with only a small part of Bremen and Verdens

In the meantime, diplomatic negotiations with George and with Peter were diligently pursued, and sincerely meant, to test where the greater advantage for Sweden lay. George, however, was suspicious enough to recall Fabrice in June 1718, confident enough to let Charles XII know that he would not resume the Lund talk. 'as long as Herr von Görtz* continued his Åland conferences', and prudent enough to leave Schrader in Sweden.

Developments certainly favoured George.[86] The Quadruple Alliance was regarded as being in business as soon as Charles VI's acceptance in principle became known in Europe; and the British-mediated peace of Passarowitz (21 July NS 1718) between the

---

* The Russian emissaries had arrived at Lövö in January 1718, but negotiations were not opened till Georg Heinrich von Görtz joined them in May.

emperor and the Turks – very much in favour of the former – further strengthened the king's position. Tsar Peter became worried enough to reinsure with George I, dropping – at least temporarily – his Jacobite contacts and showing greater caution in his negotiations with Alberoni for a 1719 invasion of Britain to promote James Edward Stuart's cause.[87] George, for his part, speedily responded to the Russian overtures by announcing a joint mission of Norris and James Jefferyes to the tsar, though he also continued his negotiations with Augustus II of Saxony-Poland and the emperor to curb Russia if the dreaded Russo-Swedish cooperation should materialize in 1719.[88]

In spreading his net wide, George was not unique. Emissaries arrived in Sweden in 1718 from Prussia, Saxony, from the Polish-Lithuanian Commonwealth and from Augustus' rival for the Polish crown, James Sobieski. This increased Charles XII's confidence that if he could achieve peace with one of his major enemies, the rest would fall into line along the snowball-effect pattern which Louis XIV's separate peace with England had produced between 1711 and 1714.[89] But given the westward direction of the Swedish initial thrust into Norway – and especially the strong detachment which was sent in early September 1718 into the Trondheim district – George was in a dangerous position.[90] From Trondheim Scotland could be threatened, and if Charles XII's main army (which began its move into southern Norway in late October) could be successfully transferred to Denmark in the spring of 1719, Hanover would be within reach of the Swedes.[91]

Yet George's luck held. Charles XII's death put a stop to the wider plans and brought the retreat of Swedish forces from Trondheim. Ironically, Charles had no real business at the siege of Frederiksten fortress (near Frederikshald), where he was hit and killed instantly at night on 11 December NS when visiting the soldiers of his new army in the trenches: he had postponed his own offensive across the river Glommen for a few days while waiting for Georg Heinrich von Görtz to arrive with the latest offers from the Russians.[92] Charles XII's successor, his sister Ulrika Eleonora, while continuing the Åland Island negotiations, was in part predisposed, and in part persuaded by her husband, Friedrich of Hesse, to seek peace with George I. George's real power had been amply demonstrated* and with his help the Russians might be forced to disgorge at least some of their conquests in the East Baltic. Friedrich, the eldest son of the landgrave of Hesse (and thus heir to the landgravate), was German enough in his thinking not to mind Swedish sacrifices in the Empire; and the rivalry for the Swedish succession

---

* In 1717 Byng who, in the absence of a Dutch squadron, convoyed the British merchantmen on his own to the East Baltic, had yet managed by his very presence to drive Swedish privateers – very active both before his arrival and after his departure – into port. In 1718 when Norris's force was perfectly free to cooperate with the Danes, thanks to the Dutch escorting the merchantmen of both nations on their own, Charles XII was obliged to plan his invasion of southern Norway for a time when the British fleet could be expected to have left northern waters: see my *Charles XII*, pp. 463 ff.

between his wife and her nephew, the young duke of Holstein-Gottorp,* made him eager rather than reluctant to gain peace with Denmark-Norway at the expense of the duke.

Here was George and Stanhope's opportunity. At the first hint from Ulrika Eleonora in the spring of 1719 that George's mediation would be welcome, Charles Whitworth – a diplomat experienced from Russian and Prussian missions – was sent to Berlin to wean Friedrich Wilhelm I from his alliance with the tsar; and young Carteret, German-speaking and with a good knowledge of con-tinental – and especially Imperial – affairs, went to Stockholm. No difficulty was expected with Frederik IV of Denmark-Norway: he and George had worked well together and the Danish king had more or less abandoned cooperation with Russia.[93] George's visit to Hanover in the summer and autumn of 1719 greatly facilitated the peace negotiations. The first objective was treaties with Sweden on behalf of Hanover, Denmark-Norway and Prussia which would isolate Russia. The second stage would be to negotiate with the emperor, Augustus of Saxony-Poland, and as many powers as possible, including France, to bring Russia to accept a peace with Sweden which left that state with a decent footing in the East Baltic, and preferably in control of both Riga and Reval. This built in part on the anti-Russian, and anti-Prussian, negotiations which Bernstorff had begun in the summer of 1718 with Augustus and Charles VI, culminating in a Hanoverian alliance with these rulers in January 1719.[94]

There was no desire, except in Sweden, to see tsar Peter excluded from the Baltic. Rather the plan envisaged partitions which would accord with a balance of power in the north: Sweden to recover Finland, Livonia and as much of Estonia as possible, and Russia to keep Karelia, Ingria and part of Estonia. In this way Sweden would lose her monopoly of trade with the East Baltic ports, while Russia would be sufficiently circumscribed not to pose a danger to Poland, Prussia and the Empire.[95]

The first stage of the northern peace plan went well. Carteret was authorized to promise Ulrika Eleonora British naval help against the tsar and, since the Russian galley-fleet was already beginning to ravage the Swedish coasts, he speedily achieved agreement that Bremen and Verden should be ceded to Hanover against a money compensation, and that Sweden's 1700 treaty with Britain should be renewed 'in the light of present conditions', a wording which hinted at the desired commercial concessions. Some influential Swedes were reluctant to sacrifice the Elbe duchies. Others were inclined, in the Charles XII tradition, to demand a detailed clarification of the

---

* Karl Fredrik (b. 1700), son of Charles XII's elder sister Hedvig Sofie (d.1708) and Friedrich IV, duke of Holstein-Gottorp (d. 1702).

'every possible' British help against Russia. Carteret, however, was able to follow his instructions and not tie George down at this stage, since Russian landings close to Stockholm created near-panic in the Swedish capital. Conventions were therefore signed and ratified with both Hanover and Britain before the end of July on Carteret's terms. He was too intelligent not to realize why he had made such speedy progress. 'Our success', he reported, 'is chiefly owing to the Czar, he at the gates of Stockholm has reasoned best for us'.[96] There was no conscious desire to cheat Sweden of the promised help, but Britain's naval resources were stretched in 1719: by the Mediterranean blockade, by the sending of detachments to the West Indies, and by the need to keep ships at home in case Alberoni should support a fresh invasion of Britain after the fiasco of that of March 1719.*

A definite deceit was, however, practised on the Swedes concerning Hanover's support for Prussian gains from Sweden. This is partly explained by George's great difficulty in detaching Friedrich Wilhelm from his Russian alliance. From the Prussian point of view Russia was close and powerful; and George's prevarications in 1715 had not been forgotten. The Prussian king's vacillation, and his insistence that Augustus of Saxony-Poland must not be brought into the peace plan for the north till he had given up his claim to Polish sovereignty over East Prussia, made for greater delays than Bernstorff's opposition to the alliance with Prussia, though there were reasons why Stanhope, in attendance on George in Hanover, and Craggs, his confidant in Whitehall, should emphasize, and even exaggerate, Bernstorff's obstinacy and selfish concern for his 'three villages'.[97] It remains true, however, that Bernstorff's distrust of Prussia was real. Prussia was so close a neighbour to Hanover in both the east and the west, that Bernstorff – in a vision which proved prophetic, if at long range – predicted its conquest of the whole of north Germany. He was therefore reluctant to see the Prussians move further into Pomerania,† even if they kept to the far side of the Peene river. He and Vienna were at one in suggesting that if Prussia were to obtain Pomerania, Friedrich Wilhelm ought to give up those western territories – Magdeburg, Halberstadt and Minden – which it had been granted in 1648 as compensation for the award of Pomerania to Sweden.[98] It was left to George to override Bernstorff and those Hanoverians who sided with him since the peace plan for the north demanded an isolation of Russia as complete as

---

* James Edward Stuart had moved from Rome to Spain; and on 28 March 1719, a Spanish squadron, under Ormonde's command, set out to invade George I's dominions, only to be scattered by a great storm in the Bay of Biscay. The ships not lost returned to Spain; but two frigates with 300 Spaniards on board evaded the British squadron lying in wait for the invasion fleet and made a landfall on the island of Lewis. A ship with Jacobites from France also arrived in Scotland. After the defeat of Glenshiel the Spaniards surrendered and the 1,000 highlanders who had joined them 'melted away'.

† At the peace of Fontainebleau (1679), Brandenburg had received a strip of Swedish Pomerania as its gain from the Dutch War.

possible if it were to succeed. With renewed British and French support for Friedrich Wilhelm's obtaining Pomerania, including Stettin, up to the Peene river, other matters were easily adjusted and the Prussian king showed his gratitude by giving up his claim to suzerainty over the 'Bernstorff villages'.

The problem remained, however, how to induce Sweden to accept the sacrifice of Stettin and the part of Pomerania guaranteed to Friedrich Wilhelm by two treaties signed between Hanover and Prussia and Hanover and Britain on 12 August 1719. Stanhope's solution was to antedate the treaties to 4 August so that George I's commitment, both as king and elector, could be presented in Stockholm as having been made before the arrival of Carteret's news of the Swedish conventions. This 'sharp practice' (to use Stanhope's biographer's term) was not in itself harmful to the Swedes; but the threats to deny them naval help against Russia until they agreed to the land cessions to Prussia demonstrated their utter dependence on Britain as well as the determination and bluntness of the George-Stanhope team. On 29 August a new Anglo-Swedish convention was signed accepting the loss of Bremen, Verden and Stettin with Pomerania east of the Peene river, against British armed help and subsidies to cope with Sweden's remaining enemies and George I's good offices in the final peace negotiations. The French ambassador to Sweden associated the regent with this convention. With the subsidies which France put at Sweden's disposal and the presence of admiral Norris in Swedish waters, the Russian threat was contained for the moment. Treaties were next worked out in detail. That between Sweden and Hanover was signed on 20 November 1719, those between Britain and Sweden and Prussia and Sweden early in 1720. A convention, ending the state of hostilities between Sweden and Augustus of Saxony-Poland, was also signed at this time.[99]

French diplomacy had helped Sweden to retain a foothold in north Germany. Bernstorff's ideas had run on the lines of Sweden's total withdrawal from the Empire, and George and Stanhope had not challenged this as their peace plan for the north envisaged Sweden regaining the major part of her East Baltic provinces. Both bowed, however, to French pressure; and when peace between Sweden and Denmark was negotiated (signed on 3 July 1720) Frederik IV, receiving an Anglo-French guarantee for the Holstein-Gottorp territories he had occupied in Sleswig, returned Pomerania west of the Peene river, with Wismar, Rügen and Stralsund to the Swedes. A money compensation to the Danish king was paid by Ulrika Eleonora from Anglo-French subsidies, and Sweden gave up its exemption from Danish Sound dues as its price for the restoration of the land lost.

To force Russia into the peace plan proved, however, impossible. In 1719 Norris's fleet had been too weak for him to act offensively in concert with the Swedes. In 1720, when he was sent to the Baltic as early as April, the tsar prudently avoided battle. Reconnaissance off the strongly defended ports of the East Baltic convinced the British admiral and his Swedish counterpart that they ought not to risk attacks from the sea unsupported by land armies. Plans discussed at George's court for such attacks (from Livonia and Finland) on the Russian positions to compel tsar Peter to negotiate did not materialize. This was in part due to conflicts within the Empire. There had long been disputes between Charles VI and the Protestant princes of Germany over religious matters and the close cooperation between Hanover and Prussia caused uneasiness at Vienna.[100] More significant was the temporary weakening of George and Stanhope's position by the South Sea bubble bursting during the late summer of 1720 while the court was in Germany. Bernstorff's correspondence shows how closely the ups and downs of the stock market were followed in Hanover. As panic gripped London the demand for George's return grew loud enough to raise the spectre of revolution.[101]

At the same time France was paralyzed by the unrest connected with the crash of Law's system (the Mississippi bubble) in combination with the outbreak of the plague in Marseilles which necessitated the major part of the French army being used as a *cordon sanitaire* to prevent the plague reaching Paris and the north.[102] It was clearly not the time to think of forceful action against Russia, and in October 1720 Sweden was told that she would have to make the best terms she could on her own with Russia: the tsar had ignored George I's offers of mediation and Britain was in no position, at the moment, to exert pressure on him.[103]

Circumstances therefore, rather than bad faith, prevented George and Stanhope from realizing in full the peace plan of the north. There was not time enough, given Sweden's plight, to achieve all that had been hoped for. Indeed, two such large-scale commitments, nearly contemporaneous, as the peace plans for the south and north would seem to have been beyond the resources even of Britain and the George-Stanhope team unless circumstances had been far more favourable than they were in the crowded and confused year 1720 to 1721. The peace plan for the south had required three years of intense negotiations and two naval squadrons to the Mediterranean to bring it to fruition. For the northern plan, stage two – that of forcing Russia, as Spain had been forced, to make concessions – was

never given a chance to develop. One might be tempted to blame
George I's caution – reflected in Norris's lack of dash in the Baltic in
1719 and 1720 – for the failure of stage two. But George had always
been cautious, not willing to act until success was within reasonable
grasp. He was a realist, and by the autumn of 1720 he faced the fact
that stage two could not be accomplished and had to be abandoned.

For George's contemporaries – apart from the Swedes, who by
the peace of Nystad of August 1721 had to give Kexholm, Karelia
and all their former East Baltic provinces to tsar Peter – the success
of stage one was a matter of strong acclaim whereas the non-fulfilment
of stage two counted for less. George was hailed as the man who had
brought to a close the long northern war on terms which served
Hanover and Britain* well and which fitted the balance of power
principle in that Sweden retained a foothold in the Empire, while
Denmark had to be satisfied with far less than she had expected when
Frederik IV forged the anti-Swedish coalition of 1699–1700. The
pacification of the north, even at the cost of Swedish losses to Russia,
was greeted with relief everywhere, even in Sweden: countries could
now turn to peaceful pursuits and the Baltic would be free for the
commerce of all nations. After twenty-one years of war, that seemed
a real watershed. In historical perspective, however, it must be
admitted that the combination of George's Hanoverian needs and
his fortuitous accession to the British throne in 1714 had contributed
greatly to that strengthening of the Russian position which removed
stage two of the peace plan for the north from the realms of the
possible.

SHIFTS OF EMPHASIS

The work on the peace plan for the north, stage one and stage two,
brought a shift in George I's relationship to his British and Hanoverian ministers decisive for the second half of his reign as king. Already
in the spring of 1718 Schulenburg had noted that the English
ministers liked to keep Bernstorff and Bothmer outside 'secret
matters'; the German ministers retaliated to some extent by 'seeking
refuge' with Melusine and by keeping Empire matters in their own
hands.[104] Thus Stanhope was not fully informed of the anti-Prussian
and anti-Russian stance of the alliance signed by George as elector
on 5 January (NS) 1719 with Charles VI and Augustus of Saxony-
Poland. The treaty had beneficial effects in loosening Friedrich
Wilhelm's attachment to and dependence on tsar Peter and thus
facilitating the withdrawal of Russian troops from Mecklenburg;
but it left distrust in Whitehall at Bernstorff's independence. The

---

* The only concession Sweden received was the return of Finland and the right to import
a given annual quantity of corn from Livonia, its former granary.

differences should not be exaggerated; British and Hanoverian ministers cooperated, as we have seen, in the peace plan for the south and reached agreement on the peace plan for the north. George did, however, increasingly take a wider view than Bernstorff of European affairs. It was natural for Stanhope and Sunderland – both of whom accompanied George I to Hanover in 1719 – to exaggerate their victory over Bernstorff;[105] but a change undeniably made itself felt in George's calculations between 1718 and 1720. The emperor and the quest for the investitures of Bremen and Verden seemed less important: 'we shall', the king-elector wrote on one occasion, 'be able to maintain our possession of those duchies whether the emperor grants the investitures or not.'[106] The French alliance had become a cornerstone of George's policy in the south as in the north; the emperor, it was argued by his British ministers, had sufficient need of Britain's support to learn to live with that fact.[107] And if Bernstorff's 'disgrace' was less complete than is usually asserted, there is proof that the German ministers after 1719 felt that their advice was less sought than formerly. Bothmer, in a letter to Bernstorff in 1724, complains that he and his London colleagues are not even consulted by the king on German [i.e. Empire] affairs.[108] The explanation lies in the fact that George had come by stages to find the specifically German outlook restrictive. He had been transformed from an elector of Hanover into a king of Great Britain who, though his keenest pleasure was still found in the scenes, sounds and scents of his electorate, neither could nor would look at European affairs except as seen from Great Britain. The change was unmistakable to those of his entourage who still felt more German than British.

The large measure of success for the peace plans had important repercussions also in British circles. Before George set out for Hanover in 1719 the prince of Wales, to judge from hints in the Schulenburg correspondence, had made certain moves to obtain the regency, but had been disappointed since the king chose to revive the system of lord justices, as in the interim period between the death of Anne and the arrival of George in 1714.[109] No doubt this was a salutary lesson. It followed closely upon the Stanhope ministry's success in the 1718–19 session in removing at least some of the disabilities on the religious dissenters in spite of the opposition of the prince, Townshend and Walpole. Argyll and his brother, who with their Scottish background sympathized with the repeal of the Occasional Conformity and Schism Acts, had helped the ministry and were rewarded, Argyll being made lord steward of the king's household in February 1719. That he accepted gave food for thought both to the prince and to the Walpolian Whigs. Sunderland's appointment – so long desired – as groom of the stole to George was another indication of the growing influence of the British ministers and a pointer to what honours the faithful could expect.

The score was to some extent evened in December 1719 when Walpole, in the most brilliant speech of his career, defeated the peerage bill introduced by the Stanhope-Sunderland ministry. This bill aimed at limiting the English peerage to the current number of families: once six more new peers had been created, a new title could be bestowed only when a vacancy occurred through the extinction of a title. At the same time it was intended that the sixteen Scotch representative peers should be replaced by twenty-five hereditary peers. The peerage bill – first attempted in 1718 but withdrawn before it reached the House of Commons – was a form of reinsurance against the ministry's losing power on George I's death. The king's ill-health in 1718, which so worried the Hanoverian courtiers, seems to have been noticed by his British ministers as well; and Sunderland in particular hoped to clip Georg August's wings in the event of a speedy succession. If the new king could not re-ward his followers, he might feel obliged to continue his father's ministers in office; at the very least he would be prevented from swamping the House of Lords with new creations to force through impeachment proceedings against Sunderland and his colleagues. George is depicted in English historiography as being heart and soul for the peerage bill, either because he wanted to revenge himself on his son or because he wished to make the nobility more exclusive. In reality he seems to have embraced the bill reluctantly, as the price he had to pay to keep his ministry content and to further the 'Whig' proposals for toleration and university reform which were meant to entice the Commons into acceptance of the peerage bill. Schulen-burg certainly regarded himself as bold, and George as forgiving, when the king did not take umbrage at his confession that he – if he had been of the English nobility – would have voted in favour of not cheapening aristocratic privileges by spreading them too widely.[110] Neither were George's Hanoverian ministers in London in favour of the peerage bill, since they realized that it would limit the king's power; and Bernstorff and Bothmer were accused by Sunderland and his supporters of having worked secretly against the bill. The bill initially brought the prince and princess of Wales to near panic, but they soon resolved to do all in their power to bring about its downfall.[111] The reintroduction of the bill in the 1719–20 session was widely interpreted as an anti-German move since the 'closed ranks' would make the ministry independent not only of the

prince of Wales but of George I's non-British advisers, and possibly
– so it was rumoured – of the king himself: a closed aristocracy
would be able to give laws to the king and his son, and 'even to
remove him [the king] when they shall think proper'.[112]

The ministry's defeat naturally raised Walpole's standing with the
court; but unless Townshend and Walpole had been sufficiently
impressed with the peacemakings of 1719–20 – north and south –
they might not have been tempted back. After all, in 1718 George
had twice approached Walpole secretly; once through a confidant
of Melusine's, the second time through a general (unnamed in the
source of our information) who can confidently be identified as
major-general von Hammerstein since there was no other general
so much in George's confidence, and it is known from the Schulenburg letters that Hammerstein and Walpole were well acquainted.[113]
We sorely miss Schulenburg's account of the 1720 reconciliation,
but he had died suddenly in January of that year.[114] From Bothmer
and Bernstorff's correspondence we find that they are congratulated
on helping to heal the breach in the Whig ranks, but – since their
correspondents are Germans – the emphasis naturally tends
to be on their services towards restoring the unity within the royal
family.[115] Professor Plumb's theory that Walpole and Townshend, by publicizing a letter addressed to the Imperial vice-chancel-
lor, purporting to be by Bernstorff, managed to scare Stanhope
and Sunderland sufficiently to make them willing to share power
is intriguing and plausible: Walpole and Townshend, so runs the
argument, gave notice of their willingness to outbid Sunderland
and Stanhope by obtaining huge sums from parliament which would
permit George to buy territories in Germany, 'which would enable
him to hold the balance between the Northern Powers better than
by sending a fleet yearly to the Baltic which gives umbrage to
the people'.[116] While the letter does not read as if written by Bernstorff, the Hanoverian minister may well have acquiesced in any
ruse to reunite the king and the prince of Wales, especially in
view of his close friendship with the Cowpers.[117] Another hypothesis, that the reconciliation was dictated by a joint interest of the
divided courts and the 'split' Whigs in the burgeoning South Sea
bubble – promoted in late 1719 and early 1720 – is less convincing:
no valid reason is given why the ministers in power should be willing
to readmit Walpole and Townshend at a time when great financial
benefits were expected, nor why Walpole and Townshend should
feel compelled to reconcile Georg August, the governor of the South
Sea Company until the election of 1718 (when the king replaced
him), with his father.[118] In my judgment, the fact that early in 1720

the balance of power was relatively even as between the Whigs in and out of office promoted that reconciliation of the two courts which by now both desired. Walpole had shown that he could baulk Sunderland's most cherished measure; Stanhope had demonstrated that his foreign policy solutions worked. Money was certainly hinted at during the negotiations which brought Walpole and Townshend back. If returned to office, it was understood that they would both facilitate paying off the accumulated debt of the civil list, now standing at £600,000.

George was his cautious self. Services to the king would have to come before rewards. On 23 April, as recounted above, the prince of Wales made his submission. The next day the Walpolian Whigs did the same. On 4 May a cleverly worded address in George's name suggested that the debts of the civil list might be paid, without the British people being burdened by 'any new aid or supply', if the House of Commons would permit George to issue letters patent to two insurance companies willing to pay handsomely for the privilege of insuring ships and merchandise. Care was taken to add that the king had received many petitions from merchants stressing the benefit they would derive from the insurance companies.[119] Walpole skilfully steered the bill for paying off the civil list debt in this manner through the House. On 11 June he was made paymaster-general with the promise that he should move to the treasury at the first suitable opportunity. Townshend was made lord president of the council in place of the duke of Kingston, who – with Argyll – was sacrificed to satisfy the prince of Wales's desire for revenge on those who had either deserted him or criticized him.

The 'harmony and unity' of George I's 1720 ministry may have been more apparent than real; but all members had learnt that a king's party, in the sense in which George interpreted it, was necessary for keeping the king's confidence. At the same time George had passed an important milestone in his reign; his British ministers, both those in office between 1718 and 1720 and those who 'came into the king's measures' in 1720, had convinced him that they would no longer tolerate Hanoverians as the king's advisers in any matter that touched on British interests. With peace restored in the north and Hanoverian objectives thus secured, it was natural that George's role as king of Great Britain should begin to count more than his position as elector of Hanover. The second stage of his reign had commenced, the one in which it became natural for him to read memoranda written in English and even put his comments on them in the language of his kingdom.

IX

Peace, its problems and achievements

THE SOUTH SEA BUBBLE

The concern expressed in the king's address in 1720 for the mercantile prospects of Britain was not feigned. Nor was that for the general economic welfare and prosperity of the country written into his speech for the opening of the 1719 parliamentary session, though its phraseology was in the grand manner: 'All I have to ask of you is, that you would agree to be a great and flourishing people, since it is the only means by which I desire to become a happy King'.[1] It was the ministry, then as now, which fashioned the king's speech and it has usually been assumed that George was uninterested in trade, industry and kindred matters.[2] It is therefore with something of a shock that one finds Townshend in 1723 urging Robert Walpole in a private letter 'to form a good scheme for the next session, by falling on some new Expedients for the Ease of the Nation, and the benefit of Trade and Credit which points His Majesty has so much at heart, that the succeeding in them will infallibly rivet us in his esteem'.[3]

It would be a mistake to deduce that George I was the initiator of plans for economic and commercial advancement and financial reform, but he was undoubtedly on the lookout for, and keen to encourage, measures in that direction. He was conversant with the details of economic and financial administration from Hanover and more alive than most of his German subjects to the possibilities arising from the Bremen and Verden acquisitions. The port of Harburg, inherited from his uncle, the duke of Celle, could now be encouraged without fear of stronger competitors; and with British collaborators George I helped to promote companies to dredge and improve the harbour, to build canals connecting the town with its German hinterland so that its trade might increase.[4]

In Britain he had taken a keen interest in the redemption scheme which Walpole had worked out, on Dutch and Venetian models,

during the spring and summer of 1716 to reduce the proportion of
the nation's annual income spent on servicing the national debt. At
George's accession that debt stood at £54 million as against £1
million in 1688; and since most of it had been taken up during the
War of the Spanish Succession, when interest rates were as high as
7 and even 9 per cent, the servicing of it consumed £3 million out
of an annual budget of some £10 million. Walpole supported a
redemption scheme (largely worked out by himself) even after he
had left the ministry, and in 1717 three acts of parliament carried
the reform into effect: a new loan was taken up at a uniform interest
of 5 per cent, old stock was forcibly redeemed, and from the resulting
savings a sinking fund was established for the gradual paying off of
the national debt.[5] The rapid over-subscription of the new loan is
evidence of the confidence of the propertied classes in the Hanoverian
regime after the Fifteen, and money continued to be cheap throughout George I's reign. A further conversion, to reduce the interest rate
from 5 to 4 per cent by 1727, was planned by the South Sea Act of
1 February 1720, but this time under circumstances and on conditions which led to speculation and to a spectacular crash within
half a year. Unsettled conditions followed which seriously hampered
government initiatives, particularly abroad, between the autumn
of 1720 and the spring of 1722, but – as modern commentators have
pointed out – wealth was not destroyed though it was redistributed.[6]

It would be difficult to explain the South Sea bubble without
taking into account the British addiction to betting and gambling
(strong enough to astonish their contemporaries on the continent
where gambling tended to be confined to card-playing), on horse-
racing, on cockfights, on the date at which a besieged town would
surrender, on incidents in people's personal lives, as well as on affairs
of state.

The English gambling mania was reinforced by the speculation
which started in France in 1718 in the shares of Law's Mississippi
company. Englishmen, Scots and Dutchmen flocked to Paris, or used
intermediaries to buy shares; indeed, the flow of capital out of
England was large enough to make George I's ministry look with
favour on the South Sea company's initiative.[7] This west-European
fever of speculation between 1718 and 1720 must be seen against the
backcloth of a near mythological belief in the inexhaustible riches of
Spanish America. Ever since Columbus's voyages pearls, gold and
silver had become synonymous with Spain's colonial possessions. This
myth gave an edge both to the late sixteenth- and early seventeenth-
century buccaneering ventures and to the late seventeenth- and early
eighteenth-century competition for entry into the South Sea trade:

indirectly through Spanish middlemen in Seville; directly by concessions, such as the contracts to import slaves; illegally by the
smuggling trade carried on with the connivance of Spanish subjects
overseas, who preferred its benefits to the monopoly of the mother-
land and therefore hindered the efforts of the Spanish authorities to
stamp it out.[8]

The very name of the South Sea Company proved irresistible to
those not well informed; and even to men of experience the circumstances of 1720 seemed promising. The gold mines of Brazil had not
been discovered and exploited till the first years of the eighteenth
century, and one-third of their output had found its way into Britain
during the War of the Spanish Succession.[9] Philip V had given commercial concessions to Britain in 1715 and 1716, and it is not surprising
that after his accession to the Quadruple Alliance early in 1720,
rumours should have spread that he was about to cede to the Company
lands rich in gold and silver.[10] After all, the Company had been
founded in 1711 in anticipation of the slave *asiento* stipulated for
Britain in the secret Anglo-French peace terms of that year.

The gains of the slave trade, even when taking into account the
semi-legal smuggling trade in British manufactured goods which
sheltered under the umbrella of the 'annual ship', had not come up to
highly pitched expectations. Yet hope sprang eternal where the
South Seas were concerned.[11] Had not Britain just won a war with
Spain and been at the expense of sending two fleets to the Mediterranean? Surely rewards must follow for the victory off Cape Passaro
in 1718 and for Byng's evacuation of Vigo (captured in 1719) on
Spain's signature of the peace plan?

It should not be forgotten, as many of the less informed speculators
forgot, that the South Sea Company was from its very formation in
1711 a finance company. It was the brainchild of lord Oxford who,
to counterbalance the Whig-dominated Bank of England, had
brought holders of the unfunded government debt – then standing at
£9 million – to exchange their securities for stock in the Company at
par. By the time of George I's accession the Company was firmly
established as one of the three pillars, with the Bank of England and
the East India Company, of the credit structure of Britain. It chafed,
however, under the Bank's continued predominance, and some of its
directors became tempted to take large risks to emulate the success of
the French Mississippi Company. It offered to take over that part of
the national debt (some £31 million) not held by its two sister
institutions and, in a tussle with the Bank between November 1719
and February 1720, secured the ministry's full support for its plans in
the House of Lords and in the Commons.

The government saw several advantages ahead. First, the conversion into South Sea Company stock would be voluntary and would therefore not invite criticism: no bond or annuity holder would be forced to convert. Second, the issue of South Sea Company stock would give scope for profitable investment at home and, it was hoped, stop the drain of money to France. Thirdly, the country would benefit by the Company's willingness to accept a uniform rate of interest of 5 per cent, less than the average interest paid hitherto, and this rate was to be further reduced by 1727 to 4 per cent. Finally, in its effort to outbid the Bank, the Company had raised its cash offer for the privileges it wanted from £3½ million to £7½ million. Optimism was in the air. Aislabie, the chancellor of the exchequer, assured the House of Commons that the deal was profitable enough to enable Britain to pay off its national debt within twenty-five years.

There were, however, several flaws in this reckoning. The Company had been empowered to issue £1 of new stock for every £1 of debt it took over, and it had been generally expected that new stock would not be issued till conversion had taken place. But the Company had not named (as had the Bank in its rejected offer) the ratio of stock to be paid for bonds and annuities on conversion. This loophole was deliberate and must have been connived at by at least some of George I's ministers, certainly by Aislabie. It was quickly exploited, as was the ambiguity of the act of 1 February which permitted the Company to 'open books or subscriptions' when it should 'think fit'. The government's loan to the Company of £1 million of exchequer bills – again procured by ministerial support – was also put to good use. Promotion techniques of various kinds were employed: payment by instalments for new stock, subscription for which was opened on 14 April 1720; loans – financed from the government loan to the Company – for subscribers; generous terms for conversion which were whittled down as soon as demand for the new stock rose. Fortuitous events, especially Law's heavy forward buying of South Sea shares early in April on the Amsterdam *bourse*, had helped to drive up the price of old stock. Shrewd operators made good profits from this, notably Thomas Guy of hospital fame (since with his gains he founded the London hospital that bears his name) and Robert Walpole who bought land. The Company was also helped in that such profits whetted public appetite for the new stock: soon bond and annuity holders – who had been wooed with offers of 375 when the market rate stood at 400 – were pleased to take less scrip than they were entitled to. The Company thus amassed a surplus for sale in the open market; but more significant was their – again deliberate – covert expansion of the agreed £2 million new stock by £250,000.[12]

The first subscription was immediately filled. Even a cautious man like Sir John Evelyn was sufficiently carried away to sell land to buy shares, arranging a private loan to pay cash at South Sea House and remaining on tenterhooks until the money realized from his Deptford estate had come through.[13] By the end of June, South Sea stock stood at 1050 and people were still clamouring for shares for the third and fourth subscriptions, using every ounce of influence they possessed to be put on the lists for new subscribers.[14] Indeed, many who had held aloof from the earlier issues were increasingly tempted to invest in the later ones.[15]

It is clear, from the subsequent investigation by a House of Commons committee and from historians' examination of private records, that ministers and members of parliament were bribed by being given new stock without payment but with full liberty to sell their shares back to the Company whenever they wanted and thus make an easy 'profit'. Many did so, but more held on to their shares and were eventually losers, if only in a technical sense. Of George's ministers Sunderland was rewarded with a notional £50,000 worth of stock which would enable him to realize £500 for every point the stock rose above 175; Craggs, the postmaster general, with £30,000 at the same rate, stood to gain £300 for every point; while Aislabie himself secured £20,000 with the right to collect £200 for every point above 130. Charles Stanhope, secretary of the treasury, received an even larger reward since, apart from a notional £50,000 worth of stock, on which he was to have £500 for every point above 250 and a further £100 for ever point above 270, another £10,000-worth was also transferred to him.[16]

In George's family the duchess of Kendal was given a notional £15,000 on which £120 would be paid for every point above £154; her two younger 'nieces' were given a notional £5,000 each; and the countess of Darlington received the same amount on the same terms as the duchess of Kendal.[17] It has been suggested that the prince and princess of Wales were bribed with a large amount of shares to enter into the reconciliation with George, but no proof of this has ever been put forward.[18] Suspicions that George I, elected governor of the Company by the court of directors in February 1718 in succession to his son, received a bribe from the Company can now be disproved. The royal archives at Windsor contain receipts for all his dealings, including payment of £20,000 for a first instalment 'in the name of Joseph Safford for Our Use', the king having arranged a subscription of £100,000 via Craggs and Aislabie.[19] The general belief that George I made a killing, selling out in mid-June for £106,400, is mistaken. Indeed, the records show that while he sold at the figure mentioned, he did so to find cash to finance later instalments. He was, with great difficulty, dissuaded from putting the whole sum into old South Sea stock and new subscriptions. Aislabie, who arranged the selling, warned the king that the stock, 'carried up to an exorbitant height by the madness of people', was bound to fall, and advised investment in land tax tallies. George, Aislabie later recalled, 'was pleased to tell me I had the character of a timorous man', and was optimistic enough to believe that the stock might well go to 1500 – as had the Mississippi Company shares. The king finally agreed to a compromise between tallies, the third subscription and old South Sea stock: after George's departure for Hanover the chancellor bought tallies for £35,950, put £25,000 into the third subscription and £45,450 into old stock, an arrangement sanctioned by his master.[20]

Both George and the duchess of Kendal assumed, however, that they had made an arrangement with Aislabie that he should realize their South Sea stock at the earliest favourable opportunity. George never blamed Aislabie directly, but the duchess of Kendal was fairly outspoken on her own and the king's behalf. Why, she demanded in a letter to the chancellor from Herrenhausen of 27 September NS, had he asked for further orders in his letter to her of 18 August OS? It was not at all necessary as she and 'the Person whose money is committed to Your Care' had left it to his judgment 'to sell or buy as you would think it the most profitable and convenient'. Given the distance between Hanover and London and the alterations that might occur at any moment in the market, she told him on the king's behalf that 'if the best occasion is missed you will be pleased to make use of those that shall offer themselves for the future without expecting any new advices'. She continued on her own account,

I and my two nieces give you many thanks for what you have been pleased to subscribe and pay on our account at the third subscription. If we had been present in England, we would not have failed to sell them out, when they were at such an advantageous Price, and I wish you had been so kind as to do it for us, the more when you judged and saw they was [sic] not to rise but fall as they have done. I am sorry our Absence made us miss that good Opportunity; and I hope you will be so kind as to take a little Care of our Interest if it is not to[o] great a disadvantage in your other Affairs.[21]

By the time this letter arrived in England (29 September OS according to Aislabie's memorandum), the price of stock had fallen to 300; and he found the confusion so great, the situation so difficult and uncertain, and 'the eyes of all people' so intent upon himself that he judged he could not dispose of the stock 'without increasing the public clamour upon myself, or without prejudice to the king's affairs'. He therefore left George's holdings, as well as those of Melusine and her 'nieces', unsold. Towards the end of his life, when he composed the memorandum referred to above, he tried to make out that a profit of £45,304 had been made for the king. He had paid the 'produce of the land tax tallies' soon after George I's return and here a small loss had been sustained (£392 to be exact). The loss on the £6,000 South Sea stock bought at £45,450 was far more severe: when the stock was sold in February 1722 'with all the dividends upon it', only £9,746 was realized. As for the £25,000 paid into the third subscription, he 'believed it was turned into [new] stock for the king's use', and hazarded a guess that 'if it remains there yet' – that is, in 1742 – it would be worth, with its dividends since 1720, £39,000. He thus contrived to show 'a gain upon the whole transaction of £45,304'. This is, however, misleading – to say the least. Seen from George I's point of view in 1722, he had (as Aislabie realized) suffered a loss of £35,704.[22] George, however, put a brave face on it: after all, the credit of Britain was at stake in a period of European speculation. He remained governor of the Company and gave support to the rescue operation. Melusine did the same. When relatives commiserated with her on her losses, she let them know that she and her 'nieces' had made a reasonable profit and were 'well content', though they had at one time feared 'to lose all'.[23]

Whether George's Hanoverian ministers received bribes of the kind that several British ministers and members of parliament had accepted from the South Sea Company cannot be ascertained with certainty. It was generally believed at the time, but no proof has come to light.[24] On the whole it seems unlikely. They were not in favour with Sunderland and had no influence in Parliament. In his will Robethon gave his losses in the South Sea bubble as a reason for his bequests to relatives being smaller than he had expected.[25] Bernstorff's correspondence from Hanover in 1720 with his London banker, Paul de la Tour, with Bothmer and with the Mecklenburg nobleman in exile, von Plessen, shows a paid-up first subscription, a desire to increase his stake and a close interest in the market. It is worth noting, since Bernstorff kept the Hanoverian court informed, that de la Tour continued optimistic long after the stock had begun to fall from its June peak. The fluctuations of August – when the rate varied between 940 and 900 – were assumed to be a passing phase even after news had come from Paris of the panic there and the plight of Law whose windows were broken if he stayed at home and whose carriage was stoned if he ventured into the streets.[26] De la Tour prided himself on having used Bernstorff's position as 'Premier Ministre d'Estat de Sa Majesté à Hanovre' to obtain £1,000 worth of stock in the third and fourth subscriptions, though the Company had ruled that £200 would be the highest allocation 'a ce qui se soit'. A newsletter (in French), dated London 9/20 September, reported a general meeting of the Company at which the directors had been received with applause and addresses of thanks for their 'sage administration'.[27]

From that date onwards, however, all correspondents proved dismal and worried. Rumours that George had sold out when the price had been at its highest were used by 'the ill-intentioned' in Britain to insinuate (falsely, as we have seen) that the king had no confidence in the Company. Agitation and cabals were the order of the day. Confusion reigned after the bankruptcy of the Sword Blade Company, closely connected with the South Sea Company. By 29 September OS South Sea stock had sunk to 190, and de la Tour – who had hitherto followed Bernstorff's instructions 'to the letter' – took fright and began to use his own discretion to save what he could.[28] On 4/15 October Bothmer sounded the alarm, conveying the 'extreme impatience' of the British ministers for the king's return: that alone would 'give them heart' to carry on, any delay would 'cause despair'. For his own part Bothmer added the following warning: 'Nous ne serons pas loin d'une révolte. Croyez moy que je n'exagère rien, on parle deja de son [the king's] absence avec une extreme liberté.'[29]

The panic-like fear of revolution in London had some effect on George and Stanhope, though both were preoccupied with foreign policy issues of importance. 'Give us a week to settle the most urgent matters', was the gist of their appeals to London. In the event, contrary winds delayed them on the Dutch coast, but they reached London in mid-November: much earlier than was George's habit on his Hanover visits.[30] Bernstorff planned to follow six months later. This probably had something to do with his disappointment that George had taken Stanhope's advice on the need for an Anglo-Hanoverian-Prussian alliance, but to countess Cowper he wrote that he had 'no heart' to return to London where everybody was miserable because of the South Sea crash. He may also have feared popular agitation against George's Hanoverian ministers even if he had nothing to hide. One of Plessen's letters to him of 17/28 March 1721 reports a debate in the House of Lords in which 'Bernstorff and Bothmer', as well as *les Dames* of George's court, had been openly accused of having received bribes from the Company. The ladies had been saved by lord Guilford who argued that, at all times, 'les Dames avoient este en droit de recevoir de pareilles faveurs'; but he had added, ominously for the king's German advisers, 'mais qu'il s'agis de savoir, si les Ministres, Monsieur Bernstorff et Monsieur Bothmer, y avoient'.[31]

George and Robert Walpole rode out the storm. Neither had been prescient on the dangers inherent in the Company's plans and procedures, but both were calm and determined to the point of ruthlessness to save what could be saved. A select committee, highly critical of the ministry, carried on its inquiry into the Company's affairs to determine the degree of guilt of directors and ministers; but George took care to rob it of the witness it clamoured loudest to cross-examine. Robert Knight, the cashier of the Company, had fled abroad, first to the Austrian Netherlands and then to Paris. Through diplomatic channels the king let prince Eugène know that he would be obliged if the privileges of the province of Brabant would be upheld so that Knight should not be extradited;[32] via the duchess of Kendal the regent was informed of George's 'personal wish' that he should ignore the British ambassador's request for Knight's forcible return to London.[33]

These were, however, dismal days for George. In February death removed his two best experts on foreign affairs: James Stanhope on 5 February, the younger Craggs on 16 February. Craggs died of smallpox; but James Stanhope's cerebral haemorrhage was generally held to be caused by a particularly trying sitting of the House of Lords during the investigation of links between the Company and ministers.[34] At the end of the debate Stanhope lost his temper at a jibe of Wharton's, answered in kind, and fell fainting to the ground.* He himself had clean hands, but he was much concerned for his favourite cousin, Charles Stanhope. The knowledge that the South Sea crash had adversely affected Great Britain's position as Europe's peacemaker also weighed upon him. He had made all arrangements to attend the congress of Cambrai, where he confidently expected the peace treaty between Charles VI and Philip V to be signed, and fretted at the domestic crisis which necessitated postponement of the opening of the congress.[35] Even worse, the northern peace plan might well be jeopardized if the crisis proved of long duration.

George's grief at Stanhope's death is well documented. The king could neither sleep nor eat. He visited lady Stanhope and 'assured her that next to her, he was the person who had suffered the greatest loss in being deprived of a good servant and good friend, that there was nothing she could ask he would not do for her and her children'. A pension of £3,000 a year was immediately awarded her.[36] Sentiment probably influenced George's active participation to ensure that Charles Stanhope was acquitted. He asked several members of the House of Commons as a personal favour to him to abstain in the

---

* Wharton's comparison of Stanhope to Sejanus slyly put the blame on the secretary of state for the late quarrel in the royal family. Stanhope's retort was more direct: if Wharton's father had been alive he would – like Brutus – have felt compelled to kill so unworthy a son.

vote whether James's cousin was guilty or not – the only occasion I have come across when George took so drastic a step.[37] Charles Stanhope's guilt was, however, sufficiently well known to make his resignation from the treasury imperative. The saving of Sunderland was essential for the depleted government. He had been fiercely attacked in the House of Lords as in the House of Commons. Plessen wrote Bernstorff that he did not dare to give him the details of the Lords' accusations beyond Sunderland being regarded as the 'promoteur et encourageur' of the later South Sea subscriptions.[38] With Robert Walpole's help Sunderland was acquitted. He retained his groomship of the stole, but resigned his first commissionership of the treasury. Aislabie was found guilty of 'the most notorious, infamous and dangerous corruption', and was – like several members of the House of Commons who had accepted South Sea stock without payment – expelled from the House. The elder Craggs committed suicide, realizing that he would also have been found guilty.

By the end of March the worst was over. Walpole's motion (suggested by his banker Robert Jacombe), which envisaged the breaking up of the South Sea Company capital so that parts of it could be engrafted into the Bank of England and the East India Company, did not pass the House of Commons;[39] but by August 1721 credit had revived and South Sea stock rose to 400. Though investors long cursed the bubble, bemoaned their losses and pointed out to their children – as Sir John Evelyn did – South Sea House 'so fatal to the nation',[40] before the end of George's reign the trading of the Company – in northern whaling as well as in the southern seas – had improved and South Sea House was admired as one of the finest buildings in London.

GEORGE, A CAPTIVE OF HIS MINISTERS?*

Sunderland's sudden death in April 1722 weakened the balancing factor within the ministry and pushed the Townshend-Walpole group into prominence. As far as domestic policies were concerned, the firm was now Walpole and Townshend rather than Townshend and Walpole, thanks to the success of the former's post-bubble rescue operation of 1721. The head of the firm even impinged on foreign policy issues because of his close watch over Jacobite conspiracies. His was the leading part in unveiling the Atterbury plot of 1722 in favour of James Edward Stuart and in fighting the battle to deprive the popular and brilliantly wily bishop of Rochester of his clerical offices and secure his banishment. Proof of treason was hard to come by, but the main outlines of the plan to take power in the name of

---

* The idea that George was a captive of his ministers has arisen because of a comment by Palm, the Imperial diplomat, who on 17 December 1726 wrote of the king as 'captivated and besieged by his English ministers' (Coxe, *Robert Walpole*, p. 509). Historians have failed to take into account, however, the element of self-justification of Palm's despatches in a period of tense relations between the Hofburg and Whitehall.

James III were pieced together from a variety of evidence (information sent from Dubois, hints in diplomatic despatches, an anonymous letter to the duchess of Kendal): George I, who had planned to go to Hanover, was to be murdered on his way there, the British ministers were to be arrested and held in the Tower while the Jacobites seized control of the Bank and the Royal Exchange. It is easy to ridicule Walpole's obsession with the threat of Jacobitism. We know that he was not above using it, or planning to use it, when it suited the ministry, but in the Atterbury affair the Stuart papers now available have proved him right in all but one surmise – the plot did not have Spanish support.[41] That he overreacted is possible. It was sensible to persuade George to postpone his Hanover visit till the following year and a wise precaution to bring the Guards regiments to London, encamping them in Hyde Park; but when the autumn session of parliament opened in October 1722 Walpole had Habeas Corpus suspended for a whole year and put a heavy fine (£10,000) on Roman Catholics with the explanation – in answer to the Catholic powers' protest at the severity of his measures – that this was to pay for the heavy expense which their support (tacit or open, or assumed even if non-existent) of James Edward Stuart had brought in its train. At the end of the day only one conspirator was executed (Layer, Atterbury's secretary) and two imprisoned for life; and Walpole's spying activities on Atterbury in exile, though deemed excessive, seem justified in view of what we now know from the Caesar correspondence of Jacobite plots between 1725 and 1727.[42] Yet it cannot be denied that Walpole made use of these plots to further his own ambitions. He took care that he alone should put 'Jacobite intelligence' before the king – thus appearing as a zealous supporter of the house of Hanover – while simultaneously attempting to isolate George by ousting the remnants of the Stanhope-Sunderland group from office. He skilfully infiltrated his own nominees into vacant posts, and aimed high in that he worked to effect the removal of Townshend's co-secretary of state, Carteret. Townshend shared Walpole's objectives, though he counselled subtlety, patience and concealment of joy at each success on the road to their common goal. Both were delighted when certain foreign policy issues* played into their hands and Carteret, as a consequence, was removed from his secretaryship to become lord lieutenant of Ireland: by the autumn of 1724 they felt safe against all British and Hanoverian rivals.

Yet what George I valued in Walpole more than his spy nets and his intrigues was his work for British prosperity and the necessary reforms which the minister planned and executed between 1721 and 1725. Home industries were protected against foreign competition

* Connected with the 'de Vrillière affair'.

and bounties were paid on a variety of exports, such as grain and spirits, sailcloth and refined sugar. The complex tariff system was brought up to date and duties were taken off export articles and imports of raw materials needed for British manufactures – for instance, raw silk, undressed flax and dyes. The land tax was reduced from 3s to 2s in the £ and the tax burden spread more fairly by emphasis on indirect taxation which, by the bonded warehouse system, did not hamper the British re-export of goods transported to Britain from overseas: the British consumption of tea, coffee, cacao and chocolate was taxed, but the same commodities escaped tax when re-exported to the continent. To make British exports competitive, wages were regulated by local justices of the peace and workmen were forbidden to 'combine' for the purpose of withholding their labour in an attempt to push up wages. Protection was enforced not only against foreign competition, but against competition from Britain's colonies (a well-known example is the prohibition against the manufacture of beaver hats in North America) and from Ireland. The role of the colonies was defined as the producers of raw materials, such as ginger and tobacco, masts and other naval stores, since the government hoped to free itself from too strong a dependence on the Baltic for the latter.[43]

In this there was nothing particularly new. What appealed to George was the sensible, systematic and rational way Walpole proceeded and the control which he had over the House of Commons. No doubt Walpole's task was made easier by the peace-time conditions after 1721. There might be investigations into what the Baltic squadrons had cost Britain between 1715 and 1721, but after the peace of Nystad between Sweden and Russia this was to some extent a closed chapter, and Norris's 1724 expedition to the Baltic – to keep an eye on tsar Peter – was one of which the vast majority of the House of Commons approved.[44] There were a variety of European issues which preoccupied George I and the two secretaries of state, but none of these played a significant role in the relationship between George and Walpole. This made for a placid, but fruitful, cooperation, removed from the tension and atmosphere of crisis which was so often the lot of the king and those of his advisers whose main field of activity was foreign policy. The king was happy to trust Walpole with the management of the House of Commons and with some patronage, though he kept an eye on what went on even in the field of minor office.[45] Because domestic affairs loomed largest in the interests of Walpole's countrymen in the post-1722 years, Walpole was thought of as the first minister and the nickname 'The Great Man' – used by friends and foes alike but with different intonation – began to be applied to him during the last years of George I's reign.

The element of specific satire, not only in *Gulliver's Travels* but even in John Gay's *The Beggar's Opera*, can easily be exaggerated. When Swift came to London in 1726 to see his book through the press he was one of the summer-party (along with Gay and Arbuthnot) at Bolingbroke's house in Dawlish that was planning a new journal (*The Craftsman*) to attack Walpole. But when his book was published, his friends assured him that the politicians, 'to a man', agreed that it was 'free from particular reflections': no 'considerable person was angry'.[46] Rereading *Gulliver's Travels* in search of comments on Walpole or George, the historian is forced to the conclusion that it is a general commentary on life in the states and societies of the time and that later editorial comments have provided more references to contemporary figures than are really there. Gay's opera, which was not staged until January 1728, is again a general commentary on society though of a more biting kind; and here certainly audiences interpreted some of the barbs as directed against Walpole. By standing up in his box to applaud and demand an encore of the song thought most damaging to himself, he earned reluctant admiration. But this is already the Walpole of the reign of George II when he was more truly prime minister than in George I's last five years. *The Craftsman*, the anti-Walpole journal, belongs mainly to George II's reign, though it is significant that it was started in that of George I. Bolingbroke had been permitted to return to England in June 1723, helped by the intercession of the duchess of Kendal, but with the willing cooperation of Townshend and Walpole even if both later became alarmed at the outcry his return raised among the Whigs.[47] His estates were subsequently restored to him, but he was not permitted to sit in the House of Lords, a circumscription of his activities for which he blamed Walpole. The invective of *The Craftsman* is evidence of the depth of his hatred and envy, though there is hardly any censure bearing on George. This is not to say that George I was not criticized inside or outside parliament. But invective against the king was beginning to be thought of as bad form in both Houses and bad tactics too: after all, it was more sensible to cast aspersions on the king's ministers rather than on the monarch, the fount of power. Printed criticism of the king was rare, for fear of punishment, but handwritten copies of poems which ridiculed the king and the house of Hanover had a lively circulation, especially in Jacobite and High Church circles. We occasionally learn, from oral evidence recorded, of popular ditties referring to George as cuckolded by Königsmarck, as in the following example:

Potatoes is a dainty dish and turnips is a-springing
And when that Jemmy [James III] comes over, we'll set the bells aringing
We'll take that cuckold by the horns and lead him unto Dover
And put him in a leather boat and send him to Hanover.[48]

If Walpole was not prime minister in George's last years, he was, as the king realized, the pillar of the ministry at home. He was trusted, honoured – by the Order of the Bath in 1725, the Garter in 1726 – and liked by the king. George felt quite at home when visiting him and his mistress* at Richmond Park. But there were wide areas of George I's duties which Walpole could not touch.

The minister had never been out of England and had no real grasp of European affairs, though he acted as secretary of state in 1723 when both Townshend and Carteret were in Hanover, and received copies of all important despatches. He took expert advice when he needed it from his brother Horatio. Again, this was more necessary to him during George II's reign. In George I's, foreign affairs were the concern of Townshend who had specialized, if geographically limited, knowledge. Both could have benefited if they had only been willing to admit their need, and share their power, with the expertise of Carteret, the fine Spanish scholar† trained in Mediterranean statecraft by Stanhope and himself an expert on Imperial and northern affairs.

GEORGE AS A PATRON OF THE ARTS

The peaceful years after 1721 gave both Walpole and George I opportunities to build, to refashion and to spend more time on their respective hobbies. For George, though foreign policy remained a daily preoccupation, there was not the urgency and danger inherent in the 1714–21 situation, nor were the problems he had to deal with so intractable.

It is difficult to tell what influence George exerted on the two important assignments which came the way of James Thornhill in October 1714, when he was chosen to commemorate pictorially the Protestant Succession in the Great Hall at Greenwich, and a year later when he was given the task of decorating the cupola of St Paul's. The two masters under whom he had studied as an assistant, the Italian Antonio Verrio and the Frenchman Louis Laguerre, had been expected to receive these commissions, Verrio – who had already done a great deal of work at Hampton Court – the former and Laguerre the latter. We know that Thornhill's promoters won the day by stressing the peculiar fitness of an Englishman, a Protestant, to undertake both tasks. Halifax secured the Greenwich

---

* Maria (Molly) Skerret (whom he married on his wife's death).
† It was Carteret who, during his banishment to Ireland (where he, incidentally, took his duties seriously and was a considerable success), commissioned an illustrated translated edition of *Don Quixote*.

commission by refusing Treasury permission to pay the bills unless Thornhill was commissioned; Tenison, the archbishop of Canterbury, was more subtle in his approach to the St Paul's commission. George would not have had religious scruples about using Catholics for the paintings, and it seems likely that he supported Thornhill because he realized the strength of feeling – and the propaganda value – of the native, Protestant appointment. On Verrio's death in 1715 George also used Thornhill to complete decorations at Hampton Court – the ceiling of the Queen's Bedroom (used by the prince and princess of Wales during the summer of 1716) is by him. It must have pleased George, for from then on he took a special interest in Thornhill's work; he made him royal history painter in 1718, took him to Hanover in 1719, and knighted him in May 1720 – the first English-born painter to be so honoured in any reign. Thornhill, for his part, returned the compliments in various ways. Notoriously tightfisted, he presented George with a free copy of his episodes from the life of St Paul (the ones he had depicted in the cupola of St Paul's cathedral); and when he had made enough money to buy back the family estate he built in its grounds an obelisk celebrating George I.

From an historical and biographical point of view, Thornhill's treatment of George and his family at Greenwich is worth studying. The painter had long wrestled with the problem of how to present (in the Upper Hall) George I's landing in England. In the end he chose an allegorical solution, with the king in a scalloped chariot, reminiscent of the huge painting of the Hanoverian family in which the electress Sophia is seated in a scalloped carriage. Thornhill would certainly have seen this when he made sketches of George I's grandson, Frederick, during his 1719 stay in the electorate. In the Painted Hall panorama of George and his family, Thornhill presented his subjects in contemporary dress, though with conventional armour for George and Georg August. Here we find Frederick placed between his grandfather and his father: he looks delicate, as if he has not fully recovered from the illness we know he suffered just before George I's visit. In a group to the left of the king we find the remaining children of the prince and princess of Wales. It is gratifying to have them all collected together and to admire the beauty of the princess of Wales as a young woman, though the age perspective between Frederick (sketched in 1719) and his youngest sisters (born in 1724 and 1725 respectively) is telescoped and nags at the historical eye. A feature worth noting is the Saxon horse which Thornhill painted in, close to his own portrait, on the pillar in the right-hand corner. The colours we now see, alas, are not as fine as the original ones, nineteenth-century retouching having dimmed the clear blues, the deep pinks, the cool browns and sea-greens, the glorious crimson and the frothy whites which contemporaries admired.[49]

George did not have a deep knowledge of painting,* but he had from youth onwards been keen on family portraits and historical painting, and all models and designs for decorations had to be submitted for his approval. That he was not impervious to changes in style is shown by his replacing Thornhill with William Kent for the decoration of the new state rooms at Kensington Palace, and the grand staircase hall, between 1722 and 1725. Kent had been recommended to him by Burlington, whose acquaintance George had made in Hanover in 1714 before his accession (when the young earl passed through the electorate en route to his first visit to Italy) and who had brought Kent from Italy to London in 1719 after his second visit. Kent is usually regarded as much inferior to Thornhill as a painter, but his decorations suit the rooms, and the portraits he included in the hall scheme give us a good idea of figures we usually know only from literary sources: there is the dwarf of Fabrice's memoirs who sometimes amused the company after the king's supper; there is the wild boy found in the Hanover forests, brought to England in 1725 and given as a present to the princess of Wales; there are Mehemet and Mustafa. Some we cannot now identify: the several yeomen of the guard (who probably were well known at court at the time) and a solitary Quaker who seems to symbolize George I's sympathy for non-conformists or to celebrate the measure of relief he brought to them.

Old Nottingham House, the kernel round which William and Mary had built Kensington Palace (or 'House' as it was called in their time), had deteriorated by the time of George I's accession and this was the reason the king had ordered a conversion which would give Wren's building a new centre, a series of state rooms. Vanbrugh's ideas proved too grandiose, suiting neither the king's purse nor purpose, though the drawings he made may have influenced the actual architect, Colin Campbell, who worked under William Benson, the surveyor-general who had succeeded Wren at the reorganization of the Board of Works. Benson had been employed by George as elector. He was with the king in Hanover in 1716 and in 1718 we find orders to Görtz that Benson's machine for pumping water for the big Herrenhausen fountain must be bought, 'whatever the cost'.[50] He seems to have been a better engineer than builder and he did not last long in his post as surveyor-general. A misleading report on the state of the Palace of Westminster caused his dismissal; and the new state rooms – the King's Drawing Room, the Cupola or

---

* The statement, attributed to George I by the author of *The Life and Times of George I* (1972), that he hated 'all boets and bainters', is by George II, and even so is quoted incorrectly and out of context.

Cube Room and the Privy Chamber – were in need of repair not long after their completion in 1722.[51] But the proportions are delightful and the successful Kent décors are matched by the redecorations – and particularly the many new ceilings – which he carried out also in other parts of the palace, giving it greater unity. Economies had to be practised, queen Mary's curtains and hangings were re-used, though their blue was dyed green – but when the whole was completed courtiers and visitors found it harmonious and exciting. The cupola ceiling with its clever perspective (influenced by Thornhill's work for the dome of St Paul's) was much admired, and the Roman style of the room praised. The Kent ceiling in the chamber leading to the Drawing Room produced a novelty, the first ceiling in England to be decorated in the Etruscan style. The great gallery – which had long housed the 'fine Pictures that adorn that long room from one end to the other' and contained several Holbeins – Erasmus, Froben the printer of Basle, and a portrait of Henry VIII 'in the flower of his age' – was 'new finisht and furnisht' by George I and won recognition from so critical a connoisseur as Sir John Evelyn. He liked the crimson damask on the walls, the fresh gilt on ceiling and cornices and thought they set off the large paintings well. He noted in his diary a 'Tintoret', a 'Basson', and the huge equestrian portrait of Charles I on a white horse on one of the end walls. The king clearly enjoyed equestrian paintings; one of Olivares was also among those Evelyn listed.[52]

By this time two charming arcaded courtyards had been added to the north of Wren's Clock Court under the aegis of the new surveyor-general, Hewett, by the resident clerk of works, Joynes: one for the granddaughters still in George's care and labelled the Princesses' Court; the other (later known as the Prince of Wales Court since Frederick lived there in the early years of George II's reign) housed the duchess of Kendal. Her apartments were also decorated by Kent, the chimney-pieces he designed for them being particularly fine. The fact that communication was arranged (though not originally provided by the architect) between her lodgings and those of the princesses indicates that there was much coming and going between the two courts and that Melusine shared George's concern for the care of his granddaughters, though the day-to-day supervision was provided by the governess chosen by George in 1718, the countess of Portland.

The gardens were close to George's heart. The parkland which had been bought by William III from Nottingham was extensive. Here the king worked with the royal gardener, Henry Wise, his assistant Charles Bridgman (who succeeded Wise after George's death), and

Kent in re-landscaping the grounds. One purpose was to create a magnificent view from the new King's Drawing Room. The Round Pond, then called the Basin, was dug and filled with water, radiating paths were constructed, and the Grand Walk, 80 feet wide and 2800 feet long, was laid out 'by His Majesty's own direction', and planted with trees at a cost of nearly £4,000. The Serpentine project, only just begun by the summer of 1727, was fully planned. Queen Caroline, who is often, though erroneously, given all credit for the remodelling of the Kensington Palace grounds, shared her father-in-law's interest and completed his plans after 1727. Anybody willing to walk was pressed into service when George, for relaxation and exercise, inspected the improvements. Melusine's brother, field marshal Johann Matthias von der Schulenburg, who visited his sister in 1726, found himself exhausted by his evening walks with George I; at times they lasted for three hours.

George I's granddaughters and his two youngest daughters by Melusine shared the same music teacher, Georg Friedrich Handel,* undoubtedly the artist who gave George the greatest and most consistent pleasure. Handel had paid a brief visit to Hanover in 1703 and was made George's *Kapellmeister* in June 1710 – an appointment which brought to an end his four years of study in Italy. Historians of music and biographers of Handel, even those who realize that there was never any quarrel between the elector and his music master, have wondered why George let Handel stay abroad so much of the time between 1710 and 1714; there were some brief visits to other German courts and music centres, and two long visits to England, one from August 1710 till the end of June 1711, and the other from the autumn of 1712 until George arrived as king of Great Britain. The first stay in England can be explained, in part anyhow, by Handel's need to fulfil promises to the earl of Manchester (queen Anne's representative in the republic of Venice) to visit London, but for the second stay these scholars have been driven, by lack of documentary evidence, to speculate. For the political historian there is no mystery: reasons of economy, imposed by the War of the Spanish Succession, had forced the elector to discontinue his own opera company. During his year-long stay in Hanover in 1712 Handel composed and conducted chamber music and wrote cantatas and duets for Caroline, the electoral princess; but until peace should come to the Empire (as it did in 1714) there would be no task at George's court commensurate with Handel's ability and Italian experience. It was, therefore, in the interests of both patron and composer that the *Kapellmeister*, whose salary of 1,000 Taler continued to be paid, return to London with its greater opportunities: Handel's

---

* To his English correspondents Handel (writing in French) signed himself George Frederic long before his naturalization in 1726; but it would be pedantic, especially as he himself used the form Handel in England, to employ the German Händel.

first opera in England, *Rinaldo*, in 1711, had been successful enough for him to be asked to have a new work ready for November 1712.[53]

As soon as George arrived in 1714, Handel became part of the court's entourage. Handel knew the whole royal family from Hanover and was a particular favourite of the Kielmanseggs, having met the baron with Steffani and prince Ernst August in Italy; he owed his original appointment in Hanover partly to their recommendation.[54] For George and the court he provided a welcome and easy introduction to the musical life of London; he knew managers like the indefatigable Heidegger, other composers such as Johann Christoph Pepusch, instrumentalists and singers. In his turn Handel benefited from royal patronage. George I asked that *Rinaldo* should be revived as part of the coronation festivities in October 1714, and when Handel's next opera, *Amadigi*, opened in May 1715, the king and his family attended several performances. Known to be in George's good graces, Handel attracted other patrons. Burlington housed and fed him, and many another artist, in Burlington House for long periods at a time between 1713 and 1718, and *Amadigi* was composed there; Chandos invited him to his seat at Canons when Burlington left for his second visit to Italy and made him his musical director as successor to Pepusch. At Canons, Handel found an alternative platform for his work when the Italian opera ran into financial difficulties at the end of the 1717 season. Here he composed the Chandos anthems and here his masque *Haman and Mordecai* – based on Racine's *Esther* – was performed in 1720.

Royal and court patronage remained, however, decisive. Handel received an annual pension from George of £200 (in addition to the £200 he had been given for life by queen Anne as a reward for his birthday ode of 1713 and his 'Te Deum' for the peace of Utrecht), and he was paid extra for his teaching activities at court. Handel was of the royal party to Hanover in 1716 and in 1719. On both occasions he did some work at court, but his main task was to search for fine Italian voices at the music centres of Germany. We owe his *Water Music* to Freiherr von Kielmansegg, who commissioned it for a river party in George's honour on 17 July 1717; the king enjoyed it so much that he commanded it to be played three times over: on the way to supper, during supper at Chelsea, and on the return journey. George I's support made possible the foundation of the Royal Academy of Music in 1719–20; the king's subscription was £1,000 per annum. The prince of Wales also subscribed a large sum and Burlington and a host of lesser patrons – British and Hanoverians – bound themselves to put one or more 'shares' of £100 each into the venture so that the Academy could call on a capital of £50,000 over ten years. Its purpose, apart from general encouragement of music, was to revive opera at the King's Theatre, Haymarket, under the musical direction of Handel. The shareholders made no profit and did not expect to do so.

Handel's regular salary (which enabled him to buy his own house in Brook Street) was not exorbitant, but singers of the calibre expected by London audiences were expensive; the male soprano Senesino, the tenors Baldassi and Bereselli, Margherita Durastanti and Francesca Cuzzoni (ugly, but with a 'nest of nightingales in her belly'), and the mezzo-soprano Faustina Bordoni commanded up to £2,000 for the season which lasted from October/November to March/April and usually brought two new operas. The Academy attracted fine instrumental players, English, Italian and German. On his visit to London in 1726–27 Quantz, the future teacher of flute-composing and -playing to George I's Prussian grandson Friedrich, praised in particular Geminiani, the famous violin virtuoso, and his English pupil Dubourg, the Castucci brothers and Mauro d'Alaia (also violinists), and the flute players Weidemann and Festing (another Geminiani pupil, and also a good violinist). The composers Buononcini and Ariosti were employed to share Handel's work. They and the singers became the idols of various groups, often politically orientated, of the audience; but the fact that the twenty directors of the Academy (with the duke of Newcastle and Fabrice particularly active) worked well together in spite of their different political views is perhaps more significant than the tittle-tattle about boos or applause bestowed according to political commitment.

The audience for Italian opera was necessarily limited to the educated classes, and normally there were only two opera evenings a week during the season. On the other evenings the King's Theatre was used for a variety of entertainments, mainly masquerades organized by Heidegger* which proved very popular, much to Schulenburg's amazement; in his correspondence with Görtz he saw the great enthusiasm for masquerades as proof of that change-ability for which the English nation was a byword on the contin-ent.[55] The masquerades, which the king and other members of the royal family sometimes attended, were much criticized by moralists: being masked made the women wanton, it was held, and cuckoldry was therefore the end product. One of Hogarth's earliest satires, 'The Bad Taste of the Town' of 1724, manages to express disapproval, in one admittedly overcrowded print, of masquerades, Burlington's architectural and artistic principles, and Italian opera.[56]

There were, of course, areas of Handel's experience in England into which George I could not enter; the composer's friendships with Gay

---

* Similar entertainments were, as can be seen by Fabrice's memoirs, at times arranged in private houses (including his own) where the servants found their profit in supplying and selling food and drink.

and Pope (both of whom worked with Handel as librettists) and other poets and writers were closed to the king because of his lack of intimate knowledge of the language; but George's enjoyment of music and singing and his patronage of them made a significant contribution to the arts in England. The Royal Academy of Music had to be wound up soon after George I's death, having used up its capital and being shaken by its patron's demise; but the heritage of the reign was not wasted. Handel was now sufficiently well established to found a less ambitious academy and to carry on, though on a more modest scale, with opera and oratorios.

UNFINISHED BUSINESS

The settlements of 1719–21 had left some issues undecided which George meant to tackle. The first was the unsatisfactory relationship between Britain and the Dutch Republic. We have seen that George had been ruthless enough to exclude the Dutch from the advantages which he had promised them in Sweden when their accession to the Quadruple Alliance had come so late as to be virtually useless. But he did not contemplate a negative policy towards the Republic, the one defender of the Protestant Succession whose willingness to act had been tested in 1715 and in 1719. George and his ministers, British and Hanoverian, deplored the inactivity of the United Provinces. They ascribed it, not to divergent interests of the two Maritime Powers, but to the fact that the Republic had been without a stadholder and captain-general since 1702, and that Heinsius – who had proved a valued member of the inner councils of the Grand Alliance during the War of the Spanish Succession – was now nearing eighty and lacking in drive. What would happen after his death? Prince Willem of Orange-Nassau, born in 1711 to Maria Louise, widow of William III's nephew, Jan Willem Friso, had been elected at birth to his father's position as stadholder and captain-general of the province of Friesland, but as long as he was not of age there was no prospect that he would be made stadholder of all seven provinces. Yet George and his ministers decided to work for the future.

It is possible that a Dutch suggestion of 1716, which George refused, that he himself might become a candidate for the stadholdership in order to 'reanimate' the Republic, may have turned the king's thoughts in the direction of support for the young prince. As early as 1717 Bernstorff had asked the Dutch agent and newswriter in London, de l'Hermitage, to sound out opinion on prince Willem's prospects during a visit to the Republic. His report was pessimistic: Dutch influential circles were on the whole anti-stad-holder, as that position was reckoned inimical to the free exercise of oligarchic power. Post-1717 experiences, and the appointment after Heinsius's death of a *raadpensionaris* (Hoornbeck) who was con-sidered anti-British, ripened George's determination to take positive measures to help remedy the situation as seen from the British point of view. A stadholder now seemed essential to root out the 'false and pernicious maxims' of the Amsterdam regents 'de ne prendre point de part aux Affaires Etrangères, de tacher de subsister sans Alliances ou Engagemens'.[57] Between September and mid-November 1721 Cadogan (who had all along been detailed to render services to the young prince and his mother) undertook a mission to the Republic to take counsel with those who wished to put an end to the second stadholderless period.* To render prince Willem more 'considerable' Cadogan was empowered to offer him one of George I's grand-daughters in marriage as soon as he should come of age. In an audience of 10 December with the king, Cadogan – married to a Dutch lady and with a wide variety of acquaintances in the Republic – reported on his journey and delivered his 'Relation de l'Etat des Affaires en Hollande', delineating the various steps by which the pro-stadholder party hoped to achieve its goal.[58] The planning paid off, though not till after George's death; the marriage between Willem and Anne, the eldest daughter of George II, took place in 1734 and was followed by the election of Willem IV as stadholder for the United Provinces in 1747.

One problem which the Dutch, in closer touch because of their barrier towns in the Southern Netherlands, spotted before the British was the threat which Charles VI's Ostend Company posed for the trade of the Maritime Powers.[59] The Southern Netherlanders had long worked to gain an entry into Europe's overseas trade but had been handicapped between 1609 and 1715 by the Castile monopoly of trade with Spain's colonial empire and by the closure of the river Scheldt to all seaborne traffic by international treaties imposed by the Dutch. Their eyes had become fixed on trade with the east, when they were still under Spanish rule, since that would not offend the Castile monopoly; and they continued their agitation for a trading company of their own after their transfer to the Austrian house of Habsburg.[60] Ostend, unlike Antwerp and the other ports on the Scheldt, was not closed, and in 1715 and 1716 ships were sent to the east to prove to Charles VI that commerce with the East Indies could be profitable.[61] Those active in promoting trading companies to the east at this time, in Vienna as in other European capitals (Stockholm and Copenhagen, for instance), were often English and

---

* The first stadholderless period was between 1650 and 1672; Willem III, born post-humously to Willem II's widow, Mary princess of Orange (daughter of Charles I of England), was made stadholder after the French attack on the Republic in 1672.

Scottish 'adventurers' who had the necessary contacts and a desire to break the Anglo-Dutch hegemony in the eastern trade.[62] By December 1722 a body of promoters had persuaded Charles VI to establish a chartered Ostend Company which would pay a given percentage of its profits to the Austrian treasury in return for its privileged position. The company was seen in Britain as a possible rival; but as the British East India Company was so well established, no real urgency was felt to tackle the problem until information was received that Spain, by the treaty of Vienna of April 1725, had given Charles VI concessions which would permit the Ostend Company to trade with the Spanish Indies.[63]

This Austro-Spanish treaty created a good deal of general un-easiness among British ministers. It was rumoured that the two Catholic monarchs had agreed by secret articles to put James Edward Stuart in George's place, and that Charles VI, in return for Spanish support for the Pragmatic Sanction of 1713 (intended to secure the succession of Charles's daughters to the Austrian Habsburg dominions in preference to the daughters of the late emperor Joseph I who had the stronger hereditary claim),* had bound himself to help Philip V reconquer Gibraltar and Minorca.

At the same time disturbing news arrived from the north. During the last years of tsar Peter's reign, information procured direct from Russia through the British diplomat Whitworth had been reassuring. The sick tsar was preoccupied with expansionist plans to the south-east; he had no inclination to meddle in Mecklenburg and Holstein affairs even though he agreed to marry his daughter to the duke of Holstein-Gottorp. But on Peter's death in 1725 his widow Catherine I (whom he had designated to succeed him) entered into negotiations for an alliance with Charles VI. This raised suspicions that she might join the Vienna treaty; the years when the late tsar – though technically an ally – had been the more or less open enemy of George I as elector and king seemed on the point of repetition. The tsaritsa's suggestion that her son-in-law Karl Fredrik of Holstein-Gottorp should be compensated with the duchies of Bremen and Verden, unless his lands in Sleswig were restored to him and those in Holstein released from Danish occupation, threatened the northern settlement of 1719–20. George had no intention of giving up Bremen and Verden, and Britain, as well as France, had guaranteed Frederik IV of Denmark's possession of the former ducal lands in Sleswig. The northern peace plan of George and Stanhope had not ignored the duke of Holstein-Gottorp. King and minister alike hoped, since the marriage of Ulrika Eleonora and Friedrich of Hesse seemed likely to remain childless, that the succession in Sweden could be stipu-

---

* Neither Joseph I nor Charles VI had sons who survived childhood.

lated for the duke as a compensation for his losses in Sleswig. A pro-Holstein group in Sweden favoured such a settlement, but time would be needed to implement it.[64]

The tsaritsa's sponsorship of the duke altered the situation. Karl Fredrik now became, in Townshend's words, George's 'worst enemy', a prospective king of Sweden who would act as Russia's puppet. If, in the meantime, Charles VI should take action along the lines advocated by Catherine – as he could do in his capacity as overlord of the duke of Holstein-Gottorp, a German prince – the whole peace settlement of the north might be endangered and in particular George's possession of the Elbe duchies.[65] Charles VI had denied George the Imperial investitures he had long sought for Bremen and Verden. Negotiations on these investitures, as on the investiture for Hadeln, had been diligently pursued after 1719; but the emperor kept pitching his price ever higher. George was told to scale down his support in the Empire for the Protestant cause. He was also expected to argue the case for the emperor at the Cambrai congress gathered to mediate between Charles VI and Philip V, though that congress had been called in 1722 to press the former to put into effect his Quadruple Alliance commitment to let neutral troops garrison don Carlos's 'expectatives'. The emperor, avoiding discussion of this topic, desired George, as king of Great Britain, to recommend to the congress that he (Charles) should be permitted to bestow on the duke of Tuscany the fief of Siena, the very one which Stanhope had realized Britain was bound to respect as a Spanish fief now transferred to don Carlos. Furthermore, the emperor wished to use the congress to obtain Austrian advantages foreign to the settlement of the Italian problems for which the congress had been called. If George wanted the investitures, British and Hanoverian ministers were told in 1724, George as king must guarantee the Pragmatic Sanction settling the Austrian succession. He must also 'finish' the Ostend affair, that is, he must accept the Ostend Company as a rival to Britain in overseas trade.

While these demands clarified Austrian objectives and therefore provided useful information for future negotiations, they were totally unacceptable at the time. Bothmer, Townshend and George himself told the Austrian negotiator in London, count Starhemberg, that, while George wished to live on good terms with the emperor and desired the investitures, he could not obtain them at the cost of sacrificing the Protestant interest in Germany; nor could he negotiate the investitures at the expense of the trade of his British subjects.[66] Irritated at Charles VI's terms, George ordered a message to be conveyed to the emperor that the king of Great Britain was confident that, as he had hitherto been able to defend Bremen and Verden, he would be able to continue to do so, come what may.[67]

Bothmer was clearly less happy about the king's firmness than Townshend. In his meetings with Starhemberg the Hanoverian minister promised to help the Austrian cause 'if he could' and excused George's actions: the king-elector would not want it to be thought that he was selling out on the religious issue for the sake of Bremen and Verden, and he could not do much in the Ostend affair since his British subjects might then argue that he was sacrificing their interests for the sake of the Hanoverian investitures. This is the period when Bothmer, and Bernstorff in Hanover, were feeling the pinch of George I's British orientation. They would have liked to come to terms with the emperor and hold Hadeln, Bremen and Verden in immaculate legal possession. In his report to Bernstorff of 14/25 April 1724, Bothmer criticized both the English government which 'monopolizes' German affairs and the king who 'connives' in this by not pressing his British ministers to consult with the Hanoverians.[68]

The fears which the treaty of Vienna aroused in British ministers, and especially in Townshend, were in part founded on insufficient and even false information. Philip V's Dutch-born confidant Ripperda had negotiated in great secrecy an alliance that was totally unexpected. Three documents had been signed; and experienced British diplomats, taken by surprise in Vienna as in Madrid, sent home mere rumours of contents of secret clauses as certainties. The Pretender was not even mentioned in any of the documents signed in April and May 1725; Charles VI had promised Spain no more than his 'good offices' for the restitution of Gibraltar and Minorca; the privileges Philip V had granted to the Ostend Company did not specifically mention trade with the Spanish Indies; the future dynastic ties between Spain and Austria were deliberately left vague and there was no mention of the marriage of the emperor's elder daughter, Maria Theresa, to Philip V's heir, the prince of Asturias, nor of that of the younger daughter to don Carlos.

Rumours of these unions had particularly worried the English court in an age when political alliances were often expressed by double marriages arranged as both proof and reinsurance of political links between two countries. George I's alliance with Prussia of 1719 was confirmed by the treaty of Charlottenburg of 1723 and a double marriage was informally agreed, one between Friedrich Wilhelm's heir, Friedrich (later Friedrich *der Grosse*, king from 1740), and the eldest granddaughter of George I, and the other between the elder son of the prince of Wales, Frederick – in direct line of succession to the throne of Great Britain – and the Prussian princess Wilhelmine. We have seen that this was a marriage alliance among first cousins which George I's daughter, Sophia Dorothea, had long wanted, but it was also the outward sign of the political alliance which Townshend valued greatly. He reported enthusiastically to Walpole on the great access of strength implied for Britain in the Charlottenburg treaty. Britain had the largest navy and to this would now be added the whole force and strength of Prussia's military power if help was ever needed.[69] It was customary on the signing of treaties to hand out presents to those who had been given extra work by the negotiations and the toil of drafting; but those distributed both from the Hanoverian and British treasuries on this occasion were particularly high. 'The King', Townshend wrote on 7/18 October, 'upon his leaving Charlottenburg made large presents out of his German Treasury, and as we had concluded so useful a Treaty it was very proper England should make a figure too on that occasion and therefore His Majesty ordered £4500 to be distributed.'* The secretary thoroughly approved: 'the money could never be employed to a more advantageous end, than this has been'.[70]

Dynastic marriage plans were, however, subject to postponement and even annulment when the political climate changed. This was the fate of the unions envisaged at Charlottenburg, though for reasons beyond George I's control. But a most dramatic and abrupt annulment of a double marriage plan – between Spain and France – in February 1724 had a considerable bearing on Philip V's decision to reach an understanding direct with Charles VI rather than through the congress of Cambrai. That such a congress should be called had been part of the unwritten bargain when Spain acceded to the Quadruple Alliance. The unrest and problems connected with the bursting of the South Sea bubble in England and Law's crash in France delayed the arrival of delegates. The Spaniards and the Savoyards were the first to arrive, then the French and the British, and finally in April 1722 the representatives of Charles VI. Talks now began though the formal congress was not opened till 1724. Contemporaries wrote scathingly about the congress 'as ever-lasting as the wars of the seventeenth century'.[71] The forum for discussing problems did, however, provide a useful service in making change by clash of arms less likely. As long as negotiations were in progress, recourse to war was less tempting. That there was resentment, particularly by the two monarchs who felt they had been forced into the Quadruple Alliance, goes without saying. Philip V hoped to overturn that part of the peace plan which declared don Carlos's expectatives Imperial fiefs; Charles VI schemed to rob don Carlos

---

* George's gifts at the signature of the Quadruple Alliance were less splendid: Pecquet was given a ring (which had belonged to queen Anne) valued at £1,000, but bought by George I for £680; to Stanhope George gave plate worth £2,000.

of one, if not all, of the Italian successions to which the Spanish signature of the Quadruple Alliance entitled him. The French and the English walked warily between the two opposite camps. Like mediators at all times they alternatively restrained and encouraged. Because of the treaty France and Britain had signed in June 1721 with Spain (to resume diplomatic relations after the brief war), neither wanted to discourage Philip V too strongly; he had, after all, guaranteed the French succession as laid down at Utrecht and had restored normal trade relations with Britain. An element of double talk was unavoidable. The regent and George I promised to promote at the congress Spanish desiderata above the terms of the Quadruple Alliance if Philip were able to gain the consent of the other participants. When Charles VI refused to admit neutral garrisons until Philip would accept that the expectatives should be Imperial fiefs (as laid down in the Quadruple Alliance), the French and the British, anxious not to offend either Spain or the emperor, refrained from any initiative – though Britain leant towards the emperor and France towards Spain, as had been the case during the Quadruple Alliance negotiations.[72]

French wooing of Spain had been intense after the limited hostilities of 1719–20. It had expressed itself in a typical double marriage project. Louis XV was affianced to the young daughter of Philip V of his second marriage and she was sent to France at the age of six to be brought up in French ways; the daughter of the duc d'Orléans was at the same time engaged to the prince of Asturias and travelled to Spain to be brought up at the Spanish court. This arrangement was upset in February 1725. Dubois had died in August 1723 and the duc d'Orléans survived him by only four months. After his death Louis XV's most important adviser (he was now past the age when he needed a formal regent) was the next closest prince of the blood, the duc de Bourbon. To him, as to most influential men in French politics, the inadvisability of postponing Louis XV's marriage until the Spanish infanta should be of childbearing age became clear when a short but sharp illness raised anxieties that the king might die without an heir of his own body. The Spanish infanta was sent back to Madrid with little ceremony or tact and Louis was married to Maria Leszczyńska, daughter of Stanislas Leszczyński, the ex-king of Poland.[73] The return of the infanta strained Franco-Spanish relations to the limit and Philip V was won over to the idea of a direct approach to Charles VI.

ALLIANCES AND COUNTER-ALLIANCES

Townshend and George found it easier than they had expected to create a counter-alliance to the Austro-Spanish treaty of Vienna. Plans were laid in England from June 1725 onwards and by 3 September a treaty was signed in Hanover between Britain, Prussia and France. During 1727 Sweden and Denmark joined the so-called Hanover alliance and so did the Dutch Republic, though without signing its secret articles. Negotiations with Friedrich Wilhelm, who came to visit his father-in-law in the electorate towards the end of July, proceeded speedily and terms were agreed early in August. At the time the Prussian king was feeling particularly aggrieved against the emperor. Resentment against Charles VI for his anti-Protestant stance had been growing for several years in the Empire and had been raised to fever pitch by the so-called blood-bath of Thorn of December 1724;[*] every German Protestant believed that Augustus II of Saxony-Poland would not have meted out such harsh punishment to his Polish Protestant subjects unless he had been encouraged or even forced to do so, in order to curry favour with Vienna. Two conditions stipulated by Friedrich Wilhelm were that the signatories of the counter-alliance should support the cause of Polish Protestantism as well as uphold the liberties of the Empire; a third was that they should guarantee his claim to the Jülich and Berg successions in the Rhineland. This last demand, embodied in a secret article, proved a stumbling-block for the Dutch who were in conflict with Friedrich Wilhelm over William III's inheritance;[74] but the support of Protestantism became an issue which was much stressed in England and with prospective signatories.

For the British ministry, and especially for Townshend, the need for the counter-alliance was caused less by the religious issue or by the grievances connected with the Ostend Company than by the threat to the balance of power.[75] The very fact that Philip V had made a separate agreement with Charles VI while the congress of Cambrai was sitting threatened to destroy the collective security system laid down in the Quadruple Alliance. In parliament ministers had stressed the danger for Britain of Spanish concessions to the Ostend Company and had obtained authorization for the king, before his departure for Hanover, to take strong counter-measures on the grounds that the treaty of Vienna was 'calculated for the entire destruction of British trade'.[76] But in the correspondence between Whitehall and British diplomats abroad, and in that between Townshend and Walpole when they were separated, we find a

---

[*] In June 1724 a quarrel between the Protestant townsfolk of Thorn and a Jesuit college had led to an attack on the college and its desecration. Ten Protestants were executed in December for their part in this outrage and, as a general punishment, Protestant churches and schools were closed down.

stronger emphasis on the danger to Britain and Europe of an Austro-Spanish hegemony of the kind that had existed when the house of Habsburg ruled both Spain and Austria.

To Townshend's relief the duc de Bourbon and his advisers shared this view and proved willing and even eager to sign the counter-alliance. Relations between Britain and France had been somewhat impaired by the deaths of Dubois and the regent in 1723. Further-more, George I had been intensely embarrassed when it was pointed out to him that the efforts of Luke Schaub and Carteret (first with the duc d'Orléans and then with the duc de Bourbon) to have the de Vrillière family elevated to the rank of *duc et pair* had amounted to pressure and had given offence.[77] The storm was blown up out of all proportion by Carteret's rivals, Townshend and the Walpole brothers, for the purpose of eliminating Carteret's influence with George I. But unless George had resented the invidious position into which he had been manoeuvred, they would not have succeeded in having Schaub recalled and his patron Carteret transferred in April 1724 from the secretaryship of the south to the lord lieutenancy of Ireland. Constant reminders in long despatches by Horatio Walpole that the duc de Bourbon and the whole corps of French *ducs et pairs* had become incensed at 'foreign interference' with French royal prerogative hit their target: the king's concern for his reputation. But George himself must take part of the blame. By implicit, if not explicit, agreement that the countess of Platen's desire to see her daughter's future husband rise in rank should be gratified by feelers at the French court, he allowed himself to become involved, however indirectly, in the factional struggle inside his ministry.[78]

Townshend and Walpole used this opportunity to make sweeping changes. Newcastle became secretary of state in Carteret's place. The duke got on well with the brothers-in-law. He enjoyed cooperating with Robert in parliamentary tactics, and he was indefatigable in his correspondence, official and private, with the diplomats in his department and with Townshend when he and his fellow secretary were parted. Newcastle's younger brother, Henry Pelham, was made secretary-at-war and Cadogan was replaced as commander-in-chief by Argyll. Robert's brother Horatio was left in sole charge of the Paris post after the recall of Schaub. He took care to cultivate all influential men at the French court (one gravamen against Schaub had been his partisanship), and was rewarded by a good working relationship with the aged abbé Fleury, Louis XV's former tutor, who replaced the duc de Bourbon as first minister in June 1726. Horatio's knowledge of foreign affairs was essential to the ministry at home; Townshend and Newcastle were both in the Lords and

Robert Walpole did not feel confident of speaking on the details of the government's foreign policy. Horatio was therefore given brief leaves from France in 1726 and in 1727 in order to put the government's case in the House of Commons. He did so, if at great length, with lucidity and commonsense.

The consensus among ministers achieved by the Townshend-Walpole coup of 1724 brought some advantages since the absence of factional strife made for relative ease of cabinet business. But all was not gain. George disliked parting with Cadogan and even more with Carteret. The changes denied him British advisers independent of each other. Gone were the days when Sunderland, Stanhope and Craggs – who had an arrangement whereby they went into the king's closet in a body* – could find themselves interrupted by Cadogan, who took it as a matter of course that he could join them in the closet, however much they resented his intrusion.[79] Carteret, though a member of the cabinet and thus with access to the closet when in London, resided mainly in Ireland where he made a success of his new office.[80] Yet the king's own strong control of foreign policy, and the keen eye he continued to keep on posts and patronage, prevented him from becoming ruled instead of ruler during the last two years of his life. When in Hanover in 1725, he went through the minutes of the meetings of the lord justices as carefully as ever and, where he deemed it necessary, disagreed with recommendations for pardons and promotions. He read all incoming despatches, opening them himself if no British secretary was present, scrutinized draft instructions and initiated negotiations with visiting diplomats and rulers.[81]

Even without Carteret, George I had some room for manoeuvre in the incipient friction between Townshend and Walpole. Walpole, though he did not trust himself to discuss the details of foreign policy issues, was determined to have his say on their bearing on parliament and the treasury. A good example of this is the disagreement which arose between the brothers-in-law during the planning stages of the king's speech from the throne for January 1726. Walpole thought Townshend overhasty and bold, too free with British money for subsidies and payment for troops, even when these were hired more for diplomatic demonstrations than from expectation or promotion of war.

The interplay between Hanoverian and British advisers also remained significant, since George listened to both sides and made up his own mind. It should be stressed that when Bothmer complained in 1724 that the king no longer ordered his British ministers to consult with his German ministers, he did not complain that the king no

---

* Or, more correctly, that each entered as he arrived, approximately near the time set, without waiting in the antechamber for the others.

longer consulted his Hanoverian ministers. And Bernstorff, for all that the British ministers thought of him as being in disgrace, particularly after 1721 when he had left England for good, was in constant attendance on George during his 1723 visit to Hanover. It was reported that he could have had permission to return with George to London for the asking; but at this stage he decided to retire to Gartow. Conscious of his advanced age, he began a long and important policy memorandum to the king with the statement that this might be a last opportunity to lay his thoughts before the master he had served so long.[82]

WAR OR PEACE?

Bernstorff's counsel was, predictably, not to forget the importance for Hanover of Imperial good-will. Of this neither George nor Towns-hend was unmindful and, indeed, recent research on the Hanover alliance has emphasized, not its warlike aspect, but its implied diplomatic pressure to prevent Charles VI from committing himself too firmly on the Spanish side.[83] Yet for those not fully in the know, and even for those in charge of affairs, at times during 1726 it looked like touch and go whether a war might break out, at least with Spain. The Hanover alliance had provoked a new Austro-Spanish treaty of November 1725, again negotiated by Ripperda, and this – since it was much more specific than the earlier ones – encouraged Philip V to take a tough line with Britain. He demanded fulfilment of George's promise to restore Gibraltar to Spain and tried to embarrass the British king by sending copies of documents to the parliamentary opposition which seemed to prove a firm royal undertaking as recent as May 1721.[84]

The ministry, partly to stem criticism of George, sent supplies and reinforcements to Gibraltar and a fleet to the Caribbean in response to complaints in parliament of Spanish attacks on British traders. George's cause was weakened when Friedrich Wilhelm of Prussia had second thoughts about the Hanover alliance. He was, as ever, given to vacillation, and as soon as he had left his father-in-law's company in 1725 began to wonder whether he had been wise in taking so anti-Vienna a stand, particularly as Charles VI now proved willing to promise him the succession to Jülich and Berg – a seemingly surer road to success than Hanoverian support. After all, George had not as yet been able to obtain investitures for Bremen and Verden for himself, nor the Prussian investiture for the parts of Swedish Pomerania ceded by Ulrika Eleonora in 1719.[85] Charles VI had no real intention of fixing the Jülich-Berg succession on Friedrich

Wilhelm and his successors (a contributory cause to the outbreak of war in 1740); but the uncertainty of Prussian attitudes in 1726 forced Townshend on the one hand to hire Hessian troops, at a hefty cost, in case matters should get out of hand in Europe and on the other to blow cold on the double-marriage project in the hope of bringing the Prussian king to his senses.[86] Attacks on George in parliament, even if not as concerted and solid as in the days of the Townshend-Walpole opposition, could not be avoided. Pulteney, disappointed not to have been given high office by Walpole, was particularly vocal; and Bolingbroke, embittered at being debarred from taking his place in the House of Lords, sharpened his arrows in the background though these were meant for Walpole rather than for the king.

In the Commons, as in the Lords, the 'Hanover treaty' was picked upon as aptly named, made solely for the benefit of the king's German dominions. Ministers had, however, little difficulty in countering such arguments. In the Commons, Robert Walpole successfully argued that in the present circumstances Hanover risked being dragged into war in defence of British trading interests: opposition to the Ostend Company – which had nothing to do with Hanover – might bring an attack on the king's electorate if Charles VI decided to stand by his Spanish ally. Both Houses, in their addresses to the king, approved the Hanover alliance and pledged parliament's support if George's German dominions should be attacked because of it. In effect, it was Hanover that proved to be at risk, and though the danger was averted in George's reign by skilful diplomacy, Hanover suffered French invasions in the 1740s and 1750s during European wars deriving basically from Anglo-French colonial rivalry.[87] Britain was never involved in any war 'for the sake of Hanover'. But an interesting point was made during the 1726 debate in the Commons by Henry Pelham on the subject of Britain's duty or otherwise to defend Hanover if the king's electoral dominions were attacked. The restraining clause of the Act of Settlement of 1701, the secretary-at-war propounded, had never been intended to deprive the king of British assistance in case his non-British possessions were attacked; it was there to ensure that he asked parliament's consent to give such help. This point is worth making since all standard accounts of the Act of Settlement assume that George I was forbidden to use British troops in defence of Hanover in any circumstances.[88]

Whatever risk there had been of war with Spain disappeared in the early spring of 1727 when Philip V – who had already opened trenches for a siege of Gibraltar – became disillusioned at lack of support of any kind from Charles VI. He dismissed and arrested Ripperda. In his turn, the emperor tired of the Spanish alliance. Philip V had promised subsidies from treasure expected from overseas and, anticipating these, Charles had contracted to pay subsidies to a variety of German allies won for the Vienna treaty. British squadrons, by patrolling close to Spain's coasts and in the Caribbean, inhibited the sailings of the Spanish galleon fleets and put Charles VI in acute embarrassment as to how to pay his lesser allies. Fleury, anxious to restore that French understanding with Spain which Dubois had achieved between 1720 and 1725, was only too willing to act as a mediator between Vienna and London. He was a supple and energetic go-between and by the so-called preliminaries of Paris of 31 May 1727 the crisis was dispelled. Philip withdrew from Gibraltar, and Charles VI agreed to suspend the Ostend Company for seven years, with a tacit understanding that this would be 'for ever' once Great Britain signed a more detailed arrangement mapped out at this time: in return for a British guarantee of the Pragmatic Sanction the Ostend Company would be disbanded, the investitures of Bremen and Verden would be given to Hanover, and don Carlos's expectatives would be furthered even to the extent of the admission of Spanish garrisons into Parma, Piacenza and Tuscany. Meanwhile, since the treaty of Vienna had virtually killed the congress of Cambrai, it was agreed that a new congress,* would meet so that Anglo-French mediation between Spain and Austria – and with it the collective security system – would be restored.[89]

---

* Aachen (Aix-la-Chapelle) was the meeting place agreed upon; this was later changed to Soissons.

X

Death of George I

GEORGE'S LAST JOURNEY

It is worth tracing George's last journey in detail mainly because no modern biography of him exists in any language and contemporary stories connected with his death have been given credence down to this day in British historiography, especially the one that he had a premonition of his death before leaving England, and that the heart attack which killed him was caused by the fright he took when he was presented with a letter from his deceased divorced wife* in which she prophesied that he would die within a year of her own death.[1]

From reliable accounts that have survived, principally those of Fabrice, from the moment George left St James's Palace at seven o'clock in the morning of 3/14 June 1727, we know that the king was in a serene mood, even if the death of Trudchen in the previous year had cast a shadow over his personal life. He had much to look forward to. At Osnabrück he would meet Ernst August, the last relative of his own generation since their half-sister Sophia Charlotte had died in 1725 and Max, who had cut himself off from the family, died in the following year;[2] the prince-bishop was to join the king and Melusine for the whole visit. At Herrenhausen George would see [Anna] Louisa settled in the Delitzsche Palais. Best of all, his daughter, the queen of Prussia, would travel from Berlin to Herrenhausen, where the double-marriage plan would be finalized. Now that the shadows of war were dispelled he had told his daughter this was the time for a public announcement: there were no obstacles and Friedrich Wilhelm's 'desertion' to the side of the emperor could be forgiven and forgotten.[3] George knew that the marriage plans would please his grandson, since Frederick, who always looked forward to his grandfather's visits (and all his life revered his memory as 'a good and great king'), had become as attached as his aunt to the idea that he should marry Wilhelmine – a bright, intelligent girl who shared

---

* Sophia Dorothea had died at Ahlden on 13 November 1726 (NS).

his interest in the arts. For her part, as her memoirs testify, Wilhelmine was also keen on the match. For both of them it was a grievous disappointment when George II and her father reversed George I's plans and forbade the planned marriages since they could not mutually agree on conditions and timing.[4]

Quite apart from meeting relatives, George looked forward to seeing what progress had been made at Herrenhausen with his latest project there; it was only in 1725 that he had ordered the planting of the linden trees which were to form a long double allée between the summer residence and the town of Hanover.

Greenwich was reached within the hour on 3/14 June. The king went on board his yacht, courtiers and officers who were not to accompany him to Hanover came to bid adieu, dinner was served, and sail was set to go with the tide to Gravesend. There the wind was found to be contrary and it was not till 16 June that the crossing to the Dutch side of the water could be effected, but then with so favourable a wind that the coast of the Republic was sighted at 8 o'clock the next morning. After passing the Holland *Diep* and Moerdijk, George transferred to a Dutch yacht sent by the States General in his honour. In the early evening of 18 June, after passing through the Kil waters, he landed at Schoonhoven where his carriage awaited him as well as a guard of Dutch cavalry to look after his security as long as he was on the Republic's soil. The baggage, including the king's bed, had gone ahead; in the king's own carriage only Hardenberg, his court marshal, and Fabrice, his Hanoverian *Kammerherr*, accompanied him while his body servants, the *Kammerdiener*, followed fairly close behind. The ladies of the party, British ministers and officials, both Hanoverian and British, set out in their own or hired carriages as and when their yachts made landfall, some ahead of the king, most behind him. George pushed on immediately on 18 June till 10 o'clock at night when he halted at a small place called Varth, an hour and a half from Utrecht.

He dined (miserably, Fabrice felt) on a single carp, and was up and about by 5 o'clock the next morning, eager to continue his journey. Contrary to custom – 'for the first time in all his journeys', Fabrice averred – he stopped to eat dinner halfway through the day's estimated stint at Appeldoorn, presumably because of the meagre supper of the previous night. At 8 in the evening he reached Delden (where, according to tradition, the fateful letter was handed to him); there he had supper and spent the night. To his entourage he seemed in good health (*völlig gesund*) and in good humour; he gave 'a kind of audience' to some five or six Dutch ladies who wanted to meet him and he conversed with them in Dutch till about midnight.

The next day, 20 June, George, Hardenberg and Fabrice, accompanied by their Dutch guard, set out at 7 o'clock in the morning. The carriage party talked of this and that for some three-quarters of an hour. Then the king revealed that he had suffered a bad night, stomach pains – which he blamed on his over-indulgence in strawberries and oranges at supper – having kept him awake.* When the two courtiers deplored George's decision to continue his journey without taking time to recover at Delden, the king assured them that he felt better. Half an hour later he bade the carriage stop that he might answer a call of nature. When he returned, Hardenberg noted that the king's face was oddly distorted and that his right hand seemed to be out of control. Just as Fabrice (who him-self had recently suffered a disjointed ankle) was asking the king whether his hand had come out of joint and if he wished Fabrice to put it back, George grew pale and fainted. It happened that, con-trary to custom, the *Kammerdiener* carriage was only two steps behind and that it contained a surgeon, lodged there at the request of Hardenberg and Fabrice with a view to their own need of assistance: Fabrice's foot was still swollen and Hardenberg was not well. Never before on George's travels had a medical man been so close and, while Hardenberg halted the king's coach to fetch the surgeon, Fabrice took smelling salts (known as 'English salt' on the continent) from his pocket and held them under the king's nose in an attempt to bring him out of the faint. The surgeon diagnosed a stroke and ordered the king to be carried out and placed on the ground to be bled; hardly two minutes, it was estimated, elapsed between the apoplexy and the bloodletting. The king recovered consciousness on being replaced in the coach and indicated with his left hand that he wished the journey to continue. He answered lucidly, if with words of one syllable, questions put to him on how he felt; but after another half hour he fell into a sleep that appeared unnatural because of the strange snoring which accompanied it. The surgeon, Hardenberg and Fabrice, who between them supported the king in their arms, began to fear the worst. The king seemed to be falling into a 'lethargy'. One of the Dutch officers was sent ahead to locate and stop the baggage with the king's bed and did so at Noordhorn. Hattorf, who had been ahead of the royal carriage, sent his secretary galloping to find the king's physician Steigerdahl far back in the royal cavalcade. Various remedies were, meanwhile, tried in the open field at Noordhorn, but neither drawing-plasters – applied to his hand (presumably the right one) and his neck – nor strong spirits had any effect. What to do? Hattorf travelled in haste to Lingen to see if he could find one of Friedrich Wilhelm's two doctors resident

* It would seem as if the fruit had given him an upset stomach; for quite apart from the reference in the text, culled from Fabrice, of the king's need to leave the carriage after only one hour and a half to answer a call of nature, Mustafa volunteered information during the night of 20–21 June to those who considered purging the king that this was not necessary: his master had left his bed several times the previous night.

there, but both were away – one at Osnabrück, the other at Amsterdam. At this news some (including Fabrice and Hattorf) were for moving George to Lingen and putting him to bed there; but Hardenberg decided to continue to Osnabrück. All approved of this once the surgeon had reassured them that the movements of the carriage would not worsen the king's condition; he was, in fact, so insensible that 'the movement of the coach would be as comfortable as the softest bed'. Hattorf and Fabrice moved ahead to apprise Ernst August of the situation, and to disperse the Hanoverian courtiers already assembled to greet George I so that he might be carried along the 'secret stairs' into his room without publicity. On arrival at Osnabrück – some time between 10 and 11 o'clock – George revived sufficiently to realize where he was; with his left hand he removed his hat in greeting and replaced it. But once in bed he sank into unconsciousness again. Blood was let during the night of 20–21 June, but to no avail. The following night between half an hour and an hour after midnight, George died. The only movement that Fabrice noted before death was the death cramps. The king's last conscious or semi-conscious movement had been the left-handed greeting to Osnabrück, his childhood home.[5]

*   *   *

Melusine and young Melusine arrived in Osnabrück on Sunday morning, 22 June. Townshend caught up the next day and returned to England on the Wednesday.[6] Fabrice had written twice to Bothmer, with the 'riding post' on the evening of 20 June and by courier on the morning of 21 June, so that he might prepare the prince of Wales for the news of the king's illness. At 4 o'clock in the morning of 22 June Fabrice wrote to George II, after consultations between Ernst August, Hattorf and himself – to give formal notification of George I's death. Fabrice – who had met Georg August fairly frequently in Hanover ever since he (Fabrice) was a lad of fourteen or fifteen and had been in correspondence with him when in Turkey – had naturally become somewhat removed from the successor when serving the father after 1718. He would have liked to ride post-haste with the news, in the hope of securing his own position and even more that of his elder brother Johann Ludwig in Hanoverian service, but his still swollen ankle prevented him from doing so. In the meantime, he regarded it as his duty to stay close to the late king's body until orders should arrive from George II.[7]

As soon as the medical men had pronounced George I dead, Fabrice and Hattorf had the gates of Osnabrück closed so that only their own couriers should be able to leave with the news; George's successor might take offence unless he was the first in England to be told. One hour after the couriers had left for London, Fabrice sent another with letters to George I's grandson, Frederick, and to the Hanoverian regency government to confirm the forebodings communicated the previous day. Another courier went to meet Townshend so that he should not be unprepared for what he would find at Osnabrück. George I's apartments at Osnabrück were locked and sealed with the seal of Ernst August, in order to keep the late king's clothes, papers and trunks with other properties – of which a list was made – undisturbed. A report on all this, written by Fabrice, was sent to England on 23 June at 6 o'clock in the morning with a *Kammerjunker* of Ernst August's. The duchess of Kendal and lady Walsingham left for Hanover on 23 June, as did all the late king's entourage with the exception of Fabrice, who – impatient to know George II's orders – travelled by slow stages towards the Dutch border to intercept the king's courier. Naturally enough, no one had wanted to take the responsibility for arrangements in connection with the late king's funeral which might conflict with the wishes of George II. The only stipulation George I had laid down was that his body should not be opened, or embalmed.[8]

George II decided that his father should be buried at Hanover, close to the late electress Sophia in the Leineschloss church.* He asked that Hattorf and the two Reiches, father and son, *Deutsche Kanzlei* officials, should return to London immediately, as he needed their services. Fabrice returned, briefly, after the funeral to hand over the jewels and valuables which the late king had taken with him on his journey, and which George II had asked that he return. He was not, and had hardly expected to be, retained in constant attendance on George II; but he hoped, and eventually succeeded, in being given a more lucrative appointment than that of *Kammerherr* to the king on his visits to Hanover. The king is dead, long live the king. The concern to retain, or gain, the favour of George II was naturally uppermost in the minds of those who enjoyed positions of power and influence or even a livelihood in administration or at court in the kingdom as in the electorate.

Many of George's old ministers, friends and servants had died before him: Stanhope in 1721, Robethon in 1722, Sophia Charlotte in 1725, Bernstorff, Cadogan and Mehemet in 1726. Of those still alive, we know from Fabrice that Hardenberg was quite broken by the king's death, to such a degree that he left all practical work that had to be done in June 1727 to Hattorf and Fabrice.[9] The countess of Schaumburg-Lippe wrote that her family had 'lost a father and never would things be as in his lifetime'.[10] Frederick mourned the

---

* The Leineschloss, with the Schlosskirche, were severely damaged during the Second World War. When rebuilding took place, the decision was made to move George's sarcophagus, and that of his mother, to the nineteenth-century mausoleum in the Herrenhausen garden.

grandfather who had been the only person to show him paternal affection and concern after 1714 and spoke of him – long afterwards – to his own children.[11] The most intense personal grief was felt by Melusine. She returned to England and in 1728 bought a house at Twickenham, close to that of Johanne Sophie of Schaumburg-Lippe.[2]* There is a story told from her Twickenham years that she believed George I had come back to her in the shape of a bird which she befriended and tamed. The reason for her belief is given as a remark, supposedly overheard during a conversation in George's lifetime, in which he had promised to return to her 'from the other side' if he should precede her in death. The original story has 'a large bird', but this was soon improved to 'a large raven'. Melusine's fondness for songbirds is well established and there may well be no more foundation for the story than this. If the legend has any basis, one would prefer to believe that the bird was a dove – since that may have reminded Melusine of the sublime *colomba* aria by Handel to which she and George had often listened. In the raven tradition, again on the supposition that the story is not totally apocryphal, the connotation might conceivably be that old European folklore belief (since proved erroneous) that the raven remains faithful all its life to its chosen mate, and that it returns to the nest to sing just once a year.[13] Sentiment one can attribute to Melusine, but not superstition.

THE BALANCE SHEET

George I was king of Great Britain for slightly less than thirteen years, from 2/13 August 1714 to 11/22 June 1727. He was elector of Hanover for twenty-nine years.

Having followed his life and career, we may wonder at the epithet 'lucky George' which his Hanoverian courtiers bestowed upon him.[14] Lucky? With the traumatic experiences of the *Prinzenstreit*, the Königsmarck affair, and the Sophia Dorothea divorce and imprisonment? 'Lucky', on a less personal level, in the serious problems which the dynastic union between Hanover and Great Britain posed: Jacobite invasions of the kingdom and growing unease in the electorate that it was being reduced to an 'Irish' dependent status?

The 'luck' uppermost in the courtiers' minds was no doubt the greater personal *gloire* which came to George by the vicissitudes of history which made an elector of Hanover king of so prosperous and powerful a state as Great Britain, and also the way in which George succeeded in his objectives. Hanover was extended to include Bremen and Verden; Britain's influence in European politics in-

---

* The Gräfin, feeling responsible for Trudchen's motherless boys, left England on her son's accession as ruling Graf of Schaumburg–Lippe, but kept up a lively correspondence with friends in England; she also promoted knowledge of the English language in Germany.

creased; what from the outside looked like his diplomatic 'gambles' paid off; and time and again he managed to extricate himself from situations that looked desperate, like the Fifteen, the South Sea bubble and the threat of war from 1725 to 1727.

With the wisdom of hindsight, and access to material which illuminates the decision-making process of George and his political advisers, the historian can focus on the determination and ruthlessness in grasping and exploiting opportunities which are so characteristic of George as a ruler, and also on the long accumulated experience which made him so effective a figure on the European scene.

Yet the historian may also judge George 'lucky' in several respects. He was 'lucky' in that he had not, like his son, grandson and great-great-grandson, been condemned to wait for the exercise of power. Frederick, prince of Wales after 1727, waited in vain; and for George II and George IV power came so late that their characters were to some extent warped by the long years when they could not exercise the office for which they were destined by birth. No wonder that each of the three joined – for a longer or shorter period – the political opposition to the ruling king in spite of the personal difficulties and even tragedies that this brought to the royal family. Only George III was spared this fate and he, it would seem, was adversely affected by losing his father (Frederick) so early; like many another prince in his position he became obsessed with his duties and with the need to set a good example.[15]

George I, while he did not escape damage to his personality from the *Prinzenstreit* and the collapse of his marriage to Sophia Dorothea, was fortunate enough to have had an alternative *métier*, that of a soldier, for most of his early manhood. From the age of fifteen he fought in wars against France and the Turks, becoming a respected and experienced officer, having a *raison d'être* independent of his father even after Ernst August's decision to introduce primogeniture in Hanover. He was fortunate in that there were many sons, so that he, in spite of his special position as first-born, could be risked without injury to the ruling house. The military career of George's only legitimate son was cut short in part by the necessity to postpone its start till he had sired an heir, and in part also because Europe entered into a prolonged period of peace after the War of the Spanish Succession. It says much for George I's understanding of his son's need to prove himself in battle that he did send him to serve under Marlborough after Frederick's birth in 1707. George's grandson, great-grandson and great-great-grandson in the legitimate line all suffered under the refusal, successively, of George II and George III to let them go to war. They felt less manly because of it – even the artistically inclined Frederick – since they had been brought up in a tradition in which martial valour was still part of the royal *métier*.[16]

George was also 'lucky' in that the Stuart malady, porphyria, transmitted to the house of Hanover via Sophia, skipped him though it affected George III and George IV.[17] His health was good. The fistula scare proved of short duration. The cure when he was at Pyrmont, his long walks both at that spa and in the grounds of Kensington Palace and Hampton Court, as well as his riding and hunting, kept him in trim. From the Göhrde hunting-season of 1723 a pleasant and evocative scene has been transferred to canvas. It shows George I, his Prussian son-in-law Friedrich Wilhelm, Ernst August, Townshend and his wife, and a host of Hanoverian courtiers and officials riding out in the early morning.[18]

The fact that after 1714 Georg August could not share the visits to Germany may have weakened the bond between father and son. There was, however, no help for it. Just as Frederick had to be left alone in Hanover while his father and grandfather resided in England, so Georg August had to stay in Britain as a symbol of the loyalty of the house of Hanover to the Protestant succession.

That George I did not make the best of his relationship with Georg August after 1716 is undeniable. Given the facts of political life in Britain after 1689, and Georg August's own ambitions, this is not surprising, but George I certainly tried, for as long as possible, to avoid open conflict with his son. Here memories not only of the *Prinzenstreit*, but of his son as a young man, affected the king. The elector and his mother Sophia had been seriously worried by Georg August's unreliability and tendency to speak impulsively on matters of state without due reflection. Their relief and joy were great when they noticed that war service had matured and improved him.[19] Buried unease burst into the open when Georg August, as prince of Wales, challenged his father's authority by refusing to attend cabinet meetings and by forming a party of his own in both houses of parliament: George I, like many another parent before and after him, could no longer cope on a rational level. Again, he was fortunate in that a variety of circumstances, not least the appetite for office of Robert Walpole and Townshend, procured the reconciliation of 1720 and thus laid the foundation for the harmonious family life of the remaining years of George I's reign.

*   *   *

On the rational level, where tense family relationships did not distort good intentions, George as elector and ruler was famed for his compassion, and for his concern with justice and equity. His mother stressed that he was 'the enemy of injustice in any form'.[20] This trait is also emphasized by other commentators, who may be assumed to be less biased, from 1698 to 1727. It took a variety of forms. He upheld the law in matters where he himself was involved. Two instances may be given. He accepted as king, without demur, the legal opinion that he was not entitled to reclaim from his son's British income (after the quarrel in the royal family) the expenses of the education of his granddaughters: the verdict ran that, as the king had the right to take care of them under English law, he had to pay the cost.[21] And, at a later date, on the death of his divorced wife Sophia Dorothea in 1726, the negative answers to his query to Hanoverian legal authorities whether he – until her will was found – would be entitled to the income from her estate, immediately put an end to his attempts to benefit from the situation.[22] When it came to the rights of others, he was especially sensitive. He paid compensation if anyone had to lose his office, at court or in the administration, for political reasons;[23] and if he thought that a moral injustice followed on legal justice – for example, when Macclesfield was dismissed with ignominy for what George regarded as a technical offence, he allocated him a pension.[24] In theory all his subjects, Hanoverian or British, had the right to seek audience with him, though it was not always easy for petitioners to get through the screen of courtiers and officials. All written petitions had to be submitted to him, since he wanted to ensure that cases which might not seem meritorious to his Hanoverian or British advisers should be decided by his personal scrutiny: a good example is the petition in 1724 of the old *gentilhomme de la chambre* of the late duchess of Celle (George's mother-in-law, with whom he had not been on the best of terms) who secured his 100 *écus*.[25] George's close-fistedness with his private Hanoverian income or his British civil list is largely a myth. He paid the debts which a certain lieutenant von Weyhe left behind on his death, presumably for sentimental reasons since the lieutenant was a relative (possibly a son of her second marriage) of the Mlle von Meysenbug who had been a companion of his youth.[26] From the *Schattullrechnungen* kept by Mehemet for his privy purse after 1714 we can see how generous he was both with benefit tickets for singers and actors (male and female), and how lavish with presents to members of his family.[27] Quite apart from pecuniary rewards, he showed sensitivity to the feelings of others. He not only arranged for a pension for Stanhope's widow, but called on her shortly after her husband's death to express his gratitude for the services of her late husband; and his choice of words of comfort bears witness to his generosity of spirit.[28] When his Hanoverian minister Görtz worried whether George would take amiss his attempts to save the life of his kinsman Georg Heinrich von Görtz, accused in Stockholm after the death of Charles XII of having 'alienated the [late] king's affection from his subjects', George could put himself in his minister's place. Hanover and Sweden were at war and Georg Heinrich von Görtz had been one of the perpetrators of the Gyllenborg plot; yet the ruler assured his minister that he found his endeavours 'on behalf of so close a member of his family natural', and that they would not in any way detract from his appreciation of his valuable work in Hanover.[*][29]

*   *   *

On a more general level, George I's concern to render justice can be seen in his attempts to secure religious toleration for his subjects. In Hanover such toleration was already in existence when George became elector, but he was not as successful as he might have wished in his later efforts to make the Hanoverian Lutheran clergy accept a reunion of Calvinism and Lutheranism.[30] In Britain George was not satisfied with the halfway house constructed in 1718, whereby dissenters were permitted to keep their positions and offices as long as they were not reported by outsiders within the first six months of their appointment for not having taken the sacrament according to the rites of the Anglican church. He hoped to procure for them worship according to their own conscience without subterfuge and uncertainty.

In this George, who was not religious by temperament, was concerned with freedom of thought. Correspondence between British ministers at the time of the peerage bill shows that for most of them – with the exception of Stanhope – the matter of conscience was less important than the deal they hoped to make with the House of Commons: if the Lower House would swallow the peerage bill, the ministers were in return willing to grant freedom for dissenters and reform which would ensure that the universities (and Oxford in particular) did not remain, as hitherto, a breeding ground for High Anglicanism.[31]

The failure of the peerage bill, the fiasco of the South Sea speculation, Stanhope's death and Walpole's unwillingness to introduce controversial measures – all contributed to the frustration of George's hopes. Walpole's success, when in opposition,[†] at nullifying the king's and Stanhope's attempts to gain a measure of religious freedom for Roman Catholics, effectively killed any prospect of relief for a long time to come.[32] Efforts to ease the position of Jews in Britain had also met sufficient opposition to make concessions minimal: individual Jews were allowed to apply for naturalization by submitting a

* The Hanoverian minister was unsuccessful in his efforts: given the anti-absolutist fervour of Sweden at this time, Georg Heinrich's execution in February 1719 was as inevitable as it was unjust.
† Walpole then insinuated that George leant towards Roman Catholicism and inferred that it was 'a good thing' for the Church of England that the next heir would not continue along his father's path.

private act to parliament, a long and costly process, which denied this freedom to the vast majority.[33]

The reasons why religious toleration was not easily established in Great Britain are not far to seek. Party loyalties and convictions were strong on religious belief and doctrine; and the struggle for power in parliament between men of great ability meant that even when these were tolerant, or religiously indifferent, as individuals, they had to take such beliefs and doctrines into account. Reform was, however, slowly prepared for by the appointment of tolerant Whig bishops whenever a see fell vacant; by the expedient, after the Hoadley controversy of 1717,[34] of proroguing, and not recalling, the High Church convocations of either York or Canterbury. Attempts were also made, though in vain, to give government control of appointments of heads and fellows of colleges. The motivation was a double one: concern for the security of the dynasty (the nipping of Jacobitism in the bud) and a desire to uproot in new generations of students the dogma of the supremacy of church over state.[35] Even bishops reckoned Whig by inclination were usually strongly anti-dissenter in their attachment to the power of the Anglican church; there was a closing of ranks in a way not dissimilar to that of Catholics of all shades of persuasion in the France of Louis XIV against the Huguenots.[36]

One of George's reforms at the universities of Oxford and Cambridge was successfully brought about: the endowment of regius professorships in history, intended to encourage the study of 'the interests of state', in the Pufendorf sense of the phrase. This emphasis on 'modern' subjects, on history and living languages to serve as a training for future diplomats and statesmen, can be seen as a measure to induce the universities to accept the wider range of subjects already studied in the dissenting academies and at the inns of court; it was thought desirable not to confine the highest educational institutions of the country to theology and the classics. Again, we can find parallels with European experiments: Louis XIV's *académie politique* of 1712 is the most obvious one, though that institution fell into disuse after the French king's death while George's regius professorships have lasted down to our own day.[37]

That George was in tune with Early Enlightenment ideas both in domestic and foreign affairs has been postulated in this study. A great deal of additional evidence could be furnished.* His administrative and financial reforms for the town of Hanover were thorough and beneficial; the state took over the care of the poor and needy in one province of the electorate after another; the university of Helmstedt (serving both Hanover and Wolfenbüttel) increased its reputation, as

---

* Two examples must suffice. First, the keen interest of George (like others who knew of the Turkish experience) in promoting inoculation against smallpox: he had his granddaughters inoculated and was pleased when Frederick chose to follow their example. Second, George's insistence that a bill put before the Irish parliament which decreed castration for Catholic priests caught proselytizing should be dropped: it would offend the Catholic allies of Britain, he argued, and it was in any case ridiculous.

did the *Gymnasium* of Göttingen which in George II's reign rose to university status. The *Oberappellationsgericht* in Celle was held in the highest regard and widely appealed to, even by non-Hanoverian courts; and the fame of Hanoverian lawyers became widespread. German historians have agreed that George's motto ('Never desert a friend, strive to do justice to every person, fear no one'*) was peculiarly appropriate to his achievement in the electorate. Minor changes to the advantage of his subjects were also effected: for instance, the opening, with certain safeguards, of the Herrenhausen gardens and the grounds of Kensington Palace,† to the public. (Visitors were bidden not to frighten the birds, or damage plants and trees, and were enjoined to follow the directions of attendants.)[38] More significantly, George was thought of in Europe as a protector of progressive views. This was not only because he had, in principle, accepted the 'mixed government' of the English system, but also because he made clear his sympathy with the freedom of expression held to be inseparable from that system. In Britain George is not thought of as a man well versed in or well disposed towards literature. This is justified to the extent that the books we know he bought for himself are on the whole factual (the *Relation des Indes Orientales, Voyage d'Espagne et de Portugal, Histoire de Louis XIV, Relation d'un Voyage de Dannemarck* are typical examples), or connected with his *métier*, such as collections of treaties and accounts of diplomatic negotiations.[39] But his reading of French authors and dramatists and his general interest in philosophical exchange of ideas had given him the reputation of a 'modern' ruler.[40] It is not accidental that Voltaire dedicated his *Henriade* to George I, sought and was permitted refuge in Britain in 1726 when he got into trouble with the French authorities, and received encouragement and financial help from the king as well as from the princess of Wales.[41] George's lack of prejudice is noteworthy and extended even to his Stuart relatives. He expressed himself mildly enough on the topic of the Pretender[42] to astonish the British; and lord Percival marvelled (according to his diary of 1716) that the king refused to attend a thanksgiving service for the defeat of the Jacobite rebellion: he reported George as saying that he did not think it fitting that he should render thanks to God for having vanquished his own subjects.[43] There was no strict censorship of the press, though British ministers retaliated, in print and by propaganda, when they were attacked.[44] Popular ditties – to well-known tunes and often with only slightly altered text – ridiculing the king and his family were tolerated. The quarrel between George and the prince of Wales was a natural target for this kind of versifying, but compared to those current in the reign of George II they were mild in

---

* *Verlasse nie einen Freund*
  Strebe, jeden Gerechtigkeit zu erwiesen
  Fürchte niemand
† Access here was only for Saturdays and Sundays if George I was in residence.

tone.[45] The best-known verse on George I, focused on the statue of
the king placed on the top of St George's church in Bloomsbury, is
of a later date;* the contemporary version poked fun at the fact that
the benefactor who had the statue cast and put in position was a
brewer.[46]

The men and women George personally met were, naturally,
drawn from a fairly narrow social range. The story that he frequented
coffee-houses incognito to hear what was being said about him is
suspect, though his presence at public plays, operas, concerts and
masquerades must have helped to foster the image of a king who
behaved like a private person.[47] That George cared for decorum is
shown by his finding it necessary to apologize to the archbishop of
Canterbury for the fact that colonel Charles Churchill had appeared
at a masquerade, where the king had been present, in the habit of a
bishop: the king would see that it did not happen again.[48] It was not
difficult, if one had a bit of nerve, was reasonably dressed and willing
to behave properly, to gain entry into the king's receptions or
'drawingrooms'. A young student, neither well-connected nor rich,
found it easy enough to be a guest at the king's birthday celebrations
at St James's once he had greased the palm of the doorkeeper; and
at Hampton Court there were gatecrashers at plays and entertainments. This did not mean, however, that these interlopers came into
personal contact with the king.[49] Vagabonds and beggars were, as
elsewhere in Europe, kept away from routes along which George
was expected to travel; but George, since he lived in London, was
probably more aware of the actual state of his British subjects than,
for instance, Louis XIV after he had moved himself and his court
to Versailles. George's accounts occasionally list sums for 'poor on
the streets', 'poor students' and 'poor prisoners'.[50]

The years of his reign, in spite of the Jacobite alarms and the
South Sea bubble, were on the whole years of prosperity and of a
rising standard of living for all sections of society. Taxes were low
(though the crisis of 1726–27 pushed the land tax up to four shillings
in the pound), and food was plentiful if monotonous for the vast
majority in town and country. The king, as we have seen, encouraged economic initiative both in Hanover and in Britain and
took a special interest in linking the kingdom and the electorate
commercially. His support for a company which aimed at bypassing
the Imperial free city of Bremen (not part of the Hanoverian
possession) and Hamburg to give easy access from Britain to the
Hanoverian parts of north Germany by the construction of a network of canals has been studied in detail. George lent his Hanoverian
army-trained surveyors for the construction of this network and

---

* When Henry the Eighth left the Pope in the lurch
  The Protestants made him head of the Church;
  But George's good subjects the Bloomsbury people
  Instead of the Church, made him head of the steeple.

helped also with gifts of money and loans.[51] One of the British directors of this company was later found to be a crook, and the company got into serious difficulties through his actions: a fact which (if we take the South Sea bubble period into account) leads one to assume that George was more trusting and less successful in picking entrepreneurs than in his choice of ministers. Financial trickery was only one aspect of vice and crime in George I's Britain. Punishment was not always carried out according to the savage letter of the law, but theft, highway robbery and poaching (including wholesale poaching in the royal forests) were severely punished to protect property;[52] while madams of 'houses of ill repute' suffered spells in prison if they too openly flouted the convention of relative discretion.[53]

*   *   *

During George's reign London took a shape still discernible to our own day. Before the death of queen Anne money had been put aside for the building of churches outside the city boundaries to cater for the population of an ever-expanding capital. The commission in charge of this programme was, for political reasons, changed on George I's accession, but the programme itself went speedily ahead. Wren, Hawksmoor, Gibbs and other skilled architects were employed, and the places of worship they created (though some have been reduced to rubble or to ruins beyond repair during the second world war of this century) form a glorious heritage: St Martin-in-the-Fields, St Anne, Limehouse, St George's, Hanover Square and St George's, Bloomsbury, a dozen in all.[54]

Many of the pleasant squares of London were laid out between 1714 and 1727, among them St James's Square, Grosvenor Square and Hanover Square, though, alas, the majority of them are now more pleasing seen on old prints than in their modified or vandalized modern state. The regularity of the Georgian houses, the open square with its trees and, usually, a statue in the centre convey that impression of order and harmony which was the aesthetic ideal of that time. The squares were, of course, not personally inspired by George, but he gave an impetus to them since his courtiers and ministers built or bought houses in these squares within easy distance of St James's Palace, and Melusine at one time owned No. 43 Grosvenor Square as well as a house in Portugal Row.[55]

We owe, however, to George's personal building initiative the extension of Kensington Palace and the layout of its grounds. Nearly all the furniture from his time has disappeared, but the decorations are intact or restored as near to the original as possible and convey the atmosphere of George's favourite residence, surely one of the most pleasant and intimate of palaces. George's patronage of William Kent won him other commissions, the most notable being Robert Walpole's magnificent Houghton Hall in Norfolk, and this added to England's architectural treasures.

British musical heritage also owes much to George. In part this was a consequence of the Hanoverian succession since George's German entourage and his whole court strengthened the bonds which had already been forged in respect of church and secular music between England and Germany: German *Kapellmeister* and German instrumentalists were found in England before George I's reign.[56] Where the king's own patronage was especially influential, however, was in his strong support for Handel in particular and for opera in general.

*   *   *

In the political field George contributed two great services to Britain. One was that he reconciled the country to Europe. The separate Tory peace with France had alienated the Dutch Republic and the Austrian Habsburg state from 'perfidious Albion'; and resentment was felt also by the German states of the Empire who had held objectives of their own in the War of the Spanish Succession. George was particularly well fitted for this reconciliation. He had publicly protested against the separate British agreement with Louis XIV, and against the Tory collusion with France in the 'restraining orders' that took the British army out of the war in a way regarded as treacherous by the allies. On his accession George took the initiative to improve relations with Dutch statesmen and with the emperor Charles VI, and achieved considerable success. But his initiatives, and those of the British ministers whom he most trusted in foreign policy matters, especially Stanhope, went beyond the old comrades-in-arms of the late war and extended also to France, the enemy of that war. His family relationship to Philippe, duc d'Orléans, was helpful here. The ideas which animated the peace plans for the south and for the north – agreements reached by mutual sacrifices and mutual advantages – are significant ones. Great patience, much ingenuity, and a fair amount of ruthless determination were needed by George, Stanhope and their foremost French partner, Dubois, to start this early eighteenth-century experiment in solving acute inter-state European problems without recourse to war. There was no undue optimism about the ease with which wars could be avoided; the expressed objective, to keep the peace 'as long as humanly possible', was, however, genuinely meant. The realism and the persistence of the three main architects of the two peace plans is remarkable, and the congress tradition which they helped to build is of more than early eighteenth-century importance. That George, by the very situation in which he found himself as elector, saw less clearly in northern affairs than Townshend in the early years of the reign is a fact that should not be glossed over. Hanover's commitment to the conquest of Bremen and Verden did rob Britain of a chance to play the forceful mediator in the north between 1715 and 1719. Conversely, George managed to restrain Townshend in the years 1725–27 when his principal secretary of state was more aggressively inclined than the king: even if Townshend did not plan for war during that period, his contingency preparations were so blatant in the diplomatic field that Europe expected war between the great powers to break out any moment. It needed all the king's expertise to guide, with French help, the British ship of state towards the Soissons congress.

The debate whether British interests suffered from George's Hanoverian ambitions ought now to be a dead one. George certainly used the trump-card of the British navy for electoral purposes, though he largely managed to conceal this from the majority of his British ministers and subjects, or – at least – not to provide them with proof. Yet British interests were also served by protection of trade to the Baltic, and commercial advantages for Britain were obtained at the peacemakings of the north. There was thus a large measure of overlap between the interests of the electorate and those of the kingdom. If a generalization can be made, it is that Hanoverian interests tended to dominate George's policy in the north between 1715 and 1718, and that British and European interests dominated that theatre – as they had always dominated the south of Europe – from the end of 1718 to George's death. George's preoccupation with the Great Northern War made him the effective advocate of a strong British navy; here again electoral and royal policies merged: the navy increased its number of fast ships during his reign.[57]

As we have seen, George became progressively more British in outlook, and when he planned for the dissolution of the dynastic union between Hanover and Great Britain, it was on the condition that his own senior line should remain kings and (if fate so decreed) queens regnant of Britain: Hanover would become secundogeniture on the European model worked out for the Italian states in the dynastic competition between Spain and Austria. That the separation of Hanover and Britain did not take place in the way George had planned, does not rob his will of 1716 with its 1720 codicil of interest. On the contrary, it is a most convincing example of his realism and rationalism. In smaller ways also George's increasing absorption into the kingdom can be demonstrated. We have already noted his growing command of the language; and it is, for instance, noteworthy that the governess he chose for his granddaughters when he took charge of their education was the countess of Portland, a highly intelligent and learned Englishwoman, the niece of William Temple who, after her husband's death, had brought up a large family of her own as well as his children of his first marriage.[58]

George's second great service to Great Britain was his contribution to the political stability of his kingdom. His military experience and his unflappability softened the impact of the Jacobite invasions and plots, while his clemency (more pronounced than that of his ministers) blunted Tory resentment after the failure of the Fifteen. He did not, as we have seen, achieve a 'mixed' government in the sense of Whig and Tory ministers cooperating with him in a 'king's party'; but he adapted to the reality of the situation and tried to balance one set of Whig ministers against another so that in the inner cabinet, where he himself presided throughout his reign, he could influence decisions. After Carteret's removal from the secretary of state's office in 1724, George may be thought to have been more of a 'captive' of the remaining powerful ministers, Townshend and Walpole, than in the days of Stanhope and Sunderland; but what evidence we have points to control by George over Townshend in foreign policy and to a smooth cooperation with Robert Walpole on domestic matters. If George ever was a captive of his ministers, it was during the peerage bill crisis which has been analyzed in this study in its chronological perspective.

The closet, where George all along saw his ministers in groups or individually, was the necessary and important venue for cooperation between king and ministers. It would, however, in my judgment be misleading to characterize George I's reign as one of 'closet government' pure and simple. The king's government was made up of the king and the whole of the inner cabinet; and the necessary presence of the ministers of the inner cabinet in the two houses of parliament, and their need to carry both Commons and Lords, made for a smoother exercise of the 'mixed' constitutional principles of England than in the years between 1640 and 1714.

George's reputation, in the sense of *gloire*, and power in Britain as in Europe, stood high in his own lifetime. In the very nature of international relations, his reconciliation of Britain to Europe and his peacetime congresses to solve European problems, could not but undergo changes; particularly as Britain, with the larger navy built during George I's reign, began to concentrate on overseas commercial expansion. In time the cooperation with France lapsed and Britain became involved in the War of the Austrian Succession in 1740, in the Seven Years War of 1756 and in the War of American Independence: by the latter period Britain was considered an 'exorbitant' state making undue use of its naval power to dictate to other nations. Nor could George have visualized that Hanover, during these wars, would become so important for Britain as a continental centre for British intelligence and for Europe as a focal point for the spread of British intellectual ideas.[59]

Understandably, George's contribution to British and European history tended to be forgotten, as the century wore on. The field was left open for the build-up of the stock picture which this study has sought to modify by going back to contemporary records beyond memoir literature and propaganda, both pro-George and anti-George. Most of the statues of George have disappeared. Of the three best-documented equestrian statues, the one which, after the Canons sale, was put up in Leicester Square was removed temporarily to make room for an exhibition. It was then forgotten for years and when remembered found to be too damaged to survive a return to the square.[60] The one put up in Dublin was taken down (at what date is not known) and resurrected from a junk-yard in the present century. It is now nicely placed outside the Barber Institute of Fine Art in Birmingham, close enough to the ground for George's finely moulded hands to be studied. Alas, recent years of student demonstrations have resulted in the loss of one hand, one stirrup and the king's baton.[61] The second surviving equestrian statue is in the grounds of Stowe school and is the only one which is in an appropriate Georgian setting, flanked by fine buildings, with space and trees around it as far as the eye can see. The interested spectator can now look more closely at George's face in the statue in Roman dress at the entrance to the Public Record Office museum, rediscovered as recently as 1954. The two, together with some of the paintings from life, illuminate the public and private figure of the elector-king.

The present study is not meant as an apologia for George I but as an illumination, from all the evidence available, of an elusive ruler, in the sense that so much of the evidence was hard to come by. When the balance sheet is made up, George turns out to be, if not the most attractive of the Hanoverian kings in Britain, the most competent and politically imaginative.

Of literary characterizations,[62] the one by a Dutch diplomat who had lived some considerable time at George's electoral court can be largely upheld by the historian: 'He is much concerned for his reputation but is not excessively ambitious; he has a special aptitude for affairs of state, a well-ordered economy, very sound brain and judgment; he does not waste his time on trifles; he keeps good discipline among his troops and good order in his finances; he does not flare up, being of a calm temperament; he bears justice in mind at all times and, withal, he is goodhearted.'

Bibliography and Notes

BIBLIOGRAPHY

No select bibliography is necessary, since there has been no biography of George in German and only two in English: that by Melville in two volumes in 1908 and the one-volume study by Terry in 1927. Popular works which deal with George I are, not unexpectedly, out of touch with modern research: this is true of the recent volume on George by Joyce Marlow in the series 'Kings and Queens of England' (1973), and the character sketch of him in Chevenix Trench's biography of George II (1975). General treatments are usually hilarious in their mixture of factual inaccuracies and uncritical reliance on contemporary anti-Hanoverian propaganda, or excessively bland in following the contemporary government line. The most perceptive remarks on George have come from Professor J. H. Plumb, who was the first scholar to stress (in his *The First Four Georges* of 1956 and in his *Growth of Political Stability* of 1967) that the king was a complex and by no means commonplace personality who by his perspicacity and firmness provided stable government; and Plumb's pupil Professor Beattie, has given us an excellent study of the administration of George I's royal court which throws light also on political issues. For those interested, I have already given an analytical survey of material, published and unpublished, of importance for an assessment of George I as a person and as a ruler in *Fürst, Bürger, Mensch* (Wiener Beiträge zur Geschichte der Neuzeit vol. 2, ed. F. Engel-Janosi, G. Klingenstein, H. Lutz, Vienna 1975): 'In search of an elusive ruler. Source material for a biography of George I as elector and king'.

To save space in the notes to the text I have chosen to give my bibliography by means of short titles, extended in full below, within three sections: unpublished documents; published documents, letters and memoirs; and secondary works. Within each section the arrangement is alphabetical and the continental ä, ö, ü and the Scandinavian a, ø and æ are, for convenience, treated as if they were a, o, u and ae. Russian transcriptions are in accordance with the Library of Congress system, without diacritical marks.

Abbreviations used for periodicals, yearbooks and works of reference cited in notes:

ADB	*Allgemeine Deutsche Biographie*
BDR	*British Diplomatic Representatives 1689–1789*, ed. D. B. Horn (1932)
BIHR	*Bulletin of the Institute of Historical Research*
DNB	*Dictionary of National Biography*
EHR	*English Historical Review*
ESR	*European Studies Review*
HJ	*Historical Journal*
HLQ	*Huntington Library Quarterly*
HT	*Historisk Tidskrift* (Sweden)
HZ	*Historische Zeitschrift*
JMH	*Journal of Modern History*
JGO	*Jahrbücher für Geschichte Osteuropas*
JSAHR	*Journal for Society of Army Historical Research*
KFÅ	*Karolinska Förbundets Årsbok* (Sweden)
NJ	*Niedersächsisches Jahrbuch für Landesgeschichte*
RH	*Revue Historique*
RHD	*Revue d'Histoire Diplomatique*
SHR	*Scottish Historical Review*
ZHVN	*Zeitschrift des Historischen Vereins für Niedersachsen*

I *Unpublished Archive Material*

BRITISH ARCHIVES

British Museum (now British Library), abbrev.
B.M.

Additional Manuscripts, abbrev. Add. MSS.

6117: Letters from William King, archbishop of Dublin, to William Wake, archbishop of Canterbury.

9078–9283: Coxe Papers. Copies in full or in extract, made by archdeacon William Coxe from a variety of papers in private ownership. Important has been vol. 9132, the papers of Horatio Walpole.

15943: Letters of princes of Germany 1559–1802.

20985: Papers (mainly Dutch) connected with the Utrecht peace congress 1712–13.

22510: Letter book of James Stanhope 1715–16.

22511–22525: Carteret Papers 1719 to 1725.

32679–32751: Newcastle Papers (up to 1728).

35349–36278: Hardwicke Papers. Especially important have been 35837 (prepared for publication but not printed) on the Quadruple Alliance period; 35886, papers which include those connected with the duchess of Kendal's inheritance from George; and 36139, which brought to light George's private will in favour of the duchess.

37156: Stepney Papers.

37361–37386: Whitworth Papers, of importance both for George's northern diplomacy and for the congress of Cambrai; includes also (in vol. 37373) copies of Stanhope's correspondence in 1719 with Dubois.

38507: Townshend Papers.

40843: Vernon Papers (the Privy Purse and Secret Service Accounts for 1721–25).

47028–47029: Egmont Papers (Percival's journal and correspondence).

Autograph volumes, Miscellaneous Papers volumes, and volumes of the diplomatic correspondence of minor figures, have not been listed here, though they have yielded good material; brief explanations of their provenance are given in the notes where they have been cited.

Stowe MSS 227–42 and 246: Hanover Papers, Robethon Papers, Castle Papers, and Craggs Papers. (Where these are copies I have preferred to use and cite the originals when extant.)

The *King's MSS* vol. 140. A collection of copies of letters which passed between members of the Hanoverian electoral family, selected and copied by the army officer Frederick Georges August Gargan. No. 49 is George's letter to his mother from London of 1681. The volume came into British royal possession in 1729.

Blenheim Archive (now deposited in the British Library)

In contrast to its great riches for the reign of queen Anne, this archive has little to offer for George I's reign. The Sunderland section has hardly anything of importance for political history (possibly because many papers were destroyed, by the Cowpers for example, in the traumatic years 1720–22; certainly some were removed at George's request on the day after Sunderland's death). A few interesting Treasury papers remain (cited in notes according to the old catalogue).

Chevening MSS (now deposited in the Kent Record Office at Maidstone)

Although thinner for George I's reign than for that of queen Anne, there is much information of vital importance, especially in documents connected with the quarrel between George and the prince of Wales, and in papers which illuminate Britain's relations with France and Spain and George's role in the decision-making process. Remnants of the original correspondence between Stanhope and Dubois, and of both with British diplomats, and some non-diplomatic documents, e.g. library lists and accounts, have also proved useful.

Cholmondeley (Houghton) MSS (now deposited in Cambridge University Library)

These papers have been used to good effect by Professor Plumb for his Robert Walpole biography; and the Walpole spy-net focused on the Jacobites has been analysed by his pupil, Professor Fritz. For me, letters sent to Walpole by George's Hanoverian entourage have been significant, as have documents connected with the South Sea bubble.

Edinburgh National Library MS 5129 (Jacobite material)

Evelyn MSS (now deposited in Christ Church Library, Oxford)

A series of journals kept by Sir John Evelyn covering George's reign, though with gaps for part of 1716–17 and 1723–24. Of the greatest importance for George and his rehanging of the paintings at Kensington Palace, highly illuminating also for the cultural interests and concerns of the diarist.

Lambeth Palace

MS 1770. The diary of archbishop Wake, consulted by kind permission of the Archbishop of Canterbury and the trustees of the Lambeth Palace library. Useful for Wake's political allies and enemies and for his connection with the king and the prince and princess of Wales.

Panshanger MSS

The MS diary of Lady Mary Cowper, which contains some entries left out of the printed version (for this see II below). Those portions of the diary (1716–20) which lady Cowper herself destroyed can, to some extent, be supplemented by correspondence kept between those dates. Of this correspondence the letters between husband and wife when they were separated by the duties of either spouse are important; and the letters to Lady Cowper from her brother, John Clavering, during his visit to Hanover in 1716, are entertaining and informative (only a few of these letters, generally in extract, have been printed in an appendix to the *Diary*). Of non-family correspondents the few letters from Caroline, princess of Wales, which escaped destruction have been most illuminating, as have those from Bernstorff and the countess of Schaumburg-Lippe in the period where the diary pages have been destroyed. The letters of Mme Robethon have been useful for the contacts between lady Cowper and the 'German ladies' at court.

Public Record Office (abbrev. P.R.O.)

State Papers Domestic (abbrev. SPD)

Regencies, incoming correspondence from Hanover and on the journeys to and from the electorate (call no. 43).

Regencies, entry books (drafts or copies of letters going to Hanover, call no. 44).

Treasury papers (call no. 35): for detailed analysis of these see Beattie, *Court*, 285. I have principally used them for accounts of expenditure.

State Papers Foreign (abbrev. SPF)

Incoming Correspondence and Foreign Entry Books for Austria, Denmark, Germany (states), France, Hanover, Holland, Italy (states), Poland, Russia, Spain and Sweden for the period of the reign.

Foreign Ministers in England Books; royal letters; treaty papers, treaties; intercepted correspondence.

Westminster Abbey Library
Funeral books and documents connected with Friedrich Wilhelm von der Schulenburg.

Windsor Castle, Royal Archives (abbrev. Windsor, R.A.)
52837–52848: Aislabie papers (sent to George II by Aislabie's son William in 1742).
53017: 'Astle' volume sent in 1771 to the royal family by Thomas Astle (for whom see *DNB*), as he held it 'not fit to be in the library of a private subject': papers and letters connected with George I's submission to legal opinion (a) on his right to educate his grandchildren, (b) on his hope to alter the succession to give absolute preference to male heirs and (c) of his plan to dissolve, by a will, the dynastic union.
Geo 57581–57583: Wardrobe account volume (one only) for 1714–27.
Geo Add MSS 1/25: George I's letter (in own hand, in French) to the regent of France 21 Jan. OS 1718.
Geo Add MSS 28: Letters in French from Caroline, princess of Wales, to her lady-in-waiting Mrs Clayton from 1716–27 with English contemporary copies and translations (for which see ch. V note 64). Nearly all her letters are undated and are not in sequence even as to years (they can, however, be roughly dated according to contents); references to them are therefore by archival numbers. The series is valuable for the attitudes and policies of the prince and princess during the quarrel with George I, and is also informative on the king's attitude to his grandchildren.

HANOVER ARCHIVES

Hannover Hauptstaatsarchiv (abbrev. Hann.)*
(i) *Calenberg Brief Archiv 24:* Letters to George from abroad, arranged by countries. Designation *England* proved the most important for

* For the losses sustained during the Second World War see G. N. Schnath, *Studia Leibnitiana* 1972, 263–67; the post-1705 foreign policy documents (Hannover 9) were then destroyed, a circumstance which enhances the value of the Bernstorff archive.

the period before 1714 with letters to and from Portland, Marlborough, Schütz, Kreienberg, Bothmer, Townshend and others. Second in importance is the correspondence between George I and Huldeberg in Vienna (Des. *Österreich*) which illuminates George's policies 1707–09.
(ii) *Calenberg Brief Archiv 16:* Kriegskanzlei (*Kriegssachen* and *Kriegsereignisse*). Letters and other documents from the periods when George, as elector, was on campaign. Letters from Marlborough and other correspondents on military affairs are there in abundance as are documents on troop dispositions, subsidies, hospitals, food rations, etc. For Hanoverian domestic affairs, *Hofmarschall* Hardenberg's correspondence from George's headquarters with the *Kammerpräsident* Friedrich Wilhelm von Görtz in Hanover is useful.
(iii) *Calenberg Brief Archiv 11E I:* A long series of files which has proved invaluable for George's foreign policy from 1714–27, as both elector and king. The files are divided by topics and each contains drafts, memoranda, letters received, some by English statesmen, which illuminate decision-making: we learn of George's sources of information and of plans discussed by him and by his advisers on a variety of problems. It is significant that exchanges and equivalents, reciprocal advantages and reciprocal sacrifices form part of many of the plans here put on paper. The most significant for me have been: Numbers 99, 177 and 258 for George's relations with the Empire and emperor; 137, 179 and 218 for religious affairs in the Empire; 167a and 186 on the Protestants in the Palatinate; 208 on plans 1720 for reunion of all Protestants; 170 on the Quadruple Alliance and 227 on the Italian fiefs problem; 272 and 274 on the congresses of Cambrai and Soissons 1727–28; 210, 213, 223 and 225 on Bremen and Verden investiture problems 1721–23; 183 on George's success in efforts from 1718 to have the house of Wolfenbüttel included in the Hanoverian electoral line.

Hannover 91:
19a, *Kürfurstin Sophie.* Letters to Sophia from 1663 onwards. The most important for me have been the 30 letters written by George to his mother. They are now being edited and published – with the letters already in print

from George to Sophia – by Professor Schnath for *NJ*.

König Georg Archiv (abbrev. K.G.) in Haus und Hofsachen, deposited by the Prince of Hanover in the Hauptstaatsarchiv

The most important for me have been the Schatullrechnungsbeläge in 27 boxes (K.G. 22 Anhang no. 3) since they contain the receipts and papers connected with George I's private expenditure from 1698 to 1726. Papers put at my disposal by H.R.H. Prince Ernst August of Hanover from his library at Calenberg have also been useful as background information.

OTHER GERMAN ARCHIVES

Bernstorff Archive (Bernstorffsches Archiv, Gartow)

The papers of Freiherr Andreas Gottlieb von Bernstorff. A very rich archive. The material of interest to English historians has been analysed by myself and a copy of this work (financed by the British Academy) is available at the L.S.E., International History Department. Between my first visit in 1971 and the second in 1973 Professor Schnath catalogued these papers (a copy of this catalogue is now in the Hanover Staatsarchiv), and I have adopted his catalogue-numbers in the analysis mentioned above as in the references in my notes. The whole Andreas Gottlieb part of the archive has been studied and has yielded a great deal of important information. References to the different sections are given in the notes in such a way that the reader can ascertain not only the sections between AG 1 and AG 84, but the correspondent or the class of document in question.

Bückeburg Archive

The marriage contract of Albert Wolfgang zu Schaumburg-Lippe and *die schöne Gertrud* deposited in the Niedersächsisches Archiv, Bückeburg.

The Görtz Archive (Gräflich Görtzisches Archiv, deposited in Darmstadt)

Letters, many in French, received by and drafts of letters written by Friedrich Wilhelm von Görtz, George's minister. The whole archive has been studied and references to all sections cited will be found in the notes. The most important section has been 121/6, the

letters written by Friedrich Wilhelm von der Schulenburg, a *Kammerherr* with diplomatic experience and political interests, who attended George in England. His unique position at court (he was the half-brother of [Ehrengard] Melusine von der Schulenburg) and the frequency of his letters for the eventful and critical years 1717–20 have made his testimony particularly significant and given new insight into George's behaviour and attitudes in these years. All his letters are in NS but I have in the text transposed to OS or given double dating where necessary in the English context.

OTHER ARCHIVES USED

Heinsius Archief (correspondence addressed to the Dutch *raadpensionaris* Antonie Heinsius) at the Hague, indicated by catalogue numbers where directly cited; a full list of the documents used is in Hatton, *Diplomatic Relations*, 261–62.

Archives des Affaires Etrangères, Paris (abbrev. AAE)

The three series 'Correspondance', 'Mémoires et Documents', and 'Supplements' have been extensively used for the whole period for Austria, the houses of Brunswick-Lüneburg, the Dutch Republic and Great Britain; in direct citations series and volume are indicated.

II *Printed Documents, Letters and Memoirs*

Place of publication is London unless stated otherwise.

Addison, *Letters: The Letters of Joseph Addison 1693–1718*, ed. Walter Graham (Oxford 1941).

Alberoni, *Letters: Lettres intimes de J. M. Alberoni au comte Rocca*, ed. E. Bourgeois (Paris 1892).

Anne, *Letters and Instructions: The Letters and Diplomatic Instructions of Queen Anne*, ed. Beatrice Curtis Brown (1933).

BDI, Denmark: British Diplomatic Instructions III *Denmark 1689–1792*, ed. J. F. Chance (1926).

BDI, France: British Diplomatic Instructions II *France 1689–1721*, ed. L. G. Wickham Legg (1925).

BDI, Sweden: British Diplomatic Instructions I *Sweden 1689–1729*, ed. J. F. Chance (1922).

Bebenbourg, *Correspondance: Correspondance du Baron Karl de Bebenbourg avec le cardinal Paolucci 1700–1719*, ed. Louis Jadin (2 vols. Rome 1968).

Bernstorff, *Autobiography:* 'Selbstbiographie', ed. A. Köcher in *Jahrbuch des Kaiser Wilhelms Gymnasiums zu Hannover* vol. 2 (Hanover 1877).

Bidrag, SNKH: Bidrag til den Store Nordiska Krigs Historie, publ. by the Danish general staff, vols. I–VIII, ed. A. P. Tuxen and vol. IX, ed. K. G. Rockstroh (Copenhagen 1899–1932).

Bolingbroke, *Letters: Letters and Correspondence, public and private, of Lord Viscount Bolingbroke*, ed. G. Parke (4 vols. 1798).

Bolingbroke, *Letters to Stair: Lettres inédites de Bolingbroke à Lord Stair 1716–20*, ed. Paul Baratier (Paris 1939).

Bothmer, *Memoirs: Aus den Erinnerungen des Hans Kaspar von Bothmer*, ed. Karl Freiherr von Bothmer and G. Schnath (Hildesheim/ Leipzig 1936).

Bothmer, *Q.A.:* 'Mémoires des Englischen Ministers Grafen von Bothmer über die Quadrupelallianz von 1718', ed. R. Doebner, in *Forschungen zur Deutschen Geschichte* vol. 26 (Göttingen 1886).

Bristol, *Diary: The Diary of John Hervey, first Earl of Bristol* (1894), ed. S.H.A.H. [i.e. Sydenham H. A. Hervey].

Boyer, *Political State:* A. Boyer, *Political State of Great Britain* (60 vols. 1711–40) vols. VIII–XXXI.

Burnet, *History:* Gilbert Burnet, *History of His Own Time* (2 vols. 1724–32, expanded ed. 6 vols. Oxford 1833).

Burnet, *Letters: The Letters of Thomas Burnet to George Duckett, 1712–22*, ed. David Nicol Smith (Oxford 1914).

Bussche, *Letters to:* 'Briefe an den kurhannoverschen Minister Albrecht Philipp von dem Bussche von der Herzogin Sophie, der Erbprinzessin Sophie Dorothea, der Abtissin von Herford, Leibniz und der Frau von Harling, aus den Jahren 1677–1697', ed. E. Bodemann, *ZHVN* 1882, 129–214.

Byng, *Papers: The Byng Papers, selected from the Letters and Papers of Admiral Sir George Byng, First Viscount Torrington*, ed. Brian Tunstall (3 vols. 1930–32).

Cantillo, A. del, *Tratados y convenios* (Madrid 1843) prints significant secret articles in Spanish treaties omitted in other treaty collections.

Chandler, *Proceedings:* Richard Chandler, *The History and Proceedings of the House of Commons, from the Restoration to the Present Times* (14 vols. 1742–44) vol. VI *1714–27* (1742).

Chesterfield, *Letters: The Letters of Philip Dormer Stanhope, 4th Earl of Chesterfield*, ed. in 6 vols. by B. Dobrée (1932).

Cibber, *Apology:* C. Cibber, *An Apology for his life* (2 vols. 1740).

Cobbet: William Cobbet, *Parliamentary History of England* vols. VI, VII and VIII, covering 1714–27 (36 vols. 1806–20).

Cowper, Mary, *Diary: The Diary of Mary, Countess Cowper 1714–1720*, ed. the Hon. C. S. Spencer Cowper (1864). Note that parts of the diary (dealing with the period from the end of October 1716 to April 1720) were destroyed by the diarist herself in 1722, but this gap is to a considerable extent filled by surviving correspondence in the Panshanger MSS (see I above).

Cowper, William, *Diary: The Private Diary of William First Lord Cowper, Lord Chancellor of England*, ed. Edward Craven Hawtrey (Eton 1833).

CTB: Calendar of Treasury Books vols. covering 1714–19, ed. W. A. Shaw (1927–57).

CTP: Calendar of Treasury Papers vol. V, ed. J. Redington (1883).

Danmark-Norges Traktater vols. VII, VIII, IX, ed. L. Laursen; X, ed. C. Christiansen (Copenhagen 1933–48).

Defoe, Daniel, *A Tour through the Whole Island of Great Britain*, ed. G. Cole (2 vols. 1927), important for stately homes.

Drögereit, *Will:* R. Drögereit, 'Das Testament König Georgs I und die Frage der Personalunion zwischen England und Hannover', *NJ* 1937 (prints George I's will with codicils).

Dubois, *Mémoires secrets: Mémoires secrets et correspondance inédite du Cardinal Dubois*, ed. Charles Louis Sevelinges (2 vols. Paris 1815).

Dumont, *Treaties:* J. Dumont, *Corps Universel Diplomatique du Droit des Gens* VII and VIII (The Hague 1731).

Ernst August, *Letters to his wife:* 'Briefe des Kurfürsten Ernst August von Hannover an seine Gemahlin, die Kurfürstin Sophie', ed. Anna Wendland, *NJ* 1930.

Ernst August II, *Letters: Briefe des Herzogs Ernst August zu Braunschweig-Lüneburg an Johann Franz Diedrich von Wendt aus den Jahren 1703 bis 1726*, ed. Erich Graf Kielmansegg (Hanover/ Leipzig 1902).

Fabrice, *Letters: Anecdotes du sejour de Roi de Suède à Render, ou Lettres de Mr. le Baron de Fabrice pour servir d'eclaircissement à l'histoire de Charles XII* (Hamburg 1760).

Fabrice, *Memoiren: Die Memoiren des Kammerherrn Friedrich Ernst von Fabrice, 1683–1750*, ed. R. Grieser (Hildesheim 1956). Note translation from the original French to German.

Friedrich III, *Letters: Aus dem Briefwechsel Friedrichs I von Preussen und seiner Familie*, ed. Ernst Berner (Berlin 1901).

London Gazette vols. for 1714–27. Useful for pin-pointing dates of events at court.

George, *Letters:* 'George I's letters to his daughter', in *EHR* 1937, ed. R. L. Arkell.

Görtz: F. C. von Moser, *Rettung der Ehre und Unschuld des Georg Heinrichs, Freiherr von Schlitz, genannt von Görtz* (Hamburg 1776).

Gourville, *Mémoires:* Jean de Gourville, *Mémoires de Gourville 1646–1702* (2 vols. Paris 1894–95).

Hamilton, *Diary: The Diary of Sir David Hamilton 1709–1714*, ed. Philip Roberts with notes by D. W. A. Speck (1976).

Harcourt, *Papers: The Harcourt Papers*, ed. Edward William Harcourt, vol. II (Oxford 1832).

Heinsius, *Briefwisseling: De Briefwisseling van Anthonie Heinsius* vol. I (March–December 1702), ed. A. J. Veenendaal, Jr (The Hague 1976).

Hervey, *Memoirs: Memoirs of the Reign of George the Second from his Accession to the Death of Queen Caroline*, ed. W. Croker (2 vols. 1848).

Hervey, *Memoirs* (Sedgwick): *Some Material towards Memoirs of the Reign of George II by John, Lord Hervey*, ed. R. Sedgwick (3 vols. 1931); one-vol. selection 1952, with paperback reprint 1963.

HMC: the reports and published papers of the Historical Manuscript Commission, followed by an abbreviated indication of the series and volumes cited: the most important for my work have been *Carlisle MSS; Downshire MSS; Dropmore MSS; Egmont MSS; Hasting MSS; House of Lords MSS; Laing MSS; Onslow MSS; Ormonde MSS; Polwarth MSS; Portland MSS; Roxburgh et al. MSS; Townshend MSS; Stuart MSS; Various MSS.*

JHC: Journals of the House of Commons vols. XVII–XXI (n.d.) for 1714–27.

JHL: Journals of the House of Lords vols. XIX–XXIII (n.d.) for 1714–27.

King, *Notes:* 'Notes on domestic and foreign affairs during the last years of the reign of George I and the early part of the reign of George II', in appendix to P. King, *Life of John Locke* vol. II (1830).

Knachtbull, *Diary: The Parliamentary Diary of Sir Edward Knachtbull 1722–1730*, ed. A. N. Newman (1963); useful as it includes information on when the House 'sat close', i.e., without admitting strangers.

Königsmarck, Aurora, *Mémoires:* 'Mémoires', fragments ed. by Anna Wendland, *ZHVN* 1882, 228–36.

Königsmarck-Sophia Dorothea, *Correspondence: Der Königsmarck-Briefwechsel: Korrespondenz der Prinzessin Sophie Dorothea von Hannover mit dem Grafen Philipp Christoph Königsmarck 1690–1694.* Kritische Gesamtausgabe in Regestenform, ed. G. Schnath (Hildesheim 1952). Note the definitive proof of the genuineness of the correspondence, in G. Schnath, 'Der Königsmarckbriefwechsel – eine Fälschung?', *NJ* 1930, 135–205.

Lamberty, *Mémoires:* Guillaume de Lamberty, *Mémoires pour servir à l'histoire du XVIII Siècle* (14 vols. 2nd ed. Amsterdam 1735–40).

Leibniz, *Anecdota:* Gottfried Wilhelm Leibniz 'Anecdota' (of 1695 on the Sophia Dorothea-Königsmarck affair), ed. A. Köcher, *HZ* 1882.

Leibniz, *Correspondence: Correspondance de Leibniz avec l'Electrice Sophie de Brunswick-Luneburg*, ed. Onno Klopp in 'Die Werke von Leibniz', vols. 7–9 (Hanover/London/Paris 1873–74).

Leibniz, *Letters to Bernstorff:* 'Leibnizens Briefwechsel mit dem Minister Bernstorff und andere Leibniz betreffende Briefe und Aktenstücke 1703–1715', ed. R. Doebner, *ZHVN* 1881, 205–308.

Leibniz, *Papers and Letters (Akademie):* Gottfried Wilhelm Leibniz, *Sämtliche Schriften und Briefe*, Reihe I: *Allgemeiner, Politischer und Historischer Briefwechsel*, publ. by the Deutsche Akademie der Wissenschaften zu Berlin (1947 onwards).

Liselotte, *Letters to Görtz:* 'Briefe der Herzogin Elisabeth Charlotte von Orleans an dem Freiherrn Friedrich Wilhelm von Schlitz genannt von Görtz 1719–22', ed. Mathilde Knoop, *Mitteilungen des Oberhess. Geschichtsvereins* (Giessen 1957).

Liselotte, *Letters to Princess of Wales: Die Briefe der Herzogin Elisabeth Charlotte von Orleans an die Prinzessin von Wales*, ed. C. Künzel (Ebenhausen 1923).

Liselotte, *Letters to Sophia: Aus den Briefen der Herzogin Elisabeth Charlotte von Orleans an die*

Kurfürstin Sophie von Hannover, ed. E. Bodemann (Leipzig/Hanover 1891), with further letters ed. Guillaume Depping in *RH* 1894 and 1895.

Liselotte, *Selected letters: Letters from Liselotte*, transl. and ed. Maria Kroll (1970), cited at times because of good translation.

Lockhart Papers: The Lockhart Papers: containing Memoirs and Commentaries upon the Affairs of Scotland from 1702 to 1715, ed. A. Aufrere (2 vols. 1817).

Loewe: V. Loewe, *Preussens Staatsverträge aus der Regierungszeit König Friedrich I* (Leipzig 1913).

Macpherson, *Original Papers*: James Macpherson, *Original papers, containing the secret history of Great Britain* II (1775), prints some papers which have since disappeared.

Mahon, *War of Succession in Spain*: Lord Mahon, *History of the War of Succession in Spain* (2 vols. 1836), useful documents in text and appendices.

Marlborough, *Letters: The Letters and Despatches of John Churchill, First Duke of Marlborough, from 1702 to 1712*, ed. Sir George Murray (5 vols. 1845).

Marlborough (Sarah), *Correspondence: Private Correspondence of Sarah, Duchess of Marlborough*, ed. Lord John Russell (2 vols. 1838).

Marlborough-Godolphin, *Correspondence: The Marlborough-Godolphin Correspondence*, ed. Henry L. Snyder (3 vols. Oxford 1975). Note that letters to and from Sarah, duchesss of Marlborough, are also included. Authoritative on dating.

Marlborough-Heinsius, *Correspondence: The Correspondence 1710–1711 of John Churchill, First Duke of Marlborough and Anthonie Heinsius, Grand Pensionary of Holland*, ed. B. van 't Hoff (The Hague 1951).

Mary, *Memoirs: Memoirs of Queen Mary of England*, ed. R. Doebner (Leipzig 1886), prints correspondence between Sophia, William and Mary.

Miège, G., *The Present State of Great Britain* (1715).

Montagu, *Letters: The Complete Letters of Lady Mary Wortley Montagu*, ed. Robert Halsband (2 vols. Oxford 1965–66).

Montagu, *Works: The Letters and Works of Lady Mary Wortley Montagu*, ed. lord Wharncliffe (1837); third ed. with additions by W. Moy Thomas, 2 vols. n.d., has been used, I, 122 ff.: 'Account of the Court of George I at his accession'. An improved ed. by R. Halsband is in preparation for *The Prose Works of Lady Mary Wortley Montagu*; he kindly put his MS at my disposal.

Motraye, *Voyages*: Aubry de la Motraye, *Voyages du Sr A. De La Motraye en Europe, Asie et en Afrique* (3 vols. 1727). Unless otherwise stated I have preferred this version to the English edition (*Travels*) of 1723 since Motraye, in the preface to the 2nd revised English edition of 1732, complains of changes and additions by his translator (Mandeville) for the first. The 2nd English edition includes a section on the Harz mines that does not appear in the first (though it does in the French edition of 1727).

Murault, M., *Letters describing the Character and Customs of the English and French Nations* (1726).

Ormonde, *Letters: Letters of James Butler, Second Duke of Ormonde, relating to Cardinal Alberoni's Project for the Invasion of Great Britain on behalf of the Stuarts*, ed. W. K. Douglas (Edinburgh 1895).

Ö.S., England: Österreichische Staatsverträge, England I, *1526–1748*, ed. A. F. Pribram (Innsbruck 1907).

Ö.S., Netherlands: Österreichische Staatsverträge, Niederlanden I, *1672–1723*, ed. Heinrich Ritter von Sbrik (Vienna 1912).

Pauli, *Aktenstücken*: Reinhold Pauli, 'Aktenstücken zur Thronbesteigung des Welfenhauses in England', *ZHVN* 1883 (prints extracts from material later destroyed).

Poems on Affairs of State. Augustan Satirical Verse 1600–1714 vol. VII *1704–1714*, ed. Frank H. Ellis (New Haven 1975).

Pope, *Letters*: Alexander Pope, *The Works and Correspondence of*, ed. J. W. Croker; *Correspondence* vols. II and IV (1871 and 1886).

Prideaux, *Life: The Life of the Reverend Humphrey Prideaux, Dean of Norwich with several tracts and letters*, ed. E. M. Thompson (1748).

Recueil: Recueil des Instructions données aux Ambassadeurs et Ministres de France depuis les Traités de Westphalie jusqu'à la Révolution Française (vols. for *Angleterre, Autriche, Espagne, Hollande, Etats Allemands*, and others as cited in notes).

Rousset: J. Rousset de Missy, *Recueil historique d'actes, négotiations, mémoires, et traités, depuis la paix d'Utrecht* (The Hague 1728–55).

Ryder, *Diary: The Diary of Dudley Ryder 1715–16*, ed. W. Matthews (1939).

Saussure, *Letters*: C. de Saussure: *A Foreign View of England in the Reigns of George I and George II*, transl. and ed. Madame van Meyden (1902).

Sbornik: Sbornik Imperatorskogo Russkogo Istoricheskogo Obshchevstva, especially vols. 3, 15, 20,

24, 40, 61 (St Petersburg, 148 vols. 1867–1916), instructions and despatches from European archives as well as Russian ones printed in the original languages.

Schaumburg-Lippe, *Letters: Briefe der Gräfin Johanne Sophie zu Schaumburg-Lippe an die Familie von Münchhausen zu Remeringhausen 1699–1734*, ed. Friedrich-Wilhelm Schaer (Rinteln 1968).

Schulenburg, *Life: Leben und Denkwürdigkeiten Johann Mathias Reichsgrafen von der Schulenburg* (2 vols. Leipzig 1834).

Sophia, *Correspondence with her brother* (some in German, most in French): *Briefwechsel der Herzogin Sophie von Hannover mit ihrem Bruder, dem Kurfürsten Karl Ludwig von der Pfalz*, ed. E. Bodemann (Leipzig 1885).

Sophia, *Letters to diplomats: Briefe der Königin Sophie Charlotte und der Kurfürstin Sophie von Hannover an hannoversche Diplomaten*, ed. R. Doebner (Leipzig 1905).

Sophia, *Letters to Mme von Harling:* 'Briefe der Herzogin späteren Kurfürstin Sophie von Hannover an ihre Oberhofmeisterin, A. K. von Harling', ed. E. Bodemann, *ZHVN* 1895.

Sophia, *Letters to the Hohenzollerns: Briefwechsel der Kurfürstin Sophie von Hannover mit dem Preussischen Königshause*, ed. G. Schnath (Berlin/Leipzig 1927).

Sophia, *Letters to the raugravines: Briefe der Kurfürstin Sophie von Hannover an die Raugräfinnen und Raugrafen zu Pfalz*, ed. E. Bodemann (Hanover/Leipzig 1888).

Sophia, *Mémoires: Memoiren der Herzogin Sophie, nachmals Kurfürstin von Hannover*, ed. A. Köcher (Leipzig 1879). Note that while editorial matter is in German, the memoirs (written in 1680) are in the original French.

Spain, *Bourbon documents: Spain under the Bourbons, 1700–1833*, a collection of documents, transl. and ed. W. N. Hargreaves Mawdsley (1973).

Spanheim, *Account:* Ezekiel Spanheim, 'Account of the English Court', *EHR* 1887.

Stair, *Annals: Annals and Correspondence of the Viscount and the First and Second Earls of Stair*, ed. John Murray Graham (2 vols. 1875).

Stanhope, *History:* Philip Henry Stanhope, *History of England 1713–1783* (7 vols. 1713–1783), vol. II has an appendix of relevant documents.

Stanhope, *Memoirs:* Hugh Stanhope, *Memoirs of the Life and Action of the Right Hon. James, Earl Stanhope* (1721).

State Papers, *Hardwicke: Hardwicke's State Papers*

1501–1726 vol. II (1778); for a projected third volume ready for the press but not printed see I, British Museum, Hardwicke Papers.

State Papers, *Kemble: State Papers and Correspondence 1688–1714*, ed. J. H. Kemble (1857).

Steele, *Correspondence: The Correspondence of Richard Steele*, ed. Rae Blanchard (Oxford 1941).

Suffolk, *Letters: Letters to and from Henrietta, Countess of Suffolk and her second husband, the Hon. George Berkeley from 1712–1767*, ed. J. W. Croker (2 vols. 1824).

Sundon, *Letters: Memoirs of Viscountess Sundon, including letters from the most celebrated persons of her time*, ed. K. Thomson (1847).

Sweden, *Treaties: Sveriges freder och fördrag 1524–1905*, ed. H. Seitz and E. Rosengren (Stockholm 1944).

Swift, *Correspondence: The Correspondence of Jonathan Swift*, ed. Harold Williams, II (Oxford 1963).

Toland, *Hanover:* John Toland, *An Account of the Courts of Prussia and Hanover, sent to a Minister of State in Holland* (1705).

Treasury (Roseveare): Henry Roseveare, *The Treasury 1660–1870. The Foundation of Control* (1973), prints documents of importance for George I's reign in section 21.

Vanbrugh, *Works: The Complete Works of Sir John Vanbrugh*, ed. B. Dobrée and C. Webb, vol. IV (1938) contains his letters.

Verney Letters: The Verney Letters of the Eighteenth Century from the Manuscripts at Claydon House, ed. Margaret Lady Verney (2 vols. 1930).

Walpole, Horace, *Memoirs: Memoirs of the Reign of George II by Horace Walpole*, ed. Lord Holland, vols. II and III (1847).

Walpole, Horace, *Reminiscences: Reminiscences written by Mr. Horace Walpole in 1788 with notes by Paget Toynbee* (1924).

Walpole, Horace, *Walpolianae: Walpolianae, Aedes Walpolianae* (2nd ed. 1752).

Walpole, Horatio, *Private Letters: An Honest Diplomat at The Hague. The private letters of Horatio Walpole 1715–16*, ed. John J. Murray (Bloomington/The Hague 1955).

Wendland, *Prinzenbriefe: Prinzenbriefe zum hannoverschen Primogeniturstreit, 1685–1701*, ed. Anna Wendland (Hildesheim 1937).

Wentworth Papers: The Wentworth Papers 1705–1739 selected from the private and family correspondence of Thomas Wentworth, lord Raby, created in 1711 earl of Strafford, ed. James J. Cartwright (1883).

Weensche Gezantschapsberichten vol. II (*1698–1720*), ed. G. von Antal and J. C. H. de Pater (The Hague 1934).

Wilhelmine, *Mémoires*: Frederike Sophie Wilhelmine, Markgräfin von Bayreuth, *Mémoires* (first published 1810, reissued Paris 1967; references are to this ed.). Note that the German translation ed. by J. Ambruster (Ebenham 1910) leaves out parts significant for Melusine.

Wilkins: W. H. Wilkins, *The love of an uncrowned Queen. Sophia Dorothea, Consort of George I, and her Correspondence with Philip Christopher Count von Königsmarck* (revised ed. 1903). The translation of these letters is good but they should not be used without Schnath's *Königsmarck-Briefwechsel* which is complete and where dating and readings are corrected.

William III and Louis XIV (Grimblot): *Letters of William III and Louis XIV and of their Ministers, and Foreign Politics of 1697–1702*, ed. Paul Grimblot (2 vols. 1848).

Wortley Montagu, *see* Montagu.

Wraxall, *Memoirs*: Sir N. W. Wraxall, *Historical and Posthumous Memoirs*, ed. H. B. Wheatley (5 vols. 1884).

III Short titles of secondary works cited or utilized

Books and articles which are cited once only are given in full in the notes. Place of publication is London unless stated otherwise.

Adamson, Donald, *Peter Beauclerk, Duke of St. Albans* (1974).

Aldridge, *Norris*: D. D. Aldridge, 'Sir John Norris and the British Naval Expeditions to the Baltic Sea, 1717–1727' (unpublished London Ph.D. thesis 1972).

Alvensleben, *Herrenhausen*: U. von Alvensleben, *Herrenhausen, die Sommerresidenz der Welfen* (Hanover 1929). New edition by Hans Reuther (Hanover 1966), revised in light of recent research but with fewer illustrations.

Anderson, R. C., *Naval Wars in the Baltic during the Sailing Ship Epoch* (1910).

André, L., *Louis XIV et l'Europe* (Paris 1950).

Andreas, M., *History of the Bank of England* (1966).

Aretin, *Joseph*: Karl Otmar, Freiherr von Aretin, 'Kaiser Joseph I zwischen Kaisertradition und österreichischer Grossmachtspolitik', *HZ* 1972.

Arkell, *Caroline*: Ruby L. Arkell, *Caroline of Ansbach* (Oxford 1939).

Armstrong, *Elisabeth Farnese*: E. Armstrong, *Elisabeth Farnese 'the Termagant of Spain'* (1892).

Armstrong, *Jewellery*: N. Armstrong, *A historical survey of British styles and jewels* (1973).

Arneth, *Eugen*: A. Arneth, *Prinz Eugen von Savoyen* (Vienna 1858).

Ashton, T. S., *Economic Fluctuations in England, 1700–1800* (Oxford 1959).

Åström: S. E. Åström, *From Stockholm to St. Petersburg* (Helsinki 1962);

—, *Cloth: From Cloth to Iron: The Anglo-Baltic Trade in the late Seventeenth Century* (2 vols. Helsinki 1963 and 1965).

Atherton, H. M., *Political Prints in the Age of Hogarth* (Oxford 1974).

Atkinson, *Army*: C. T. Atkinson, 'The Army under the early Hanoverians', *JSAHR* 1931.

Aubertin, Charles, *L'Esprit public au XVIIIᵉ Siècle* (Paris 1873).

Avery, *London Stage*: ed. Emmet L. Avery, *The London Stage 1660–1800*, part II: *1700–1729* (South Illinois University Press 1961).

Ayling, S., *George the Third* (1972).

Bagger: Hans Bagger, *Ruslands alliancepolitik efter freden i Nystad* (Copenhagen 1974), an important contribution for Russian foreign policy, 1721–32.

Baker, *Chandos*: C. H. and M. Baker, *The Life and Circumstances of James Brydges, First duke of Chandos, Patron of the Liberal Arts* (Oxford 1947).

Ballantyne, *Carteret*: Archibald Ballantyne, *Lord Carteret, a Political Biography 1690–1763* (1887);

—, *Voltaire*: *Voltaire's Visit to England 1726–1729* (1893).

Ballschmieter, *Bernstorff and Mecklenburg*: Hans Joachim Ballschmieter, *Andreas Gottlieb von Bernstorff und der mecklenburgische Ständekampf 1680–1720* (Cologne 1962).

Bandorf, Franz, *Wolf Philipp von Schrottenberg (1640–1715) und der Friede von Rijswijk* (Bamberg 1975).

Baraudon, *Savoy*: Alfred Baraudon, *La Maison de Savoie et la Triple Alliance, 1713–1722* (Paris 1896).

Barlow, *Toleration*: Richard G. Barlow, 'The Struggle for Religious Toleration in England, 1685–1719', *The Historian* 1960.

Baudrillart: Alfred Baudrillart, *Philippe V et la Cour de France* (3 vols. Paris 1892–99).

Baugh, Daniel A., *British naval administration in the Age of Walpole 1739–1748* (1965), an important study also for George I's reign, demonstrating the king's interest in the navy and promotion of its growth.

Baxter, *Treasury:* Stephen B. Baxter, *The Development of the Treasury 1660–1702* (1957);

—, *William III: William III and the Defence of European Liberty, 1650–1702* (1966).

Baynes, *1715:* John Baynes, *The Jacobite Rising of 1715* (1970).

Beattie, *Court:* J. M. Beattie, *The English Court in the Reign of George I* (Cambridge 1967), a work of outstanding importance based on the archives of the royal household departments;

—, *Crime:* 'The Pattern of Crime in England, 1660–1800', *Past and Present* 1974.

Beckett, *Ireland:* J. C. Beckett, *The Making of Modern Ireland 1603–1923* (1966).

Benedikt, *Italy:* H. Benedikt, *Kaiseradler über den Apenninen. Die Österreicher in Italien 1700 bis 1865* (Vienna/Munich 1964);

—, *Neapel: Das Königreich Neapel unter Kaiser Karl VI* (Vienna 1927).

Bennett, *Atterbury:* G. V. Bennett, *The Tory Crisis in Church and State, 1688–1730: The Career of Francis Atterbury, Bishop of Rochester* (Oxford 1975);

—, *Jacobitism:* 'Jacobitism and the Rise of Walpole', in *Historical Perspectives: Studies in English Thought and Social History in Honour of J. H. Plumb*, ed. N. McKendrick (1974);

—, *Kenneth: White Kenneth, 1660–1728, Bishop of Peterborough* (Cambridge 1957).

Béranger, Jean, *Les Hommes de Lettres et la Politique en Angleterre de la Revolution de 1688 à la Mort de George I* (Bordeaux 1968).

Bérenger: J. Bérenger, 'La monarchie autrichienne au XVIIe siècle, 1650–1700', *Information Historique* 1971;

—, *Hongrie:* 'La Hongrie des Habsbourgs au XVIIe siècle', *RH* 1967.

Berger, *Karl VI:* Ana Berger, *Karl VI und Friedrich Wilhelm von Preussen 1716–1730* (Vienna 1935).

Béthencourt Massieu, *Patiño:* Antonio Béthencourt Massieu, *Patiño en la politice internacional de Felipe V* (Valladolid 1954).

Beuleke, *Huguenots:* Wilhelm Beuleke, *Hugenotten in Niedersachsen* (Hildesheim 1960).

Bezobras, P. V., *Otnoseniiakh Rossii s Frantsiei* (Moscow 1892).

Bingham, *Vanbrugh:* Madeleine Bingham, *Masks and Facades. Sir John Vanbrugh. The Man in his Setting* (1974).

Bliard, *Dubois:* P. Bliard, *Dubois, cardinal et premier ministre* (2 vols. Paris 1901–02);

—, *Gibraltar:* 'La question de Gibraltar au temps du Régent d'après les correspondances officielles 1720–1', *Revue des questions historiques* 1895.

Bodemann, *Ilten:* E. Bodemann, 'Jobst Hermann von Ilten, Ein hannoverscher Staatsmann des 17. and 18. Jahrhunderts', *ZHVN* 1879, pp. 1–256;

—, *Sophie:* 'Herzogin Sophie von Hannover', *Historische Taschebücher* (Hanover 1888, good quotes from documents not cited elsewhere).

Borgmann, K., *Der deutsche Religionsstreit der Jahre 1719–1720* (Berlin 1937).

Bourgeois: Emile Bourgeois, *La diplomatie secrète au XVII siècle* vol. I *Le Secret du Régent et la Politique de l'Abbé Dubois* (Paris 1907), vol. II *Le Secret des Farnèse, Philippe V, et la Politique d'Alberoni* (Paris 1909).

Bossy, *Catholic Community:* J. Bossy, *The English Catholic Community* (Cambridge 1975).

Bowley: Marian Bowley, *Studies in the History of Economic Theory before 1870* (1973).

Brandt, *Schleswig-Holstein:* O. Brandt, *Geschichte Schleswig-Holsteins* (Kiel 1941).

Braubach: M. Braubach, *Versailles und Wien von Ludwig XIV bis Kaunitz* (Bonn 1952);

—, *Barrier:* 'Die Reichsbarriere', *Zeitschrift für Geschichte Oberrheins*, 1936, reprinted more accessibly in his collected essays, *Diplomatie und Geistiges Leben im 17. und 18. Jahrhundert* (Bonn 1969);

—, *Eugen: Prinz Eugen von Savoyen* (5 vols. Vienna 1963–65);

—, *Geheimediplomatie: Die Geheimediplomatie des Prinzen Eugen von Savoyen* (Cologne 1962).

Brauer, *Subsidien:* Gert Brauer, *Die hannoversch-englischen Subsidienverträge 1702–48* (Aalen 1962).

Breuil, *Pretender:* Comte Jean de Hamel de Breuil, 'Le Mariage du Prétendent 1719', *RHD* 1895.

Brewer, John, *Party ideology and popular politics at the accession of George III* (Cambridge 1976).

Brisco, N. A., *The Economic Policy of Robert Walpole* (New York 1907).

Brooke, John, *King George III* (1972).

Browning, *Newcastle:* Reed Browning, *The Duke of Newcastle* (New Haven 1975).

Bruce, *Jacobites:* Maurice W. Bruce, 'Jacobite relations with Peter the Great', *Slavonic Review* XIV (1935–36).

Burton, Elizabeth, *The Georgians At Home* (1967).

Busch, Siegfried, *Hannover, Wolfenbüttel und Celle* (Hildesheim 1969).

Campana de Cavalli, Marquise, *Les Derniers Stuarts à Saint Germain-en-Laye* (2 vols. Paris 1871).

Campbell, *Lord Chancellors:* J. Lord Campbell, *Lives of the Lord Chancellors and Keepers of the Great Seal of England* IV (1846).

Campbell, Judith, *Royalty on Horseback* (1974).

Cannon, J., *Parliamentary Reform, 1640–1832* (Cambridge 1973).

Carlsson, *Nystad:* Einar Carlsson, *Freden i Nystad: Fredrik I's personliga politik och des betydelse för förhållandet mellan Sverige och England sommaren 1720* (Uppsala 1932).

Carpenter, *Tenison:* Edward Carpenter, *Thomas Tenison, Archbishop of Canterbury, His Life and Times* (1948).

Carpio, *Stuarts:* M. Carpio, *España y los Ultimos Estuardos* (Madrid 1952).

Carswell: John Carswell, *The South Sea Bubble* (1960).

Castagnoli, *Alberoni:* Pietro Castagnoli, *Il Cardinale Giulio Alberoni* (3 vols. Rome 1929–32).

Chalkin, G. W., *The Provincial Towns of Georgian England* (1974).

Chance, *Great Northern War:* J. F. Chance, *George I and the Great Northern War* (1909), useful for documents cited or printed;

—, *Hanover alliance: The alliance of Hanover. A study of British foreign policy in the last years of George I* (1923), useful for documents cited or printed.

Chandler, *Marlborough:* David Chandler, *Marlborough as a Military Commander* (1973);

—, *Warfare: The Art of Warfare in the Age of Marlborough* (1976).

Chaunu, *Civilisation:* P. Chaunu, *La civilisation de l'Europe classique* (Paris 1966).

Chrysander, *Händel:* Friedrich Chrysander, *G. F. Händel* (3 vols. Leipzig 1856–1867).

Clapham, *Bank:* Sir John Clapham, *The Bank of England. A History* (2 vols. 1944).

Colley, Linda J., 'The Tory Party 1727–1760' (unpublished Cambridge doctoral thesis 1976; cp. her article in *HJ* 1977). I understand that in preparing her thesis for publication Dr Colley is paying attention also to the period 1714–1727.

Colshorn, C. H., *Die Hospitalkassen der hannoverschen Armee* (Hildesheim 1970).

Colvin, H. M., *Royal Buildings* (1968);

— et al., *The History of the King's Works*, vol. V:

1660–1782 (1976). This important volume was published in time for some references to be made to it in the notes.

Conn, *Gibraltar:* Stetson Conn, *Gibraltar in British Eighteenth Century Diplomacy* (New Haven 1942).

Coombs, D., *The Conduct of the Dutch. British opinion and the Dutch alliance during the War of the Spanish Succession* (The Hague 1958).

Coomer, D., *English Dissent under the Hanoverians* (1946).

Coxe, *Austria:* William Coxe, *History of the House of Austria* (2 vols. 1807);

—, *Spain: Memoirs of the Kings of Spain of the House of Bourbon* (2 vols. 1788);

—, *Horatio Walpole: Memoirs of Horatio Lord Walpole* (2nd ed., 2 vols. 1808), based on the MSS collection at Wolterton and on other original papers;

—, *Robert Walpole: Memoirs of the Life and Administration of Robert Walpole* (3 vols. 1789; 4 vols. 1820), important letters to and from Robert Walpole. The four-volume ed. has some additional material and is at times cited.

Cragg, G. R., *From Puritanism to the Age of Reason* (Cambridge 1966).

Cruickshanks, *1714:* Eveline G. Cruickshanks, 'The Tories and the Succession to the Crown in the 1714 Parliament', *BIHR* 1973.

Dalton, *George I's Army:* Charles Dalton, *George the First's Army 1714–1727* (2 vols. 1910–12).

Davies, *German Thought and Culture:* Gerald Davies, *German Thought and Culture in England 1700–1770* (Chapel Hill 1967), a most perceptive study.

Davillé, *Pretender:* Louis Davillé, 'Le séjour du Prétendant Jacques-Edouard Stuart à Bar-le-Duc 1713–16', *Pays Lorrain* 1928 (Professor Gregg kindly drew my attention to this article).

Davis, *Commercial revolution:* Ralph Davis, *A Commercial Revolution; English Overseas Trade in the Seventeenth and Eighteenth Centuries* (1967);

—, *Shipping: The Rise of the English Shipping Industry in the Seventeenth and Eighteenth Centuries* (1963).

Dehio, *Gleichgewicht:* L. Dehio, *Gleichgewicht oder Hegemonie* (English transl., *The Precarious Balance* 1963).

Deutsch, *Handel:* O. R. Deutsch, *Handel, A Documentary biography* (1955), a most useful selection of documents.

Dickinson, *Bolingbroke:* H. T. Dickinson, *Bolingbroke* (1970);

—, *Politics and Literature: Politics and Literature in the Eighteenth Century* (1974);

—, *Sovereignty:* 'The Eighteenth Century debate on the Sovereignty of Parliament', *TRHS* 1976;

—, *Walpole: Walpole and the Whig Supremacy* (1973).

Dickson, *Argyll:* Patricia Dickson, *Red John of the Battles, John Second Duke of Argyll and First Duke of Greenwich* (1973).

Dickson, *Financial Revolution:* P. G. M. Dickson, *The Financial Revolution in England: A Study in the Development of Public Credit 1688–1756* (1967).

Dickson, W. K., *The Jacobite attempt of 1719* (Edinburgh 1894).

Donaldson, *Scotland:* Gordon Donaldson, *Scotland: The Shaping of a Nation* (1974).

Drodtloff, *Pentenriedter:* Anneliese Drodtloff, *Johann Christoph Pentenriedter, Freiherr von Adelhausen* (Vienna 1964).

Drögereit, *Will:* 'Das Testament König Georgs I und die Frage der Personal-union zwischen England und Hannover', *NJ* 1937; cp. II above.

Duchhardt, *Kaisertum:* H. Duchhardt, *Protestantisches Kaisertum und altes Reich* (Wiesbaden 1976).

Dureng: J. Dureng, *Le Duc de Bourbon et l' Angleterre 1723–1726* (Paris 1911).

Edwards, *Frederick Louis:* Averyl Edwards, *Frederick Louis, Prince of Wales 1707–1751* (1947).

Ellis, *Administration:* Kenneth L. Ellis, 'The Administrative Connection between Britain and Hanover', *Journal of the Society of Archivists* II (1965–69).

Engel, *Le Régent:* Claire-Elaine Engel, *Le Régent* (Paris 1969).

Esebeck, *Kurwürde:* Frieda, Freiin von Esebeck, *Die Begründung der hannoverschen Kurwürde* (Hildesheim 1935).

Every, G., *The High Church Party, 1688–1718* (1956).

Eves, *Prior:* Charles Kenneth Eves, *Matthew Prior* (1939).

Fay, *Brandenburg-Prussia:* S. B. Fay, *The Rise of Brandenburg-Prussia to 1785* (ed. of 1964 revised by Klaus Epstein).

Fayard: Janine Fayard, 'Attempts to Build a Third Party in North Germany 1690–1694' in *Louis XIV and Europe*, ed. Ragnhild Hatton (1976), translated from 'Les tentatives de constitution d'un tiers party en Allemagne du Nord 1690–1694', *RHD* 1965.

Feigina: S. Feigina, *Alandskii kongress* (Moscow 1959).

Feiling, *Tory Party:* Keith Feiling, *The Second Tory Party, 1717–1892* (Oxford 1928).

Ferguson, *Scotland:* William Ferguson, *Scotland from 1689 to the Present* (1968).

Finke, *Bothmer:* Hans-Joachim Finke, 'Hans Caspar von Bothmer und die Hannoversche Erbfolge in England 1714–1718', *NJ* 1973.

Fischer, *Musik:* Georg Fischer, *Musik in Hannover* (Hanover/Leipzig 1903).

Fisher, *Portugal Trade:* H. E. S. Fisher, *The Portugal Trade. A study of Anglo-Portuguese commerce 1700–1770* (1972).

Flinn, M. W., *British Population Growth, 1700–1850* (1970).

Flovorskii, A. V., *Russko-avstriiskie otnoseniia v epokhu Petra Velikogo* (Prague 1955).

Foord, *Opposition:* Archibald S. Foord, *His Majesty's Opposition 1715–1830* (Oxford 1964).

Foss, *Judges:* E. Foss, *The Judges of England* (9 vols. 1848–64) vol. VIII.

Francis, *Peninsular War:* A. D. Francis, *The First Peninsular War 1702–13* (1975);

—, *Portugal:* *The Methuens and Portugal* (Cambridge 1966);

—, *Wine Trade: The Wine Trade* (1972).

Fransen, *Leibniz:* Petronella Fransen, *Leibniz und die Friedenschlüsse von Utrecht und Rastatt-Baden* (Purmerend 1933).

Fricke, *Leibniz:* Waltraut Fricke, *Leibniz und die englische Sukzession des Hauses Hannover* (Hildesheim 1957).

Friis, *The Bernstorffs:* Aage Friis, *Bernstorffene og Danmark* vol. I (Copenhagen 1903), with a German translation of 1905.

Fritz, *Jacobitism:* Paul S. Fritz, *The English Ministers and Jacobitism between the Rebellions of 1715 and 1745* (Toronto 1975); based on his (more informative for George I's reign) Cambridge Ph.D. thesis 'Jacobitism and the English government 1717–1731' (1966).

Gehling, *Saint Saphorin:* T. Gehling, *Ein europäischer Diplomat am Kaiserhof zu Wien. François Louis de Pesme, Seigneur de Saint-Saphorin, als englischer Resident am Wiener Hof 1718–1727* (Bonn 1964).

Geikie and Montgomery, *Barrier:* R. Geikie and I. Montgomery, *The Dutch Barrier 1705–1719* (Cambridge 1930).

Genzel, F., 'Studien zur Geschichte des Nordischen Krieges 1714–1720 unter besonderer Berücksichtigung der Personalunion zwischen Grossbritannien und Hannover' (Bonn doctoral dissertation 1951, used on microfilm).

George, *Political Caricature:* M. D. George, *English Political Caricature to 1792. A Study of Opinion and Propaganda* (2 vols. 1959).

Gerhard, *Russland:* Dietrich Gerhard, *England und der Aufstieg Russlands* (Munich/Berlin 1933).

Gerig, *Hervey:* H. Gerig, *Die Memoiren des Lord Hervey als historische Quelle* (Freiburg 1936).

Geyl, *Low Countries:* Pieter Geyl, *History of the Low Countries: Episodes and Problems* (1964);

—, *Nederlandse Stam: Geschiedenis van de Nederlandse Stam*, Deel III *1688–1781* (Amsterdam 1937).

Gibbs, *Hanover Alliance:* G. C. Gibbs, 'Britain and the Alliance of Hanover April 1725–February 1726', *EHR* 1958, reprint 1966 as ch. 12 in *Essays in Eighteenth Century History from the English Historical Review*, ed. R. Mitchison;

—, *Newspapers:* 'Newspapers, Parliament and Foreign Policy in the Age of Stanhope and Walpole', *Mélange offerts à G. Jacquemyns* (Brussels 1968);

—, *Parliament:* 'Parliament and Foreign Policy in the Age of Stanhope and Walpole', *EHR* 1962, reprint as ch. 15 in the *EHR* collection cited above;

—, *Quadruple Alliance:* 'Parliament and the Treaty of Quadruple Alliance' in *William III and Louis XIV. Essays 1680–1720 by and for Mark A. Thomson*, ed. Ragnhild Hatton and J. S. Bromley (Liverpool/Toronto 1968);

—, *Treaties:* 'Laying Treaties before Parliament in the Eighteenth Century' in *Studies in Diplomatic History. Essays in Memory of David Bayne Horn*, ed. Ragnhild Hatton and M. S. Anderson (1970).

Goodwin, A., 'Wood's Halfpence', *EHR* 1936.

Goslinga, *Slingelandt:* A. Goslinga, *Slingelandt's Efforts towards European Peace* (The Hague 1915).

Grandis, *Musik:* Renato de Grandis: 'Musik in Hannover zur Leibniz-zeit' in *Leibniz*, ed. Wilhelm Totok and Carl Haase (Hanover 1966).

Green, *Henry Wise:* D. Green, *Gardener to Queen Anne. Henry Wise 1683–1738 and the formal garden* (Oxford 1956).

Greenwood, *William King:* David Greenwood, *William King. Tory and Jacobite* (Oxford 1969)

Gregg, *Marlborough:* E. G. Gregg, 'Marlborough in Exile, 1712–1714', *HJ* 1972;

—, *Protestant Succession:* 'The Protestant Succession in International Politics 1710–1716' (unpublished London Ph.D. thesis 1972);

—, *Queen Anne:* 'Was Queen Anne a Jacobite?', *History* 1972.

Grew, *Saint-Germain:* Edwin and Marion Grew, *The English Court in Exile. James II at Saint-Germain* (1911).

Grieser, *Deutsche Kanzlei:* Rudolph Grieser, 'Die Deutsche Kanzlei in London, Ihre Entstehung und Anfänge', *Blätter für deutsche Landesgeschichte* 1952.

Grönroos: H. Grönroos, 'England, Sverige och Ryssland 1719–1727' (Finnish), *Historisk Tidskrift* 1946.

Grote: Erich Freiherr Grote, *Familiengeschichte der Grafen und Freiherren Grote* (Hanover 1891).

Grotefend, *The Oeynhausens:* V. Grotefend, *Geschichte des Geschlecht Oeynhausen* (2 vols. Hanover 1899).

Gunnis, Rupert, *A Dictionary of British Sculptors* (1953).

Habbakuk, 'England': H. T. Habbakuk's chapter in *The European Nobility in the Eighteenth Century*, ed. A. Goodwin (1967).

Hahlweg, *Barrier:* W. Hahlweg, 'Barriere-Gleichgewicht-Sicherheit 1646–1715', *HZ* 1959;

—, *Dutch Barrier:* 'Untersuchungen zur Barrierepolitik Wilhelms III von Oranien und der Generalstaaten im 17. und 18. Jahrhundert', *Westfälische Forschungen* 1961.

Halsband, *Hervey:* Robert Halsband, *Lord Hervey, Eighteenth Century Courtier* (Oxford 1973);

—, *Lady Mary: The Life of Lady Mary Wortley Montagu* (Oxford 1956).

Hamilton, *Scotland:* Henry Hamilton, *An Economic History of Scotland in the Eighteenth Century* (Oxford 1963).

Handover, *Gazette:* P. M. Handover, *A history of the London Gazette* (1965).

Hanson, *The Press:* Laurence Hanson, *Government and the Press 1695–1763* (1936).

Hantsch, *Schönborn:* H. Hantsch, *Reichsvizekanzler Friedrich Karl Graf von Schönborn* (Augsburg 1929).

Harcourt-Smith, *Alberoni:* Simon Harcourt-Smith, *Alberoni and the Spanish Conspiracy* (1943).

Hare, J. P., *The History of the Royal Buckhounds* (1895).

Hart, *Bolingbroke:* Jeffrey Hart, *Viscount Bolingbroke, Tory Humanist* (1965).

Hassinger, *Brandenburg-Preussen:* E. Hassinger,

Brandenburg-Preussen, Schweden und Russland 1700–1713 (Munich 1953).

Hatton, *Charles XII*: R. M. Hatton, *Charles XII of Sweden* (1968, USA 1969);

—, *Diplomatic Relations*: *Diplomatic Relations between Great Britain and the Dutch Republic 1714–1721* (1950);

—, *Drummond*: 'John Drummond in the War of the Spanish Succession' in *Studies in Diplomatic History. Essays in memory of David Bayne Horn*, ed. Ragnhild Hatton and M. S. Anderson (1970);

—, *Electorate*: 'The Beggarly Electorate', in *The Hanoverians*, no. 65 of the Purnell part-edition of Winston Churchill, *History of the English Speaking Peoples* (1971);

—, *Europe*: *Europe in the Age of Louis XIV* (1969);

—, *Gratifications*: 'Gratifications and Foreign Policy' in *William III and Louis XIV. Essays 1680–1720 by and for Mark A. Thomson*, ed. Ragnhild Hatton and J. S. Bromley (Liverpool/Toronto 1968);

—, *Louis XIV and His World* (1972);

—, *Louis and Fellow Monarchs*: 'Louis XIV and his Fellow Monarchs' in *Louis XIV and the Craft of Kingship*, ed. John C. Rule (Ohio University Press 1969), reprinted in *Louis XIV and Europe*, ed. Ragnhild Hatton (1976);

—, *Search*: 'In Search of an Elusive Ruler'. Source material for a biography of George I as elector and king in *Fürst, Bürger, Mensch*, ed. Friedrich Engel-Janosi, Grete Klingenstein, Heinrich Lutz (Vienna 1975);

—, *War and Peace*: *War and Peace 1680–1720*, inaugural lecture 1968 (published 1969).

Hauck, *Karl Ludwig*: Hauck, *Karl Ludwig, Kurfürst von der Pfalz* (Leipzig 1903).

Hayes, *Army*: James Hayes, 'The Royal House of Hanover and the British Army 1714–1760', *Bulletin of the John Rylands Library* 1958;

—, *Colonelcies*: 'The Purchase of the Colonelcies in the Army 1714–63', *JSAHR* 1961.

Hayes, *Kensington Palace*: J. Hayes, *Kensington Palace* (1971).

Hazard, *La Crise*: P. Hazard, *La Crise de la conscience européene 1680–1715* (Paris 1935), English transl.: *The European Mind* (1952).

Hedley, *Royal Palaces*: Olwen Hedley, *Royal Palaces* (1972).

Heer, Friedrich, *Das Heilige Römische Reich* (Munich 1967).

Henderson, A. F., *London and the National Government 1721–40* (Durham N.C. 1945).

Hennel, Sir R., *History of the King's Bodyguard of Yeomen of the Guard* (1974).

Henriques, Henry, *The Return of the Jews to England; being a chapter in the history of English Law* (1905).

Hertz, *Ostend Company*: Gerald B. Hertz, 'England and the Ostend Company', *EHR* 1907.

Hibbert, *London*: Christopher Hibbert, *London. The Biography of a City* (1969).

Hills, *Gibraltar*: G. Hills, *Rock of Contention. A History of Gibraltar* (1974).

Hinrichs, *Preussen*: C. Hinrichs, *Preussen als historisches Problem* (Berlin 1964).

Höfler, *Soissons*: C. Höfler, *Der Congress von Soissons nach den Instruktionen des kaiserlichen Cabinets und den Berichten des kaiserlichen Botschafter Stefan Grafen Kinsky* (Vienna 1871).

Holdsworth, *English Law*: William Holdsworth, *A History of the English Law* (12 vols. 1922–38), last three volumes.

Hole, Christina, *English Sports and Pastimes* (1949).

Holmes: G. Holmes, *British Politics in the Age of Queen Anne* (1967).

Holmes, *Regalia*: Martin Holmes, *English Regalia. Their History, Custody and Display* (1972).

Holst, *Fredrik I*: Walfrid Holst, *Fredrik I* (Stockholm 1953);

—, *Ulrika*: *Ulrika Eleonora, Karl XIIs syster* (Stockholm 1956).

Horn, D. B., *Great Britain and Europe in the Eighteenth Century* (Oxford 1967);

—, *Diplomatic Service*: *The British Diplomatic Service 1689–1789* (Oxford 1964).

Horwitz, *Nottingham*: Henry Horwitz, *Revolution Politicks, The Career of Daniel Finch, Second Earl of Nottingham 1647–1730* (Cambridge 1968).

House of Commons 1715–54: *History of Parliament. The House of Commons 1715–1754*, ed., R. Sedgwick (2 vols. 1970), to be used with review by G. C. Gibbs in *The Welsh History Review* 1973.

Howard, Philip, *The Royal Palaces* (1970).

HSL, followed by volume and author: *Het Staatse Leger*, the collective history of the Dutch army, vol. VII (1950) by J. G. Ten Raa and vol. VIII in four parts (1956–64) by J. Wijn.

Huber, Norbert, *Österreich und der Heilige Stuhl vom Ende des Spanischen Erbfolgekrieges bis zum Tode Papst Klemens XI, 1714–1721* (Vienna 1967).

Hudson, *Kensington Palace*: Derek Hudson, *Kensington Palace* (1950).

Huisman: Michael Huisman, *La Belgique Commerciale sous l'Empereur Charles VI: La Compagnie d'Ostende* (Brussels 1902).

Hüttl, Ludwig, *Max Emanuel. Der Blaue Kurfürst. Eine politische Biographie* (Munich 1976).

Hyamson, A. M., *History of the Jews in England* (1908).

Insh, *Jacobites:* George Pratt Insh, *The Scottish Jacobite Movement* (1952).

Jackson, *Bolingbroke:* Sydney W. Jackson, *Man of Mercury* (1958).

Jacob, Ilse, *Beziehungen Englands zu Russland und zur Türkei in den Jahren 1718–1727* (Basel 1945).

Jägerskiöld: Stig Jägerskiöld, *Sverige och Europa 1716–1718* (Stockholm 1937).

Jarnut-Derbolav, Elke, *Die Österreichische Gesandtschaft in London 1701–1711* (Bonn 1972).

Jesse, *Memoirs:* James Heneage Jesse, *Memoirs of the Court of England from the Revolution in 1688 to the death of George II* vol. III (1867); useful as a source for tracing anecdotes.

Jones, *Jacobitism:* George Hilton Jones, *The Mainstream of Jacobitism* (Cambridge, Mass. 1954).

Jordan, Ruth, *Sophia Dorothea* (1971).

Jourdain, *Kent:* Margaret Jourdain, *The Work of William Kent* (1948).

Junge: W. Junge, *Leibniz und der Sachsen Lauenburgische Erbfolgestreit* (Hildesheim 1964).

Kalisch and Gierowski, *Poland:* J. Kalisch und J. Gierowski ed., *Um die Polnische Krone, Sachsen und Polen während des Nordischen Krieges 1700–21* (Berlin 1962).

Kalthoff, Edgar, 'Die englische Könige des Hauses Hannover im Spiegel der britischen Geschichts-schreibung', *NJ* 1958.

Kamen: Henry Kamen, *The War of Succession in Spain 1700–1715* (1969).

Keens-Soper, Maurice, 'The Académie Politique, 1712–1721', *ESR* 1972.

Kelch, *Newcastle:* Ray R. Kelch, *Newcastle. A. Duke without Money. Thomas Pelham Holles 1793–1768* (1974).

Kellenbenz, Hermann, *Die Herzogtümer von Kopenhagener Frieden bis zum Wiedervereiningung Schleswigs 1660–1721* (Neumünster 1960).

Kemp, *King and Commons:* Betty Kemp, *King and Commons 1660–1832* (1957);

—, *Robert Walpole:* Sir Robert Walpole (1976). More useful for the reign of George II than that of George I.

Kielmansegg, Familien-Chronik: Erich Graf von Kielmansegg, *Familien-Chronik der Herren,*

Freiherren und Grafen von Kielmansegg (2nd ed. Vienna 1910).

King, P., *The Development of the English Economy to 1750* (1971).

Klaveren, *Corruption:* J. van Klaveren. 'Die historische Erscheinung der Korruption in ihrem Zusammenhang mit der Staats und Gesellschafts Struktur', *Vierteljahrschrift für Sozial und Wirtschaftsgeschichte* 1937.

Klopp: Onno Klopp, *Der Fall des Hauses Stuart und die Succession des Hauses Hannover in Gross-Britannien und Irland,* vols. VIII and XIV (Vienna 1888).

Knoop, *Sophie:* Mathilde Knoop, *Die Kurfürstin Sophie von Hannover* (Hildesheim 1964).

Kobbe, *Lauenburg:* Peter von Kobbe, *Geschichte des Herzogtums Lauenburg* vol. III (Altona 1837).

Köcher: Adolf Köcher, *Geschichte von Hannover und Braunschweig 1648–1674* (2 vols. Leipzig 1894–95).

Kramnick, *Bolingbroke:* Isaac Kramnick, *Bolingbroke and his Circle. The Politics of Nostalgia in the Age of Walpole* (Cambridge, Mass. 1968).

Krieger, *Pufendorf:* L. Krieger, *The Politics of Discretion: Pufendorf and the acceptance of Natural Law* (Chicago 1965).

Kroll, *Sophie:* Maria Kroll, *Sophie Electress of Hanover. A personal portrait* (1973).

Lambert, Sheila, *Bills and Acts, Legislative procedure in eighteenth century England* (Cambridge 1971).

Lampe: Joachim Lampe, *Aristokratie, Hofadel und Staatspatriziat in Kurhannover. Die Lebenskreise der höheren Beamten an den Kurhannoverschen Zentral- und Hofbehörden 1714–1760* (2 vols. Hildesheim 1963).

Lang, *Handel:* Paul Henry Lang, *George Frideric Handel* (1966).

Lapeure, *Colonial Trade:* H. Lapeure, 'De L'Atlantique au Pacifique. Les trafics maritimes de l'empire colonial espagnol', *RH* 1962.

Laprade, *Public Opinion:* William Thomas Laprade, *Public Opinion and Politics in eighteenth century England to the fall of Walpole* (New York 1936).

Leadam, *England:* I. S. Leadam, *The History of England from the Accession of Anne to the Death of George II* (1912).

Lecky, *Rationalism:* W. E. H. Lecky, *History of the Rise and Influence of the Spirit of Rationalism in Europe* (2 vols. 1897).

Leclerq: H. Leclerq, *Histoire de la Régence pendant le minorité de Louis XV* (3 vols. Paris 1921–22).

Legrelle: A. Legrelle, *La Diplomatie Française et la Succession d'Espagne* vol. IV: *La Solution 1700–1725* (2nd ed., Braine-le-comte 1892).

Leibniz (collection of essays), ed. Wilhelm Totok and Carl Haase (Hanover 1963).

Leitsch: Walther Leitsch, 'Der Wandel der österreichischen Russlands politik in den Jahren 1724–1726', *JGO* 1962.

Lémontey: P. E. Lémontey, *Histoire de la Régence et de la minorité de Louis XV jusque au ministère du Cardinal de Fleury* (2 vols. Paris 1832).

Leys, *Catholics:* M. D. R. Leys, *Catholics in England 1559–1829* (1952).

Lindeberg, G., *Svensk ekonomisk politik under den Görtzska perioden* (Lund 1941).

Lodge, Sir Richard, *Great Britain and Prussia in the Eighteenth Century* (Oxford 1923).

Longrigg, Roger, *The History of Horse Racing* (1972).

Macalpine and Hunter, *Mad Business:* Ada Macalpine and Richard Hunter, *George III and the Mad Business* (1969).

MacInnes, *Harley:* Angus MacInnes, *Robert Harley, Puritan Politician* (1970).

Malortie, *Beiträge:* Carl Ernst von Malortie, *Hannoversche Geschichts-Kalender. Beiträge zur Braunschweig-Lüneburgischen Geschichte* (5 vols. Hanover 1860–72);

—, *Court:* *Der Hannoversche Hof unter dem Kurfürsten Ernst August und der Kurfürstin Sophie* (Hanover 1847).

Mandrou: R. Mandrou, *Staatsräson und Vernunft, 1649–1775,* vol. 3 of the new ed. of the 'Propyläen Weltgeschichte' (Berlin 1976).

Marshall, *England:* Dorothy Marshall, *Eighteenth Century England* (1962).

Marshall, *Hooper:* William Marshall, *George Hooper Bishop of Bath and Wells, 1640–1727* (1976).

Martin: Miguel Martin, 'Great Britain and Spain 1711–1714', London Ph.D. thesis 1962, published in Spanish *España entre Inglaterra y Francia 1711–1714* (Panama 1964);

—, *Spain and Italy:* 'The Secret Clause, Britain and Spanish ambitions in Italy 1712–31', *ESR* 1976.

Massini, Schaub: R. Massini, *Sir Luke Schaub 1690–1758* (Basel 1953).

McGuiness, Rosamund, *English Court Odes 1620–1820* (Oxford 1971).

McKay: Derek McKay, 'Diplomatic Relations between George and the Emperor Charles VI, 1714–1719', unpublished London Ph.D. thesis 1971;

—, *North 1718–1719:* 'The Struggle for Control of George I's Northern policy 1718–19', *JMH* 1973;

—, *Utrecht Settlement:* 'Bolingbroke, Oxford and the defence of the Utrecht settlement in southern Europe', *EHR* 1971.

McLachlan: Jean McLachlan, *Trade and Peace with Old Spain 1667–1750* (Cambridge 1940).

Mediger: W. Mediger, *Mecklenburg, Russland und England-Hannover 1706–21* (2 vols. Hildesheim 1967);

—, *Bremen-Verden:* 'Die Gewinnung Bremens und Verdens durch Hannover im Nordischen Kriege', *NJ* 1971;

—, *Moskau: Moskaus Weg nach Europa* (Brunswick 1952).

Meier, *Verfassung:* Ernst von Meier, *Hannoversche Verfassungs und Verwaltungsgeschichte 1680–1866* (2 vols. Leipzig 1898).

Melville, *George:* Lewis Melville, *The First George in Hanover and England* (2 vols. 1908);

—, *Wharton: The Life and Writings of Philip, Duke of Wharton* (1913).

Meyer, *Herrenhausen garden:* Karl Heinz Meyer, *Königliche Gärten. 300 Jahre Herrenhausen* (Hanover 1966).

Mezgolich: E. Mezgolich, *Graf Johann Wenzel Wratislaw von Mitrowiz. Sein Wirken während des Spanischen Erbfolgekrieges* (Vienna 1967).

Michael: Wolfgang Michael, *Englische Geschichte im 18. Jahrhundert* (5 vols. Berlin/Basel and Berlin/Leipzig 1896–1955) with a second unchanged ed. of vol. I of 1921. Note English (abbreviated) translations of vol. I: *England under George I. The Beginnings of the Hanoverian Dynasty* (1936) and vol. II: *England under George I. The Quadruple Alliance* (1939). These translations have caused English historians to neglect the early German volumes. Generally speaking, the later volumes are more satisfactory than the earlier ones, though for diplomatic history all are valuable;

—, *1709:* 'Ein schwieriger Fall aus dem Jahre 1709', *HZ* 1902.

Millar, *Royal Collection:* Oliver Millar, *Tudor, Stuart and Early Georgian Pictures in the Royal Collection* (2 vols. 1952).

Minchinton, W. E., ed., *The Growth of English Overseas Trade in the Seventeenth and Eighteenth Centuries* (1969).

Mingay, G. E., *English Landed Society in the Eighteenth Century* (1956);

—, *The Gentry: the Rise and Fall of a Ruling Class* (1976).

Morgan, *1715 election:* William T. Morgan, 'Some sidelights upon the General Election of 1715', *Essays in Modern English History in honour of Wilbur Cortez Abbott,* ed. Charles Seymour (Cambridge, Mass. 1941).

Morrah, *Rupert:* Patrick Morrah, *Prince Rupert of the Rhine* (1976).

Murray: John J. Murray, *George I, The Baltic and the Whig Split of 1717* (Chicago and London 1969);

—, *Baltic 1715:* 'Sjömakternas expedition till Östersjön 1715', *KFA* 1953;

—, *Görtz and Gyllenborg:* 'The Görtz-Gyllenborg arrests, a problem in diplomatic immunity', *JMH* 1956.

Murray-Baillie, Hugh, 'Etiquette and the Planning of State Apartments in Baroque Palaces', *Archaeologia* 1967.

Naylor, *Peerage Bill:* John F. Naylor, *The British Aristocracy and the Peerage Bill of 1719* (Wisconsin 1968), useful selection of documents with introductions to the various sections.

Narotchnitzky, A., 'Russie et France, XVIe siècle à 1789', *RH* 1967.

Naumann: M. Naumann, *Österreich, England und das Reich 1719–1732* (Berlin 1933).

Nekrasov: G. A. Nekrasov, 'Baltiiskii vopros i evropeiskaia politika Russii posle Nistadtskogo mira', *Ocherki istorii* 1957;

—, *Suedo-Russian relations: Russko-skvedskie otnosheniia i politika 1721–26* (Moscow 1964).

Newman, *The Stanhopes:* Aubrey Newman, *The Stanhopes of Chevening. A family biography* (1969).

Nicholson and Turberville: T. C. Nicholson and A. S. Turberville, *Charles Talbot Duke of Shrewsbury* (Cambridge 1930).

Nicolini, *War of Spanish Succession:* F. Nicolini, *L'Europa durante la guerra di successione de Spagna* (2 vols. 1938) deals mainly with Naples.

Nicoll, *Theatre:* Allardyce Nicoll, *The Development of the Theatre. A study of theatrical art from the beginnings to the present day* (1927).

Nikiforov: L. A. Nikiforov, *Russko-angliiskie otnosheniia pri Petre I* (Moscow 1950) with German ed. of 1954;

—, *Nystad: Vneshnaia politika Rossii v poslednie gody Severnoj voiny. Nistadkii mir* (Moscow 1959).

Nöldeke, *Kunstdenkmäler:* Arnold Nöldeke, *Die Kunstdenkmäler der Provinz Hannover* (2 parts Hanover 1932).

Noorden: Carl von Noorden, *Europäische Geschichte im achtzehnten Jahrhundert* (vols. III and IV Düsseldorf 1870–72).

Nordmann: Claude Nordmann, *La crise du Nord au début de XVIIIe siècle* (Paris 1962);

—, *Jacobites:* 'Louis XIV and the Jacobites', in *Louis XIV and Europe,* ed. Ragnhild Hatton (1976).

Nulle, *Newcastle:* H. Stebelton Nulle, *Thomas Pelham-Holles, Duke of Newcastle. His early Political Career, 1693–1724* (Philadelphia 1931).

Oakley, *Interception:* S. P. Oakley, 'The interception of Posts in Celle, 1697–1700', in *William III and Louis XIV,* ed. Ragnhild Hatton and J. S. Bromley (1968).

O'Callaghan: J. C. O'Callaghan, *History of the Irish Brigades in the service of France* (Glasgow 1870).

Odenthal, J., *Österreichische Türkenkrieg 1700–1718* (Cologne 1938).

Oliver, F. S., *The Endless Adventure* (3 vols. 1930–35).

Otruba G., 'Die Bedeutung englischen Subsidien und Antizipationen für die Financen Österreichs 1701 bis 1748', *Vierteljahrschrift für Sozial- und Wirtschaftsgeschichte* 1964.

Owen, *Country attitudes:* J. B. Owen, 'The survival of Country attitudes in the eighteenth-century House of Commons in Great Britain', *Britain and the Netherlands* vol. 4, ed. J. S. Bromley and E. Kosmann (The Hague 1971);

—, *Political Patronage:* 'Political Patronage in 18th Century England', *The Triumph of Culture: 18th Century Perspectives,* ed. Paul Fritz and David Williams (Toronto 1972).

Pagès, *Germany:* G. Pagès, *Louis XIV et l'Allemagne 1661–1715* (Paris 1937);

—, *Money:* 'Notes sur le rôle d'argent dans la politique française en Allemagne', *Contributions à l'histoire de la politique française en Allemagne sous Louis XIV* (Paris 1905).

Parry, *Spanish Empire:* J. H. Parry, *The Spanish Seaborne Empire* (1966).

Paulson, *Hogarth:* Ronald Paulson, *Hogarth. His Life and Times* (2 vols. 1971).

Pemberton, *Carteret:* N.W.B. Pemberton, *Carteret, the brilliant Failure of the Eighteenth Century* (1936).

Perkins, *Saint-Pierre:* Merle Perkins, *The moral and political philosophy of the Abbé de Saint-Pierre* (Geneva/Paris 1959).

Perry, Thomas W., *Public Opinion, Propaganda and Politics in Eighteenth Century England: A Study of the Jewish Naturalization Act of 1753* (Cambridge, Mass. 1962)

Petrie, *Jacobite Activities:* Sir Charles Petrie, 'Jacobite Activities in South and West

England in the Summer of 1715', *TRHS* 1935;

—, *Jacobitism: The Jacobite Movement* (1959).

Pfeffinger, *Historie*: Johann Friedrich Pfeffinger, *Historie des Braunschweig-Lüneburgischen Hauses bis auf das Jahr 1733* (3 vols. Hamburg 1734), good factual information; helpful for dates in Hanoverian OS.

Plumb, *Cabinet*: J. H. Plumb, 'The Organization of the Cabinet in the reign of Queen Anne', *TRHS* 1957;

—, *Four Georges: The First Four Georges* (1956);

—, *Stability: The Growth of Political Stability 1675–1725* (1967);

—, *Walpole: Sir Robert Walpole. The Making of a Statesman* I (1956) and *The King's Minister* II (1960).

Polievktov: M. A. Polievktov, *Baltiisskii vopros v russkoi politike posle Nistadskogo mira 1721–1725* (Moscow 1959).

Postlethwayt, James, *The History of the Public Revenue* (1759).

Prüser, *Göhrde*: Jürgen Prüser, *Die Göhrde. Ein Beitrag zur Geschichte des Jagd- und Forstwesens in Niedersachsen* (Hildesheim 1969).

Pryde, *Union 1707*: George S. Pryde, *The Treaty of Union of Scotland and England 1707* (1950).

Püster: K. Püster, *Möglichkeiten und Verfehlungen merkantiler Politik im Kurfürstentum Hannover unter Berücksichtigung der Personalunion mit dem Königreich Grossbritannien* (Hamburg 1966).

Pyne, *Hampton Court*: W. H. Pyne, *History of Royal Hampton Court* (2 vols. 1819).

Quazza, *Equilibrium*: G. Quazza, *Il problema italiano e l'equilibrio europeo 1720–1738* (Turin 1965);

—, *Italia*: 'L'Italia e l'Europa durante la guerra di successione 1700–48', in *Storia d'Italia*, ed. N. Valeri (2nd ed. Turin 1965).

Radzinowics, Leon, *A History of English Criminal Law and its Administration from 1750* (1948).

Realey: Charles B. Realey, *The Early Opposition to Sir Robert Walpole 1720–27* (Philadelphia 1931).

Redlich, O., *Österreich von 1700 bis 1740* (Baden bei Wien 1938).

Redman, *Hanover*: Alvin Redman, *The House of Hanover* (1960).

Reese, *Historie*: Armin Reese, *Die Rolle der Historie beim Aufstieg des Welfenhauses 1680–1714* (Hildesheim 1967), important for Leibniz as a historian.

Reese, H. M., *The Royal Office of Master of the Horse* (1976).

Richmond: Sir Herbert Richmond, *The Navy as an instrument of Policy 1558–1727* (Cambridge 1953).

Riley: P. W. J. Riley, *The English Ministers and Scotland 1707–1727* (1964).

Risk: James C. Risk, *The History of the Order of the Bath and its Insignia* (1972).

Robb, *William III*: Nesca Robb, *William of Orange, a personal portrait*, II: *1674–1702* (1966).

Roberts, Clayton, *The Growth of Responsible Government in Stuart England* (Cambridge 1966).

Roseveare, Henry, *The Treasury. The Evolution of a British Institution* (1969).

Roth, William, 'L'affaire de Majorque', *RHD* 1972.

Rothenburg, G. E., *The Austrian Military Border in Croatia 1522–1747* (Urbana 1960).

Rothert, *Hannover*: Wilhelm Rothert, *Hannover unter dem Kurhut 1646–1815* (Hanover 1916).

Rubinstein, Samuel, *Historians of London* (1968).

Rudé, *Hanoverian London*: George Rudé, *Hanoverian London 1714–1808* (1971).

Sadie, Stanley, *Handel* (1968).

Saint-Léger, *Dunkerque*: A. de Saint-Léger, *La Flandre Maritime et Dunkerque sous la Domination Française 1659–1789* (Paris 1900).

Sainty, J. C., *Officials of the Secretaries of State 1660–1782* (1973).

Salomon: Felix Salomon, *Geschichte des letzten Ministeriums Königin Annas von England und der englischen Thronfolgefrage* (Gotha 1894).

Schaer: B.H.O. Schaer, *Der Staatshaushalt des Kurfürstentums Hannover unter dem Kurfürsten Ernst August 1680–1698* (Hanover 1912).

Schaer, *Schaumburg-Lippe*: Friedrich-Wilhelm Schaer, *Graf Friedrich Christian zu Schaumburg-Lippe als Mensch und Repräsentant des kleinstaatlichen Absolutismus um 1700* (Bückeburg 1966).

Schartau: S. Schartau, *Förhallåndet mellan Sverige och Hanover 1709–15* (Lund 1905).

Schazmann, Paul-Emile, *The Bentincks. The history of a European family* (English transl. 1976).

Schmidt, *Schulenburg family*: G. Schmidt, *Das Geschlecht von der Schulenburg* (3 vols., the 2nd and 3rd bound together, Beetzendorf 1899).

Schmidt, H. D., 'The establishment of "Europe" as a political expression', *HJ* 1966.

Schnath, *Hannover I*: G. Schnath, *Geschichte Hannovers im Zeitalter der Neunten Kur und der englischen Sukzession 1674–1714* (Hildesheim

1938); *Hannover* II, covering 1692 to 1698 (Hildesheim 1976), has also been consulted; —, *Leineschloss*: section in Schnath, Hildebrecht, Plath, *Das Leineschloss. Kloster, Fürstensitz, Landtagsgebäude* (Hanover 1962);

—, *Sophia-Dorothea Trilogy*: The so-called Sophia Dorothea trilogy, three articles (two reprinted) most easily accessible in *Ausgewählte Beiträge zur Landesgeschichte Niedersachsens*, abbrev. AB (Hildesheim 1968), chapters 6, 7 and 8 dealing respectively with 'Der Fall Königsmarck. Leben, Ende und Nachlass des Grafen Philipp Christoph von Königsmarck im Licht neuer Funde' from *Hann. Geschichtsblätter* 1953; 'Eleonore v. d. Knesebeck, die Gefangene von Scharzfels' from *NJ* 1955; and 'Die Prinzessin in Ahlden: Sophie Dorotheas Gefangenschaft 1694–1726';

—, *Wolfenbüttel*, 'Die Überwaltigung Braunschweig-Wolfenbüttels durch Hannover und Celle zu Beginn des Spanischen Erbfolgekrieges, März 1702', *Braunschweigisches Jahrbuch* 1975.

Schnee, *NJ*: Heinrich Schnee, 'Der Hof- und Kammeragent Leffmann Behrens als Hoffinanzier der Welfen', *NJ* 1951.

Scholes: P. M. Scholes, 'Parliament and the Protestant Dissenters 1702–19', unpublished London M.A. thesis 1962.

Schryver, *Barrier*: Reginald de Schryver, 'De eerste staatse barriere in de Zuidelijke Nederlanden 1697–1701', *Bijdragen voor de Geschiedenis der Nederlanden* 1963–64;

—, *Bergeyck*: *Jan van Brouchoven, Graaf van Bergeyck 1644–1725* (Brussels 1965).

Schulte: A. Schulte, *Markgraf Ludwig Wilhelm von Baden und der Reichskrieg gegen Frankreich 1693–1697* (2nd ed., 2 vols. Heidelberg 1901).

Schuster, *Kunst und Künstler*: Edward Schuster, *Kunst und Künstler in den Fürstentümern Calenberg und Lüneburg in der Zeit von 1636 bis 1727* (Hanover 1905).

Schwarte: Clemens Schwarte, *Die neunte Kur und Braunschweig-Wolfenbüttel* (Münster 1905).

Schwenke: Alexander Schwenke, *Geschichte der hannoverschen Truppen im spanischen Erbfolgekrieg 1710–1714* (Hanover 1862).

Scott, *Joint Stock Companies*: W. R. Scott, *The Constitution and Finance of English, Scottish and Irish Joint Stock Companies to 1720* (3 vols. Cambridge 1910–12).

Seiler: Harald Seiler, 'Bilder zu Leibniz Zeit am hannoverschen Hof', in *Leibniz*, ed. Wilhelm Totok and Carl Haase (Hanover 1966).

Shapiro, S.S., 'The Relations between Louis XIV and Leopold of Austria from the Treaty of Nymwegen to the truce of Ratisbon' (UCLA doctoral thesis 1966).

Sheppard, *St. James's Palace*: Edgar Sheppard, *Memorials of St. James's Palace* (2 vols. 1894).

Sichart, *Army*: G. Sichart, *Geschichte der Hannoverschen Armee*, vols. I–II (1866).

Sievers, *Musik*: Heinrich Sievers, *Die Musik in Hannover* (Hanover 1961).

Silbener, *War*: E. Silbener, *La guerre dans la pensée économique de XVIe au XVIIe siècle* (Paris 1939).

Simms, *Confiscation*: J. G. Simms, *The Williamite Confiscation in Ireland 1690–1703* (1936).

Sitwell, H. D. W., *The Crown Jewels and other regalia in the Tower of London* (ed. Clarence Winchester, 1953).

Skinner, Q., 'The Principles and Practice of Opposition: the case of Bolingbroke and Walpole', in ed. N. McKendrick, *Historical Perspectives* (Plumb Festschrift 1974).

Smithers, P., *Life of Joseph Addison* (1954).

Snyder, *Queen Anne*: Henry L. Snyder, 'The Last Days of Queen Anne. The Account of Sir John Evelyn examined', *HLQ* 1971.

Soler: A. M. Soler, *Die spanisch-russischer Beziehungen im 18. Jahrhundert* (Wiesbaden 1970).

Somerville, *Shrewsbury*: D. H. Somerville, *The King of Hearts, Charles Talbot, Duke of Shrewsbury* (1962).

Sörensson, P., 'Keijsaren, Sverige och de nordiska allierade från Karl XII:s hemkomst från Turkiet till alliansen i Wien' (four parts in *KFÅ* 1926, 1927, 1928, 1929).

—, *Sverige och Frankrike 1715–1718* (three parts, Stockholm 1909, 1916, 1921).

Speck, *Elections*: W. A. Speck, *Tory and Whig: the Struggle in the Constituencies 1701–1715* (1970);

—, *Stability and Strife*: *Stability and Strife. England 1714–1760* (1976);

Sperling: J. Sperling, *The South Sea Company* (Boston, Mass. 1962).

Spittler: Ludwig Spittler, *Geschichte des Fürstentums Hannover* vol. II (Göttingen 1786).

Srbik: Heinrich Ritter von Srbik, *Wien und Versailles 1692–1697* (Munich 1944), useful for the secret negotiations of the Nine Years War in which Hanover was also involved.

Stamm, *Theatre*: Rudolf Stamm, *Geschichte des englischen Theaters* (Berne 1951).

Starkey, *Cambrai*: A. M. Starkey, 'La diplomatie Britannique au Congrès de Cambrai 1722–25', *RHD* 1971.

Steele, I. K., *The Politics of Colonial Policy. The Board of Trade and Colonial Administration 1696–1720* (Oxford 1968).

Stern, Selma, *The Court Jew* (Philadelphia 1950).

Steuart, *Jacobites 1719–20*: A. F. Steuart, 'Sweden and the Jacobites 1719–1720', *SHR* 1926.

Stevens, David H., *Party Politics and English Journalism 1702–42* (Wisconsin 1916).

Stille: Åke Stille, *Studier över Bengt Oxenstiernas politiska system och Sveriges förbindelser med Danmark och Holstein-Gottorp 1689–1692* (Uppsala 1947).

Storch: Dietmar Storch, *Die Landstände des Fürstentums Calenberg-Göttingen 1680–1714* (Hildesheim 1972).

Stork-Penning, *1705–10*: J. Stork-Penning, *Het Grote Werk, Vreedesonderhandelingen 1705–1710* (Groningen 1958);

—, *1711*: 'Het Gedrag van de Staten 1711', *Bijdragen voor de Geschiedenis der Nederlanden* 1963–4.

Stoye, *Charles VI*: J. H. Stoye, 'Emperor Charles VI: The early years of the reign', *TRHS* 1962;

—, *Siege*: *The Siege of Vienna 1683* (1964).

Strich, *Bavaria*: M. Strich, *Das Kurhaus Bayern im Zeitalter Ludwigs XIV und die europäische Mächte* (2 vols. Munich 1933).

Stromberg, R. N., *Religious Liberalism in Eighteenth Century England* (Oxford 1954).

Stuwe, J. E., *Geschichte des Hochstifts Osnabrück* (Osnabrück 1789).

Summerson, Sir John, *Georgian London* (1945, reprint 1962).

SUPH (followed by vol., part and author): the collective history of Swedish foreign policy, *Svenska Utrikespolitikens Historia*.

Sutherland, L., *The East India Company in eighteenth century politics* (1952).

Sykes: Norman Sykes, *Church and State in England in the Eighteenth Century* (Cambridge 1934);

—, *Gibson*: *Edmund Gibson, Bishop of London* (1926);

—, *Wake*: *William Wake, Archbishop of Canterbury 1657–1737* (2 vols. Cambridge 1957).

Symcox, G., 'Louis XIV and the War in Ireland. A Study in his strategic thinking and decision making' (UCLA doctoral thesis 1967).

Syveton, *Ripperda*: F. Syveton, *Une cour et un aventurier au XVIIIᵉ siècle: le baron de Ripperda* (Paris 1896).

Tardito-Amerio, Rosalba, 'Italienische Architekten, Stukkatoren und Bauhandwerker in den Welfischen Ländern und im Bistum Hildesheim', *Nachrichten von der Akademie der Wissenschaften in Göttingen* (Philosophische und Historische Klasse) 1968.

Tarle, *Great Northern War*: E. Tarle, *Svernaya voyna is shvedkoye nashestvye na Rosniyi* (Moscow 1958).

Tayler, *1715*: Alaistair and Henrietta Tayler, *1715. The Story of the Rising* (1936).

Terry, *George I*: Sir Imbert Terry, *A Constitutional King, George the First* (1927).

Thiele, *Wilhelmine*: Heinrich Thiele, *Wilhelmine von Bayreuth, die Lieblingsschwester Friedrichs des Grossen* (Munich 1967).

Thomas, P. D. G., *The House of Commons in the Eighteenth Century* (Oxford 1971);

—, *Jacobitism*: 'Jacobitism in Wales', *Wales Historical Review* 1963.

Thompson, *Hunters*: E. P. Thompson, *Whigs and Hunters. The Origin of the Black Act* (1975).

Thompson, *Mainz*: Richard H. Thompson: *Lothar Franz von Schönborn and the Diplomacy of the Electorate of Mainz* (The Hague 1973).

Thomson, *Rupert*: George Malcolm Thomson, *Warrior Prince. The Life of Prince Rupert of the Rhine* (1976).

Thomson, *Secretaries*: M. A. Thomson, *The Secretaries of State, 1681–1782* (Oxford 1932);

—, *Constitution*: *A Constitutional History of England, 1642–1801* (1938);

—, *Protestant Succession*: 'The Safeguarding of the Protestant Succession 1702–18', *History* 1954, reprinted in *William III and Louis XIV* (ed. Hatton and Bromley 1968).

Torntoft, P., 'William III and Denmark-Norway 1697–1700', *EHR* 1966.

Torrens, *Cabinets*: W. M. Torrens, *History of Cabinets* I (1894).

Trench, *George II*: Charles Chenevix Trench, *George II* (1975).

Trevelyan, *England*: G. M. Trevelyan, *England under Queen Anne* (3 vols. 1930–1934).

Turberville, *House of Lords*: A. S. Turberville, *The House of Lords in the Eighteenth Century* (Oxford 1927).

Überhorst: G. Überhorst, *Der Sachsen-Lauenburgische Erbfolgestreit bis zum Bombardement Ratzeburgs 1689–1693* (Berlin 1915).

Veenendaal, *Condominium*: A. J. Veenendaal, *Het Engels-Nederlands Condominium in de Zuidelijke Nederlanden Tijdens de Spaanse Successioorlog* (Utrecht 1945).

Vehse, *Court*: Eduard Vehse, *Geschichte der Höfe des Hauses Braunschweig in Deutschland und England* (5 vols. Hamburg 1853).

Vietsch, *Balance*: E. von Vietsch, *Das europäische Gleichgewicht* (Leipzig 1942).

Wagner, *Heralds*: A. Wagner, *Heralds of England* (1968).

Walcott, Robert, *English Politics in the early Eighteenth Century* (Oxford 1956).

Walker, *Music*: Ernest Walker, *A History of Music in England* (3rd ed. 1952).

Wallbrecht, *Theatre*: Rosenmarie Wallbrecht, *Das Theater des Barockzeitalters an den welfischen Höfen Hannover und Celle* (Hildesheim 1974).

Walters, *Frederick*: John Walters, *The Royal Griffin, Frederick, Prince of Wales 1707-51* (1972).

Ward: A. W. Ward, *Great Britain and Hanover. Some Aspects of the Personal Union* (Oxford 1899);

—, *Sophia*: *The Electress Sophia and the Hanoverian Succession* (2nd ed. 1909).

Ward, *University Politics*: W. R. Ward, *Georgian Oxford, University Politics in the Eighteenth Century* (Oxford 1959).

Waterhouse, E. K., *Painting in Britain 1630-1790* (1953).

Weber, *Quadruple Alliance*: Ottocar Weber, *Die Quadrupel-Allianz vom Jahre 1718* (Vienna 1887);

—, *Utrecht*: *Der Friede von Utrecht* (Gotha 1891).

Wensheim, *Nystad*: Göran Wensheim, *Studier kring freden i Nystad* (Lund 1973).

Westermann: Herbert Westermann, 'Brand Westermann', *Hannoversche Geschichtsblätter* 1974.

Whiting, *Medals*: J. R. S. Whiting, *Commemorative Medals* (1972).

Wiesener: Louis Wiesener, *Le Régent, L'Abbé Dubois et les Anglais* (3 vols. Paris 1891-99).

Wilkins, *Sophia Dorothea*: W. H. Wilkins, *The love of an uncrowned Queen. Sophia Dorothea, Consort of George I, and her Correspondence with Philip Christopher Count von Königsmarck* (1900, 2nd ed. 1903); cp. II above.

Wilks, *Pelham*: John W. Wilks, *A Whig in power. The political career of Henry Pelham* (1964).

Williams, *Carteret and Newcastle*: Basil Williams, *Carteret and Newcastle* (Cambridge 1943);

—, *Stanhope*: *Stanhope. A study in eighteenth century war and diplomacy* (Oxford 1932, reprint 1966);

—, *Whig Supremacy*: *The Whig Supremacy* (Oxford 1939).

Williams, *Constitution*: E. N. Williams, *The eighteenth century Constitution 1688-1815* (Cambridge 1960), introductions to documents edited.

Wilson, *Fleury*: A. M. Wilson, *French Foreign Policy during the Administration of Fleury, 1726-1743* (Cambridge, Mass. 1936).

Wilson, Charles, *England's Apprenticeship, 1603-1763* (1965);

—, *Commerce*: *Anglo-Dutch Commerce and Finance in the Eighteenth Century* (Cambridge 1941);

—, *Profit and Power*: *Profit and Power. A Study of England and the Dutch Wars* (1957).

Wimes, *Imperial Circles*: Roger Wimes, 'The Imperial Circles, Princely Diplomacy and Imperial Reform 1681-1714', *JHM* 1967.

Wittram: R. Wittram, *Peter I. Czar und Kaiser* (2 vols. Göttingen 1964).

Woker, F. W., *Geschichte der katholischen Kirche und Gemeinde in Hannover und Celle* (Paderborn 1889).

Wolf et al., *Die Reichsidee*: Julius Wolf, Konrad J. Heilig, Herman M. Görgen, *Österreich und die Reichsidee* (1936).

Woodbridge, *Temple*: H. Woodbridge, *Sir William Temple, The Man and his World* (Oxford 1940).

Wrangel: H. Wrangel, *Kriget i Östersjöen 1719-1721* (2 vols. Stockholm 1906-07).

Wright, Thomas, *England under the House of Hanover* (2 vols. 1848), useful for satire and caricatures.

Young, *London Churches*: Elizabeth and Wayland Young, *Old London Churches* (no date).

Young, *Poor Fred*: Sir George Young, *Poor Fred, The People's Prince* (1937).

Young, Percy M., *Handel* (1965 rev. ed.).

Younghusband, Sir G., *The Jewel House* (1921).

Zeller, *Equilibrium*: G. Zeller, 'Le principe d'équilibre dans la politique internationale avant 1789', *RH* 1956.

Zernack: Klaus Zernack, *Von Stolbova nach Nystad. Russland und die Ostsee in der Politik des 17. and 18. Jahrhundert* (Giessen 1958).

Notes to the text

Chapter I: Parents and childhood

This chapter is based on the printed *Mémoires* of Sophia, on the many volumes of her printed correspondence and of the equally voluminous volumes of Liselotte's letters, and of printed memoirs of the period. Knoop, *Sophie*, has been useful for information drawn from unprinted correspondence, especially Friedrich August's letters to his mother. Köcher till 1674, and Schnath, *Hannover* I, from that date till 1692, have provided essential background information.

1 For the *Reichsidee* and the Empire in general see Heer; Wolf *et al.*; and the studies by Bandorf and Richard Thompson. For the most recent account of the 1519 election, see Manuel Fernández Alvarez, *Charles V. Elected Emperor and Hereditary Ruler* (1974), ch. 3.

2 For a good example of this, see P. Höynck, *Frankreich und seine Gegner auf dem Nymwegener Friedens-Kongress* (Bonn 1960) 49 ff. For a more detailed treatment of the unsuccessful attempt of the Brunswick dukes to obtain equal status with the electors see Schnath, *Hannover* I, 106 ff.

3 Sophia, *Correspondence with her brother*: Karl Ludwig's letter of 6/16 Apr. 1678.

4 Sophia, *Mémoires*, 121.

5 *Ibid.*, 52.

6 *Ibid.*, 58–61 for the mission of Georg Christoph von Hammerstein and the wording of the convention.

7 *Ibid.*, 59. For her later realization that Karl Ludwig had been told this of Georg Wilhelm to make him consent to the substitution of bridegrooms, see Sophia, *Correspondence with her brother*: to Karl Ludwig 8 April 1666.

8 Ernst August, *Letters to his wife*, 13 Nov. [1671]; cp. Sophia, *Mémoires*, 64 and

Correspondence with her brother: to Karl Ludwig 6 Feb. 1659.

9 Sophia, *Mémoires*, 68 and Sophia, *Correspondence with her brother*: to Karl Ludwig 15 Aug. [1661]. Liselotte agreed; at a time when George was already a grandfather, she recalled his birth and childhood 'as if it were yesterday ... he was a beautiful child with large eyes': Liselotte, *Selected Letters* (Kroll translation), 128 note 1.

10 Sophia, *Correspondence with her brother*: to Karl Ludwig 12 Dec. 1661.

11 Knoop, *Sophie*, 63.

12 Sophia, *Mémoires*, 71.

13 *Ibid.*, 74, and Sophie, *Letters to Mme von Harling*, passim, for the duration of the Italy visit.

14 Ernst August, *Letters to his wife*: 26 Aug. [1670].

15 Sophia, *Correspondence with her brother*: to Karl Ludwig 12 Dec. 1661, 3 Aug. 1663, 15 June 1669 and 19 Sept. 1675.

16 For Sophia's comments on Karl Philipp, see her *Letters to the raugravines*: to Caroline 2/12 March 1690, and to Louise 10/20 March 1690. For the comments quoted on the other children see Bodemann, *Sophie*, 85.

17 Sophia, *Correspondence with her brother*: to Karl Ludwig, e.g. 19 Sept. 1675, 6 July 1679. It should be noted that the stress on this trait was intended to comfort her brother, who had similar problems with his son and heir.

18 Sophia's closeness to George is well demonstrated in her *Letters to the Hohenzollerns*, passim.

19 Sophia, *Mémoires*, 104. She explains the nickname by a parenthesis in her copying of Ernst August's letter: 'Vostre Benjamin (c'est ainsi que M. le duc appelloit mon fils aisne) ...'

20 Sophia, *Correspondence with her brother*: to Karl Ludwig 13 June 1675; Sophia, *Letters to the raugravines*: to Louise 10/20 Jan. 1689; Sophia, *Letters to diplomats*: to Schütz 20 June 1702.

21 For Sophia's wonder see *Letters to the raugravines*: to Louise 7 Jan. 1703; for her comment on Christian Heinrich: to Louise 8 Dec. 1702; for Karl Philipp's gambling debts see Schnath, *Hannover* I, 564.

22 Sophia, *Correspondence with her brother*: to Karl Ludwig 24 Nov. 1667; for the Herford visit see Knoop, *Sophie*, 81.

Chapter II: The electoral cap

The principal printed sources for this chapter are Sophia's *Mémoires* and her various correspondences, to which should be added Leibniz's letters and papers, Wendland's selection of *Prinzenbriefe* (illustrating the family strife caused by the primogeniture decree of Ernst August), and Schnath's superb 'register' edition of the Königsmarck-Sophia Dorothea letters, *Der Königsmarck-Briefwechsel*. Specialized monographs, in particular Schnath's well-documented Sophia Dorothea trilogy, have been invaluable. Older works on Brunswick-Lüneburg history by Havemann, Malortie, Meier, Pfeffinger, Rothert and Sichart, have proved useful; while Esenbeck and Schnath, *Hannover* I, have given the necessary background for the achievement of the electoral bonnet.

1 Sophia, *Mémoires*, 88–89.

2 *Ibid.*, 107–08: copy of Georg Wilhelm's letter of 30 Jan./9 Feb. 1676 to Sophia in answer to hers of 1 Feb. 1676.

3 For the Osnabrück negotiations and commitments of this period see Schnath, *Hannover* I, 50 ff.; for Sweden's involvement in the Dutch War see *SUPH* I, part 3: *1648–1697*, by Georg Landberg, 175 ff.

4 See the significant comment in Sophia, *Correspondence with her brother*: Karl Ludwig's letter of 23 Sept./3 Oct. 1676: 'Je crois les ris et les pleurs de mon nevue [George] et de la Freilein [*i.e.*, Fräulein] Sophie se determineront selon la volonté de leur parents et selon les conjonctures.'

5 Bussche, *Letters to*: Sophia's of 4 March 1682.

6 For George's behaviour under fire see (apart from the Ernst August letter cited in chapter 1 note 19) Sophia, *Correspondence with her brother*: to Karl Ludwig 23 Aug. 1675. For Louis XIV's praise see Sophia, *Mémoires*, 43.

7 Sophia, *Letters to the raugravines*: to Louise 3 Dec. 1702, authorizing her to spend money to have Maximilian and Christian mentioned in the gazettes. Cp. her letter to Louise of 29 Aug. 1704.

8 Books bought after 1699 can be traced in K.G., Schatullrechnungsbeläge. George's command of French is sufficiently demonstrated in his surviving correspondence; for his command of Latin see e.g. B.M., Add. MSS 6117, bishop of Dublin to archbishop Wake, 26 June 1717 and *HMC*, *Laing MSS* II, 194, letter from D. Wilkins (who was present at George I's visit to Cambridge) of 15 Oct. 1717; for the king's ability to converse fluently in Dutch in 1727 see Fabrice, *Memoiren*, 146 (report of 12 July 1727).

9 Görtz Archive: 121/6, Schulenburg's letter of 27 July 1717.

10 *Ibid.*: 126/2, Weber's letter with draft of Görtz's reply of 15 July 1721; they show that George had read the diplomat's account of Russia with satisfaction and approval. Cp. George's questioning de la Motraye in 1727 on his travels in Russia and Poland: Motraye, *Travels* (2nd ed.) I, x, reporting his conversation with the king the night he landed in the Netherlands en route for Hanover.

11 Sophia, *Correspondence with her brother*: to Karl Ludwig 15 Oct., 5 Nov., 24 Dec. 1676 and 21 Jan. 1677. All that is known for certain is the lady's Christian name, Anne.

12 Hatton, *Louis XIV*, 38. Cp. for George's daughter assuming that her nephew Frederick had mistresses at the age of sixteen: Trench, *George II*, 127.

13 For a rumoured brief relationship with a more distant relative of the father's mistress, see Leibniz, *Anecdota*, 23. The duration of George's affair with Maria Katharine is uncertain. Assumptions in the diplomatic reports from Hanover that it was resumed after the death of her first husband (1693) may not be well founded, given George's close attachment to Melusine from 1691.

14 Sophia, *Mémoires*, 110–11; for documentary details of the long drawn-out marriage negotiations see Schnath, *Hannover* I, 146 ff.

15 Sophia, *Correspondence with her brother*: to Karl Ludwig 20 June 1679.

16 Bernstorff Archive: AG 25, Sophia's letter (from France) to Georg Wilhelm of 4 Sept. 1679.

17 Sophia, *Mémoires*, 124–25.

18 Prüser, *Göhrde*, 44 ff.

19 For Sophia's reaction to the death of Wartenberg, bishop of Osnabrück, see her *Mémoires*, 70; for Ernst August's and her own to Johann Friedrich's death, *ibid.*, 134.

20 Phrases quoted by Sichart, *Army* I, 20–21. The Swedish commander was Otto Vellingk who fought during the Dutch war on the side of France as an officer in Louis XIV's Swedish regiment.

21 For Rupert's suggestion of Jan. 1680 see Knoop, *Sophie*, 102–03; for Sophia's positive response see *Correspondence with her brother*: to Karl Ludwig 18 Apr. 1680. For William III's favouring an English marriage for George as early as 1677 see P. L. Müller, *Wilhelm III von Oranien und Georg Friedrich von Waldeck* I (The Hague 1873) 109 ff; for his disappointment at the negative outcome see Conway's instructions (cited in Skelton's letter to Conway of 19 Jan. 1682/3 from Hamburg) that 'the king doth not intend to answer the Dukes of Brunswick upon the notification they have given of the marriage lately consomated here between their children [i.e. George and Sophia Dorothea]'. This disappointment may have been a contributory cause for William III's denying Ernst August the Garter which Sophia so diligently solicited for him: for her efforts see Skelton's letters to Blathwayt of 22 Dec. 1682, 16 and 22 Jan., 23 Feb. and 2 March 1682/3; Skelton's copy of his letter to Sophia of 10 Jan. 1682/3 and his letter to Conway of 26 Jan. 1682/3: all in B.M., Add. MSS 37984.

22 Those modern writers who stress the enmity of Anne towards George follow Spanheim, *Account* and Burnet, *History*; those who deduce a grudge on George's part rely on contemporary gossip committed to paper. With the lack of reliable evidence, historians have been reduced to assumptions; e.g. Knoop, *Sophie*, 103, holds that George himself decided against a marriage to Anne because of his dislike of 'everything foreign', while Chandler, *Marlborough*, 125–26, looks upon George as

ardent but unsuccessful: 'Anne with difficulty fended off George as a suitor for her hand.'

23 The well-informed Skelton (in a letter to Blathwayt, 16 Jan. 1682/3 from Hamburg: B.M., Add. MSS 37984) states categorically that 'there never was any proposal of marriage on either side'. It is worth noting that Sophia told Liselotte, even before George left for London, to disregard rumours that the Hanoverian heir would propose to Anne of York (Liselotte, *Letters*: 27 Sept. 1680). George's letter to his mother from London of 30 Dec. 1680/10 Jan. 1681 has survived in a contemporary copy in B.M., King's MSS 140 (see section I of my Bibliography) and has been printed in *Archiv des Historischen Vereins für Niedersachsen* (1846); George's letter to Margaret Hughes of 26 Oct. 1682 is in B.M., Add. MSS 38091, fol. 242 r and v.

24 *Newdigate*, 256.

25 Bernstorff Archive: AG 24, Sophia to Georg Wilhelm, an undated letter (the one first quoted in my text), and two others on this topic of 4/14 Sept. and 13/23 Sept. 1682.

26 Sophia, *Letters to diplomats*: to the abbé Ballati 10/20 Sept. 1682.

27 Sophia, *Mémoires*, 97: 'le prince electoral vouloit voir sa maitresse avant que de l'épouser': see also Sophia, *Correspondence with her brother*: to Karl Ludwig 10 Sept. 1670 and 8 July 1671.

28 Evidence that George was in love with Sophia Dorothea has been available since 1938 when Schnath, *Hannover* I, 721–30, printed the report of d'Arcy Martel: the French diplomat noted that George 'a un fils de sa femme, laquelle il aime, quoyque sans démonstration extérieure'.

29 A copy of this horoscope, made by an Italian courtier, was generously put at my disposal by Professor Schnath; the original is in the Niedersächsisches Landesbibliothek (Hs XXXIII).

30 The part of Hoya ceded consisted of the *Ämter* Stolzenau, Diepenau, Harpstedt, Steyerberg, Siedenburg, Barenburg and Heiligenrode; the remaining *Ämter* (Syke, Bruchhausen and Ehrenburg, and the town of Nienburg) came to Hanover in 1705. For the marriage contract, see Schnath, *Hannover* I, 164–65. During

31 George's reign other North German territories, long desired, were bought from Hanover's neighbours: in 1700 the district of Wildeshausen (from the Swedish king), and in 1711 (from the king of Denmark) the town and district of Delmenhorst and four smaller Oldenburg districts.

31 Schnath, in his introduction to Sophia, *Letters to the Hohenzollerns* (1927), was the first to realize this. He has been followed by Knoop, *Sophie*, 152 ff.

32 For Ernst August's fondness for his daughter-in-law see *Letters to his wife*: 2/12 November 1684; for Friedrich August's appreciation of Sophia Dorothea see Knoop, *Sophie*, 113 and Schnath, *Hannover* I, 567–78 and 746; for Maximilian's paying court to her see a great many references in the *Königsmarck-Briefwechsel*, e.g. nos. 78, 212, 215; for Karl Philipp's role: *ibid.*, introduction.

33 The first stage of the *Prinzenstreit* (1682–87) is dealt with by Schnath, *Hannover* I, 274–97. The *Prinzenbriefe*, selected letters between Ernst August, Sophia and those sons who opposed the primogeniture decree of the father, published by Anna Wendland in *NJ* 1937, illustrate the personal aspect of all stages (the second starting in 1691 and the third in 1698) of the *Prinzenstreit*.

34 Wendland, *Prinzenbriefe*, 9.

35 *Ibid.*, Friedrich August's letters to his mother, *passim*; for Karl Philipp's dragoon regiment (bought for him in May 1688 as soon as he had signed the primogeniture clause), see Schnath, *Hannover* I, 564. For Maximilian's military career with the Hanoverian troops, see Alexander Schwenke, *Geschichte der hannoverschen Truppen in Griechenland 1685–89* (Hanover 1854), and, more briefly, Schnath, *Hannover* I, 375–76 and 396–99.

36 For the second stage of the *Prinzenstreit* see Schnath, *Hannover* I, 557–91, where he (582) judges Sophia's activities treasonable. For Sophia's side of the story see Bussche, *Letters to*: 15/25 Feb. 1692.

37 Maximilian signed on 23 Feb./5 March 1689.

38 For Ernst August's exploitation of the situation see Schnath, *Hannover* I, 500 ff. and 592 ff.

39 Sophia, *Letters to the raugravines*, gives many details about the changes; cp. Schnath,

Leineschloss, and Seiler, *passim*. Note that the identification of the figures in the composite family picture (our illustration no. 6) varies. I have followed Schnath, *Hannover* I, ill. V. for the groupings and for the assumption that Sophia Charlotte is depicted by Sophia's side. I have further deduced that in the left group (the soldier sons) George, as *Erbprinz*, has the position of pre-eminence close to his father. A different (but still tentative) interpretation can be found in Kroll, *Sophie*, who regards the young female figure as that of Sophia Dorothea, George's wife, with George on her right; and the childlike figure as their son Georg August, not (as in Schnath) the commemorative symbolic representation of Maximilian's dead twin.

40 For the opera see Wallbrecht, *Theatre*, 45–60, and, for the *Historia Domus*, Reese, *Historie*, 18 ff., 161–90.

41 Bernstorff Archive: AG 28, Beyrïe's letter from London 3/13 Jan. 1699.

42 For Sophia's friendship with Spanheim see Knoop, *Sophie*, 43–44; his letters to her after she left Heidelberg are in Hann.: 91, Kurfürstin Sophie, 6.

43 For Sophia's remark on Sophia Charlotte see Gourville, *Mémoires* II, 127, reinforced by Bussche, *Letters to*: Sophia's of 8 May 1682. It should be noted, since historians have frequently misinterpreted Sophia's expression, that what she intended to convey was not that her daughter was an atheist but that, with a view to future marriage prospects, her options between Calvinism and Lutheranism were kept open.

44 For the position of the Huguenots see Beuleke's monograph; for the Catholic church built in Ernst August's reign see Woker's study; for the German Calvinist church, urged by Sophia, promised by Ernst August, and established by George see Sophia, *Letters to the raugravines*: 1 Nov. 1699, 2 Apr. and 12 Oct. 1702.

45 For the Hanoverian summer residence see Alvensleben, *Herrenhausen* (1966 ed.); Meyer, *Königliche Garten*; and *Westermann*.

46 For the carnivals in Ernst August's reign see Malortie, *Court*, and numerous references throughout Sophia's correspondence; for a fine one in George's reign see Sophia, *Letters to the raugravines*: 12 Feb. 1708.

47 Bothmer, *Mémoires*, 22.

48 Schnath, 'Sophia-Dorothea trilogy': *A.B.*, *Knesebeck*, 135.

49 Schnath, *Königsmarck-Briefwechsel*, introduction.

50 Königsmarck (Aurora), 'Mémoires', ed. Anna Wendland, *ZVHN* 1910.

51 The history of the family can be followed in Schmidt, *Schulenburgs*, especially entry no. 616 for [Ehrengard] Melusine's father. Cp. Johann Matthias's letter of 12 Nov. 1726 in Schulenburg, *Leben* II, 263, in which he quotes the king of Prussia's remark to him: 'vous êtes tous de bonne race'.

52 Pictorial evidence in the Kielmansegg collection shows that Sophia Charlotte was slim and beautiful as a young woman. To call her 'grossly obese' in her mature years (as in most English modern works, e.g. *Burton*, 239) is exaggerated, though not surprising in view of contemporary stories that George preferred 'German trulls and fat trulls at that'. More bothersome may be the fact that English historians at times muddle up who was the plump and who the slim of 'George's ladies' (Williams, *Whig Supremacy*, 146, who is followed e.g. by Young, *Poor Fred*). For Sophia's reference to Melusine's tall and thin figure (in conversation with Mrs Howard) see Coxe, *Robert Walpole* (1816 ed.) I, 151; for the late Melusine's portrait, now in the Landesgalerie of Hanover, see Schnath, *Hannover* II, ill. 15.

53 For Melusine's taking the initiative to meet influential Englishwomen see Panshanger MSS: Mme Robethon's undated letter of 1714; and Halsband, *Lady Mary*, 240–41, for the presence of letters from Melusine in the Wortley MSS. For Melusine being used as a go-between, there is ample evidence in the Panshanger MSS for 1718 and in the Görtz Archive: 121/6, Schulenburg correspondence; see also Beattie, *Court*, 247–48. For the duchess of Marlborough being granted an audience with George I in 1720 through Melusine's intercession see David Green, *Sarah Duchess of Marlborough* (1967), 219–20.

54 Wilhelmine, *Mémoires*, 57. For English contemporary rumours of a morganatic marriage see Montagu, *Works* I, 75; and Coxe, *Robert Walpole* (1816 ed.) I, 150 and II, 258.

55 Schaumburg-Lippe, *Letters*: 12/23 June 1724.

56 This gift was twisted by contemporaries to suggest that she (and/or George) spent much of their time inanely cutting out 'paper dolls'.

57 See Windsor, R.A.: 52884, letter to Aislabie, from Herrenhausen 27 Sept. NS 1720; Coxe, *Robert Walpole* II, 668, letter to Walpole of 18 Feb. 1729/30.

58 For the good looks of the daughters see Ernst August II, *Letters*: 20 Jan. [1708]; Fabrice, *Memoiren*, 133–34 and Palm's letter to Charles VI of 17 Dec. 1726: Coxe, *Robert Walpole* (1816 ed.) III, 509. This is supported by pictorial evidence in Alvensleben, *Herrenhausen* (1923 ed.), for the two elder daughters and for *die schöne Gertrud* in Fabrice, *Memoiren*, ill. no. 10 (the copy by Mercier). The present illustration no. 32, also from the Bückeburg collection, seems to be of a later date when she was already marked by illness. For the three daughters being present at Pyrmont and Herrenhausen and generally sharing George and Melusine's life between 1707 and 1714 see Ernst August II, *Letters*, for these years. The references to [Ehrengard] Melusine and the two elder girls are easily gathered via the index, for those to Gertrud (whom the editor has not been able to identify beyond Trudchen, a *Vertraute* of George's, and whom he does not connect with the Fräulein von Oeynhausen mentioned in the letter of 16 Apr. 1713) see letters of 23 June [1707], 16 May [1709], 16 Apr. and 12 July 1713. Evidence for the closeness of these family links after 1714 can be found e.g. in Panshanger MSS: Mme Robethon's letter of 18 Aug. 1716; and Fabrice, *Memoiren*, 134, 136.

59 Ernst August II, *Letters*: from a comparison of those of 19 Aug. [1707], 20 Jan. [1708] and 16 May [1709].

60 Schnath feels confident about the two elder girls (*A.B.*, *Sophie Dorothea*, 174 note 22) and near-certainty for Gertrud (*Hannover* II, 490). Contemporaries assumed George's paternity in the case of the two younger girls; e.g. for [Petronella] Melusine: Coxe, *Robert Walpole* (1816 ed.) II, note 257; and for Gertrud: Fabrice, *Memoiren*, 125–26. The first printed German reference to George's paternity of [Petronella] Melusine,

in the *ADB*, is not accepted by Schmidt, *Schulenburgs*, no. 860.

61 These wills of 1743, 1773 and 1778 are all in the P.R.O., Probate. For the veiled references to Gertrud see Schaumburg-Lippe, *Letters*: 13/24 Oct. 1721; 25 Sept./6 Oct. 1722; 7/18 Jan. 1724.

62 *Königsmarck-Briefwechsel*: Sophia Dorothea's letter of 30 June 1693. Buccolini's mother was the dancer Zenobia Buccolini, and he rose to the position of *Oberjägermeister* in Celle.

63 Schulenburg, *Leben* I, 381, for Maurice's reception in Hanover in 1709 and for his position after the legitimization in 1711.

64 Cp. Sophia and George's interest in Maximilian's illegitimate daughter and her 'princely' marriage festivities: Sophia, *Letters to the raugravines*: to Louise 10 Dec. 1711.

65 Königsmarck-Sophia Dorothea, *Correspondence*: his letters undated [March 1692] and 10 Sept. OS 1692; her letters of 28 and 29 Aug. OS 1692 show that she was aware of the gossip surrounding George and Melusine.

66 For the fate of the surviving correspondence see Schnath's introduction to the *Königsmarck-Briefwechsel*, and his *A.B.*, *Königsmarck*, 89–96. For the letters found at the Leineschloss apartments of Sophia Dorothea see his *A.B.*, *Knesebeck*, 133, 135, 169 and his *NJ* article of 1930.

67 Wilkins published the Lund letters in English translation in 1901; Ward in appendix B to his *Sophia* of 1909 printed, both in the original languages used (French with some German) and in English translation, the Prussian letters. Biographers of Sophia Dorothea have continued to use these translations even after 1952 when Schnath's *Königsmarck-Briefwechsel* gave scholars a complete edition which also corrects dating and readings, particularly in Wilkins. For Sophia Dorothea and Knesebeck's public stances see Schnath, *A.B.*, *Sophie Dorothea*, 201–02 and *ibid.*, *Knesebeck*, 151.

68 Sympathy for Sophia Dorothea is not, of course, restricted to those, like Wilkins, who feel convinced that George's wife did not commit adultery. For the sake of historical accuracy it should be said that the Sophia Dorothea-Königsmarck corre-

spondence leaves no doubt of full sexual intercourse. Dislike of prying into the private relationship of two lovers of the past, more than was essential for the purposes of the biography of George, made me restrict my references to the physical aspect of the love-affair in the text. Quite apart, however, from the polite contemporary euphemism, cited in my footnote on page 57 (and frequently employed in the correspondence), the following more explicit remarks can be noted: no. 38 [March 1692] in which Königsmarck sends a thousand kisses to her *bocqua sensa dente*; those of 10 and 18 Aug. and 12 Sept. 1692 which conjure up for the princess *une prison qui attend vostre prisonnier avec bien de l'impatience*, express the hope that on his return he will find no sentinel before the prison, and urge her to take care that the prison will always be open to him, but *fermée pour toute la terre*; that of 29 Dec. 1692 – after George has become an electoral prince – in which Königsmarck contemptuously refers to the *minces* and *médiocres plaisirs électoraux* when compared to *den unsrigen*; that of 19 July 1693 in which he swears he'll take leave of his senses if the princess should *monter à cheval* with anyone else as passionately as she has done with him; and that of 29 Sept. 1693, when he recalls the joy in her eyes *à me voir mourir sous eux* and her cry *Mon scher Koenigs, je – faisons le ensamble!*, adding for his own part, *Ah, si je pouway baiser ses petis millieux qui m'a tans donné de plaisir!* For Sophia Dorothea's reference to her own passionate feelings see her letters of 20 June, 30 July and 22 Aug. 1693; and, by inference, Königsmarck's letter of 10 July 1692.

69 For Sophia Dorothea's references to and citations from George's letters see the *Königsmarck-Briefwechsel*, nos. 81, 83, 91, 92, 112, 128, 201 and 230; for the Lucretia quote and the count's debts, *ibid.*, 23 June 1693; for Sophia Dorothea riling Königsmarck on the frequency of George's letters, *ibid.*

70 Sophia, *Letters to the raugravines*: to Louise 15/25 July 1694.

71 Schnath, *A.B.*, *Knesebeck*, 133–36, for her interrogation; cp. *A.B.*, *Königsmarck*, 77.

72 *Ibid.*, 83–89. For the details of Montalban's reward, and an earlier gift of 50,000 Taler,

see Schnath, *Hannover* II, 173–74. Luise Gilde, in a rejoinder to Schnath's review of her *Die Reichweite der Prinzessin von Ahlden* of 1966 (both in *NJ* 1968), disputes Schnath's deductions on the subject of Königsmarck's murder, but without supporting evidence.

73 Knesebeck's letter of 26 Feb. 1710: Schnath, *A.B., Knesebeck*, 159–60.

74 Sophia, *Letters to the raugravines:* to Louise 3/13 and 25 Aug., and 5 Sept. 1694. For diplomats and their dilemma see e.g. Bernstorff Archive; AG 28 vol. viii: Beyriё's 1694 letters from London of 31 July/10 Aug. (on the *éclat* of the affair); 3/13 Aug. (acknowledging instructions of 27 July to plead ignorance); 7/17 and 14/24 Aug. (reporting rumours still current and his own attempts to lessen William III's concern).

75 Anti-Hanoverian propaganda took advantage of British ignorance of the roles played by Ernst August and Georg Wilhelm in the divorce proceedings to make George the central figure; on Königsmarck's presumed fate it could utilize sensational manuscript and printed material circulating in Germany from 1695 onwards, for an analysis of which see Schnath, *A.B., Königsmarck*, 68–74.

76 For the 1826 reconstruction (after vain searches between 1816 and 1821 for the original papers, occasioned by George IV's desire for a divorce) see Schnath, *A.B., Sophie Dorothea*, 175; for Louis XIV's attitude in 1694–99 see *ibid., Königsmarck*, 81 and *Sophie Dorothea*, 205; and for the efforts of Sophia Dorothea's mother with William III and queen Anne, see *A.B., Sophie Dorothea*, 206–11.

77 For Jacobite efforts to gain the support of the Swedish king see Hatton, *Charles XII*, 404, 416–17, 438, 445, 449, 474; and *Nordmann*, 84 ff.

78 For these gentlemen who wanted 'to greet their Queen', and for George I's countermeasures, see Schnath, *A.B., Sophie Dorothea*, 194–95.

79 *Ibid.*, 198–99, 212–20, 251–56 for George's behaviour towards Sophia Dorothea after 1698 and the Bar mission of 1725.

80 For the former *Kammerjungfer* turning against Sophia Dorothea see *A.B., Knesebeck*, 155 ff: her praise of George is on 160–

61. On the letters offered for sale (and later preserved in Lund) see Schnath, *Hannover* II, 143, who characterizes the refusal of Sophia Dorothea's mother in 1710, and of Sophia Dorothea herself in 1724, to buy them as 'nearly inexplicable'. In 1727 the same letters were offered to the Hanoverian government for 100,000 Taler but no sale took place – the response being as negative as that to an earlier offer (in 1724 on behalf of the heirs of Königsmarck's former *Hofmeister*) of another bundle of Sophia Dorothea and Königsmarck letters, which have since disappeared.

81 Coxe, *Robert Walpole* (1816 ed.) III, 261–62, based on the reminiscences (not reliable) of Horace Walpole. John Brooke, in his contribution to the *Festschrift* for Dame Lucy Sutherland (1973), 263, makes a wise distinction between Walpole's facts of truth and truth of feeling.

82 Hervey, *Memoirs* (Sedgwick, 1-vol. ed.), 353.

83 See Schmidt, *Schulenburgs*, no. 742 for Melusine's *Reichsfürstin* status of 17 Apr. 1722.

84 Cowper (Mary), *Diary*, 132 (note that in the index this remark is erroneously attributed to Horatio Walpole).

85 For her court and daily life see Schnath, *A.B., Sophie Dorothea*, 221–30. A fine portrait of George which I noted in the Osnabrück *Rathaus* probably formed part of Sophia Dorothea's collection, since it is the property of the Bar family.

86 For George reminding his uncle (in 1703) that Sophia Dorothea had *denigrirt* him in her letters to Königsmarck, see Schnath, *A.B., Sophie Dorothea*, 212. For the expressed desire of Sophia Dorothea, her mother, and Königsmarck for George's death, see *Königsmarck-Sophia Dorothea, Correspondence*: e.g. her letter of 22 June 1683, his letters of 22 Aug. and 14 Sept. 1693; for the lovers' contempt for George's looks and ability see nos. 18, 71, 78, 172, 272, 280, 282.

Chapter III: Experience gained

The main documentation for this chapter comes from Sophia's published letters, George's letters to his mother in the Hanover Haupstaatsarchiv, and correspondence in the Bernstorff archive.

Of printed archive material the William III and Louis XIV documents edited by Grimblot and the so-called Queen Mary 'memoirs' (which also includes letters from William III) are the most significant. Gregg's doctoral thesis on the Protestant Succession, building *i.a.* on the Calenberg Brief Archiv, England, has been particularly useful for one section of the chapter, as has Holmes' study of queen Anne's reign. Schnath's Sophia-Dorothea trilogy remains important for the whole chapter, as does his *Geschichte Hannovers*, supplemented for the period after 1692 by studies by Schaer (administration), Brauer and Schwenke as well as Sichart (army) and Esebeck, Fricke and Schwarte (foreign policy). For the Holstein-Gottorp issue I have drawn on Scandinavian works noted in my *Charles XII* and the doctoral thesis of Oakley on William III's northern policy. For European issues in general I have utilized (but not specifically annotated for reasons of space) my researches into the Louis XIV period from British, French, Dutch and Austrian archives.

1   The full text of this note addressed to Albert Philipp von dem Bussche, ed. by E. Bodemann, is in *ZHVN* 1882, 169.

2   See e.g. Jordan, *Sophia Dorothea*, 206–08, lending support to these accounts 'sanctioned by tradition' by her choice of endpapers: the drawings by Rex Whistler for A. E. W. Mason's *Königsmarck*; and Trench, *George II*, 3–4, who takes for gospel at least some of the stories related in Horace Walpole's *Letters* I and *Memoirs* III.

3   The original title was *Octavia. Römische Geschichte*, but it would be pedantic not to use the better-known title of post-1714 editions.

4   It should be noted that Professor Schnath, for whose work I have the greatest respect, deduces from the Königsmarck-Sophia correspondence and from diplomatic reports that the count had been Gräfin Platen's lover and that the Gräfin was extremely jealous of Sophia Dorothea. He therefore allocates more responsibility than I am inclined to do to the Gräfin for the Königsmarck murder.

5   Cited by Schnath, *A.B., Knesebeck*, 150, from Danish archive material. Cp. the so-called Knesebeck, *Memoiren*, copied from the writings of Eleanore found on the doors and walls of her prison cell.

6   The Linden palace and garden, destroyed in the Second World War, are described in *Lampe* I, 164 ff.

7   For Sophia's reference to Ernst August's 'weak nerves' see *Letters to the raugravines*: to Louise 22 May/6 June 1697; *ibid.*, nos. 131, 146, 152, 158, 164, 171, 174, 181 for other symptoms of her husband's illness; for countess Platen's stroke *ibid.*, letter of 18/28 Feb. 1699.

8   For these vexations see Schnath, *A.B., Knesebeck*, 145–52.

9   Sophia, *Letters to the raugravines*: to Louise 26 Aug./5 Sept. 1694.

10   For rumours of a duel with a count Lippe see Schnath, *A.B., Knesebeck*, 134.

11   *Ibid.*, 151 note 74. From Sophia, *Letters to the raugravines*, no. 152, it is clear that Ernst August had begun by the end of August 1696 to hand over much of his work to George.

12   *Ibid.*: to Louise 20 Feb./2 March 1698.

13   For the Cresset intrigues and their consequences see Schnath, *A.B., Sophie Dorothea*, 207–16. His wife, Louise Marie de la Motte, a Huguenot from Poitou, was the Mlle de la Motte who had been a lady-in-waiting of the princess of Tarente. Cresset returned to represent William III with the Brunswick-Lüneburg dukes after Ernst August's death, and from then on abandoned the cause of the duchess of Celle and her daughter.

14   Bernstorff Archive: AG 32 contains the Portland letters of 1688–1705; AG 9, 10, 12, 18, 26, 27, 28, 42 and 50, cover Bernstorff's correspondence with a large number of Celle and non-Celle diplomats and agents and span most of Europe for the period 1675 to 1722. English news looms large, Beyrie's letters between 1685 and 1708 (AG 28) filling nine large volumes.

15   Schnath, *A.B., Sophie Dorothea*, 209–10.

16   The traditional view derives mainly from Klopp, Michael and Trevelyan and needs to be tested against a wider range of Hanoverian material, as in Gregg, *Protestant Succession*.

17   Fricke, *Leibniz*, 13 ff.

18   For Hanoverian complaints see Schnath, *A.B., Sophie Dorothea*, 198–99; for Eléonore's letter to queen Anne of 20 Sept. 1702 *ibid.*, 211.

19   George expressed *estime*, however, for

Christian's consistent attitude when compared to Maximilian's vacillation: Sophia, *Letters to the raugravines*: to Louise 18 Jan. 1703. The letters George wrote to his mother after Christian's death (Hann.: 91, Kurfürstin Sophie, no. 19a) on 23 and 29 Aug. 1703 show sympathy and concern and refer also to his own *chagrin*.

20 The domestic and foreign aspects of the third stage of the *Prinzenstreit* (1698–1701) will be fully covered in Schnath's third volume of *Geschichte Hannovers*. Suffice it here to say that Maximilian and Christian lost their appeal to the *Reichshofrat* (to have Ernst August's will declared illegal) and failed to get effective political support from foreign princes.

21 It is significant that Maximilian agreed to accept his father's will by a fresh signature of the primogeniture clause only after the Grand Alliance had been signed on 7 Sept. 1701 and while negotiations were in progress for Hanover's formal accession. Note that the allowance was to be increased, again in accordance with Ernst August's will, to 24,000 Taler on the death of Georg Wilhelm since the union with Celle would give George a larger income. Christian, who refused to sign, had to be content with 6,000 Taler a year (Sophia, *Letters to the raugravines*: to Louise 20 Dec. 1701 and 3 Dec. 1702).

22 Liselotte's letters to Sophia of 24 July 1701 and 8 Jan. 1702 printed in extract by Bodemann in Sophia, *Letters to the raugravines*, 240, note 1. For Sophia's hatred of the Jesuit père Wolf see *ibid.*: letters to Louise of 14 and 28 Dec. 1702, 14 and 18 Jan. 1703, and 14 Jan. 1712.

23 Schnath, *A.B.*, *Sophie Dorothea*, 210, from Eltz's reports.

24 The Liselotte quote in footnote on page 75 is from Ernst August II, *Letters*, 19; homosexuality has been inferred, e.g. by Kroll, *Sophie Dorothea*, 225.

25 See e.g. Bernstorff Archive: AG 34 vol. iii, Schütz's letter from London of 24 Feb. 1699 and one undated [1700].

26 *Ibid.*: AG 29 vol. iv, Bothmer's letter of 23 Nov. 1700 from The Hague on the effect of Sophia's talk of George's 'indifference'; cp. AG 34 vol. iii, for Schütz reporting on 13/24 Dec. 1700 from London a conversation with William III on the

same subject. Sophia's letter to Stepney is printed in *Klopp* VIII, 208.

27 For the initiatives of 1688–89 see Schnath, *Hannover* I, 493–96; for Sophia's disappointment see Mary, *Memoirs*, William III's letter of 10/20 Dec. 1689.

28 Bernstorff Archive: AG 34 vol. iii, Schütz's letter of 13/24 Dec. 1700 from London reporting the English view that Sophia had shown herself 'trop affectionée' to king James and his son.

29 This idea had been aired already during the Nine Years War in secret peace negotiations between Austrian and French diplomats: *Srbik*, 100–08, 129–32; for knowledge of it in Hanover, see Gregg, *Queen Anne*, note 51.

30 Sophia, *Letters to the raugravines*: to Louise 25 Oct. 1701.

31 For this embassy see Knoop, *Sophie*, 196 ff., and Toland, *Account*, 58–62.

32 Sophia, *Letters to the raugravines*: to Louise 8 Feb. 1703. That Sophia also had hopes of saving Maximilian from his Jesuit (père Wolf) by greater financial support from an English income is shown by a copy of her letter to Maximilian of 2 June 1701 (B.M., Add. MSS 15943, fol. 54), promising to help him: 'ou que je vivois seulement assez pour etre deux ans Reyne'.

33 Sophia, *Letters to diplomats*: to Schütz 25 May 1701.

34 Ward, *Sophia*, 323–24, citing her letter to Burnet of 22 June 1701 (on being 'too old'); for her allusions to her expected death see *Letters to the raugravines*: 29 Aug. 1702 and 27 Nov. 1709.

35 Toland, *Hanover*, 65–66.

36 For Rupert's relationship to Margaret Hughes (to whom he was not legally married) see Morrah, *Rupert*, 413–17.

37 That Harley understood the real position is clear from his letter of 1/12 March 1706 to Howe (printed in *Salomon*, 8 note 1): 'some people [in England] are so busy and so troublesome, what would they be, if any of that family [the electoral one] were brought into England during the Queen's life and in this heat of faction?'

38 For written, as opposed to oral evidence noted down, see her letter to Marlborough of 22 July OS 1708 (Anne, *Letters and Instructions*): 'I cannot bear to have any successor here, though it were but for a week.'

39 *Holmes*, 83.

40 The pamphlet printed the Gwynne letter as well as Sophia's letter of Nov. 1705 to Tenison (archbishop of Canterbury), intimating that she was keen to be invited to England. For Sophia's approval and justification of both, see her *Letters to diplomats*: to Schütz 29 Jan. and 30 March 1706.

41 Gregg, *Protestant Succession*, 14–24, has two brief but important sections on 'The role of Georg Ludwig' and 'The invitation crisis' (of 1702) to which I am much indebted. For Sophia telling Schütz to follow George's orders see e.g. *Letters to diplomats*: 4 Nov. 1708.

42 See Waldemar Röhrbein, 'Wirtschaftspolitik in den Hannoverschen Kurlanden zur Zeit des deutschen Frühmerkantilismus', *Neues Archiv für Niedersachsen* 1962.

43 Bernstorff Archive: AG 34, Schütz from London 3/13 March 1699.

44 For the details of the exchange of territory plan see Schnath, *Hannover* I, 422–23; and for the exchange and equivalent concept, Hatton, *War and Peace*, 13 ff. For the barrier plan against Denmark in its various stages see Schnath, *Hannover* I, 390 ff. and 421 ff.; and for the barrier concept in general Hahlweg, *Barrier*; Hahlweg, *Dutch Barrier*; and Schryver, *Barrier*.

45 For the Altona recess and the negotiations leading up to it see L. Stavenow, 'Sveriges politik 1686–89', *HT* 1895; L. Laursen, *Danmark-Norges Traktater* VIII, 480 ff.; Schnath, *Hannover* I, 437–47; and S.P. Oakley, 'William III and the Northern Crowns during the Nine Years War 1688–1697' (unpublished London Ph.D. thesis 1961).

46 For the events leading up to the peace of Travendal, see Hatton, *Charles XII*, 133–37.

47 The only evidence for this is the diplomatic report of Gourville (see Schnath, *Hannover* I, 307 note 4); that Ernst August also gave his son written instructions is clear from evidence given by *Schaer*, 44 (destroyed in 1943).

48 For Ernst August's system of government see Schnath, *Hannover* I, 298–339.

49 See the 1685 report by the French diplomat René d'Arcy-Martel printed in full *ibid.*, 721–30: opinion on George, 726. Cp. Toland, *Account*, 70, that George is opposed to France's 'intended universal monarchy'.

50 For Louis XIV's third-party efforts see *Fayard*, 213–40 and Hatton, *Gratifications*, 68–74; cp. Pagès, *Money*, passim.

51 For the secretly arranged scaling down of the treaty commitment of 500,000 Taler to 500,000 gulden, see Schnath, *Hannover* I, 607.

52 For the details of the 72,900 *livres* paid to Ernst August's advisers see *Fayard*, 230 and Schnath, *Hannover* I, 521. There is less certainty of the sums actually paid out in Vienna, but Schnath, *Hannover* I, 598 and 638, shows that Ernst August authorized the expenditure of 77,000 Taler.

53 Bernstorff Archive: AG 34 vol. iii, Schütz's letters of 6/16 Jan. 1699 to 17/28 Dec. 1700; for earlier information see *ibid.*: AG 44, Robethon's letter from The Hague, 29 Oct. 1697, and B.M., Add. MSS 371561, Stepney to Vernon from Celle, 11/24 Oct. Oct. 1968.

54 For Louis having hinted at advantages to be gained and having pressed the Brunswick-Lüneburg dukes to sign the second partition treaty see Bernstorff Archive: AG 29 vol. iv, Bothmer's letter from Paris of 15/25 Apr. 1698, and AG 34 vol. iii, Schütz's letter from Het Loo 2 Aug. 1700. For the disappointment when Louis XIV accepted the will of Carlos II, see AG 29 vol. iv, Bothmer's letter, The Hague, 23 Nov. 1700.

55 See Hatton, *Louis XIV and Fellow Monarchs*, 37 ff.

56 For William's determination to get the war against France moving in the Empire (until he could bring England and the Dutch Republic to go to war with Louis XIV) see Bernstorff Archive: AG 34 vol. iii, Schütz's letters of 12/23 Nov., 3/14, 13/24 and 17/28 Dec. 1700.

57 See Schnath, *Wolfenbüttel*, for an excellent study of the 1702 offensive in its diplomatic and military aspects.

58 For the troop negotiations see Sichart, *Army* I, 243 ff. and Brauer, *passim*. The first convention was signed as early as March 1702.

59 Sophia, *Letters to the Hohenzollerns*, 90.

60 Toland, *Hanover*, 53. There are numerous references to Karl Moritz's drinking problem in Sophia, *Letters to the raugravines*: to Amalie 28 March/7 Apr. 1689; to Louise 19/29 Oct. 1699; 22 Dec. 1700; 31 July, 18 Oct. and 27 Nov. 1701.

61 Hann.: 91, Kurfürstin Sophie 19a: George's letters of 29 May and 24 June 1702, both from Herrenhausen.

62 For Sophia Charlotte's deathbed see Sophia, *Letters to the Hohenzollerns*: to Friedrich I, 11 Feb. 1705. This attitude seems to have been common among George's closest friends: see e.g. that Johann Adolf von Kielmansegg refused to see a pastor on his deathbed: Görtz Archive: 121/6, Schulenburg's letter of 26 Nov. 1717.

63 Hatton, *Charles XII*, 411. For George's attitude to doctors see e.g. George, *Letters*, 495: to Sophia Dorothea 16 July [1714]; and Windsor R.A.: Geo. Add. MSS 28, no. 20; for Sophia's see *Letters to the raugravines*: e.g. to Louise 27 Nov. 1701 and 3 March 1712.

64 Cowper (Mary), *Diary*, 149, quoting Mehemet.

Chapter IV: The royal crown

The basic background material for this chapter is the Calenberg Brief Archiv, Des. 24, England, and the Kriegssachen papers in the Hanover Hauptstaatsarchiv, complemented by the Bernstorff and Görtz archives. Of older works Ward, *Sophia*, is still useful, though Klopp (who prints many documents) is misled by unreliable material into assuming that queen Anne was a Jacobite. Recent studies of the succession issue, Fricke, Shennan and, in particular, Gregg's doctoral thesis and his two published articles have been a great help to me, as have biographies of Harley and Bolingbroke by McInnes and Dickinson. For Hanoverian advisers and court life in general, family histories as well as the books by Lampe and Prüser have yielded much. They have been supplemented by a variety of archival material from the Public Record Office and the British Museum. For the war of the Spanish Succession I am indebted to Braubach's *Eugene* and Chandler's Marlborough biographies, to Mezgolich's study of Wratislaw, and to works on the Hanoverian and Dutch armies. Of printed material for the war the Snyder edition (with corrections and redating where necessary) of the Marlborough-Godolphin correspondence, the van't Hoff edition of the Marlborough-Heinsius correspondence and Veenendaal's first volume of the Heinsius Archief have lightened my labours.

1 Schnath, *Hannover* I, 648–50, assesses the total sum spent by 1694 for the electoral dignity in ready cash and indirect expenses (e.g. two years campaigning with a Hanoverian army at Ernst August's own cost) as 2,000,000 Taler; and estimates the budget deficits for the years 1690–94 at 768,420 Taler.

2 For Lefmann Berens-Cohen, see Schnee's long and well-documented article, *NJ* 1951.

3 Schnath, *Hannover* II, 408–09, while praising his late pupil's work, stresses that Lampe's thesis is less applicable for Ernst August's reign than for the eighteenth century.

4 For Bernstorff's Mecklenburg position and the complications which followed, see the studies by Ballschmieter and *Mediger* I. For Bernstorff's villages see *Michael* II, 640 ff.

5 For information about these members of the Schulenburg family see Schmidt's genealogical volumes: Johann Matthias no. 740, Bodo no. 741, [Ehrengard] Melusine no. 742, and Friedrich Wilhelm no. 750.

6 See e.g. the unsigned and undated letter, most informative on affairs in Hanover (possibly intercepted), placed with the post of 3/14 Sept. 1723 in P.R.O., SPD Regencies 43 vol. 5: 'As to Mr. Bernstorff's capacity in business hardly anyone ever disputed it with him.' The one exception I have come across is Craggs, who in his private letters to Stair complains of Bernstorff's ignorance and muddleheadedness: Stair, *Annals* II, 406, letter of 1 Oct. 1719.

7 Though not immediately: after the death of the elder Schütz (Ludwig Justus) in Feb. 1710, Hanover sent a resident, Kreienberg, who remained in London from Sept. 1710 until George I's accession. A new envoy, Thomas Grote, arrived in 1712 and died in 1713. Bothmer was next accredited to both the Dutch Republic and England, and made several brief visits to London before the arrival as extraordinary envoy of the younger Schütz (Georg Wilhelm) in Sept. 1713; Bothmer took over when Schütz was recalled in Apr. 1714.

8 For the Grote family see E. Grote, *Familien-Geschichte der Grafen und Freiherren Grote* (Hanover 1897); for Bothmer's will of 1723 see P.R.O. Probate, with codicil of 1728.

9 On a more exalted level, in January 1725

George I had to make a speedy and emphatic refusal of the offer of a marriage between king Louis XV of France and his eldest granddaughter: her conversion to Catholicism (an obvious necessity) could not be contemplated without compromising the king's commitment to the Protestant cause.

10 P.R.O., 31/14/159 vol. XXIV, letters from Giacomo Quirini to Inquisitor of State, Venice, from London 3/14 and 10/21 June 1715.

11 Schnath, in his ed. work for the *Hohenzollern correspondence*, 16 note 7, has shown that the older Herrenhausen garden was largely modelled on the Dutch gardens of Sophia's childhood and youth; and that, when George became elector, it was remodelled on the French pattern, in which fountains played a dominant role. Cp. Schnath, *Hannover* II, 399–400 and the article by Irmgard Lange-Kohte, 'Die Wasserkunst in Herrenhausen', *Hannoversche Geschichtsblätter* 1960.

12 See e.g. Schnee, *NJ* 1951, 121 ff.

13 For the building and decoration of Göhrde, 1706–10, see Prüser, *Göhrde*, ch. 5, and Meier I, 244 ff.; for entertainment see Malortie, *Beiträge* II, 148 ff.

14 P.R.O., SPD Regencies 43 vol. 5, Tilson to Delafaye, 30 Nov./11 Dec. 1723, on the recent stay at Göhrde, where the king had lived truly *en Roy*, 'at the rate of 3000 Dollars [i.e. Talers] a day'; with servants Tilson reckoned that George had 'above 1100 in his family' to pay and feed from his 'patrimonial Estate'.

15 Sophia, *Letters to the raugravines*: to Louise 24 Sept. 1702. In conversation with Mrs Howard she was more outspoken: 'Do you see that malkin? You would scarcely believe that she has captivated my son' (Coxe, *Robert Walpole* (1816 ed.) I, 151).

16 Hann.: Cal. Brief 16 (Kriegssachen), 756, at George's headquarters, Hofmarschall Hardenberg (draft) to Görtz 4 Oct. 1709, with the elector's reasoned decision in two questions, one of precedence and one of allocation of apartments, both going against 'Mad la Raugraffe'; cp. Sophia, *Letters to the raugravines*: to Louise 2 Apr. 1702, in which she fondly, but erroneously, imagines that Ernst August would have been easier in such matters.

17 Kielmansegg, *Familien-Chronik*, 443 ff.

18 The family tradition (see *Familien-Chronik*, 454) is that he held this English court office from the time of George I's coronation (this has been followed e.g. by Schaer in the Schaumburg-Lippe *Letters*, 49 note 129); but Beattie's ascertaining that the salary of the Master of the Horse was saved after Somerset's resignation is conclusive (*Court*, 245 note 1). Note that though Kielmansegg was treated in London as George's Hanoverian Master of the Horse, he was in reality Vice-Master of the Horse, Harling holding the Master's office till his death in 1724; see the comment in Schaumburg-Lippe, *Letters*: 24 Jan. and 4 Feb. 1718, that Kielmansegg had died without having obtained the *Oberstallmeister* title.

19 Schmidt, *Schulenburgs*, no. 750.

20 Fabrice, *Memoiren*, 128–29.

21 For this young Turk see Ernst August, *Letters to his wife*: no. 37, Sophia's letter of 6/16 Jan. 1686. For the common misconception about Mehemet and Mustafa being captured by George, see e.g. Trench, *George II*, 53. Percival notes in his diary for 26 Jan. 1715 (B.M., Add. MSS 47028) the libel that 'the King keeps two Turks for abominable uses'; from this presumably derives the legend, still repeated in English works, that George had 'depraved tastes' or, more ambiguously, that the 'backstairs duty' of Mehemet and Mustafa was 'to organise the King's strenuous sex life' (Howard, *The Royal Palaces*, 155).

22 Mehemet rose to be 'keeper of the king's closet'; Mustafa's title remained that of *Leibdiener* (body servant).

23 Wratislaw's role is known from the 1967 study by Mezgolich and is noted in Chandler, *Marlborough*, 124–25. Francis, *Peninsular War* (416 and as indicated in index) has independently examined part of Wratislaw's correspondence.

24 Bernstorff Archive: AG 52, Georg Ludwig's letter to Bothmer, 7 Feb. 1704, with information to be passed on to Marlborough in answer to his request for George's views on the coming campaign.

25 For Sophia's pride in George see her letter to Leibniz, *Correspondence*, 18 Aug. 1700; for her hopes of a command see *Letters to the raugravines* between 1700 and 1702. For a Dutch suggestion of George as 'most

suited' to be allied commander see van der Meer's letter to Heinsius of 30 March 1702: Heinsius, *Briefwisseling* I, 55.

26 Görtz Archive: 126/4, letter from baron Voigt, 14 Nov. 1705.

27 The offer of the *Reichsfeldmarschall* baton was made by Joseph I on 10 July and accepted on 16 July by George who took command of the *Reichsarmee* in September of that year: Calenberg Brief Archiv 24, *Österreich*, Huldeberg's letters to George, 8 and 25 June and 9 and 27 July 1707 and George's drafts of letters to Huldeberg, 11 and 26 June, and 26 Aug. 1707. For George's share in the 1707 campaign until Villars broke off the campaign in November see *HSL* (Wijn) Deel VIII, vol. II (*1706–10*) 257 ff., and Bebenbourg, *Correspondance* I, letters from 17 Sept. 1707 onwards.

28 For the deceit see Braubach, *Eugen* II, 221–38; Marlborough-Godolphin *Correspondence* II, no. 961: 5 May 1708. *HSL* (Wijn) Deel VIII, vol. II (*1706–10*) 269 ff. shows that Heinsius was at least partially in the know. For George's letter to Joseph I reporting the deceit, though with assurances that he would remain at his post, serving the *Vaterland* even if his own honour should be besmirched, see Schulenburg, *Leben* I, 439. Eugene, unaware that a general in the Austrian service had betrayed the allied *dessein* to the French, suspected someone in the *Reichsarmee* of careless talk. He was well aware, however, of Joseph's appropriation of money earmarked for George's command, though this did not restrain him from scathing remarks on the elector's slowness in taking the field ('Un fantôme de Prince qui doit commander l'armée): Braubach, *Eugen* III, 313–15 and note 184. For the Jacobite propaganda (note that Chandler, *Marlborough*, 250, has been misled by it into assuming that George was in command at Rumersheim) see my text page 173 and note 10.

29 Hann.: Cal. Brief 16 (Kriegssachen), 756, Hardenberg (draft) to Mauro, 5 Sept. 1709, and Görtz to Hardenberg, 9 Sept. 1709, expressing fear that Mercy's defeat would put obstacles in the way of the 'glorieuses enterprises de S.A.S. notre auguste Maitre'. For George's good opinion of Mercy see Sophia, *Letters to the*

raugravines: to Louise 16 May 1709; for his continued concern see Görtz Archive: 121/6, Schulenburg's letter of 16 Aug. 1717, reporting that 'L'accident du C. de Mercy Lui [George I] effraya à un tel point, qu'il me demanda en sursaut de la chaise, est il possible?' For the general conviction that George would not accept the field-marshal task unless he was assured of Hanover's entry into the electoral college see Bebenbourg, *Correspondance* I: his letter of 3 Aug. 1707.

30 For George's reward in 1718 of Robert Pringle, secretary of the 1702 commission, see Gregg, *Protestant Succession*, 16 note 21; for the negotiations which led to the 1707 union see the works of Pryde (1950) and Riley (1964).

31 Macpherson, *Original Papers* II, 93; George did, however, employ Scott after 1719 as a diplomat in Poland and Saxony (the courts of which he knew from a previous mission in queen Anne's reign) and Prussia: *BDR*, 88–89, 106 and Horn, *Diplomatic Service*, 115. For his being sent by George in 1717 on a secret mission, see below ch. VIII note 35.

32 *Michael* (English ed.) I, 13 ff.

33 Macpherson, *Original Papers* II, 192 prints George's letter to queen Anne of 24 Sept. 1710 (the date as corrected by Gregg, *Protestant Succession*, 331 note 72, who in his text 71 ff. deals with the elector's efforts to support Marlborough).

34 Handover, *Gazette*, 48, for Samuel Buckley's publishing George's memorial against the separate Anglo-French peace in the *Daily Courant* 5 Dec. 1711.

35 For James's declaration and its effect see J. H. and Margaret Shennan, 'The Protestant Succession, April 1713–September 1715', in *William III and Louis XIV. Essays 1680–1720 by and for Mark A. Thomson*, ed. Hatton and Bromley (Liverpool/Toronto 1968), 257 ff.

36 Gregg, *Protestant Succession*, 233 ff. has convincingly demonstrated George's complicity in the writ demand and has also, *ibid.*, 215 ff., and in his *Marlborough*, passim, covered the political and military preparations of George and his advisers. For Anglo-Dutch cooperation at this time see Hatton, *Diplomatic Relations*, 13–15 and 48 ff.; and for the English measures directed against the Pretender, A. New-

man, 'Proceedings in the House of Commons March–June 1714', *BIHR* 1960.

37 Anne's letters to Sophia, to George and to
Georg August are printed in Anne, *Letters
and Instructions* (ed. Brown); both recent
biographers of Sophia (Knoop, *Sophie*,
212–13 and Kroll, *Sophie*, 245–46) read a
good deal into her impetuous comment,
J'y succomberai, to the countess of Schaumburg-Lippe, on receipt of Anne's letter to
herself; but we also have evidence which
suggests that her agitated state passed
quickly.

38 The trustworthiness of Hamilton on this
point is enhanced by independent proof
that the doctor carried out the order noted
in his diary as received from the queen on
the day of Oxford's dismissal: to establish
a secret line of communication with
George via the correspondence of the
London Palatine agent Steingens with
Johann Matthias von der Schulenburg (see
the latter's *Leben* I, letter to, from London,
of 7 July OS 1714).

39 Snyder, *Queen Anne's Last Days*, passim.

40 Diarists tended to note down where they
heard the proclamation, whether in
London or in the rural market towns, e.g.
Evelyn MSS, journal entry of 1 August
1714: 'I saw it performed between four and
five in the afternoon at the Royal Exchange.'

Chapter V: Settling down

In this chapter I have benefited from excellent
recent treatments of English, Scottish and Irish
history: Beckett and Simms on Ireland; Davis,
Dickson, King, Plumb and Charles Wilson on
England; Donaldson, Hamilton and Ferguson
on Scotland. While some older works are still
valuable (Campbell on the lord chancellors,
Foss on the judges, Holdsworth on English law),
Michael's pioneer work has become outdated
for George as a ruler since he relied too much on
unverified diplomatic reports and on English
memoir literature. This memoir literature is
important for 'attitudes', but must be critically
examined. The much-quoted 'Account' of lady
Mary Wortley Montagu has proved to be a
superficial sketch from the early months of
George I's reign and not (as formerly held) a
considered analysis from her later years. Her
letters are, however, more rewarding, as is the

famous diary of lady Mary Cowper. Of German
letters, those of the countess of Schaumburg-
Lippe, on the best of terms with George I as well
as the prince and princess of Wales, have
brought new information to light, not only for
this chapter but for the whole period after 1714.
Of unprinted source material, the letters of
Friedrich Wilhelm von der Schulenburg,
Melusine's half-brother and George's *Kammerherr*, never before examined, have been invaluable. The Dutch archives have yielded
much information (documented in my *Diplomatic Relations*), and so have scattered documents
in the less well known collections of the British
Museum. A search of printed treasury books and
papers (and of treasury papers in the P.R.O.)
has proved rewarding for background information. Biographies of English statesmen and
office-holders have been of great help: Plumb's
Robert Walpole and Dickinson's brief study of
the same minister; Williams on Stanhope;
Horwitz on Nottingham; the Bakers on Brydges;
Sykes, Marshall and Bennett on several bishops;
and the many studies of Bolingbroke (particularly those by Hart, Kramnic and Dickinson).
For the court of George I as king I owe much
to Beattie's fine work of 1967. Studies of the
House of Commons which cover or refer to the
period of George's reign (Kemp, Ford, Owen,
Plumb's *Stability*, P. D. G. Thomas, Walcott,
E. N. Williams) have been most useful, as have
the biographical entries of members of the
House 1714–54, published in 1970. The House
of Lords has been neglected since the pioneer
work of Turberville of that chamber in the
eighteenth century; and it is to be hoped that
research on the Upper Chamber will become,
if not fashionable, respectable.

1 B.M., Add. MSS 20985, fols 56 ff.:
Drummond's letter to Buys, 25 Jan. 1712
reporting a conversation, often verbatim,
with Oxford and St John.

2 See Baxter, *Treasury*, and Dickson,
Financial Revolution; and (for the comparison with Louis XIV's France) J.
Bouvier and H. Germain-Martin, *Finance
et financiers de l'Ancien Régime* (Paris 1964).

3 William III to Shrewsbury in July 1696:
cited in Somerville, *Shrewsbury*, 115.

4 See Hatton, *Drummond*, 69–96; for the
Bank's policy towards the new ministry,
and the foundation of the South Sea
Company see Dickson, *Financial Revo-*

lution, 19–26 and Carswell, *South Sea Bubble*, 49 ff.

5 For the manipulation of the navigation acts of 1651 and 1660 see N. Japikse, *Verwikkelingen tusschen de Republiek en Engeland van 1660–1665* (Leiden 1900), Wilson, *Profit and Power*, and S. E. Åström, 'The English Navigation Laws, and the Baltic trade 1660–1700', *Scandinavian Economic History Review* 1960.

6 Francis, *Wine Trade*, 139–41 and Fisher, *Portugal Trade*, 26 ff.

7 *McLachlan*, 46 ff.

8 Fisher, *Portugal Trade*, 30 ff.

9 See Hatton, *Europe*, 46–47 and references given there.

10 J. L. Price, *The Dutch Republic during the Seventeenth century* (1974), 215 ff.; Hatton, *Diplomatic Relations*, 10 ff.

11 I am indebted for recent research in the field of Austrian administrative history to a seminar paper read in London in 1973 by Grete Klingenstein; for the slightly earlier period see John P. Spielman, *Leopold I of Austria* (1977), ch. 1 and references under 'Government', 206–07.

12 Leibniz's letter to Davenant, printed in State Papers, *Kemble*, 451.

13 For the political reasons which dictated this policy (fear that the Habsburg powers might support the exiled James II) see Hatton, *Louis and Fellow Monarchs* (London ed.) 43 and authorities there cited. For William's Irish campaign see Baxter, *William III*, and Symcox's thesis of 1967.

14 See Claude Nordmann, 'Louis XIV and the Jacobites', in *Louis XIV and Europe*, ed. Hatton (1976), 82 ff. I am further indebted to a seminar paper given by Nordmann in London in 1970 on the absorption of the Jacobites in French society.

15 For French policy on the North American continent see W. J. Eccles, *Canada under Louis XIV* (Oxford 1964); M. Giraud, *Histoire de la Louisiane française* (Paris 1952). For British fear of French competition see e.g. P.R.O., SPD Regencies 43 vol. 3, Stanhope to Delafaye, Hanover 14 Sept. 1720, the purpose of which is to convey George's approval of directions by the Lords Justices to enquire carefully 'whether there is any foundation for the Report that the Squadron of French Men

of War lately sail'd on a secret expedition under the Command of Mons Cassart, is intended to go and make a settlement upon the Borders of Carolina, on the River Allabahama', and the king's opinion that 'no time should be lost' to prevent this if the report should prove true.

16 For this epithet, common at the time, see e.g. the anonymous pamphlet, *The Most Christian Turk: Or a View of the Life and Bloody Reign of Louis XIV* (1690).

17 They echo to a remarkable degree the similar sentiments after the Nine Years War expressed by Newdigate (*Newdigate*, 325 ff.) during his visit to France, July to Oct. 1699. For post-1713 improvement see e.g. Montagu, *Letters* II, 142.

18 Hatton, *Diplomatic Relations*, 54 and note 4; McKay, *Utrecht Settlement*, passim.

19 For the Tory view of Charles XII after 1709, see Bolingbroke, *Letters*, 55–56 (to Drummond); for the plans for a 1714 squadron to the Baltic see Hatton, *Diplomatic Relations*, 39 ff.

20 See George's written answer of 18 Oct. 1710 to a memorial presented by earl Rivers: *Klopp* XIII, 556–57.

21 His proposal for this change was submitted to a legal commission in 1717: see my text page 167.

22 Hatton, *Louis and Fellow Monarchs* (1976 ed.), 6.

23 Kent to Prior, 26 July 1710: *HMC, Bath MSS* III, 438–39.

24 *Trevelyan* III, 299 note 1; *Holmes*, 227.

25 The change was, however, to be kept secret until the king's arrival, barring an emergency: Pauli, *Aktenstücke*, 56.

26 Evelyn MSS: Journal, entry for 22 Apr. 1722, looking back on Sunderland's career on the day of that minister's death.

27 This can, in the main, be traced to Chance's somewhat misleading article on Robethon and the Robethon papers in *EHR* 1898, and to the fact that Bothmer was well known to contemporary Englishmen because of his several missions to Whitehall and his prolonged stay after young Schütz's recall.

28 Bernstorff Archive: this paper is in AG 23.

29 Panshanger MSS: Bernstorff's first preserved letter to lady Cowper [1714], in F 198.

30 See Cowper (Mary), *Diary*, 7 and 32, for

this treatise being prepared for the king, for his having read it 'several times', and lent it to the princess of Wales. A copy, adorned with Bernstorff's seal, is in Bernstorff Archive: AG 23. For Görtz remaining in England at least until Volkra's arrival (10 Nov. 1715) as Charles VI's representative, see Görtz Archive: 124/5, letter (on Volkra's behalf) of 6 Jan. 1723 in which the Austrian diplomat and statesman recalls the *bons diners et repas delicieux* with which Görtz had regaled him in London. He goes on to ask Görtz to choose him a good Hanoverian *cuisinier*.

31 Heinsius Archief: 1869, Duyvenvoorde's undated report (in Dutch) that Bernstorff had discussed with him 'the characters of most of the English noblemen I know personally, and I was asked about the Dukes of Devonshire and Shrewsburi, the Lords Sommers, Couper, Halifax, Townsand and some others'.

32 Hatton, *Diplomatic Relations*, 54–55.

33 For the post-1689 development of the cabinet see Jennifer Carter, 'Cabinet Records of the Reign of William III', *EHR* 1963; Stephen B. Baxter, 'The Age of Personal Monarchy in England', in *Eighteenth-Century Studies presented to Arthur Wilson*, ed. Peter Gay (New York 1972); and Plumb, *Cabinet*, where the distinction between cabinet councils and meetings of the lords of the committee in queen Anne's reign is clearly delineated. In his *Stability*, 103–07, Plumb persuasively develops the argument that the faction-ridden cabinets of William III and Anne 'had been a major factor in the political instability of their reigns', and that 'it required a monarch of George I's perspicacity and firmness to reduce their significance and so take a major step forward towards political stability.'

34 See Mark A. Thomson, *Secretaries of State*, 2 ff., 90 ff. There was no official representative in Rome after Henry VIII's break with the pope, but agents were increasingly employed; for these in George I's reign see Lesley Lewis, *Connoisseurs and secret agents in eighteenth century Rome* (1961), 27 ff.

35 See Veenendaal, *Condominium*, and Geikie and Montgomery, *The Dutch Barrier*, for the treaties of Barrier and Succession of 1709 and 1713.

36 Hatton, *Diplomatic Relations*, 56.

37 McKay, *Utrecht settlement*, passim.

38 Gregg, *Marlborough*, 599, 601–02.

39 For Stanhope's youth and early career before 1714 see Williams, *Stanhope*; for George sending Friedrich Wilhelm von der Schulenburg to Spain see Schmidt, *Schulenburgs*, no. 750.

40 For Dutch humiliation and annoyance see Hatton, *Drummond*, 81 ff., and Stork-Penning, *1711* (mission of Buys), passim; for Eugène's visit see Braubach, *Eugen* III, 77–98.

41 For George's dislike of Oxford see B.M., Add. MSS 47028: lord Percival's journal, entry for 14 March 1717. There is an intriguing piece of information by Schulenburg in his letter to Görtz of 16 July 1717 (Görtz Archive: 121/6) to the effect that the House of Commons requested George to exclude Oxford from any act of pardon, 'pour donne par la occasion aux Communs de le [Oxford] poursuivre une autre fois par les voyes Parlementaires'. For George buying Oxford's town house and making it into four apartments for his Hanoverian high officials (Hattorf, Reiche, Hammerstein) and Dr Steigerthal, his German physician, *ibid.*, letters of 27 July and 1 Oct. 1717.

42 George's views were well known to contemporaries; see e.g. B.M., Add. MSS 47028: lord Percival's journal for 26 Jan. 1715, 'that the King was inclined to think that only the great men of the last Ministry were his Enemies and resolved to continue as many of them as would be contented to accept of the Employment he offer'd them'.

43 To Kenneth L. Ellis' study of *The Post Office in the Eighteenth Century* (1958) should be added, for this period, the same author's *Administration*. For the feeling of security in government circles when Craggs replaced Evelyn, see Panshanger MSS: duchess of Marlborough's letter of Oct. 1715: 'One may write anything by the Post very safe as long as Mr. Craggs is in the Office' (F 203).

44 *Wentworth Papers*, 424, Peter Wentworth to his brother, 1 Oct. 1714, reporting George's unexpected visit to Kensington

to see the gardens and look over the palace. *Verney Letters* I, 18 and 20 Sept. and 6 Nov. 1714, tell of the king's visit to the ruins of Whitehall Palace and his walks (with the prince and princess of Wales) in St James's Park. For the refurbishings in general of all the palaces (including Windsor) there is much evidence in the entries in the *Treasury Books*, in the P.R.O., Treasury papers, and in Windsor, R.A.: Wardrobe account volume for the whole reign. Hedley and Hudson have made good use of plans and other documents of the Board of Works, the older volumes by Sheppard (for St James's) and Pyne (for all the residences, but especially for Hampton Court) are still invaluable. For the major reconstruction and changes at Kensington Palace see my text pages 262–65 and notes thereto.

45 Wallbrecht, *Theatre*, 23–24, 108.

46 For the ceremony and its symbolism see Sitwell, 1 ff., 47 ff., 69 ff., and for the new crown Holmes, *Regalia*, 18–20 and plates 12 and 13. The recent biography of George Hooper, bishop of Bath and Wells, adds to earlier accounts of George I's coronation: Marshall, *Hooper*, 130 ff.

47 Cowper (William), *Diary*, 56–58, entry for 21 Sept. 1715.

48 Plumb, *Cabinet*, 156; cp. his *Walpole* I, 201 ff.

49 Marshall, *England*, 127; Redman, *Hanoverians*, 59; Walters, *Frederick*, 36.

50 Görtz Archive: 121/6, Schulenburg's letter of 3 Aug. 1717 (read in conjunction with his letters of 2 March, 2 and 6 Apr. 1717). Corroborative evidence is found in Panshanger MSS: 6 Oct. 1717 Cowper writes to his wife to say that he has to leave home tomorrow: he has had a letter from Sunderland informing him that the king wants a [cabinet] council to meet next Tuesday at Hampton Court (Family Letter Books vol. 4, 282). For the prince attending cabinet councils (and Thursday being the usual day of meeting) during 1716 see P.R.O., SPD Regencies 44 vol. 269, Methuen's letters of 13 and 17 July and 9, 25, 28 Aug. It is worth stressing that, from the letters in this volume for the whole of the period when George was in Hanover, the distinction between meetings of the cabinet council and

meetings of the lords of the committee is scrupulously made, thus showing that the system developed in queen Anne's reign persisted.

51 P.R.O., SPD Regencies 43 vol. 4: Carteret to Stanyan 16/27 July 1723.

52 Gwynne's letter to George of 2 Apr. 1707, cited, from Stowe MSS 223, fols. 25 ff., by Gregg, *Protestant Succession*, 315 note 24.

53 For this piece of flattery by Harley (as he then was) see Macpherson, *Original Papers* II, 197: letter to George of 1/12 Nov. 1710.

54 Cowper (William), *Diary*, 56–58, entry for 21 Sept. 1714.

55 Cited in Campbell, *Lord Chancellors* IV, 351. Later evidence that the king conversed freely in English when need arose comes from Saussure, *Letters*: no. V (151) 14 June 1727; he stood close enough to George during the traditional birthday ceremony (when the king was presented with a nosegay by the oldest male inhabitant of London of those who were fit enough to perform the task of delivering a brief speech) to overhear the king's conversation with that year's performer, a 'common soldier', who had first served in Charles I's reign.

56 Cowper (Mary), *Diary*, e.g. 10, 12 (1714), 43–44 (1715).

57 *Ibid.*, 146. I have checked with the original in the Panshanger MSS to make sure that the plural was not due to a printer's error. The goods and chattels story derives from Horace Walpole and is repeated in Jesse, *Memoirs* III, 138–39.

58 K.G., Schatullrechnungsbeläge, where the entries in English increase from 1717 onwards and become more or less the rule in the 1720s. There is also evidence for George's fluency in reading more testing material in English: I owe to Peter Barber (engaged on a study of the congress of Cambrai under my supervision) the information that during this congress important despatches meant for the king were not accompanied by translations into French, as had been customary in the early years of the reign.

59 For these performances in 1718, and the £200 received from George see Cibber, *Apology* II, 214–19.

60 Görtz Archive: 121/6, Schulenburg's

letter of 6 Apr. 1717. For London performances during George's reign see Avery, *London Stage*, part II. Some performances were by French players, but the majority were by English companies.

61 P.R.O., SPD Regencies 43 vol. 5, undated, but placed with letters of 10 and 11 Dec. 1723. I am greatly indebted to Professor S. Baxter for drawing my attention to this document during a conversation about the king's English. Scholars have long realized that George had a smattering of English, e.g. *Michael* (English ed.) I, 114; but recent books on the period still persist in the 'not a word of the language' legend (e.g., *Burton*, 1, in 1967 and Trench, *George II*, 51–52, in 1975).

62 They were translated into German, however, by the editor, R. Grieser, to make them accessible to a wider public; for the original French see his ill. no. 2.

63 For Georg August being taught English, see Toland, *Account*, 73. For the ridicule, see the 'boet and bainter' quote in note on my page 262; and his equally well-known 'Yarmany', often quoted.

64 Windsor, R. A.: Geo I Add. MSS 28, contains Caroline's letters in French to Mrs Clayton (with a few written by Caroline's daughters, in English). Caroline's French was no odder in spelling than that of most of her contemporaries but very hard to decipher because of her open flowing hand. Mrs Clayton remonstrated and attempted copies (which she also translated into English) in her own neat hand, and these are included in the R.A. file. They are at times incorrect, but they contain occasional marginalia which help to identify people and to date Caroline's letters (nearly all undated). This convinced me that the copyist, hitherto unidentified, was Mrs Clayton herself. Mrs Clayton's objections did her little good. The princess passed on the complaints of her lady-in-waiting to the prince (who commented, according to Caroline, 'I always said you wrote like a cat'), but no improvement is noticeable.

65 For letters written in English by Melusine see e.g. those to Aislabie of 27 Sept. 1720 in Windsor, R.A. 52844, and to Robert Walpole of 18 Feb. 1729/30 in Coxe, *Robert Walpole* II, 668; for Sophia Charlotte see her letters, e.g. to Mrs Clayton, in Sundon, *Memoirs* I, 15–16, and to Robert Walpole, undated, from the period 1720–22, in Cholmondeley (Houghton) MSS; Corr. 994. That Melusine could read English is stressed in Townshend's private letter to Walpole of 29 June 1723; P.R.O., SPD Regencies 43 vol. 4.

66 Suffolk, *Letters* II, 23, for J. W. Croker's praise: he prints her letters of 16 Oct. 1731 and 21 Aug. 1732 as 'samples'.

67 Schaumburg-Lippe, *Letters*: 21 Nov./2 Dec. 1727. For this not being unusual see Cowper (Mary), *Diary*, 38 on princess Anne, 'who at five years old speaks, reads and writes both German and French to Perfection . . . speaks English very prettily and dances very well.'

68 Schaumburg-Lippe, *Letters*: 28 Dec. 1716/8 Jan. 1717.

69 Hann.: Cal. Brief 16 (Kriegssachen), 756, Hardenberg's draft letter from George's headquarters to Görtz, 27 Sept. 1709: 'S.A.S. n'aimera pas d'avoir des ceremonies, ne batter les timbales ou sonner les trompettes'. The cost of the electoral coronation is noted in Görtz Archive: 88/8, 16 March 1712 in two sums: 46760,9,6 and 2992,30,5 (both in Marks and its lesser dominations).

70 Fabrice, *Memoiren*, 125–26.

71 Görtz Archive: 121/6, Schulenburg's letter of 24 Sept. 1717.

72 George's interest in painting (often thought to be non-existent) was considerable, especially in portraits. In 1711 he ordered for the Rittersaal copies of those of his ancestors hanging in the Lüneburg *Rathaus* (Sophia, *Letters to the raugravines*, 326); and he arranged for 500 paintings to embellish the palace he built at Göhrde (Prüser, *Göhrde*, 60 and authorities there cited); for his rehanging of those at Kensington Palace see my text page 263. Evidence of his visits to the houses of ministers and courtiers, and for his special interest in paintings and in the layout of gardens, is plentiful in Schulenburg's letters to Görtz for 1717: to Peterborough's home (27 July), to Cranborn (24 Sept.), to Claremont (2 Nov.), to Cliveden (12 Nov.). Other references abound, in a variety of source

material, for the king's viewing houses and gardens and taking dinner with even minor figures at court or in office. For his pride in the princesses see Schaumburg-Lippe, *Letters*: 13/24 Jan. 1719; and for the role of the countess of Portland, see Schazmann, *The Bentincks*, 127 ff. with a charming illustration of the governess with the princesses and their entourage at a tea party, Handel at the harpsichord.

73 Money for bell-ringing is regularly entered in K.G., Schatullrechnungsbeläge.

74 Cowper (Mary), *Diary*, 13, entry for 8 Nov. 1714.

75 Kielmansegg, when publishing the Ernst August II, *Letters*, 59–68 (a long footnote), established the position of Sophia Charlotte vis-à-vis George I as early as 1902; and in his *Familien-Chronik* (1910 ed.), 762–72, printed the documents relating to her Irish (1720) and English (1721) naturalization, her elevation to the Irish peerage as countess of Leinster (1721) and to the English peerage as countess of Darlington (1722) and the subsequent granting of arms (1723). The original parchment for the Irish title, decorated with a miniature portrait of George I, embodies the phrase *consanguineam nostram*, and is still kept framed on the walls of the study of the present Graf Kielmansegg. The phrase is also embodied in the parchment for her Darlington title. Note that Wilhelmine, *Mémoires*, 58, states outright that the countess of Darlington was the natural daughter of Ernst August.

76 Beattie, *Court*, 136 and note 1. Beattie, like Plumb (neither of whom has used Kielmansegg's works), accepts the tradition (which can be traced back to Horace Walpole's conversations and written reminiscences in old age) that Sophia Charlotte was George's mistress; *Burton*, 239, revives (from the same sources) the story that one of her daughters – who became Lady Howe – was George I's child.

77 Sophia, *Correspondence with the Hohenzollerns*, 265, in a letter to her granddaughter of 29 Apr. 1713, declares untrue the rumours in Berlin that Sophia Charlotte's sister-in-law was George's mistress. The countess of Platen and her husband lived apart even before 1714, when he went as *Oberkam-*

merherr with George to London and she remained in Hanover. Young Platen is hardly ever mentioned in material that has survived from George's period of kingship (I have found only two brief references to him in the Schulenburg letters); but there is evidence before that time of his being a problem to his family. Johann Adolf von Kielmansegg had been sent in 1698 to keep him out of mischief in London and Paris (*Familien-Chronik*, 435–36 and 459–62); and Sophia, in the letter cited above, felt he deserved to be cuckolded; he drank, gambled and wenched. Ernst August had favoured young Platen, had provided the dowry for his bride and paid his debts (Sophia, *Letters to the raugravines*: to Louise 12/22 Feb. 1697). This, and the dissatisfaction of the elder Platen with son as well as daughter, may hint at Ernst August's feeling a paternal responsibility for both of Klara von Platen's children. For the dowry (£3000) paid by George I for the daughter of the younger Platens, see P.R.O., SPD Regencies 43 vol. 5, Townshend to Robert Walpole, 15 Nov. 1723.

78 Walpole (Horace), *Reminiscences* cxii. Stories of George I's 'harem' usually fail to stand up to examination; see e.g. Halsband, *Hervey*, 54–59, showing that Hervey's wife, Molly Lepell, was not (as is often assumed) the mistress of the king.

79 Hervey, *Memoirs* (Sedgwick) III, 558–59.

80 For the expression 'the apples of his eyes' see Schaumburg-Lippe, *Letters*: 13/24 Jan. 1719; for Gertrud's marriage and her children see *ibid.*, letters of 13/24 Oct. 1721, 25 Sept./6 Oct. 1722, 7/18 Jan. 1724.

81 This is specifically stated in the marriage contract of 19/30 Oct. 1721 which I examined in Niedersächsisches Archiv, Bückeburg: Des. L.Oc. vol. 12, no. 233: I am grateful for courtesies extended by Prince Philipp Ernst of Schaumburg-Lippe during my stay at Bückeburg to work in this archive.

82 Schaumburg-Lippe, *Letters*: 12/23 March, 24 May/4 June and 12/23 June 1724; 25 May/5 June, 14/25 Sept. 1725; 24 June/5 July 1726.

83 For their inseparability *ibid.*, letter of 2/13 Apr. 1728. Young Melusine's marriage seems to have made little difference: there

is hardly a mention of her in Chesterfield, *Letters*, and her husband's biographers have concluded that, though he behaved towards her with great politeness in society, they lived more or less apart. The duchess of Kendal could not have approved of him; in her will of 1743 she makes sure that he cannot touch any of the money left to the younger Melusine.

84 P.R.O., SPD Regencies 43 vol. 5, Townshend to Walpole, Hanover, 17 and 25 Sept. NS 1723 on the money order composed of two bills of £500 each drawn on the treasury. It is clear from the letters that Robert Walpole had not, at this time, met Lousie.

85 It is now known as the *Fürstenhaus* and is used to exhibit paintings and furniture illustrating the history of the house of Hanover.

86 Marginal note to the letter of 17 Sept. NS 1723 mentioned in note 84 above: 'A most agreeable woman about 67 years of age.' Cp. Hervey, *Memoirs* (Sedgwick) II, 558–59, describing her as handsome, if now somewhat declined, and witty.

87 Ernst August II, *Letters*: 19 Aug. [1707], 20 Jan. [1708], 16 May [1709]. These also show that George sided with her in promoting her marriage, which took place on 31 Dec. 1707. Note that the editor of this collection, on p. 109, by a slip gives the year of her marriage as 1708: it is clear from a letter of 13 Jan. 1708 that she is already married.

88 Hervey, *Memoirs* (Sedgwick) II, 558–59.

89 Schmidt, *Schulenburgs*, no. 859.

90 I take the opportunity to correct my mistake in 'George I as an English and a European Figure', *The Triumph of Culture: 18th Century Perspectives*, ed. Paul Fritz and David Williams (Toronto 1972), 195 note 18 where I married her to a non-existent Graf Delitz.

91 For Horace Walpole's character sketch of Chesterfield see his *Memoirs* I, 51 ff.

92 For Sophia Charlotte's envy of Melusine's title see extract of letter from lady Cowper's brother, John Clavering, dated Hanover 7 July 1716, printed in Cowper (Mary) *Diary*, Appendix E, 193; for the tension between the 'Platen clique' and Melusine see *ibid.*, 193 and Wilhelmine, *Mémoires*, 60 ff.; for Melusine's conver-

sation with Townshend see PRO, SPD Regencies 43 vol. 5: Townshend's letter to Robert Walpole of 30 Oct. NS 1723.

93 For the de Vrillière affair and the use made of it by Horatio Walpole, see Plumb, *Walpole* II, 63, 65–66, 70, 74 and Coxe, *Horatio Walpole* I, 64 ff. Cp. my text page 275.

94 For such presents see K.G., Schatullrechnungsbeläge after 1714: e.g. 13 Apr. 1720 (paid 19 May) – fans for the queen of Prussia.

95 The original is in the Kielmansegg archive; the text is printed in *Familien-Chronik*, 731. I am greatly indebted to Carl Graf Kielmansegg and his wife for courtesies extended to me when I was permitted to see this and other documents in their archive.

96 Portraits of her English women friends are among those still in the Kielmansegg collection, and deserve the attention of English art historians.

97 See Beattie, *Court*, 241–42 for ministers; for courtiers see Vanbrugh, who writes of 'speaking softly to die Schulenberg': *Bingham*, 300. Among the foreign diplomats Melusine dined we note Dubois: Görtz Archive: 121/6, Schulenburg's letter of 22 Feb. 1718; for her being used by George to give messages to Destouches see my text page 255 and note 53.

98 Beattie, *Court*, 244–47.

99 For the Twickenham House see below ch. X, note 12; for Louise living in Paddington see the marginal note in the P.R.O. document referred to in note 86 above.

100 Kielmansegg, *Familien-Chronik*, 456, 467–68. This daughter, Sophie Charlotte Marie, married in 1719 Emanuel Scrope, viscount Howe. A younger daughter, Caroline Wilhelmine, was only 13 years old at the time of her mother's death and returned to Hanover, where she married Friedrich von Spörcken in 1729.

101 Beattie, *Court*, 258–59 correcting Ward; Verney, *Letters* II, 14–15, lists the Hanoverian ministers and court officials who came with George and is (in spite of the odd German spelling) most useful for the grooms and gentlemen of the bedchamber.

102 For Hammerstein's action in 1693 see

Sichart, *Army* I, 238 ff.; for Jorry the dwarf, a skilled entertainer, having been presented to George by a baron Schack see Fabrice, *Memoiren*, 126: presumably the George Schack who was given a present from the privy purse of £330 4s 6d: B.M., Add. MSS 40843. For Jorry's clothes and expenses being paid by George see Beattie, *Court*, 259. For Ulrich (Jorry) taking part in the royal hunt in 1725 see Millar, *Royal Collection*, no. 616.

103   Proof of this is found in the Lafontaine portrait painted between 1725 and 1726, illustration no. 40.

104   Liselotte, *Letters to Görtz*: e.g. of 4 May 1719; 4 Apr. and 23 June 1720; 15 May 1721.

105   For praise of the Hanover grapes see Sophia, *Letters to the raugravines*: to Louise 11 Nov. 1708. Lady Mary Wortley Montagu's praise of the Hanover hothouse pineapples is well known, and it is interesting to note that pineapples were (with oranges, bananas, truffles and sausages) sent to George from Hanover in 1720: see the charge for transport (£3 3s 8d) in K.G. Schatullrechnungsbeläge vol. xiii. From lady Mary Cowper, who had the information from Melusine, we know of another preference of George I's: he ate 'le Pain le plus noir' (Panshanger MSS: F 230, 121–22).

106   Görtz Archive: 121/6, Schulenburg's letter of 16 July 1717. There may well have been something in this taunt; for George seems to have preferred wine. In Sophia, *Letters to the Hohenzollerns*, there are references to his enjoyment of the Neuchâtel wine sent him from Berlin; he bought French wine (Görtz Archive: 121/6, Schulenberg's letter of 2 Nov. 1717); and Townshend asked Walpole to have some malmsey sent to Hanover since the king had developed a taste for it: P.R.O., SPD Regencies 43 vol. 4: letters from Pyrmont 4/15 July 1723.

107   Görtz Archive: 121/6, Schulenberg's letter of 22 March 1718.

108   For the gentlemen of the bedchamber see Beattie, *Court*, 59 ff: for their duties, especially at Hampton Court, Schulenburg's letters of 1717 and 1718 are informative.

109   Selkirk is mentioned by name as one of the

seigneurs who attended George at Hampton Court (Görtz Archive: 121/6, Schulenburg's letter of 10 Sept. 1718). Two others mentioned as serving at the same time were the French Huguenot officer marquis de Miremont and a comte de Brandenbourg (whom I have not been able to identify but who, from his name, may have been an illegitimate member of the Hohenzollern family).

110   Of the musicologists Percy M. Young, in his *Handel* (1965 revised ed.) 28 ff., is unique in having realized the lack of enmity of George towards Handel; but historians are indebted to the musicologists in general for their demonstration that the Water Music as we now know it was not identical with the performance of 1717: Handel expanded it at a later date.

111   For a list of the court offices see Beattie, *Court*, 279–82. One, that of the ode-maker, has been investigated by McGuiness, and George I's reign is covered.

112   K.G., Schatullrechnungsbeläge, *passim* for the period 1714–1726.

113   *HMC, Polwarth MSS* I, 316.

114   Hann.: Cal. Brief 16 (Kriegssachen), 718 giving list of gentlemen in attendance, officials and servants, and the number of horses for the campaign of 1707.

115   Beattie, *Court*, 117. Schnath, in his review of Beattie's study (*NJ* 1968), has drawn attention to the fact that the cost of the Hanoverian court in relation to the electorate's *Kammereinkünfte* was also roughly one-third.

116   For this revival see Risk's history of the Order.

117   Boscawen's accompanying George to Hanover in 1716, Cowper (Mary), *Diary*, 118, I incline to see as an indication of the king's liking for him as now attested by the Schulenburg letters (see page 203 of my text), and not as a possible indication of the significance of the duties of the comptroller's office: Beattie, *Court*, 69.

118   This story derives from Horace Walpole and may be apocryphal; if so, like the goods and chattels story related on my page 131, it is *ben trovato*. For the difficulty of reform of the household as late as the 1770s and '80s see John Norris, *Shelborne and Reform* (1963), 102 ff., 176 ff., 189 ff.:

reorganization had to wait until 1816–41.

119 Windsor, R.A.: Geo 57044, 'An Abstract of the Expenses of the Civil List of the late Queen Anne and his Present Majesty stated and compared'. Pensions granted by George I between 1715 and 1718 are listed, with the sums involved, in Sunderland's treasury papers: Blenheim Archive, D II 2/3.

120 B.M., Add. MSS 40843, Privy Purse and Secret Service Pensions and Bounties Account, 25 March 1721 to 1725.

121 Beattie, *Court*, 80, 127–28.

Chapter VI: Two issues of principle

This chapter is largely based on unpublished material from the Bernstorff and Görtz archives, from wills and the Regencies papers in the Public Record Office, and on the 'Astle' volume in the Royal Archives at Windsor and the Evelyn journals at Christ Church, Oxford. Letters printed in Coxe's works have eliminated references to the sources which he used, but checks have convinced me (as well as other historians) how accurate he was in his copying and how unerring was his appreciation of significant material. Of printed German letters and memoirs, those of the countess of Schaumburg-Lippe and Fabrice have been most useful. Essential has been Drögereit's research, known since 1937, on George's will, but it is here put into a wider context provided by the 'Astle' volume. For the background, constitutional historical works by Thomson (1938), Kemp (1957), Plumb, *Stability* (1967), Cannon (1973) and Dickinson, *Sovereignty* (1976) have been of great help.

1 See e.g. one verse of the 1715 poem *Blessings attending George's accession* (*Poems on Affairs of State* VII, cited 623 note 4);
Hither he brought the dear Illustrious House:
That is *Himself*, his *Pipe, Close-stool* and *Louse,*
Two Turks, three W[hores], and half a dozen Nurses,
Five hundred *Germans*, all with empty Purses.
For recent works see e.g. Young, *Poor Fred*, 18: 'the incursion of hungry Hanoverian courtiers and courtesans', and *Burton*, 2, to

the effect that George's rapaciousness was only exceeded by that of his mistresses.

2 Schaumburg-Lippe, *Letters*: 13/24 Jan. 1716.

3 Estimate by Schnath, *Hannover* I, 522.

4 Friis, *The Bernstorffs* I, 10 ff.

5 Görtz Archive: 126/6, Vanbrugh's letter of 23 Nov. 1715. Görtz had made Vanbrugh's acquaintance when he, as Clarenceux king of arms, visited Hanover in 1706 to present the order of the Garter to Georg August (deputizing for the aged Garter king of arms): for this ceremony and the visit in general see the excellent description in Bingham, *Vanbrugh*, 133–41, based on the manuscript report of Samuel Stebbing in B.M., Add. MSS 6231.

6 For the sums spent by Brydges, see Baker, *Chandos*, 112 and note 1. For the sale of office in England see *Swart*, 46 ff.

7 Jacques Levron, *Les Courtisans* (Paris 1961), an extract of which has been translated in *Louis XIV and Absolutism*, ed. Hatton, 130–53, under the title 'Louis XIV's Courtiers'.

8 *The Memoirs of the Duchess of Marlborough*, ed. William King (1930), 217.

9 For George being against the sale of offices see P.R.O., SPD Regencies 43 vol. 6: Townshend to Delafaye 22 June/3 July 1725. For the filling of office of all kinds, military, ecclesiastical and political, *ibid.*, vols. 2–7 (1719–25) have a great many examples of George scrutinizing all suggestions sent to Hanover during his absences from England: he frequently objected to the names put forward either on the grounds that he had already promised the post to someone else or that seniority claims were being ignored. Cp. Beattie, *Court*, 165–67 for suggestion that sale of office declined in the reign of George.

10 *Wentworth Papers*, 436, Peter Wentworth to his brother 5 Nov. 1714 to the effect that the king had himself read the memorial he had presented and had sent through G[örtz] this fairly negative message.

11 Görtz Archive: 124/23, Strafford to Görtz 14 March 1716.

12 *Ibid.*: 121/6, Schulenburg's letter of 23 July 1717.

13 Burnet, *Letters*: editor's introduction and letters between Oct. 1714 and May 1719. All bishop Burnet's sons were provided for

by George. The slowness in giving Thomas a post may have been due to doubts about his suitability; in any event he did not last long in Lisbon, returning home after a quarrel with the British diplomatic representative there.

14 Evelyn MSS: journal entries for 16 March (when he kisses hands on his appointment), 21 Aug., 16 and 18 Oct. 1721.

15 Townshend's complaint to Stanhope is in a private letter of 16/27 Oct. 1716: Coxe, *Robert Walpole* II, 115–119; for the story spread in 1717 see Görtz Archive: 121/6, Schulenburg's letter of 12 Feb. 1717.

16 Craggs to Stanhope 30 June 1717: Stanhope, *History* II, appendix.

17 For Townshend's comment on Bothmer: Coxe, *Robert Walpole* II, 119.

18 Coxe, *Robert Walpole* I, 55, based on the reminiscences of lord Orford.

19 P.R.O., SPD Regencies 43 vol. 5: unsigned, undated letter placed with post of 3/14 Sept. 1723 (possibly copy of an intercepted letter); and Tilson to Delafaye 13/24 Sept. 1723.

20 Fabrice, *Memoiren*, 137.

21 P.R.O., Probate: Robethon's will of 19 Feb. 1721/2.

22 *Ibid.*: Bothmer's will of 8 Dec. 1723, at a time when his daughter was a widow (she remarried before the end of the year), with codicil 3/14 Dec. 1728: both translated into English 26 March 1732.

23 Kielmansegg, *Familien-Chronik*, 458 ff. for her will and the sale of her effects. The will of 3 Dec. 1723 was made and deposited in Hanover, with a codicil dated 18/29 April 1725 in London, where she died two days later. She was buried in Westminster Abbey and the cost of the burial service is recorded in the MS funeral books of the abbey as £100.

24 Montague, *Works* I: 'Account', 128.

25 Kielmansegg, *Familien-Chronik*, 457–58, to which I am indebted for Sophia Charlotte's circumstances as a widow in London.

26 *Ibid.*, 458; for the real position see Barker, *Chandos*, 112 and note 1; *Carswell*, 115 and Dickinson, *Financial Revolution* II, both from *JHC* XIX, 425 ff. (For the misleading name used by both see below, ch. IX, n. 17.)

27 Fabrice (*Memoiren*, 137) believed the rumours in respect of Kent's Garter, but

has nothing to say of the gifts Melusine or young Melusine are assumed to have accepted from Newcastle and Bolingbroke (or his second wife). Kent has not attracted a biographer; but Nulle, Kelch and Browning for Newcastle, and Hart, Dickinson and Kramnick for Bolingbroke do not touch on the topic of the rumoured money-presents; one must therefore deduce that they have not come across material to substantiate contemporary talk. Support for Melusine's desire to influence (or at least of her habit of conveying that she might be able to influence) promotions is, however, found in Görtz Archive: 114/20, Norris' letter of 1 July 1725 (the duchess has promised to help him speed up his entry into the peerage); and *HMC, Polwarth MSS* IV, 139, her letter of 20 Aug. 1724 to Marchmont: she regrets that the death of his father (for whom he had solicited an English peerage) has prevented her from being of service. This is in sharp contrast to George I's firm answer (*ibid.*, 147, letter of 25 Aug. 1724, conveyed through Townshend) that he cannot grant the request 'without putting his affairs in the House of Lords in the utmost confusion'.

28 For the difficulty of tracing money-presents bordering on bribes see Hatton, *Gratifications*, 68 ff. Rumours in respect of the Hanoverians have been followed up, but can usually not be traced beyond the assertions of interested parties: e.g. the story in Cowper (Mary), *Diary*, 31, of Sophia Charlotte von Kielmansegg accepting 500 guineas in cash and the promise of an annual pension of £200 from Chetwynd for a place on the Board of Trade derives from a disappointed candidate; and the note that she has received from Chetwynd a pair of 'fine Brilliant Ear-rings' comes from an anonymous 'another Hand'. In any case lady Cowper was biased against Sophia Charlotte because of the dislike which her mistress, the princess of Wales, felt for George's half-sister.

29 Letter from Johann Matthias von der Schulenburg to Fabrice, from Venice, 12 March 1728, printed in Fabrice, *Memoiren*, 153–59 (cited portion from 156–57). An alternative interpretation of the phrase might be that the family had urged her to demand a morganatic marriage with George; but

30 this would also have a bearing on her financial circumstances.

30 Palm to Emperor, from London, 17 Dec. 1726: Coxe, *Robert Walpole* II, 509.

31 For the coinage affair see Plumb, *Walpole* II, 67 ff. Its aftermath gave a great deal of trouble. Townshend wrote to Delafaye on 20/31 Aug. 1724 of the king's relief when Wood surrendered the patent and Ireland became quiet once more: P.R.O., SPD Regencies 43 vol. 7.

32 Rudé, *Hanoverian London*, 40, listing holdings of 1721; Dickson, *Financial Revolution*, 279, listing holdings of 1723–24.

33 Schmidt, *Schulenburgs*, no. 742: she bought the estate at Emkendorf for 116,000 Danish *riksdaler* and sold it in 1729 for 120,000 *Reichstaler*.

34 B.M., Add. MSS 36139 fols. 80–83: a copy of George's last will and testament of 25 May 1723 witnessed by Robert Walpole and Mehemet. This leaves Melusine all the stock in the South Sea Company of which George was possessed, namely £10,000; as well as a further £12,986 2s 2d of the same stock left in trust by the king with Robert Walpole on the understanding that the sum and all dividends, products and profit thereof should go to Melusine. A document to this effect, signed by Robert Walpole on 24 May 1723, is appended.

35 The story derives from Horace Walpole and has several variants: some say that young Melusine was left £40,000 and that Chesterfield settled for half that sum; others that Chesterfield's demand was for £20,000 and that George II settled in full out of court. I have searched diligently for another private will, since Fabrice, *Mem-oiren*, 149 refers to George I's having laid down in his testament that his body should not be opened after death or embalmed. Hervey, *Memoirs* (Sedgwick) III, 839, quotes queen Caroline that George's will 'said nothing on bequests to individuals' (and which may therefore refer to the political will now published by Drögereit). The last will and testament, hitherto unknown, cited in note 34 above and discussed on my text page 154 is, however, the only one I have found.

36 For the demand see duchess of Kendal to Robert Walpole of 18 Feb. 1729/30: Coxe, *Robert Walpole* II, 668; B.M., Add. MSS 36139 fol. 83 r and v, reveals that the £12,986 2s 2d kept in trust by Robert Walpole since 1723 fetched in 1730 only £6,493 1s 1d (made up of £6,103 9s 6d for the stock and £389 11s 7d for the dividends): Melusine accepted this sum in full settlement from Walpole and his heirs.

37 She did not immediately, as stated by the ed. of the Schaumburg-Lippe, *Letters*, 93 note 230, move to Twickenham; the intermediate move was to 'a house here in London' (*ibid.*, letter of 2/13 Apr. 1728), probably No. 43 Grosvenor Square, which we know was her home at one time (Hibbert, *London*, 117), or possibly the house she owned in Portugal Row and which in 1728 had a rentable value of £90 a year (Rudé, *Hanoverian London*, 146).

38 Schmidt, *Schulenburgs*, no. 742 mentions the will briefly, and notes her other charitable bequests: to the hospital at Hyde Park and to German orphans and widows.

39 P.R.O., Probate: will of 1778.

40 This daughter, Charlotte Sophie, had in 1705 married Joachim Engelche von Bernstorff (a cousin of her father's), and it was in the interest of Joachim and the sons of their marriage (Andreas Gottlieb, 1708–68, and Johann Hartwig Ernst, 1712–72) that Bernstorff in 1720 made his estate into a fideikommis (since he had by that date lost his five sons as well as one of his five daughters): Friis, *The Bernstorffs* I, 11 ff.

41 See e.g. Panshanger MSS, for letters of Bernstorff to lady Cowper accompanying such gifts (F 198 and 199).

42 See Hatton, *Gratifications*, 80 and Hatton, *Charles XII*, 224 for the significant distinction between a present divulged to the ruler and one that was kept secret.

43 The Tory arrears amounting to £65,022 were paid, with other army debts, in Aug. 1715: *Treasury Books* XXIX, part I (1957), assent by George I 21 Aug. 1715.

44 For the characterization of Kent and the rumoured bribe see Raby's 'Caractères': *Wentworth Papers*, 134. For Kent's career in Anne's reign see *Holmes*, 227–28.

45 Bernstorff Archive: AG 29 vol. iv, Bothmer to Bernstorff, 2/13 Oct. 1716; cp. Walpole to Stanhope 28 Sept./9 Oct. 1716: Coxe, *Robert Walpole* I (1816 ed.), 296–98, reporting conference with Bothmer.

46 Schmidt, *Schulenburgs*, no. 860.

47 For the *Graf* rank for Sophia Charlotte's sons (of 23 Feb. 1723) see Kielmansegg, *Familien-Chronik*, 736–42. Her own Leinster title was in the Irish peerage, the Darlington one in the English peerage. Both peerages were, like those of Melusine, for life, an innovation by George I which is noteworthy since the public discussion of life peerages did not begin till the second half of the nineteenth century: Reginald Lucas, *George II and his Ministers* (1910), 14.

48 P.R.O., SPD Regencies 43 vol. 4: Townshend to Robert Walpole 12 July 1723; for the rivalry with Carteret see e.g. *ibid.*, Townshend's private letters to Robert Walpole of 29 June and 6 Aug. 1723.

49 Work on this will and its codicils (beyond Michael's deductions) has been done by Drögereit and published, with the relevant documents, in *NJ* 1937, 84–199; a brief summary in English, 'The Testament of King George I and the Problem of the Personal Union between England and Hanover', is in *Research and Progress* (Berlin 1939). What I have been able to supplement is the English dimension of the discussion, principally from the 'Astle' volume in Windsor, R.A.: 53017.

50 George, *Letters*, 496: 29 Aug. [1714]. Cp. Panshanger MSS: lady Cowper's brother, John Clavering, from Hanover 28 Sept. 1716, tells of 'the joy the king was in when he saw her [his daughter] first, everybody took notice of it, to see his Majesty who is commonly mighty grave and thoughtfull, as gay and merry as any young Fellow of twenty year old, running about the Drawing Room, jesting and laughing at everybody' (F 196 and F 231, 67).

51 For reports of the crossing and the arrival in Rye see P.R.O., SPD Regencies 43 vol. 7, Townshend to Newcastle 3 and 6 Jan. OS 1725/6 (informing us *inter alia* that Melusine and young Melusine are with George in Rye, and that the return journey will be slow because of the newly fallen snow); and Tilson to Delafaye of 4 Jan. OS 1725/6 giving the proposed stages of the king's journey to London. See the *National Trust Guide*, ed. R. Fedden and R. Joekes (1973), for Lamb House, Rye, and George's stay there; the house had been completed in 1723 and the owner, James Lamb, was the mayor of the town.

52 For Liselotte's early impression of George see her *Letters to Sophia*: 15 March 1687, 20 Nov. 1692, 22 May 1695; her surprise at reports that he could be *lustig* are frequent, the first time e.g. *ibid.*, letter of 21 May 1699.

53 Fabrice, *Memoiren*, 134–35. His account of festivities in Hanover and Göhrde is confirmed by P.R.O., SPD Regencies 43 vol. 3, letters between 2 May and 16 Nov. 1720 from Delafaye and Payzant to G. Tilson. Indeed, the correspondence of the men who went with the secretaries of state to Hanover at one time and another (Balaguier, Couraud, Delafaye, Payzant and Tilson) tells us a great deal about the daily routine, the entertainments laid on for George and his guests, and also of the work of the king, the secretaries of state and of the men themselves, who at times were too busy copying despatches and drafting documents to go to church, to say nothing of time for leisure pursuits.

54 *Ibid.*, 135–36.

55 For the most recent and authoritative accounts of the 1722 crisis see Bennett's contribution to the Plumb *Festschrift* of 1974 and his 1976 study of Atterbury. Cp. Fritz, *Jacobitism* (thesis), 295 ff. The many progresses planned for George, several of which he undertook, indicates the seriousness of the situation; the king also reviewed the soldiers stationed in Hyde Park and visited encampments outside London.

56 For George's mode of travelling fast and alone see P.R.O., SPD Regencies 43 vol. 5, Townshend's letter of 28 Sept./9 Oct. 1723: the king 'according to his custom' had covered 18 German miles, 'which is more than 100 English miles', the previous day without stopping to eat or rest. There is evidence in this volume and in others of the series that the king's preference for speedy travel caused the British secretary (or secretaries) in attendance in Hanover to set out on journeys, even brief ones, well in advance of George.

57 *Ibid.* 43 vol. 5: Townshend and Carteret's letters to Robert Walpole of 28 Sept./9 Oct. 1723 mention the 'fainting-fit' and deny *apoplexie*.

58 For these plans see Schnath, *A.B.*, *Sophie Dorothea*, 214. As negotiations progressed Amalie, the second daughter of the prince of Wales, was more seriously considered as

she was closer in age to Friedrich. The early negotiations can be followed in Wilhelmine, *Mémoires*, 33 ff., 60 ff., built on what she herself remembered and what she had been told by her mother. For the later negotiations see my text pages 280–81 and notes thereto.

59 For Melusine's conversation with Townshend see his letter to Robert Walpole of 5 Oct. NS 1723: P.R.O., SPD Regencies 43 vol. 5. For Melusine's illness in 1724 (chest pains and fever) see Schaumburg-Lippe, *Letters*: 12/23 June 1724.

60 P.R.O., SPD Regencies 43 vol. 8, Tilson to Delafaye, Göhrde, 1/2 Nov. 1725: after the hunt the king galloped home; 'his strength of Constitution was wonderfull to see'. For George walking five hours every morning at Pyrmont see Tilson's letter of 9/20 July 1725 from the spa: *ibid.* 43 vol. 6. It is clear from vols 6, 7 and 8 that the king worked hard as well, once the Pyrmont cure was completed.

61 Görtz Archive: 126/12, Görtz (draft) to baron Waldeck 15 Jan. 1717.

62 For this petition of 25 Apr. 1716, signed Etienne de Bonnivet de Villiers, see Görtz Archive: 126/2; for other petitions see e.g. *ibid.*: 125/43, that of 31 March 1716 for a musician (François Venturini) who had served four years in Hanover.

63 Görtz Archive: 121/6, Schulenburg's letters of 8/19 and 12/23 March, 20 July, 10 and 17 Aug. 1717; and Görtz's draft to Schulenburg 8 Feb. 1718.

64 *Ibid.*: Schulenburg's letters of 5/16 March and 6/17 Apr. 1717.

65 This title fits the younger Hattorf better (for whom see my text page 96); he had the necessary discreetness as well as ability. He is the only Hanoverian who was not criticized by George's British ministers; indeed, he was even praised: see e.g. Hervey, *Memoirs* (Sedgwick) II, 342–43.

66 That British men in office who received these orders used some discretion in carrying them out is indicated by admiral Norris telling the Russians that in 1716 he had not acted on instructions received, since he was not 'd'humeur de porter sa tête sur un échafaud pour l'amour de M. Bernstorff': letter of 8 Aug. 1718 from G.H. Görtz (who had the story from the Russian diplomat Ostermann) cited by

Nordmann, 175 note 15. Confirmation for this can be found in the Bernstorff Archive: AG 18, general Bothmer's letter from Copenhagen (undated but, from the context, of the autumn of 1716) accusing Norris of being a 'veritable procureur pour le Czar' and quoting the admiral to the effect that George could not order him to prevent tsar Peter quartering Russian troops in Mecklenburg 'sans la connaissance de l'Engletaire', adding for good measure that he, as a member of parliament, knew what he was talking about.

67 Görtz Archive: 121/6, Schulenburg's letter of 11 Feb. 1718. Robethon was not totally disgraced, however. The following year George granted him a pension for life of £600 a year (*ibid.*: letter of 9 May 1719); and in 1720 we find him entrusted with sending George's orders on high policy to Stanhope when need arose: Chevening MSS 84/11, letter of 3 Jan. 1720 (on northern affairs) with a postscript of 4 Jan. 1720 (on affairs in Italy).

68 For the English desire to have Frederick come either to Oxford or Cambridge see e.g. B.M., Add. MSS 6117 fol. 40: William, bishop of Dublin to Wake from Bath, 26 June 1717.

69 His courtier beginnings (for which see text page 49) may have had something to do with this: see his *Mémoires* for his early career.

70 For Bernstorff's presence in England in 1720 and his influence with George, acting as a go-between between Wake and the king in the former's work for a reconciliation between Lutherans and Calvinists, see report of July 1720 cited in Syke, *Wake* II, 70. Bernstorff seems initially to have intended a return to London early in 1721: *ibid.*, 72, for Bernstorff's secretary having arrived in February and Bernstorff being expected in April. In May 1721 Bernstorff wrote to lady Cowper that he would delay his return since he expected to find England 'a sad place' while the South Sea bubble agitation lasted: Panshanger MSS: F 233, 3. From Friis, *The Bernstorffs* I, ch. 1, it is clear that arrangements for the fideikommis and the composition of a general directive for his heirs occupied him greatly from the autumn of 1720 onwards.

71 For Bothmer's letters from London after

1720 see Bernstorff Archive: AG 29 vol. iv; for those of Whitworth, mainly from Berlin, between 1722 and 1725 see AG 72. It is worth noting that in the summer of 1722, when Bernstorff was indisposed, Whitworth, then in Hanover, signalled his intention to visit Gartow to discuss foreign affairs and to give Bernstorff by word of mouth 'delicate' news of Prussian policies; for the moment he had to reserve it for the King's ear: letter of 22 June 1722.

72   P.R.O., SPD Regencies 43 vol. 5, Townshend to Newcastle 27 Nov. 1723, reporting success after a long campaign (mirrored in earlier letters) for Hardenberg's candidature. Cp. Beattie, *Court*, 244 for Newcastle's approval.

73   For Stanhope's and his colleagues' joy at their 'complete victory' over Bernstorff see Stanhope, *History* II, appendix, letter from Stanhope to Craggs of 10 July 1719 and Stair, *Annals* II, 405, private letter Craggs to Stair 1 Oct. 1719; cp. Williams, *Stanhope*, 366–72 and McKay, *North 1718–1719*, passim. For Townshend's report of the 1723 struggle, and his own victory, see P.R.O., SPD Regencies 43 vol. 4: his private letters to Robert Walpole of 6 Aug. and 2 Oct. 1723.

74   For a slower procedure, lopping off one day every leap year (begun in Sweden in 1700, but abandoned in 1712 since the Great Northern War had made the administration 'forget' the procedure laid down for 1704 and 1708), see Hatton, *Charles XII*, 349.

75   This idea is still entertained: Trench, *George II*, 52, regards George I's refusal to touch for the king's evil as at least 'partial confirmation' of the contention that he felt himself an usurper. For the history of touching see Marc Bloch, *Les Rois Thaumaturges* (Strasbourg 1924), passim; for the post-1689 period in England and at the exiled Stuart courts, 388 ff.

76   The reference to the Pufendorfian 'the general good is the highest law' in George's will has already been noted by Drögereit, *Will*, 107, 126. For George's enjoyment of the conversation of Karl Moritz and of Leibniz see my text pages 90–91, and for his support of Bucquoy and Voltaire see my text page 291 and ch. X notes 40 and 41.

77   Liselotte, *Selected Letters* (Kroll translation),

181: to raugravine Louise 16 Feb. 1716.

78   See Frederick's 'Instructions for my son George, drawn by my-Self for His Good, that of the Family, and for that of his People, according to the ideas of my Grandfather, and best friend, George I', dated 13 Jan. 1748/9. These instructions, usually called the political testament of Frederick, prince of Wales, are in Windsor R.A. and have been printed by Sedgwick in the editorial introduction to Hervey, *Memoirs* I, xxxiv ff. They have been reprinted by Young, *Poor Fred*, 172–76; but note that Young in his text, 184, reverses George I's intentions. Young, as well as Segwick, was handicapped in interpreting the will since both wrote before its discovery and publication by Drögereit, though Sedgwick was aware of Michael's assumption that a political will existed which envisaged separation of kingdom and electorate.

79   For George's proposals and the answers to them see Windsor, R.A.: 53017 ('Astle' volume).

80   George's persistence is, in part, explained by the Imperial Constitution: the Golden Bull did not preclude an elector abdicating of his own free will, though it was laid down that he could not be forced to do so.

81   Bernstorff Archive: AG 29 vol. iv, Bothmer's letter 17/28 Apr. 1724.

82   King, *Notes*: entry in his diary for 24 June 1725, based on what Robert Walpole had told him.

83   Walpole (Horace), *Memoirs* III, 307–08: see Hervey, *Memoirs* (Sedgwick) I, 27–28, for a slightly different version.

84   For concessions to the emperor Charles VI in the form of an offer in Jan. 1731 for the guarantee of the Pragmatic Sanction, leading to the treaty of Vienna of May 1731, see Williams, *Whig Supremacy*, 192, and Drögereit, *Will* for this, as well as for success with Wolfenbüttel. For George II's intense preoccupation with the will see B.M., Add. MSS 32751 fols. 24, 26, 121 and 122, two drafts by Newcastle to Horatio Walpole of July [undated] 1727 marked 'very private' in which Walpole is asked to sound cardinal Fleury as to whether George II could count on French help to defeat 'any attempt that may be made to enforce the Execution of it [the late King's will]', which, it was stressed, George II's

Hanoverian ministers held to be illegal and invalid. That at least the first of these letters was sent is clear from Horatio Walpole's acknowledgment of 31 July NS marked 'secret': *ibid.* fol. 125 r and v.

85 See e.g. Charles Grant Robertson, *The Hanoverians* (13th ed. 1944), 56: 'The father had been the only person in Great Britain to dispute the title of the son, George II, to the throne'; conversely Redman, *Hanover*, 54, who also stresses the hatred, assumes that George I attempted to deprive his son of the succession to Hanover.

Chapter VII: Three crises

The section on George's image is based on a systematic viewing of portraits, engravings, busts and statues. Those which proved to be posthumous (like Rysbrack's bust at Christ Church and the profile wax medallion by Isaac Gosset at Windsor) I have taken as less reliable than those which can be shown to have been done from life. I have received courteous help from the Queen's Librarian, Sir Robin Mackworth-Young, in respect of portraits and engravings, as also from the owners and custodians of the many collections which I have visited, in Britain, Germany and France. I owe much to the generous interest of H.R.H. the Princess of Hanover, who has permitted me to study the Marienburg, Calenberg and Herrenhausen collections with her as guide on three separate occasions. For the crises which form the main topics of this chapter the importance of the Schulenburg letters can hardly be exaggerated: they have added greatly to our knowledge both of the ministerial crisis and the quarrel in the royal family and have forced a reinterpretation of George's role in both. For the background material the many works on the 1715–16 Jacobite rebellion (referred to in note 16 below) and the biographies and other studies which cover the period of the ministerial crisis, both in its domestic and foreign aspects (especially Plumb, *Walpole* I, Williams, *Stanhope*, and Mediger) have been particularly useful.

1 In the report of d'Arcy-Martel, printed by Schnath, *Hannover* I, 726.

2 This derives from a superficial reading of Cowper (Mary), *Diary*, 12, in which she recounts the duchess of Shrewsbury's criticism of a medal (in which the king has

'un Nez long comme le Bras') in an attempt to persuade him to have his portrait painted. Profile medals show the shape of George's nose well, as do the statues (most easily observed in those in the Gartentheater at Herrenhausen and in the anteroom to the Public Record Office Museum).

3 There is one piece of literary evidence which indicates corpulence: Saussure, *Letters*, 45 (17 Sept. 1725), but it is possible that the young man only intended to convey the undoubted stockiness of the king. For George making a good figure on horseback see Addison, *Letters*, 336: to Delafaye 7 June 1715.

4 Sophia, *Correspondence with her brother*: her letter of 21 Jan. 1677 mentions both George's fair hair as a child and its present dark colour.

5 Montagu, *Works* I, 'Account', 125.

6 Görtz Archive: 121/6 Schulenburg letter of 12 Feb. 1717 (for the contemporary connotation of *monter à cheval*, see asterisk note, text page 57). For George's conversation when ladies were present see Cowper (Mary), *Diary*, 12: 'He said a world of sprightly things.'

7 For George's concern to keep promises made in this matter see Görtz Archive: 121/6, Schulenburg's letters of 2 April and 12 May 1717.

8 For examples of this see Hatton, *Charles XII*, 11 and Hatton, *Louis XIV*, 41. For George's splendid reception in 1714 by the well-to-do both at Greenwich and in London (more than 200 carriages took part in the procession) see Bristol, *Diary*: 20 Sept. 1714; and for the huzzas, and people thronging to kiss the king's stirrup, see Addison, *Letters*, 336: letter of 7 June 1715.

9 This is also the case in verses directed to or in commemoration of the king, and in letters which touch on plans for statues of him: see e.g. B.M., Add. MSS 38507 fol. 179 r and v, letter to Townshend from Paris 13 Dec. 1715, from a correspondent to whom Townshend has entrusted the discussion with the royal French sculptor-in-chief of an equestrian statue of George I. The suggestion is that the king's valour and heroic actions should be celebrated as well as his concern for justice and religion. The 1715 rebellion put a stop to this particular project.

10 See *The Character of Sultan Gaga, the present Cham of Tartary Drawn by a Walachian who had been his favourite for several years*: 'Not clear if he hath Personal Courage ... [he and his troops] fled scandalously in the Beginning of a Battle, almost before they were attack'd.'

11 For the Jacobite attempts to gain Swedish military support at this period see Hatton, *Charles XII*, 416–17; for Louis XIV's Swedish policy at this time see Sörensson, *KFÅ* 1910; for the proposed Stuart marriage see Edinburgh National Library, MS 5129.

12 For Louis XIV's attitude towards the Jacobites see Nordmann, *La Crise*, 45 ff. and Gregg, *Protestant Succession*, 276 ff.; the money actually sent by Philip V has recently been investigated by L.B. Smith (for his London Ph.D. thesis, 'Spain and Britain 1715–1719. The Jacobite Issue'). It amounted to £43,500 in English money, the largest pecuniary help given for the Jacobites in 1715–16. I am indebted to him for this information as also for the unravelling of the motives which prompted the Spanish support for James.

13 Williams, *Whig Supremacy*, 149 ff.; for an analysis of impeachment processes in England see Clayton Roberts' study, 383 ff.

14 For this imprisonment of 1712 and its resultant rancour see Plumb, *Walpole* I, 180–81, 213–17.

15 P.R.O., SPF France vol. 160 for Stair's reports; for preparations at home by the purging of Jacobites from civil and army office, and military preparations in general, see Plumb, *Walpole* I, 213–14 (based *i.a.* on Townshend cabinet minute of 30 May 1715); Dalton, *History of the British Army* II, 10–16.

16 For good studies of the 1715 rising see Alastair and Henrietta Tayler, *The Story of the Rising* (1936); Jones, *Jacobitism* (1954); Petrie, *The Jacobite Movement* (3rd ed. 1959); Thomas, 'Jacobitism in Wales', *Welsh Historical Review* 1963; Baynes, *1715* (1970) and Christopher Sinclair-Stevenson, *Inglorious Revolution* (1971).

17 Gregg, *Protestant Succession*, 272 ff. and 295 for the importance of Ormonde and Oxford, and the reinsurance policies of Marlborough and Shrewsbury.

18 For the 'Salvador' epithet see Heinsius Archive: 1930, Duyvenvoorde's letters from London of 13 and 16 Aug. 1715; for the earlier vilification see Coombs' study of 1958, chs. x and xi. For the troops see Hatton, *Diplomatic Relations*, 81–86, 102.

19 *Ibid.*, 84 ff. for the barrier negotiations; for text of the Nov. 1715 Barrier treaty see *Ö.S. Netherlands*.

20 Note that the battle of Sheriffmuir was on 13 Nov. according to the English calendar, but on 14 Nov. according to the Scottish (James V having dropped one day from OS in the year 1600). For the secret request of George's see Hatton, *Diplomatic Relations*, 94 based on Heinsius Archive: 1930.

21 Williams, *Whig Supremacy*, 157.

22 For Shrewsbury being forced to resign (5/16 July 1716) through pressure from the Whig ministers see Gregg, *Protestant Succession*, 275; for Nottingham's dismissal on 27 Feb. OS 1716 see *Horwitz*, 250. Somerset had resigned his position as Master of the Horse in Oct. 1715 when his son-in-law (Sir William Wyndham) was arrested for suspected Jacobite activities: Beattie, *Court*, 101.

23 Schaumburg-Lippe, *Letters*: 22 Nov. 1715 and 13/24 Jan. 1716.

24 For the London incidents see Rudé, *Hanoverian London*, 206–08 based on the unpublished Edinburgh Ph.D. thesis by D.C.G. Isaac, 'A Study of Popular Disturbances in Britain, 1714–1754'; Ward, *University Politics*, 54 ff. deals with outbreak of violence and hooliganism in Oxford.

25 Frederick's 'Instructions for my son George', cited in ch. VII note 78; cp. Schaumburg-Lippe, *Letters*: 13/24 Jan. 1716.

26 See *Wentworth Papers*, 436 for George closely questioning a visitor who had recently measured the Dunkirk canals and pronouncing his verdict after consultation with lord Berkeley. For the Mardyk issue in Anglo-French relations at this time see Hatton, *Diplomatic Relations*, 63–64, 100, 118.

27 For Townshend's argument see Heinsius Archive: 1972, cited in Hatton, *Diplomatic Relations*, 100.

28 See Fransen, *Leibniz*, passim.

29 Hatton, *Diplomatic Relations*, 98–99, 106 for the *simul-et-semel* policy and Townshend's interpretation of the Anglo-Imperial treaty.

30 See Hatton, *Charles XII*, 395–96, 402 ff. and Mediger, *Bremen and Verden*, 42 ff.

31 See, for the various treaties, Stoerk (Hanover), *Danmark-Norges Traktater* (Denmark), Loewe (Prussia) and Bantys-Kamensky (Russia).

32 The former school derives from contemporary anti-George propaganda; the latter from ministerial defence of the king's northern policies.

33 *Mediger* (1967), in his notes, has printed extensive extracts which prove that George made direct use of the British navy for electoral purposes in 1715, but concludes that it is not possible to say if the squadron of that year rendered any real help to the anti-Swedish alliance: I, 240. Murray (1953 and 1969), from Dutch and Danish sources, has been more positive for the 1715 squadron. Hatton, from a wide variety of material, has shown that the naval support, which was withheld or granted according to George's relations at any one time with individual members of the northern alliance, operated for the whole period of the Great Northern War, though within finely judged limits of what he could and could not manage to 'get away with' as king: see *Charles XII*, 403 ff., 424 ff., 463, 478 ff., 512–13. Cp. Lindeberg, 46–47, and Sörensson, *KFÅ* 1929, 196–97. During the whole 1714–21 period there was only one minor direct Anglo-Swedish skirmish, on 17 July 1717, when four British men-of-war attacked and captured a Swedish frigate; see E. Holmberg, *KFÅ* 1915, 1920. British tactics in the Baltic were to use their squadrons for blockades of Sweden and for junctions with Danish and Russian fleets to overawe the Swedes and prevent their navy from leaving port and risking battle.

34 The decision to fit out a strong squadron in 1715 was indeed taken before the privateering edict of Charles XII; but—as a compromise—the British admiralty managed then, and in later years, to keep ammunition to peacetime rations in order to prevent large-scale battle involvement.

35 Hatton, *Charles XII*, 416 ff., 460, 474–75, 493.

36 Hatton, *Diplomatic Relations*, 173–74, 201–03, 233–34, 241.

37 This promise was on 'Our Royal Faith and Troth'; it is frequently cited, e.g. by Williams, *Stanhope*, 232. Cp. from Russian archives *Nikiforov* (German ed.), 161, for

promises of a strong British naval presence. The draft instructions for Norris and Hopson of 11/22 March to 25 Oct./5 Nov. 1715 are in the Hanover archives and have been analyzed by *Mediger* II, notes to ch. 5.

38 For the Scania invasion plan see Hatton, *Charles XII*, 406, 417, 420–28 and references there given.

39 Bernstorff Archive: AG 29 vol. iv: Bothmer's letter from Hampton Court of 25 Sept./6 Oct. 1716.

40 For the Mecklenburg issue see *Mediger* I, ch. 2.

41 *HMC, Polwarth MSS* I, 97: Robethon to Polwarth 1/12 Oct. 1716.

42 Coxe, *Robert Walpole* II, 84–85, Stanhope to Townshend 25 Sept. NS 1716.

43 *Ibid.*, 86, Townshend to Stanhope 23 Sept./4 Oct. 1716.

44 For Horatio Walpole explaining his difficult position, see his letter to Stanhope 12 Dec. 1716: Coxe, *Robert Walpole* II, 146. For his mission in general see Hatton, *Diplomatic Relations*, 130 ff., supported by the private letters of Horatio Walpole to Townshend ed. by J. J. Murray (1955).

45 For Townshend being kept informed see P.R.O., SPD Regencies 43 vol. 1: Stanhope's letters from The Hague and Hanover of 8 July, 14 and 21 Aug. NS 1716; for Townshend's argument see Hatton, *Diplomatic Relations*, 139–40, strengthened by Murray's edition of Horatio Walpole's private letters to Townshend.

46 For Dubois' reports of the negotiations see his *Mémoires secrets*, 210 ff. Stanhope's reports to Townshend are in *Wiesener* I, 469 ff. For George's own share see Chevening MSS: 83/17, correspondence between the king and duc d'Orléans. For the negotiations see Hatton, *Diplomatic Relations*, 128–43, where reasons are given for not fully accepting the earlier versions by *Bourgeois* I, 116 ff. and *Wiesener* I, 312 ff. The treaty was formally signed at The Hague by Dubois and Cadogan on 28 Nov.; but both copies were burnt on 4 Jan. 1717 when the Dutch acceded to the Anglo-French alliance, which thus became the Triple Alliance.

47 Townshend's letter to Stanhope of 16/27 Oct. 1716 is printed by Coxe, *Robert Walpole* I (1816 ed.), 302–05.

48 Their correspondence and other relevant letters between 30 July OS 1716 and 16 Jan. NS 1717 were printed by Coxe, *Robert Walpole* II, in 1789; they fill pp. 285–321 in vol. I of the 1816 ed.

49 Görtz Archive: 121/6, Schulenburg's letter of 12 Feb. 1717.

50 *Ibid.*: 124/1, Görtz (drafts) to Stanhope of 29 June and 2 July 1717, referring to conversations when Stanhope was in Hanover.

51 For Horatio Walpole's visit to Hanover see his letter to Stanhope of 11 Dec. 1717: Coxe, *Robert Walpole* II, 308.

52 For Robert Walpole's letter to Stanhope of 2/13 Dec. 1716 see Coxe, *Robert Walpole* II, 192–94; for Stanhope's letters to Robert Walpole of 15 Dec. 1716 and 1 Jan. 1717 see *ibid.*, 308, 314.

53 Stanhope to Robert Walpole 16 Jan. 1717 from The Hague: Coxe, *Robert Walpole* I (1816 ed.), 319.

54 Görtz Archive: 121/6, Schulenburg letters of 12 and 19 Feb. 1717.

55 *Ibid.*: 121/6, letters of 23 Feb. and 2/13 and 5/16 March 1717. Cp. for diplomatic reports Hatton, *Diplomatic Relations*, 147.

56 Görtz Archive: 121/6, Schulenburg's letters of 12/23 and 15/26 March and 2 April 1717.

57 *Ibid.*: 121/6, letter of 12/23 March 1717.

58 *Ibid.*: 121/6, letters of 2 March NS and, for the French court, of 12/23 March 1717.

59 *Ibid.*: 121/6, letters of 12/23 and 15/26 March and 6 April NS 1717.

60 It should be noted that in popular works the prince's position is usually misinterpreted: the title of guardian of the realm was traditional and was later used for queen Caroline during George II's absences from England. There was therefore no slight implied in Georg August not being named 'regent', though a grievance was assumed by the prince's officials and advisers. For the latest treatment of Argyll's dismissal see Dickson, *Argyll*, 148 ff.

61 Robert Walpole to Stanhope, 30 July/10 Aug. 1717: Coxe, *Robert Walpole* I (1816 ed.), quote from p. 287.

62 Görtz Archive: 121/6, Schulenburg's letters of 2 and 6 Apr. 1717.

63 *Ibid.*: 121/6, Schulenburg's letter of 20 Apr. 1717. For the Gyllenborg plot see Hatton, *Diplomatic Relations*, 147 ff. and Hatton, *Charles XII*, 436 ff. with references to the

contributions by Westin (1898), Jägerskiöld (1937), Murray (1956) and Nordmann (1962).

64 *Ibid.*: 121/6, Schulenburg's letter of 6 Apr. 1717; this letter is of crucial importance, proving that it was the prince of Wales, and not George, who absented himself from cabinet meetings.

65 *Ibid.*: 121/6, Schulenburg's letter of 6 Apr. 1717. For Stanhope's marriage to Pitt's daughter see Newman, *Stanhope*, 91 ff.; for the Pitt diamond being offered in 1714 successively to George and to the prince of Wales, but refused see *HMC, Dropmore MSS* I, 150: for its sale to the regent in 1717 see *ibid.*, 62: Thomas Pitt to his son Robert Pitt 29 June 1717.

66 Görtz Archive: 121/6, Schulenburg's letter of 20 Apr. 1717; for further, equally vain, efforts by Bernstorff and Bothmer with the prince and princess see his letter of 23 July 1717. Owen, *Country attitudes*, estimates that there were 73 'country' members, 50 of whom were Tories, in the 1715–22 House of Commons.

67 Görtz Archive: 121/6, Schulenburg's letters of 7, 23 and 29 Apr. 1717, which show the king as trying hard to achieve reconciliation both with his son and with Townshend and Walpole. Cp. Schulenburg's letters of 18 and 25 Nov. 1718 for the king being less tough with the prince than his ministers.

68 *Ibid.*: 121/6, a loose list sent with letter of 12 Feb. 1717.

69 *Ibid.*: 121/6, Schulenburg's letter of 27 Apr. 1717.

70 Plumb, *Walpole* I, 251 ff.; for the worry and subsequent relief of the court when supply was voted see Görtz Archive: 121/6, Schulenburg's letter of 20 Apr. 1718; for previous concern see letters of 26 Oct. and 19 Nov. 1717.

71 *Ibid.*: 121/6: Schulenburg's letters of 1 June, 2, 5, 9, 11 and 20 July 1717. On the reasons for Oxford's discharge see Clayton Roberts' study, 414–19.

72 Görtz Archive: 121/6, Schulenburg's letters of 23 and 27 July 1717.

73 *Ibid.*: 121/6, Schulenburg's letters of 6 (Stanhope's visit) and 20 Apr. and 23 and 27 July 1717. For the differing attitude to Melusine of the prince and princess of Wales at this time, *ibid.*, letter of 20 Aug. 1717. For respect and favours from both after

74 George's death see Schaumburg-Lippe, *Letters*: 2/13 Apr. 1728.

74 Görtz Archive: 121/6, Schulenburg's letters of 3 Aug. (from Hampton Court) and 24 Sept. (from Windsor) 1717. Beattie, *Court*, 264 ff., was the first to realize the political significance of George's spending so much money on entertainment in 1717 and 1718.

75 Görtz Archive: 121/6; Schulenburg's letters of 3, 13, 17 Aug., 21 Sept. and 22 Oct. 1717. For Pope's comments see *Letters* IV, 395 (n.d.) (to lady Wortley Montagu), and ed. note for a slightly different wording dated 13 Sept. 1717.

76 Görtz Archive: 121/6, Schulenburg's letters of 11 and 20 July, 3 and 28 Sept. 1717, giving evidence which has necessitated revision of the accepted views on the king's attitude to his son.

77 For the king's disappointment see Panshanger MSS: F 231, 89, Bernstorff to lady Cowper, Hanover, letter of 3 Dec. NS 1716. For George II's characterization of his father see Hervey, *Memoirs* (Sedgwick) I, 69; III, 918.

78 Görtz Archive: 121/6, Schulenburg's letters of 20, 27, 31 Aug. and 7, 9 and 10 Sept. 1717. At least one Englishman suspected that George was ill: *HMC, Stuart MSS* V, 44, letter to Mar of 15 Sept. 1717, reporting the duke of Shrewsbury as saying that the king was not in good health, indeed he thought him 'agoing'.

79 Görtz Archive: 121/6, Schulenburg's letters of 20 Aug., 24 Sept., 22 Oct. and 7 Dec. 1717. While George did not go to the races often, he was keen on the breeding of horses and was interested in the studs both at Newmarket and Hampton Court: see Longrigg, *The History of Horse Racing*, 260. For his introduction of the famous cream Hanoverian carriage-horses to Britain see Campbell, *Royalty on Horseback*, 31. For Robert Walpole being 'extrêmement animé' at the king's treatment of him at Newmarket see Görtz Archive: 121/6, Schulenburg's letter of 7 Dec. 1717.

80 Stair, *Annals* II, 38, Craggs to Stair, 5 Sept. 1717.

81 For George's joy at the birth of the grandson, see Panshanger MSS: Bernstorff to lady Cowper from Hampton Court 3 Nov. 1717 (F 231, 287–88). For the 'opposition'

threats see Görtz Archive: 121/6, Schulenburg's letter of 16 Nov. 1717.

82 *Ibid.*: 121/6, Schulenburg's letters of 16, 19, 23, 30 Nov. and 3 Dec. 1717.

83 The report by Kingston, Kent and Roxburghe of their first meeting is in Chevening MSS: 84/10 and part of it is quoted verbatim in the note to my text page 215. For the second meeting see Görtz Archive: 121/6, Schulenburg's letters of 10 and 14 Dec. 1717. The correspondence subsequently exchanged between George and his son was widely circulated and is printed by *Michael* I, 309–10, from copies in the Vienna archives. For the king's disappointment at Caroline leaving see Görtz Archive: 121/6, Schulenburg's letter of 14 Dec. 1717.

84 George's instructions (in his own hand) to his son, to be transmitted by Coke, the vice-chamberlain, have been printed from the Panshanger MSS by Plumb, *Walpole* I, 260. Schulenburg's letters in Görtz Archive: 121/6, are uniquely informative (and explain hints in the Schaumburg-Lippe *Letters*) on George's concern to ease the difficult position of the princess: on 28 Jan. 1718 he reports that the king has given Caroline permission to visit her children; and on 26 Apr. 1718 that she sees her daughters by royal connivance 'every day', usually in the late afternoon when she plays with them, stays for their supper and puts them to bed.

85 The papers connected with this legal issue are in Windsor, R.A.: 53017 ('Astle' volume); see also Görtz Archive: 121/6, Schulenburg's letters of 8 and 11 Feb. 1718.

86 For their move to the house of Portman Seymour see *ibid.*: 121/6, Schulenburg's letter of 8 Feb. 1718.

87 The notification was printed in the *London Gazette* for 24 Dec. OS 1717. For the problems created see Görtz Archive: 121/6, Schulenburg's letter of 4 Feb. 1718, and Schaumburg-Lippe, *Letters*: 24 Jan./4 Feb., 4/15 March, 27 May/7 June, 25 Nov./6 Dec. 1718 and 13/24 Jan. 1719, though she herself remained in a privileged position between the two courts. So did lady Cowper. Thanks to Melusine's intercession, following strong protests by both the Cowpers who blamed Sunderland for their dilemma, lady Cowper was told (via the

countess of Schaumburg-Lippe) that she
had 'nothing to fear from Sunderland,' and
that George I 'n'insistera pas sur cette
article [i.e. Sunderland's letter of 2 Dec.
1717 forbidding lady Cowper to see the
princess of Wales], mais qu'on laissera tout
en *status quo*, jusqu'à un accomodement':
Panshanger MSS, 'Family Books', vol. 4,
entered with other copies from pages 296
onwards. For the subterfuges by which Mrs
Clayton and lady Cowper saw the princess
even in public, see Windsor R.A.: Geo Add.
MSS 28, nos. 32, 39 and Panshanger MSS:
F 203, letters of Mrs Clayton to lady Cowper.

88 For George and the Cowper resignation
    see Görtz Archive: 121/6, Schulenburg's
    letters of 11 and 29 Feb. and 19 April 1718.
    Schulenburg surmised that Cowper had
    been urged to resign by his wife who was
    'much loved by the young court'. The
    correspondence between Cowper and his
    wife, however, shows tension between him
    and his fellow ministers on a variety of
    issues throughout his period of office. Foord,
    Opposition, 74 has added a Jacobite element
    based on the Caesar papers, but these (if
    they can be trusted) date from the 1720–22
    period.

89 Görtz Archive: 121/6, Schulenburg's letters
    of 28 Dec. 1717, 4 Jan., 8 March and 5 Apr.
    1718. The Kneller portrait, stored at
    Marienburg, is not at present in a state to be
    reproduced.

90 Görtz Archive: 121/6, Schulenburg's letters
    of 23 Apr. 1717 and 10 March 1718.

91 *Ibid.*: 121/6, Schulenburg's letter of 10
    March 1718.

92 *Ibid.*: 121/6, Schulenburg's letter of 4
    March 1718; cp. letter of 1 Aug. 1718 (from
    Emden).

93 *Ibid.*: 121/6, Schulenburg's letters 2 Apr.
    1717 (for marriage rumours) and 6 March
    1718 (for George and Sunderland).

94 Bothmer, *Q.A.*, though noting that Sunder-
    land was a good linguist and knew German
    well. For Sunderland's 'great Ability in
    Parliament' see *HMC*, *Onslow MSS* I, 509.

Chapter VIII: The watershed 1718–21

Where domestic affairs have been touched on,
the correspondence printed either in the

Historical Manuscript Commission volumes or
in privately edited collections of letters have
been important. Constitutional and political
histories and biographies have been a great help.
For foreign policy issues I have, over the years,
gone through all the State Papers Foreign,
instructions to diplomats and dispatches from
diplomats for all the countries involved in the
two 'peace plans' which occupied so much of
George's time, supplemented by foreign archive
material, especially French and Dutch. Indeed,
my unpublished material is so rich that only the
top of the iceberg emerges in the notes. The
Austrian unprinted documents have been so
well utilized for this period and for that of the
following chapter by doctoral dissertations
which – if they do not always sufficiently
consider non-Austrian material – make independent research in the Vienna archives hardly
worth while; though it is still necessary to
use the university library there to consult the
printed theses which do not seem to find their
way to British libraries. Conversely, the
Hanover archives have yielded material that
has not been used before and, for the same
reason, the Bernstorff archive has been invaluable.

1 Scotland has in recent years been well
   served by excellent histories which give
   much space to the first half of the eighteenth century: Donaldson and Ferguson
   have been particularly useful to me.

2 For the drawbacks of the Triennial Act of
   1694 see Holmes, 218–19; Marshall,
   England, 85.

3 Plumb, *Stability*, 173–74; Kemp, *King and
   Commons*, 37 ff.

4 Foord, *Opposition*, 8–11, 54–77.

5 For Anne's position in William III's reign
   see Baxter, *William III*, 296, 300; for
   George II's reign see the biography of
   Frederick by Edwards. Biographies of
   queen Anne (by E. G. Gregg) and of
   George II (by S. B. Baxter) are in the
   making and we can hope for further
   enlightenment.

6 The standard accounts build on Cowper
   (Mary), *Diary*, 145, entry of 23 Apr. 1720
   (to the effect that none of the Germans,
   apart from Melusine, knew of the reconciliation); and (from *ibid.*, 52–53, 56,
   59–61) the assumption that the close
   cooperation between the Cowpers and

Bernstorff came to an end in Oct. 1715 when they took umbrage at Bernstorff's criticism that lord Cowper was *trop vif* and his wife *beaucoup trop vive* in promoting their own views. The correspondence in the Panshanger MSS, however, shows that Bernstorff's efforts (visible already in the *Diary*, 66, 69, 98, 101, 105 ff.) to restore the friendship were successful, and that all three worked together to reunite the royal family in late 1717 and early 1718: see the copies of letters sent and received in F 231 and 232 after 2 Dec. 1717, in particular Cowper's letters to George I, Bernstorff and the duchess of Munster (Melusine) with answers from Bernstorff and the countess of Schaumburg-Lippe (on Melusine's behalf). She refers to Bernstorff's efforts behind the scenes for the *bon Accord* they all strive for. There are also interesting letters from Caroline, princess of Wales, in which she appeals to lady Cowper to use as a go-between her *Amy* (most probably Bernstorff); and a letter from the archbishop of Canterbury (Wake) which openly refers to his seeing both the princess and Bernstorff in the hope of furthering reconciliation.

7 Schaumburg-Lippe, *Letters*: 24 Jan./4 Feb., 4/15 March and 27 May/7 June 1718, 13/24 Jan. 1719. For the funeral from Kensington Palace of George William on 14 Feb. 1718/19, with the King's coaches and yeomen of the guard and horseguards, see *London Gazette*.

8 Hervey, *Memoirs*. The Croker ed. (II, 478–79) has the original French; the Sedgwick ed. (III, 848–49) gives the French version and an English translation, and both are printed in his one-vol. selection of 1952, 309–10. Croker and Sedgwick alike read Hervey as giving 'Earl Stanhope' as the author of the first extract in my note page 214, though it is possible that Charles Stanhope (Sunderland's secretary) penned it. While Hervey mentions both James Stanhope and Sunderland as enemies of the prince at this time, our corroborative evidence shows Sunderland as the advocate of violent action; see Görtz Archive: 121/6, Schulenburg's letter of 28 Sept. 1717. Cp. letters of 3 Sept. and 16 Nov. 1717 for the

general ministerial pressure for firm measures against the prince.

9 For joy at the birth of William see Schaumburg-Lippe, *Letters*: 9/20 May 1721; for the christening of Trudchen's son, Georg August, 25 Sept./6 Oct. 1722; for family affairs in general, 26 Oct./6 Nov. 1722; 12/23 March 1723; 7/18 Jan., 21 Apr./4 May and 12/23 June, 1/12 Dec. 1724; 2/13 Feb. 1725; 24 June/5 July 1726. For Melusine's illness *ibid.*: letter of 12/23 June 1724; for Amalie's illness in 1726, see Windsor, R.A.: Geo Add. MSS 28, nos. 20–28. The dating of this illness is made possible by a marginal reference (in Mrs Clayton's transcripts) to Mary Toft, who claimed to have given birth to rabbits. For the sensation this caused, George I's disbelief and her being proved an impostor by one of the royal physicians sent by the king to examine her case, see article in *DNB*. Trench, *George II*, 125 assumes Amalie's illness to date from George II's reign and therefore attributes George I's attitude to his granddaughter's illness to George II.

10 For the relevant quotation from Ernst August's letter to Friedrich August of 3/13 Apr. 1685 see my text page 44; for the sentence by George here cited see his letter to the prince of Wales printed in full as appendix D to Cowper (Mary), *Diary*, 191–92.

11 The secret pleasure can be deduced from the tone of Caroline's letter to Mrs Clayton of 22 Apr. [1720]: Windsor, R.A.: Geo Add. MSS 28 no. 59; she expressed her pleasure openly to her sister-in-law, the queen of Prussia, and George judged her sentiment sincere: George, *Letters*, 497 (to Sophia Dorothea of 9 July 1720). For George's broken words, his being 'dismayed and pale', and the reconciliation in general see Cowper (Mary), *Diary*, 142 ff. For the extension of the reconciliation to ministers' wives see Jane Pitt to the Hon. Mrs Pitt 7 May [1720], commenting on 'Townshend and Walpole's Ladys going to see lady Stanhope': *HMC, Dropmore MSS*, 64–65.

12 George, *Letters*, 497: to Sophia Dorothea of 9 July 1720.

13 Bernstorff Archive: AG 62, Flemming to Bernstorff, Dresden, 27 Sept. 1717 (the

resident was Vernon, for whom see *DNB*).

14 Görtz Archive: 121/6, Schulenburg's letters of 24 and 27 Aug., 9 Nov. and 3 Dec. 1718 compared with Fabrice, *Memoiren*, 117–22.

15 Görtz Archive: 121/6, Schulenburg's letters of 22 Oct. and 14 Dec. 1717 and 22 Feb. 1718 compared with Dubois, *Mémoires secrets*, *Wiesener*, and other secondary authorities based solely on French archives.

16 Görtz Archive: 121/6, Schulenburg's letter of 20 Apr. 1717 for the *faux pas*; cp. Williams, *Stanhope*, 249.

17 Hatton, *Diplomatic Relations*, 160–61.

18 For the arrest, custody and release of Görtz see Hatton, *Diplomatic Relations*, 147–59.

19 *Ibid.*, 152–56 for the Dutch refusal to prohibit trade with Sweden and for the 'lye-still' of the Dutch navy; *Lindeberg*, 336 ff. for the great increase in Dutch-Swedish trade.

20 For the protest made on behalf of the London diplomatic corps by the Spanish diplomat, Isidor de Cassado, marques de Monteleón, see *Wiesener* II, 4; for White-hall's vigorous counter-propaganda see *Murray*, 337 ff.

21 For Charles XII's disavowal and the regent's offices see Hatton, *Diplomatic Relations*, 157–58 and Hatton, *Charles XII*, 449; for the Swedish diplomatic initiatives see *Jägerskiöld* (1937), supplemented by *Feigina* from Russian archival material (1959), and Hatton, *Charles XII*, 425 ff., 451 ff.

22 *Ibid.*, for the Turkey period, 372–76; based *i.a.* on Charles' letter to his sister Ulrika Eleonora of 2 Sept. 1714 printed in *Konung Karl XII:s egenhändiga bref*, ed. E. Carlson (Stockholm 1893).

23 See Hatton, *Charles XII*, 445–50 for the policy and the men employed.

24 For their correspondence see Görtz Archive: 125/40; for Vellingk's role in the negotiations after 1716 see Fabrice, *Memoiren*, 117–18, 121, 125; and Hatton, *Charles XII*, 375, 449, 455.

25 For Ranck being sent to Bender in 1713 by Friedrich of Hesse see Holst, *Fredrik I*, 31 ff.; for his role in the diplomacy here discussed see Hatton, *Charles XII*, 447–79.

26 For Fabrice's stay with Charles XII in

Turkey (and in Stralsund) see *ibid.*, 319–21, 361, 376; and, more fully, in Fabrice, *Letters*, passim, for the period; cp. his *Memoiren*, 42–115. For Fabrice having met George in Hanover in 1707 and 1708 (in the latter instance in his capacity as a Holstein-Gottorp diplomat) and being well received at his court, see *ibid.*, 25–26, 29–30.

27 Görtz Archive: 121/6, Schulenburg's letter of 27 Aug. 1717; Fabrice, *Memoiren*, 117–21.

28 For the Russian decision to leave see *Feigina*, 115 ff., and *Mediger* I, 366 ff. Some years after George's death a Russian diplomat (who, in Vienna, had been instrumental in obtaining proofs of the king's strong commitment in this matter) had a conversation with viscount Percival in which he stressed that the tsar was sufficiently vexed to revenge himself by support for the Pretender; he eventually 'cooled off' since he admired George and was impressed by the fact that the king had 'boldly maintained the share he had in that transaction': *HMC*, *Egmont Diary* I, 114–16, entry for 5 Nov. 1730.

29 For the negotiations between tsar Peter and the regent see Sörensson, *Sverige och Frankrike 1715–1718* I, 91 ff.; Vicomte de Guichen, *Pierre le Grand et le premier traité franco-russe* (Paris 1908).

30 Hatton, *Charles XII*, 449.

31 Görtz Archive: 121/6, Schulenburg's letter of 1 October 1717, reporting arrival two days earlier and the failure of his mission to the tsar.

32 See Bruce, *Jacobites*; *Jägerskiöld*, 42 ff.; *Feigina*, 153 ff.

33 For Fabrice's second visit (arrival in October 1717), see his *Memoiren*, 121–122, and Görtz Archive: 121/6, Schulenburg's letters of 19 Nov. and 3 Dec. 1717.

34 For his mission see Hatton, *Charles XII*, 453–55 and Fabrice, *Memoiren*, 122–25.

35 Bernstorff Archive: AG 62, Flemming to Bernstorff 27 Sept. 1717 with (undated) draft answer in Robethon's hand. The 'secretary' sent to replace Richard Vernon was the James Scott who had been in disgrace in 1707 but who had, towards the end of queen Anne's reign and the early months of George's, been a regular diplomat in Saxony and Poland. He was,

however, taken seriously ill after his arrival in Dresden (only one letter from him, Dresden 27 Oct. 1717, is on the file); and a variety of experienced Hanoverian diplomats were therefore brought on to the fringes of the negotiations. Their letters or copies of them are in AG 62. George's control is evident not only from expressions in the several draft answers and from Flemming's letter of 30 Dec. 1717 addressed directly to the king; but also from George's later use of the Saxon minister for secret negotiations: see Stair, *Annals* II, 397–98 for George's letter to the French regent, dated Hanover 7 Nov. 1719, in which he tells of his meeting and secret negotiations with Flemming. Scott, incidentally, recovered from his illness (though Flemming reported him dying at the end of 1717) and was later employed on an official mission to Saxony, Poland and Prussia.

36 *Ibid.*, Bernstorff's draft answers, especially those of 7 Jan. (with postscript of 8 Jan.) and 14 June 1718.

37 *Ibid.*, Flemming's letter to the king cited in note 35 above, and Bernstorff (draft) to Flemming of 7 Jan. 1718.

38 Görtz Archive: 121/6, Schulenburg's letter of 29 Dec. 1717.

39 For Victor Amadeus' hint see Stanhope to Stair of 3 Feb. 1716: P.R.O., SPF France vol. 160, supported by Baraudon, *Savoy*, 124 ff. For the power and ambition of the emperor, see G. Quazza, 'Italy's role in the European problems of the first half of the eighteenth century', *Studies in Diplomatic History. Essays in memory of David Bayne Horn*, ed. Ragnhild Hatton and M.S. Anderson (1970), 140 ff. and authorities there cited.

40 For the Hanover stage of the negotiations between Stanhope and Dubois see Hatton, *Diplomatic Relations*, 134–35; for Pentenrriedter's mission see Drodtloff's biography, 48 ff.

41 For the plan, the project of settlement as it was at first called, see Stanhope's letters to Robert Walpole and Townshend of 6 and 9 Oct. 1716: Coxe, *Robert Walpole* II, 100–02, also Weber, *Quadruple Alliance*, 28 ff.; *Baudrillart* II, 269 ff.; Hatton, *Diplomatic Relations*, 166 ff.

42 For the influence of Pufendorf's ideas in general see Krieger, *Pufendorf*, 255 ff.; for his ideas on international relations and for the various editions and translations of his works see Hatton, *War and Peace*, 13 ff. See *ibid.*, 7, 23–24 for Callières' work of 1716, translated into English in 1716 with the title, *The Art of Negotiating with Princes*. I have not been able to trace a direct link between this book and either George or Stanhope, but it seems certain (from phrases used in diplomatic instructions at the time) that Callières' development of Pufendorf's ideas and especially his slogan of reciprocal advantages and reciprocal sacrifices is significant for the period of Anglo-French close cooperation 1716–1731.

43 Chevening MSS: library ms. catalogue lists Pufendorf's *History*, and the acquisition accounts note expenditure for the two *Accounts*.

44 A copy of this letter in its original French, from George I to Philip V, dated St James's 1 June 1721 was sent to the regent of France and is now in AAE, Angleterre, Suppl. vol. 7 (1721–26); there is an English version in P.R.O., SPF Spain vol. 90. The letter remained secret in England till 1728; after that time it was frequently committed to paper, see e.g. *HMC, Roxburgh et al.*, 196–97 (the MSS of the dowager countess of Seafield). For the Gibraltar issue in general see the pioneer work by Conn, *Gibraltar*, 31 ff.; Gibbs, *Treaties*, 125–29 and Hills, *Gibraltar*, 249 ff., based on Spanish material.

45 See P.R.O., SPD Regencies 43 vol. 7 for Townshend's letter (copy) to William Stanhope of 14/25 Sept. 1725; for his outspoken letter to Newcastle (quoted in the text) of 24 Sept./7 Oct. 1725; and for his letter to the same of 28 Oct./8 Nov. 1725, showing realization that a promise had been made and transmitting George's orders that a search for an entry on promises in respect of Gibraltar should be made in the secretary of state's office. Townshend suggests that Carteret ought to be consulted. For proof of verbal promises made see Williams, *Stanhope*, 307, and Martin, *Spain and Italy*, 417, based on British and Spanish documents; cp. Massini, *Schaub*, 26, for conditional promises in 1720.

46 For the grievances, and rectifications and concessions, see *McLachlan*, 3–29, 46–67 and Williams, *Stanhope*, 207–08.

47 B.M., Add. MSS 37364, Whitworth to Sunderland (draft, private) 18 May 1717; cp. Hatton, *Diplomatic Relations*, 160.

48 Harcourt-Smith, *Alberoni*, 159 ff. For the Austrian ambitions in Italy see K.O. von Aretin, 'Der Heimfall des Herzogtums Mailand an das Reich im Jahre 1700', *Gedenkschrift Martin Göhring* (Wiesbaden 1968); the same author's larger study on Joseph's reign in *HZ* 1972; and Huber's monograph covering the period from 1700 onwards.

49 Martin, *Spain and Italy*, 412. For Patiño's work (he was particularly active in preparing the navy for the Italian descents 1717–1718) see the study by Béthencourt Massieu, *passim*.

50 For the Molinez affair see *Wiesener* II, 89–90.

51 B.M., Add. MSS 37364, Whitworth to Sunderland (draft, private) 3 Aug. 1717 from The Hague; cp. for context Hatton, *Diplomatic Relations*, 163.

52 B.M., Add. MSS 37365, Stair to Whitworth 30 July 1717.

53 Görtz Archive: 121/6, Schulenburg's letters of 3 and 10 Aug. 1717.

54 *Ibid.*: 121/6, Schulenburg's letter of 18 Jan. 1718.

55 *Ibid.*: 121/6, Schulenburg's letter of 3 Sept. 1717.

56 The arrears claimed was £900,000; what George offered (it was accepted) was £130,000: P.R.O., SPF Foreign Entry Books, Empire vol. 42; for payment taking place on 11 Jan. 1718 see *Wiesener* II, 49; cp. for context Hatton, *Diplomatic Relations*, 163.

57 For Stanhope's illness see Görtz Archive: 121/6, Schulenburg's letter of 26 Oct. 1717; for Dubois' arguments to George, Melusine and Schulenburg see *ibid.*, letters of 22 Oct. 1717 and 22 Feb. 1718.

58 The regent, however, took a decision to support Great Britain if Philip V (as a consequence of Byng's orders in 1718) should declare war: Chevening MSS:88/7, Stair to Stanhope 26 July 1718 with assurance that Louis XV would in that case 'faire cause commun' with George. For the strength of British opposition to the

sacrifice of Gibraltar, even against an equivalent, see Stair, *Annals* II 145, Craggs to Stair 18 February 1720: 'And therefore tho' His Majesty were ever so much disposed to part with it [Gibraltar] it may well be doubted whether he would have it in his power so to do.'

59 The citation is from the original preamble to the peace project, printed in French by *Michael* II, 626 and in English translation by Williams, *Stanhope*, 314. For the negotiations that followed see Weber, *Quadruple Alliance*, chs. i and ii; Baraudon, *Savoy*, livre 3; *Bourgeois* I, 241 ff.; *Michael* I, 787 ff.; *Ö.S.*, *England* I, 352 ff.

60 Chevening MSS: 81/8, Stanhope to Stair, 1 February 1717/18. For the secret English commitment referred to by Stanhope see Martin, *Spain and Italy*, 407–11.

61 Görtz Archive: 121/6, Schulenburg's letter of 22 Feb. 1718.

62 Massini, *Schaub*, 20–27 (based on Schaub's papers from the autumn of 1717, when he became Stanhope's secretary, until Stanhope's death).

63 Chevening MSS: 87/8, Stair to Stanhope, Paris, 7 July 1717, reporting assurances given, as ordered, to the regent.

64 Victor Amadeus signed on 8 Nov. 1718, while the Dutch resolution to sign was not taken until 16 Dec. 1719 (repeated 31 Jan. 1720) and was then not accepted by Great Britain: Hatton, *Diplomatic Relations*, 166–74, 176–205.

65 Williams, *Stanhope*, 284–85.

66 For Schaub's participation in the conferences see Chevening MSS: 81/8, Stanhope to Stair, 23 Jan. 1717/18; cp. *ibid.*, Dubois to Schaub, London 1 March 1718, that the latter's task was to convince Charles VI and prince Eugène of the merits of 'the plan'.

67 Chevening MSS: 83/17, George's correspondence (copies and originals) with the regent between 1716 and 1719; cp. Windsor, R.A.: Geo Add. MSS I/25, George's letter (in his own hand) to the regent of 21 Jan. 1718, assuring him that he can have 'une foy entière' in what Schaub shall tell him 'de ma part'. The clinching proof that George was in control throughout the foreign policy negotiations also comes from the Chevening MSS: 84/11, George's orders to Stanhope via

Robethon (of 3 and 4 Jan. 1720 at a time when the secretary of state was not in London) on what action to take both in Italian affairs and in those of the North.

68 Bothmer, *Q.A.*, passim.

69 Görtz Archive: 121/6, e.g. Schulenburg's letters of 28 Dec. 1717, 31 March, 3, 15 and 18 Apr. 1718. In the event George had to stay at his post and Schulenburg, who had permission to visit his family in Germany, followed events closely from Emden (see e.g. his letters of 1, 11, 18, 28 Aug. and 15 Sept. 1718).

70 Gibbs, *Quadruple Alliance*, 293 for Walpole's warning; for the court's relief at supply see Görtz Archive: 121/6, Schulenburg's letter of 31 March 1718 (for worry see *ibid.*, letters of 26 Oct. and 19 Nov. 1717).

71 Gibbs, *Quadruple Alliance*, 296 ff.

72 Williams, *Stanhope*, 302.

73 For Byng's orders of 26 May and 7 Aug. see T.C. [Thomas Corbett], *Account of the Expedition of the British Fleet to Sicily* (3rd ed. 1739, 91 ff.), and for his account of the Passaro incident *HMC, Polwarth MSS* I, 587–89; cp. for context Williams, *Stanhope*, 302 ff.

74 The answer is printed (from the Chevening MSS) *ibid.*, 452 dated the Escurial, 15 July 1718; it was signed by Alberoni and began 'Sa Majesté Catholique m'a fait l'honneur de me dire que . . .'

75 The fullest account of Stanhope's Madrid mission is in Williams, *Stanhope*, 306–08, with quotations also from *The History of Alberoni* (anon., published in Genoa in 1719 and translated into English the same year), a pamphlet which gives Alberoni's side of the story.

76 According to this convention the final prolongation of grace for the Italian expectancies was to run from not later than 15 Oct. 1719 until not later than 25 Jan. 1720: Hatton, *Diplomatic Relations*, 197. For the war in Spain see Williams, *Stanhope*, 329 ff.

77 Görtz Archive: 121/6, Schulenburg's letter from Emden of 11 Aug. 1718.

78 *Baraudon*, 318 ff.

79 Hatton, *Diplomatic Relations*, 176 ff.

80 Robethon to Polwarth 4 July 1719: *HMC Polwarth MSS* II, 1976–98; Hatton, *Diplomatic Relations*, 198–205.

81 Hatton, *Louis XIV and Fellow Monarchs* (London ed.), 39.

82 Hatton, *War and Peace*, 21 ff.; Hatton, *Europe in the Age of Louis XIV*, 208–09.

83 Görtz Archive: 121/6, Schulenburg's letter from Emden of 11 Aug. 1718.

84 Hatton, *Diplomatic Relations*, 173–75.

85 *Ibid.*, 203–05.

86 It is necessary to stress this, since modern Russian historians (Nikoforov, Feigina), tend to underestimate the importance of favourable conjunctures in tsar Peter's success. The tsar and George both used their opportunities well, but both also benefited from circumstances which they themselves had not been in a position to influence.

87 *HMC, Stuart MSS* VII, 189 ff.: Jerningham's letters of Aug. 1718; *Feigina*, 325; Hatton, *Charles XII*, 459.

88 For Jefferyes' mission (he left London on 15 Oct. 1718) see Hatton, *Jefferyes*, 26 and his instructions and dispatches in *Sbornik*, vol. 61, 451 ff. In the event Norris did not sail to meet the tsar, his instructions reaching him after he had already left the Baltic: *BDR*, Russia entry; for the negotiations with Augustus II and Charles VI, see *Mediger* I, 399 ff.

89 Hatton, *Charles XII*, 461.

90 *Ibid.*, 474–77, 485–86.

91 *Ibid.*, 475.

92 *Ibid.*, 483–84.

93 *Ibid.*, 479; *Bidrag, SNKH*, 180 ff.

94 For the alliance of 5 Jan. 1719 see Sörensson, *KFÅ* 1929; *Mediger* I, 410 ff., and McKay, *North 1718–1719*.

95 For the operational plan envisaged against tsar Peter, dated Hanover 12 Nov. 1719, see B.M., Add. MSS 37385, Whitworth's private letter to Townshend of 16/27 July 1721.

96 Cited by Williams, *Stanhope*, 377.

97 The most balanced account of the 'three villages' issue is by *Mediger* I, 419–20: the Prussian king had undertaken in his Hanover treaty of 1715 to hand over the documents on which he based his claim (see my text page 95), but had failed to do so.

98 For Bernstorff's prediction see his letter to Saint Saphorin of 15 Feb. 1719 cited by *Michael* II, 489.

99 Williams, *Stanhope*, 343 for the 'sharp

practice' judgment. The Prussian treaties of 1719 with Britain and Hanover are printed in *Loewe*, 210–22. For the negotiations which led to the peace treaties between Sweden and Hanover and Sweden and Prussia (21 Jan. 1720) as well as the commercial treaty between Britain and Sweden (2 Feb. 1720) see J. Rosén, *Svensk Historia* (Stockholm 1967), 610 ff.; Chance, *Great Northern War*, 340 ff.; and, more briefly, Hatton, *Charles XII*, 511–13 and 622 note 5 (the advantages for Britain) and 623 (the peace with Poland which was not signed until 1731). For the Dano-Swedish peace treaty, and the Sleswig guarantees (the British of 23 July and the French of 20 Oct. 1720) see *ibid.*, 622, note 8.

100 For the strategic and tactical difficulties in 1720 see Aldridge, *Norris*; for the religious tension see *Naumann*, passim and Duchhardt, *Kaisertum*, 273 ff.; for the genuineness (which has been doubted) of British and Prussian planning and negotiations in July 1720 see *Mediger* I, 425 ff.

101 Bernstorff Archive: AG 70 contains papers and letters connected with the South Sea Company and Bernstorff's shares in it from Bothmer, Plessen and the banker Paul de la Tour from 28 June/9 July 1720 to 18/29 Apr. 1721; for the spectre of revolution see Bothmer's letter of 4/15 Oct. 1720.

102 Claude Sturgill, 'La Municipalité de Mende et la peste de 1721–1722', *Bulletin du centre d'études et de recherches littéraires et scientifiques de Mende* 1974, 12–15.

103 *BDI, Sweden* I, 146–50; cp. Williams, *Stanhope*, 427.

104 Görtz Archive: 121/6, Schulenburg's letter of 11 Apr. 1718.

105 See e.g. Stanhope to Newcastle from Hanover 27 Oct. 1719 (B.M., Add. MSS 32686): 'I may safely assure your Grace … the King will doe whatever shall be proposed to him.'

106 Hann.: Cal. Brief 11 E I, 213 (Bremen and Verden investitures), unsigned letter from Vienna of 15 Apr. 1722 (possibly by Saint-Saphorin) reporting that the writer had told prince Eugène 'un Roy de la Grande Bretagne trouveroit toujours les moyens de se conserver un lieu qu'il avoit si justement acquis, qu'oy qu'il n'en eut pas

les Investitures.' It is clear from the context of this and other (undated) letters in the same hand that this phrase had been authorized by George.

107 Charles VI needed the guarantee of Great Britain for the Italian settlement: only its naval power kept Philip V quiescent.

108 Bernstorff Archive: AG 29 vol. iv, Bothmer's letter from London of 17/28 Apr. 1724. Cp. *ibid.*: AG 63 vol. iv for Huldeberg's complaint of 17 Feb. 1720 that Saint-Saphorin objected to his dealing even with *Reich* matters; cp. his letters of 13 Sept. 1721 and 23 Jan. 1723.

109 Görtz Archive: 121/6, Schulenburg's letters of 1 and 11 Aug. 1718 from Emden.

110 *Ibid.*: 121/6, Schulenburg's letter of 20 July 1717 (after discussing with the king the prerogatives of the *seigneurs* in general).

111 For the accusations against the Germans see e.g. Craggs' private letter to Stair of 1 Oct. 1719 in which he relates that Bernstorff 'last year underhand gave out the king was against the peerage bill': Stair, *Annals* II, 399; cp. Williams, *Stanhope*, 409. For the attitude of the prince and princess of Wales see Windsor, R.A.: Geo Add. MSS 28, Caroline's letters to Mrs Clayton, especially nos. 49, 50, 51, 52, 54.

112 See Plumb, *Walpole* I, 283–84. For the peerage bill in general and its connection with relief of dissenters and university reform see Williams, *Stanhope*, 403–16 and Plumb, *Walpole* I, 266–82.

113 *Ibid.*, 264–65 printing extract from lady Cowper's letter to her husband of June 1718; for Walpole's knowing Hammerstein see Görtz Archive: 121/6, Schulenburg's letter of 6 Apr. 1717 reporting that he and Hammerstein had dined with Walpole the previous Sunday.

114 The newspaper accounts show that he went to bed in good health and died during the night; a note in *HMC, Portland MSS* II, 432 informs us that death was due to 'apoplexie'. He is buried in Westminster Abbey where the plate (which has since disappeared) on his coffin is copied in the Burial book of expenses: its Libri Baronis (*Freiherr*) proves, incidentally, that Johann Matthias' half-brother was not comprised (as Schmidt, *Schulenburgs* no. 750 assumes) in the promotion to *Reichsgraf*.

115 See e.g. Bernstorff Archive: AG 63, Huldeberg to Bernstorff, Vienna, 21 May 1720, reporting that Cadogan has told him how much Bernstorff had contributed with 'advice and management'.

116 Plumb, *Walpole* I, 208–85, listing three copies of the alleged letter. One of these, in *HMC, Portland* V, 594–96, has *ibid.*, 596–97, the unsigned letter of 7 May 1720 to 'Dear Sir' (possibly Edward Harley), which explains the reason for the delay in sending the copy. It also relates what the writer has heard of events since Sunderland had received the letter: when that minister, after the reconciliation, charged Walpole, Townshend and the duke of Devonshire with responsibility for the plot, they all denied it, though they freely admitted they had had a project in mind for overturning the Sunderland-Stanhope ministry; they also maintained that the Germans were now engaged in a new project 'deeper than this'.

117 The original of the alleged letter was searched for by Michael in the Vienna archives but was not found: see Michael, *Quadruple Alliance*, 303. For Bernstorff's cooperation with the Cowpers, see note 6 above.

118 *Carswell*, 128–31.

119 The address is printed in Chandler, *Proceedings* VI, 214–15.

Chapter IX: Peace, its problems and achievements

While this chapter is fundamentally based on new material from the State Paper Domestic, Regencies volumes, the several correspondences of the Bernstorff Archive, and on a variety of documents from the Royal Archives at Windsor, it is also heavily indebted to the published works of other scholars. Older books, particularly on French diplomatic and political history (by Leclerq, Lémontey, Syveton, Dureng, Wilson), have retained their usefulness. More recent studies by Austrian, Danish, Spanish, Swedish and Russian historians on European issues have proved of great importance, notably those by Bagger, Berger, Drodtloff, and Wensheim. Of British scholars I have found Gibbs especially stimulating on the Hanover alliance, and I have benefited from talks with him and with my own present and former doc-

toral students (David Aldridge, Peter Barber, Hugh Dunthorne, Edward Gregg, Derek McKay, Stewart Oakley, Hamish Scott and L. B. Smith) on a variety of points connected with British relations to Europe. For the South Sea bubble Carswell's book and Dickinson, *Financial Revolution*, have been a great help. For British affairs in general the biographies by Plumb, Browning and Bennett have been most useful, as have works dealing with particular topics, such as Fisher's on Anglo-Portuguese trade and Naylor on the peerage bill, which brought significant newspaper articles by Steele and Addison to my attention. In connection with the latter bill, studies relating to the Anglican church and its bishops, to dissenters and to the universities and education in a wide sense, have proved important.

1 Chandler, *Proceedings* vol. VI, 200.

2 The king naturally left the details to those who knew the interests of specific manufactures and trades best, but did not hesitate to give advice. A typical example is in Stanhope's letter to Craggs from Hanover 22 May 1719, on two Russian memorials. He reports: 'As they wholly relate to the British Trade, his Majesty leaves it to the Lords Justices to make what answer they shall think proper to them, tho' it is his opinion that the more steady and vigorous their Answer is, the better effect it will have touching the Freedom and Liberty of our Commerce in those parts' (P.R.O., SPD Regencies 43 vol. 2).

3 P.R.O., SPD Regencies 43 vol. 4, letter of 28 July 1723; cp. *ibid.*, Townshend's letter of 8 Sept. 1723: 'I must again repeat to you that nothing will gain the King's heart more than the striking out of some good Plan for the benefit of Trade and Credit.'

4 For such plans in general see *Püster*, 155 ff. There are many references to George's personal interest and orders to surveyors, etc., in unpublished correspondence, e.g. B.M., Add. MSS 37387, Tilson's letter of 5 Dec. 1721 from Whitehall and Whitworth's answer of 16/27 Dec. 1721; and P.R.O., SPD Regencies 43 vol. 5, Tilson's letter to Delafaye from Hanover of 26 Oct./6 Nov. 1723.

5 Plumb, *Walpole* I, 246 ff.

6 *Carswell*, 194 ff.

7 For one example of capital going out

(£40,000 of it coming from Chandos) see Ragnhild Hatton, 'John Drummond of Quarrel', *The Scottish Genealogist* 1970, 9, based on Scottish Record Office, Abercairney MSS: 487.

8 For the growing economic prosperity and initiative of the Spaniards overseas see John Lynch, *Spain under the Habsburgs* II (Oxford 1969), 160 ff., 194 ff.

9 Fisher, *Portugal Trade*, 92 ff.

10 The mood of the English after the war with Spain is shown by two letters from Craggs to Stair of 18 Feb. 1720: the one in French – so that it might be read by the regent – argues, firstly, that the war had rendered null and void whatever promises had been made regarding Gibraltar before December 1718, and, secondly, that the nation was now clamouring for advantages to be gained at the peacemaking; the other letter (for Stair's eyes alone) stresses that 'tho'' his Majesty were ever so much disposed to part with it [Gibraltar], it may be doubted whether he would have it in his powers to do so' (Stair, *Annals* II, 413–16, 145). For Anglo-Spanish tension over trade matters, see Gibbs, *Quadruple Alliance*, 296 ff.

11 *MacLachlan*, 44–76; *Carswell*, 65 ff.

12 For the most comprehensive accounts of the South Sea Company and the speculations that resulted in the bubble bursting, see Plumb, *Walpole* I, 295 ff.; *Carswell*, passim; and, from the financial point of view the most complete, Dickson, *Financial Revolution*, 90–109. I have also benefited from the unpublished London M.A. thesis (1934) by Eric Wagstaff, 'The Political Aspects of the South Sea Bubble'.

13 Evelyn MSS: journal entries for 17 Feb., 3, 7, 11, 17 March 1719/20; 28, 29 March, 15, 29 Apr. 1720. For his decision not to take up the third subscription *ibid.*: entry for 16 June 1720, and for a desire to sell but persuaded otherwise, 8 July 1720.

14 Evelyn successfully used lord Harcourt as a go-between for the second subscription (journal entry for 15 Apr. 1720). Cp. my text pages 253–54 for the difficulty Bernstorff's banker had in obtaining stock for him for the last two subscriptions.

15 Of late investors, apart from Evelyn, we can note Robert Molesworth, who borrowed £2,000 and found to his horror that the shares fell two days after he had

secured them: *HMC, Various* VIII, 150, letter to his son John 20 Oct. 1722 (in a summary of his 1720 experiences).

16 See *Carswell*, 216–17, 229–31 (Sunderland), 115, 217, 231 (Craggs), 217, 224–25, 240 (Aislabie), 212, 217, 229, 232, 240 (Charles Stanhope); and, more generally, Dickson, *Financial Revolution*, 109–11, 171 ff.

17 *Carswell*, 115, 128–29, 231, 240. Note that Carswell and Dickson name Sophia Charlotte 'countess von Platen' or 'Madame von Platen', based on *JHC* XIX, 426–28 (though Carswell correctly identifies her in the index as Platen, Sophia Charlotte Kielmansegg, Countess von). The contemporary use of Sophia Charlotte's maiden name in the period of her widowhood from 1717 to her naturalization and creation as countess of Leinster in the Irish peerage (1721) and countess of Darlington (1722) is curious: it may have come into use because of its higher rank, since strictly speaking she was Freiin von Kielmansegg. To avoid confusion with her sister-in-law I have in my text, when touching on her connection with the South Sea Company, used, a little prematurely, the Darlington title (a contemporary was indeed misled: *HMC, Portland MSS* V, 615, Thomas Harley to the earl of Oxford 17 Feb. 1720/21).

18 *Carswell*, 126.

19 For a categorical statement that George received 'a large sum' from the company see Redman, *Hanover*, 57; for a surmise that he did so see *Carswell*, 126. The real state of affairs can be studied in Windsor, R.A.: 52538–52548 in papers which were presented to George II on 23 Aug. 1742 by the son of Aislabie, to justify his father: 'making him speak as from the grave'.

20 For the belief that George made 'a very tidy profit', see e.g. Trench, *George II*, 100. The true state of affairs, deduced from the Windsor papers 52841–47, is confirmed by a memorandum in Robert Walpole's own hand dated 16 Sept. 1721 in which he notes that George had told him that tallies were bought for £35,950, but that for the rest of the £106,400 Mr Aislabie was (under his own signature) accountable to the king 'for ye South Sea stock and ye money paid to ye third Subscription': Cholmondeley (Houghton) Papers 36 a/1. *Ibid.* a/2 con-

sists of the copies made from George I's originals by Walpole (at the king's request on 16 Sept. 1721) of the receipt of 13 June 1720 for the £106,400 paid by Robert Knight and the reallocation of that sum on 16 June 1720.

21 Windsor, R.A.: 52844, copy of the duchess of Kendal's letter of 27 Sept. NS 1720, marked rec. 29 Sept. OS.

22 *Ibid.*: 52538–40, Aislabie's memorandum and 52837, William Aislabie's letter of 23 Aug. 1742.

23 Görtz Archive: 121/2, drafts of 30 Aug. 1720 and 21 Feb. 1721 to Johann Matthias von der Schulenburg.

24 For the contemporary belief see Bernstorff Archive: AG 70, Plessen's letter from London of 17/28 March 1721: cp. quotation from this letter in my text pages 254–55.

25 P.R.O., Probate: Robethon's will of 1721/22.

26 Bernstorff Archive: AG 70, Plessen's letters of 12/23 July, 2/13 Aug. and 24 Aug./3 Sept. 1720.

27 *Ibid.*, Plessen's letters of 5/16, 8/19, 12/23 July and 2/13 Aug. 1720; the newsletter in French of 9/20 Sept. is enclosed with Bothmer's letter of that date.

28 *Ibid.*, de la Tour's letters of 27 Sept. and 18 Oct. 1720; Plessen's letters of 16/27 Sept. and 20 Sept./1 Oct. 1720.

29 *Ibid.*, Bothmer's letter of 4/15 Oct. 1720.

30 For George's concern see P.R.O., SPD Regencies 43 vol. 3, Stanhope's letters to Delafaye 1, 8 and 18 Oct. 1720 from Hanover; for the eleven-days' delay at Helvoetsluys see Fabrice, *Memoiren*, 135–36.

31 Bernstorff Archive: AG 70, Plessen's letter of 17/28 March 1720.

32 I owe this information to Peter Barber. In public the British government insisted on its desire to have Knight brought to justice: see Hatton, *Diplomatic Relations*, 218, for Cadogan asking for Dutch help once Knight had escaped from his prison in the castle of Antwerp.

33 This appeal, via the French diplomat Destouches, came after it was known that Knight had fled to France: see *Carswell*, 266.

34 For Stanhope's illness and death see *JHL* XXI, 417–18 and *Parl. History* VII, 705–06. Contemporaries noted down Stanhope's exchange of words with Wharton: e.g.

Evelyn MSS, journal entry for 5 Feb. 1720/21.

35 See Windsor R. A.: Wardrobe acount volume for Stanhope being issued on 29 Sept. with all the appurtenances (cloth of state and state bible among them) as ambassador to the congress of Cambrai. See also Stanhope asking that his wife's advice should be taken on the ambassadorial plate: his letter to Delafaye of 7 Sept. 1720 in P.R.O., SPD Regencies 43 vol. 3.

36 My quotation is from B.M., Add. MSS 47209, Percival to Charles Dering, 17 Feb. 1720/21. Cp. for George I's grief Williams, *Stanhope*, 442 and Newman, *Stanhopes*, 99.

37 *House of Commons, 1715–54* II: entries for Sir Joseph Jekyll and Robert Molesworth based on unpublished Stuart MSS. A third member, William Sloper (like these two a member of the committee of inquiry and strongly opposed to the ministry), also abstained, though in his case no evidence has come to light which indicates intervention by George. Since the Commons found Charles Stanhope not guilty by three votes only, these three abstentions created a sensation. See e.g. *HMC, Various* VIII, 300, letter to John Molesworth of 2 March OS 1721.

38 Bernstorff Archive: AG 70, Plessen's letter 17/28 March 1721.

39 Plumb, *Walpole* I, 325 ff.

40 Evelyn MSS: journal entry for 3 Apr. 1721.

41 For the most authoritative account of this period see Bennett, *Atterbury*, passim. An interesting newsletter of 22 May 1722 was sent to John Molesworth, who was accredited to several Italian courts 1720–25. He was one of the diplomats who had informed Whitehall of the plot to kill the king. The newsletter lists the countermeasures taken to safeguard George; among them was the closure of the backstairs in St James's Palace to visitors: *HMC, Various* VIII, 342. For Walpole's spying and the use he made of it see Plumb, Walpole II, 40 ff.

42 *House of Commons, 1715–54* I: entry for Charles Caesar; and Fritz, *Jacobitism* (thesis), using Caesar's papers from 1716 onwards.

43 For economic policy in general see Plumb, *Walpole* II, 234 ff., based largely on unpublished material, Brisco's study having proved misleading. Dickson, *Financial Revo-*

lution, is also critical of Brisco's work but values Walpole's initiatives in economic and financial matters more highly than Plumb. Evelyn, after his appointment in 1721, took a keen interest in the customs; see e.g. his brief but good summary of the changes in Evelyn MSS: journal entry of 8 Jan. 1721/22.

44 For the 1724 Baltic squadron see the chapter in Aldridge, *Norris*.

45 Walpole, though he had much influence on ecclesiastical appointments, working closely with Gibson, bishop of London, found even here that the king kept a watchful eye: many examples of this in P.R.O., SPD Regencies 43.

46 See Swift, *Correspondence* III, 181, letter from Pope of 16 Nov. 1726. Kramnick, *Bolingbroke*, 140 ff. and Skinner, *passim*, have shown that the concerted attacks on Robert Walpole belong to the next reign.

47 See e.g. P.R.O., SPD Regencies 43 vol. 4: Bolingbroke to Townshend 28 June 1723 and 43 vol. 5: Bolingbroke's letter to the same of 17 Sept. 1723.

48 Anti-Hanoverian poems, most of them not in print, abound in a variety of manuscript collections in the B.M., and there are some also in the Portland Papers deposited in Nottingham University Library; the ditty cited is printed by Thompson, *Whigs and Hunters*, 200, from evidence of 4 Jan. 1725 by a tailor (William Preston).

49 Paulson, *Hogarth* I, 85 ff. has an excellent chapter on Thornhill (Hogarth's father-in-law) entitled 'The presence of Sir James Thornhill'.

50 Görtz Archive: 121/6, Schulenburg's letter of 11 Nov. 1718: for Benson's success see P.R.O., SPD Regencies 43 vol. 4: Tilson to Delafaye 18/29 June 1723, informing him that the forty pumps and five wheels of the Herrenhausen engine produced a water height of 120 feet for the big fountain. For George's early interest see his letter to Sophia of 15 Nov. [1704] (Hann.: 91, Kurfürstin Sophie, 19a) in which he light-heartedly links his belief in progress to news of a good English mining pump, hoping that it could be used to perfect the Herrenhausen fountains.

51 For Benson's period as surveyor-general see Colvin *et al.*, *The History of the King's Works* V, 59 ff.

52 For the paintings as rearranged by George I in the grand gallery see Evelyn MSS: entry of 11 Oct. 1729; cp. his entries of 8 May and 3 Sept. 1721 for the Kensington pictures in general. For the dyeing of curtains see Windsor R.A.: Wardrobe account volume (1724). For general information about the rebuilding of Kensington Palace see Colvin, *Royal Buildings*; Jourdan, *Kent*; Hudson, *Kensington Palace*; and Christopher Hussey's three articles in *Country Life* (1928) which are especially useful for the duchess of Kendal's apartments. For George's enjoyment of Kensington there is much evidence in Vanbrugh, *Works* IV: e.g. letter of 19 July 1722.

53 For Johann Matthias' walks with George I see Schulenburg, *Leben* II, 256: letter of 26 July 1726. For the gardens in general see Green, *Henry Wise*. George's failure to restart the Hanoverian opera after the customary year of discontinuation on his father's death was caused not only by the outbreak of the War of the Spanish Succession and his later preoccupation with the Great Northern War, but also (as Schnath, *Hannover* II, 392, has shown) by the fact that from 1698 the Osnabrück income which Ernst August had enjoyed, and from which he had defrayed the expenses of the Hanover opera, ceased.

54 See Kielmansegg, *Familien-Chronik*, 447 for the circumstances under which Handel obtained his post at Hanover. For Handel's London operas in the reigns of Anne and George I see the biographies by Deutsch (1955), Lang (1966), and Sadie (1968). For the Academy of Music and George's strong appreciation of opera see Fabrice, *Memoiren*, 129–33.

55 Görtz Archive: 121/6, Schulenburg's letter of 4 March 1718.

56 Paulson, *Hogarth* I, 111 ff. For the ecclesiastical opposition to masquerades and the king's support of them see Vanbrugh, *Works* IV, letter of 18 Feb. 1724.

57 Hatton, *Diplomatic Relations*, 221.

58 *Ibid.*, 250–57, the *Relation* printed from P.R.O., SPF Holland vol. 274 fols. 235–51.

59 For the Ostend Company during George I's reign see Huisman's indispensable study.

60 For the early agitation see Schrijver, *Bergeyck*, 155 ff.

61 The Ostend Company caught the imagination of Charles VI, who, from his ten years in Spain, had become interested in trade and shipping; see Stoye, *Charles VI* for innovations in the early years of his reign.

62 Jacobites were also active in promoting the Ostend Company; Fritz, *Jacobitism* (thesis), 33 ff.

63 The Dutch were more alarmed by the Ostend Company than the English: for their pamphlets against it see Gibbs, *Hanover Alliance*, 264 note 5 in collected *EHR* volume. Robert Walpole kept an early warning that the company 'ought to be ruined' among his papers: Cholmondeley (Houghton) MSS, Corr. 1147, extract from a letter to Bothmer by Renard of Amsterdam dated 7 July 1724. For the Vienna treaties of 1725 see Armstrong, *Elisabeth Farnese*, 169 ff.; Arneth, *Eugen* III, 170 ff.; Syveton, *Ripperda*, 52 ff.; *Baudrillart* III, 130 ff.; *Dureng*, 235 ff.; and *Michael* III, 410 ff.

64 See, for a recent valuable treatment of Russian policies, *Bagger*, ch. 7, which covers the period 1724–32. Cp., briefly, for the Swedish party in favour of the duke of Holstein-Gottorp, Ragnhild Hatton, *New Cambridge Modern History* VII (1957), 355 ff. For George's desire to do something for the duke see B.M., Add. MSS 37377, extract of letter from Stanhope to Carteret of 17 Nov. 1719.

65 For Townshend's expression see P.R.O., SPD Regencies 43 vol 8: letter to Poyntz 22 Oct./2 Nov. 1725.

66 Bernstorff Archive: AG 29 vol. iv, Bothmer's letter, marked secret, of 14/25 April 1725, conveying Charles VI's terms as proposed by Starhemberg to Bothmer and Townshend, and reporting their answers.

67 See ch. VIII note 106 above.

68 Bernstorff Archive: AG 29 vol. iv, Bothmer's letter of 14/25 Apr. 1724; cp. letter of 17/28 Apr. 1724 in which Bothmer expresses his regret that the opportunity to obtain speedy investitures for Bremen and Verden will not be taken. For the desire to obtain Hadeln and negotiations on this issue see *ibid*: AG 63 vol. ii, Huldeberg's letters of 9 Jan. 1715, 24 Apr. 1717; vol. iv, 17 Feb., 15 and 29 May, 27 July and 31 Aug. 1720. Huldeberg had authorization to give liberal gratifications for the Hadeln investiture (as for those of Bremen and Verden), but Hanoverian efforts were not crowned with success in George I's reign.

69 P.R.O., SPD Regencies 43 vol. 5: Townshend to Robert Walpole 7/18 Oct. 1723. His joy at the Prussian alliance is reminiscent of Stanhope's in 1719 as expressed in his letter to Newcastle of 27 Oct. 1719: B.M., Add. MSS 32686 fol. 156.

70 For Townshend's approval of the gratifications see the letter of 7/18 Oct. 1723 cited in note 69 above; for the present of politeness to Pecquet in 1718, a ring (given by queen Anne to lady Masham who had subsequently sold it) which 'His Majesty desires him to wear for his sake, as a small token of His Majesty's sense of the great pains and trouble he has had in all this affair', see Chevening MSS: 86/6, Craggs to Stanhope and Stair 10 July 1718 and Craggs to Stanhope 17 July 1718.

71 See also Görtz Archive: 121/4, Johann Matthias von der Schulenburg's letter of 10 June 1724, 'Le Congres de Cambrai paroit encore absent, et au lieu d'une paix il pourroit bien nous produire une guerre.' Historians have until recently judged these congresses useless: see e.g. Williams, *Stanhope* 185; but for more positive views see the article by J. H. Plumb, 'In Defence of Diplomacy', *The Spectator*, 11 Apr. 1969; Hatton, *Europe*, 209; and Hatton, *War and Peace*, 22.

72 There is a good treatment of the congress, as seen from the Austrian point of view, in Drodtloff's work on Pentenrriedter, 133 ff. Starkey's brief article in *RHD* 1971 on the British side is very slight; and the rich material in the Whitworth and Polwarth papers will be further exploited by Peter Barber in his study of the congress.

73 For the considerations which led to the marriage see Paul de Raynal, *Le Mariage d'un Roi, 1721–1725* (Paris 1887), and Wilson, *Fleury*, 29 ff.

74 For the Dutch position (they finally acceded on 9 Aug. 1726) see P.R.O., SPD Regencies 43 vol. 7, Townshend to Horatio Walpole 23 Aug./3 Sept. 1725; cp. Goslinga, *Slingelandt*, 95 ff., and G. J. Rive, *Schets der staatkundige betrekkingen tusschen de Republiek der Vereenigde Nederlanden en het koningrijk*

Pruissen, 1701–1767 (Amsterdam 1873), *passim*. For the religious issues see *Naumann*, 31 ff., and *Recueil, Diète Germanique*, ed. B. Auerbach (Paris 1912), 127 ff. For the Hanover Alliance in general see Chance, *Hanover Alliance*, and Gibbs, *Hanover Alliance*; and for its text Rousset II, 189 ff. For the accession of Sweden and Denmark in 1727 see Ragnhild Hatton, *New Cambridge Modern History* VII (1957), 347, 355.

75 This has been shown in the perceptive study by Gibbs, *Hanover Alliance*, *passim*.

76 *Parl. History* VII, 492, cited by Williams, *Whig Supremacy*, 188.

77 For the origins of the de Vrillière affair see my text pages 137–38.

78 See Coxe, *Horatio Walpole* I, 132 ff. For George I's permission that Horatio Walpole should investigate the role played by Schaub in Paris see B.M., Stowe MSS vol. 251, Townshend to Robert Walpole 24 Sept. 1713 marked 'Most secret'. For the ensuing struggle and the changes that followed the Townshend-Walpole victory see Plumb, *Walpole* II, 74 ff.; Browning, *Newcastle*, 25 ff.; Kelch, *Newcastle*, 69 ff.; and J. B. Owen, *The Rise of the Pelhams* (1957), 46 ff. for Henry Pelham rising with his brother.

79 Craggs to Stair 31 March 1719: Stair, *Annals* II, 105–06.

80 For George I's continued friendly relations with Carteret see Ballantyne, *Carteret*, 98, 101; and for Carteret's six years of service in Ireland *ibid.*, 89 ff. and Williams, *Carteret and Newcastle*, 75 ff.

81 His initiatives in all these matters are amply illustrated in P.R.O., SPD Regencies 43 for the whole time he spent outside Britain. For policy decisions in 1725 see vols. 7 and 8: e.g. vol. 7, Townshend's letter to Newcastle of 31 Aug./11 Sept. on relations with Portugal; of 3/14 Sept. for insistence not only that Roxburghe shall have a pension but that he shall be told of the king's 'regard and tenderness' for him; vol. 8, of 31 Nov./11 Dec. on three Russian ships that are wintering in Ireland; and Townshend to Poyntz 22 Oct./2 Nov. on relations with the Russian tsaritsa and the duke of Holstein-Gottorp.

82 For growing tension between Walpole and

Townshend see Plumb, *Walpole* II, 132 ff.; for Bernstorff's continued influence see Sykes, *Wake* II, 70 ff. quoting letters of May 1720 to July 1721; and P.R.O., SPD Regencies 43 vol. 4: Tilson to Robert Walpole of 26 June/7 July 1723; for Bernstorff's memorandum to George I dated 6 Nov. 1723, see Hann.: Cal. Brief 11 EI, 3.

83 Gibbs, *Hanover Alliance*, 280 ff. in collected *EHR* volume.

84 B.M., Add. MSS 32744, Newcastle to Horatio Walpole 19/30 Nov. 1725.

85 For Friedrich Wilhelm moving closer to Charles VI in 1726 see Berger's study, which covers 1716 to 1730.

86 I am indebted for information about Townshend's general bellicosity to Hugh Dunthorne, whose doctoral thesis 'The Alliance of the Maritime Powers 1721–1740' will deal with Townshend's energetic contingency plans for war in 1726; for George's attitude to the Prussian marriage negotiations see my text pages 280–81 and ch. X, note 4.

87 For the risk to Hanover in 1726–27 see Gibbs, *Hanover Alliance* (*EHR* collected ed.), 281, 284 and Gibbs, *Parliament*, 330 note 1; for the situation in the 1740s and 1750s see *Mandrou*, 320 ff.

88 Pelham cited from *Boyer* XXXI, 204 in Gibbs, *Hanover Alliance* (*EHR* collected ed.), 284.

89 Fleury's mediation (for which see Wilson, *Fleury*, 164–69) was essential, given Spain's indignation at Hosier's blockade of the Spanish-American coast and islands (well explained in *Richmond*, 382 ff.) and the impasse reached in Anglo-Austrian relations: accusations in George's speech from the throne that Charles VI gave support to the Pretender provoked the publication of an Austrian memorial in London deemed offensive enough to cause the expulsion from Britain of Palm, the emperor's diplomatic representative. The peace preliminaries are printed in *Ö.S. England* I, 457–64, with a good introduction by the editor. For the Aix-la-Chapelle meeting place see P.R.O., SPD Regencies 43 vol. 9, Townshend's letter to Newcastle from The Hague 8/19 June 1727.

Chapter X: Death of George I

The first part of this chapter is based on Fabrice's memoirs and on two letters which he wrote to George II in June 1727 printed with the *Memoiren* by R. Grieser. The 'Balance sheet' draws on a wide variety of material, both unpublished and published, in which I have attempted a summing-up of George as a ruler of the Early Enlightenment, influenced by the intellectual climate of the age, and also of George as a person. I was tempted, because of the abundant documentation, to extend this chapter but resisted temptation in order to preserve the balance of a relatively brief biography. Much material has been destroyed, by George himself, by his son and successor, by request of those who had written letters to him (e.g. his daughter, the queen of Prussia), and by damage to Hanover archives during the Second World War. More will certainly be learnt about George as the ruler of Hanover when the third volume of Schnath's *Geschichte Hannovers* is published, at least up to 1714 which is the terminal date for Professor Schnath's great venture. There is other material that ought to be examined for the post-1714 period both in Hanover and in Britain: further analysis of the Schatullrechnungsbeläge, of entries for expenditure of many kinds in the treasury collections of the Public Record Office and in various Additional Manuscript volumes of the British Museum, and in the Sunderland treasury papers (now with the Blenheim archive in the British Museum) might prove worth while.

I derived stimulus, as well as information, from the specialist works and the biographies I read to throw light on George I's cultural interests and musical tastes. To walk round Kensington Palace and its gardens with George and his family in mind, and to be permitted to view the various courts and rooms he built or redecorated was a special delight, as were the small discoveries I made through my own researches which added to our knowledge of the physical surroundings of the king and court. The two that pleased me most were the finely drawn and coloured design which I came across in the Wardrobe account volume at Windsor for Vanbrugh's tabard as Clarenceaux king of arms in George I's reign, showing – for the first time – the Saxon horse; and the comment which Evelyn penned in his journal when he noticed the coal fires at court in the next reign (entry of 22 Nov. 1728): in George I's time the king had insisted on wood fires in all his palaces.

1   See e.g. Jordan, *Sophia Dorothea*, 267 and 271–73; and Trench, *George II*, 127. Cp. Young, *Poor Fred*, 27 for misinformation about the place and cause of death: 'George had a happy end on his return to Herrenhausen and Madame von Platen, as a result of his first repast of gherkins and pickled herring.'

2   For Maximilian suffering a serious stroke (in Vienna in 1725) see Bernstorff Archive: AG 63 vol. iv, Huldeberg's letters of 3 and 7 Feb. 1725.

3   The relaxation of tension was in part due to the fact that Friedrich Wilhelm, in his alliance with Russia of 10/21 Aug. 1726, went no further than a promise of strict neutrality if Russia and Austria should use force to restore the duke of Holstein-Gottorp: *Bagger*, 233–35.

4   From Wilhelmine's *Mémoires*, 67 ff., 73ff., it is clear that in 1725 George had told his daughter that she must be patient a while before the first half of the plan (the match between Frederick and Wilhelmine, who were now of a suitable age to marry) could be realized. Interestingly, he used the excuse that he 'needed time to inform parliament'. But before starting his journey in 1727 George let Sophia Dorothea know that 'everything was now in order' and that the marriage would be solemnized in Hanover during his stay. On the memoir evidence the disappointment of Sophia Dorothea and Wilhelmine was intense; and Frederick's biographers have stressed both his keenness on the match and his prolonged if unsuccessful efforts, after George I's death, to obtain permission from his father to marry Wilhelmine.

5   The fullest account of the king's last journey and illness is in Fabrice, *Memoiren*, 146–49 and in his letters to George II of 22 June NS and 12/23 June 1727 printed *ibid.*, 150–53; cp. P.R.O., SPD Regencies 43 vol. 9: 'Documents concerning the King's last journey and death June 8/19 – 13/24 1727.' For George's feeling for Osnabrück see Sophia, *Letters to the raugravines*: to Louise 1 Jan. 1708: George recognized 'everything' in the Schloss on

his visit in 1707, the first since the family's move to Hanover.

6 Fabrice, *Memoiren*, 149. For Townshend's movements see also his letters to Newcastle of 8/19 June 1727 (from the Hague) and of 11/22 June (from Bentheim): P.R.O., SPD Regencies 43, vol. 9.

7 Fabrice, *Memoiren*, 150 ff. For his disappointment that Johann Ludwig was not appointed a *Geh. Rat* in the new reign, see *ibid.*, 153, letter from Johann Matthias von der Schulenburg of 12 March 1978.

8 Fabrice, *Memoiren*, 148–49.

9 *Ibid.*, 151.

10 Schaumburg-Lippe, *Letters*: 14/25 July 1727 from St James's.

11 After 1714 Frederick had never seen his parents, but had been much in his grandfather's company during all George I's visits to Hanover. The king had supervised his education; and it is typical of their relationship that when George in 1725 hoped to have his grandson inoculated against smallpox he left the decision to Frederick, since he was 'now of an age to make his own decision'. He let him know, however, of the successful inoculation of two of his sisters (Anne had suffered a relatively light attack of smallpox in 1722 and therefore needed no inoculation).

12 Caroline, now queen, acknowledged in a letter dated Kensington 23 June OS 1727 Melusine's strong attachment to George: Schulenburg, *Leben* II, 290; for Melusine's grief see Schaumburg-Lippe, *Letters*: 2/13 Apr. 1728; for her house at Twickenham see *Michael* II, 513 and *Victoria County History* III: *Middlesex* (1962), 91–92.

13 Horace Walpole, *Memoirs* III, 3/5 has 'a large bird, I forget what sort'. For the east European folklore on the raven see Galina von Meck, *As I remember them* (1973), 369. For Handel's frequent use of birdsong themes see Lang, *Handel*, 266–67.

14 Görtz Archive: 121/6, Schulenburg's letter of 18 Jan. 1718; cp. his letter of 2 July 1717.

15 Cp. the similar obsession of the Swedish king Charles XII who was fourteen years old at the time of his father's death: Hatton, *Charles XII*, 522.

16 For this tradition see Hatton, *Louis and Fellow Monarchs* (London ed.), 21 ff. The frustration suffered in the post-George II generations is well documented: for Freder-

ick in 1743, see e.g. Walters, *Frederick*, 185–86; for George III as prince of Wales in 1759 see e.g. Ayling, *George the Third*, 51; and for George IV when prince of Wales see e.g. C. Hibbert, *George IV as Prince of Wales 1762–1811* (1972), 117.

17 Macalpine and Hunter, *Mad Business*, 195 ff., 250 ff., discuss the incidence of porphyria transmitted via Elizabeth of Bohemia and Sophia. They are convinced that George III and 'all his children' had the illness, and surmise that George II and Frederick, prince of Wales, were sufferers as also were Friedrich Wilhelm I and several of his children by George's daughter, among them Wilhelmine and Friedrich (later *der Grosse*).

18 It has been reproduced, though without the key to all the figures, from a photograph in the Bomann Museum in Prüser, *Göhrde*, ill. no. 9. The full key to the numbered figures is painted at the bottom of the picture (and is printed in Millar, *Royal Collection*, no. 661). The painting is inscribed 'Göhrde anno 1725' and is now at Windsor Castle, having been sent to England from Hanover in 1819; however, Prüser, p. 69, has shown conclusively that the hunt in question took place in 1723. Unfortunately it does not reproduce well, but it might be mentioned that of the characters that appear in my text (apart from those mentioned on page 287) the following are represented: George's grandson prince Frederick; Hardenberg; Fabrice; 'Buckeburg', i.e. Schaumburg-Lippe, Gertrude's husband; Mehemet, Mustafa, and Jorry; 'Finsch' (Edward Finch, groom of the bedchamber) and 'Albemarle', called lord of the bedchamber, though gentleman of the bedchamber would be correct.

19 Sophia, *Letters to the raugravines*: to Louise 6 May 1709.

20 *Ibid.*: to Amalie 19 Dec. 1708.

21 A copy of this decision of 1 July 1718 is in B.M., Add. MSS 35886 fols. 398 ff.; and a report of the discussion on the issue in Windsor, R.A.: 53017. Schulenburg, in a letter of 18 Nov. 1718 (Görtz Archive: 121/6), surmised that this decision might bring back to the king's party at least some of those who had sided with the prince on this matter only.

22 Schnath, *A.B.*, *Sophie Dorothea*, 244. The

long-drawn legal tussle about her will (*ibid.*, 241–42) had no connection with George I.

23 Examples: a yearly pension of £1,600 to Addison when he had to leave his office as secretary of state (*House of Commons* I, 408); of £600 a year for life to Robethon when he was asked to retire (Görtz Archive: 121/6, Schulenburg's letter of 9 May 1719); provision was also made for Bernstorff after 1719; he was naturalized in Ireland and arrangements made so that he and his family could enjoy for a period of 31 years an annual pension of £2,500 on the Irish civil list: Friis, *The Bernstorffs* I, 9.

24 Campbell, *Lord Chancellors* IV, 70 ff. and Foss, *Judges* VIII, 47 ff.; the king's sympathy was well known in informed circles; see e.g. *HMC, Various* VIII, 382 and 387, letters to John Molesworth of 28 Jan. and 15 March 1724/25: 'It is hard to judge of his [Macclesfield's] fate as yet, although the Court love that man; we have seen guiltier men find out a back door'. It is worth noting that after Macclesfield had been found guilty George contributed to the fine imposed on him.

25 Görtz Archive: 125/8, letter from David de Vaux of 17 May 1724, and Görtz's draft answer 30 May 1724.

26 K.G., Schatullrechnungsbeläge for 1723: the debts amounted to £2,200.

27 *Ibid.*: passim for 1714–26.

28 His words are cited in my text page 255.

29 Görtz Archive: 121/6, Schulenburg's letter of 21 March 1719.

30 Sykes, *Wake* II, 80–88.

31 For the 'deal' element in peerage bill see Williams, *Stanhope*, 403–15.

32 For the position of the Catholics see the studies by Leys (1952) and Bossy (1975).

33 For the position of the Jews see the history by Hyamson of 1908 and the study by Perry of 1962; and, for the legal issues, Henriques' monograph of 1905.

34 For the Hoadley controversy see Williams, *Whig Supremacy*, 386 ff.; Bennett, *Kenneth*, 83 ff., 132 ff. The fact that Hoadley, bishop of Bangor, had expressed his latitudinarian views in a sermon (subsequently published 'by authority') preached before George I in March 1717, involved the king in some measure; Schulenburg notes specifically that the king was blamed for the prorogation of convocation (Görtz Archive: 121/6, letter of 12 May 1717).

35 Plans to reform the universities started early in George I's reign: see the interesting letter to Townshend in 1715 from Humphrey Prideaux: Prideaux, *Life*, 188 ff., discussing, at Townshend's suggestion, the situation in Oxford. By 11 March 1717, however, Schulenburg reports Townshend as no longer keen on tackling the university problem while George still desires reform (Görtz Archive: 121/6).

36 See Sykes, *Wake* II, 115 ff.

37 The documents between 1720 and 1725 dealing with the foundation of the professorships in modern history and modern languages are conveniently found in B.M., Add. MSS 5843 (Rev. W. Cole copies) fols. 255 ff. For the special efforts made to welcome and entertain the Oxford University delegation that came to London to give thanks for the establishment of the regius chair see the letters in *HMC, Portland MSS* VII, 389–90, from Dr William Stratford to Edward, Lord Harley of 12 and 17 Nov. 1724. He stressed that faction and parties were not mentioned and George I's speech was 'full of grace and favour'. For George's continued close interest in professorships see P.R.O., SPD Regencies 43 vol. 8; Townshend's letters to Newcastle of 22 Oct./2 Nov. and 8/19 Nov. 1725. For the French experiment see Keens-Soper's article, *ESR* 1972.

38 For the reforms and innovations in Hanover see the older histories of the electorate, most succinctly in Rothert, *Hannover*. A modern treatment can be expected in Schnath's continuation of his *Geschichte Hannovers*. The bronze plaque with the Herrenhausen instructions is still *in situ* at the garden entrance.

39 K.G., Schatullrechnungsbeläge between 1699 and 1714. George I was often presented with books, especially those dedicated to him, when he invariably made a present to the author; Motraye, for example, received a gift of £200. Among the many volumes dedicated to the king it is interesting to note Giacomo Leone's edition of Palladio: Rudolf Wittkower, *Palladio and English Palladianism* (1974).

40 For George's familiarity with the works of Molière, Corneille and Racine there is

evidence in his own letters to his mother and in his brother Ernst August's letters to Wendt; cp. also Wallbrecht, *Theatre*, 135 ff. For his partiality for and financial support of the French writer Bucquoy, a skilled conversationalist who had been brought to Hanover in 1711 by Johann Matthias von der Schulenburg, there is also evidence in Ernst August's letters and Sophia's correspondence: he was reckoned so much a favourite with George that Villiers, in a letter to Görtz of 8 July 1715 asked the king's pardon for having written a satire on the 'abbé Bucquo': Görtz Archive: 126/2.

41 For George's relationship with and presents to Voltaire from 1718 onwards see Theodore Besterman, *Voltaire* (1969), 79–82, 104, 110 ff. and Voltaire's 'Autobiography', printed, in English translation, *ibid.*, 548–49. I have come across an earlier reference, P.R.O., SPD Regencies 43 vol. 11: Stanhope to Townshend of 21 Aug. NS 1716, in which he conveys George I's request that Voltaire be assisted with money. For Voltaire being received by George at court during his stay and writing an ode in his honour see Ballantyne, *Voltaire*, 61 ff. George's donation of money to buy specific libraries for Cambridge University should also be noted: see e.g. *Wake* II, 132 for 600 guineas to buy the late bishop of Ely's library.

42 Anecdotes to this effect abound in the memoir literature; a much-quoted one is of George entering a house (without previous warning), noticing a picture of the Pretender, examining it closely and remarking politely and pleasantly on the strong Stuart family likeness, much to his host's relief.

43 B.M., Add. MSS 47028 fol. 156: letter to Charles Dering of 4 June 1716.

44 *Stevens*, 28 has reckoned out that during the reign of George I 'there were only thirty-six cases of people held to bail for libels'.

45 For these see the works of George and Wright. Some of these lampoons have been frequently reprinted, see e.g. Trench, *George II*, 155, 184, 187–89, 203, 205.

46 For the contemporary version see *Rubinstein*, 215:
The King of Great Britain was reckoned before,

The 'Head of the Church' by all
    Christian People,
But this brewer has added still one title
    more
To the rest, and has made him the 'Head
    of the Steeple'.

47 B.M., Add. MSS 47028 fol. 7, lord Percival's journal entry (undated) on current gossip about George's incognito visits to chocolate and coffee houses.

48 B.M., Add. MSS 47028 fol. 182, lord Percival's journal entry for 1 March 1717/18.

49 Ryder, *Diary*, 356, entry 30 Oct. 1716 for giving a servant a shilling to watch the ball at court; *ibid.*, 66, entry 1 Aug. 1715 for gate-crashing at George's annual accession celebrations.

50 K.G., Schatullrechnungsbeläge regularly lists sums after 1714 given to the poor, to poor students and similar. The highest sum given, £1,000 to 'poor prisoners', was on the occasion of George's first ceremonial dinner in the City: see *Verney Letters*, 19.

51 For British appreciation see P.R.O., SPD Regencies 43 vol. 3: Townshend to Robert Walpole 3/14 Sept. 1723, pointing out that the king's plan for a new port at the mouth of the Elbe was very useful 'not only to his dominions here, but also to the Trade of his Kingdoms'.

52 Thompson, *Whigs and Hunters*, passim, for poaching; for the criminal law see the works of Radzinowicz and of Beattie.

53 See Paulson, *Hogarth* I, 251–52.

54 For the churches see e.g. Young, *London Churches*, and Rudé, *Hanoverian London*, 100 ff.

55 For the London squares laid out during George I's reign see Hibbert, *London*, 113 ff., and Rudé, *Hanoverian London*, 13 ff. For Melusine's London houses see above, ch. VI note 37.

56 Davies, *German Thought and Culture*, 64 ff.

57 For the growth in the navy and improvement in naval administration in George's reign see *Baugh*, 495 ff. Though detailed work still remains to be done, much can be gathered from tables published in books dealing with the reign of queen Anne and on the navy in general.

58 For the countess see Schazmann, *The Bentincks*, 127 ff.

59 Both points have been made by *Mandrou*,

213 ff. and 328 ff.; Schaer, in his editorial work for the Schaumburg-Lippe *Letters*, has stressed the intellectual impact made by those, who like the countess, returned to Germany after the end of George I's reign.

60 For the history of the Canons statue see Gunnis, *Dictionary*, 70 ff.

61 This statue was unveiled in 1722 at Essex bridge in Dublin: see B.M., Add. MSS 47029 fol. 27, letter to lord Percival from Dublin 22 July 1722: 'On Thursday next the king's Equestrian statue is to be uncovered and exposed to view. The Several Companys will ride the fringes on that day and our Magistrates appear in their utmost magnificence. I hear 6 guineas are given for a floor to see the show.'

62 See Christopher Goodwin, 'Kent and the Eastern Gardens', *The History of Stowe* XIII, 266. A third surviving statue which I have not had the opportunity to see is at Hackwood Park, Northumberland, put up by the 2nd duke of Bolton, who had been made a knight of the Garter by George I in Dec. 1714. One, listed in Gunnis as 'still in the Royal Exchange', I have failed to gain access to and have therefore not been able to ascertain if it is from life. The Rysbrack bust in Christ Church by Hogarth is very fine and justly admired, but it should be noted that George did not sit for it: see W. G. Hiscock, *A Christ Church Miscellany* 1946, 83.

63 Albert van der Meer to Heinsius, from Frankfurt 30 March 1702: Heinsius, *Briefwisseling* I, 55.

Table I GEORGE'S BRUNSWICK-LÜNEBURG DESCENT

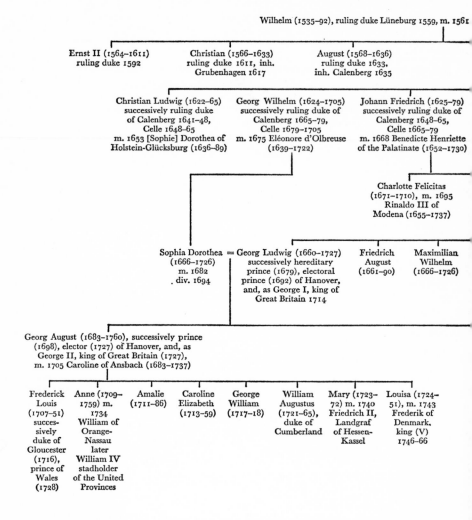

(Children who died in infancy and daughters of no political importance for this book have generally been omitted.)

Dorothea of Denmark (d. of Christian III) (1546–1617)

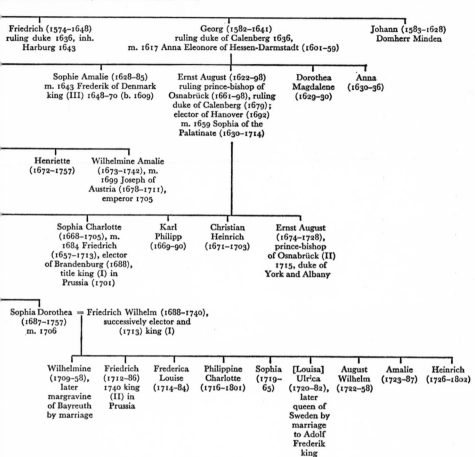

Friedrich (1574–1648) ruling duke 1636, inh. Harburg 1643

Georg (1582–1641) ruling duke of Calenberg 1636, m. 1617 Anna Eleonore of Hessen-Darmstadt (1601–59)

Johann (1583–1628) Domherr Minden

Sophie Amalie (1628–85) m. 1643 Frederik of Denmark king (III) 1648–70 (b. 1609)

Ernst August (1622–98) ruling prince-bishop of Osnabrück (1661–98), ruling duke of Calenberg (1679); elector of Hanover (1692) m. 1659 Sophia of the Palatinate (1630–1714)

Dorothea Magdalene (1629–30)

Anna (1630–36)

Henriette (1672–1757)

Wilhelmine Amalie (1673–1742), m. 1699 Joseph of Austria (1678–1711), emperor 1705

Sophia Charlotte (1668–1705), m. 1684 Friedrich (1657–1713), elector of Brandenburg (1688), title king (I) in Prussia (1701)

Karl Philipp (1669–90)

Christian Heinrich (1671–1703)

Ernst August (1674–1728), prince-bishop of Osnabrück (II) 1715, duke of York and Albany

Sophia Dorothea (1687–1757) m. 1706 = Friedrich Wilhelm (1688–1740), successively elector and (1713) king (I)

Wilhelmine (1709–58), later margravine of Bayreuth by marriage

Friedrich (1712–86) 1740 king (II) in Prussia

Frederica Louise (1714–84)

Philippine Charlotte (1716–1801)

Sophia (1719–65)

[Louisa] Ulrica (1720–82), later queen of Sweden by marriage to Adolf Frederik king 1751–71

August Wilhelm (1722–58)

Amalie (1723–87)

Heinrich (1726–1802)

Table II GEORGE I'S PALATINATE RELATIVES

Elizabeth (1596–1662) d. of James I of England = Frederick (1596–1632) elector Palatine (V), and elected king of Bohemia 1619–21

Heinrich Friedrich (1614–29)

Karl Ludwig (1617–80) elector Palatine 1648 m. Charlotte of Hesse-Cassel

1 Karl II (1651–85) m. Wilhelmine Ernestine of Denmark (1650–1706) (line died out)

Elizabeth (1618–80)

Rupert (1619–82)

Moritz (1621–52)

Louise Hollandine (1622–1709)

Ludwig (1624–25)

Anne Henriette (1648–1709)

Edward (1625–63) m. Anna Gonzaga

Henrietta (1626–51)

Philip (1627–50)

Benedicte Henriette (1652–1730) (for issue of her m. to Johann Friedrich, see Table I)

Charlotte (1628–31)

Sophia (1630–1714) (for issue from her m. to Ernst August, see Table I)

Gustavus Adolphus (1632–41)

Elisabeth Charlotte (1652–1722) m. 1671 Philippe I of Orléans (1640–1701)

Philippe (1674–1723), II from 1701)

Elisabeth Charlotte (1676–1744), m. 1698 Leopold-Joseph-Charles (1690–1729), duke of Lorraine

2 Issue from Karl Ludwig's morganatic marriage to Louise von Degenfeld (1634–77), all with titles Raugraf or Raugräfin (three d. in infancy)

Karl Ludwig (1658–88)

Caroline (1659–96) m. 1683 Meinhard von Schomberg, later 2nd duke of Leinster (1641–1719)

Louise (1661–1733)

Amalie Elisabeth (1663–1709)

Georg Ludwig (1664–1665)

Friederike (1665–74)

Friedrich Wilhelm (1666–67)

Karl Edward (1668–90)

Karl Moritz (1670–1702)

Karl August (1672–1702)

Karl Casimir (1675–91)

Table III THE PROTESTANT SUCCESSION AND THE HOUSE OF HANOVER

(ruling kings in bold type)

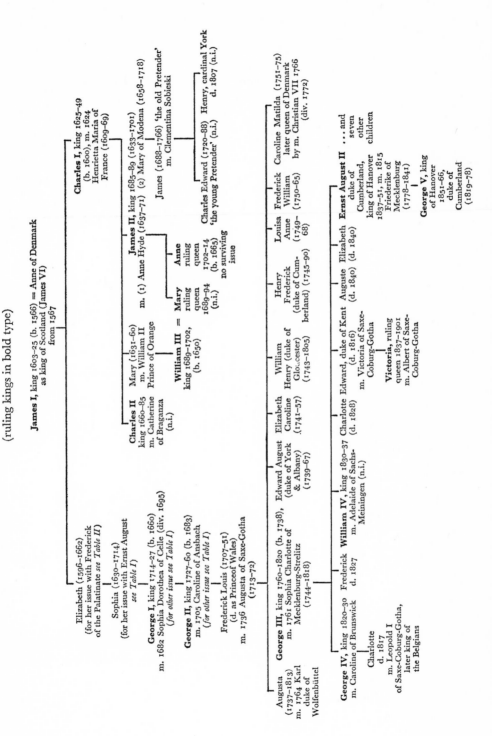

Table IV THE ELDER BRANCH OF THE HOUSE OF BRUNSWICK, THAT OF WOLFENBÜTTEL

This table is meant to show the splitting off into the two branches of Brunswick-Wolfenbüttel and Brunswick-Lüneburg and relatives of the senior branch who played a significant role in George's lifetime

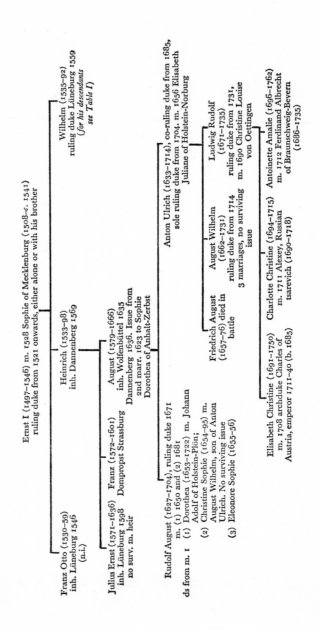

Ernst I (1497–1546) m. 1528 Sophie of Mecklenburg (1508–c. 1541)
ruling duke from 1521 onwards, either alone or with his brother

Franz Otto (1530–59)
inh. Lüneburg 1546
(n.i.)

Heinrich (1533–98)
inh. Dannenberg 1569

Wilhelm (1535–92)
ruling duke Lüneburg 1559
(for his descendants see Table I)

Julius Ernst (1571–1636)
inh. Lüneburg 1598
no surv. m. heir

Franz (1572–1601)
Dompropst Strassburg

August (1579–1666)
inh. Wolfenbüttel 1635
Dannenberg 1636. Issue from
2nd marr. 1623 to Sophie
Dorothea of Anhalt-Zerbst

Rudolf August (1627–1704), ruling duke 1671
ds from m. 1   m. (1) 1650 and (2) 1681
(1) Dorothea (1653–1722) m. Johann
     Adolf of Holstein-Plön;
(2) Christine Sophie (1654–95) m.
     August Wilhelm, son of Anton
     Ulrich. No surviving issue
(3) Eleonore Sophie (1655–56)

Anton Ulrich (1633–1714), co-ruling duke from 1685,
sole ruling duke from 1704. m. 1656 Elisabeth
Juliane of Holstein-Norburg

Friedrich August
(1657–76) died in
battle

August Wilhelm
(1662–1731)
ruling duke from 1714,
3 marriages, no surviving
issue

Ludwig Rudolf
(1671–1735)
ruling duke from 1731,
m. 1690 Christine Louise
von Oettingen

Elisabeth Christine (1691–1750)
m. 1708 archduke Charles of
Austria, emperor 1711–40 (b. 1685)

Charlotte Christine (1694–1715)
m. 1711 Alexey, Russian
tsarevich (1690–1718)

Antoinette Amalie (1696–1762)
m. 1712 Ferdinand Albrecht
of Braunschweig-Bevern
(1686–1735)

George's Hanoverian dominions and the near neighbours of his Electorate

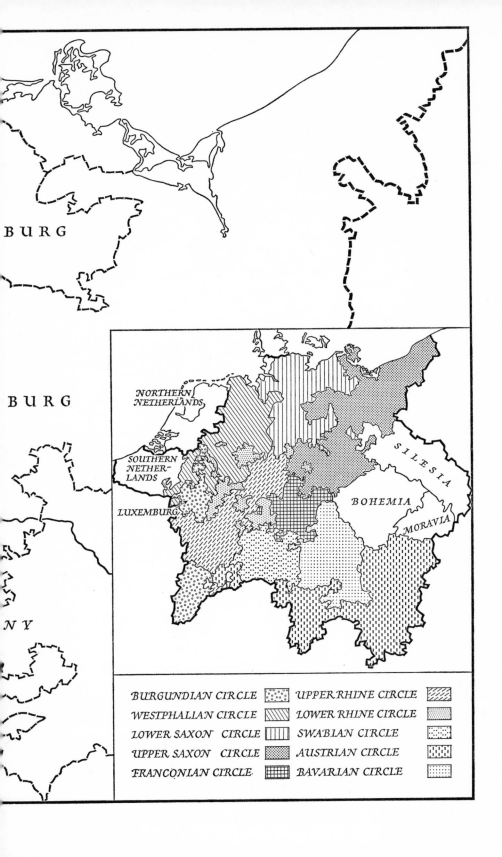

BURG

BURG

N Y

NORTHERN
NETHERLANDS

SOUTHERN
NETHER-
LANDS

LUXEMBURG

SILESIA

BOHEMIA

MORAVIA

BURGUNDIAN CIRCLE

WESTPHALIAN CIRCLE

LOWER SAXON CIRCLE

UPPER SAXON CIRCLE

FRANCONIAN CIRCLE

UPPER RHINE CIRCLE

LOWER RHINE CIRCLE

SWABIAN CIRCLE

AUSTRIAN CIRCLE

BAVARIAN CIRCLE

The Baltic area of importance for George I: the peace plan for the North

FINLAND

Nystad

land
Islands

GULF OF FINLAND

KARELIA

LAKE LADOGA

Neva St.Petersburg

INGRIA (Russ.1721)

Narva

RUSSIA

Reval

DAGÖ
(Russ.
1721)

ESTONIA
(Russ. 1721)

OSEL

LIVONIA
(Russ. 1721)

Riga

COURLAND

Dvina

Smolensk

EAST
PRUSSIA

Königs-
berg

POLISH-
LITHUANIAN
COMMON-
WEALTH

| 0 | 50 | 100 | 150 | 200 | Mls |

Kms

| 0 | 100 | 200 | 300 |

The Mediterranean area of importance for George I: the peace plan for the South

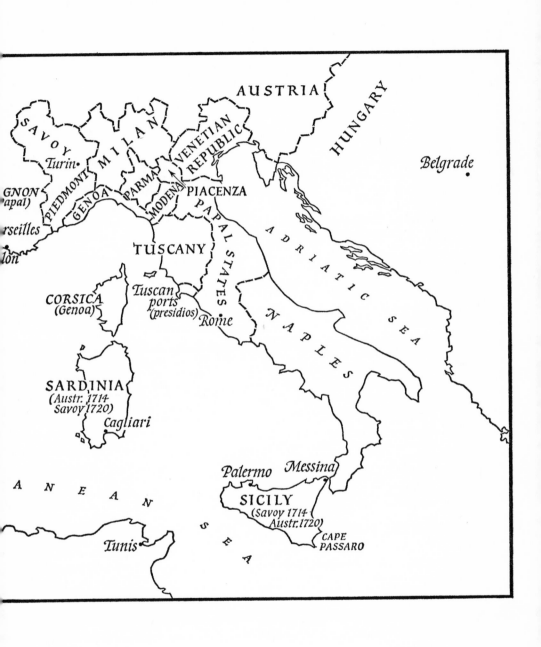

AUSTRIA

HUNGARY

SAVOY

M I L A N

VENETIAN
REPUBLIC

Belgrade

Turin

GNON
(apal)

rseilles

PIEDMONT

GENOA

PARMA

MODENA

PIACENZA

lon

PAPAL STATES

TUSCANY

A D R I A T I C

CORSICA
(Genoa)

*Tuscan
ports
(presidios)*

Rome

N A P L E S

S E A

SARDINIA
*(Austr. 1714
Savoy 1720)*

Cagliari

A N

E A N

Palermo

Messina

SICILY
*(Savoy 1714
Austr. 1720)*

S E A

Tunis

CAPE
PASSARO

LIST OF ILLUSTRATIONS

Index